A COBOL Book of Practice and Reference

Prentice-Hall Software Series

Brian W. Kernighan, advisor

A COBOL Book of Practice and Reference

ROBERT T. GRAUER, Ph.D.
University of Miami

PRENTICE-HALL, INC.
Englewood Cliffs, New Jersey 07632

Library of Congress Cataloging in Publication Data

Grauer, Robert T
    A COBOL book of practice and reference.

    (Prentice-Hall software series)
    Includes index.
      1. COBOL (Computer program language)   I. Title.
II. Series.
QA76.73.C25G725   001.64'24   80-26112
ISBN 0-13-139717-6 (paper)
        0-13-139725-7 (case)

Editorial/production supervision
    and interior design by Kathryn Gollin Marshak
Cover design by Alon Jaediker
Manufacturing buyer: Joyce Levatino

© 1981 by Prentice-Hall, Inc., Englewood Cliffs, NJ 07632

All rights reserved. No part of this book
may be reproduced in any form or by any means
without permission in writing from the publisher.

Printed in the United States of America

10 9 8 7 6 5 4 3 2 1

Prentice-Hall International, Inc., *London*
Prentice-Hall of Australia Pty. Limited, *Sydney*
Prentice-Hall of Canada, Ltd., *Toronto*
Prentice-Hall of India Private Limited, *New Delhi*
Prentice-Hall of Japan, Inc., *Tokyo*
Prentice-Hall of Southeast Asia Pte. Ltd., *Singapore*
Whitehall Books Limited, *Wellington, New Zealand*

To Marion

The love of my life

Contents

PREFACE

SECTION 1: GETTING STARTED IN COBOL   1

   Overview   1

      Capsule Summary: Skeletal COBOL Outline *2*
      Capsule Summary: Guidelines for a COBOL Program *3*
      Exercise 1.1: Fill in the Blanks *3*
      Exercise 1.2: Fill in the Blanks *5*
      Solutions *6*

   Introduction to Debugging   7

      Programming Tip: Compilation Errors to Avoid *9*

   Tuition Billing Problem   12

      Exercise 1.3: Tuition Billing with Compilation Errors *12*
      Exercise 1.4: Tuition Billing with Logic Errors *17*
      Solutions to Tuition Billing Problem *19*

   Employee Selection Problem   23

      Exercise 1.5: Employee Selection with Compilation Errors *23*
      Exercise 1.6: Employee Selection with Logic Errors *27*
      Solutions to Employee Selection Problem *30*

   Payroll Problem   33

      Exercise 1.7: Payroll Program with Compilation Errors *34*
      Exercise 1.8: Payroll Problem with Logic Errors *38*
      Solutions to Payroll Problem *41*

SECTION 2: THE COBOL LANGUAGE   45

Overview   45

    Capsule Summary: COBOL Syntax *46*

Topic 2.1: Elementary Input-Output   47

COBOL Syntax *47*
Exercise 2.1: Coding COBOL Statements *47*
Exercise 2.2: Checking COBOL Syntax *48*
Exercise 2.3: Group versus Elementary Items *49*
Exercise 2.4: Self-Checking Examination *50*
Solutions for Topic 2.1 *52*

Topic 2.2: Arithmetic   55

COBOL Syntax *55*
Capsule Summary: ADD, SUBTRACT, MULTIPLY, DIVIDE, and COMPUTE Statements *56*
Exercise 2.5: Checking COBOL Syntax *57*
Exercise 2.6: Evaluating Arithmetic Statements *58*
Exercise 2.7: Coding COBOL Statements *58*
Exercise 2.8: Self-Checking Examination *59*
Solutions for Topic 2.2 *62*

Topic 2.3: MOVE, MOVE CORRESPONDING, Qualification, and Editing   64

COBOL Syntax *64*
Capsule Summary: The MOVE Statement *65*
Exercise 2.9: The MOVE Statement *65*
Capsule Summary: Editing *66*
Exercise 2.10: Editing *67*
Capsule Summary: The MOVE CORRESPONDING Statement *68*
Exercise 2.11: The MOVE CORRESPONDING Statement *69*
Exercise 2.12: Self-Checking Examination *70*
Solutions for Topic 2.3 *73*

Topic 2.4: The IF Statement   75

COBOL Syntax *75*
Exercise 2.13: Condition Names *76*
Exercise 2.14: Compound and Implied Conditions *76*
Exercise 2.15: The ELSE Clause *77*
Exercise 2.16: Nested IFs *78*

Exercise 2.17: Self-Checking Examination *80*
Solutions for Topic 2.4 *82*

Topic 2.5: The PERFORM Statement 85

COBOL Syntax *85*
Exercise 2.18: Performing Sections and Paragraphs *85*
Exercise 2.19: PERFORM VARYING *87*
Exercise 2.20: Self-Checking Examination *88*
Solutions for Topic 2.5 *91*

Topic 2.6: Table Processing 93

COBOL Syntax *93*
Capsule Summary: Storage Allocation and Hierarchial References *94*
Exercise 2.21: Hierarchical References *95*
Exercise 2.22: The OCCURS Clause *95*
Capsule Summary: The SEARCH Verb *96*
Exercise 2.23: Coding COBOL Statements *96*
Exercise 2.24: Self-Checking Examination *97*
Solutions for Topic 2.6 *100*

Topic 2.7: Sorting and Merging 103

COBOL Syntax *103*
Capsule Summary: INPUT PROCEDURE/OUTPUT PROCEDURE *104*
Capsule Summary: USING/GIVING *105*
Exercise 2.25: Vocabulary Associated with Sorting *106*
Exercise 2.26: USING/GIVING Option *107*
Exercise 2.27: Coding COBOL Statements *108*
Exercise 2.28: Self-Checking Examination *108*
Solutions for Topic 2.7 *112*

Topic 2.8: Indexed Files 114

COBOL Syntax *114*
Exercise 2.29: Concepts of ISAM Organization *115*
Exercise 2.30: Concepts of VSAM Organization *116*
Capsule Summary: ISAM/VSAM COBOL Differences *116*
Exercise 2.31: ISAM/VSAM Differences *117*
Exercise 2.32: Coding COBOL Statements *118*
Exercise 2.33: Self-Checking Examination *118*
Solutions for Topic 2.8 *121*

Contents

Topic 2.9: Report Writer   124

    COBOL Syntax *124*
    Exercise 2.34: Identifying Report Groups *126*
    Exercise 2.35: Coding Report Groups *126*
    Exercise 2.36: Coding Other Report Writer Statements *126*
    Exercise 2.37: Self-Checking Examination *127*
    Solutions for Topic 2.9 *130*

SECTION 3: SOURCE LEVEL DEBUGGING   134

Overview   134

    Programming Tip: Execution Errors to Avoid *135*
    Exercise 3.1: Compilation Errors and Report Writer *139*
    Exercise 3.2: Execution Errors and Report Writer *143*
    Exercise 3.3: Execution Errors and Control Breaks *146*
    Exercise 3.4: Compilation Errors and SORT *151*
    Exercise 3.5: Execution Errors and SORT *155*
    Exercise 3.6: Subprograms: 1 *158*
    Exercise 3.7: Subprograms: 2 *166*
    Exercise 3.8: Sequential File Maintenance *171*
    Exercise 3.9: Nonsequential File Maintenance *174*
    Exercise 3.10: Two File Merge: 1 *177*
    Exercise 3.11: Two File Merge: 2 *179*
    Exercise 3.12: Incorrect Use of Group Move *181*
    Exercise 3.13: Incorrect Use of the SEARCH Verb *182*
    Exercise 3.14: Incorrect Use of Signed Numbers *183*
    Exercise 3.15: Incorrect Use of Output Buffers *185*
    Exercise 3.16: Table Processing *186*
    Exercise 3.17: Procedure Division Potpourri *190*
    Solutions *195*

SECTION 4: TOP DOWN TESTING   217

Overview   217

Case Study Requirements   217

    Sequential Versus Nonsequential Processing *219*

Sequential File Maintenance   220

    Pseudocode *220*
    Hierarchy Charts *221*

Testing 223

The Sequential Maintenance Program (With Stubs) *225*
The Completed Maintenance Program *230*

Sequential Maintenance—A Review 235

Nonsequential File Maintenance 236

The Nonsequential Maintenance Program (With Stubs) *238*
The Completed Nonsequential Maintenance Program *242*

Summary 246

SECTION 5: GOOD PRACTICES AND BAD 247

Overview 247

Use Appropriate Comments 248

Eliminate 77-Level Entries 249

Choose Meaningful Names 249

Indent 251

Space Attractively 253

Avoid Commas 254

Restrict Switches and Subscripts to a Single Use 254

Use 88-Level Entries 255

Perform Paragraphs, not Sections 256

Use the COMPUTE Verb for Multiple Arithmetic Operators 257

Keep it Simple 258

Use the Appropriate Search Technique 259

Initialize Tables Dynamically 260

Avoid Constants 261

Contents

    Avoid Literals   262

    Use READ INTO, WRITE FROM, and WS BEGINS HERE   264

    Pass a Single 01 Parameter to a Subprogram   265

    Consider Report Writer   266

SECTION 6: PROGRAMMING PROJECTS   267

    Overview   267

    Student Information System   269

        Project 6.1: Student Selection *269*
        Project 6.2: Grade Point Listing *270*
        Project 6.3: Tuition Billing *272*
        Project 6.4: Student Transcripts *274*
        Project 6.5: Student Course Cards *277*
        Project 6.6: Student Profiles *278*
        Project 6.7: Student Profiles with Table Lookups *279*
        Project 6.8: Grade Distributions *282*
        Project 6.9: Student Credit Hours *283*
        Projects 6.10a and b: File Maintenance (Sequential and Non-sequential) *285*
        Record Descriptions and Test Data for the Student Information System *288*

    Personnel Information System   293

        Project 6.11: Employee Selection *293*
        Project 6.12: Annual Compensation Analysis *293*
        Project 6.13: Payroll *295*
        Project 6.14: Benefit Statement *297*
        Project 6.15: Employee Profiles *299*
        Project 6.16: Employee Profiles With Table Lookups *302*
        Project 6.17: EEO Reporting *304*
        Project 6.18: Salary Totals *305*
        Project 6.19: Salary Distribution *307*
        Projects 6.20a and b: File Maintenance (Sequential and Non-sequential) *309*
        Record Descriptions and Test Data for the Personnel Information System *311*

SECTION 7: ABEND DEBUGGING — 315

Overview — 315

Warmup Exercises — 316

Solutions to Warmup Exercises *320*
Capsule Summary: Elementary ABEND Debugging Procedure *322*
Programming Tip: A List of Common ABENDs *323*

Problem Statement: Employee Selection Problem — 331

Exercise 7.1: Dump Reading *337*
Exercise 7.2: Dump Reading *340*

Problem Statement: Employee Profiles — 344

Exercise 7.3: Dump Reading *358*
Exercise 7.4: Dump Reading *363*
Solutions to ABEND Debugging Excercises 1, 2, 3 and 4 *370*

INDEX — 377

Preface

The ability to detect and correct programming errors is highly praised by the professional programmer, instructor, trainee, and student alike, yet students and trainees rarely have adequate opportunity to develop this vital skill. The typical programming curriculum, in both education and industry, is centered (and justifiably so) on individual programming projects. An individual is given an assignment and judged on his or her ability to produce a working COBOL program. True, the novice programmer is responsible for debugging that program, but no individual will ever approach the diversity of errors possible with a language as rich as COBOL. The project leader, on the other hand, is privy to the work of many people and often obtains more debugging exercise than expected. Although much of it is mundane, a significant amount is often challenging, and this author is grateful to his students who through their unique programming problems have done much to enhance a mutual learning experience. It is in this spirit that *A COBOL Book of Practice and Reference* was initially conceived.

Another impetus came from the author's initial experience with a commercial programming project. Having just learned all there was to know about COBOL (or so he thought), he was rudely awakened by stringent testing requirements, installation standards, coding conventions, and the dump he received when his first job failed to run. He quickly realized there was more to COBOL than the language itself.

The final thrust for the project came from the many practitioners who have seen fit to adopt this author's previous work (*COBOL: A Pragmatic Approach, The COBOL Environment, COBOL: A Vehicle for Information Systems,* and *Structured COBOL: A Pragmatic Approach,* all by Prentice-Hall.) It seems that no matter how many questions, exercises, problems or projects were included, the cry always came for "problems, more problems!".

Hence, the objectives of *A COBOL Book of Practice and Reference* are:

1. To provide the requisite variety and quantity of problems needed for *mastery* of the language by the professionals,
2. To provide a series of meaningful debugging exercises on programs going

to a normal end of job, but which produce results that are unexpected or unintended,
3. To provide an understandable and commercially acceptable approach to testing, program development, and standards, and
4. To provide a reasonable set of ABEND debugging exercises and associated guidelines for use by the professional.

With these goals in mind, *A COBOL Book of Practice and Reference* is designed specifically for the programmer trainee in industry. It can also accompany *any* text in the academic *two* semester COBOL sequence, as organization is by COBOL topic and not by the chapters in a particular book. The large number of *structured* COBOL listings (over 30) is seen as a major strength. Any individual who completes the book will in the process have established a manual to which he or she can continually refer as a practitioner.

A COBOL Book of Practice and Reference is divided into seven sections:

Section 1 begins with completed programs, and is aimed at the first time programmer to help get his or her feet wet. The reader is asked to correct both compilation and execution errors in heading, detail, and summary line programs.

Section 2 on the COBOL language, contains exercises aimed at mastery of the language. The reader is asked to code individual statements for specific tasks, to state the effects of supplied COBOL statements, and to answer true/false and multiple choice questions. The section is generally involved with *details* of the language.

Section 3 is the author's favorite, and one which many professionals have enjoyed and continually contribute to. It consists of seventeen listings, all of which fail to execute as intended. The reader is asked simply to find and correct the errors. Collectively, these exercises embrace most, if not all of the major language features including: SORT, subprograms, Report Writer, table processing, and indexed files.

Section 4 discusses techniques of program development, including: top down testing, hierarchy charts, and pseudocode. A case study approach is used, focusing on a rather complex maintenance program. The processing requirements are presented and the necessary logic is developed for both sequential and nonsequential processing. A partially completed stubs program is developed for both sequential and nonsequential versions to stress the advantages of top down testing. This section is more pedagogic in nature than its predecessors and provides substantial coverage of the complexities of file maintenance.

Section 5 offers a series of succinct programming strategies to accomplish everyday tasks in COBOL. The author begins with commonly acceptable COBOL code, critiques it, and then establishes a better way to accomplish the objective. He is especially grateful to many individuals in the COBOL community for their contributions in this area.

Section 6 contains specifications for two information systems, each consisting of ten programming projects. The author has found that a *unified* set of projects, with common COPY clauses and data files, promote a sense of continuity, and hence are superior to isolated programming projects. The areas chosen are those with which individuals can easily identify. The first is a personnel system for a medium-sized company; the second is a student data system for a university. Each project has in its specifications a detailed description of incoming records, report formats, and test data. Either system, i.e., set of ten projects, is ample work for a one-year training sequence.

Section 7 deals with ABEND debugging, and as such is limited to IBM compatible systems. Nevertheless, the author believes there is sufficient interest in the material to warrant its inclusion in a generalized set of COBOL problems. The first set of examples are relatively simple and pertain to invalid decimal data. The second set considers debugging in a subprogram with associated mention of link-edit maps, BL and BLL cells, etc.

Although the emphasis throughout is on problems, rather than pedagogy, the author has included several "programming tips" and "capsule summaries" which are instructional in nature. Moreoever, the solutions to *all* exercises are provided, and the author cannot refrain from expanding on subtleties of the language. The summary information in conjunction with the completed exercises form the basis for a *personal reference manual,* containing multiple examples to illustrate the precise function of COBOL statements.

Finally, since experience is the best teacher, completion of the exercises does more for the reader than any other activity. This is especially true in Section 3 on debugging, which consists entirely of seventeen listings that produce erroneous results. It is one thing to read and/or talk about the importance of, for example, indentation, a missing period, or the order of arguments in a subprogram. The effect is far more lasting if the points are made directly by the trainee through debugging *realistic production programs.* This participation enables the reader to maintain interest, gain confidence, and reach a higher level of competence in a much shorter period.

The author warmly thanks his editor, Steve Cline of Prentice-Hall, for his guidance and encouragement. He is especially grateful to Kathy Marshak, Production Editor, for her patience and creativity in bringing the project to fruition. He appreciates Herb Daehnke's fine job of preparing the artwork. He thanks his reviewers, Allan Buttles, Brian W. Kernighan, Ralph A. Szweda, Richard J. Weiland, and Jerry D. Wethington for their positive comments, and appreciates the thoroughness of Marilu Ambros and Joseph Durnell in reading galleys. He commends his typists, Teri Rodriguez, Deborah Miller, and Edith Butler, for their ability to decipher his handwriting. Finally, and most important, he thanks his many colleagues and students for their contributions over the years.

The following information is reprinted from COBOL Edition 1965, published by the Conference on Data Systems Languages (CODASYL), and printed by the U.S. Government Printing Office:

Any organization interested in reproducing the COBOL report and specifications in whole or part, using ideas taken from this report as the basis for an instructional manual or for any other purpose is free to do so. However, all such organizations are requested to reproduce this section as part of the introduction to the document. Those using a short passage, as in a book review, are requested to mention "COBOL" in acknowledgment of the source, but need not quote this entire section.

COBOL is an industry language and is not the property of any company or group of companies, or of any organization or group of organizations.

No warranty, expressed or implied, is made by any contributor or by the COBOL Committee as to the accuracy and functioning of the programming system and language. Moreover, no responsibility is assumed by any contributor, or by the committee, in connection therewith.

Procedures have been established for the maintenance of COBOL. Inquiries concerning the procedures for proposing changes should be directed to the Executive Committee of the Conference on Data Systems languages.

The authors and copyright holders of the copyrighted material used herein:

FLOWMATIC (Trade mark of the Sperry Rand Corporation), Programming for the Univac (R) I and II, Data Automation Systems copyrighted 1958, 1959, by Sperry Rand Corporation; IBM Commercial Translator Form No. F28-8013, copyrighted 1959 by IBM; FACT, DSI 27A5260-2760, copyrighted 1960 by Minneapolis-Honeywell

have specifically authorized the use of this material in whole or in part, in the COBOL specifications. Such authorization extends to the reproduction and use of COBOL specifications in programming manuals of similar publications.

1 Getting Started in COBOL

OVERVIEW

There are two commonly held views on how COBOL should be taught. The first holds that students need significant background in COBOL before they start coding. The second suggests that students begin coding as soon as possible, and without spending weeks on syntactical variations.

This book leans heavily toward the second approach. The author believes that once students have a basic knowledge of program logic and how a program is intended to function; that is, accept input, process it, and produce output, COBOL programming can and should begin immediately. This author begins his COBOL course by presenting a complete program in the first lecture or two, with an eye toward an overall view of what the program is attempting to accomplish. The students are not yet to be concerned with precise syntactical rules of the COBOL language. This approach is consistent with the way a baby first learns the English language. The baby mimics sounds, then words, and finally sentences, and only learns about grammar several years later.

With this philosophy in mind, this section begins by presenting a capsule summary containing a skeletal COBOL outline for a typical card-to-print program, followed by general guidelines for writing a complete program. The first two exercises present simple programs in which the reader is asked to supply the missing information.

The subject of debugging is entered next, with exercises in both compilation and execution errors. There is a brief discussion on debugging, followed by specifications for three programs, each requiring heading, detail, and summary logic. Two listings are associated with each program, for compilation and execution errors, respectively. *Solutions to all exercises appear with appropriate discussion.*

Capsule Summary: Skeletal COBOL Outline
(A card-to-print program)

```
IDENTIFICATION DIVISION.
PROGRAM-ID.    8 character name.
AUTHOR.        your name.
ENVIRONMENT DIVISION.
CONFIGURATION SECTION.
SOURCE-COMPUTER. computer-name.
OBJECT-COMPUTER. computer-name.
INPUT-OUTPUT SECTION.
FILE-CONTROL.
     SELECT CARD-FILE ASSIGN TO ...             Two files, one for input and one for
     SELECT PRINT-FILE ASSIGN TO ...            output are defined in the Environ-
                                                ment Division.
DATA DIVISION.
FILE SECTION.
FD   CARD-FILE
     LABEL RECORDS ARE OMITTED                  Typical FD for a card-file.
     RECORD CONTAINS 80 CHARACTERS
     DATA RECORD IS STUDENT-CARD.
01   STUDENT-CARD.
     05 etc.
FD   PRINT-FILE
     LABEL RECORDS ARE OMITTED
     RECORD CONTAINS 133 CHARACTERS             Typical FD for print-file.
     DATA RECORD IS PRINT-LINE.
01   PRINT-LINE.
     05 etc.
WORKING-STORAGE SECTION.
01   EOF-SWITCH    PIC XXX    VALUE SPACES.     Switch controls performed routine.

PROCEDURE DIVISION.
MAINLINE.
     OPEN INPUT CARD-FILE OUTPUT PRINT-FILE.    Housekeeping consists of opening
     READ CARD-FILE                             files and the initial read.
         AT END MOVE 'YES' TO EOF-SWITCH.
     PERFORM PROCESS-RECORDS                    Routine is performed until there is
         UNTIL EOF-SWITCH = 'YES'.              no more data.
     CLOSE CARD-FILE, PRINT-FILE.               Termination includes closing files
     STOP RUN.                                  and stop run.
PROCESS-RECORDS.
     your logic here
     READ CARD-FILE                             Last line of performed routine is a
         AT END MOVE 'YES' TO EOF-SWITCH.       read.
```

Capsule Summary: Guidelines for a COBOL Program

1. The four divisions must appear in the specified order: Identification, Environment, Data, and Procedure. Division headers begin in the A margin (columns 8 to 11) and always appear on a line by themselves.
2. The Environment and Data Divisions contain sections with fixed names. The Identification Division does not contain any sections. (The Procedure Division may contain programmer defined sections; however, this is usually not done in beginning programs.) Section headers begin in the A margin and are on a line by themselves.
3. The Data Division is the only division without paragraph names. In the Identification and Environment Divisions the paragraph names are fixed. In the Procedure Division, they are determined by the programmer. Paragraph names begin in the A margin.
4. Any entry not required to begin in the A margin may begin in or past column 12.
5. The COBOL program executes instructions sequentially as they appear in the Procedure Division, unless a transfer of control, or PERFORM, is encountered.
6. Every file must be opened and closed. A file name appears in at least four statements: SELECT, FD, OPEN, and CLOSE. In addition, the READ statement will contain the *file* name of an input file while the WRITE statement contains the *record* name of an output file.
7. Every program must contain at least one STOP RUN statement.
8. The skeletal COBOL outline (page 2) makes reference to a mainline routine which "drives" the entire program. It consists of, at least an OPEN, an Initial READ, a PERFORM, a CLOSE, and a STOP RUN. The performed routine contains the program's logic and ends with a READ (for every record but the first). Note also the definition of the switch in Working-Storage and its use in the READ and PERFORM statements.

Exercise 1.1: Fill in the Blanks

The listing in Fig. 1-1 is a COBOL program that will process a file of employee records and print the names of programmers under 30. Restore the missing information so that the program will run as intended.

```
00001            IDENTIFICATION DIVISION.
00002            PROGRAM-ID.  'FIRSTTRY'.                          (1)
00003            [        ]. MARION MILGROM.
00004
00005            ENVIRONMENT DIVISION.
00006            CONFIGURATION SECTION.
00007            SOURCE-COMPUTER.    IBM-370.
00008            OBJECT-COMPUTER.    IBM-370.                       (2)
00009            INPUT-OUTPUT SECTION.
00010            FILE-CONTROL.
00011                SELECT CARD-FILE ASSIGN TO UT-S-SYSIN.
00012                   [    ] PRINT-FILE ASSIGN TO UT-S-SYSOUT.
00013                                                               (3)
00014            [         ].
00015            FILE SECTION.
00016            FD  CARD-FILE
00017                LABEL RECORDS ARE OMITTED
00018                RECORD CONTAINS 80 CHARACTERS
00019                DATA RECORD IS EMPLOYEE-CARD.
00020            01  EMPLOYEE-CARD.
00021                05  CARD-NAME        PIC X(25).
00022                05  CARD-TITLE       PIC X(10).
00023                05  CARD-AGE         PIC 99.
00024                05  FILLER           PIC XX.
00025                05  CARD-SALARY      PIC 9(5).
00026                05  FILLER           PIC X(36).                (4)
00027            FD  PRINT-FILE
00028                   [          ] ARE OMITTED
00029                RECORD CONTAINS 133 CHARACTERS
00030                DATA RECORD IS PRINT-LINE.
00031            01  PRINT-LINE.
00032                05  FILLER           PIC X(1).
00033                05  PRINT-NAME       [      ]                  (5)
00034                05  FILLER           PIC X(2).
00035                05  PRINT-AGE        PIC 99.
00036                05  FILLER           PIC X(3).
00037                05  PRINT-SALARY     PIC 9(5).
00038                05  FILLER           PIC X(95).
00039                                                               (6)
00040            [          ].
00041            77  END-OF-DATA-FLAG     PIC XXX.
00042
00043            PROCEDURE DIVISION.
00044            MAINLINE-ROUTINE.                                  (7)
00045           *HOUSEKEEPING ROUTINE
00046                [    ] INPUT CARD-FILE, OUTPUT PRINT-FILE.
00047                MOVE SPACES TO PRINT-LINE.
00048                MOVE ' SALARY REPORT FOR PROGRAMMERS UNDER 30' TO PRINT-LINE.
00049                WRITE PRINT-LINE AFTER ADVANCING 2 LINES.
00050                READ CARD-FILE
00051                    AT END MOVE 'YES' TO END-OF-DATA-FLAG.     (8)
00052
00053                   [      ] PROCESS-EMPLOYEE-RECORDS
00054                    UNTIL END-OF-DATA-FLAG = 'YES'.
00055                CLOSE CARD-FILE, PRINT-FILE.
00056                STOP RUN.
00057                                                               (9)
00058            PROCESS-EMPLOYEE-RECORDS.
00059                IF CARD-TITLE = 'PROGRAMMER' AND CARD-AGE < 30
00060                    MOVE [     ] TO PRINT-LINE
00061                    MOVE CARD-NAME   TO PRINT-NAME             (10)
00062                    MOVE [     ]     TO PRINT-AGE
00063                    MOVE CARD-SALARY TO PRINT-SALARY
00064                    WRITE PRINT-LINE AFTER ADVANCING 2 LINES.
00065                READ CARD-FILE
00066                    AT END MOVE [   ] TO END-OF-DATA-FLAG.     (11)
```

Figure 1.1 Program Listing with Missing Elements.

4

Exercise 2.2: Fill in the Blanks

The listing in Fig. 1.2 represents a COBOL program to process a file of student records and print the names of engineering majors with 110 credits or more. Restore the missing information so the program will run as intended.

```
00001           IDENTIFICATION DIVISION.
00002           PROGRAM-ID.     FIRSTTRY.
00003           AUTHOR.         CRAWFORD.            ①
00004           ▢.
00005           CONFIGURATION SECTION.
00006           SOURCE-COMPUTER.    IBM-370.
00007           OBJECT-COMPUTER.    IBM-370.
00008           INPUT-OUTPUT SECTION.              ②
00009           FILE-CONTROL.
00010               SELECT ▢      ASSIGN TO UT-S-SYSIN.
00011               SELECT PRINT-FILE ASSIGN TO UT-S-SYSOUT.
00012           DATA DIVISION.
00013           ▢.                       ③
00014           FD  CARD-FILE
00015               LABEL RECORDS ARE OMITTED
00016               RECORD CONTAINS ▢ CHARACTERS
00017               DATA RECORD IS CARD-IN.     ④
00018           01  CARD-IN.
00019               05  CARD-NAME           PICTURE IS A(25).
00020               05  CARD-CREDITS        PICTURE IS 9(3).
00021               05  CARD-MAJOR          PICTURE IS A(15).
00022               05  FILLER              PICTURE IS X(37).
00023       ⑤  ▢   PRINT-FILE
00024               LABEL RECORDS ARE OMITTED
00025               RECORD CONTAINS 133 CHARACTERS
00026       ⑥  ▢   DATA RECORD IS PRINT-LINE.
00027               PRINT-LINE.
00028               05  FILLER              PICTURE IS X(8).
00029               05  PRINT-NAME          PICTURE IS X(25).
00030               05  FILLER              PICTURE IS X(100).
00031           WORKING-STORAGE SECTION.
00032       ⑦  ▢   DATA-REMAINS-SWITCH     PICTURE IS X(2).
00033           PROCEDURE DIVISION.         ⑧
00034           MAINLINE.
00035               OPEN ▢  CARD-FILE, OUTPUT PRINT-FILE.
00036               READ CARD-FILE,
00037                   AT END MOVE 'NO' TO DATA-REMAINS-SWITCH.
00038               PERFORM PROCESS-CARDS
00039                   UNTIL DATA-REMAINS-SWITCH = 'NO'.
00040       ⑨  ▢       CARD-FILE, PRINT-FILE.
00041               STOP RUN.
00042
00043       ▢   .                   ⑩
00044               IF CARD-CREDITS NOT < 110 AND CARD-MAJOR = 'ENGINEERING'
00045                   MOVE SPACES TO PRINT-LINE
00046                   MOVE CARD-NAME TO PRINT-NAME
00047                   WRITE PRINT-LINE.
00048               READ ▢                                    ⑫
00049       ⑪       AT END MOVE 'NO' TO ▢                  .
```

Figure 1.2 Program Listing with Missing Elements.

Solutions

Exercise 1.1: Fill in the Blanks

1. AUTHOR: This is an optional paragraph in the Identification Division.
2. SELECT: Every file is first defined in a SELECT statement.
3. DATA DIVISION: The File Section marks the beginning of this division.
4. LABEL RECORDS: This clause is required in all FDs.
5. PIC X(25): The picture clauses in lines 32 through 38 sum to 133 (see line 29).
6. WORKING-STORAGE SECTION: This section contains all data names which were not defined in the File Section.
7. OPEN: All files must be opened before processing.
8. PERFORM: The PERFORM verb is used to establish a loop.
9. SPACES: All print lines should be blanked out initially.
10. CARD-AGE: The corresponding field from the input record is moved to the output record.
11. 'YES': The PERFORM statement in line 53 is intended to loop until there is no more data in the input file (until END-OF-DATA-FLAG = 'YES'), hence the AT END and UNTIL conditions must be consistent.

Exercise 1.2: Fill in the Blanks

1. ENVIRONMENT DIVISION: The Configuration Section marks the beginning of the Environment Division.
2. CARD-FILE: The file name in the SELECT statement is the same file name appearing in an FD (line 14), OPEN statement (line 35), and CLOSE statement (line 40).
3. FILE SECTION: This is the first section in the Data Division.
4. 80: The total number of characters in a record is equal to the sum of the picture clauses (lines 19-22).
5. FD: Files are defined in an FD.
6. 01: Records are defined in an 01 entry.
7. 01 (or 77): either level number can be used to define an independent data name, but current practice is leaning away from 77.
8. INPUT: CARD-FILE is an input file.
9. CLOSE: All files must be closed before processing terminates.

10. PROCESS-CARDS: The paragraph name must match the one in the PERFORM statement of line 38.
11. CARD-FILE: The READ statement contains a file name which previously appeared in SELECT, FD, and OPEN statements.
12. DATA-REMAINS-SWITCH: The data name in the UNTIL condition of the PERFORM statement should match the one in the AT END clause of the READ.

INTRODUCTION TO DEBUGGING

Very few computer programs run successfully on the first attempt. Indeed, the programmer is realistically expected to make errors, and an important "test" of a good programmer is not whether he or she makes mistakes but how quickly he or she can detect and correct the errors that invariably occur. (Structured techniques can reduce the number of logic errors, but it is unrealistic to think that every program can be made error-free on the first attempt.) Since debugging is such an integral part of programming, three sections are devoted to the subject. In the present section we shall consider errors in compilation, and simple errors in execution in which the program goes to a normal end of job. In Sect. 3 we present 17 programs with more complex logic requirements that also produce errors in execution. Finally, in Sect. 7 we shall consider errors resulting in an ABEND, or abnormal end-of-job condition.

Compilation errors occur in the translation of COBOL to machine language and result because the programmer has violated a rule of the COBOL grammar; for example, omitted a period, misspelled a word, placed an entry in a wrong column, etc. *Execution* errors result after the program has been successfully translated to machine language and are generally of two types:

1. The computer was able to execute the entire program, but results are different from that which the programmer expected or intended, or
2. The computer is unable to execute a particular instruction and comes to an abnormal end of job; for example, division by zero, addition of nonnumeric data, etc.

Execution errors of the first type may be caused by an incorrect translation of the flowchart or pseudocode to the programming language or by a correct translation of incorrect logic. (A list of common execution errors is contained in the Programming Tip for Sect. 3.) In either case, there is an error in logic which is generating incorrect output.

Execution errors of the second type are deferred to Sect. 7. At that point we shall introduce the memory print or core dump as an important debugging tool. For the present, however, we shall restrict our discussion to compilation errors and execution errors of the first type.

IBM systems specify four types of COBOL compiler error messages or diagnostics. These are listed in order of increasing severity.

W-Warning diagnostic: Calls attention to what may cause a potential problem. A program can compile and execute with several W-level diagnostics present; however, ignoring these messages could lead to errors in execution.

C-Conditional diagnostic: Requires the compiler to make an assumption in order to complete the compilation. Execution is typically suppressed, and if not, usually is inaccurate.

E-Error diagnostic: A severe error in the sense that the compiler cannot make corrections and, therefore, cannot generate object instructions. Execution will not take place. Any statement flagged as an E-level error is ignored and treated as if it were not present in the program.

D-Disaster diagnostic: An error of such severity that the compiler does not know what to do and cannot continue. D-level diagnostics are extremely rare, and one practically has to submit a FORTRAN program to the COBOL compiler to cause a D-level message.

The COBOL compiler tends to rub salt in a wound in the sense that an error in one statement can cause error messages in other statements which appear correct. For example, should you have an E-level error in a SELECT statement, the compiler will flag the error, ignore the SELECT statement, then flag any other statement which references that file even though those other statements are otherwise correct.

Often simple mistakes such as omitting a statement or misspelling a reserved word can lead to a long and sometimes confusing set of error messages. The only consolation is that compiler errors can disappear as quickly as they occurred. Correction of the misspelled word or insertion of the missing statement will often eliminate several errors at once.

Proficiency in debugging comes from experience. The more programs you write, the better you become. As an indication of what to expect, and as an aid to the forth-coming exercises, consider the Programming Tip: Compilation Errors to Avoid on pages 9 to 11.

Given this brief introduction to debugging, consider exercises 1.3 through 1.8. The exercises occur in pairs. The first problem pertains to compilation errors and the second to logic or execution errors. Exercises 1.3 and 1.4 relate to tuition billing, exercises 1.5 and 1.6 to employee selection, and exercises 1.7 and 1.8 to payroll. *Solutions follow each pair of problems.*

Programming Tip: Compilation Errors to Avoid

1. *Nonunique Data Names:* Occurs because the same data name is defined in two different records or twice within the same record. For example, NAME might be specified as input data in a CARD-FILE, and printed as output in a PRINT-FILE. To avoid the problem of nonunique data names, it is best to prefix every data name within a file by a short prefix. CARD could be established as a prefix for CARD-FILE, and PRINT as the prefix for PRINT-FILE as shown below. This also helps locate data names while writing and debugging programs.

```
        .
        .
    FD  CARD-FILE
        .
        .
        DATA RECORD IS CARD-RECORD.
    01  CARD-RECORD.
        05   CARD-NAME              PIC X(20).
        05   CARD-SOC-SEC-NO        PIC 9(9).
        .
        .
    FD  PRINT-FILE
        .
        .
        DATA RECORD IS PRINT-RECORD.
    01  PRINT-RECORD.
        05   PRINT-NAME             PIC X(20).
        05   FILLER                 PIC X(5).
        05   PRINT-SOC-SEC-NO       PIC 9(9).
        .
        .
```

2. *Omitted Periods:* Every COBOL sentence should have a period and omission usually results in the compiler's assumption of a period. Realize, however, that the period has special significance with respect to the IF statement where its omission (or inclusion) does not cause compiler errors, but significantly alters the program's logic.

3. *Omitted Space Before/After an Arithmetic Operator:* The arithmetic operators **, *, /, +, and − all require a blank before and after them. (A typical error for FORTRAN or PL/I programmers since the space is not required in those languages.)

4. *Invalid Picture for Numeric Entry:* All data names used in arithmetic statements must have numeric pictures. Permissible entries include: a sign(S), 9's, and a V. Any other entry in a picture clause is invlaid.

Programming Tip, cont.

5. *Conflicting Picture and Value Clause:* Numeric pictures must have numeric values (no quotes); non-numeric pictures must have non-numeric values (must be enclosed in quotes). Both entries below are *invalid*.

    05   TOTAL   PIC 9(3)   VALUE '123'.
    05   TITLE-WORD   PIC X(3)   VALUE 123.

Another common error is to use value and picture clauses of different lengths. The entry:

    05   EMPLOYEE-NAME   PIC X(4)   VALUE 'R BAKER'.

causes a diagnostic for just that reason.

6. *Inadvertent Use of COBOL Reserved Word:* COBOL has a list of some 300 reserved words which can only be used in their designated sense; any other use results in one or several diagnostics. Some reserved words are obvious; e.g. WORKING-STORAGE, IDENTIFICATION, ENVIRONMENT, DATA, and PROCEDURE. Others such as CODE, DATE, START, and REPORT are less obvious. Instead of memorizing the list or continually referring to it, try this simple rule of thumb. Always use a hyphen in every data name you create. This will work better than 99% of the time.

7. *Conflicting RECORD CONTAINS Clause and FD Record Description:* A recurrent error, even for established programmers. It stems from sometimes careless addition in that the sum of the pictures in an FD does not equal the number of characters in the RECORD CONTAINS clause. It can also result from other errors within the Data Division, namely when an entry containing a PICTURE clause is flagged. If an E-level diagnostic is present, that entry will be ignored and the count is thrown off. This is often one of the last errors to disappear before a clean compile.

8. *Receiving Field Too Small to Accommodate Sending Field:* An extremely common error, often associated with edited pictures. Consider the entries:

    05   PRINT-TOTAL-SALARIES   PIC $$,$$$.
    .
    .
    05   TOTAL-SALARY-YOUNG-PROGRAMMERS   PIC 9(5).
    .
    .
    MOVE TOTAL-SALARY-YOUNG-PROGRAMMERS TO PRINT-TOTAL-SALARIES.

The MOVE statement would generate the warning that the receiving field may be too small to accommodate the sending field. The greatest possible value for TOTAL-SALARY-YOUNG-PROGRAMMERS is 99,999;

Programming Tip, cont.

the largest possible value that could be printed by PRINT-TOTAL-SALARIES is $9,999. Even though the print field contains five $'s, one $ must always print and hence the warning.

9. *Omitted Hyphen in a Data Name:* A careless error, but one that occurs entirely too often. If in the Data Division we define PRINT-TOTAL-PAY, and then try to reference PRINT TOTAL-PAY, the compiler objects violently. It doesn't state that a hyphen was omitted, but it flags both PRINT and TOTAL-PAY as undefined.

10. *Misspelled Data Names or Reserved Words:* Too many COBOL students are poor spellers. Sound strange? How do you spell environment? One or many errors can result, depending on which word was spelled incorrectly.

11. *Reading a Record Name or Writing a File Name:* The COBOL rule is very simple. One is supposed to read a file and write a record; many people get it confused. The entries below should clarify the situation:

```
FD   CARD-FILE
     .
     .
     .
     DATA RECORD IS CARD-RECORD.
     .
     .
     .
FD   PRINT-FILE
     .
     .
     .
     DATA RECORD IS PRINT-RECORD.
```

Correct entries:

```
READ CARD-FILE....
WRITE PRINT-RECORD....
```

Incorrect entries:

```
READ CARD-RECORD....
WRITE PRINT-FILE....
```

12. *Going Past Column 72:* This error can cause any of the preceding errors as well as a host of others to occur. A COBOL statement must end in column 72 or before; columns 73-80 are left blank or used for program identification. If one goes past column 72 in a COBOL statement, it is very difficult to catch because the COBOL listing contains columns 1 to 80 although the compiler only interprets columns 1 to 72. (The 72 column restriction does not apply to data cards.)

TUITION BILLING PROBLEM

This problem description is to be used for Exercises 1.3 and 1.4. The Bursar has requested a COBOL program to process a set of student records and calculate the amount due from each student. Incoming records have the following format:

Card Columns	Field	Picture
1-20	Student Name	A(20)
21-29	Social Security Number	9(9)
30-31	Credits Taken	99
32	Union Member	A
33-36	Scholarship Amount	9(4)

Student bills are calculated as follows:

Tuition:	$80 per credit
Union Fee:	$25 for members, $0 for nonmembers (members have a "Y" in column 32)
Activity Fee:	$25 for 6 credits or less $50 for 7-12 credits $75 for more than 12 credits
Scholarship:	The amount, if any, is punched in columns 33-36

The net bill, therefore, is tuition plus union fee plus activity fee minus scholarship.

In the first exercise derived from this problem, you are asked to correct various compilation errors. The second exercise shows a program which compiles cleanly, but produces unexpected and erroneous results.

Exercise 1.3: Tuition Billing with Compilation Errors

Correct the compilation errors found in the listing of Fig. 1.3.

```
00001           IDENTIFICATION DIVISION.
00002           PROGRAM-ID.    'TUITION'.
00003           AUTHOR.       THE BURSAR.
00004
00005           ENVIRONMENT DIVISION.
00006           CONFIGURATION SECTION.
00007           SOURCE-COMPUTER.   IBM-370.
00008           OBJECT-COMPUTER.   IBM-370.
00009           INPUT-OUTPUT SECTION.
00010           FILE-CONTROL.
00011               SELECT CARD-FILE ASSIGN TO UT-S-SYSIN.
```

Figure 1.3 Tuition Program with Compilation Errors.

```
00012            SELECT PRINT-FILE ASSIGN TO UT-S-SYSOUT.
00013
00014        DATA DIVISION.
00015        FILE SECTION.
00016        FD  CARD-FILE
00017            RECORD CONTAINS 80 CHARACTERS
00018            DATA RECORD IS STUDENT-CARD.
00019        01  STUDENT-CARD.
00020            05  STUDENT-NAME         PICTURE IS A(20).
00021            05  SOC-SEC-NO           PICTURE IS 9(9).
00022            05  CREDITS              PICTURE IS 9(2).
00023            05  UNION-MEMBER         PICTURE IS A.
00024            05  SCHOLARSHIP          PICTURE IS 9(4).
00025            05  FILLER               PICTURE IS X(44).
00026        FD  PRINT-FILE
00027            LABEL RECORDS ARE OMITTED
00028            RECORD CONTAINS 133 CHARACTERS
00029            DATA RECORD IS PRINT-LINE.
00030        01  PRINT-LINE.
00031            05  FILLER               PICTURE IS X.
00032            05  PRINT-STUDENT-NAME   PICTURE IS A(20).
00033            05  FILLER               PICTURE IS X(2).
00034            05  PRINT-SOC-SEC-NO     PICTURE IS 999B99B9999.
00035            05  FILLER               PICTURE IS X(4).
00036            05      CREDITS          PICTURE IS 99.
00037            05  FILLER               PICTURE IS X(3).
00038            05  PRINT-TUITION        PICTURE IS $$$$,$$9.
00039            05  FILLER               PICTURE IS X.
00040            05  PRINT-UNION-FEE      PICTURE IS $$$$,$$9.
00041            05  FILLER               PICTURE IS X(3).
00042            05  PRINT-ACTIVITY-FEE   PICTURE IS   $$,$$9.
00043            05  FILLER               PICTURE IS X(3).
00044            05  PRINT-SCHOLARSHIP    PICTURE IS $$$$,$$9.
00045            05  FILLER               PICTURE IS X(5).
00046            05  PRINT-IND-BILL       PICTURE IS $$$$,$$9.
00047            05  FILLER               PICTURE IS X(38).
00048
00049        WORKING-STORAGE SECTION.
00050        77  DATA-REMAINS-SWITCH      PICTURE IS X(2)  VALUE SPACES.
00051        77  TUITION                  PICTURE IS 9(4)  VALUE ZEROS.
00052        77  ACTIVITY-FEE             PICTURE IS 9(2)  VALUE ZEROS.
00053        77  UNION-FEE                PICTURE IS 9(2)  VALUE ZEROS.
00054        77  INDIVIDUAL-BILL          PICTURE IS 9(6)  VALUE ZEROS.
00055        77  TOTAL-TUITION            PICTURE IS 9(6)  VALUE ZEROS.
00056        77  TOTAL-SCHOLARSHIP        PICTURE IS 9(6)  VALUE ZEROS.
00057        77  TOTAL-ACTIVITY-FEE       PICTURE IS 9(6)  VALUE ZEROS.
00058        77  TOTAL UNION FEE          PICTURE IS 9(6)  VALUE ZEROS.
00059        77  TOTAL-IND-BILL           PICTURE IS X(6)  VALUE ZEROS.
00060        01  DASHED-LINE.
00061            05  FILLER         PICTURE IS X      VALUE SPACES.
00062            05  FILLER         PICTURE IS X(97)  VALUE ALL '-'.
00063            05  FILLER         PICTURE IS X(35)  VALUE SPACES.
00064        01  HEADER-LINE.
00065            05  FILLER         PICTURE IS X.
00066            05  HDG-NAME       PICTURE IS X(12)  VALUE 'STUDENT NAME'.
00067            05  FILLER         PICTURE IS X(10)  VALUE SPACES
00068            05  HDG-SOC-SEC    PICTURE IS X(11)  VALUE 'SOC SEC NUM'.
00069            05  FILLER         PICTURE IS X(2)   VALUE SPACES.
00070            05  HDG-CREDITS    PICTURE IS X(7)   VALUE 'CREDITS'.
00071            05  FILLER         PICTURE IS X(2)   VALUE SPACES.
00072            05  HDG-TUITION    PICTURE IS X(7)   VALUE 'TUITION'.
00073            05  FILLER         PICTURE IS X(2)   VALUE SPACES.
00074            05  HDG-UNION-FEE  PICTURE IS X(9)   VALUE 'UNION FEE'.
00075            05  FILLER         PICTURE IS X(2)   VALUE SPACES.
00076            05  HDG-ACTIVITY   PICTURE IS X(7)   VALUE 'ACT FEE'.
```

Figure 1.3 *cont.*

```
00077            05  FILLER           PICTURE IS X(2)   VALUE SPACES.
00078            05  HDG-SCHOLAR      PICTURE IS X(11)  VALUE 'SCHOLARSHIP'.
00079            05  FILLER           PICTURE IS X(2)   VALUE SPACES.
00080            05  HDG-TOTAL-BILL   PICTURE IS X(10)  VALUE 'TOTAL BILL'.
00081            05  FILLER           PICTURE IS X(36)  VALUE SPACES.
00082        PROCEDURE DIVISION.
00083        START.
00084            OPEN INPUT CARD-FILE, OUTPUT PRINT-FILE.
00085            MOVE HEADER-LINE TO PRINT-LINE.
00086            WRITE PRINT-LINE AFTER ADVANCING PAGE.
00087            MOVE DASHED-LINE TO PRINT-LINE.
00088            WRITE PRINT-LINE AFTER ADVANCING 1 LINE.
00089            READ CRD-FILE
00090                AT END MOVE 'NO' TO DATA-REMAINS-SWITCH.
00091            PERFORM PROCESS-A-CARD
00092                UNTIL DATA-REMAINS-SWITCH = 'NO'.
00093            PERFORM WRITE-UNIVERSITY-TOTALS.
00094            CLOSE CARD-FILE, PRINT-FILE.
00095            STOP RUN.
00096
00097        PROCESS-A-CARD.
00098            COMPUTE TUITION = 80* CREDITS.
00099            MOVE ZERO TO UNION-FEE.
00100            IF UNION-MEMBER = 'Y' MOVE 25 TO UNION-FEE.
00101            MOVE 25 TO ACTIVITY-FEE.
00102            IF CREDITS > 6 MOVE 50 TO ACTIVITY-FEE.
00103            IF CREDITS > 12 MOVE 75 TO ACTIVITY-FEE.
00104            COMPUTE INDIVIDUAL-BILL = TUITION + UNION-FEE + ACTIVITY-FEE
00105               - SCHOLARSHIP.
00106
00107        *** INCREMENT UNIVERSITY TOTALS
00108            ADD TUITION TO TOTAL-TUITION GIVING TOTAL-TUITION.
00109            ADD UNION-FEE TO TOTAL-UNION-FEE.
00110            ADD ACTIVITY-FEE TO TOTAL-ACTIVITY-FEE.
00111            ADD INDIVIDUAL-BILL TO TOTAL-IND-BILL.
00112            ADD SCHOLARSHIP TO TOTAL-SCHOLARSHIP.
00113
00114        *** WRITE DETAIL LINE
00115            MOVE SPACES TO PRINT-LINE.
00116            MOVE STUDENT-NAME TO PRINT-STUDENT-NAME.
00117            MOVE SOC-SEC-NO TO PRINT-SOC-SEC-NO.
00118            MOVE CREDITS TO PRINT-CREDITS.
00119            MOVE TUITION TO PRINT-TUITION.
00120            MOVE UNION-FEE TO PRINT-UNION-FEE.
00121            MOVE ACTIVITY-FEE TO PRINT-ACTIVITY-FEE.
00122            MOVE SCHOLARSHIP TO PRINT-SCHOLARSHIP.
00123            MOVE INDIVIDUAL-BILL TO PRINT-IND-BILL.
00124            WRITE PRINT-FILE AFTER ADVANCING 1 LINE.
00125
00126            READ CARD-FILE
00127                AT END MOVE 'NO' TO DATA-REMAINS-SWITCH.
00128
00129        WRITE-UNIVERSITY-TOTALS.
00130            MOVE DASHED-LINE TO PRINT-LINE.
00131            WRITE PRINT-LINE AFTER ADVANCING 1 LINE.
00132            MOVE SPACES TO PRINT-LINE.
00133            MOVE TOTAL-TUITION TO PRINT-TUITION.
00134            MOVE TOTAL-UNION-FEE TO PRINT-UNION-FEE.
00135            MOVE TOTAL-ACTIVITY-FEE TO PRINT-ACTIVITY-FEE.
00136            MOVE TOTAL-SCHOLARSHIP TO PRINT-SCHOLARSHIP.
00137            MOVE TOTAL-IND-BILL TO PRINT-IND-BILL.
00138            WRITE PRINT-LINE AFTER ADVANCING 2 LINES.
```

Figure 1.3 *cont.*

CARD	ERROR MESSAGE	
11	IKF2133I-W	LABEL RECORDS CLAUSE MISSING. DD CARD OPTION WILL BE TAKEN.
12	IKF2146I-C	RECORD SIZE IN RECORD-CONTAINS CLAUSE DISAGREES WITH COMPUTED RECORD SIZE. 00131 ASSUMED.
58	IKF1037I-E	UNION INVALID IN DATA DESCRIPTION. SKIPPING TO NEXT CLAUSE.
68	IKF1043I-W	END OF SENTENCE SHOULD PRECEDE 05 . ASSUMED PRESENT.
83	IKF1067I-W	' START ' SHOULD NOT BEGIN A-MARGIN.
83	IKF4050I-E	SYNTAX REQUIRES QISAM-FILE WITH NOMINAL KEY . FOUND END-OF-SENT . STATEMENT DISCARDED.
89	IKF3001I-E	CRD-FILE NOT DEFINED. STATEMENT DISCARDED.
98	IKF1007I-W	ASTERISK NOT PRECEDED BY A SPACE. ASSUME SPACE.
98	IKF3002I-E	CREDITS NOT UNIQUE. DISCARDED.
102	IKF3002I-E	CREDITS NOT UNIQUE. TEST DISCARDED.
103	IKF3002I-E	CREDITS NOT UNIQUE. TEST DISCARDED.
108	IKF4005I-W	SUPERFLUOUS TO FOUND IN ADD STATEMENT. IGNORED.
109	IKF3001I-E	TOTAL-UNION-FEE NOT DEFINED. SUBSTITUTING TALLY .
111	IKF4019I-E	DNM=2-412 (AN) MAY NOT BE USED AS ARITHMETIC OPERAND IN ADD STATEMENT. ARBITRARILY SUBSTITUTING TALLY .
118	IKF3002I-E	CREDITS NOT UNIQUE. DISCARDED.
118	IKF3001I-E	PRINT-CREDITS NOT DEFINED.
124	IKF4050I-E	SYNTAX REQUIRES RECORD-NAME . FOUND DNM=1-244 . STATEMENT DISCARDED.
134	IKF3001I-E	TOTAL-UNION-FEE NOT DEFINED. DISCARDED.

Figure 1.3 *cont.*

```
STUDENT NAME          SOC SEC NUM   CREDITS   TUITION   UNION FEE   ACT FEE   SCHOLARSHIP   TOTAL BILL
------------          -----------   -------   -------   ---------   -------   -----------   ----------
JOHN SMITH            123 45 6789     15      $1,200      $25         $75         $0          $1,300
HENRY JAMES           987 65 4321     15      $1,200       $0         $75       $500            $775
SUSAN BAKER           111 22 3333     09        $720       $0         $50       $500            $270
JOHN PART-TIMER       456 21 3546     03        $240      $25         $25         $0            $290
PEGGY JONES           456 45 6456     15      $1,200      $25         $75         $0          $1,300
H. HEAVY-WORKER       789 52 1234     18      $1,440       $0         $75         $0          $1,515
BENJAMIN LEE          876 87 6876     18      $1,440       $0         $75         $0          $1,515

                                              $7,440      $75        $450     $1,000          $6,965
```

Figure 1.4 Correct Report. (See Exercise 1.4)

```
                                                                    Activity fee should be $75
STUDENT NAME          SOC SEC NUM   CREDITS   TUITION   UNION FEE   ACT FEE   SCHOLARSHIP   TOTAL BILL
------------          -----------   -------   -------   ---------   -------   -----------   ----------
JOHN SMITH            123 45 6789     15      $1,200      $25         $50         $0          $1,275
HENRY JAMES           987 65 4321     15      $1,200       $0         $50         $0            $750
SUSAN BAKER           111 22 3333     09        $720       $0         $50         $0            $270
JOHN PART-TIMER       456 21 3546     03        $240      $25         $25         $0            $290
PEGGY JONES           456 45 6456     15      $1,200      $25         $50         $0          $1,275
H. HEAVY-WORKER       789 52 1234     18      $1,440       $0         $50         $0          $1,490
BENJAMIN LEE          876 87 6876     18      $1,440       $0         $50         $0          $1,490
BENJAMIN LEE          876 87 6876     18      $1,440       $0         $50         $0          $1,490

                                              $8,880       $0        $375        $0          $1,490
         Row of dashes is missing                                                       Total is not correct
                                    Union fee was not summed      Scholarship should be $500
Last student appears twice
```

Figure 1.5 Actual Report. (See Exercise 1.4)

16

Exercise 1.4: Tuition Billing with Logic Errors

The listing in Fig. 1.6 compiled cleanly, but produced execution errors resulting in an incorrect report. Page 16 contains the desired report (Fig. 1.4) followed by the erroneous report (Fig. 1.5) that was actually produced. Find and correct all errors.

```
00001              IDENTIFICATION DIVISION.
00002              PROGRAM-ID.  'TUITION'.
00003              AUTHOR.      THE BURSAR.
00004
00005              ENVIRONMENT DIVISION.
00006              CONFIGURATION SECTION.
00007              SOURCE-COMPUTER.  IBM-370.
00008              OBJECT-COMPUTER.  IBM-370.
00009              INPUT-OUTPUT SECTION.
00010              FILE-CONTROL.
00011                  SELECT CARD-FILE ASSIGN TO UT-S-SYSIN.
00012                  SELECT PRINT-FILE ASSIGN TO UT-S-SYSOUT.
00013
00014              DATA DIVISION.
00015              FILE SECTION.
00016              FD  CARD-FILE
00017                  LABEL RECORDS ARE OMITTED
00018                  RECORD CONTAINS 80 CHARACTERS
00019                  DATA RECORD IS STUDENT-CARD.
00020              01  STUDENT-CARD.
00021                  05  STUDENT-NAME          PICTURE IS A(20).
00022                  05  SOC-SEC-NO            PICTURE IS 9(9).
00023                  05  CREDITS               PICTURE IS 9(2).
00024                  05  UNION-MEMBER          PICTURE IS A.
00025                  05  SCHOLARSHIP           PICTURE IS 9(4).
00026                  05  FILLER                PICTURE IS X(44).
00027              FD  PRINT-FILE
00028                  LABEL RECORDS ARE OMITTED
00029                  RECORD CONTAINS 133 CHARACTERS
00030                  DATA RECORD IS PRINT-LINE.
00031              01  PRINT-LINE.
00032                  05  FILLER                PICTURE IS X.
00033                  05  PRINT-STUDENT-NAME    PICTURE IS A(20).
00034                  05  FILLER                PICTURE IS X(2).
00035                  05  PRINT-SOC-SEC-NO      PICTURE IS 999B99B9999.
00036                  05  FILLER                PICTURE IS X(4).
00037                  05  PRINT-CREDITS         PICTURE IS 99.
00038                  05  FILLER                PICTURE IS X(3).
00039                  05  PRINT-TUITION         PICTURE IS $$$$,$$9.
00040                  05  FILLER                PICTURE IS X.
00041                  05  PRINT-UNION-FEE       PICTURE IS $$$$,$$9.
00042                  05  FILLER                PICTURE IS X(3).
00043                  05  PRINT-ACTIVITY-FEE    PICTURE IS $$$$,$$9.
00044                  05  FILLER                PICTURE IS X(8).
00045                  05  PRINT-SCHOLARSHIP     PICTURE IS      $$9.
00046                  05  FILLER                PICTURE IS X(5).
00047                  05  PRINT-IND-BILL        PICTURE IS $$$$,$$9.
00048                  05  FILLER                PICTURE IS X(38).
00049
00050              WORKING-STORAGE SECTION.
00051              77  DATA-REMAINS-SWITCH   PICTURE IS X(2)  VALUE SPACES.
00052              77  TUITION               PICTURE IS 9(4)  VALUE ZEROS.
00053              77  ACTIVITY-FEE          PICTURE IS 9(2)  VALUE ZEROS.
00054              77  UNION-FEE             PICTURE IS 9(2)  VALUE ZEROS.
```

Figure 1.6 Tuition Program with Logic Errors.

```
00055           77   INDIVIDUAL-BILL            PICTURE IS 9(6)   VALUE ZEROS.
00056           77   TOTAL-TUITION              PICTURE IS 9(6)   VALUE ZEROS.
00057           77   TOTAL-SCHOLARSHIP          PICTURE IS 9(6)   VALUE ZEROS.
00058           77   TOTAL-ACTIVITY-FEE         PICTURE IS 9(6)   VALUE ZEROS.
00059           77   TOTAL-UNION-FEE            PICTURE IS 9(6)   VALUE ZEROS.
00060           77   TOTAL-IND-BILL             PICTURE IS 9(6)   VALUE ZEROS.
00061           01   DASHED-LINE.
00062                05   FILLER           PICTURE IS X        VALUE SPACES.
00063                05   FILLER           PICTURE IS X(97)    VALUE ALL '-'.
00064                05   FILLER           PICTURE IS X(35)    VALUE SPACES.
00065           01   HEADER-LINE.
00066                05   FILLER           PICTURE IS X.
00067                05   HDG-NAME         PICTURE IS X(12)    VALUE 'STUDENT NAME'.
00068                05   FILLER           PICTURE IS X(10)    VALUE SPACES.
00069                05   HDG-SOC-SEC      PICTURE IS X(11)    VALUE 'SOC SEC NUM'.
00070                05   FILLER           PICTURE IS X(2)     VALUE SPACES.
00071                05   HDG-CREDITS      PICTURE IS X(7)     VALUE 'CREDITS'.
00072                05   FILLER           PICTURE IS X(2)     VALUE SPACES.
00073                05   HDG-TUITION      PICTURE IS X(7)     VALUE 'TUITION'.
00074                05   FILLER           PICTURE IS X(2)     VALUE SPACES.
00075                05   HDG-UNION-FEE    PICTURE IS X(9)     VALUE 'UNION FEE'.
00076                05   FILLER           PICTURE IS X(2)     VALUE SPACES.
00077                05   HDG-ACTIVITY     PICTURE IS X(7)     VALUE 'ACT FEE'.
00078                05   FILLER           PICTURE IS X(2)     VALUE SPACES.
00079                05   HDG-SCHOLAR      PICTURE IS X(11)    VALUE 'SCHOLARSHIP'.
00080                05   FILLER           PICTURE IS X(6)     VALUE SPACES.
00081                05   HDG-TOTAL-BILL   PICTURE IS X(10)    VALUE 'TOTAL BILL'.
00082                05   FILLER           PICTURE IS X(36)    VALUE SPACES.
00083           PROCEDURE DIVISION.
00084           MAINLINE.
00085                OPEN INPUT CARD-FILE, OUTPUT PRINT-FILE.
00086                MOVE HEADER-LINE TO PRINT-LINE.
00087                WRITE PRINT-LINE AFTER ADVANCING PAGE.
00088                MOVE DASHED-LINE TO PRINT-LINE.
00089                WRITE PRINT-LINE AFTER ADVANCING 1 LINE.
00090                PERFORM PROCESS-A-CARD
00091                    UNTIL DATA-REMAINS-SWITCH = 'NO'.
00092                PERFORM WRITE-UNIVERSITY-TOTALS.
00093                CLOSE CARD-FILE, PRINT-FILE.
00094                STOP RUN.
00095
00096           PROCESS-A-CARD.
00097                READ CARD-FILE
00098                    AT END MOVE 'NO' TO DATA-REMAINS-SWITCH.
00099                COMPUTE TUITION = 80 * CREDITS.
00100                MOVE ZERO TO UNION-FEE.
00101                IF UNION-MEMBER = 'Y' MOVE 25 TO UNION-FEE.
00102                MOVE 25 TO ACTIVITY-FEE.
00103                IF CREDITS > 12 MOVE 75 TO ACTIVITY-FEE.
00104                IF CREDITS > 6 MOVE 50 TO ACTIVITY-FEE.
00105                COMPUTE INDIVIDUAL-BILL = TUITION + UNION-FEE + ACTIVITY-FEE
00106                    - SCHOLARSHIP.
00107
00108           *** INCREMENT UNIVERSITY TOTALS
00109                ADD TUITION TO TOTAL-TUITION.
00110
00111                ADD ACTIVITY-FEE TO TOTAL-ACTIVITY-FEE.
00112                ADD INDIVIDUAL-BILL TO TOTAL-IND-BILL.
00113                ADD SCHOLARSHIP TO TOTAL-SCHOLARSHIP.
00114
00115           *** WRITE DETAIL LINE
00116                MOVE SPACES TO PRINT-LINE.
00117                MOVE STUDENT-NAME TO PRINT-STUDENT-NAME.
00118                MOVE SOC-SEC-NO TO PRINT-SOC-SEC-NO.
```

Figure 1.6 *cont.*

```
00119            MOVE CREDITS TO PRINT-CREDITS.
00120            MOVE TUITION TO PRINT-TUITION.
00121            MOVE UNION-FEE TO PRINT-UNION-FEE.
00122            MOVE ACTIVITY-FEE TO PRINT-ACTIVITY-FEE.
00123            MOVE SCHOLARSHIP TO PRINT-SCHOLARSHIP.
00124            MOVE INDIVIDUAL-BILL TO PRINT-IND-BILL.
00125            WRITE PRINT-LINE AFTER ADVANCING 1 LINE.
00126
00127        WRITE-UNIVERSITY-TOTALS.
00128            MOVE DASHED-LINE TO PRINT-LINE.
00129
00130            MOVE SPACES TO PRINT-LINE.
00131            MOVE TOTAL-TUITION TO PRINT-TUITION.
00132            MOVE TOTAL-UNION-FEE TO PRINT-UNION-FEE.
00133            MOVE TOTAL-ACTIVITY-FEE TO PRINT-ACTIVITY-FEE.
00134            MOVE TOTAL-SCHOLARSHIP TO PRINT-SCHOLARSHIP.
00135            MOVE INDIVIDUAL-BILL TO PRINT-IND-BILL.
00136            WRITE PRINT-LINE AFTER ADVANCING 2 LINES.
```

Figure 1.6 *cont.*

Solutions to Tuition Billing Problems

Exercise 1.3: Compilation Errors

Card 11 W   LABEL RECORDS CLAUSE MISSING. DD OPTION WILL BE TAKEN...
Card 11 is the SELECT statement for CARD-FILE. The diagnostic, however, refers to the FD for this file in lines 16-18 and, sure enough, the LABEL RECORDS clause has been omitted. Since this a W-level diagnostic, the compiler indicates what action it is taking; in this case it will extract the necessary information from the DD card, a JCL statement (on IBM systems.)

Correction: Insert a statement LABEL RECORDS ARE OMITTED between lines 16 and 17.

Card 12 C   RECORD SIZE IN RECORD-CONTAINS CLAUSE DISAGREES WITH COMPUTED RECORD SIZE...
Card 12 points to the SELECT statement for PRINT-FILE and as before the error is actually in the FD for this file. Line 28 states there are 133 characters in a record, but the actual computed record size from lines 31-47 is 131, hence the message.

Correction: Increase the number of print positions by two, from 131 to 133 by expanding a picture clause; for example, FILLER in line 47.

Card 58 E   "UNION" INVALID IN DATA DESCRIPTION...
Note that in TOTAL UNION FEE in line 58, the -'s between the parts of the name are missing. In COBOL, a data

name is followed by a blank, and the compiler does not know how to handle what it thinks are three data names in a row (TOTAL, UNION, FEE) in line 58.

Correction: Insert -'s to read TOTAL-UNION-FEE.

Card 68 W
END OF SENTENCE SHOULD PRECEDE 05 ...
Any level number must follow a completed statement, but there is no period ending line 67. In this instance, the compiler assumes that the period is present, so no harm is done, but it is poor programming to permit such W-level diagnostics to remain. Moreover, there are situations in which a missing period can be very damaging.

Correction: Insert a period at the end of card 67.

Card 83 E
"START SHOULD NOT BEGIN A-MARGIN ...
A subtle error and one which typically sends the beginner for help. START is intended as a paragraph name, and paragraph names must begin in the A-MARGIN, so what's the problem? START, however, is a reserved word in COBOL, and its usage is severely restricted. It may not be used as a paragraph name.

Correction: Choose another paragraph name; for example, START-THE-PROGRAM.

Card 83 E
SYNTAX REQUIRES QISAM-FILE WITH NOMINAL KEY ...
A most perplexing error and an example of how one mistake can cause several other diagnostics to appear. This error stems from the previous error concerning the word START.

Correction: No action required other than the previous correction.

Card 89 E
CRD-FILE NOT DEFINED. STATEMENT DISCARDED.
Perhaps your initial reaction is that the compiler made a mistake. CARD-FILE is defined with a SELECT statement in line 11 and an FD beginning in line 16. Take another look. Lines 11 and 16 define CARD-FILE, not CRD-FILE. You know they are the same, but the compiler does not.

Correction: Change CRD-FILE to CARD-FILE in statement 89.

Card 98 W
ASTERISK NOT PRECEDED BY A SPACE. ASSUME SPACE.
An easy error to fix. Remember all arithmetic operators,

+, –, *, /, and **, must be preceded and followed by a blank.

Correction: Insert a space before the *.

Card 98 E
102 E
103 E
118 E

CREDITS NOT UNIQUE ...

A message of "not unique" means that there is more than one data item with the same name. In this case, we find CREDITS is defined in line 22 and again in line 36 (it should be PRINT-CREDITS), and the compiler does not know which is which.

Correction: Restore uniqueness to the data name; for example, PRINT-CREDITS in line 36 or use qualification.

Card 108 W

SUPERFLUOUS TO FOUND IN ADD STATEMENT IGNORED ...

Check the syntax of the COBOL ADD verb in Sect. 2 and observe that the TO option is not permitted with the GIVING option.

Correction: Eliminate TO in line 108.

Card 109 E
134 E

TOTAL-UNION-FEE NOT DEFINED ...

Another example of how one error can cause several others. In line 58 the -'s were omitted in the definition of TOTAL-UNION-FEE, thus insofar as the compiler is concerned this data name (TOTAL-UNION-FEE) does not exist.

Correction: These diagnostics will disappear with the correction to line 58.

Card 111 E

DNM=2-412 MAY NOT BE USED AS AN ARITHMETIC OPERAND IN ADD STATEMENT ...

This error becomes easy to understand once we guess that DNM=2-412 refers to TOTAL-IND-BILL in line 111. (In Sect. 7, we shall introduce the data division map, which relates compiler names such as DNM=2-412 to programmer-defined data names.) Observe that in the definition of TOTAL-IND-BILL in line 59 a picture X(6) was specified. This is not a numeric picture which is required in arithmetic operations, hence the error.

Correction: Change X(6) to 9(6) in line 59.

Card 118 E

PRINT-CREDITS NOT DEFINED ...

This diagnostic pertains to the nonunique message from lines 98, 102, 103, and 118.

Correction: If the previous diagnostic is eliminated by distinguishing between CREDITS and PRINT-CREDITS, this message will also disappear.

Card 124 E   SYNTAX REQUIRES RECORD-NAME . . .
Statement 124 is WRITE PRINT-FILE . . . The problem here is that PRINT-FILE is a file-name, not a record-name. Remember, in COBOL one reads a file, but writes a record.

Correction: Statement 124 should read WRITE PRINT-LINE . . .

Exercise 1.4: Logic Errors

The execution errors associated with the Tuition Billing Problem are explained as follows:

1. Missing row of dashes: DASHED-LINE is defined in lines 61-64 and moved to PRINT-LINE in line 128. It is never written, however, as there is no WRITE statement on line 129, PRINT-LINE is cleared in line 130 and eventually a total line is written.
2. The total of all individual bills is incorrect in the total line: TOTAL-IND-BILL is defined in line 60 and correctly incremented for each record in line 112; so far so good. However, when the total line is cleared in line 130, and built in lines 131-135, INDIVIDUAL-BILL rather than TOTAL-IND-BILL is moved to PRINT-IND-BILL in line 135.
3. The total for UNION-FEE is wrong: TOTAL-UNION-FEE is defined and initialized in line 59. However, when the other counters are incremented in lines 109-113, an ADD statement for TOTAL-UNION-FEE is conspicuously absent. (Unlike the previous error, TOTAL-UNION-FEE is moved to PRINT-UNION-FEE in line 132, except TOTAL-UNION-FEE never budged from its initial value of zero, due to the missing ADD statement.)
4. The last record was processed twice: Recall that the skeletal COBOL outline shows an initial READ statement in the mainline paragraph, and a second READ, as the *last* statement in the performed routine. That structure is *correct*. In this exercise the initial READ statement was eliminated, and the second READ *incorrectly* moved to the beginning of the performed routine. To understand the effect, consider a file with only a single record, which is read as the performed routine is entered for the first time. When the end of the routine is reached, the end of file has not yet been sensed; hence, PROCESS-A-CARD is entered a *second* time, even though there is only a single record. The end of file is sensed immediately in line 98, but the perform is not terminated until line 125. Consequently, the intermediate statements are executed a second time for the previous (last) record. The error is corrected by rearranging the READ statements.

5. ACTIVITY-FEE computations are incorrect: Consider the case of John Smith and his 15 credits. The value of ACTIVITY-FEE is initially set to 25 in line 102. Since Smith has more than 12 credits, ACTIVITY-FEE is reset to 75 in line 103 and again reset to 50 in line 104. The problem is simply that lines 103 and 104 are inverted, causing anyone with 6 credits or more to be charged $50. Reversing lines 103 and 104 will set the activity fee to $50 for students with 7-12 credits, and $75 for anyone with more than 12 credits.

6. Individual SCHOLARSHIP is incorrect: This is the *only* error caught by the compiler which flagged lines 123 and 134 with the message: AN INTERMEDIATE RESULT OR A SENDING FIELD MAY HAVE ITS HIGH ORDER DIGIT POSITION TRUNCATED. In line 123, SCHOLARSHIP with picture 9(4) is moved to PRINT-SCHOLARSHIP with picture $$9. The largest value that can appear in the latter field is $99; hence, any scholarship amounts in excess of $99 will have the high order digit eliminated.

EMPLOYEE SELECTION PROBLEM

A personnel administration officer has requested a COBOL program be developed to process a file of employee records and select programmers under 30. Incoming employee records have the following format:

Card Columns	Field	Picture
1-15	Last Name	X(15)
16-24	First Name	X(9)
25	Middle Initial	X
26-35	Job Title	X(10)
36-37	Birth Month	99
38-39	Birth Year	99
40-44	Present Salary	9(5)
45-48	Filler	X(4)
49-53	Previous Salary	9(5)
54-80	Filler	X(27)

The resulting report is to contain only selected employees; programmers under 30. It is to have a suitable heading line(s) and in addition, contain the following fields: last name, age, present salary, previous salary, and percent salary increase. Finally, the total salary for all selected employees is to appear at the report's conclusion.

In the first exercise derived from this problem, you are asked to correct various compilation errors. The second exercise shows a program which compiles cleanly, but produces unexpected and erroneous results.

Exercise 1.5: Employee Selection with Compilation Errors

Correct the compilation errors found in the listing of Fig. 1.7.

```
00001            IDENTIFICATION DIVISION.
00002            PROGRAM-ID.  "SECOND"
00003            AUTHOR.
00004                MARION MILGROM.
00005
00006            ENVIRONMENT DIVISION.
00007            CONFIGURATION SECTION.
00008            SOURCE-COMPUTER.    IBM-370.
00009            OBJECT-COMPUTER.    IBM-370.
00010
00011            INPUT-OUTPUT SECTION.
00012            FILE-CONTROL.
00013                SELECT CARD-FILE ASSIGN TO UT-S-SYSIN.
00014                SELECT PRINT-FILE ASSIGN TO UT-S-SYSOUT.
00015
00016            DATA DIVISION.
00017            FILE SECTION.
00018            FD  CARD-FILE
00019                LABEL RECORDS ARE OMITTED
00020                RECORD CONTAINS 80 CHARACTERS
00021                DATA RECORD IS EMPLOYEE-CARD.
00022            01  EMPLOYEE-CARD.
00023                05  CARD-NAME.
00024                    10   LAST-NAME            PIC X(15)
00025                    10   FIRST-NAME           PIC X(9).
00026                    10   MIDDLE-INITIAL       PIC X.
00027                05  CARD-TITLE                PIC X(10).
00028                05  DATE-OF-BIRTH.
00029                    10   BIRTH-MONTH          PIC 99.
00030                    10   BIRTH-YEAR           PIC 99.
00031                05  PRESENT-SALARY            PIC 9(5).
00032                05  FILLER                    PIC X(4).
00033                05  FORMER-SALARY             PIC 9(5).
00034                05  FILLER                    PIC X(26).
00035            FD  PRINT-FILE
00036                LABEL RECORDS ARE OMITTED
00037                RECORD CONTAINS 133 CHARACTERS
00038                DATA RECORD IS PRINT-LINE.
00039            01  PRINT-LINE                    PIC X(133).
00040
00041            WORKING-STORAGE SECTION.
00042            77  END-OF-DATA-FLAG              PIC XXX     VALUE SPACES.
00043            77  EMPLOYEE-AGE                  PIC 99V9.
00044            77  PERCENT-SALARY-INCREASE       PIC 99V9.
00045            77  TOTAL-SALARY-YOUNG-PROGRAMMERS PIC 9(6)   VALUE ZEROS.
00046            01  DATE-WORK-AREA.
00047                05  TODAYS-YEAR               PIC XX.
00048                05  TODAYS-MONTH              PIC 99.
00049                05  TODAYS-DAY                PIC 99.
00050            01  DASHED-LINE.
00051                05  FILLER                    PIC X(57)   VALUE ALL "-".
00052                05  FILLER                    PIC X(76)   VALUE SPACES.
00053            01  HEADING-LINE.
00054                05  FILLER                    PIC X(10)   VALUE SPACES.
00055                05  FILLER                    PIC X(4)    VALUE "NAME".
00056                05  FILLER                    PIC X(7)    VALUE SPACES.
00057                05  FILLER                    PIC X(3)    VALUE "AGE".
00058                05  FILLER                    PIC X(4)    VALUE SPACES.
```

Figure 1.7 *Cont.*

```
00059              05  FILLER                    PIC X(8)    VALUE "PRES SAL".
00060              05  FILLER                    PIC X(3)    VALUE SPACES.
00061              05  FILLER                    PIC X(7)    VALUE "OLD SAL".
00062              05  FILLER                    PIC X(3)    VALUE SPACES.
00063              05  FILLER                    PIC X(6)    VALUE "% INCR".
00064              05  FILLER                    PIC X(78)   VALUE SPACES.
00065          01  DETAIL-LINE.
00066              05  FILLER                    PIC X(1)    VALUE SPACES.
00067              05  PRINT-LAST-NAME           PIC X(15).
00068              05  FILLER                    PIC X(5)    VALUE SPACES.
00069              05  PRINT-AGE                 PIC 99.9.
00070              05  FILLER                    PIC X(4)    VALUE SPACES.
00071              05  PRINT-PRESENT-SALARY      PIC $99,999.
00072              05  FILLER                    PIC X(3)    VALUE SPACES.
00073              05  PRINT-FORMER-SALARY       PIC $9,999.
00074              05  FILLER                    PIC X(4)    VALUE SPACES.
00075              05  PRINT-PERCENT-INCREASE    PIC ZZ.9.
00076              05  FILLER                    PIC X(81)   VALUE SPACES.
00077          01  TOTAL-LINE.
00078              05  FILLER                    PIC X(12)   VALUE SPACES.
00079              05  FILLER                    PIC X(17)
00080                      VALUE "TOTAL SALARIES =".
00081              05  PRINT TOTAL-SALARIES      PIC  $99,999.
00082              05  FILLER                    PIC X(86)   VALUE SPACES.
00083
00084          PROCEDURE DIVISION.
00085          MAINLINE-ROUTINE.
00086              OPEN INPUT CARD-FILE
00087                   OUTPUT PRINT-FILE.
00088              ACCEPT DATE-WORK-AREA FROM DATE.
00089              MOVE SPACES TO PRINT-LINE.
00090              MOVE "             SALARY REPORT FOR PROGRAMMERS UNDER 30
00091                  TO PRINT-LINE.
00092              WRITE PRINT-LINE AFTER ADVANCING PAGE.
00093              MOVE HEADING-LINE TO PRINT-LINE.
00094              WRITE PRINT-LINE AFTER ADVANCING 3 LINES.
00095              WRITE PRINT-LINE FROM DASHED-LINE.
00096              READ EMPLOYEE-CARD
00097                  AT END MOVE "YES" TO END-OF-DATA-FLAG.
00098              PERFORM PROCESS-EMPLOYEE-RECORDS
00099                  UNTIL END-OF-DATA-FLAG = "YES".
00100              WRITE PRINT-LINE FROM DASHED-LINE AFTER ADVANCING 2 LINES.
00101              MOVE TOTAL-SALARY-YOUNG-PROGRAMMERS TO PRINT-TOTAL-SALARIES.
00102              WRITE PRINT-FILE FROM TOTAL-LINE.
00103              CLOSE CRD-FILE, PRINT-FILE.
00104              STOP RUN.
00105
00106          PROCESS-EMPLOYEE-RECORD.
00107              COMPUTE EMPLOYEE-AGE
00108                  = TODAYS-YEAR - BIRTH-YEAR
00109                  + (TODAYS-MONTH - BIRTH-MONTH) / 12.
00110              COMPUTE PERCENT-SALARY-INCREASE
00111                  = 100 * (PRESENT-SALARY - FORMER-SALARY) / FORMER-SALARY.
00112              IF CARD-TITLE = "PROGRAMMER" AND EMPLOYEE-AGE < 30
00113                  MOVE SPACES                  TO PRINT-LINE
00114                  MOVE CARD-NAME               TO PRINT-LAST-NAME
00115                  MOVE EMPLOYEE-AGE            TO PRINT-AGE
00116                  MOVE PRESENT-SALARY          TO PRINT-PRESENT-SALARY
00117                  MOVE FORMER-SALARY           TO PRINT-FORMER-SALARY
00118                  MOVE PERCENT-SALARY-INCREASE TO PRINT-PERCENT-INCREASE
00119                  WRITE PRINT-LINE FROM DETAIL-LINE AFTER ADVANCING 2 LINES
00120                  ADD PRESENT-SALARY TO TOTAL-SALARY-YOUNG-PROGRAMMERS.
00121              READ CARD-FILE
00122                  AT END MOVE "YES" TO END-OF-DATA-FLAG.
```

Figure 1.7 *Cont.*

CARD	ERROR MESSAGE	
13	IKF2146I-C	RECORD SIZE IN RECORD-CONTAINS CLAUSE DISAGREES WITH COMPUTED RECORD SIZE. 00079 ASSUMED.
25	IKF1043I-W	END OF SENTENCE SHOULD PRECEDE 10 . ASSUMED PRESENT.
81	IKF1037I-E	TOTAL-SALARIES INVALID IN DATA DESCRIPTION. SKIPPING TO NEXT CLAUSE.
90	IKF1098I-C	ALPHA LITERAL NOT CONTINUED WITH HYPHEN AND QUOTE. END LITERAL ON LAST CARD.
91	IKF1007I-W	TO NOT PRECEDED BY A SPACE. ASSUME SPACE.
96	IKF4050I-E	SYNTAX REQUIRES FILE-NAME . FOUND DNM=1-108 . STATEMENT DISCARDED.
98	IKF3001I-E	PROCESS-EMPLOYEE-RECORDS NOT DEFINED. STATEMENT DISCARDED.
101	IKF3001I-E	PRINT-TOTAL-SALARIES NOT DEFINED. DISCARDED.
102	IKF4050I-E	SYNTAX REQUIRES RECORD-NAME . FOUND DNM=1-384 . STATEMENT DISCARDED.
103	IKF3001I-E	CRD-FILE NOT DEFINED. DELETING TILL LEGAL ELEMENT FOUND.
107	IKF4004I-E	DNM=2-67 (AN) IS ILLEGALLY USED IN COMPUTE STATEMENT. DISCARDED.
122	IKF4001I-C	OUTCOME OF A PRECEDING CONDITION LEADS TO NON-EXISTENT 'NEXT SENTENCE'. 'GOBACK' INSERTED.

Figure 1.7 *Cont.*

Exercise 1.6: Employee Selection With Logic Errors

The listing of Fig. 1.8 compiled cleanly, but produced execution errors resulting in an incorrect report. Page 29 contains the desired report (Fig. 1.9) followed by the erroneous report (Fig. 1.10) that was actually produced. Find and correct all errors.

```
00001             IDENTIFICATION DIVISION.
00002             PROGRAM-ID.  "SECOND"
00003             AUTHOR.
00004                 MARION MILGORM.
00005
00006             ENVIRONMENT DIVISION.
00007             CONFIGURATION SECTION.
00008             SOURCE-COMPUTER.    IBM-370.
00009             OBJECT-COMPUTER.    IBM-370.
00010
00011             INPUT-OUTPUT SECTION.
00012             FILE-CONTROL.
00013                 SELECT CARD-FILE ASSIGN TO UT-S-SYSIN.
00014                 SELECT PRINT-FILE ASSIGN TO UT-S-SYSOUT.
00015
00016             DATA DIVISION.
00017             FILE SECTION.
00018             FD  CARD-FILE
00019                 LABEL RECORDS ARE OMITTED
00020                 RECORD CONTAINS 80 CHARACTERS
00021                 DATA RECORD IS EMPLOYEE-CARD.
00022             01  EMPLOYEE-CARD.
00023                 05  CARD-NAME.
00024                     10  LAST-NAME              PIC X(15).
00025                     10  FIRST-NAME             PIC X(9).
00026                     10  MIDDLE-INITIAL         PIC X.
00027                 05  CARD-TITLE                 PIC X(10).
00028                 05  DATE-OF-BIRTH.
00029                     10  BIRTH-MONTH            PIC 99.
00030                     10  BIRTH-YEAR             PIC 99.
00031                 05  PRESENT-SALARY             PIC 9(5).
00032                 05  FILLER                     PIC X(4).
00033                 05  FORMER-SALARY              PIC 9(5).
00034                 05  FILLER                     PIC X(27).
00035             FD  PRINT-FILE
00036                 LABEL RECORDS ARE OMITTED
00037                 RECORD CONTAINS 133 CHARACTERS
00038                 DATA RECORD IS PRINT-LINE.
00039             01  PRINT-LINE                     PIC X(133).
00040
00041             WORKING-STORAGE SECTION.
00042             77  END-OF-DATA-FLAG               PIC XXX       VALUE SPACES.
00043             77  EMPLOYEE-AGE                   PIC 99.
00044             77  PERCENT-SALARY-INCREASE        PIC 99V9.
00045             77  TOTAL-SALARY-YOUNG-PROGRAMMERS PIC 9(6)      VALUE ZEROS.
00046             01  DATE-WORK-AREA.
00047                 05  TODAYS-YEAR                PIC 99.
00048                 05  TODAYS-MONTH               PIC 99.
00049                 05  TODAYS-DAY                 PIC 99.
00050             01  DASHED-LINE.
00051                 05  FILLER                     PIC X(57)     VALUE ALL "-".
00052                 05  FILLER                     PIC X(76)     VALUE SPACES.
00053             01  HEADING-LINE.
00054                 05  FILLER                     PIC X(10)     VALUE SPACES.
00055                 05  FILLER                     PIC X(4)      VALUE "NAME".
```

Figure 1.8 Selection Program with Logic Errors.

27

```
00056              05  FILLER                    PIC X(7)    VALUE SPACES.
00057              05  FILLER                    PIC X(3)    VALUE "AGE".
00058              05  FILLER                    PIC X(4)    VALUE SPACES.
00059              05  FILLER                    PIC X(8)    VALUE "PRES SAL".
00060              05  FILLER                    PIC X(3)    VALUE SPACES.
00061              05  FILLER                    PIC X(7)    VALUE "OLD SAL".
00062              05  FILLER                    PIC X(3)    VALUE SPACES.
00063              05  FILLER                    PIC X(6)    VALUE "% INCR".
00064              05  FILLER                    PIC X(78)   VALUE SPACES.
00065          01  DETAIL-LINE.
00066              05  FILLER                    PIC X(1)    VALUE SPACES.
00067              05  PRINT-LAST-NAME           PIC X(15).
00068              05  FILLER                    PIC X(5)    VALUE SPACES.
00069              05  PRINT-AGE                 PIC 99.9.
00070              05  FILLER                    PIC X(4)    VALUE SPACES.
00071              05  PRINT-PRESENT-SALARY      PIC $99,999.
00072              05  FILLER                    PIC X(3)    VALUE SPACES.
00073              05  PRINT-FORMER-SALARY       PIC $99,999.
00074              05  FILLER                    PIC X(4)    VALUE SPACES.
00075              05  PRINT-PERCENT-INCREASE    PIC ZZ.9.
00076              05  FILLER                    PIC X(81)   VALUE SPACES.
00077          01  TOTAL-LINE.
00078              05  FILLER                    PIC X(12)   VALUE SPACES.
00079              05  FILLER                    PIC X(17)
00080                      VALUE "TOTAL SALARIES =".
00081              05  PRINT-TOTAL-SALARIES      PIC $999,999.
00082              05  FILLER                    PIC X(86)   VALUE SPACES.
00083
00084       PROCEDURE DIVISION.
00085       MAINLINE-ROUTINE.
00086           OPEN INPUT CARD-FILE
00087               OUTPUT PRINT-FILE.
00088           ACCEPT DATE-WORK-AREA FROM DATE.
00089           MOVE SPACES TO PRINT-LINE.
00090           MOVE "              SALARY REPORT FOR PROGRAMMERS UNDER 30"
00091               TO PRINT-LINE.
00092           WRITE PRINT-LINE AFTER ADVANCING PAGE.
00093           MOVE HEADING-LINE TO PRINT-LINE.
00094
00095           WRITE PRINT-LINE FROM DASHED-LINE AFTER ADVANCING 1 LINE.
00096           READ CARD-FILE
00097               AT END MOVE "YES" TO END-OF-DATA-FLAG.
00098           PERFORM PROCESS-EMPLOYEE-RECORDS
00099               UNTIL END-OF-DATA-FLAG = "YES".
00100           WRITE PRINT-LINE FROM DASHED-LINE AFTER ADVANCING 2 LINES.
00101           MOVE TOTAL-SALARY-YOUNG-PROGRAMMERS TO PRINT-TOTAL-SALARIES.
00102           WRITE PRINT-LINE FROM TOTAL-LINE.
00103           CLOSE CARD-FILE, PRINT-FILE.
00104           STOP RUN.
00105
00106       PROCESS-EMPLOYEE-RECORDS.
00107           COMPUTE EMPLOYEE-AGE
00108               = TODAYS-YEAR - BIRTH-YEAR
00109               + (TODAYS-MONTH - BIRTH-MONTH) / 12.
00110           COMPUTE PERCENT-SALARY-INCREASE
00111               = (PRESENT-SALARY - FORMER-SALARY) / FORMER-SALARY.
00112           IF CARD-TITLE = "PROGRAMMER" AND EMPLOYEE-AGE < 30
00113               MOVE SPACES              TO PRINT-LINE
00114               MOVE CARD-NAME           TO PRINT-LAST-NAME
00115               MOVE EMPLOYEE-AGE        TO PRINT-AGE
00116               MOVE PRESENT-SALARY      TO PRINT-PRESENT-SALARY
00117               MOVE FORMER-SALARY       TO PRINT-FORMER-SALARY
00118               MOVE PERCENT-SALARY-INCREASE TO PRINT-PERCENT-INCREASE
00119               WRITE PRINT-LINE FROM DETAIL-LINE AFTER ADVANCING 1 LINE.
00120               ADD PRESENT-SALARY TO TOTAL-SALARY-YOUNG-PROGRAMMERS.
00121           READ CARD-FILE
00122               AT END MOVE "YES" TO END-OF-DATA-FLAG.
```

Figure 1.8 *Cont.*

```
            SALARY REPORT FOR PROGRAMMERS UNDER 30

            NAME            AGE     PRES SAL    OLD SAL     % INCR
    ------------------------------------------------------------------

    SMITH                   25.0    $15,000     $14,100      6.3

    SUPERPROGRAMMER         23.5    $39,000     $34,000     14.7

    LEE                     27.7    $12,000     $11,000      9.0

    MILGROM                 25.0    $10,000     $08,500     17.6
    ------------------------------------------------------------------
                TOTAL SALARIES = $076,000
```

Figure 1.9 Correct Report.

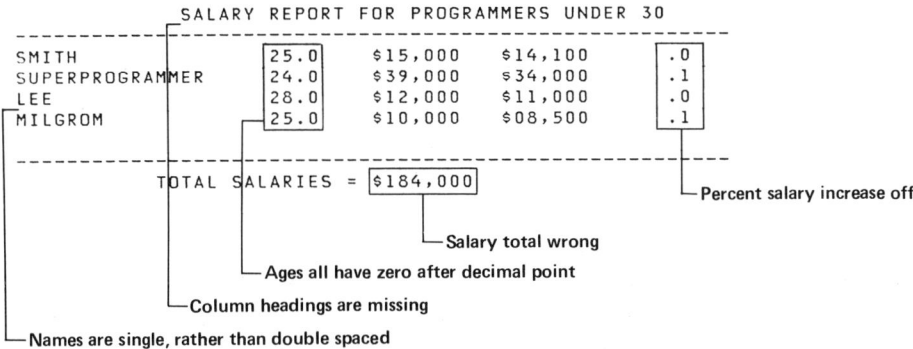

Figure 1.10 Actual Report

Solutions to Employee Selection Problem

Exercise 1.5: Compilation Errors

Card 13 C   RECORD SIZE IN RECORD CONTAINS CLAUSE DIS-AGREES WITH COMPUTED RECORD SIZE.
Statement 13 is the SELECT statement for CARD-FILE, but the error is actually in the FD for the file. Line 20 says that EMPLOYEE-CARD contains 80 characters, but the associated picture clauses sum to 79, hence the problem.

Correction: Change the PICTURE clause in line 34 to PIC X(27).

Card 25 W   END OF SENTENCE SHOULD PRECEDE 10. ASSUMED PRESENT.
Any level number must follow a completed statement, but there is no period to end line 24. In this instance, the compiler assumes that the period is present, so no harm is done, but it is poor programming to permit W-level diagnostics to remain. Moreover, there are situations in which a missing period can be very damaging.

Correction: Insert a period at the end of line 24.

Card 81 E   TOTAL-SALARIES INVALID IN DATA DESCRIPTION.
Line 81, like so many other lines in the Data Division, merely defines an elementary item. Why then was it flagged? The answer is that the data name itself is invalid, a hyphen was omitted and hence the compiler thinks it has two data names for a single level number and picture.

Correction: Insert a hyphen between PRINT and TOTAL in line 81.

Card 90 C   ALPHA LITERAL NOT CONTINUED WITH HYPHEN AND QUOTE. END LITERAL ON LAST CARD.
This message refers to a non-numeric (alpha) literal in statement 90. There is a beginning quote, but no ending quote. The compiler looks for continuation of the literal on the next card, line 91, but fails to find a hyphen in column 7 and a continuing quote, hence the error.

Correction: Put a closing quote on line 90.

Card 91 W   TO NOT PRECEDED BY A SPACE. ASSUME SPACE.
A rather puzzling error, caused by the error in the previous statement.

Correction: None required beyond fixing line 90.

Getting Started in COBOL **31**

Card 96 E	SYNTAX REQUIRES FILE-NAME. FOUND DNM=1–108 STATEMENT DISCARDED.
Line 96 is a READ statement and COBOL requires that one read a file, not a record. In other words, READ should be followed by a file-name, CARD-FILE, rather than the associated record-name. (The rather cryptic note, DNM=1–108 is the way the compiler references EMPLOYEE-CARD.)
Correction: Change EMPLOYEE-CARD to CARD-FILE in line 96.

Card 98 E	PROCESS-EMPLOYEE-RECORDS NOT DEFINED. STATEMENT DISCARDED.
Line 98 is a PERFORM statement for PROCESS-EMPLOYEE-RECORDS, but the compiler was unable to find the referenced paragraph. What about line 106? Look again-it's missing the letter S after RECORD. A person would assume that the PERFORM is in fact referring to line 106, but the compiler does not make assumptions. It requires total 100% agreement.
Correction: Make lines 98 and 106 consistent either by adding the S in line 106, or deleting it in line 98.

Card 101 E	PRINT-TOTAL-SALARIES NOT DEFINED. DISCARDED.
A good example of how one error can cause other errors in otherwise perfect statements. Statement 81 was previously flagged because of the omitted hyphen; hence PRINT-TOTAL-SALARIES was not defined as intended in line 81 and any subsequent reference to it is invalid.
Correction: None required besides the fix for line 81.

Card 102 E	SYNTAX REQUIRES RECORD-NAME. FOUND DNM=1–384. STATEMENT DISCARDED.
Analogous to the error in line 96. COBOL requires that one read a file, but write a record. All WRITE statements, therefore, should specify a record-name (PRINT-LINE), rather than a file name. (DNM=1–384 is the compiler's way of referring to PRINT-FILE.)
Correction: Change PRINT-FILE to PRINT-LINE in line 102.

Card 103 E	CRD-FILE NOT DEFINED. DELETING TILL LEGAL ELEMENT FOUND.
Another case of the compiler doing exactly what it is told, and nothing more. A person would realize that CRD-FILE

in line 103 refers to CARD-FILE previously defined in a SELECT and FD. The compiler doesn't, because CRD-FILE and CARD-FILE are different.

Correction: Substitute CARD-FILE for CRD-FILE in line 103.

Card 107 E   DNM=2-67 (AN) IS ILLEGALLY USED IN COMPUTE STATEMENT. DISCARDED.

Arithmetic should logically be done only on numeric fields: those data names with pictures of 9's and an optional implied decimal point or sign. The presence of any other character in a picture clause implies that the field is non-numeric, and therefore ineligible for inclusion in a COMPUTE statement. The compiler is flagging DNM=2-67 as having an alphanumeric (AN) picture. A little checking shows that TODAYS-YEAR is the offender.

Correction: Change the picture of TODAYS-YEAR in line 47 from XX to 99.

Card 122 C   OUTCOME OF A PRECEDING CONDITION LEADS TO NON-EXISTENT NEXT SENTENCE. ...

This is a rather perplexing error as nothing is wrong with the READ statement of line 122. Recall however that the PERFORM statement of line 98 was previously flagged and discarded. Consequently line 122 is no longer part of a PERFORM and hence there is no next statement to execute.

Correction: None required beside the previous fix to line 98.

Exercise 1.6: Logic Errors

The execution errors associated with the Employee Selection Problem of Fig. 1.8 are corrected as follows:

1. Missing column headings: Column headings are defined in the 01 entry HEADING-LINE, COBOL statements 53-64. HEADING-LINE in turn is moved to PRINT-LINE in line 93, but the statement to actually write this line is missing. In other words, a print line was built by the MOVE statement but never written. Notice that line 94 is blank in the exercise and is where the missing statement should go.

2. Incorrect salary total: Errors of this kind are fairly easy to spot when only four records are included in the total, but extremely difficult with sums consisting of many records. This particular problem is due to the presence of an *extra* period in line 119 which terminates

the IF. Accordingly, the salaries of *all* records in the file, not just those of programmers under 30, are included in the total. The problem is easily corrected by removing the period in line 119.

3. Incorrect age calculation: PRINT-AGE, defined in line 69 as PIC 99.9 contains the printed value of age. EMPLOYEE-AGE, defined in line 43 as PIC 99, holds the calculated value for age as determined by the COMPUTE statement of line 107. The problem arises because of an inconsistency between the two picture clauses. In effect we are printing a field containing a decimal point, PRINT-AGE (PIC 99.9) *without* having calculated a decimal value; EMPLOYEE-AGE has a picture of 99, but *should* have had a picture of 99V9 instead. The computer is not a mind reader and follows instructions to the letter. It was not told to retain a decimal for EMPLOYEE-AGE, so it didn't. The fact that this field is subsequently moved to one containing a decimal point is immaterial.

4. Incorrect percent salary increase: A similar error, but quite common. Percent salary increase is defined as the difference between an employee's present salary and previous salary, divided by his previous salary. To convert this fraction to a percent, requires multiplication by 100, hence the error. The COMPUTE statement of lines 110-111 omitted the multiplication.

5. Names are single, rather than double spaced—a fairly trivial error, but nonetheless an important one to the end user who requested the report in the first place. It is corrected by specifying 2 LINES in the WRITE statement of line 119.

PAYROLL PROBLEM

Use this description for Exercises 1.7 and 1.8. A COBOL program is required to compute a company payroll. Incoming data for each employee are punched on cards according to the format:

Columns	Field	Picture
1-25	Employee-Name	A(25)
26-30	Hours-Worked	9(3)V99
31-35	Hourly-Rate	9(3)V99

An individual receives straight time for the first 40 hours worked, time and a half for the next 8 hours, and double time for each hour over 48. For example, an employee earning $7.00/hour and working 49 hours would receive $378 as calculated on page 34.

Straight time	40 hours @ $ 7.00	$280
Time and a half	8 hours @ $10.50	$ 84
Double time	1 hour @ $14.00	$ 14
	Gross Pay	$378

Federal income taxes are computed according to the schedule:

	Gross Pay	Tax
	$240 or less	16% of Gross
More than	$240, but less than $300	$42 + 20% of amount over $240
	$300 or more	$60 + 22% of amount over $300

Thus, individuals with gross wages of $200, $276, and $378, would pay $32.00, $49.20, and $77.16 respectively.

The completed program is to process a file of employee records and for each employee, compute, and print: gross pay, federal tax, and net pay. Company totals are also required for these fields as is a suitable heading line.

The first exercise associated with this problem asks you to correct various compilation errors. The second exercise shows both intended and actual output of a correctly compiled program. You are asked to identify and correct the logic errors. Finally, review the program specifications and see if you can find an inconsistency.

Exercise 1.7: Payroll Program with Compilation Errors

Correct the compilation errors found in the listing in Fig. 1.11.

```
00001          IDENTIFICATION DIVISION.
00002          PROGRAM-ID. 'PAYROLL'.
00003          AUTHOR.
00004              MARION MILGROM.
00005
00006          ENVIRONMENT DIVISION.
00007          CONFIGURATION SECTION.
00008          SOURCE-COMPUTER.    IBM-370.
00009          OBJECT-COMPUTER.    IBM-370.
00010
00011          INPUT-OUTPUT SECTION.
00012          FILE-CONTROL.
00013              SELECT CARD-FILE ASSIGN TO UT-S-SYSIN.
00014              SELECT PRINT-FILE ASSIGN TO UT-S-SYSOUT.
00015
00016          DATA DIVISION.
00017          FILE SECTION.
00018          FD  CARD-FILE
00019              LABEL RECORDS ARE OMITTED
```

Figure 1.11 Payroll Program with Compilation Errors.

```
00020               RECORD CONTAINS 80 CHARACTERS
00021               DATA RECORD IS CARD.
00022           01  CARD.
00023               05  CARD-NAME               PIC A(25).
00024               05  CARD-HOURS              PIC 9(3)V99.
00025               05  CARD-RATE               PIC 9(3)V99.
00026               05  FILLER                  PIC X(44).
00027
00028           FD  PRINT-FILE
00029               LABEL RECORDS ARE OMITTED
00030               RECORD CONTAINS 133 CHARACTERS
00031               DATA RECORD IS PRINT-LINE.
00032           01  PRINT-LINE.
00033
00034               05  FILLER                  PIC X.
00035               05  PRINT-NAME              PIC X(25).
00036               05  FILLER                  PIC X(3).
00037               05  PRINT-HOURS             PIC ZZZZV99.
00038               05  FILLER                  PIC X(3).
00039               05  PRINT-RATE              PIC $$$$.99.
00040               05  FILLER                  PIC X(3).
00041               05  PRINT-GROSS             PIC $$$$$.99
00042               05  FILLER                  PIC X(5).
00043               05  PRINT-FED-TAX           PIC $$$$$.99.
00044               05  FILLER                  PIC X(4).
00045               05  PRINT-NET               PIC $$$$$.99.
00046               05  FILLER                  PIC X(51).
00047           WORKING-STORAGE SECTION.
00048           01  DATA-REMAINS-SWITCH         PIC X(3)    VALUE 'YES'.
00049
00050           01  INDIVIDUAL-COMPUTATIONS.
00051               05  IND-GROSS-PAY           PIC 9(4)V99.
00052               05  IND-FED-TAX             PIC 9(4)V99.
00053               05  IND-NET-PAY             PIC 9(4)V99.
00054
00055           01  COMPANY-TOTALS.
00056               05  COMP-GROSS-PAY          PIC 9(5)V99 VALUE ZEROS.
00057               05  COMP-FED-TAX            PIC 9(5)V99 VALUE ZEROS.
00058               05  COMP-NET-PAY            PIC 9(5)V99 VALUE ZEROS.
00059
00060           01  HEADING-LINE.
00061               05  FILLER                  PIC X(8)    VALUE SPACES.
00062               05  FILLER                  PIC X(4)    VALUE 'NAME'.
00063               05  FILLER                  PIC X(19)   VALUE SPACES.
00064               05  FILLER                  PIC X(5)    VALUE 'HOURS'.
00065               05  FILLER                  PIC X(5)    VALUE SPACES.
00066               05  FILLER                  PIC X(4)    VALUE 'RATE'.
00067               05  FILLER                  PIC X(6)    VALUE SPACES.
00068               05  FILLER                  PIC X(9)    VALUE 'GROSS PAY'.
00069               05  FILLER                  PIC X(5)    VALUE SPACES.
00070               05  FILLER                  PIC X(7)    VALUE 'FED TAX'.
00071               05  FILLER                  PIC X(5)    VALUE SPACES.
00072               05  FILLER                  PIC X(7)    VALUE 'NET PAY'.
00073               05  FILLER                  PIC X(50)   VALUE SPACES.
00074
00075           01  TOTAL-LINE.
00076               05  FILLER                  PIC X(34)   VALUE SPACES.
00077               05  FILLER                  PIC X(13)   VALUE 'TOTAL'.
00078               05  PRINT-CO-GROSS          PIC $$$,$$$.99.
00079               05  FILLER                  PIC X(3)    VALUE SPACES.
00080               05  PRINT-CO-FED-TAX        PIC $$$,$$$.99.
00081               05  FILLER                  PIC X(3)    VALUE SPACES.
00082               05  PRINT-CO-NET            PIC $$$,$$$.99.
00083               05  FILLER                  PIC X(48)   VALUE SPACES.
00084           PROCEDURE DIVISION.
```

Figure 1.11 *Cont.*

```
00085           MAINLINE.
00086               OPEN INPUT CARD-FILE
00087                   OUTPUT PRINT-FILE.
00088               READ CARD-FILE
00089                   AT END MOVE 'NO' TO DATA-REMAINS-SWITCH.
00090               MOVE HEADER-LINE TO PRINT-LINE.
00091               WRITE PRINT-LINE AFTER ADVANCING PAGE.
00092               PERFORM PROCESS-CARDS
00093                   UNTIL DATA-REMAINS-SWITCH = 'NO'.
00094               PERFORM WRITE-TOTAL-LINE.
00095               CLOSE CARD-FILE
00096                   PRINT-FILE.
00097               STOP RUN.
00098
00099           PROCESS-CARD.
00100               COMPUTE IND-GROSS-PAY = CARD-HOURS * CARD-RATE.
00101               IF CARD-HOURS>40
00102                   COMPUTE IND-GROSS-PAY =
00103                       IND-GROSS-PAY + (CARD-HOURS  - 40) * .5 * CARD-RATE.
00104               IF CARD-HOURS > 48
00105                   COMPUTE IND-GROSS-PAY =
00106                       IND-GROSS-PAY + (CARD-HOURS  - 48) * .5 * CARD-RATE.
00107               IF IND-GROSS-PAY > 300
00108                 COMPUTE IND-FED-TAX = 60 + .22 * (IND-GROSS-PAY - 300)
00109               ELSE
00110                   IF IND-GROSS-PAY > 240
00111                       COMPUTE IND-FED-TAX = 42 + .20 * (IND-GROSS-PAY - 240)
00112                   ELSE
00113                       COMPUTE IND-FED-TAX = .16 * IND-GROSS-PAY.
00114
00115               SUBTRACT IND-FED-TAX FROM IND-GROSS-PAY
00116                   GIVING IND-NET-PAY.
00117
00118               ADD IND-GROSS-PAY TO COMP-GROSS-PAY.
00119               ADD IND-FED-TAX TO COMP-FED-TAX.
00120               ADD IND-NET-PAY TO COMP-NET-PAY.
00121
00122               MOVE SPACES TO PRINT LINE.
00123               MOVE CARD-NAME TO PRINT-NAME.
00124               MOVE CARD-HOURS TO PRINT-HOURS.
00125               MOVE CARD-RATE TO PRINT-RATE.
00126               MOVE IND-GROSS-PAY TO PRINT-GROSS.
00127               MOVE IND-FED-TAX TO PRINT-FED-TAX.
00128               MOVE IND-NET-PAY TO PRINT-NET-PAY.
00129               WRITE PRINT-LINE
00130                       ADVANCING 2 LINES.
00131
00132               READ CARD
00133                   AT END MOVE 'NO' TO DATA-REMAINS-SWITCH.
00134
00135           WRITE-TOTAL-LINE.
00136               MOVE COMP-GROSS-PAY TO PRINT-CO-GROSS.
00137               MOVE COMP-FED-TAX TO PRINT-CO-FED-TAX.
00138               MOVE COMP-NET-PAY TO PRINT-CO-NET.
00139               MOVE TOTAL-LINE TO PRINT-LINE.
00140               WRITE PRINT-FILE
00141                   AFTER ADVANCING 2 LINES.
```

Figure 1.11 *Cont.*

CARD	ERROR MESSAGE	
13	IKF2146I-C	RECORD SIZE IN RECORD-CONTAINS CLAUSE DISAGREES WITH COMPUTED RECORD SIZE. 00079 ASSUMED.
14	IKF2146I-C	RECORD SIZE IN RECORD-CONTAINS CLAUSE DISAGREES WITH COMPUTED RECORD SIZE. 00132 ASSUMED.
42	IKF1043I-W	END OF SENTENCE SHOULD PRECEDE 05 . ASSUMED PRESENT.
90	IKF3001I-E	HEADER-LINE NOT DEFINED. DISCARDED.
92	IKF3001I-E	PROCESS-CARDS NOT DEFINED. STATEMENT DISCARDED.
102	IKF1007I-W	GREATER NOT PRECEDED BY A SPACE. ASSUME SPACE.
102	IKF1007I-W	40 NOT PRECEDED BY A SPACE. ASSUME SPACE.
128	IKF3001I-E	PRINT-NET-PAY NOT DEFINED. DISCARDED.
129	IKF4003I-E	EXPECTING NEW STATEMENT. FOUND ADVANCING . DELETING TILL NEXT VERB OR PROCEDURE-NAME.
132	IKF4050I-E	SYNTAX REQUIRES FILE-NAME . FOUND DNM=1-112 . STATEMENT DISCARDED.
140	IKF4050I-E	SYNTAX REQUIRES RECORD-NAME . FOUND DNM=1-198 . STATEMENT DISCARDED.

Figure 1.11 *Cont.*

Exercise 1.8: Payroll Program with Logic Errors

The listing of Fig. 1.12 compiled cleanly, but produced execution errors resulting in an incorrect report. Page 40 contains the desired report (Fig. 1.13) followed by the erroneous report (Fig. 1.14) which was actually produced. Find and correct all errors.

```
00001           IDENTIFICATION DIVISION.
00002           PROGRAM-ID. 'PAYROLL'.
00003           AUTHOR.
00004               MARION MILGROM.
00005
00006           ENVIRONMENT DIVISION.
00007           CONFIGURATION SECTION.
00008           SOURCE-COMPUTER.    IBM-370.
00009           OBJECT-COMPUTER.    IBM-370.
00010
00011           INPUT-OUTPUT SECTION.
00012           FILE-CONTROL.
00013               SELECT CARD-FILE ASSIGN TO UT-S-SYSIN.
00014               SELECT PRINT-FILE ASSIGN TO UT-S-SYSOUT.
00015
00016           DATA DIVISION.
00017           FILE SECTION.
00018           FD  CARD-FILE
00019               LABEL RECORDS ARE OMITTED
00020               RECORD CONTAINS 80 CHARACTERS
00021               DATA RECORD IS CARD.
00022           01  CARD.
00023               05  CARD-NAME              PIC A(25).
00024               05  CARD-HOURS             PIC 9(3)V99.
00025               05  CARD-RATE              PIC 9(3)V99.
00026               05  FILLER                 PIC X(45).
00027
00028           FD  PRINT-FILE
00029               LABEL RECORDS ARE OMITTED
00030               RECORD CONTAINS 133 CHARACTERS
00031               DATA RECORD IS PRINT-LINE.
00032           01  PRINT-LINE.
00033
00034               05  PRINT-NAME             PIC X(25).
00035               05  FILLER                 PIC X(3).
00036               05  PRINT-HOURS            PIC ZZZZ.99.
00037               05  FILLER                 PIC X(3).
00038               05  PRINT-RATE             PIC $$$$.99.
00039               05  FILLER                 PIC X(3).
00040               05  PRINT-GROSS            PIC $$$$$.99.
00041               05  FILLER                 PIC X(5).
00042               05  PRINT-FED-TAX          PIC $$$$$.99.
00043               05  FILLER                 PIC X(5).
00044               05  PRINT-NET-PAY          PIC $$$$$.99.
00045               05  FILLER                 PIC X(51).
00046           WORKING-STORAGE SECTION.
00047           01  DATA-REMAINS-SWITCH        PIC X(3)    VALUE 'YES'.
00048
00049           01  INDIVIDUAL-COMPUTATIONS.
00050               05  IND-GROSS-PAY          PIC 9(4).
00051               05  IND-FED-TAX            PIC 9(4).
00052               05  IND-NET-PAY            PIC 9(4).
00053
00054           01  COMPANY-TOTALS.
00055               05  COMP-GROSS-PAY         PIC 9(5)V99 VALUE ZEROS.
00056               05  COMP-FED-TAX           PIC 9(5)V99 VALUE ZEROS.
```

Figure 1.12 Payroll Program with Logic Errors.

```
00057              05  COMP-NET-PAY          PIC 9(5)V99 VALUE ZEROS.
00058
00059          01  HEADING-LINE.
00060              05  FILLER                PIC X(8)    VALUE SPACES.
00061              05  FILLER                PIC X(4)    VALUE 'NAME'.
00062              05  FILLER                PIC X(19)   VALUE SPACES.
00063              05  FILLER                PIC X(5)    VALUE 'HOURS'.
00064              05  FILLER                PIC X(5)    VALUE SPACES.
00065              05  FILLER                PIC X(4)    VALUE 'RATE'.
00066              05  FILLER                PIC X(6)    VALUE SPACES.
00067              05  FILLER                PIC X(9)    VALUE 'GROSS PAY'.
00068              05  FILLER                PIC X(5)    VALUE SPACES.
00069              05  FILLER                PIC X(7)    VALUE 'FED TAX'.
00070              05  FILLER                PIC X(5)    VALUE SPACES.
00071              05  FILLER                PIC X(7)    VALUE 'NET PAY'.
00072              05  FILLER                PIC X(50)   VALUE SPACES.
00073
00074          01  TOTAL-LINE.
00075              05  FILLER                PIC X(34)   VALUE SPACES.
00076              05  FILLER                PIC X(13)   VALUE 'TOTAL'.
00077              05  PRINT-CO-GROSS        PIC $$$,$$$.99.
00078              05  FILLER                PIC X(3)    VALUE SPACES.
00079              05  PRINT-CO-FED-TAX      PIC $$$,$$$.99.
00080              05  FILLER                PIC X(3)    VALUE SPACES.
00081              05  PRINT-CO-NET          PIC $$$,$$$.99.
00082              05  FILLER                PIC X(48)   VALUE SPACES.
00083          PROCEDURE DIVISION.
00084          MAINLINE.
00085              OPEN INPUT CARD-FILE
00086                   OUTPUT PRINT-FILE.
00087              READ CARD-FILE
00088                   AT END MOVE 'NO' TO DATA-REMAINS-SWITCH
00089              MOVE HEADING-LINE TO PRINT-LINE
00090              WRITE PRINT-LINE AFTER ADVANCING PAGE.
00091              PERFORM PROCESS-CARDS
00092                   UNTIL DATA-REMAINS-SWITCH = 'NO'.
00093              PERFORM WRITE-TOTAL-LINE.
00094              CLOSE CARD-FILE
00095                    PRINT-FILE.
00096              STOP RUN.
00097
00098          PROCESS-CARDS.
00099              COMPUTE IND-GROSS-PAY = CARD-HOURS * CARD-RATE.
00100              IF CARD-HOURS > 40
00101                  COMPUTE IND-GROSS-PAY =
00102                     IND-GROSS-PAY + (CARD-HOURS  - 40) * 1.5 * CARD-RATE.
00103              IF CARD-HOURS > 48
00104                  COMPUTE IND-GROSS-PAY =
00105                     IND-GROSS-PAY + (CARD-HOURS  - 48) * 2.0 * CARD-RATE.
00106              IF IND-GROSS-PAY > 300
00107                  COMPUTE IND-FED-TAX = 60 + .22 * (IND-GROSS-PAY - 300)
00108              ELSE
00109                  IF IND-GROSS-PAY > 240
00110                      COMPUTE IND-FED-TAX = 42 + .20 * (IND-GROSS-PAY - 240)
00111                  ELSE
00112                      COMPUTE IND-FED-TAX = .16 * IND-GROSS-PAY.
00113
00114              SUBTRACT IND-FED-TAX FROM IND-GROSS-PAY
00115                  GIVING IND-NET-PAY.
00116
00117              ADD IND-GROSS-PAY COMP-GROSS-PAY GIVING COMP-GROSS-PAY.
00118              ADD IND-FED-TAX TO COMP-FED-TAX.
00119              ADD IND-NET-PAY TO COMP-NET-PAY.
00120
00121              MOVE SPACES TO PRINT-LINE.
00122              MOVE CARD-NAME TO PRINT-NAME.
```

Figure 1.12 *Cont.*

```
00123            MOVE CARD-HOURS TO PRINT-HOURS.
00124            MOVE CARD-RATE TO PRINT-RATE.
00125            MOVE IND-GROSS-PAY TO PRINT-GROSS.
00126            MOVE IND-FED-TAX TO PRINT-FED-TAX.
00127            MOVE COMP-NET-PAY TO PRINT-NET-PAY.
00128            WRITE PRINT-LINE
00129                AFTER ADVANCING 2 LINES.
00130
00131            READ CARD-FILE
00132                AT END MOVE 'NO' TO DATA-REMAINS-SWITCH.
00133
00134        WRITE-TOTAL-LINE.
00135            MOVE COMP-GROSS-PAY TO PRINT-CO-GROSS.
00136            MOVE COMP-FED-TAX TO PRINT-CO-FED-TAX.
00137            MOVE COMP-NET-PAY TO PRINT-CO-NET.
00138            MOVE TOTAL-LINE TO PRINT-LINE.
00139            WRITE PRINT-LINE
00140                AFTER ADVANCING 2 LINES.
```

Figure 1.12 *Cont.*

NAME	HOURS	RATE	GROSS PAY	FED TAX	NET PAY
SMITH	40.00	$5.00	$200.00	$32.00	$168.00
JONES	44.00	$6.00	$276.00	$49.20	$226.80
PETERS	49.00	$7.00	$378.00	$77.16	$300.84
HANSEN	36.00	$5.55	$199.80	$31.96	$167.84
MILGROM	42.00	$10.14	$436.02	$89.92	$346.10
TATAR	40.00	$4.33	$173.20	$27.71	$145.49
TOTAL			$1,663.02	$307.95	$1,355.07

Figure 1.13 Correct Report.

ACTUAL REPORT:

— 1st character of name is missing   Gross pay incorrect   Net pay is wrong

MITH	40.00	$5.00	$200.00	$32.00	$168.00
ONES	44.00	$6.00	$300.00	$54.00	$414.00
ETERS	49.00	$7.00	$451.00	$93.00	$772.00
ANSEN	36.00	$5.55	$199.00	$31.00	$940.00
ILGROM	42.00	$10.14	$455.00	$94.00	$1301.00
ATAR	40.00	$4.33	$173.00	$27.00	$1447.00
TOTAL			$1,778.00	$331.00	$1,447.00

Heading line is missing

Gross pay has cents missing

Figure 1.14 Actual Report.

Solutions to Payroll Problems

Exercise 1.7: Compilation Errors

Card   13 C   RECORD SIZE IN RECORD CONTAINS CLAUSE DISAGREES WITH COMPUTED RECORD SIZE . . .
Statement 13 is the SELECT statement for CARD-FILE but the error is actually in the FD for the file. Line 20 says that CARD contains 80 characters, but the associated picture clauses sum to 79, hence the problem.

Correction: Change the PICTURE clause in line 26 to PIC X(45).

Card   14 C   RECORD SIZE IN RECORD CONTAINS CLAUSE DISAGREES WITH COMPUTED RECORD SIZE . . .
Similar problem as previous diagnostic, except the problem is with the FD for PRINT-FILE. The picture clauses sum to 132, rather than 133. The most likely problem is in line 37, with PIC ZZZZV99, where the V is an *implied* decimal point and doesn't count as a position. Since this is a print file, the V should be changed to a decimal point.

Correction: Change PIC ZZZZV99 to PIC ZZZZ.99 in line 37.

Card   42 W   END OF SENTENCE SHOULD PRECEDE 05. ASSUMED PRESENT . . .
Any level number must follow a completed statement, but there is no period to end line 41. Since the compiler has assumed the period was present, no harm was done but the correction should still be made.

Correction: Insert a period at the end of line 41.

Card   90 E   HEADER-LINE NOT DEFINED. STATEMENT DISCARDED . . .
Line 60 defined an 01 entry HEADING-LINE, whereas line 90 referenced HEADER-LINE. The programmer understands the entries to be the same, but the compiler requires *identical* data names.

Correction: Be consistent; change line 90 to HEADING-LINE *or* line 60 to HEADER-LINE.

Card   92 E   PROCESS-CARDS NOT DEFINED. STATEMENT DISCARDED . . .
Similar to the previous diagnostic, except the problem relates to a paragraph name. Line 99 defines the paragraph PROCESS-CARD rather than PROCESS-CARDS.

Correction: Be consistent.

Card 102 W   GREATER NOT PRECEDED BY A SPACE. ASSUME SPACE...
A space is required before and after the relational symbols >, <, and =.

Correction: Insert spaces before and after the greater than sign.

Card 102 W   40 NOT PRECEDED BY A SPACE. ASSUME SPACE...
This diagnostic will disappear when the previous correction is made.

Correction: None required beyond the previous correction.

Card 128 E   PRINT-NET-PAY NOT DEFINED. DISCARDED...
Again, a case of inconsistency. The definition in line 45 is for PRINT-NET, whereas line 128 refers to PRINT-NET-PAY.

Correction: Be consistent.

Card 129 E   EXPECTING NEW STATEMENT. FOUND ADVANCING...
The reserved word ADVANCING is optional in a WRITE statement. However, if it is used, it must be preceded by BEFORE or AFTER to indicate the desired spacing.

Correction: Since line 141 specified AFTER ADVANCING, the AFTER option should also be specified in line 129.

Card 132 E   SYNTAX REQUIRES FILE-NAME. FOUND DNM=1-112. STATEMENT DISCARDED...
Line 132 is a READ statement and COBOL requires that one read a file, not a record. READ should be followed by a file-name, CARD-FILE, rather than the associated record-name. (The rather cryptic note, DNM=1-112, is the way the compiler references CARD.)

Correction: Change CARD to CARD-FILE in line 132.

Card 140 E   SYNTAX REQUIRES RECORD-NAME. FOUND DNM=1-198. STATEMENT DISCARDED.
Similar to previous diagnostic, except that a WRITE statement requires a record-name, rather than a file-name.

Correction: Change PRINT-FILE to PRINT-LINE in line 140.

Exercise 1.8: Logic Errors

The execution errors associated with exercise 1.8 are analyzed and corrected, beginning on page 43.

1. Heading line is missing: HEADING-LINE is properly established in Working-Storage in lines 59-72. It is moved to PRINT-LINE in line 89, and apparently written in line 90. What then is the problem? Look *carefully* at the AT END clause in line 88 following the initial read, and discover that the period is missing. Hence, the MOVE and WRITE statements of lines 89 and 90 are incorporated into the AT END clause of the initial read and are not executed. The required correction is to place a period at the end of line 88.

2. First character missing: A fairly common error and typical of beginning programmers. IBM systems use the first character of a print line for carriage control. If the programmer fails to specifically allocate this position, then the compiler generates instructions to usurp whatever is there; the first character of the last name is taken as the carriage control character. The problem is solved by inserting a one-byte filler entry in line 33, and simultaneously adjusting the picture clause in line 45, to retain 133 characters in the record description.

3. Gross pay incorrect: The gross pay calculation stretches over three COMPUTE statements in lines 99-105. According to the problem statement, employees are to receive straight time for the first 40 hours, time and a half for the next 8 hours, and double time for any hours over 48. The COMPUTE statement of line 99 pays straight time for every hour worked, *including* overtime hours. The COMPUTE in lines 100-102 pays time and a half for all hours over 40, so that the net effect of the two statements is to pay employees 2½ times the hourly rate for every hour over 40. In similar fashion, employees are paid 4½ times the hourly rate for every hour over 48. The problem is easily corrected by changing 1.5 and 2.0 in lines 102 and 105, to .5 in both. Note well that the alternative correction of changing CARD-HOURS to 40 in line 99 is *incorrect*. That change would overpay those working less than 40 hours and more than 48 hours.

4. Cents missing in gross pay: GROSS-PAY is calculated in the data name IND-GROSS-PAY, defined in line 50 with picture 9(4), and printed as PRINT-GROSS, defined on line 40 with picture $$$$.99. The problem is that calculations are made in a field with no decimals, so that all cents are lost. The picture clause in line 50 (and also lines 51 and 52) should be changed to 9(4)V99.

5. Net pay is wrong and appears as a running total: IND-NET-PAY is calculated correctly by the SUBTRACT statement of lines 114 and 115. It is correctly added to COMP-NET-PAY, a company total in line 119. The problem occurs in line 127 where COMP-NET-PAY, rather than IND-NET-PAY is moved to PRINT-NET-PAY.

Finally, there is an inconsistency in the program specifications for Federal Income Tax. According to the specifications given, an individual earning $276 would pay $49.20 ($42 + 20% of $36).

However, an employee earning exactly $240 would pay only $38.40 (16% of $240). Consequently, anyone earning between $240 and $300 should pay only $38.40 (not $42) plus 20% over $240. In similar fashion, individuals earning over $300 should pay $50.40 ($38.40 + 20% of $60.00) + 22% over $300.

This problem might come to light in a structured walkthrough during which the programmer/analyst presented his design to the user, who should then realize that the original specifications were poor.

2 The COBOL Language

OVERVIEW

This section is concerned with the details of COBOL. It is divided into nine topics, each dealing with a major language feature; sorting, table processing, report writer, etc. Each topic begins with presentation, in reference form, of the precise syntax (extracted from the 74 ANS standard) for associated COBOL elements. All syntactical elements for a given topic appear together. For example, in Topic 2.1 on elementary I-O operations, the COBOL syntax for FD, OPEN, CLOSE, READ, and WRITE are grouped together at the beginning of the unit. This in turn avoids the page turning required in ordinary reference manuals where language features are listed by COBOL division, and alphabetically within division.

In addition to syntax requirements, many of the topics contain "capsule summaries" to illustrate the exact function of COBOL statements. For example, in Topic 2.3 on moving and editing, the summary shows the different outcomes generated by various moves: a longer sending field to a shorter receiving field, a numeric sending field with an implied decimal point to a receiving field without a decimal point, etc. The summaries do require a basic knowledge of the statements in question. They are however, *example oriented,* and succinctly illustrate the often complex rules of COBOL, without unnecessary verbiage.

Each topic is rich in a variety of COBOL exercises. The reader is asked to code individual statements, to state the effect of statements provided, to check on COBOL syntax, etc. Each topic concludes with a self-checking examination in the form of multiple choice questions. The section begins with a Capsule Summary on the COBOL syntax.

Capsule Summary: COBOL Syntax

COBOL is an "English-like" language. As such, it has inherent flexibility in the way a particular entry may be expressed; i.e., there are a number of different, but equally acceptable ways to say the same thing. Accordingly, a standard notation is used to express permissible COBOL formats and is listed:

1. COBOL reserved words appear in uppercase (capital) letters.
2. Reserved words which are required are underlined; optional reserved words are not underlined.
3. Lowercase words denote programmer-supplied information.
4. Brackets ([ ]) indicate optional information.
5. Braces ({ }) indicate that one of the enclosed items must be chosen.
6. Three periods (. . .) mean that the last syntactical unit can be repeated an arbitrary number of times.

This notation is clarified by example; consider the IF statement:

$$\underline{IF} \begin{Bmatrix} \text{identifier-1} \\ \text{literal-1} \end{Bmatrix} \begin{Bmatrix} IS\ [\underline{NOT}]\ \underline{GREATER}\ THAN \\ IS\ [\underline{NOT}]\ \underline{LESS}\ THAN \\ IS\ [\underline{NOT}]\ \underline{EQUAL\ TO} \end{Bmatrix} \begin{Bmatrix} \text{identifier-2} \\ \text{literal-2} \end{Bmatrix}$$

The format for the IF statement has IF underlined and in uppercase letters; thus IF is a required reserved word. The first set of braces means that either a literal or identifier must appear; both are in lowercase letters, indicating they are programmer supplied. The next set of braces forces a choice among one of three relationships: greater than, less than, or equal to. In each case, IS appears in capital letters but is not underlined; hence its use is optional. Brackets denote NOT as an optional entry. THAN is an optional reserved word which may be added to improve legibility. Finally a choice must be made between literal-2 or identifier-2.

Consider an example in which the data-name CARD-MAJOR is compared to the literal ENGINEERING. All the following are acceptable:

    IF CARD-MAJOR IS EQUAL TO 'ENGINEERING' . . .
    IF CARD-MAJOR EQUAL TO 'ENGINEERING' . . .
    IF 'ENGINEERING' IS EQUAL CARD-MAJOR . . .
    IF 'ENGINEERING' EQUAL CARD-MAJOR . . .

TOPIC 2.1: ELEMENTARY INPUT/OUTPUT

COBOL Syntax

DATA DIVISION.
FD file-name

$\left[\underline{BLOCK} \; CONTAINS \; [integer\text{-}1 \; \underline{TO}] \; integer\text{-}2 \; \begin{Bmatrix} \underline{RECORDS} \\ \underline{CHARACTERS} \end{Bmatrix} \right]$

[RECORD CONTAINS [integer-3 TO] integer-4 CHARACTERS]

$\underline{LABEL} \; \begin{Bmatrix} RECORD \; IS \\ RECORDS \; ARE \end{Bmatrix} \; \begin{Bmatrix} \underline{STANDARD} \\ \underline{OMITTED} \end{Bmatrix}$

$\left[\underline{VALUE} \; \underline{OF} \; implementor\text{-}name\text{-}1 \; IS \; \begin{Bmatrix} data\text{-}name\text{-}1 \\ literal\text{-}1 \end{Bmatrix} \right.$

$\left. \left[implementor\text{-}name\text{-}2 \; IS \; \begin{Bmatrix} data\text{-}name\text{-}2 \\ literal\text{-}2 \end{Bmatrix} \right] \ldots \right]$

$\left[\underline{DATA} \; \begin{Bmatrix} \underline{RECORD} \; IS \\ \underline{RECORDS} \; ARE \end{Bmatrix} \; data\text{-}name\text{-}3 \; [,data\text{-}name\text{-}4 \ldots] \right]$

PROCEDURE DIVISION.

$\underline{OPEN} \; \begin{Bmatrix} \underline{INPUT} \; file\text{-}name\text{-}1 \; [, file\text{-}name\text{-}2] \ldots \\ \underline{OUTPUT} \; file\text{-}name\text{-}3 \; [, file\text{-}name\text{-}4] \ldots \\ \underline{I\text{-}O} \; file\text{-}name\text{-}5 \; [, file\text{-}name\text{-}6] \ldots \end{Bmatrix} \ldots$

$\underline{CLOSE} \; file\text{-}name\text{-}1 \; [WITH \; \underline{LOCK}] \quad [, file\text{-}name\text{-}2 \; [WITH \; \underline{LOCK}]] \ldots$

$\underline{READ} \; file\text{-}name \; RECORD \; [\underline{INTO} \; identifier] \quad [AT \; \underline{END} \; imperative\text{-}statement]$

$\underline{WRITE} \; record\text{-}name \; [\underline{FROM} \; identifier\text{-}1]$

$\left[\begin{Bmatrix} \underline{BEFORE} \\ \underline{AFTER} \end{Bmatrix} \; ADVANCING \; \begin{Bmatrix} \begin{Bmatrix} identifier\text{-}2 \\ integer \end{Bmatrix} \begin{bmatrix} LINE \\ LINES \end{bmatrix} \\ \begin{Bmatrix} mnemonic\text{-}name \\ PAGE \end{Bmatrix} \end{Bmatrix} \right]$

$\left[AT \; \begin{Bmatrix} \underline{END\text{-}OF\text{-}PAGE} \\ \underline{EOP} \end{Bmatrix} \; imperative\text{-}statement \right]$

Exercise 2.1: Coding COBOL Statements

Supply Procedure Division statements as indicated:

1. Code the statement(s) necessary to open the input and output files, EMPLOYEE-FILE and PRINT-FILE respectively.

47

2. Code a statement to read a record from EMPLOYEE-FILE. Include a provision to move NO to the switch EMPLOYEE-DATA-REMAINS-SWITCH when the end of file is reached.
3. Code a *single* statement to accomplish everything in part (2) above, and in addition, move the incoming record to the field, WS-INPUT-WORK-AREA.
4. Code *two* statements (a MOVE and a WRITE) to print HEADING-LINE on top of a new page. (Assume PRINT-LINE is the record name for PRINT-FILE.)
5. Code *one* statement to accomplish the identical function as part (4).
6. Code the necessary statements to build, and subsequently double space, DETAIL-LINE. (Assume the output record DETAIL-LINE is to contain PRT-NAME, PRT-SOC-SEC-NUMBER, and PRT-SALARY).
7. Code a single statement to close the files EMPLOYEE-FILE and PRINT-FILE when processing is completed.

Exercise 2.2: Checking COBOL Syntax

Indicate whether each of the COBOL entries below is valid or invalid. State the reason and/or correction for any invalid entry. Assume FILE-ONE and FILE-TWO are file names, for an input and output file, respectively, and RECORD-ONE is a record name.

1. OPEN FILE-ONE FILE-TWO.
2. OPEN INPUT FILE-ONE FILE-TWO.
3. OPEN INPUT FILE-ONE OUTPUT FILE-TWO.
4. CLOSE INPUT FILE-ONE OUTPUT FILE-TWO.
5. READ FILE-ONE.
6. READ FILE-ONE.
   AT END PERFORM END-OF-JOB-ROUTINE.
7. READ RECORD-ONE
   AT END PERFORM END-OF-JOB-ROUTINE.
8. WRITE FILE-ONE
   AFTER ADVANCING PAGE.
9. WRITE RECORD-ONE.
10. WRITE RECORD-ONE
    AFTER ADVANCING TOP-OF-PAGE.
11. WRITE RECORD-ONE
    AFTER ADVANCING 2.
12. WRITE RECORD-ONE
    AFTER ADVANCING TWO LINES.

Exercise 2.3: Group versus Elementary Items

1. Indicate the starting and ending column for *every* field in the given record description:

```
01  STUDENT-RECORD.
    05  STUDENT-NAME.
        10  LAST-NAME           PIC X(15).
        10  FIRST-NAME          PIC X(10).
        10  MIDDLE-INIT         PIC X.
    05  MAJOR                   PIC X(10).
    05  ACHIEVEMENT-SCORES.
        10  MATH-ITEMS.
            15  ALGEBRA         PIC 9(5).
            15  CALCULUS        PIC 9(5).
        10  ENGLISH-ITEMS.
            15  COMPOSITION     PIC 9(5).
            15  LITERATURE      PIC 9(5).
            15  READING-COMP    PIC 9(5).
    05  FILLER                  PIC X(19).
```

2. Indicate whether each of the COBOL entries is valid or invalid. State the reason and/or correction for any invalid entry. (Assume that all entries are elementary items.) Indicate also those entries which are syntactically valid, but which would produce results different from what was intended.

```
05  PRINT-SALARY         PIC '$$,$$$'.
05  BLANK-LINE           PIC X(133)   VALUE 'SPACES'.
05  ROW-OF-DASHES        PIC X(10)    VALUE ALL -.
05  LAST-NAME            PIC 9(15).
05  PRINT-SALARY         PIC $$$,$$$V99.
05  PRINT-YEAR           PIC X(4)     VALUE 1980.
05  PRINT-MONTH          PIC 9(12)    VALUE 'JANUARY'.
05  SOCIAL-SEC-NUMBER    PIC 9(8).
```

3. Given the following record description:

```
01  FIELD-ONE
    05  FIELD-TWO
    05  FIELD-THREE
        10  FIELD-FOUR
        10  FIELD-FIVE
        10  FIELD-SIX
    05  FIELD-SEVEN
    05  FIELD-EIGHT
        10  FIELD-NINE
        10  FIELD-TEN
```

49

Indicate True or False as appropriate (assume the record ends with FIELD-TEN).

a. FIELD-TWO is an elementary item.
b. FIELD-THREE is an elementary item.
c. FIELD-SIX should have a picture clause.
d. FIELD-TWO *must* be larger than FIELD-FOUR.
e. FIELD-THREE *must* be larger than FIELD-FOUR.
f. FIELD-THREE and FIELD-FOUR begin in the same position.
g. FIELD-THREE and FIELD-SIX end in the same position.
h. FIELD-NINE *could* be larger than FIELD-SEVEN.
i. FIELD-NINE *could* be larger than FIELD-EIGHT.
j. FIELD-EIGHT requires a picture clause.

Exercise 2.4: Self-Checking Examination

1. The WRITE statement:
   a. Must be used with the AFTER ADVANCING option.
   b. Must be used with the BEFORE ADVANCING option.
   c. Must be used with either the AFTER or BEFORE ADVANCING options.
   d. None of the above.

2. The type of file (INPUT or OUTPUT) is:
   a. Specified in an OPEN statement.
   b. Specified in a CLOSE statement.
   c. Specified in both an OPEN and CLOSE statement.
   d. Specified in neither an OPEN nor CLOSE statement.

3. In describing a record layout (entries under an 01 record), the programmer may choose any level numbers from:
   a. 02 to 49 inclusive.
   b. 02 to 77 inclusive.
   c. 02 to 49 inclusive and 77.
   d. The set 05, 10, 15, 20, 25, 30, 35, 40, 45, 50.

4. All of the following clauses belong under a COBOL FD *except:*
   a. LABEL RECORD.
   b. TYPE OF FILE.
   c. RECORD CONTAINS.
   d. DATA RECORD IS.

5. A file-name appears in all of the following statements *except:*
   a. OPEN.
   b. CLOSE.
   c. SELECT.
   d. READ.
   e. WRITE.

6. A group item:
   a. Never has a picture clause.
   b. Must be an 01 entry.
   c. May sometimes have both a picture and a value clause.
   d. Will always have at least four data names defined under it.

7. An elementary item:
   a. Never has a picture clause.
   b. Can never be an 01 entry.
   c. May sometimes have both a picture and value clause.
   d. May sometimes have additional data names defined under it.

8. The following are all valid picture clauses *except:*
   a. PIC 999.
   b. PIC $$$.
   c. PIC $99.
   d. PIC 99¢.

9. Which is true as regards the syntax of the READ and WRITE verbs:
   a. Read a file and write a record.
   b. Read a record and write a file.
   c. Read a file and write a file.
   d. Read a record and write a record.

10. An entry prefixed by the level number 05 will:
    a. Always have a picture clause.
    b. Always be an elementary item.
    c. Always appear in the File Section.
    d. All of the above.
    e. None of the above.

11. An OPEN statement:
    a. Must contain the word INPUT.
    b. Must contain the word OUTPUT.
    c. Can not contain both INPUT and OUTPUT.
    d. May contain both INPUT and OUTPUT.

12. Given the statement, WRITE PRINT-LINE FROM HEADING-LINE, all of the following are true *except:*
    a. It is equivalent to two statements, a MOVE and a WRITE.
    b. PRINT-LINE is defined as a record name in an FD.
    c. PRINT-LINE is a file name.
    d. HEADING-LINE is probably defined in Working-Storage.

13. All of the following are valid numeric literals *except:*
    a. 123.
    b. 123.45.
    c. '$123.45'.
    d. 0123.45.

14. Non-numeric literals may contain:
    a. Numbers.
    b. Letters.
    c. Special characters.
    d. Reserved words.
    e. All of the above.

15. The statement: 'READ CARD-FILE INTO WS-CARD-AREA. . .':
    a. Will cause the input record to appear in two places.
    b. Will cause the input record to appear in WS-CARD-AREA only.
    c. Combines the effects of both a READ and a MOVE statement.
    d. Both (a) and (c) above.
    e. Both (b) and (c) above.

16. Reports can be forced to begin on a new page if:
    a. One uses the clause WRITE . . . AFTER ADVANCING TOP-OF-PAGE LINES.
    b. One uses the clause WRITE . . . AFTER ADVANCING TOP-OF-PAGE LINES and TOP-OF-PAGE is equated to an implementor-name; for example, C01, in the SPECIAL-NAMES paragraph.
    c. One uses the clause WRITE . . . AFTER ADVANCING PAGE.
    d. Both (b) and (c) above.

Solutions for Topic 2.1

Exercise 2.1: Coding COBOL Statements

1. OPEN INPUT EMPLOYEE-FILE
       OUTPUT PRINT-FILE.
2. READ EMPLOYEE-FILE
       AT END MOVE 'NO' TO EMPLOYEE-DATA-REMAINS-SWITCH.

3. READ EMPLOYEE-FILE INTO WS-INPUT-WORK-AREA
      AT END MOVE 'NO' TO EMPLOYEE-DATA-REMAINS-SWITCH.
4. MOVE HEADING-LINE TO PRINT-LINE.
   WRITE PRINT-LINE
      AFTER ADVANCING PAGE.
5. WRITE PRINT-LINE FROM HEADING-LINE
      AFTER ADVANCING PAGE.
6. MOVE CARD-NAME TO PRT-NAME.
   MOVE CARD-SOC-SEC-NUMBER TO PRT-SOC-SEC-NUMBER.
   MOVE CARD-SALARY TO PRT-SALARY.
   WRITE PRINT-LINE FROM DETAIL-LINE
      AFTER ADVANCING 2 LINES.
7. CLOSE EMPLOYEE-FILE
         PRINT-FILE.

Exercise 2.2: Checking COBOL Syntax

   1. Invalid: should be OPEN INPUT FILE-ONE OUTPUT FILE-TWO.

   2. Syntactically valid, but logically *invalid,* as both FILE-ONE and FILE-TWO will be opened as input.

   3. Valid

   4. Invalid: should be CLOSE FILE-ONE FILE-TWO.

   5. Syntactically valid, but rather unusual to code a READ statement without the AT END clause.

   6. Invalid: the period after FILE-ONE should be removed.

   7. Invalid: one reads a file, not a record.

   8. Invalid: one writes a record, not a file.

   9. Valid

   10. Valid, provided TOP-OF-PAGE was defined in the SPECIAL-NAMES paragraph of the Environment Division.

   11. Valid

   12. Invalid: TWO should be replaced by 2.

Exercise 2.3: Group Versus Elementary Items

   1. STUDENT-RECORD (columns 1-80)
      STUDENT-NAME (columns 1-26)
      LAST-NAME (columns 1-15)
      FIRST-NAME (columns 16-25)
      MIDDLE-INIT (column 26)
      MAJOR (columns 27-36)
      ACHIEVEMENT-SCORES (columns 37-61)

MATH-ITEMS (columns 37-46)
ALGEBRA (columns 37-41)
CALCULUS (columns 42-46)
ENGLISH-ITEMS (columns 47-61)
COMPOSITION (columns 47-51)
LITERATURE (columns 52-56)
READING-COMP (columns 57-61)
FILLER (columns 62-80)

2. PRINT-SALARY - Invalid: picture clause should not have quotes.
BLANK-LINE - Valid syntactically, but invalid logically. As written, the literal 'SPACES' will appear in BLANK-LINE, rather than 133 blanks as intended. (SPACES should not be in quotes.)
ROW-OF-DASHES - Invalid: quotes are required around the hyphen.
LAST-NAME - Valid syntactically, but will probably cause problems during execution. The picture clause should be alphabetic or alphanumeric.
PRINT-SALARY - Invalid: an actual decimal point, rather than the V should be used.
PRINT-YEAR - Invalid: alphanumeric pictures require value clauses with quotes.
PRINT-MONTH - Invalid: the picture clause should be X(12).
SOCIAL-SEC-NUMBER - Valid syntactically, but invalid logically as social security number is a nine-digit field.

3. a. True
   b. False: It is a group item as three fields are defined under it.
   c. True
   d. False: There is no discernible relationship between the two fields.
   e. True
   f. True
   g. True
   h. True
   i. False: FIELD-EIGHT consists of FIELD-NINE and FIELD-TEN.
   j. False: FIELD-EIGHT is a group item and consequently can never have a picture clause.

Exercise 2.4: Self-Checking Examination

1. D	5. E	9. A	13. C
2. A	6. A	10. E	14. E
3. A	7. C	11. D	15. D
4. B	8. D	12. C	16. D

TOPIC 2.2: ARITHMETIC

COBOL Syntax

ADD $\begin{Bmatrix} \text{identifier-1} \\ \text{literal-1} \end{Bmatrix}$ $\begin{bmatrix} \text{, identifier-2} \\ \text{, literal-2} \end{bmatrix}$ ... TO identifier-m [ROUNDED]
[, identifier-n [ROUNDED]] ... [ON SIZE ERROR imperative-statement]

ADD $\begin{Bmatrix} \text{identifier-1} \\ \text{literal-1} \end{Bmatrix}$ $\begin{Bmatrix} \text{identifier-2} \\ \text{literal-2} \end{Bmatrix}$ $\begin{bmatrix} \text{, identifier-3} \\ \text{, literal-3} \end{bmatrix}$ ...
GIVING identifier-m [ROUNDED] [, identifier-n [ROUNDED]] ...
[ON SIZE ERROR imperative-statement]

COMPUTE identifier-1 [ROUNDED] [, identifier-2 [ROUNDED]] ...
= arithmetic - expression [ON SIZE ERROR imperative-statement]

DIVIDE $\begin{Bmatrix} \text{identifier-1} \\ \text{literal-1} \end{Bmatrix}$ INTO identifier-2 [ROUNDED]
[, identifier-3 [ROUNDED]] ... [ON SIZE ERROR imperative-statement]

DIVIDE $\begin{Bmatrix} \text{identifier-1} \\ \text{literal-1} \end{Bmatrix}$ $\begin{Bmatrix} \text{BY} \\ \text{INTO} \end{Bmatrix}$ $\begin{Bmatrix} \text{identifier-2} \\ \text{literal-2} \end{Bmatrix}$ GIVING identifier-3 [ROUNDED]
[, identifier-4 [ROUNDED]] ... [ON SIZE ERROR imperative-statement]

DIVIDE $\begin{Bmatrix} \text{identifier-1} \\ \text{literal-1} \end{Bmatrix}$ $\begin{Bmatrix} \text{BY} \\ \text{INTO} \end{Bmatrix}$ $\begin{Bmatrix} \text{identifier-2} \\ \text{literal-2} \end{Bmatrix}$ GIVING identifier-3 [ROUNDED]
REMAINDER identifier-4 [ON SIZE ERROR imperative-statement]

MULTIPLY $\begin{Bmatrix} \text{identifier-1} \\ \text{literal-1} \end{Bmatrix}$ BY identifier-2 [ROUNDED]
[, identifier-3 [ROUNDED]] ... [ON SIZE ERROR imperative-statement]

MULTIPLY $\begin{Bmatrix} \text{identifier-1} \\ \text{literal-1} \end{Bmatrix}$ BY $\begin{Bmatrix} \text{identifier-2} \\ \text{literal-2} \end{Bmatrix}$ GIVING identifier-3 [ROUNDED]
[, identifier-4 [ROUNDED]] ... [ON SIZE ERROR imperative-statement]

SUBTRACT $\begin{Bmatrix} \text{identifier-1} \\ \text{literal-1} \end{Bmatrix}$ $\begin{bmatrix} \text{, identifier-2} \\ \text{, literal-2} \end{bmatrix}$ ... FROM identifier-m [ROUNDED]
[, identifier-4 [ROUNDED]] ... [ON SIZE ERROR imperative-statement]

SUBTRACT $\begin{Bmatrix} \text{identifier-1} \\ \text{literal-1} \end{Bmatrix}$ $\begin{bmatrix} \text{, identifier-2} \\ \text{, literal-2} \end{bmatrix}$ ... FROM $\begin{bmatrix} \text{identifier-m} \\ \text{literal-m} \end{bmatrix}$
GIVING identifier-n [ROUNDED] [, identifier-o [ROUNDED]] ...
[ON SIZE ERROR imperative-statement]

Capsule Summary: MULTIPLY, DIVIDE, and COMPUTE Statements

The ADD Instruction

Data name	A	B	C
Value *before* execution	5	10	30
Value *after* execution of*			
ADD A TO C.	5	10	35
ADD A B TO C.	5	10	45
ADD A 18 B GIVING C.	5	10	33
ADD A 18 B TO C.	5	10	63
ADD 1 TO B, C.	5	11	31

The SUBTRACT Instruction

Data name	A	B	C	D
Value *before* execution	5	10	30	100
Value *after* execution of*				
SUBTRACT A FROM C.	5	10	25	100
SUBTRACT A B FROM C.	5	10	15	100
SUBTRACT A B FROM C GIVING D.	5	10	30	15
SUBTRACT 10 FROM C, D.	5	10	20	90

The MULTIPLY Instruction

Data name	A	B	C
Value *before* execution	5	10	30
Value *after* execution of*			
MULTIPLY B BY A GIVING C.	5	10	50
MULTIPLY A BY B GIVING C.	5	10	50
MULTIPLY A BY B.	5	50	30
MULTIPLY B BY A.	50	10	30
MULTIPLY A BY 3 GIVING B, C.	5	15	15

The DIVIDE Instruction

Data name	A	B	C
Value *before* execution	5	10	30
Value *after* execution of*			
DIVIDE 2 INTO B, C.	5	5	15
DIVIDE 2 INTO B GIVING C.	5	10	5
DIVIDE B BY 5 GIVING A.	2	10	30
DIVIDE A INTO B, C.	5	2	6
DIVIDE A INTO B GIVING C.	5	10	2

*Note: In each case, value after is derived by considering the *initial* value of all variables.

Capsule Summary, cont.

The COMPUTE Instruction

Data name	A	B	C
Value *before* execution	2	3	10
Value *after* execution of			
COMPUTE C = A + B.	2	3	5
COMPUTE C = A + B * 2.	2	3	8
COMPUTE C = (A + B) * 2.	2	3	10
COMPUTE C = A ** B.	2	3	8
COMPUTE C = B ** A.	2	3	9

Exercise 2.5: Checking COBOL Syntax

Indicate whether the following COBOL entries are valid or invalid. State the reason and/or correction for any invalid entry.

1. ADD X TO Y GIVING Z.

2. ADD A B C D GIVING E ROUNDED
       ON SIZE ERROR PERFORM OVERFLOW-ROUTINE.

3. SUBTRACT N FROM 1.

4. SUBTRACT A B FROM C
       ON NEGATIVE-ANSWER PERFORM SHORTAGE.

5. MULTIPLY 10 BY A GIVING B ROUNDED.

6. MULTIPLY X BY 10
       ON SIZE ERROR PERFORM OVERFLOW-ROUTINE.

7. DIVIDE A BY B GIVING C REMAINDER D.

8. DIVIDE A INTO B.

9. COMPUTE N + 1 = N.

10. COMPUTE X = (A + B) / (C + D)
        ON SIZE-ERROR PERFORM ERROR-ROUTINE.

11. COMPUTE Y = 2(A + B).

12. COMPUTE X ROUND = A ** B ** C.

Exercise 2.6: Evaluating Arithmetic Statements

Complete the following table showing *only* those values which change. In each case refer to the *initial* values of W, X, Y, and Z.

Data Name Picture Clause:	W S999	X S999	Y S999	Z S999
Initial Value	8	16	24	2
Value After Execution				
1. ADD 1 TO X.	___	___	___	___
2. ADD W X Y GIVING Z.	___	___	___	___
3. ADD W X Y TO Z.	___	___	___	___
4. ADD 1 TO W X.	___	___	___	___
5. SUBTRACT W X FROM Y.	___	___	___	___
6. SUBTRACT W X FROM Y GIVING Z.	___	___	___	___
7. SUBTRACT 10 X FROM Z.	___	___	___	___
8. SUBTRACT 10 FROM Y GIVING X Z.	___	___	___	___
9. MULTIPLY 10 BY X.	___	___	___	___
10. MULTIPLY 10 BY X GIVING Y.	___	___	___	___
11. MULTIPLY 10 BY X GIVING Y Z.	___	___	___	___
12. MULTIPLY X BY 10 GIVING W.	___	___	___	___
13. DIVIDE W INTO Y.	___	___	___	___
14. DIVIDE Y INTO W.	___	___	___	___
15. DIVIDE Y INTO W GIVING X REMAINDER Z.	___	___	___	___
16. DIVIDE Y BY W GIVING X REMAINDER Z.	___	___	___	___
17. COMPUTE Z = W + Y / 2 * X.	___	___	___	___
18. COMPUTE Z = (W + Y) / X * 2.	___	___	___	___
19. COMPUTE Z = (W + Y) / (X * 2).	___	___	___	___
20. COMPUTE Z = W + Y / (X * 2).	___	___	___	___

Exercise 2.7: Coding COBOL Statements

Supply Procedure Division statements as indicated:

1. Code two equivalent statements, an ADD and a COMPUTE to add 1 to the counter NUMBER-QUALIFIED-EMPLOYEES.

2. Code a COBOL statement to add the contents of five fields, MONDAY-SALES, TUESDAY-SALES, WEDNESDAY-SALES, THURSDAY-SALES, and FRIDAY-SALES, storing the result in WEEKLY-SALES.

3. Code a COBOL statement to subtract the fields FED-TAX, STATE-TAX, FICA, and VOLUNTARY-DEDUCTIONS, from GROSS-PAY, and put the result in NET-PAY.

4. Code a single COBOL statement to calculate NET-AMOUNT-DUE, which is equal to the GROSS-SALE minus a two percent discount.

5. Recode part 4 using *two* statements (a MULTIPLY and a SUBTRACT).

6. Code a COBOL statement to compute GROSS-PAY, which is equal to HOURS-WORKED times HOURLY-RATE.

7. Code a *single* COBOL statement to compute GROSS-PAY, which is equal to REG-HOURS-WORKED times HOURLY-RATE plus OVERTIME-HOURS times HOURLY-RATE times 1.5.

8. Code a COBOL statement to determine AVERAGE-SALARY by dividing TOTAL-SALARY by NUMBER-OF-EMPLOYEES.

9. Code a COBOL COMPUTE equivalent to the algebraic statement:

$$x = \frac{(a+b)c}{de}$$

10. Code a COBOL COMPUTE equivalent to the algebraic statement:

$$x = \frac{-b + \sqrt{b^2 - 4ac}}{2a}$$

Note that raising a number to the .5 power is equivalent to calculating its square root.

Exercise 2.8: Self-Checking Examination

1. In a COMPUTE statement, the order of arithmetic operations (in the absence of parentheses) is:
   a. From left to right, regardless of which operations are present.
   b. From right to left, regardless of which operations are present.
   c. Exponentiation, multiplication or division, addition or subtraction, (and from left to right if a tie).
   d. Multiplication or division, addition or subtraction, exponentiation, (and from left to right if a tie).

2. All of the following verbs have two or more distinct syntactical forms *except:*
   a. ADD.
   b. SUBTRACT.
   c. MULTIPLY.
   d. DIVIDE.
   e. COMPUTE.

3. All of the following are valid as arithmetic operations in COBOL *except:*
   a. + and −.
   b. * and /.
   c. **.
   d. X and ÷.

4. The statement ADD A B TO C:
   a. Is syntactically invalid.
   b. Will change the values of B and C.
   c. Takes the value of A, adds it to the value of B, and puts the answer in C.
   d. Both (b) and (c) above.
   e. None of the above.

5. The ROUNDED clause is:
   a. Available for any arithmetic verb.
   b. Mandatory if the SIZE ERROR clause is also used.
   c. Available for the COMPUTE verb only.
   d. Valid only if two decimal places appear in the picture clause.

6. The ADD, SUBTRACT, MULTIPLY and DIVIDE statements *all:*
   a. Have at least two distinct syntactical forms.
   b. Can change the value of more than one data name in a statement.
   c. Permit the use of both constants and variables in the same statement.
   d. All of the above.
   e. None of the above.

7. The following are all syntactically valid forms of the ADD statement *except:*
   a. ADD X Y TO Z.
   b. ADD X Y GIVING Z.
   c. ADD X TO Y GIVING Z.
   d. ADD X Y Z TO Z.

8. The following are all syntactically valid forms of the SUBTRACT statement *except:*
   a. SUBTRACT X FROM Y.
   b. SUBTRACT X FROM Y GETTING Z.
   c. SUBTRACT X Y FROM Z.
   d. SUBTRACT X Y FROM Z GIVING A.

9. The following are all valid forms of the DIVIDE statement *except:*
   a. DIVIDE 2 INTO A.
   b. DIVIDE A INTO 2.
   c. DIVIDE A INTO 2 GIVING B.
   d. DIVIDE 2 INTO A GIVING B REMAINDER C.

10. The following are all valid forms of the MULTIPLY statement *except:*
    a. MULTIPLY 10 BY A B.
    b. MULTIPLY A BY B GIVING C ROUNDED D.

c. MULTIPLY X BY 5 ON SIZE ERROR PERFORM ERROR-RTN.
d. MULTIPLY A BY B.

11. Removal of parentheses would affect all of the following *except:*
    a. COMPUTE X = (A + B) / (C + D).
    b. COMPUTE X = (A + B) / C.
    c. COMPUTE X = A + (B ** 2) / C.
    d. COMPUTE X = (A + B) / (C ** 2).

12. The use of parentheses in a COMPUTE statement:
    a. Is prohibited.
    b. Clarifies, but *never* alters, the order of operation.
    c. Clarifies, and *always* alters, the order of operation.
    d. Clarifies, and *sometimes* alters, the order of operation.

13. Which of the following statements is not logically equivalent to the others:
    a. DIVIDE 2 INTO B.
    b. COMPUTE B = B / 2.
    c. MULTIPLY .5 BY B.
    d. DIVIDE B INTO 2 GIVING B.

14. Data names on which arithmetic is to be performed:
    a. Cannot be handled in ADD and SUBTRACT statements, and must therefore use a COMPUTE statement.
    b. Must be defined with an S in their picture clause.
    c. Must not contain an actual decimal point.
    d. Must not be defined with an implied decimal point.

15. Given the following definitions for the variables A and B:

    05   A   PIC 9   VALUE 2.
    05   B   PIC S9   VALUE -3.

    The COBOL statement ADD B TO A:
    a. Is syntactically invalid because B is signed and A is not.
    b. Will put +1 in A as the result of the addition.
    c. Will put −1 in A as the result of the addition.
    d. None of the above.

16. Use the same definitions for A and B as in question 15. The COBOL statement ADD A TO B:
    a. Is syntactically invalid because B is signed and A is not.
    b. Will place +1 in B as a result of the addition.
    c. Will place −1 in B as a result of the addition.
    d. None of the above.

Solutions for Topic 2.2

Exercise 2.5: Checking COBOL Syntax

1. Invalid: GIVING and TO should not appear in the same statement.
2. Valid
3. Invalid: The statement would leave the result of the subtraction in the literal 1, an impossible situation.
4. Invalid: The ON condition can only test for SIZE ERROR. A separate IF Statement would be required to test for a negative number following the subtraction.
5. Valid
6. Invalid: The statement would leave the result of the multiplication in the literal 10, an impossible situation.
7. Valid
8. Valid
9. Invalid: The left hand side of the equal sign *must* contain a data name; expressions are required to appear on the right.
10. Invalid: There should not be a hyphen between SIZE and ERROR.
11. Invalid: An operator, probably *, is required between the 2 and left parenthesis.
12. Invalid: ROUNDED, rather than ROUND, should be used.

Exercise 2.6: Evaluating Arithmetic Statements

	W	X	Y	Z
1.		17		
2.				48
3.				50
4.	9	17		
5.			0	
6.				0
7.				-24
8.		14		14
9.		160		
10.			160	
11.			160	160
12.	160			
13.			3	

	W	X	Y	Z
14.		0 (see note 2)		
15.		0		8
16.		3		0
17.				200
18.				4
19.				1
20.				8 (see note 2)

Notes: 1. Only the entries whose values change are shown.
2. The fractional answers of 1/3 and 8 3/4 in parts 14 and 20 are truncated, as the receiving fields were defined without decimal points.

Exercise 2.7: Coding COBOL Statements

1. ADD 1 TO NUMBER-QUALIFIED-EMPLOYEES.
   COMPUTE NUMBER-QUALIFIED-EMPLOYEES =
      NUMBER-QUALIFIED-EMPLOYEES + 1.
2. ADD MONDAY-SALES TUESDAY-SALES WEDNESDAY-SALES
      THURSDAY-SALES FRIDAY-SALES
      GIVING WEEKLY-SALES.
3. SUBTRACT FED-TAX STATE-TAX FICA VOLUNTARY-DEDUCTIONS
      FROM GROSS-PAY GIVING NET-PAY.
4. COMPUTE NET-AMOUNT-DUE = GROSS-SALE − .02 * GROSS-SALE.
5. MULTIPLY GROSS-SALE BY .02 GIVING DISCOUNT.
   SUBTRACT DISCOUNT FROM GROSS-SALE GIVING NET-AMOUNT-DUE.
6. COMPUTE GROSS-PAY = HOURS-WORKED * HOURLY-RATE.
7. COMPUTE GROSS-PAY = REG-HOURS-WORKED * HOURLY-RATE
      + OVERTIME-HOURS * HOURLY-RATE * 1.5.
8. COMPUTE AVERAGE-SALARY = TOTAL-SALARY / NUMBER-OF-EMPLOYEES.
9. COMPUTE X = (A + B) * C / (D * E).
10. COMPUTE X = (-B + (B ** 2 - 4 * A * C) ** .5) / (2 * A).

Exercise 2.8: Self-Checking Examination

1. C	5. A	9. B	13. D
2. E	6. D	10. C	14. C
3. D	7. C	11. C	15. B
4. E	8. B	12. D	16. C

TOPIC 2.3: MOVE, MOVE CORRESPONDING, QUALIFICATION, AND EDITING

COBOL Syntax

Editing Characters

Digit replacement:

9	numeric character
Z	zero suppression (replaced by blanks)
*	zero suppression (replaced by asterisks)

Insertion:

$	dollar sign
,	comma
.	decimal point
B	blank
0	zero
/	slash

Sign:

+	plus sign
−	minus sign
CR	credit sign
DB	debit sign

Qualification:

$$\begin{Bmatrix} \text{data-name-1} \\ \text{condition-name} \end{Bmatrix} \left[\begin{Bmatrix} \underline{OF} \\ \underline{IN} \end{Bmatrix} \text{data-name-2} \right] \ldots$$

PROCEDURE DIVISION:

$$\underline{MOVE} \begin{Bmatrix} \text{identifier-1} \\ \text{literal} \end{Bmatrix} \underline{TO} \text{ identifier-2 [, identifier-3]} \ldots$$

$$\underline{MOVE} \begin{Bmatrix} \underline{CORRESPONDING} \\ \underline{CORR} \end{Bmatrix} \text{identifier-1 } \underline{TO} \text{ identifier-2}$$

Capsule Summary: The MOVE Statement

Source Field		Receiving Field	
Picture	Contents	Picture	Contents
X(5)	| A | B | C | D | E |	X(5)	| A | B | C | D | E |
X(5)	| A | B | C | D | E |	X(4)	| A | B | C | D |
X(5)	| A | B | C | D | E |	X(6)	| A | B | C | D | E | |
9(5)	| 1 | 2 | 3 | 4 | 5 |	9(5)	| 1 | 2 | 3 | 4 | 5 |
9(5)	| 1 | 2 | 3 | 4 | 5 |	9(4)	| 2 | 3 | 4 | 5 |
9(5)	| 1 | 2 | 3 | 4 | 5 |	9(6)	| 0 | 1 | 2 | 3 | 4 | 5 |
9(3)V99	| 1 | 2 | 3 | 4 | 5 |	9(5)	| 0 | 0 | 1 | 2 | 3 |
9(5)	| 1 | 2 | 3 | 4 | 5 |	9(3)V99	| 3 | 4 | 5 | 0 | 0 |

Exercise 2.9: The MOVE Statement

Complete the following table.

	Source Field		Receiving Field	
	Picture	Contents	Picture	Contents
1.	A(5)	| C | O | B | O | L |	X(5)	
2.	A(5)	| C | O | B | O | L |	A(4)	
3.	A(5)	| C | O | B | O | L |	X(6)	
4.	9(4)	| 1 | 2 | 3 | 4 |	9(3)	
5.	9(4)	| 1 | 2 | 3 | 4 |	9(5)	

	Source Field		Receiving Field	
	Picture	Contents	Picture	Contents
6.	999V9	|1|2|3|4|	9(4)	
7.	999V9	|1|2|3|4|	9(4)V9	
8.	999V9	|1|2|3|4|	9(3)V99	
9.	999V9	|1|2|3|4|	99V99	

Capsule Summary: Editing

Table 1: $ and Decimal Alignment

	Source Field		Receiving Field	
	Picture	Value	Picture	Edited Result
(a)	9(4)V99	456789	$9(5).99	$04567.89
(b)	9(4)V99	456789	$9,999.99	$4,567.89
(c)	9(4)V99	456789	$9(5).00	$04567.00
(d)	9(6)	000008	$9(6)	$000008
(e)	9(6)	000008	$$$$$9	$8
(f)	9(6)	000008	$$$$9.99	$8.00

Table 2: B and Z, and * Edit Characters

	Source Field		Receiving Field	
	Picture	Value	Picture	Edited Result
(a)	9999V99	000123	9999.99	0001.23
(b)	9999V99	000123	ZZZZ.99	1.23
(c)	9999V99	000123	$$$$.99	$1.23
(d)	9999V99	000123	$ZZZZ.99	$ 1.23
(e)	9999V99	000123	$****.99	$***1.23
(f)	9(6)	103173	99B99B99	10 31 73
(g)	9(9)	123456789	9(3)B99B9(4)	123 45 6789

Capsule Summary, cont.

Table 3: CR and DB Symbols

	Source Field		Receiving Field	
	Picture	Value	Picture	Value
(a)	S9(5)	98765	$$$,999CR	$98,765
(b)	S9(5)	−98765	$$$,999CR	$98,765CR
(c)	S9(5)	98765	$$$,999DB	$98,765
(d)	S9(5)	−98765	$$$,999DB	$98,765DB

Table 4: Floating + and − Characters

	Source Field		Receiving Field	
	Picture	Value	Picture	Edited Result
(a)	S9(4)	1234	++,+++	+1,234
(b)	S9(4)	0123	++,+++	+123
(c)	S9(4)	−1234	++,+++	−1,234
(d)	S9(4)	1234	−−,−−−	1,234
(e)	S9(4)	0123	−−,−−−	123
(f)	S9(4)	−1234	−−,−−−	−1,234

Exercise 2.10: Editing

Complete the following table, showing the value of the edited result.

	Source Field		Receiving Field	
	Picture	Value	Picture	Edited Result
1.	9(6)	345678	9(6)	
2.	9(6)	345678	9(4).99	
3.	9(4)V99	345678	9(6)	
4.	9(4)V99	345678	9(6).99	
5.	9(3)V99	12345	$$$,$$$.99	
6.	9(5)	12345	$99,999.99	
7.	S9(3)V99	−12345	$99,999CR	
8.	S9(3)V99	12345	$99,999CR	
9.	S9(5)	−12345	$99,999DB	

	Source Field		Receiving Field	
	Picture	Value	Picture	Edited Result
10.	S9(5)	12345	$99,999DB	
11.	9(3)V99	12345	$*,***.99	
12.	9(6)	012168	99B99B99	
13.	S9(6)	−003456	++++,+++	
14.	S9(6)	−003456	---,---	
15.	S9(6)	003456	++++,+++	
16.	S9(6)	003456	---,---	
17.	9(4)V99	123456	$ZZZ,ZZZ.99	
18.	9(6)	000005	$ZZZ,ZZZ.99	
19.	9(4)V99	000005	$ZZZ,ZZZ.	

Capsule Summary: The MOVE CORRESPONDING Statement

Given the Data Division entries:

```
01  CARD-IN.
    05  STUDENT-NAME              PIC X(20).
    05  SOCIAL-SECURITY-NUM       PIC 9(9).
    05  STUDENT-ADDRESS.
        10  STREET                PIC X(15).
        10  CITY-STATE            PIC X(15).
    05  ZIP-CODE                  PIC X(5).
    05  CREDITS                   PIC 999.
    05  MAJOR                     PIC X(10).
    05  FILLER                    PIC X(3).
      .
      .
      .
01  PRINT-LINE.
    10  STUDENT-NAME              PIC X(20).
    10  FILLER                    PIC X(2).
    10  CREDITS                   PIC ZZ9.
    10  FILLER                    PIC X(2).
    10  TUITION                   PIC $$,$$9.99.
    10  FILLER                    PIC X(2).
    10  STUDENT-ADDRESS.
        15  STREET                PIC X(15).
        15  CITY-STATE            PIC X(15).
        15  ZIP-CODE              PIC X(5).
    10  FILLER                    PIC X(2).
    10  SOCIAL-SECURITY-NUM       PIC 999B99B9999.
    10  FILLER                    PIC X(47).
```

> **Capsule Summary, cont.**
>
> and the Procedure Division statement:
>
> MOVE CORRESPONDING CARD-IN TO PRINT-LINE.
>
> the following individual MOVES are generated:
>
> MOVE STUDENT-NAME OF CARD-IN   TO STUDENT-NAME OF PRINT-LINE.
> MOVE SOCIAL-SECURITY-NUM OF CARD-IN   TO SOCIAL-SECURITY-NUM OF PRINT-LINE.
> MOVE STREET OF CARD-IN   TO STREET OF PRINT-LINE.
> MOVE CITY-STATE OF CARD-IN   TO CITY-STATE OF PRINT-LINE.
> MOVE CREDITS OF CARD-IN   TO CREDITS OF PRINT-LINE.
>
> The rules governing the MOVE CORRESPONDING are:
>
> 1. At least one item in each pair of CORRESPONDING items must be an elementary item for the MOVE to be effective. Thus, in the example, STUDENT-ADDRESS of CARD-IN is *not* moved to STUDENT-ADDRESS of PRINT-LINE. (The elementary items STREET and CITY-STATE are moved instead.)
>
> 2. Corresponding elementary items will be moved only if they have the same name and qualification up to but not including identifier-1 and identifier-2. Thus ZIP-CODE will *not* be moved.
>
> 3. Any elementary item containing a REDEFINES, RENAMES, OCCURS, or USAGE IS INDEX clause is not moved.

Exercise 2.11: The MOVE CORRESPONDING Statement

Given the following Data Division entries, and the statement: MOVE CORRESPONDING RECORD-ONE TO RECORD-TWO, indicate whether the following statements are True or False (with respect to the receiving field).

```
01    RECORD-ONE.
      05    FIELD-ONE              PIC X(10).
      05    FIELD-TWO.
            10    FIELD-THREE      PIC X(10).
            10    FIELD-FOUR       PIC X(5).
      05    FIELD-FIVE             PIC X(15).
```

```
            01  RECORD-TWO.
                04  FIELD-FIVE       PIC X(10).
                04  FIELD-FOUR       PIC X(10).
                04  FIELD-THREE      PIC X(10).
                04  FIELD-TWO        PIC X(10).
                04  FIELD-ONE        PIC X(10).
                04  FIELD-ZERO       PIC X(10).
```

1. The value of FIELD-ZERO is unchanged.
2. FIELD-THREE and FIELD-FOUR will be changed.
3. The value of FIELD-FIVE is unchanged since its picture clause is different in RECORD-ONE and RECORD-TWO.
4. No moves at all will take place since level numbers are different in RECORD-ONE and RECORD-TWO.
5. FIELD-ONE will not be changed since it is the first entry in RECORD-ONE and the next to last entry in RECORD-TWO.
6. Code longhand the several individual moves which will take place when the statement, MOVE CORRESPONDING RECORD-ONE TO RECORD-TWO is executed.

Exercise 2.12: Self-Checking Examination

1. The editing symbols + and −:
   a. Suppress the printing of high order insignificant zeros.
   b. Are never associated with signed fields.
   c. Appear only if the source field is negative and are blanked out otherwise.
   d. Appear to the right of the last significant digit.

2. All of the following edit characters can appear in the same picture *except:*
   a. $ *.
   b. CR $.
   c. Z $ 9 0.
   d. CR DB.

3. The largest dollar amount that can appear in an edit picture of $$$$ is:
   a. 9999
   b. 10000
   c. 999
   d. 1000

4. All of the following moves are valid *except:*
   a. A numeric field to an edited numeric field.
   b. An alphanumeric field to a numeric field.
   c. A numeric field (integers only) to an alphanumeric field.
   d. An alphabetic field to an alphanumeric field.

5. The CORRESPONDING option:
   a. Is not used with the MOVE statement.
   b. Requires that at least one item in each pair of corresponding items be an elementary item for the move to be effective.
   c. Is effective even when REDEFINES or OCCURS clauses are present.
   d. Will cause at least one move even if every data name in a COBOL program is unique.

6. Data names within the same COBOL program:
   a. Must be unique.
   b. May be qualified by OF only.
   c. May be qualified by IN only.
   d. May be qualified by either OF or IN.

7. When an alphanumeric field is moved to an alphanumeric field:
   a. The fields must be of the same length.
   b. The characters within the sending field are moved one at a time, from right to left.
   c. The receiving field will be padded on the right with blanks, if it is larger than the sending field.
   d. The receiving field will be padded with high order zeros if it is larger than the sending field.

8. When a numeric field is moved to a numeric field:
   a. The fields must be of the same length.
   b. The digits within the sending field are moved one at a time, from right to left, *without* regard for the decimal point.
   c. The receiving field will be padded on the right with blanks, if it is larger than the sending field.
   d. The receiving field will be padded with high order zeros if it is larger than the sending field.

9. The symbols CR and DB:
   a. Represent positive and negative numbers, respectively.
   b. Represent negative and positive numbers, respectively.
   c. Appear only if the sending field is negative.
   d. Cannot appear with a dollar sign or comma.

10. The picture clause S999V99:
   a. Denotes a five-position field.
   b. Indicates two-positions to the right of the decimal point.
   c. Will hold either positive or negative numbers.
   d. All of the above.

11. If a numeric source field with picture of 9(3)V99 has the digits 12345, the value of a receiving field with picture 9(5) is:
   a. 12345
   b. 00123
   c. 00345
   d. 12300

12. If a numeric source field with picture of 9(5) has the digits 65432, the value of a receiving field with picture 9(3)V99 is:
   a. 65432
   b. 65400
   c. 43200
   d. 00432

13. Which of the following would *preclude* an individual move from taking place in a MOVE CORRESPONDING statement:
   a. The picture clauses of the sending and receiving fields are different.
   b. The level numbers of the sending and receiving fields are different.
   c. The qualification of the sending and receiving fields is different. (Not counting qualification at the 01 level.)
   d. All of the above.

14. Given the following requirements for an edited field: a dollar sign in the leftmost position, replacement of insignificant digits with asterisks, indication of dollars and cents with a maximum amount of $999.99. The required picture clause is:
   a. $$$$.99
   b. $$$$*.99
   c. $**9.99
   d. $***.*9

15. Given the following requirements for an edited field: a floating dollar sign, and indication of dollars and cents with a maximum amount of $9,999.99. The required picture clause is:
   a. $,$$$.99
   b. $$,$$$V99

c. $$,$$$.$9
d. $$,$$$.99

16. If a numeric field is moved to a numeric field, but the latter is a *group* item:

   a. The rules for an alphanumeric move are followed.
   b. Decimal alignment will be maintained.
   c. The statement will be flagged, because the receiving field must always be an elementary item.
   d. None of the above.

17. The statement MOVE A TO B C D.

   a. Is syntactically invalid.
   b. Will change the contents of A, B, C, D.
   c. Will move the contents of A to B, C, *and* D.
   d. Will follow the rules of an alphanumeric move, regardless of the pictures of the individual fields.

18. The statement MOVE ALL '–' TO DASHED-LINE.

   a. Is syntactically invalid.
   b. Will move 133 dashes to the field DASHED-LINE.
   c. Will move as many dashes to the field DASHED-LINE as there are characters in its picture clause.
   d. Is equivalent to MOVE '–' TO DASHED-LINE.

Solutions for Topic 2.3

Exercise 2.9: The MOVE Statement

1. |C|O|B|O|L|
2. |C|O|B|O|
3. |C|O|B|O|L| |
4. |2|3|4|
5. |0|1|2|3|4|
6. |0|1|2|3|
7. |0|1|2|3|4|
8. |1|2|3|4|0|
9. |2|3|4|0|

Exercise 2.10: Editing

1. 345678
2. 5678.00
3. 003456
4. 003456.78
5. $123.45
6. $12,345.00
7. $ 123CR
8. $ 123
9. $12,345DB
10. $12,345
11. $**123.45
12. 01 21 68
13. -3,456
14. -3,456
15. +3,456
16. 3,456
17. $ 1,234.56
18. $ 5.00
19. $

Exercise 2.11: The MOVE CORRESPONDING Statement

1. True

2. False: FIELD-THREE and FIELD-FOUR will *not* be changed as they are qualified differently in RECORD-ONE and RECORD-TWO.

3. False: FIELD-FIVE will be changed, but the five rightmost bytes in RECORD-ONE will be truncated.

4. False: Several moves will take place (see part 6).

5. False: Position within a record does not affect MOVE CORRESPONDING so long as the other rules are met.

6. The MOVE CORRESPONDING is equivalent to:

```
MOVE FIELD-ONE  OF  RECORD-ONE  TO FIELD-ONE OF RECORD-TWO.
MOVE FIELD-TWO  OF  RECORD-ONE  TO FIELD-TWO OF RECORD-TWO.
MOVE FIELD-FIVE OF  RECORD-ONE  TO FIELD-FIVE OF RECORD-TWO.
```

Exercise 2.12: Self-Checking Examination

1. A	6. D	11. B	15. D
2. D	7. C	12. C	16. A
3. C	8. D	13. C	17. C
4. B	9. C	14. C	18. C
5. B	10. D		

TOPIC 2.4: THE IF STATEMENT

COBOL Syntax

$$\underline{\text{IF}} \text{ condition} \begin{Bmatrix} \text{statement-1} \\ \underline{\text{NEXT SENTENCE}} \end{Bmatrix} \begin{Bmatrix} \underline{\text{ELSE}} \text{ statement-2} \\ \underline{\text{ELSE NEXT SENTENCE}} \end{Bmatrix}$$

General Format for Conditions

Relation condition:

$$\begin{Bmatrix} \text{identifier-1} \\ \text{literal-1} \\ \text{arithmetic-expression-1} \\ \text{index-name-1} \end{Bmatrix} \begin{Bmatrix} \text{IS [\underline{NOT}] \underline{GREATER} THAN} \\ \text{IS [\underline{NOT}] \underline{LESS} THAN} \\ \text{IS [\underline{NOT}] \underline{EQUAL} TO} \\ \text{IS [\underline{NOT}] >} \\ \text{IS [\underline{NOT}] <} \\ \text{IS [\underline{NOT}] =} \end{Bmatrix} \begin{Bmatrix} \text{identifier-2} \\ \text{literal-2} \\ \text{arithmetic-expression-2} \\ \text{index-name-2} \end{Bmatrix}$$

Class condition:

$$\text{identifier IS [\underline{NOT}]} \begin{Bmatrix} \underline{\text{NUMERIC}} \\ \underline{\text{ALPHABETIC}} \end{Bmatrix}$$

Sign condition:

$$\text{arithmetic-expression IS [\underline{NOT}]} \begin{Bmatrix} \underline{\text{POSITIVE}} \\ \underline{\text{NEGATIVE}} \\ \underline{\text{ZERO}} \end{Bmatrix}$$

Condition-name condition:

$$\text{88 condition-name:} \begin{Bmatrix} \underline{\text{VALUE}} \text{ IS} \\ \underline{\text{VALUES}} \text{ ARE} \end{Bmatrix} \text{literal-1} \left[\begin{Bmatrix} \underline{\text{THROUGH}} \\ \underline{\text{THRU}} \end{Bmatrix} \text{literal-2} \right]$$

$$\left[\text{literal-3} \left[\begin{Bmatrix} \underline{\text{THROUGH}} \\ \underline{\text{THRU}} \end{Bmatrix} \text{literal-4} \right] \right] \ldots$$

Negated simple condition:

NOT simple-condition

Combined condition:

condition $\left\{\begin{array}{c}\underline{AND}\\ OR\end{array}\right\}$ condition ...

Abbreviated combined relation condition:

relation-condition $\left\{\begin{array}{c}\underline{AND}\\ OR\end{array}\right\}$ [NOT] [relational-operator] object ...

Exercise 2.13: Condition Names

Establish condition names for a two position numeric code, YEAR-IN-SCHOOL, which can assume values from 1 to 12. Accommodate all of the following:

Group	Values
ELEMENTARY-SCHOOL	1-6
JUNIOR-HIGH-SCHOOL	7-9
HIGH-SCHOOL	10-12
VALID-CODES	1-12

Exercise 2.14: Compound and Implied Conditions

Indicate whether the skeletal IF statements in each pair have the same effect.

1. IF A = B AND C = D OR E = F ...
   IF (A = B AND C = D) OR E = F ...
2. IF A = B OR A = C OR A = D ...
   IF A = B OR C OR D ...
3. IF X = 10 OR X = 20 OR X = 30 AND Y = 40 ...
   IF (X = 10 OR 20 OR 30) AND Y = 40 ...
4. IF A = B AND A = C ...
   IF A NOT = B OR A NOT = C ...
5. IF A NOT > B ...
   IF A < B OR A = B ...
6. IF X > Y ...
   IF X NOT < Y ...

Exercise 2.15: The ELSE Clause

1. Consider the two sets of COBOL code shown, which differ only in their indentation and the presence of an extra period in the second example. Discuss the differences in resulting action caused by the presence of the extra period.

Example 1:

```
IF UNION-MEMBER
    PERFORM MAIL-UNION
ELSE                                    No Period
    ADD 1 TO NON-MEMBER-TOTAL
    PERFORM MAIL-COMPANY.
```

Example 2:

```
IF UNION-MEMBER
    PERFORM MAIL-UNION
ELSE                                    Extra period
    ADD 1 TO NON-MEMBER-TOTAL.
    PERFORM MAIL-COMPANY.
```

2. Consider the COBOL code of Figure 2.1. The intent is to give customers with orders of $2,000 or more a 2% discount (Customers with orders of less than $2,000 are *not* to receive any discount.) Explain the rather surprising output shown in Fig. 2.1 (Hint: count columns.)

```
COBOL code:
IF AMOUNT-ORDERED-THISWEEK < 2000
    MOVE ZEROS TO CUSTOMER-DISCOUNT
ELSE
    COMPUTE CUSTOMER-DISCOUNT = AMOUNT-ORDERED-THISWEEK * .02.
COMPUTE NET = AMOUNT-ORDERED-THISWEEK − CUSTOMER-DISCOUNT.
```

Output:

Amount Ordered	Discount	Net
3000	60	2940	— Correct calculation
4000	80	3920
1000	0	3920	— Net is incorrect
5000	100	4900	and equal to value
1500	0	4900	of previous order

Figure 2.1 COBOL Code and Associated Output.

Exercise 2.16: Nested IFs

1. Recode the following statements to show the ELSE clause on a line by itself, and indented under its associated IF. In addition, indent detail clauses four columns under their associated IF or ELSE.

    a. IF X > Y IF R > S
       MOVE E TO F ELSE MOVE A TO B.
    b. IF X > Y IF R > S MOVE E TO F
       ELSE MOVE A TO B ELSE MOVE C TO D.
    c. IF R > S MOVE X TO Y MOVE W TO Z
       ELSE IF T > V MOVE X TO Z
       ELSE IF A > B ADD 1 TO N MOVE X TO Y
       ELSE ADD 1 TO X.

2. Insert or remove periods so that the compiler interpretation will correspond with the given alignment.

    a. IF A > B
         MOVE C TO D
         MOVE E TO F
       MOVE G TO H.
    b. IF A > B
         ADD 1 TO COUNT-FIELD.
         IF C > D
            ADD 1 TO SECOND-FIELD.
       MOVE X TO Y.
    c. IF A > B
         MOVE C TO D.
         MOVE E TO F.
    d. IF A > B
         ADD 1 TO X
       ELSE
         IF C > D
            ADD 1 TO Y.
            ADD 1 TO Z
       ADD 20 TO W.

3. Given the flowchart of Fig. 2.2, answer True or False as appropriate:
    a. IF X < Y and R > S, then *always* add 1 to H.
    b. IF X < Y and R = S then *always* add 1 to J.
    c. IF X = Y and R > S and T = V then *always* add 1 to H.
    d. IF X > Y then *always* add 1 to G.
    e. IF X < Y and R > S and T < V, then *always* add 1 to I.

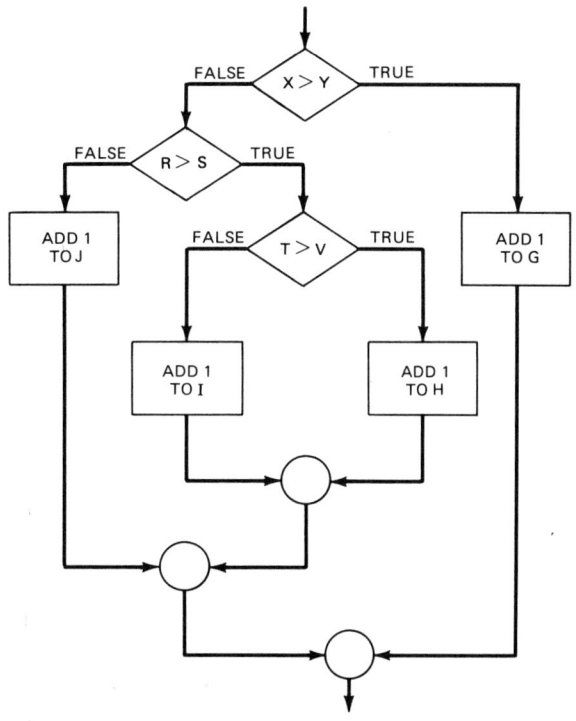

Figure 2.2

4. Are the following IF statements logically equivalent?

   Statement 1:

           IF A > B
             IF C > D
                 ADD 1 TO X
           ELSE
                 ADD 1 TO Y.

   Statement 2:

           IF A > B AND C > D
               ADD 1 TO X
           ELSE
               ADD 1 TO Y.

   Try the following sets of values to aid in answering the question:
   a. A = 5, B = 1, C = 10, D = 15
   b. A = 1, B = 5, C = 10, D = 15

Exercise 2.17: Self-Checking Examination

1. The clause IF X > Y OR X = Z AND X < W is considered true if:
   a. X > Y.
   b. X = Z AND X < W.
   c. X = Z.
   d. All of the above.
   e. Either (a) or (b) above.

Use the IF statement below to answer questions 2, 3, and 4.

```
            IF A > B
               IF C > D
                  MOVE X TO Y
                  MOVE S TO T
            ELSE
               MOVE X TO Z.
```

2. The IF statement:
   a. Is syntactically invalid.
   b. Is syntactically valid, but misleading because the ELSE is not shown under the appropriate IF.
   c. Will move X to Z if A not greater than B.
   d. Will always move X to Y if A is greater than B.

3. X will be moved to Y if:
   a. A is greater than B and C is greater than D.
   b. A is greater than B or C is greater than D.
   c. C is greater than D regardless of the relationship between A and B.
   d. A is less than or equal to B.

4. X will be moved to Z if:
   a. A is greater than B.
   b. A is greater than B and C is not less than D.
   c. A is greater than B and C is less than or equal to D.
   d. A is not greater than B.

5. When comparing two alphanumeric fields 'ADAMS' and 'ADAMSON':
   a. ADAMS will always come first.
   b. ADAMS will come first only under EBCDIC.
   c. ADAMS will come first only under ASCII.
   d. The comparison is invalid because the lengths of the two fields are different.

6. When comparing two alphanumeric fields, 'ABC12' and '56DEF':

a. 'ABC12' will *always* come first.
b. 'ABC12' will come first only under EBCDIC.
c. 'ABC12' will come first only under ASCII.
d. The comparision is invalid because both letters and numbers are contained in the same field.

7. The NEXT SENTENCE clause of the IF statement:
    a. Is mandatory if the ELSE clause is used.
    b. Is always mandatory.
    c. Directs control to the statement immediately following the first period.
    d. Cannot be used in nested IF statements.

8. The statement 'IF EXEMPT, PERFORM EXEMPT-ROUTINE' is:
    a. Syntactically invalid.
    b. Valid only if EXEMPT is defined as an 88 level entry.
    c. Valid regardless how EXEMPT is defined.
    d. None of the above.

9. The clause IF A = B OR C OR D is:
    a. Syntactically invalid.
    b. Equivalent to the clause IF A = B OR B = C OR C = D.
    c. Equivalent to the clause IF A = B OR A = C OR A = D.
    d. Both (b) and (c) above.

10. Proper indentation in a nested IF is:
    a. Required by the compiler.
    b. Strongly suggested as a programming standard to aid programmer interpretation.
    c. A waste of time, since indentation (or lack thereof) does not affect compiler interpretation.
    d. Increases compiler efficiency.

11. Which of the following is logically different from the rest:
    a. IF A IS NOT > THAN B. . .
    b. IF A IS LESS THAN B OR A IS EQUAL TO B. . .
    c. IF A IS NOT GREATER THAN B. . .
    d. IF B IS LESS THAN A. . .

Use the code below for questions 12 and 13.

```
05   YEAR-IN-SCHOOL      PIC 9.
     88   FRESHMAN        VALUE 1.
     88   SOPHOMORE       VALUE 2.
     88   JUNIOR          VALUE 3.
     88   SENIOR          VALUE 4.
     88   VALID-CODES     VALUES ARE 1 THRU 4.
```

12. All of the following are equivalent *except:*
    a. IF VALID-CODES...
    b. IF YEAR-IN-SCHOOL = 1 OR 2 OR 3 OR 4...
    c. IF YEAR-IN-SCHOOL > 0 AND < 5...
    d. IF FRESHMAN OR SOPHOMORE OR JUNIOR...

13. The entry IF SOPHOMORE...
    a. Is equivalent to IF YEAR-IN-SCHOOL = 2.
    b. Is an example of a RENAMES or 66 level entry.
    c. Is more efficient in terms of generated object code.
    d. All of the above.

Use the code below to answer questions 14 and 15.

```
IF A = B
    MOVE C TO D
ELSE
    MOVE E TO F.
    MOVE X TO Y.
```

14. All of the following are true *except:*
    a. The statements are syntactically correct, but misleadingly indented.
    b. X will be moved to Y only if A is not equal to B.
    c. X will be moved to Y regardless of the values of A and B.
    d. E will be moved to F whenever A is not equal to B.

15. All of the following are true *except:*
    a. Removing the period after MOVE E TO F will make the indentation match compiler interpretation, and will change the original meaning.
    b. Removing the period after MOVE E TO F will make the indentation match compiler interpretation, and will *not* change the original meaning.
    c. Aligning MOVE X TO Y directly under IF A = B will cause the new indentation to match compiler interpretation and leave the latter unchanged.
    d. The statements could be compressed into a single line *without* affecting compiler interpretation.

Solutions for Topic 2.4

Exercise 2.13: Condition Names

```
05  YEAR-IN-SCHOOL                    PIC 99.
    88  ELEMENTARY-SCHOOL     VALUES ARE 1 THRU 6.
```

```
        88    JUNIOR-HIGH-SCHOOL          VALUES ARE 7, 8, 9.
        88    HIGH-SCHOOL                 VALUES ARE 10, 11, 12.
        88    VALID-CODES                 VALUES ARE 1 THRU 12.
```

Exercise 2.14: Compound and Implied Conditions

1. Yes

2. Yes

3. No: The first statement is true if X = 10 or X = 20 *regardless* of the value of Y. The second statement *requires* Y = 40.

4. No: The first statement is true only when A = B = C. The second statement is false *only when* A = B = C.

5. Yes

6. No: X > Y is equivalent to X NOT < Y *and* X NOT = Y.

Exercise 2.15: The ELSE CLAUSE

1. In the first example, MAIL-COMPANY is performed only for non-union members. In the second example, the period terminates the IF statement, hence MAIL-COMPANY is performed for *all* records.

2. The logic is apparently straightforward. An order of $2000 or more receives a discount of 2% on the entire order. The amount due (NET) is equal to the amount ordered minus the discount. The code seems correct, yet the calculated net amounts are wrong for any order less than $2000. Notice that the net amount printed for these orders equals the net for the previous order (the net for an order of 1000 is incorrectly printed as 3920, which was the correct net for the preceding order of 4000). The net amount for an order of 1500 was printed as 4900, and so on.

The only possible explanation is that the COMPUTE NET statement is not executed for net amounts less than 2000. The *only* way that can happen is if the COMPUTE NET statement is taken as part of the ELSE clause, and that can happen only if the ELSE is not terminated by a period. The period is "present" however, so we are back at ground zero-or are we? The period is present, *but in column 73,* which is ignored by the compiler. Hence the visual code does not match the compiler interpretation and hence the bug.

Exercise 2.16: Nested IF Statements

```
1. a.   IF X > Y
            IF R > S
                MOVE E TO F
            ELSE
                MOVE A TO B.
```

b. IF X > Y
      IF R > S
           MOVE E TO F
      ELSE
           MOVE A TO B
  ELSE
      MOVE C TO D.

c. IF R > S
      MOVE X TO Y
      MOVE W TO Z
  ELSE
      IF T > V
           MOVE X TO Z
      ELSE
           IF A > B
                ADD 1 TO N
                MOVE X TO Y
            ELSE
                ADD 1 TO X.

2. a. Insert a period after MOVE E TO F.
   b. Remove the period after ADD 1 TO COUNT-FIELD.
   c. Remove the period after MOVE C TO D.
   d. Remove the period after ADD 1 TO Y *and* insert a period after ADD 1 TO Z.

3. a. False, only if T > V.
   b. True
   c. False, always add 1 to I.
   d. True
   e. True

4. No, they are not equivalent. The first set of values does produce identical results, namely, ADD 1 TO Y. The second set of values (A = 1, B = 5, C = 10, and D = 15) causes *different* outcomes. In statement 1 with the second set, A is not greater than B. Since there is no ELSE clause associated with IF A > B, no further action will be taken. In statement 2, A is again not greater than B, but there is an ELSE clause associated with the compound IF; hence, the statement ADD 1 TO Y is executed.

Exercise 2.17: Self-Checking Examination

1. E	5. A	9. C	13. A
2. B	6. B	10. B	14. B
3. A	7. C	11. D	15. B
4. C	8. B	12. D	

TOPIC 2.5: THE PERFORM STATEMENT

COBOL Syntax

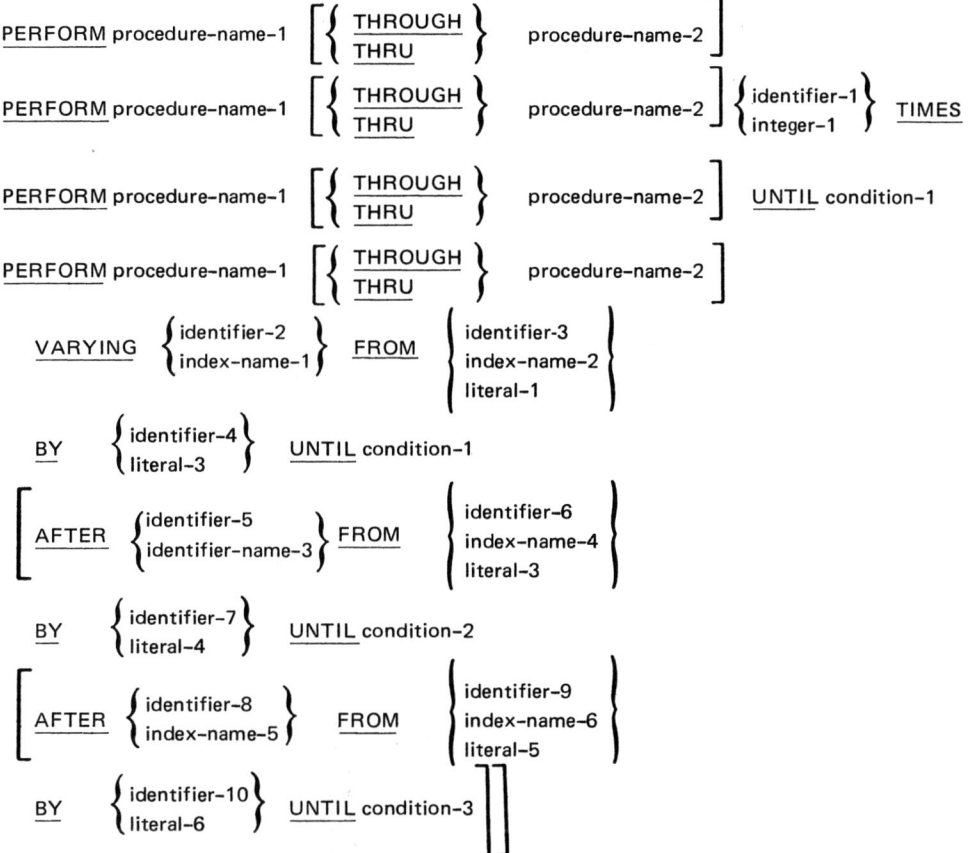

Exercise 2.18: Performing Sections and Paragraphs

1. Given the code:

        PROCEDURE DIVISION.
        MAINLINE SECTION.
        FIRST-PARAGRAPH.
            PERFORM A.
            PERFORM PAR-B 3 TIMES.
            PERFORM PAR-C THRU PAR-E.
            PERFORM PAR-F VARYING SUB FROM 1 BY 1
                UNTIL SUB = 5.

```
A SECTION.
PAR-A.
    .
PAR-B.
    .
    .
PAR-C.
    .
    .
PAR-D.
    .
    .
PAR-E.
    .
    .
B SECTION.
PAR-F.
```

Indicate how many times each paragraph has been executed *after all four* PERFORMS are completed.

2. Given the code:

```
PROCEDURE DIVISION.
MAINLINE SECTION.
FIRST-PARAGRAPH.
    PERFORM SEC-A.
    PERFORM PAR-C THRU PAR-E.
    MOVE ZERO TO N.
    PERFORM PAR-G UNTIL N > 2.
SEC-A SECTION.
PAR-A.
    ADD 10 TO X.
    ADD 10 TO Y.
    ADD 10 TO Z.
PAR-B.
    ADD 20 TO X.
PAR-C.
    ADD 30 TO X.
PAR-D.
    ADD 40 TO Y.
    ADD 50 TO Z.
PAR-E.
    EXIT.
PAR-F.
    MOVE 2 TO N.
PAR-G.
    ADD 1 TO N.
    ADD 50 TO X.
```

a. How many times is each paragraph executed?
b. What is the final value of X, Y, and Z? (Assume they were all initialized to 0.)
c. What would happen if the statement ADD 1 TO N were removed from PAR-G?

Exercise 2.19: PERFORM VARYING

1. Indicate the 12 pairs of values that will be assumed by SUB-1 and SUB-2 as a result of the statement:

```
PERFORM PROCESS-EMPLOYEE-RECORDS
    VARYING SUB-1 FROM 1 BY 1
        UNTIL SUB-1 > 6
    AFTER SUB-2 FROM 1 BY 1
        UNTIL SUB-2 > 2.
```

2. Indicate the 24 sets of values that will be assumed by INDEX-1 INDEX-2, and INDEX-3, as a result of the statement:

```
PERFORM INITIALIZE-TABLE
    VARYING INDEX-3 FROM 1 BY 1
        UNTIL INDEX-3 > 2
    AFTER INDEX-2 FROM 1 BY 1
        UNTIL INDEX-2 > 3
    AFTER INDEX-1 FROM 1 BY 1
        UNTIL INDEX-1 > 4.
```

3. Assume the 50 entries in the table, EMPLOYEE-TABLE, defined below, are to be modified by the routine PROCESS-EMPLOYEE-RECORDS:

```
01   EMPLOYEE-TABLE.
    05   LOCATION            OCCURS 5 TIMES.
        10   DEPARTMENT      OCCURS 10 TIMES   PIC 9(5).
```

In other words, the routine PROCESS-EMPLOYEE-RECORDS is to be called 50 times, once for each LOCATION/DEPARTMENT combination. The first time the routine is executed, it is to modify the table entry for (LOCATION 1, DEPARTMENT 1), then (LOCATION 2, DEPARTMENT 1), (LOCATION 3, DEPARTMENT 1), etc. The sixth time it is to modify (LOCATION 1, DEPARTMENT 2), the eleventh time (LOCATION 1, DEPARTMENT 3), and so on. Code the required PERFORM VARYING statement.

4. Use the information from part 3 except alter the sequence of execution. This time use the order: (LOCATION 1, DEPARTMENT 1), (LOCATION 1, DEPARTMENT 2), . . . (LOCATION 1, DEPARTMENT 10),

(LOCATION 2, DEPARTMENT 1), etc. Code the PERFORM VARYING statement.

5. How many times will the routine INCREMENT-TABLE be performed as a result of the following statements:

>PERFORM INCREMENT-TABLE
>   VARYING SUB FROM 1 BY 1
>   UNTIL SUB > 10.
>
>PERFORM INCREMENT-TABLE
>   VARYING SUB FROM 1 BY 1
>   UNTIL SUB = 10.
>
>PERFORM INCREMENT-TABLE
>   VARYING SUB FROM 1 BY 1
>   UNTIL SUB < 10.
>
>PERFORM INCREMENT-TABLE
>   VARYING SUB FROM 1 BY 2
>   UNTIL SUB > 10.
>
>PERFORM INCREMENT-TABLE
>   VARYING SUB FROM 7 BY 3
>   UNTIL SUB > 13.
>
>PERFORM INCREMENT-TABLE
>   VARYING SUB FROM 1 BY 1
>   UNTIL SUB = NUMBER-ENTRIES.

Exercise 2.20: Self-Checking Examination

1. The following are all valid forms of the PERFORM verb *except:*
   a. PERFORM PAR-A NUMBER-TRANSACTION TIMES.
   b. PERFORM PAR-A.
   c. PERFORM PAR-A TWICE.
   d. PERFORM PAR-A VARYING WS-SUB FROM 1 BY 1 UNTIL WS-SUB = 10.

2. The PERFORM verb:
   a. Can specify only sections.
   b. Can specify only paragraphs.
   c. Must have an associated THRU clause.
   d. Cannot cause the execution of more than a single paragraph.
   e. None of the above.

3. The statement:
   PERFORM PAR-A
       VARYING WS-SUB FROM 1 BY 1 UNTIL WS-SUB = 10 will:

a. Execute PAR-A 10 times.
  b. Execute PAR-A 9 times.
  c. Execute PAR-A once.
  d. Is an invalid form of the PERFORM verb.

4. The statement:
   PERFORM PAR-A
     VARYING SUB-1 FROM 1 BY 1 UNTIL SUB-1 > 4
       AFTER SUB-2 FROM 1 BY 1 UNTIL SUB-2 > 3.
   a. Will perform PAR-A 12 times.
   b. Will keep SUB-1 at 1 while incrementing SUB-2 from 1 to 3, after which SUB-1 will be incremented to 2 and SUB-2 will be reset to 1.
   c. Will keep SUB-2 at 1 while incrementing SUB-1 from 1 to 4, after which SUB-1 will be reset to 1 and SUB-2 incremented to 2.
   d. Both (a) and (b) above.
   e. Both (a) and (c) above.

5. The statements: MOVE 10 TO N.
                   PERFORM PAR-A UNTIL N = 10.
   a. Will execute PAR-A 10 times.
   b. Will execute PAR-A 9 times.
   c. Will not execute PAR-A at all.
   d. None of the above.

6. The PERFORM verb can:
   a. Manipulate subscripts only.
   b. Manipulate indexes only.
   c. Can manipulate both subscripts and indexes.
   d. Can manipulate neither subscripts nor indexes.

7. A single PERFORM statement can cause the execution of many different paragraphs:
   a. If a THRU clause is specified.
   b. If a section name appears as the designated procedure.
   c. Both (a) and (b) above.
   d. Neither (a) nor (b) above as only a single paragraph is executed as the result of a PERFORM.

8. A single PERFORM statement can cause the *same* paragraph to be executed many times:
   a. If the TIMES option is used.
   b. If the UNTIL clause is included.
   c. If VARYING/FROM/BY is specified.
   d. All of the above.

9. The PERFORM statement has how many distinct syntactical formats:
   a. One.
   b. Two.
   c. Three.
   d. Four.

10. The statement: PERFORM PROCESS-RECORDS
                       UNTIL END-OF-FILE.
    a. Is syntactically incorrect.
    b. Must execute the routine PROCESS-RECORDS at least once.
    c. Is syntactically correct provided END-OF-FILE is an 88-level entry.
    d. Both (b) and (c) above.

11. Given that the statement, PERFORM PAR-A THRU PAR-A-EXIT, is in effect, one may safely do all of the following *except:*
    a. PERFORM PAR-B, where PAR-B is outside the range from PAR-A through PAR-A-EXIT.
    b. GO TO PAR-B where PAR-B is outside the range from PAR-A through PAR-A-EXIT.
    c. Execute a forward GO TO to PAR-A-EXIT.
    d. Call a subprogram.

12. The THRU option:
    a. Is required if more than one paragraph is to be executed as a result of a single PERFORM.
    b. Is required if the UNTIL option is specified.
    c. Is not available with the VARYING option.
    d. None of the above.

Use the skeletal code below for questions 13-15.

```
MAINLINE.
    .
    .
    PERFORM PAR-A 5 TIMES.
    STOP RUN.
PAR-A.
    PERFORM PAR-B 10 TIMES.
    .
    .
PAR-B.
    PERFORM PAR-C 3 TIMES.
    .
PAR-C.   .
```

13. PAR-A will be executed:

a. 5 times.
b. 50 times.
c. 150 times.
d. 6 times.
e. None of the above.

14. PAR-B will be executed:
    a. 5 times.
    b. 10 times.
    c. 50 times.
    d. 51 times.
    e. None of the above.

15. PAR-C will be executed.
    a. 18 times.
    b. 150 times.
    c. 151 times.
    d. 30 times.
    e. None of the above.

16. Given the code:
```
MAINLINE.
    .
    .
    .
    READ TRANSACTION-FILE
        AT END MOVE 'NO' TO RECORDS-REMAINING-SWITCH.
    PERFORM PROCESS-RECORDS
        UNTIL RECORDS-REMAINING-SWITCH = 'NO'.
    .
    .
PROCESS-RECORDS.
```

The procedure PROCESS-RECORDS:
a. Requires a second read statement, identical to the initial read, as its *first* statement.
b. Requires a second read statement, identical to the initial read, as its *last* statement.
c. Does not require any read statements.
d. Should be a section, rather than a paragraph.

Solutions for Topic 2.5

Exercise 2.18: Performing Sections and Paragraphs

1. PAR-A: Once   PAR-D: Twice
   PAR-B: Four times   PAR-E: Twice
   PAR-C: Twice   PAR-F: Four times

Notes: 1. The statement PERFORM A invokes a *section, consisting of five paragraphs* causing each paragraph to be executed once.

2. The PERFORM statement *increments, tests, and then branches.* Accordingly, VARYING SUB FROM 1 BY 1 UNTIL SUB = 5 executes the performed routine *four* times.

2. a. PAR-A: Once PAR-E: Twice
   PAR-B: Once PAR-F: Once
   PAR-C: Twice PAR-G: Four times
   PAR-D: Twice

Note: The statement PERFORM SEC-A invokes a section, consisting of seven paragraphs.
   b. X = 290, Y = 90, Z = 110
   c. PAR-G would execute indefinitely, causing an infinite loop.

Exercise 2.19: Perform Varying

1. (1,1) (1,2) (2,1) (2,2) (3,1) (3,2)
   (4,1) (4,2) (5,1) (5,2) (6,1) (6,2)

2. (1,1,1) (2,1,1) (3,1,1) (4,1,1)
   (1,2,1) (2,2,1) (3,2,1) (4,2,1)
   (1,3,1) (2,3,1) (3,3,1) (4,3,1)
   (1,1,2) (2,1,2) (3,1,2) (4,1,2)
   (1,2,2) (2,2,2) (3,2,2) (4,2,2)
   (1,3,2) (2,3,2) (3,3,2) (4,3,2)

3. PERFORM PROCESS-EMPLOYEE-RECORDS
       VARYING DEPARTMENT–SUB FROM 1 BY 1
           UNTIL DEPARTMENT–SUB > 10
       AFTER LOCATION–SUB FROM 1 BY 1
           UNTIL LOCATION–SUB > 5.

4. PERFORM PROCESS-EMPLOYEE-RECORDS
       VARYING LOCATION–SUB FROM 1 BY 1
           UNTIL LOCATION–SUB > 5
       AFTER DEPARTMENT–SUB FROM 1 BY 1
           UNTIL DEPARTMENT–SUB > 10.

5. 10 times
   9 times
   0 times (the condition is satisfied immediately)
   5 times (For SUB = 1, 3, 5, 7, and 9)
   3 times (For SUB = 7, 10, and 13)
   One less than the value of NUMBER-ENTRIES.

Exercise 2.20: Self-Checking Examination

1. C	5. C	9. D	13. A
2. E	6. C	10. C	14. C
3. B	7. C	11. B	15. B
4. D	8. D	12. D	16. B

TOPIC 2.6: TABLE PROCESSING

COBOL Syntax

DATA DIVISION:

OCCURS $\begin{Bmatrix} \text{integer-1 } \underline{\text{TO}} \text{ integer-2 TIMES } \underline{\text{DEPENDING}} \text{ ON data-name-1} \\ \text{integer-2 TIMES} \end{Bmatrix}$

$\left[\begin{Bmatrix} \underline{\text{ASCENDING}} \\ \underline{\text{DESCENDING}} \end{Bmatrix} \text{ KEY IS data-name-2 [, data-name-3] } \dots \right]$

[<u>INDEXED</u> BY index-name-1 [, index-name-2] ...]]

PROCEDURE DIVISION:

<u>SEARCH</u> identifier-1 $\left[\underline{\text{VARYING}} \begin{Bmatrix} \text{identifier-2} \\ \text{index-name-1} \end{Bmatrix} \right]$ [AT <u>END</u> imperative-statement-1]

<u>WHEN</u> condition-1 $\begin{Bmatrix} \text{imperative-statement-2} \\ \underline{\text{NEXT SENTENCE}} \end{Bmatrix}$

$\left[\underline{\text{WHEN}} \text{ condition-2} \begin{Bmatrix} \text{imperative-statement-3} \\ \underline{\text{NEXT SENTENCE}} \end{Bmatrix} \right]$ ...

<u>SEARCH ALL</u> identifier-1 [AT <u>END</u> imperative-statement-1]

<u>WHEN</u> $\begin{Bmatrix} \text{data-name-1} \\ \text{condition-name-1} \end{Bmatrix} \begin{Bmatrix} \text{IS } \underline{\text{EQUAL TO}} \\ \text{IS =} \end{Bmatrix} \begin{Bmatrix} \text{identifier-3} \\ \text{literal-1} \\ \text{arithmetic-expression-1} \end{Bmatrix}$

$\left[\underline{\text{AND}} \begin{Bmatrix} \text{data-name-2} \\ \text{condition-name-2} \end{Bmatrix} \begin{Bmatrix} \text{IS } \underline{\text{EQUAL TO}} \\ \text{IS =} \end{Bmatrix} \begin{Bmatrix} \text{identifier-4} \\ \text{literal-2} \\ \text{arithmetic-expression-2} \end{Bmatrix} \right]$

$\begin{Bmatrix} \text{imperative-statement-2} \\ \underline{\text{NEXT SENTENCE}} \end{Bmatrix}$

<u>SET</u> $\begin{Bmatrix} \text{indentifier-1 [, identifier-2] } \dots \\ \text{index-name-1 [, index-name-2] } \dots \end{Bmatrix}$ <u>TO</u> $\begin{Bmatrix} \text{identifier-3} \\ \text{index-name-3} \\ \text{integer-1} \end{Bmatrix}$

<u>SET</u> index-name-4 [, index-name-5] ... $\begin{Bmatrix} \underline{\text{UP BY}} \\ \underline{\text{DOWN BY}} \end{Bmatrix} \begin{Bmatrix} \text{identifier-4} \\ \text{integer-2} \end{Bmatrix}$

Capsule Summary: Storage Allocation and Hierarchical References

COBOL Code

```
01    ENROLLMENTS.
   05    COLLEGE OCCURS 3 TIMES.
      10    SCHOOL OCCURS 5 TIMES.
         15    YEAR OCCURS 4 TIMES    PIC S9(4).
```

Storage Allocation

ENROLLMENTS						
COLLEGE - 1					COLLEGE - 2
School - 1	School - 2	School - 3	School - 4	School - 5	School - 1
yr-1 yr-2 yr-3 yr-4	yr-1 yr-2 yr-3 yr-4	yr-1 yr-2 yr-3 yr-4	yr-1 yr-2 yr-3 yr-4	yr-1 yr-2 yr-3 yr-4	yr-1 yr-2 yr-3 yr-4

Figure 2.3   Storage Schematic for Three Level Table.

Hierarchical References

YEAR (1, 2, 3)   refers to the enrollment in college 1, school 2, year 3. YEAR must always be used with three subscripts.

YEAR (3, 4, 5)   refers to the enrollment in college 3, school 4, year 5. It is valid syntactically in that three subscripts are specified, but *invalid logically* as YEAR occurs only four times.

SCHOOL (1, 2)   refers to the enrollment in college 1, school 2; in effect it references the four years of college 1, school 2 collectively. SCHOOL must always be used with two subscripts.

COLLEGE (3)   refers to the enrollment in the third college; it references the 20 fields of the third college collectively. COLLEGE must always be used with one subscript.

ENROLLMENTS   refers to the entire table of 60 elements. ENROLLMENTS may not be referenced with a subscript.

Exercise 2.21: Hierarchical References

Given the COBOL definition:

```
01   CORPORATION.
    05   REGION OCCURS 4 TIMES.
        10   STATE OCCURS 3 TIMES.
            15   SALESMAN OCCURS 5 TIMES   PIC 9(5).
```

indicate whether the following references are valid or invalid. In addition, for each valid entry indicate the specific positions in the table which are being referenced; and finally, for each invalid entry indicate your objection.

1. SALESMAN (1, 2, 3)
2. SALESMAN (3, 4, 5)
3. SALESMAN (1, 2)
4. REGION (1)
5. STATE (4, 3)
6. STATE (3, 4)
7. CORPORATION

Exercise 2.22: The OCCURS Clause

Show an appropriate schematic indicating storage assignment for each table.

```
1. 10   CITY-TABLE.
       15   CITY-NAME OCCURS 10 TIMES                    PIC X(10).
       15   CITY-POPULATION OCCURS 10 TIMES              PIC 9(7).

2. 10   CITY-TABLE OCCURS 10 TIMES.
       15   CITY-NAME                                    PIC X(10).
       15   CITY-POPULATION                              PIC 9(7).

3. 10   CITY-TABLE OCCURS 10 TIMES.
       15   CITY-NAME                                    PIC X(10).
       15   CITY-POPULATION-GROUP OCCURS 4 TIMES         PIC 9(7).

4. 10   CITY-CODE-TABLE OCCURS 10 TIMES
       ASCENDING KEY IS CITY-CODE
       INDEXED BY CITY-INDEX.
       15   CITY-CODE                                    PIC 9(3).
       15   CITY-NAME                                    PIC X(10).
```

95

5. 01 SALES-TOTALS.
   05 REGION OCCURS 5 TIMES.
       10 CITY OCCURS 2 TIMES.
           15 SALESMAN OCCURS 3 TIMES   PIC 9(5).

6. 01 SALES-TOTALS.
   05 REGION OCCURS 5 TIMES.
       10 CITY OCCURS 3 TIMES   PIC 9(6).
       10 SALESMAN OCCURS 3 TIMES   PIC 9(4).

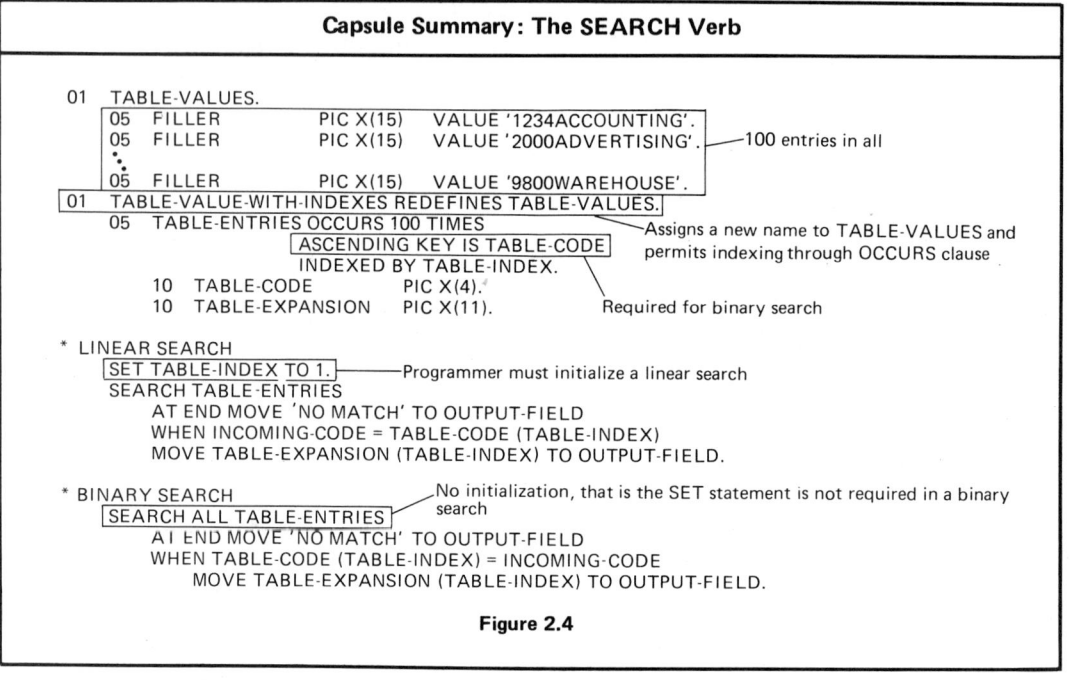

Figure 2.4

Exercise 2.23: Coding COBOL Statements

1. Code an OCCURS clause and related entries, to establish a variable length table consisting of up to 100 pairs of 2-position numeric location codes and 15-position expanded location names. The OCCURS clause should permit a binary search to be applied to the table in the Procedure Division. Note, however, that your solution is merely to allocate space for the table, without assigning any specific values.

2. Code a SEARCH verb (and any associated statement needed) to sequentially search the table of part 1. If the value of INPUT-LOCATION-CODE appears in the table, move the corresponding location name to OUTPUT-LOCATION-NAME; otherwise move UNKNOWN to OUTPUT-LOCATION-NAME.

3. Modify part 2 to use a binary, rather than a sequential search.

4. Code COBOL statements to allocate space *and* assign values to a table of job titles and codes. (Each title and corresponding code are 3 and 10 positions respectively.) Use the following four sets of titles and codes for illustration, but make your table large enough to accommodate 50 different codes.

Job Code	Job Title
010	Accountant
015	Analyst
020	Auditor
025	Bookkeeper
etc.	etc.

Finally, include the necessary entries to enable a binary search against your table.

5. Code COBOL statements to allocate space and assign values for the two-dimensional table of hourly pay rates shown below. (Note that an individual's rate is a function of both skill and experience levels. An individual with an experience level of 4 and a skill level of 1 earns $3.75. An individual at experience level 1 and skill level 4 earns $6.00.)

		Skill level					
		1	2	3	4	5	6
	1	$3.00	$4.00	$5.00	$6.00	$6.75	$10.00
	2	$3.25	$4.50	$5.50	$7.00	$7.50	$11.50
Experience	3	$3.50	$5.00	$6.00	$8.00	$8.25	$13.00
level	4	$3.75	$5.50	$6.50	$9.00	$9.00	$14.50
	5	$4.00	$6.00	$7.00	$10.00	$9.75	$16.00

Exercise 2.24: Self-Checking Examination

1. Two-dimensional tables:
   a. Are not permitted in COBOL.
   b. Require two OCCURS clauses in their definition.
   c. Can be referenced by indexes only.
   d. Can be referenced by binary subscripts only.

2. The SEARCH verb requires that:
   a. An index be present in the definition of the corresponding table.
   b. The clause ASCENDING KEY be present in the definition of the corresponding table.
   c. The AT END clause be included.
   d. No more than a single WHEN condition be used.
   e. All of the above.

3. Given:
   ```
   01 ENROLLMENTS.
      05 COLLEGE OCCURS 3 TIMES.
         10 SCHOOL OCCURS 5 TIMES.
            15 YEAR OCCURS 4 TIMES   PIC 9(4).
   ```
   all of the following are true *except:*
   a. A total of 240 bytes are defined in the table, ENROLLMENTS.
   b. Positions 1-80 of the table refer to the first college, positions 81-160 to the second college, and positions 161-240 to the third college.
   c. Any reference to YEAR requires 3 subscripts.
   d. Any reference to COLLEGE requires 3 subscripts.

4. Concerning question 3, which of the following are valid references:
   a. COLLEGE (2).
   b. SCHOOL (1, 2).
   c. YEAR (1, 2, 3).
   d. All of the above.

5. All of the following are true about the SEARCH verb *except:*
   a. It may contain more than one WHEN clause.
   b. It must contain an AT END clause.
   c. It passes control to the sentence immediately following, when either the WHEN or AT END conditions are satisfied.
   d. It must be used on a table that was defined with an index.

6. Given the entries:
   ```
   05 SALES-TABLE OCCURS 12 TIMES.
      10 SALES-VOLUME  PIC 9(6).
      10 SALES-MONTH   PIC X(10).
   ```
   a. A total of 16 bytes is defined in storage for SALES-TABLE.
   b. A total of 192 bytes is defined in storage for SALES-TABLE.
   c. The first 72 bytes of SALES-TABLE relate to SALES-VOLUME, the last 120 bytes relate to SALES-MONTH.
   d. Both (b) and (c) above.

7. Given the entries:
   ```
   05 SALES-TABLE.
      10 SALES-VOLUME OCCURS 12 TIMES    PIC 9(6).
      10 SALES-MONTH OCCURS 12 TIMES     PIC X(10).
   ```
   a. SALES-TABLE is a two-dimensional table because it has two OCCURS clauses defined under it.
   b. SALES-TABLE will have the same *amount* of space as was allocated in question 6, although the arrangement will be different.
   c. Any subsequent Procedure Division references to the 05 entry SALES-TABLE require a subscript.
   d. Any subsequent Procedure Division reference to SALES-MONTH requires two subscripts.

8. All of the following are true about a binary search *except:*
   a. It is implemented by SEARCH ALL.
   b. It requires a maximum of 10 comparisons for a 1000 entry table.
   c. It will *always* take fewer comparisons than the corresponding linear search.
   d. It requires a table whose keys are in ascending *or* descending order.

9. Which of the following is required in the OCCURS clause?
   a. DEPENDING ON.
   b. INDEXED BY.
   c. ASCENDING KEY.
   d. DESCENDING KEY.
   e. None of the above.

10. The SET verb is used:
    a. To initialize the value of an index.
    b. To alter the value of an index either up or down.
    c. To alter the value of a subscript either up or down.
    d. Both (a) and (b) above.
    e. Both (b) and (c) above.

11. The statement: SET TABLE-INDEX TO 2:
    a. Is invalid unless TABLE-INDEX has been defined as an index.
    b. Moves a 2 to the internal value of TABLE-INDEX.
    c. Both (a) and (b) above.
    d. None of the above.

12. The SET verb:
    a. Has two distinct syntactical forms.
    b. Is required prior to a binary search.
    c. Can manipulate only subscripts.
    d. None of the above.

13. Tables in COBOL:
    a. Are always fixed length.
    b. Are defined with an OCCURS clause.
    c. Must be processed via the SEARCH and SEARCH ALL verbs whenever a table lookup is performed.
    d. Can be 1, 2, 3, or 4 dimensions.

14. Direct access to table entries:
    a. Requires no comparisons whatsoever.
    b. Requires a numeric key.
    c. Often results in wasted storage space.
    d. All of the above.

15. The keys of a table are not required to be in sequence for:
   a. A binary search.
   b. A linear search.
   c. Direct access to table entries.
   d. None of the above.

16. After a SEARCH verb has been executed, and no match has been found, control passes to:
   a. The statement immediately following, provided the AT END clause does not contain a "GO TO."
   b. The statement immediately following, regardless of the AT END clause.
   c. The statement immediately following if there is no AT END clause.
   d. Both (a) and (c) above.

17. The REDEFINES clause:
   a. Allocates additional storage and assigns another name to previously defined storage locations.
   b. Can be used at the 01 level in Working-Storage.
   c. Is associated only with 77-level entries.
   d. None of the above.

18. All of the following are true about searching a table of 500 elements *except:*
   a. A binary search will *always* be faster than a sequential search.
   b. A sequential search could require 500 "guesses."
   c. A binary search will never take more than 9 guesses.
   d. A sequential search will require 250 guesses on the average.

Solutions for Topic 2.6

Exercise 2.21: Hierarchical References

1. Valid: refers to the 3rd salesman, in the 2nd state, in the 1st region.

2. Valid syntactically, but *invalid* logically; SALESMAN (3, 4, 5) refers to the 5th salesman, in the 4th state in the 3rd region. Since the COBOL definition specified only 3 states, an execution error will result.

3. Invalid: any reference to SALESMAN requires three subscripts.

4. Valid: refers collectively to the 3 states and 15 salesmen (5 per state) in the first region.

5. Valid: refers collectively to the 5 salesmen in the 3rd state of the 4th region.

6. Valid syntactically, but *invalid* logically as there are only 3 states. The reference in question is to the 4th state of the 3rd region.

7. Valid: refers collectively to the 60 elements in the entire table.

Exercise 2.22: The OCCURS Clause

1. CITY-TABLE: NAME (1), NAME (2), ... NAME (10), POP (1), ... POP (10)

2. CITY-TABLE (1): NAME (1), POP (1); CITY-TABLE (2): NAME (2), POP (2); ...

3. CITY-TABLE (1): NAME (1), GRP (1), GRP (2), GRP (3), GRP (4); ...

4. CITY-CODE (1): CD (1), NAME (1); CITY-CODE (2): CD (2), NAME (2); ...

5. SALES-TOTALS: REGION (1) [CITY (1): SL (1), SL (2), SL (3); CITY (2): SL (1), SL (2), SL (3)]; REGION (2) [CITY (1): SL (1), SL (2), SL (3)] ...

6. SALES-TOTALS: REGION (1) [CITY (1), CITY (2), CITY (3), SL (1), SL (2), SL (3)]; REGION (2) ...

Exercise 2.23: Coding COBOL Statements

1.
```
05  LOCATION-TABLE
        OCCURS 1 TO 100 TIMES DEPENDING ON NUMBER-OF-LOCATIONS
        ASCENDING KEY IS LOCATION-CODE
        INDEXED BY LOCATION-INDEX.
    10  LOCATION-CODE            PIC 99.
    10  LOCATION-NAME            PIC X(15).
```

2.
```
SET LOCATION-INDEX TO 1.
SEARCH LOCATION-TABLE
    AT END MOVE 'UNKNOWN' TO OUTPUT-LOCATION-NAME
    WHEN LOCATION-CODE (LOCATION-INDEX) = INPUT-LOCATION-CODE
        MOVE LOCATION-NAME (LOCATION-INDEX) TO OUTPUT-LOCATION-NAME.
```

3. Change SEARCH to SEARCH ALL. (In addition, the SET statement is *not* required.)

4.
```
01 TITLE-TABLE-AND-VALUES.
    05  TITLE-VALUES.
        10  FILLER        PIC X(13) VALUE '010 ACCOUNTANT'.
        10  FILLER        PIC X(13) VALUE '015 ANALYST'.
        10  FILLER        PIC X(13) VALUE '020 AUDITOR'.
        10  FILLER        PIC X(13) VALUE '025 BOOKKEEPER'.
              .
              .
              .
    05  TITLE-TABLE REDEFINES TITLE-VALUES.
        10  TITLE-CODE-NAME OCCURS 50 TIMES
                ASCENDING KEY TITLE-CODE INDEXED BY TITLE-INDEX.
            15  TITLE-CODE PIC 9(3).
            15  TITLE-NAME PIC X(10).
```

5.
```
01 HOURLY-RATE-VALUES.
    05  FILLER    PIC X(24)    VALUE '030004000500060006751000'.
    05  FILLER    PIC X(24)    VALUE '032504500550070007501150'.
    05  FILLER    PIC X(24)    VALUE '035005000600080008251300'.
    05  FILLER    PIC X(24)    VALUE '037505500650090009001450'.
    05  FILLER    PIC X(24)    VALUE '040006000700100009751600'.
01 HOURLY-RATE-TABLE REDEFINES HOURLY-RATE-VALUES.
    05  EXPERIENCE-LEVEL OCCURS 5 TIMES.
        10  SKILL-LEVEL OCCURS 6 TIMES PIC 99V99.
```

Exercise 2.24: Self-Checking Examination

1. B	6. B	11. A	16. D
2. A	7. B	12. A	17. B
3. D	8. C	13. B	18. A
4. D	9. E	14. D	
5. B	10. D	15. B	

TOPIC 2.7: SORTING AND MERGING

COBOL Syntax

DATA DIVISION:

SD file-name
 [RECORD CONTAINS [integer-1 TO] integer-2 CHARACTERS]
 $\left[\text{DATA} \begin{Bmatrix} \text{RECORD IS} \\ \text{RECORDS ARE} \end{Bmatrix} \text{data-name-1 [, data-name-2]} \ldots \right]$

PROCEDURE DIVISION:

MERGE file-name-1 ON $\begin{Bmatrix} \text{ASCENDING} \\ \text{DESCENDING} \end{Bmatrix}$ KEY data-name-1 [, data-name-2] ...

$\left[\text{ON} \begin{Bmatrix} \text{ASCENDING} \\ \text{DESCENDING} \end{Bmatrix} \text{KEY data-name-3 [, data-name-4]} \ldots \right] \ldots$

 [COLLATING SEQUENCE IS alphabet-name]
 USING file-name-2, file-name-3 [, file-name-4] ...

$\begin{Bmatrix} \text{OUTPUT PROCEDURE IS section-name-1} \left[\begin{Bmatrix} \text{THROUGH} \\ \text{THRU} \end{Bmatrix} \text{section-name-2} \right] \\ \text{GIVING file-name-5} \end{Bmatrix}$

RELEASE record-name [FROM identifier]

RETURN file-name RECORD [INTO identifier], AT END imperative-statement

SORT file-name-1 ON $\begin{Bmatrix} \text{ASCENDING} \\ \text{DESCENDING} \end{Bmatrix}$ KEY data-name-1 [, data-name-2] ...

$\left[\text{ON} \begin{Bmatrix} \text{ASCENDING} \\ \text{DESCENDING} \end{Bmatrix} \text{KEY data-name-3 [, data-name-4]} \ldots \right] \ldots$

[COLLATING SEQUENCE IS alphabet-name]

$\begin{Bmatrix} \text{INPUT PROCEDURE IS section-name-1} \left[\begin{Bmatrix} \text{THROUGH} \\ \text{THRU} \end{Bmatrix} \text{section-name-2} \right] \\ \text{USING file-name-2 [, file-name-3]} \ldots \end{Bmatrix}$

$\begin{Bmatrix} \text{OUTPUT PROCEDURE IS section-name-3} \left[\begin{Bmatrix} \text{THROUGH} \\ \text{THRU} \end{Bmatrix} \text{section-name-4} \right] \\ \text{GIVING file-name-4} \end{Bmatrix}$

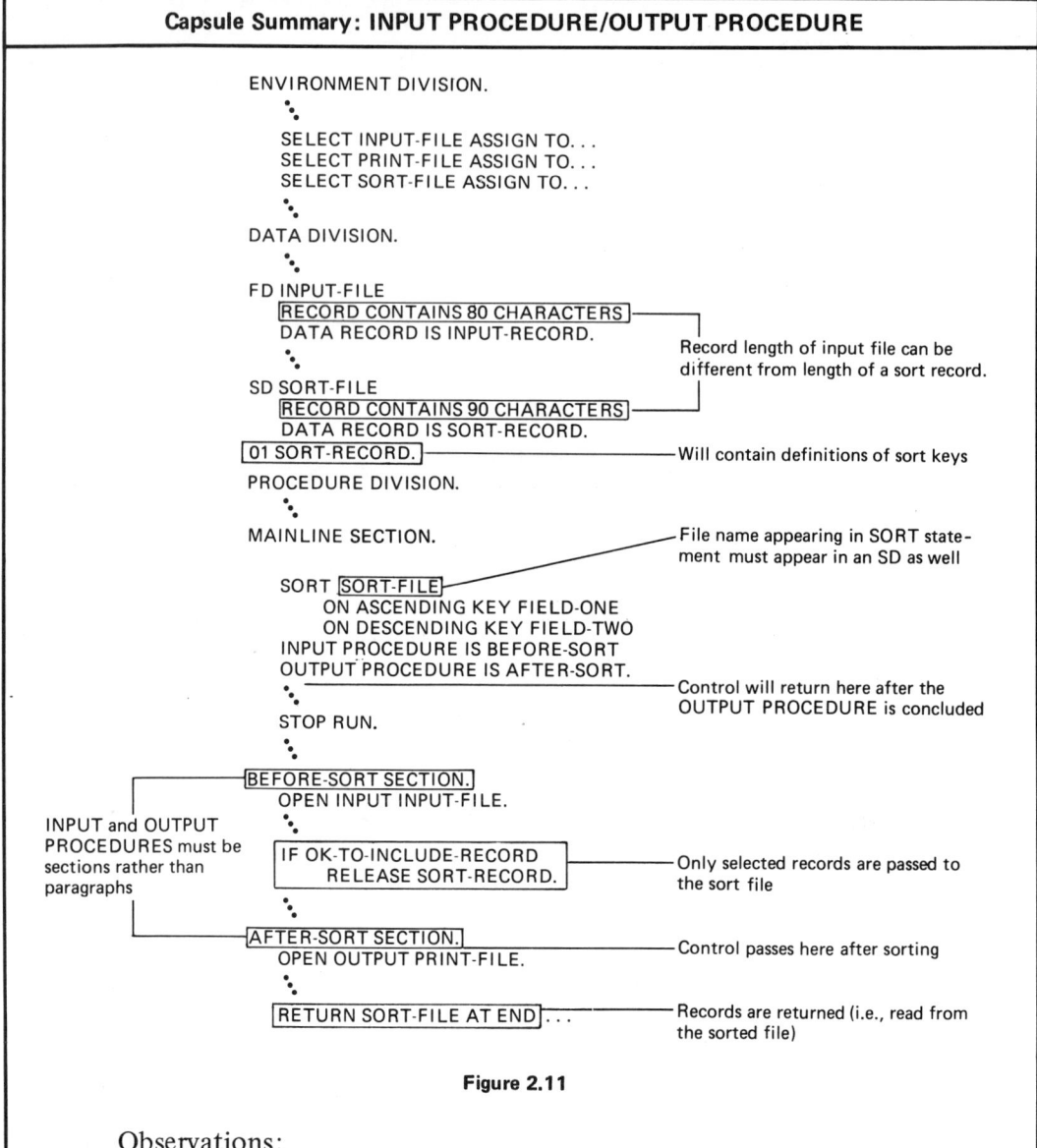

Figure 2.11

Observations:

1. The INPUT PROCEDURE option is required to sort on a calculated field; it also permits the sort record to have a different record description than the incoming record. Further, only a *limited* number of designated records in the incoming file need to be passed to sort.

2. Both the INPUT and OUTPUT PROCEDURE *must* designate section names.

Capsule Summary, cont.

3. RELEASE is an analogous to WRITE, and appears in the INPUT PROCEDURE to send a record to sort.

4. RETURN is analogous to READ, and appears in the OUTPUT PROCEDURE to read a record from the sorted file.

5. STOP RUN should appear in the "mainline" of the Procedure Division and it must *not* appear in the OUTPUT PROCEDURE. When the SORT statement is executed, it transfers control to the INPUT PROCEDURE, after which control goes to the sort utility, and then to the OUTPUT PROCEDURE. When the latter is concluded, control returns to the statement under SORT. If STOP RUN is *wrongly* included in the OUTPUT PROCEDURE, control will *still* be transferred to the statement under the SORT verb and the program will not terminate correctly.

Capsule Summary: USING/GIVING

```
ENVIRONMENT DIVISION.
   ...
   SELECT INPUT-FILE ASSIGN TO...
   SELECT SORT-FILE ASSIGN TO...
   SELECT ORDERED-FILE ASSIGN TO...     ← Extra file required to hold results from sort
DATA DIVISION.
   ...
   FD  INPUT-FILE
       RECORD CONTAINS 80 CHARACTERS
       DATA RECORD IS INPUT-RECORD.
   FD  ORDERED-FILE                     ← All three files must have identical record layouts
       RECORD CONTAINS 80 CHARACTERS
       DATA RECORD IS ORDERED-RECORD.
   SD  SORT-FILE
       RECORD CONTAINS 80 CHARACTERS
       DATA RECORD IS SORT-RECORD.
   01  SORT-RECORD.                     ← Will contain definitions of sort keys
   ...
PROCEDURE DIVISION.
   ...
   SORT SORT-FILE
       ON ASCENDING KEY FIELD-ONE
       ON DESCENDING KEY FIELD-TWO
       USING INPUT-FILE
       GIVING ORDERED-FILE.
```

Observations:

1. The sort itself handles the I-O associated with the incoming file, and hence the RELEASE and RETURN verbs do *not* appear with the USING/GIVING option. The programmer must not open or close the incoming file.

> **Capsule Summary, cont.**
>
> 2. The record descriptions for the input, sort-work, and ordered files must be identical; hence, the USING option *cannot* be used for a calculated field. Further, *every* record in the incoming file is automatically passed to sort.
>
> 3. Control passes directly to the sort utility which automatically reads records from the input file, and releases them to sort. When the sort is complete, control returns to the statement immediately under the SORT verb.
>
> 4. Sections are optional in the Procedure Division.

Exercise 2.25: Vocabulary Associated With Sorting

Given the following data:

Name	Location	Department
Milgrom	New York	1000
Samuel	Boston	2000
Isaac	Boston	2000
Chandler	Chicago	2000
Lavor	Los Angeles	1000
Elsinor	Chicago	1000
Tater	New York	2000
Craig	New York	2000
Borow	Boston	2000
Kenneth	Boston	2000
Renaldi	Boston	1000
Gulfman	Chicago	1000

1. Rearrange the data according to the sort: Major Field-Department (Descending); Minor Field-Name (Ascending).

2. Rearrange the data according to the sort: Primary Field-Name; Secondary Field-Location; Tertiary Field-Department.

3. The following code is intended to sort an employee file in order of age, listing the *oldest* first. There are two distinct reasons why the intended code will not work. Find and correct the errors.

```
PROCEDURE DIVISION.
    SORT SORT-FILE
        DESCENDING KEY BIRTH-MONTH BIRTH-YEAR
        USING EMPLOYEE-FILE
        GIVING ORDERED-FILE.
```

Exercise 2.26: USING/GIVING Option

1. Given the statement:

   ```
   SORT SORT-FILE
       ASCENDING KEY STUDENT-NAME
       DESCENDING YEAR-IN-SCHOOL
       ASCENDING MAJOR
   USING FILE-ONE
   GIVING FILE-TWO.
   ```

   a. What is the major key?
   b. What is the minor key?
   c. Which file will be specified in an SD?
   d. Which file will contain the sorted output?
   e. Which file(s) will be specified in a SELECT?
   f. Which file contains the input data?
   g. Which file must contain the data names: STUDENT-NAME, YEAR-IN-SCHOOL, and MAJOR?

2. Given the statement:

   ```
   MERGE WORKFILE
       ASCENDING ACCOUNT-NUMBER
       ASCENDING AMOUNT-OF-SALE
   USING
       JANUARY-SALES
       FEBRUARY-SALES
       MARCH-SALES
   GIVING
       FIRST-QUARTER-SALES.
   ```

   a. Which file(s) is specified in an SD?
   b. Which file(s) is specified in an FD?
   c. Which file(s) contains the key ACCOUNT-NUMBER?
   d. What is the primary key?
   e. What is the secondary key?
   f. If a record on the JANUARY-SALES file has the identical ACCOUNT-NUMBER as a record on the FEBRUARY-SALES file, which record would come first on the merged file?
   g. If a record on the JANUARY-SALES file has the identical AMOUNT-OF-SALE as a record on the FEBRUARY-SALES file, which record would come first on the merged file?
   h. If a record on the JANUARY-SALES file has the identical AMOUNT-OF-SALE and ACCOUNT-NUMBER as a record on the FEBRUARY-SALES file, which record would come first on the merged file?

Exercise 2.27: Coding COBOL Statements

1. Code an SD and record description for the file SORT-FILE, with records of 80 bytes. Include explicit specification of the social security number (positions 1-9), last name (positions 10-24), location (positions 30-40), and salary (positions 51-55) for subsequent use as sort keys.

2. Code a SORT statement that will order an incoming EMPLOYEE-FILE by alphabetical location and last name within location, putting the results into ORDERED-FILE. Refer to the SD developed for part 1 and assume that EMPLOYEE-FILE has the identical record layout as SORT-FILE.

3. Code a SORT statement that will list the employees in EMPLOYEE-FILE in order of decreasing salaries. Employees with identical salaries should be listed in order of ascending social security numbers. Refer to the SD from part 1 and assume that EMPLOYEE-FILE has the identical record layout as SORT-FILE.

4. Code a SORT statement to order employees by increasing SR-PER-CENT-SALARY-INCREASE. (Employees with duplicate percent increases should be listed alphabetically.) Assume the field SR-PERCENT-SALARY-INCREASE is present in the record description of SORT-WORK-FILE, but that it is a *calculated* field. Assume further that a report is to be prepared after sorting, so that INPUT PROCEDURE/OUTPUT PROCEDURE is required. Finally, indicate the statements needed to read and write records to SORT-WORK-FILE, the location of these statements (in the INPUT or OUTPUT procedure), and appropriate headers for the procedures themselves.

5. Code a MERGE statement, and corresponding SD and record description for a MERGE-WORK-FILE. The object is to combine five daily files, MONDAY-SALES, TUESDAY-SALES, etc., into a single file called WEEKLY-SALES in ascending order by WK-CUSTOMER-ACCOUNT-NUMBER. All input files have 80-character records and have been sorted on the field WK-CUSTOMER-ACCOUNT-NUMBER in columns 6-10. Records with the same account number in the merged file are to appear in decreasing order of WK-SALES-AMOUNT, columns 15-20.

Exercise 2.28: Self-Checking Examination

1. The INPUT PROCEDURE of the SORT verb:
   a. Specifies a section name or names.
   b. Specifies a paragraph name or names.
   c. Must use the "THRU" option.
   d. Either (a) or (b) above.

2. RELEASE is most likely to appear in:
   a. The INPUT PROCEDURE.
   b. The OUTPUT PROCEDURE
   c. Both (a) and (b) above.
   d. Neither (a) nor (b) above.

3. RETURN is most likely to appear in:
   a. The INPUT PROCEDURE.
   b. The OUTPUT PROCEDURE.
   c. Both (a) and (b) above.
   d. Neither (a) nor (b) above.

4. An SD:
   a. Appears in the File Section.
   b. Is tied to a SELECT statement.
   c. Will be followed by an 01 entry.
   d. All of the above.

5. Given the statement:

   ```
   SORT EMPLOYEE-FILE
       ASCENDING KEY EMPLOYEE-LOCATION, EMPLOYEE-NAME
       USING FILE-ONE
       GIVING FILE-TWO.
   ```

   a. EMPLOYEE-LOCATION is the major key and EMPLOYEE-NAME is the minor key.
   b. EMPLOYEE-LOCATION is the minor key and EMPLOYEE-NAME is the major key.
   c. There is only one key, since the clause "ASCENDING KEY" appears only once.
   d. EMPLOYEE-NAME is the primary key and EMPLOYEE-LOCATION the secondary key.
   e. The sorted file will contain all employees in strict alphabetical order.

6. Using the SORT statement from question 5:
   a. FILE-ONE is input to the sort, and FILE-TWO is output.
   b. FILE-TWO is input to the sort, and FILE-ONE is output.
   c. It is not possible to determine which file is which.
   d. Both FILE-ONE and FILE-TWO should be defined in an SD.

7. All of the following are valid formats of the SORT verb *except:*
   a. INPUT PROCEDURE ... OUTPUT PROCEDURE.
   b. USING ... GIVING.

c. INPUT PROCEDURE ... GIVING.
d. USING ... OUTPUT PROCEDURE.
e. INPUT PROCEDURE ... USING.

8. If an input file contained 1000 records, and the "same" file after sorting contained only 900:
    a. Several errors must have occurred.
    b. The INPUT PROCEDURE option was used.
    c. The USING option was used.
    d. The situation is not possible.

9. If an input file contained records of 120 characters each, and the "same" file after sorting had records of 140 characters:
    a. Several errors must have occurred.
    b. The INPUT PROCEDURE option was used.
    c. The USING option was used.
    d. The situation is not possible.

10. An SD:
    a. May contain variable length records.
    b. Is required for the first file name mentioned in a SORT statement.
    c. Both of the above.
    d. Neither of the above.

11. Given the statement:

    ```
    SORT STUDENT-FILE
        ON  DESCENDING KEY STUDENT-YEAR
            ASCENDING KEY STUDENT-NAME
        INPUT PROCEDURE READ-CARDS
        OUTPUT PROCEDURE WRITE-RECORDS.
    ```

    a. READ-CARDS and WRITE-RECORDS *must be section* names.
    b. READ-CARDS and WRITE-RECORDS *must be paragraph* names.
    c. READ-CARDS and WRITE-RECORDS may be either section or paragraph names.

12. Using the SORT statement of question 11, the records appearing as output in STUDENT-FILE will:
    a. Be unsorted.
    b. Be in strict alphabetical order.
    c. List all the students in the highest STUDENT-YEAR first.
    d. None of the above.

13. Using the SORT statement of question 11, the data names STUDENT-YEAR and STUDENT-NAME:

    a. Appear in the record description for STUDENT-FILE.
    b. Appear in the record description for the input file.
    c. Appear in the record description for the output file.
    d. All of the above.

14. A SORT statement may contain:

    a. As many as three file names or as few as one.
    b. As many as four section names.
    c. One or more keys.
    d. All of the above.

15. Use of the MERGE statement:

    a. Requires specification of an MD in the Data Division.
    b. Requires specification of an SD in the Data Division.
    c. Allows for the INPUT PROCEDURE/OUTPUT PROCEDURE option.
    d. Both (a) and (c) above.

16. The MERGE statement:

    a. Allows a maximum of four files.
    b. Requires that all files have identical record descriptions.
    c. Does not require that incoming records be presorted by the specified keys.
    d. None of the above.

17. All of the following are true about COLLATING SEQUENCE *except:*

    a. It is an optional clause in both the SORT and MERGE statements.
    b. IBM systems default to ASCII if the clause is not specified.
    c. A supporting entry is required in the SPECIAL-NAMES paragraph if COLLATING SEQUENCE is specified.
    d. Its specification as ASCII or EBCDIC may result in a different ordering of the output file for an alphanumeric key.

18. The SORT verb can operate on a calculated field if:

    a. INPUT PROCEDURE is specified.
    b. USING is specified.
    c. Either INPUT PROCEDURE or USING is specified.
    d. OUTPUT PROCEDURE is specified.

Solutions for Topic 2.7

Exercise 2.25: Vocabulary Associated with Sorting

1. Department (Descending), Name (Ascending)

Name	Location	Department
Borow	Boston	2000
Chandler	Chicago	2000
Craig	New York	2000
Isaac	Boston	2000
Kenneth	Boston	2000
Samuel	Boston	2000
Tater	New York	2000
Elsinor	Chicago	1000
Gulfman	Chicago	1000
Lavor	Los Angeles	1000
Milgrom	New York	1000
Renaldi	Boston	1000

2. Name (Ascending), Location (Ascending), Department (Ascending)

Name	Location	Department
Borow	Boston	2000
Chandler	Chicago	2000
Craig	New York	2000
Elsinor	Chicago	1000
Gulfman	Chicago	1000
Isaac	Boston	2000
Kenneth	Boston	2000
Lavor	Los Angeles	1000
Milgrom	New York	1000
Renaldi	Boston	1000
Samuel	Boston	2000
Tater	New York	2000

Note: Usually when name is a primary sort, the secondary sorts have little or no effect.

3. If the oldest employee is to appear first, then the sort should put birth dates in *ascending* order, that is, employees born in 1940 should appear before those in 1941, who should appear before those in 1942, and so on. Secondly, BIRTH-YEAR is a more important field than BIRTH-MONTH and should be the major key.

Exercise 2.26: USING/GIVING Option

1. a. STUDENT-NAME is the major key.
   b. MAJOR is the minor key.
   c. SORT-FILE is specified in an SD.
   d. FILE-TWO will contain the sorted output.

e. SORT-FILE, FILE-ONE, and FILE-TWO are all specified in SELECT statements.
f. FILE-ONE contains the input data.
g. SORT-FILE must contain all keys within its record description.

2. a. WORKFILE.
b. JANUARY-SALES, FEBRUARY-SALES, MARCH-SALES, and FIRST-QUARTER-SALES.
c. WORKFILE.
d. ACCOUNT-NUMBER
e. AMOUNT-OF-SALE
f. The record with the lower AMOUNT-OF-SALE.
g. The record with the lower ACCOUNT-NUMBER.
h. The record from JANUARY-SALES.

Exercise 2.27: Coding COBOL Statements

1.
```
    SD  SORT-FILE
        RECORD CONTAINS 80 CHARACTERS
        DATA RECORD IS SORT-RECORD.
    01  SORT-RECORD.
        05  SR-SOCIAL-SECURITY-NUMBER   PIC 9(9).
        05  SR-LAST-NAME                PIC X(15).
        05  FILLER                      PIC X(5).
        05  SR-LOCATION                 PIC X(11).
        05  FILLER                      PIC X(10).
        05  SR-SALARY                   PIC 9(5).
        05  FILLER                      PIC X(25).
```

2. SORT SORT-FILE
        ASCENDING KEY SR-LOCATION SR-LAST-NAME
        USING EMPLOYEE-FILE
        GIVING ORDERED-FILE.

3. SORT SORT-FILE
        DESCENDING KEY SR-SALARY
        ASCENDING KEY SR-SOCIAL-SECURITY-NUMBER
        USING EMPLOYEE-FILE
        GIVING ORDERED-FILE.

4. SORT SORT-WORK-FILE
        ON ASCENDING KEY SR-PERCENT-SALARY-INCREASE
        ON ASCENDING KEY SR-EMPLOYEE-NAME
    INPUT PROCEDURE IS A-PROCESS-INPUT
    OUTPUT PROCEDURE IS B-PREPARE-REPORT.

A RELEASE statement, RELEASE SORT-WORK-RECORD, writes a record to the sort work file and is present in the INPUT PROCEDURE. A RETURN statement, RETURN SORT-WORK-FILE, reads records from the sorted file and appears in the OUTPUT PROCEDURE. Both the INPUT and OUTPUT PROCEDURES *must be sections* rather than paragraphs.

```
5.      SD  MERGE-WORK-FILE
            RECORD CONTAINS 80 CHARACTERS
            DATA RECORD IS MERGE-WORK-RECORD.
        01  MERGE-WORK-RECORD.
            05  FILLER                          PIC X(5).
            05  WK-CUSTOMER-ACCOUNT-NUMBER      PIC 9(5).
            05  FILLER                          PIC X(4).
            05  WK-SALES-AMOUNT                 PIC 9(6).
            05  FILLER                          PIC X(60).
```

The MERGE statement itself is coded as follows:

```
        MERGE  MERGE-WORK-FILE
               ON ASCENDING KEY WK-CUSTOMER-ACCOUNT-NUMBER
               ON DESCENDING KEY WK-SALES-AMOUNT
            USING  MONDAY-SALES
                   TUESDAY-SALES
                   WEDNESDAY-SALES
                   THURSDAY-SALES
                   FRIDAY-SALES
            GIVING  WEEKLY-SALES.
```

Exercise 2.28: Self-Checking Examination

1. A	6. A	11. A	15. B
2. A	7. E	12. C	16. B
3. B	8. B	13. A	17. B
4. D	9. B	14. D	18. A
5. A	10. C		

TOPIC 2.8: INDEXED FILES

COBOL Syntax

ENVIRONMENT DIVISION:*

SELECT file-name
    ASSIGN TO implementor-name-1 [, implementor-name-2] ...

$$\left[\underline{\text{RESERVE}}\ \text{integer-1} \begin{Bmatrix} \text{AREA} \\ \text{AREAS} \end{Bmatrix} \right]$$

    ORGANIZATION IS INDEXED

$$\left[\underline{\text{ACCESS}}\ \text{MODE IS} \begin{Bmatrix} \text{SEQUENTIAL} \\ \text{RANDOM} \\ \text{DYNAMIC} \end{Bmatrix} \right]$$

*The format shown is taken from the ANS 74 standard and corresponds to the IBM VSAM syntax. Differences in IBM implementation of ISAM and VSAM can be seen in Exercise 2.31 of this topic.

RECORD KEY IS data-name-1
[ALTERNATE RECORD KEY IS data-name-2 [WITH DUPLICATES]] ...
[FILE STATUS IS data-name-3].

PROCEDURE DIVISION:

OPEN $\begin{Bmatrix} \text{INPUT file-name-1 [, file-name-2] ...} \\ \text{OUTPUT file-name-3 [, file-name-4] ...} \\ \text{I-O file-name-5 [, file-name-6] ...} \end{Bmatrix}$ ...

READ file-name [NEXT] RECORD [INTO identifier]
   [AT END imperative-statement]

READ file-name RECORD [INTO identifier]
   [KEY IS data-name]
   [INVALID KEY imperative-statement]

REWRITE record-name [FROM identifier]   [INVALID KEY imperative-statement]

START file-name $\left[\text{KEY} \begin{Bmatrix} \text{IS EQUAL TO} \\ \text{IS =} \\ \text{IS GREATER THAN} \\ \text{IS >} \\ \text{IS NOT LESS THAN} \\ \text{IS NOT <} \end{Bmatrix} \text{data-name} \right]$

[INVALID KEY imperative-statement]

WRITE record-name [FROM identifier]   [INVALID KEY imperative-statement]

Exercise 2.29: Concepts of ISAM Organization

Figure 2.5 represents the track index and record keys for a particular cylinder in an ISAM file.

	Prime		Overflow					
	Track	Key	Track	Key	Actual Record Keys			
	1	289	T8,R3	312	251	269	280	289
	2	345	T9,R1	346	316	318	327	345
	3	400	T8,R4	449	377	380	394	400
	4	598	4	598	469	500	502	598
	5	627	T9,R2	642	617	618	619	627
	6	700	T9,R3	717	658	675	680	700
	7	748	T8,R2	800	722	730	746	748
		Key	Link	Key	Link	Key	Link	Key	Link
Overflow	8	449	★★★	800	★★★	312	★★★	410	T8,R1
	9	346	★★★	642	★★★	717	★★★		

Figure 2.5 ISAM File.

1. List the record keys of the *six* records which logically belong to track 3.

2. What is the effect of adding a record with key 689?

Exercise 2.30: Concepts of VSAM Organization

Figure 2.6 represents records in a VSAM set.

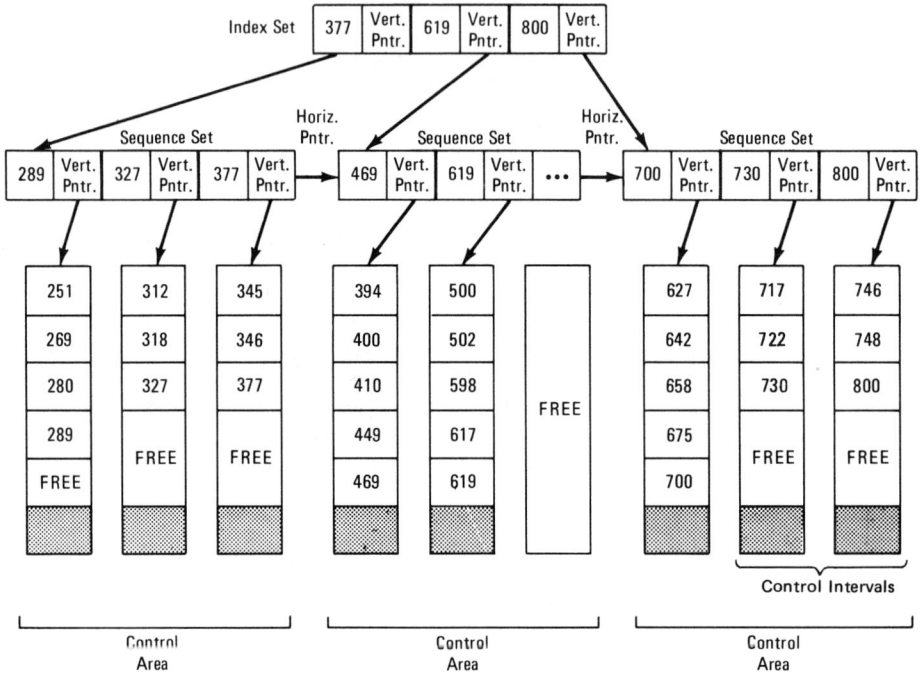

Figure 2.6 VSAM File.

1. What is the effect of adding a record with key 618?

2. What is the effect of adding a record with key 680?

Capsule Summary: ISAM/VSAM COBOL Differences

1. IBM implementation of VSAM conforms to the ANS 74 standard; IBM implementation of ISAM does not.
2. VSAM requires the clause ORGANIZATION IS INDEXED in the SELECT statement; ISAM does not use the clause at all.
3. VSAM permits DYNAMIC ACCESS (the file may be accessed both

---

Capsule Summary, cont.

sequentially and nonsequentially in the same program). VSAM also permits the use of ALTERNATE RECORD KEY and FILE STATUS in the SELECT statement, ISAM does not.

4. ISAM utilizes both NOMINAL and RECORD KEY clauses in the SELECT statement for random access. VSAM uses RECORD KEY only.

5. VSAM *physically* deletes inactive records through the DELETE verb. ISAM *logically* deletes inactive records by moving HIGH-VALUES to the first byte. (Consequently, active records in an ISAM file require the presence of LOW-VALUES in the first byte, VSAM has no such requirement.)

Exercise 2.31: ISAM/VSAM Differences

Indicate whether the following statements apply to ISAM only, VSAM only, or both:

1. Uses the first byte to denote active or inactive status.
2. Removes inactive records through the DELETE verb.
3. Requires the RECORD KEY clause in its SELECT statement.
4. Has the NOMINAL KEY clause in its SELECT statement.
5. Requires ORGANIZATION IS INDEXED in its SELECT statement.
6. Conforms to the ANS 74 standard.
7. Can access records either sequentially or nonsequentially.
8. Can *access* records either sequentially or nonsequentially in the *same* program.
9. Can be opened as an I-O file.
10. Uses the REWRITE verb to change existing records.
11. Uses control areas and control intervals.
12. Uses track and cylinder indexes.
13. Can be accessed through the START verb.
14. Can have an ALTERNATE RECORD KEY.
15. Requires a "virtual" operating system.
16. Can specify ACCESS IS DYNAMIC.

Exercise 2.32: Coding COBOL Statements

Assume the file INDEXED-FILE is in sequence according to the key SOC-SEC-NUMBER which appears in each record. Further, assume that the first byte of each record is known as ACTIVITY-CODE and indicates the status of each record under ISAM. (The byte has no meaning under VSAM.)

1. Code a COBOL SELECT statement to access the file sequentially. (Assume ISAM organization.)

2. What changes (if any) are required to part 1 if the organization is VSAM rather than ISAM?

3. Code a COBOL SELECT statement to access the file nonsequentially. (Assume ISAM organization.) Indicate any additional data names which may be required in Working-Storage.

4. What changes (if any) are required to part 3 if the organization is VSAM rather than ISAM?

5. Assume the data name, INPUT-SOC-SEC-NUMBER contains the key of a record to be read randomly from INDEXED-FILE. Show the necessary COBOL statements to access the file and perform the routine RECORD-NOT-FOUND if appropriate. Assume ISAM organization and refer to part 3 above if necessary.

6. Code statements to accomplish the same function as in part 5, except assume VSAM organization and refer to part 4 above if necessary.

7. Code statement(s) required to delete the last record accessed. (Assume ISAM organization.)

8. Code statement(s) required to delete the last record accessed. (Assume VSAM organization and refer to part 4).

9. Code the OPEN statement which would be used for either ISAM or VSAM organization that would permit subsequent modifications to existing records.

Exercise 2.33: Self-Checking Examination

1. The INVALID KEY clause:
   a. Can be used with the AT END clause in the *same* READ.
   b. Can be specified in a REWRITE statement.
   c. Can be used in a READ statement if the AT END clause is not used.
   d. All of the above.
   e. Only (b) and (c) above.

2. Records in an ISAM file:
   a. Are stored in physically sequential order.
   b. Are stored in logically sequential order.
   c. Both (a) and (b) above.
   d. Neither (a) nor (b) above.

3. An ISAM file (which does not have a master index) will have:
   a. One track index and one cylinder index.
   b. One track index and many cylinder indexes.
   c. Many track indexes and many cylinder indexes.
   d. Many track indexes and one cylinder index.

4. "Inactive" records in an ISAM file:
   a. Must be physically deleted from the file.
   b. Are denoted by HIGH-VALUES in the first byte.
   c. Are denoted by LOW-VALUES in the first byte.
   d. Are denoted by either HIGH-VALUES or LOW-VALUES in the first byte.

5. "Inactive" records in a VSAM file:
   a. Are deleted immediately by moving HIGH-VALUES to the first byte and rewriting the record.
   b. Are deleted immediately through the DELETE verb.
   c. Are moved to a new control area.
   d. Are moved to an overflow control interval.

6. The START verb:
   a. Is available under VSAM only.
   b. Can move to the middle of an indexed file, after which the file will be accessed sequentially.
   c. Is required for nonsequential access of an indexed file.
   d. Is required for sequential access of an indexed file.

7. The NOMINAL KEY clause:
   a. Is required any time an ISAM or VSAM file is processed.
   b. Is required only when an ISAM file is processed nonsequentially.
   c. Specifies a data name which is contained in the ISAM record.
   d. Appears in the File Section.

8. The RECORD KEY clause:
   a. Is required any time an indexed file is processed.
   b. Specifies a data name containing either HIGH-VALUES or LOW-VALUES for an ISAM record.
   c. Specifies a data name which is *not* contained in an indexed record.
   d. Specifies a data name which *must* be defined in Working-Storage.

9. An indexed file:
   a. May be processed either sequentially or randomly.
   b. May be both an input and output file in the same run.
   c. Requires the RECORD KEY clause in its SELECT statement.
   d. All of the above.

10. The clause: ORGANIZATION IS INDEXED:
    a. Is for documentation only.
    b. Is required to achieve device independence for indexed files.
    c. Is required for ISAM files.
    d. Is required for VSAM files.
    e. Both (c) and (d) above.

11. If two records are located on different tracks of the same recording surface:
    a. They are in the same cylinder.
    b. The access time for the second record is zero.
    c. They will both be read using the same read/write head.
    d. None of the above.

12. As the number of concentric circles on a recording surface increases:
    a. The number of tracks per cylinder increases.
    b. The number of bytes per track increases.
    c. The number of cylinders increases.
    d. All of the above.

13. The terms control area and control interval:
    a. Are associated with any type of indexed file.
    b. Are associated with ISAM files if they are implemented on a virtual operating system.
    c. Are associated with VSAM only.
    d. Are synonymous with cylinder and track index, respectively.

14. Given the COBOL FD entries:

    BLOCK CONTAINS 300 TO 900 CHARACTERS
    RECORD CONTAINS 60 TO 180 CHARACTERS:

    a. A block can contain no more than 5 records.
    b. A block could contain as many as 15 records.
    c. A block must contain from 1 to 5 records.
    d. A block must contain at least 5 records.

15. Blocking has *no* effect on:
    a. The number of logical records in a file.
    b. The number of physical records in a file.

c. The total time required to sequentially read a file.
d. The space required to store a file.

16. The RESERVE ALTERNATE AREAS clause:
    a. Has no effect on processing efficiency.
    b. Is part of the COBOL FD for a given file.
    c. Is used for blocked files only.
    d. Is required by COBOL whenever indexed files are processed.
    e. None of the above.

Solutions for Topic 2.8

Exercise 2.29: Concepts of ISAM Organization

1. 377, 380, 394, 400, 410, and 449 (The latter two records are in the overflow area.)

2. Record key 689 logically belongs in track 6. It would be added to the prime area of track six, causing record key 700 to be bumped into overflow (TR, R4). The prime area of track 6 contains 658, 675, 680, and 689. The track index is adjusted to show record key 689 as the highest entry in the prime area. The overflow area would point to T9, R4, which in turn would have a link to T9, R3.

Exercise 2.30: Concepts of VSAM Organization

1. The addition of record key 618 causes a control interval split in the second control area.

2. The addition of record key 680 causes a control area split.

The effects of the changes in both parts 1 and 2 are best discussed by examining Fig. 2.7.

Exercise 2.31: ISAM/VSAM Differences

1.	ISAM	9.	Both
2.	VSAM	10.	Both
3.	Both	11.	VSAM
4.	ISAM (for random access only)	12.	ISAM
5.	VSAM	13.	Both
6.	VSAM	14.	VSAM
7.	Both	15.	VSAM
8.	VSAM	16.	VSAM

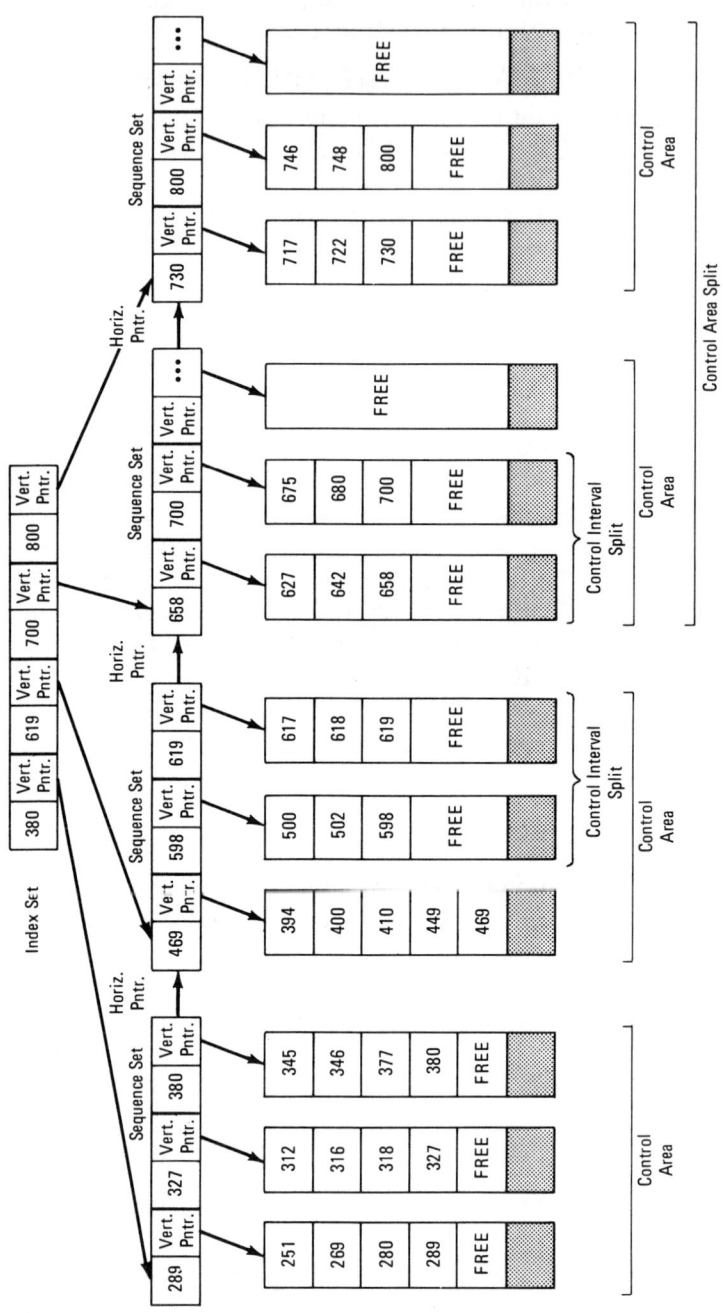

Figure 2.7 Additions to a VSAM File (See Exercise 2.30)

122

Exercise 2.32: Coding COBOL Statements

1. SELECT INDEXED-FILE
    ASSIGN TO DA-I-INPUT
    ACCESS IS SEQUENTIAL
    RECORD KEY IS SOC-SEC-NUMBER.

2. SELECT INDEXED-FILE
    ASSIGN TO DA-INPUT
    ACCESS IS SEQUENTIAL
    ORGANIZATION IS INDEXED
    RECORD KEY IS SOC-SEC-NUMBER.

3. SELECT INDEXED-FILED
    ASSIGN TO DA-I-INPUT
    ACCESS IS RANDOM
    NOMINAL KEY IS WS-KEY-AREA
    RECORD KEY IS SOC-SEC-NUMBER.

    01 WS-KEY-AREA   PIC 9(9). (Defined in Working-Storage)

4. SELECT INDEXED-FILE
    ASSIGN TO DA-INPUT
    ACCESS IS RANDOM
    ORGANIZATION IS INDEXED
    RECORD KEY IS SOC-SEC-NUMBER.

5. MOVE INPUT-SOC-SEC-NUMBER TO WS-KEY-AREA.
   READ INDEXED-FILE
        INVALID KEY PERFORM RECORD-NOT-FOUND.

6. MOVE INPUT-SOC-SEC-NUMBER TO SOC-SEC-NUMBER.
   READ INDEXED-FILE
        INVALID KEY PERFORM RECORD-NOT-FOUND.

7. MOVE HIGH-VALUES TO ACTIVITY-CODE.
   REWRITE ISAM-RECORD.

8. DELETE INDEXED-FILE.

9. OPEN I-O INDEXED-FILE.

Exercise 2.33: Self-Checking Examination

1. E	5. B	9. D	13. C
2. B	6. B	10. D	14. B
3. D	7. B	11. C	15. A
4. B	8. A	12. C	16. E

TOPIC 2.9: REPORT WRITER

COBOL Syntax

```
REPORT SECTION.
RD report-name
   [CODE literal-1]
   [ {CONTROL IS  }  {data-name-1 [, data-name-2] ...                      } ]
     {CONTROLS ARE}  {FINAL [, data-name-1 [, data-name-2] ...]            }
   [ PAGE  [LIMIT IS  ]  integer-1  [LINE ]  [, HEADING integer-2]
           [LIMITS ARE]              [LINES]
       [FIRST DETAIL integer-3]   [, LAST DETAIL integer-4]
       [FOOTING integer-5] ]
```

General Format for Report Group Description Entry

Format 1:

```
01  [data-name-1]
    [ LINE NUMBER IS   {integer-1 [ON NEXT PAGE]} ]
                       {PLUS integer-2           }

    [ NEXT GROUP IS    {integer-3     }
                       {PLUS integer-4}
                       {NEXT PAGE     } ]

    TYPE IS  { {REPORT HEADING }                          }
             { {RH             }                          }
             { {PAGE HEADING   }                          }
             { {PH             }                          }
             { {CONTROL HEADING}  {data-name-2}           }
             { {CH             }  {FINAL      }           }
             { {DETAIL         }                          }
             { {DE             }                          }
             { {CONTROL FOOTING}  {data-name-3}           }
             { {CF             }  {FINAL      }           }
             { {PAGE FOOTING   }                          }
             { {PF             }                          }
             { {REPORT FOOTING }                          }
             { {RF             }                          }
```

Format 2:

level-number [data-name-1]
$$\left[\underline{\text{LINE}} \text{ NUMBER IS} \begin{Bmatrix} \text{integer-1 [ON } \underline{\text{NEXT PAGE}}\text{]} \\ \underline{\text{PLUS}} \text{ integer-2} \end{Bmatrix} \right]$$
[[USAGE IS] DISPLAY].

Format 3:

level-number [data-name-1]
   [BLANK WHEN ZERO]
   [GROUP INDICATE]
$$\left[\begin{Bmatrix} \underline{\text{JUSTIFIED}} \\ \underline{\text{JUST}} \end{Bmatrix} \text{RIGHT} \right]$$
$$\left[\underline{\text{LINE}} \text{ NUMBER IS} \begin{Bmatrix} \text{integer-1 [ON } \underline{\text{NEXT PAGE}}\text{]} \\ \underline{\text{PLUS}} \text{ integer-2} \end{Bmatrix} \right]$$
   [COLUMN NUMBER IS integer-3]
$$\begin{Bmatrix} \underline{\text{PICTURE}} \\ \underline{\text{PIC}} \end{Bmatrix} \text{IS character-string}$$
$$\begin{Bmatrix} \underline{\text{SOURCE}} \text{ IS identifier-1} \\ \underline{\text{VALUE}} \text{ IS literal} \\ \underline{\text{SUM}} \text{ identifier-2 [, identifier-3] } \dots \\ [\underline{\text{UPON}} \text{ data-name-2 [, data-name-3] } \dots] \dots \\ \left[\underline{\text{RESET}} \text{ ON } \begin{Bmatrix} \text{data-name-4} \\ \underline{\text{FINAL}} \end{Bmatrix} \right] \end{Bmatrix}$$
[[USAGE IS] DISPLAY].

PROCEDURE DIVISION

$$\underline{\text{GENERATE}} \begin{Bmatrix} \text{data-name} \\ \text{report-name} \end{Bmatrix}$$

<u>INITIATE</u> report-name-1 [, report-name-2] ...

<u>TERMINATE</u> report-name-1 [, report-name-2] ...

Exercise 2.34: Identifying Report Groups

The report in Fig. 2.8 is the result of a COBOL program utilizing Report Writer. The program processes a file which has been sorted by location, and title within location. Salary totals are provided for all employees with similar titles. In addition, a salary total of all employees in one location was also calculated.

Identify the boxed entries in the report of Fig. 2.8 as to report group type: control heading, control footing, etc.

Exercise 2.35: Coding Report Groups

Complete the 01 entries in parts 1 to 5 to produce the report shown in Exercise 2.34. Use EMP-NAME, EMP-SALARY, EMP-TITLE, and EMP-LOCATION as data-names in incoming records. Adhere to the horizontal and vertical spacing indicated in the report of Exercise 2.34, and assume that the first character of EMP-NAME appears in column 2.

1. 01 TYPE IS PAGE HEADING.
2. 01 TYPE IS CONTROL HEADING EMP-LOCATION.
3. 01 EMPLOYEE-LINE TYPE IS DETAIL.
4. 01 TYPE IS CONTROL FOOTING EMP-TITLE.
5. 01 TYPE IS CONTROL FOOTING EMP-LOCATION.

Exercise 2.36: Coding Other Report Writer Statements

1. With reference to the report from exercise 2.34, code the FD for PRINT-FILE, the file to which the report SALARY-TOTALS will be written.

2. Code the associated RD for the report from part 1. Use appropriate controls consistent with your answers in Exercise 2.35.

3. Code the Procedure Division statements uniquely associated with Report Writer to correspond to previous answers in exercises 2.35 and 2.36.

Exercise 2.37: Self-Checking Examination

1. All of the following report groups exist except:
   a. Report Heading.
   b. Page Heading.
   c. Control Heading.
   d. Detail Heading.

2. Report Writer has how many different kinds of report groups:
   a. Five
   b. Six
   c. Seven
   d. Eight

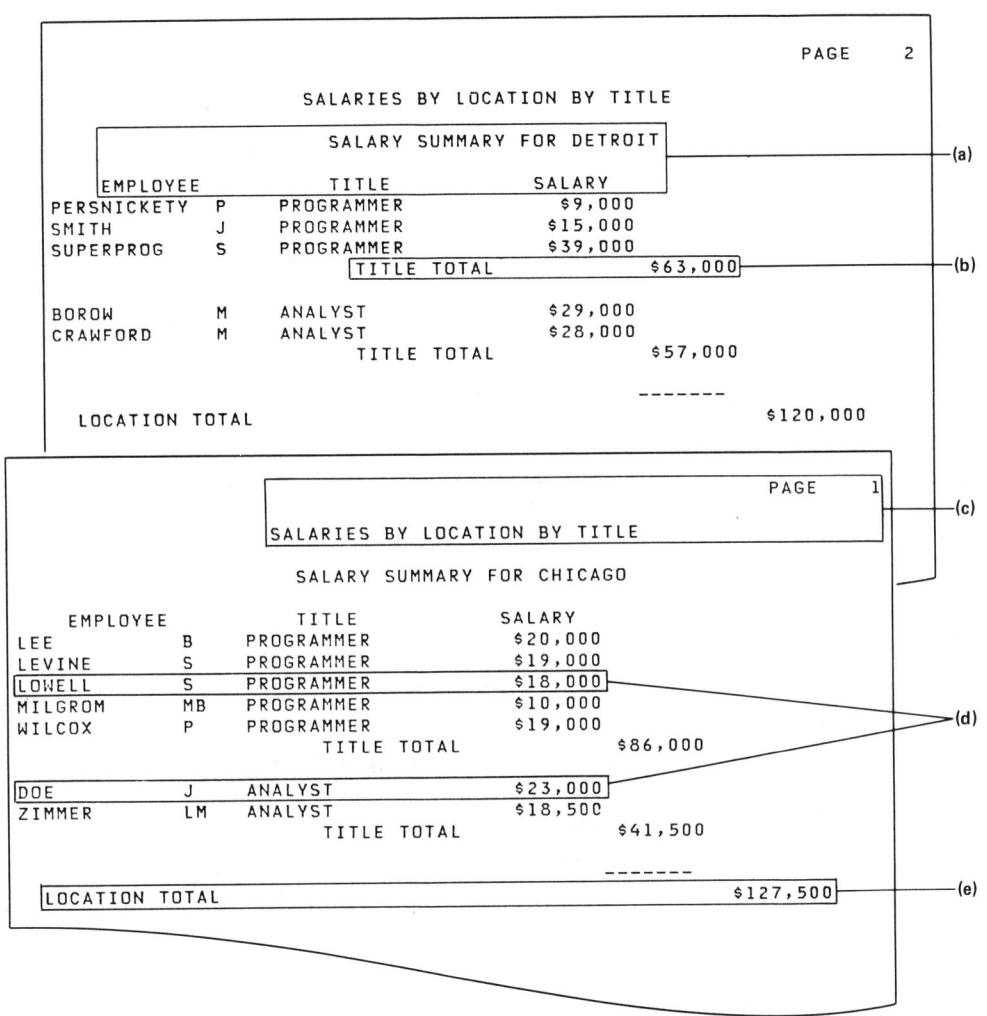

Figure 2.8 Report Groups.

3. All of the following are Report Writer verbs, appearing in the Procedure Division, except:
   a. INITIATE.
   b. GENERATE.
   c. PROPAGATE.
   d. TERMINATE.

4. All of the following are clauses in the RD except:
   a. HEADING.
   b. FIRST DETAIL.
   c. LAST DETAIL.
   d. COLUMN.

5. The type of the Report Group most likely to be identified by a data name is:
   a. Report Heading.
   b. Page Heading.
   c. Control Heading.
   d. Detail.

6. The value of a data name in a report description entry can be specified in all of the following ways except:
   a. SOURCE.
   b. VALUE.
   c. TOTAL.
   d. SUM.

7. If a report name, rather than a data name, is specified in a GENERATE statement:
   a. Detail lines will not appear in the report.
   b. The compiler will flag the statement as invalid.
   c. Only detail lines will appear in the report.
   d. None of the above.

8. A report name *must* appear in all of the following statements except:
   a. RD.
   b. INITIATE.
   c. GENERATE.
   d. TERMINATE.

9. Which of the following is a *true* statement about report groups?
   a. A given report must contain at least one of each type.
   b. Control headings and control footings must occur in pairs.
   c. A report group cannot produce more than a single line of output.
   d. None of the above.

10. Which of the following is a *false* statement about Report Writer?
    a. Report Writer requires that its input files be sorted to correspond to the designated control breaks.
    b. The Procedure Division of a Report Writer program is generally much shorter than its Data Division.
    c. Report Writer is probably the most widely used COBOL feature, and consequently is well known by all COBOL programmers.
    d. A Report Writer program will contain the four divisions of any COBOL program.

11. Given the entry:
    01 TYPE IS CONTROL FOOTING EMPLOYEE-LOCATION.
    a. EMPLOYEE-LOCATION will be specified as a control field in the RD for the report.
    b. EMPLOYEE-LOCATION will be the data name of a subsequent detail report group.
    c. The statement will be flagged because it does not have a data name.
    d. The statement will be flagged because it does not have a picture clause.

12. An 01 entry does *not* appear in:
    a. The FD specifying the name of a report to be generated by Report Writer.
    b. The RD detailing the report specifications.
    c. Any of the seven report groups.
    d. None of the above.

13. The COBOL entry: LINE NUMBER PLUS 1:
    a. Is equivalent to the entry LINE NUMBER 1.
    b. Will always cause output to begin on a new page.
    c. Can have several COLUMN entries defined under it.
    d. Can appear only in a detail report group.

Use the following code to answer questions 14 through 17.

```
01    TYPE IS CONTROL FOOTING EMPLOYEE-LOCATION.
  05    LINE NUMBER 46.
    10    COLUMN NUMBER 15
          PIC X(30)    VALUE ALL '-'.
  05    LINE NUMBER PLUS 1.
    10    COLUMN NUMBER 15
          PIC X(15)    VALUE 'LOCATION TOTAL'.
    10    COLUMN NUMBER 40
          PIC $$$$,$$$ SUM EMPLOYEE-SALARY.
```

14. The output generated by this Report Group:
   a. Will appear on every page of the report, but the starting line number will vary.
   b. Will appear on line 46 of every page in the report.
   c. Will not necessarily appear on every page, but will always begin on line 46.
   d. Will not necessarily appear on every page, and further its position on the page will vary.

15. The output generated by this report group:
   a. Consists of two lines, both beginning in column 15.
   b. Consists of two lines, which will appear as lines 46 and 47 when the report group itself is generated.
   c. Will consist of a row of hyphens, followed by a second line containing the literal LOCATION TOTAL, followed by a numeric value.
   d. All of the above.

16. In order to accurately produce the desired report, all of the following are required except:
   a. The input file is sorted on EMPLOYEE-LOCATION.
   b. The data name EMPLOYEE-LOCATION begins in position 15 of each incoming record.
   c. That EMPLOYEE-SALARY contains a valid numeric value for each incoming record.
   d. That EMPLOYEE-SALARY and EMPLOYEE-LOCATION are both defined in each incoming record.

17. The value of EMPLOYEE-SALARY will be summed for each incoming record and.
   a. The sum will be automatically reset to zero whenever there is a break on EMPLOYEE-LOCATION.
   b. The sum will be automatically reset to zero whenever there is a break on EMPLOYEE-SALARY.
   c. The sum will be reset to zero only if the RESET clause is included.
   d. Either (a) or (b) above.

Solutions for Topic 2.9

Exercise 2.34: Identifying Report Groups

a. Control Heading (on Employee Location)
b. Control Footing (on Employee Title)
c. Page Heading

d. Detail lines

e. Control Footing (on Employee Location)

Exercise 2.35: Coding Report Groups

1. 01 TYPE IS PAGE HEADING.
       05 LINE NUMBER 1.
          10 COLUMN NUMBER 61
             PIC X(4)
             VALUE 'PAGE'.
          10 COLUMN NUMBER 66
             PIC ZZZ9
             SOURCE PAGE-COUNTER.
       05 LINE NUMBER PLUS 2.
          10 COLUMN NUMBER 22
             PIC X(33)
             VALUE 'SALARIES BY LOCATION BY TITLE'.

2. 01 TYPE IS CONTROL HEADING EMP-LOCATION.
       05 LINE NUMBER 5.
          10 COLUMN NUMBER 24
             PIC X(19)
             VALUE 'SALARY SUMMARY FOR'.
          10 COLUMN NUMBER 43
             PIC X(13)
             SOURCE EMP-LOCATION.
       05 LINE NUMBER 7.
          10 COLUMN NUMBER 6
             PIC X(8)
             VALUE 'EMPLOYEE'.
          10 COLUMN NUMBER 24
             PIC X(5)
             VALUE 'TITLE'.
          10 COLUMN NUMBER 40
             PIC X(7)
             VALUE 'SALARY'.

3. 01 EMPLOYEE–LINE TYPE IS DETAIL.
       05 LINE NUMBER PLUS 1.
          10 COLUMN NUMBER 2
             PIC X(15)
             SOURCE EMP-NAME.
          10 COLUMN NUMBER 20
             PIC X(18)
             SOURCE EMP-TITLE.
          10 COLUMN NUMBER 41
             PIC $$$,$$$
             SOURCE EMP-SALARY.

4. 01 TYPE IS CONTROL FOOTING EMP-TITLE.
       05 LINE NUMBER PLUS 1.
           10 COLUMN NUMBER 26
               PIC X(20)
               VALUE 'TITLE TOTAL'.
           10 TITLE-TOTAL
               COLUMN NUMBER 48
               PIC $$$$,$$$
               SUM EMP-SALARY.
       05 LINE NUMBER PLUS 1.
           10 COLUMN NUMBER 61
               PIC X(7)
               VALUE ALL ' '.

5. 01 TYPE IS CONTROL FOOTING EMP-LOCATION.
       05 LINE NUMBER PLUS 1.
           10 COLUMN NUMBER 48
               PIC X(7)
               VALUE ALL '-'.
       05 LINE NUMBER PLUS 1.
           10 COLUMN NUMBER 4
               PIC X(14)
               VALUE 'LOCATION TOTAL'.
           10 COLUMN NUMBER 58
               PIC $$$$,$$$
               SUM TITLE-TOTAL.

Exercise 2.36: Coding Other Report Writer Statements

1. FD PRINT-FILE
     REPORT IS SALARY-TOTALS
     LABEL RECORDS ARE OMITTED
     RECORD CONTAINS 133 CHARACTERS.

(Note well, there is no 01 record specified.)

2. RD SALARY-TOTALS
       CONTROLS ARE FINAL EMP-LOCATION EMP-TITLE
       PAGE LIMIT 50 LINES
       HEADING 1
       FIRST DETAIL 5
       LAST DETAIL 45
       FOOTING 48.

3. INITIATE SALARY-TOTALS. (specifies report-name)
   GENERATE EMPLOYEE-LINE. (specifies data name of detail report group from exercise 2.35(3)).
   TERMINATE SALARY-TOTALS

Exercise 2.37: Self-Checking Examination

1. D
2. C
3. C
4. D
5. D
6. C
7. A
8. C
9. D
10. C
11. A
12. A
13. C
14. C
15. D
16. B
17. A

3 Source Level Debugging

OVERVIEW:

The beginning COBOL programmer is primarily concerned with the many compilation errors that accompany his or her first few attempts. When these errors disappear, he or she typically assumes that the execution results are correct. While this is often the case with early assignments that are logically simple, the initial euphoria disappears quickly with advanced assignments and unexpected results. Although there are those in the programming community who argue that programs can be made to run correctly on the first attempt, this author believes that logic errors will remain with us for the foreseeable future. This section is designed to provide realistic debugging experience over a wide range of programming projects.

The exercises in this book are designed to cover the spectrum of the *two*-semester COBOL sequence. The reader will find problems involving: signed numbers, control breaks, sorting and merging, table lookups, sequential and nonsequential file maintenance, and subprograms. In addition to execution errors, two listings have been included to illustrate compilation errors associated with Report Writer and SORT, two advanced language features. In all cases there are only a few statements, in programs of one or two hundred statements, which cause the problems in output. The errors are subtle but not contrived, and typical of beginning (and practicing) programmers.

The section begins with a programming tip on common execution errors, reasons for their occurrence, and ways to prevent them. The author believes that the same kinds of errors continually occur, albeit in different disguises, and that the debugging skill of the individual is enhanced by knowing what to look for. Accordingly, errors on the list are tied to specific exercises in the section to provide meaningful examples, and correspondingly to increase the pedagogical nature of the exercises. Not every problem in this section (or the real world) can be traced to the list, but it is a good starting place.

Every attempt has been made to simulate field conditions as closely as possible. The programs are of modest length, neither trivial nor unduly complex. The errors are noted objectively, with no hint as to what the problem may be. There is one major difference, between this book and the real world, in that solutions appear at the conclusion of the section beginning on page 195. The author thought long and hard about whether to include the answers, and in the end felt he had to in fairness to the reader. No peeking, however, at least not until you have made an *honest* effort at finding the problem.

Programming Tip: Execution Errors to Avoid

1. *Failure to initialize (reinitialize) a counter.* All programmers have at one time forgotten to initialize a data-name used as a counter. The usual result is an 0C7 ABEND (data exception on IBM systems) which is relatively easy to find and is discussed in Sect. 7. A more subtle error is the failure to *reinitialize* counters when control breaks are called for. Consider the following sales report, sorted by location first, then by salesman within location.

LOCATION:	ATLANTA	
	SALESMAN	YEAR-TO-DATE-SALES
	ADAMS	$10,000
	BAKER	$50,000
	SMITH	$40,000
	TOTAL SALES FOR ATLANTA = $100,000	

LOCATION:	BOSTON	
	SALESMAN	YEAR-TO-DATE-SALES
	BROWN	$15,000
	JONES	$20,000
	TURNER	$ 8,000
	YOUNG	$60,000
	TOTAL SALES FOR BOSTON = $203,000	

The correct total for Boston should be $103,000, *not* $203,000. The problem is caused by failure to reinitialize the location sales total when a new location was encountered. See exercise 3.3.

2. *Errors in looping.* The establishment of a loop requires four basic steps:
    a. Initialization of a counter
    b. Incrementing of a counter
    c. Comparison of the counter to a predetermined value
    d. An appropriate branch

Programming Tip, cont.

Regardless of whether the programmer establishes his own loop or utilizes various features of COBOL to do it for him, these four basic steps must be accomplished in one way or another.

A frequent error occurs when a loop is executed an improper number of times; often one too many or too few. Consider the PERFORM statement:

```
PERFORM COMPUTE-YEAR-TOTAL
    VARYING MONTH-SUB FROM 1 BY 1 UNTIL MONTH-SUB = 12.
```

The routine COMPUTE-YEAR-TOTAL will be performed 11 times, *not* 12, because COBOL does the comparison *before* the branch. Thus, after the routine has been performed 11 times, MONTH-SUB is incremented from 11 to 12. Then since MONTH-SUB = 12, the perform is terminated.

An associated error occurs when the last record in a file is processed twice. This can happen if the initial (or priming) read of a structured program is not handled correctly. See exercises 3.6 and 3.7.

3. *Improper use of the SEARCH verb*. SEARCH and SEARCH ALL, for linear and binary searches, respectively, greatly simplify life for the COBOL programmer. SEARCH requires that the starting search position be initialized through a SET statement, while SEARCH ALL requires codes in a table to be in sequence. Failure to conform causes erroneous results. See exercises 3.6, 3.7, and 3.13.

4. *Incorrect use of MOVE*. The MOVE is perhaps the most frequently used statement in COBOL. It is apparently quite simple yet misunderstandings can occur, particularly when the sending and receiving fields have different lengths and/or decimal alignments. Another problem arises when the receiving field is a group item which causes the entire move to be treated as alphanumeric even though the elementary items may be numeric. See exercises 3.12 and 3.17.

5. *Difficulty with signed numbers*. Negative numbers can only be held by *signed* numeric data names. Consider:

```
05    FIELD-A    PIC 99     VALUE 10.
05    FIELD-B    PIC S99    VALUE -12.
05    FIELD-C    PIC 99     VALUE 10.
05    FIELD-D    PIC S99    VALUE -12.

ADD FIELD-A TO FIELD-B.
ADD FIELD-D TO FIELD-C.
```

Programming Tip, cont.

Numerically one expects the sum of 10 and −12 to be −2. The value of FIELD-B is indeed −2, but the value of FIELD-C will *incorrectly* be 2, because FIELD-C was defined without a sign. See exercise 3.14.

6. *Improper use of nested IF statements.* A nested IF occurs when there are two or more IFs within a period. The compiler associates the ELSE clause with the closest previous IF which is not already paired with another ELSE. Consistent indentation in coding is essential if the programmer is to understand what is going on. A related problem is the misuse of Boolean functions in the condition portion of an IF. See exercises 3.6, 3.7, 3.8, 3.9, and 3.17.

7. *Missing and/or extra period.* When the IF statement is used without an ELSE, it is terminated by the period, that is, all statements between the condition and the period are executed whenever the condition is satisfied. When a period is omitted, it results in additional statements being executed, and conversely, if a period is added fewer statements are executed. While this sounds simple, it may not be easy to tell whether a period is actually present. Periods sometimes wind up in column 73, which makes them appear present, but in reality they are absent, as the compiler does not interpret columns 73-80.

The period also terminates the ELSE clause, AT END and IN-VALID KEY clauses in a READ or WRITE, and the SIZE ERROR clause in a COMPUTE. Similar cautions apply here as well. Exercises 3.5, 3.7, 3.10, and 3.17 contain *subtle* errors dealing with the presence or absence of a period.

8. *Access of an FD area after a WRITE.* Simply stated, one may not access an I-O area after a WRITE as the buffer pointers are switched. This is an error that many beginners make once and then learn not to do again. See exercise 3.15.

9. *Improper exit from a performed routine.* One may perform out of a PERFORM, or one may GO TO an exit paragraph within a range of performed paragraphs (PERFORM PAR-A THRU PAR-A-EXIT with a *forward* GO TO to PAR-A-EXIT). One may *not use GO TO to leave a performed routine* as this results in object code being altered. No example of this is shown, however, as this error so violates structured programming as to be unconscionable in today's environment.

10. *Failure to set/reset switches.* This is a common difficulty in structured programs since these are heavily dependent on logic switches. Errors of this type are usually difficult to find, because their effects can take many forms. There is not much the author can offer in the way of ad-

> **Programming Tip, cont.**
>
> vice, except a rule of thumb: whenever specific action is taken because a switch is turned on, the switch should be immediately turned off. Bear in mind, however, this is only a rule of thumb and undoubtedly has many exceptions. See exercises 3.8 and 3.9.
>
> 11. *Improper linkage to a subroutine.* Although the COBOL statement to call a subprogram presents no great difficulty in and of itself, improper linkage often leads to trouble. Specifically, the arguments in both the calling and called program must appear in the same order and should usually have identical pictures. Moreover, if a group item, for example, an 01 record, is passed as a parameter, it is essential that the elementary items in the group item be defined identically in both programs. See exercises 3.6 and 3.7.
>
> 12. *End and/or beginning file conditions.* These errors are prevalent in file maintenance applications, particularly where multiple input files are used. The author has seen untold examples of complex maintenance programs which "work" 99 percent of the time but fail if a unique combination of events occur; for example, the key of the last record on the transaction file is higher than the last record in the old master file, etc. A common error is that processing ceases prematurely when using multiple input files whenever the first file becomes empty. Another common error involves processing the last record twice. See exercises 3.7 and 3.11.
>
> 13. *Invalid subscript or index.* One of the most common errors, and most difficult to find, because the result of this error can take many forms. For example, one can exceed the bounds of a table during a table lookup. One can also exceed the declared size of a table during its initialization and thereby overlay a portion of code. Both problems stem from the freedom permitted by the compiler generated instructions. Consider:
>
>   05   TABLE-ENTRY OCCURS 20 TIMES   PIC X(10).
>
> The OCCURS clause sets aside a 200 (20 x 10) byte table in storage. Logically, one should be permitted to reference only entries with subscripts of 1 to 20. Most compilers, however, *do not* insert machine code to check on the validity of a subscript. Thus, if one tried to reference TABLE-ENTRY (21) one would access the first 10 bytes of storage beyond the table. In similar fashion, TABLE-ENTRY (0) points to the 10 bytes immediately before the actual table. The best defense against errors of this sort is for the programmer to insert Procedure Division code to check on the validity of subscripts, with appropriate error messages. Errors of this kind frequently result in an ABEND in which the program fails to go to a normal end of job. See exercise 3.16 and Sect. 7.

> **Programming Tip, cont.**
>
> 14. *Improper use of comments.* Comments in COBOL (denoted by an asterisk in column 7) are non-executable, but the presence (or absence) of these statements can adversely affect a program in two ways.
>
> First many individuals tend to overcomment, especially when writing initial code. As a program goes into production and eventually into maintenance, subtle changes are made, but the comments are usually left alone. The unhappy result is that the comments and source code are no longer consistent, causing obvious problems in maintenance. (The author knows a veteran programmer who actually removes all comments in any program he has been assigned to maintain).
>
> A second difficulty arises when a programmer "asterisks out" executable code. This happens when statements in a program are no longer deemed necessary. Of course all such statements should be deleted, but the programmer may have reason to believe that the statements will again be required at a future date. Accordingly they are turned into comments and made non-executable (and easily recallable). The resulting code is extremely difficult to read and often leads to subsequent errors.

Exercise 3-1: Compilation Errors and Report Writer

Correct the compilation errors in Fig. 3-1.

```
00001              IDENTIFICATION DIVISION.
00002              PROGRAM-ID.    TWOLEVEL.
00003              AUTHOR.      R GRAUER.

00005              ENVIRONMENT DIVISION.
00006              CONFIGURATION SECTION.
00007              SOURCE-COMPUTER.      IBM-370.
00008              OBJECT-COMPUTER.      IBM-370.
00009              INPUT-OUTPUT SECTION.
00010              FILE-CONTROL.
00011                  SELECT SALES-FILE ASSIGN TO UT-S-SYSIN.
00012                  SELECT PRINT-FILE ASSIGN TO UT-S-SYSOUT.

00014              DATA DIVISION.
00015              FILE SECTION.

00017              FD  SALES-FILE
00018                  RECORDING MODE IS F
00019                  LABEL RECORDS ARE OMITTED
00020                  RECORD CONTAINS 80 CHARACTERS
00021                  DATA RECORD IS TRANSACTION-RECORD.
00022              01  TRANSACTION-RECORD          PIC X(80).

00024              FD  PRINT-FILE
00025                  REPORT IS CONTROL-BREAK
00026                  RECORDING MODE IS F
00027                  LABEL RECORDS ARE OMITTED
00028                  RECORD CONTAINS 133 CHARACTERS.
```

Figure 3.1 Report Writer Program with Compilation Errors.

```
00030              WORKING-STORAGE SECTION.
00031              77  FILLER                    PIC X(14)
00032                      VALUE 'WS BEGINS HERE'.
00033              77  WS-DATA-FLAG              PIC X(3)    VALUE SPACES.
00034                  88  NO-MORE-DATA                      VALUE 'NO'.

00036              01  TRANSACTION-AREA.
00037                  05  TR-SALESMAN-NAME      PIC X(20).
00038                  05  TR-AMOUNT             PIC S9(4).
00039                  05  FILLER                PIC XX.
00040                  05  TR-NUMBER             PIC X(6).
00041                  05  TR-SALESMAN-REGION    PIC X(18).
00042                  05  TR-SALESMAN-LOCATION  PIC X(20).
00043                  05  FILLER                PIC X(10).

00045              01  FILLER                    PIC X(12)
00046                      VALUE 'WS ENDS HERE'.

00048              REPORT SECTION.
00049              RD  CONTROL-BREAK
00050                  CONTROLS ARE FINAL TR-SALESMAN-LOCATION
00051                  PAGE LIMIT 50 LINES
00052                  HEADING 1
00053                  FIRST DETAIL 5
00054                  LAST DETAIL 45
00055                  FOOTING 48.
00056              01  TYPE IS PAGE HEADING.
00057                  05  LINE NUMBER 1.
00058                      10  COLUMN NUMBER 61
00059                          PIC A(4)
00060                          VALUE 'PAGE'.
00061                      10  COLUMN NUMBER 66
00062                          PIC ZZZ9
00063                          SOURCE PAGE-COUNT.
00064                  05  LINE NUMBER PLUS 2.
00065                      10  COLUMN NUMBER 22
00066                          PIC X(31)
00067                          VALUE 'TWO LEVEL CONTROL BREAK EXAMPLE'.
00068              01  TYPE IS CONTROL HEADING TR-SALESMAN-LOCATION.
00069                  05  LINE NUMBER 5.
00070                      10  COLUMN NUMBER 25
00071                          PIC X(18)
00072                          VALUE 'SALES ACTIVITY FOR'.
00073                      10  COLUMN NUMBER 44
00074                          PIC X(10)
00075                          SOURCE TR-SALESMAN-LOCATION.
00076                  05  LINE NUMBER 7.
00077                      10  COLUMN NUMBER 6
00078                          PIC X(8)
00079                          VALUE 'SALESMAN'.
00080                      10  COLUMN NUMBER 24
00081                          PIC X(13)
00082                          VALUE 'TRANSACTION #'.
00083                      10  COLUMN NUMBER 40
00084                          PIC X(7)
00085                          VALUE 'AMOUNT'.
00086              01  TYPE IS DETAIL.
```

Figure 3.1 *cont.*

```
00087                   05  LINE NUMBER PLUS 1.
00088                       10  COLUMN NUMBER 2
00089                           PIC X(20)
00090                           SOURCE TR-NAME.
00091                       10  COLUMN NUMBER 27
00092                           PIC X(6)
00093                           SOURCE TR-NUMBER.
00094                       10  COLUMN NUMBER 41
00095                           PIC $ZZZ9
00096                           SOURCE TR-AMOUNT.
00097               01  TYPE IS CONTROL FOOTING TR-SALESMAN-NAME.
00098                   05  LINE NUMBER PLUS 1.
00099                       10  COLUMN NUMBER 4
00100                           PIC X(15)
00101                           VALUE 'SALESMAN TOTAL'.
00102                       10  SALESMAN-TOTAL
00103                           COLUMN NUMBER 48
00104                           PIC $$$$,999
00105                           SUM TR-AMOUNT.
00106               01  TYPE IS CONTROL FOOTING TR-SALESMAN-LOCATION.
00107                   05  LINE NUMBER PLUS 2.
00108                       10  COLUMN NUMBER 48
00109                           PIC X(10)
00110                           VALUE ALL '-'.
00111                   05  LINE NUMBER PLUS 1.
00112                       10  COLUMN NUMBER 4
00113                           PIC X(14)
00114                           VALUE 'LOCATION TOTAL'.
00115                       10  COLUMN NUMBER 48
00116                           PIC $$$$,999
00117                           SUM SALESMAN-TOTAL.
00118               01  TYPE IS CONTROL FOOTING.
00119                   05  LINE NUMBER IS PLUS 5.
00120                       10  COLUMN NUMBER 10
00121                           PIC X(28)
00122                           VALUE '***FINAL TOTAL ALL LOCATIONS'.
00123                       10  COLUMN NUMBER 40
00124                           PIC $ZZZ,999
00125                           SUM SALESMAN-TOTAL.

00127           PROCEDURE DIVISION.
00128           0010-CREATE-REPORTS.
00129               OPEN INPUT SALES-FILE
00130                   OUTPUT PRINT-FILE.
00131               INITIATE PRINT-FILE.
00132               READ SALES-FILE INTO TRANSACTION-AREA
00133                   AT END MOVE 'NO' TO WS-DATA-FLAG.
00134               PERFORM 0020-PROCESS-ALL-TRANSACTIONS UNTIL NO-MORE-DATA.
00135               END CONTROL-BREAK.
00136               CLOSE SALES-FILE
00137                   PRINT-FILE.
00138               STOP RUN.

00140           0020-PROCESS-ALL-TRANSACTIONS.
00141               GENERATE TRANSACTION-LINE.
00142               READ SALES-FILE INTO TRANSACTION-AREA
00143                   AT END MOVE 'NO' TO WS-DATA-FLAG.
```

Figure 3.1 *cont.*

CARD	ERROR MESSAGE	
61	IKF3001I-E	PAGE-COUNT NOT DEFINED. DISCARDED.
86	IKF1170I-E	DETAIL REPORT GROUP SPECIFIED WITH NO DATA-NAME. CONTINUING.
88	IKF3001I-E	TR-NAME NOT DEFINED. DISCARDED.
97	IKF1104I-E	CONTROL NAME NOT SPECIFIED IN RD. SKIPPING TO NEXT 01.
118	IKF1069I-E	INVALID TYPE CLAUSE. SKIPPING TO NEXT 01.
131	IKF1054I-E	OPERAND FOR INITIATE NOT FOUND OR ILLEGAL. OPERAND DROPPED.
134	IKF4003I-E	EXPECTING NEW STATEMENT. FOUND END . DELETING TILL NEXT VERB OR PROCEDURE-NAME.
134	IKF3020I-E	REPORT NAME ILLEGAL AS USED. DISCARDED.
141	IKF1068I-E	OPERAND FOR GENERATE NOT FOUND. CLAUSE DROPPED.

Figure 3.1 *cont.*

Exercise 3.2: Execution Errors and Report Writer

The program in Fig. 3.2 is intended to illustrate the use of Report Writer with programs requiring double control breaks. It processes a file of transaction records which have been *presorted* by location by salesman (there can be several transactions for the same salesman). The objective is simply to provide salesman and location totals. The *desired* report is shown in Fig. 3.3. The *actual* report that was produced is shown in Fig. 3.4.

```
00001              IDENTIFICATION DIVISION.
00002              PROGRAM-ID.    TWOLEVEL.
00003              AUTHOR.       R GRAUER.

00005              ENVIRONMENT DIVISION.
00006              CONFIGURATION SECTION.
00007              SOURCE-COMPUTER.       IBM-370.
00008              OBJECT-COMPUTER.       IBM-370.
00009              INPUT-OUTPUT SECTION.
00010              FILE-CONTROL.
00011                  SELECT SALES-FILE ASSIGN TO UT-S-SYSIN.
00012                  SELECT PRINT-FILE ASSIGN TO UT-S-SYSOUT.

00014              DATA DIVISION.
00015              FILE SECTION.

00017              FD  SALES-FILE
00018                  RECORDING MODE IS F
00019                  LABEL RECORDS ARE OMITTED
00020                  RECORD CONTAINS 80 CHARACTERS
00021                  DATA RECORD IS TRANSACTION-RECORD.
00022              01  TRANSACTION-RECORD        PIC X(80).

00024              FD  PRINT-FILE
00025                  REPORT IS CONTROL-BREAK
00026                  RECORDING MODE IS F
00027                  LABEL RECORDS ARE OMITTED
00028                  RECORD CONTAINS 133 CHARACTERS.

00030              WORKING-STORAGE SECTION.
00031              77  FILLER                    PIC X(14)
00032                  VALUE 'WS BEGINS HERE'.
00033              77  WS-DATA-FLAG              PIC X(3)  VALUE SPACES.
00034                  88  NO-MORE-DATA                    VALUE 'NO'.

00036              01  TRANSACTION-AREA.
00037                  05  TR-SALESMAN-NAME      PIC X(20).
00038                  05  TR-AMOUNT             PIC S9(4).
00039                  05  FILLER                PIC XX.
00040                  05  TR-NUMBER             PIC X(6).
00041                  05  TR-SALESMAN-REGION    PIC X(18).
00042                  05  TR-SALESMAN-LOCATION  PIC X(20).
00043                  05  FILLER                PIC X(10).

00045              01  FILLER                    PIC X(12)
00046                  VALUE 'WS ENDS HERE'.

00048              REPORT SECTION.
00049              RD  CONTROL-BREAK
00050                  CONTROLS ARE FINAL TR-SALESMAN-LOCATION TR-SALESMAN-NAME
00051                  PAGE LIMIT 50 LINES
00052                  HEADING 1
```

Figure 3.2 Report Writer Program with Execution Errors.

```
00053                   FIRST DETAIL 5
00054                   LAST DETAIL 45
00055                   FOOTING 48.
00056              01 TYPE IS PAGE HEADING.
00057                   05 LINE NUMBER 1.
00058                      10 COLUMN NUMBER 61
00059                         PIC A(4)
00060                         VALUE 'PAGE'.
00061                      10 COLUMN NUMBER 66
00062                         PIC ZZZ9
00063                         SOURCE PAGE-COUNTER.
00064                   05 LINE NUMBER PLUS 2.
00065                      10 COLUMN NUMBER 22
00066                         PIC X(31)
00067                         VALUE 'TWO LEVEL CONTROL BREAK EXAMPLE'.
00068              01 TYPE IS CONTROL HEADING TR-SALESMAN-LOCATION.
00069                   05 LINE NUMBER 5.
00070                      10 COLUMN NUMBER 25
00071                         PIC X(18)
00072                         VALUE 'SALES ACTIVITY FOR'.
00073                      10 COLUMN NUMBER 44
00074                         PIC X(10)
00075                         SOURCE TR-SALESMAN-LOCATION.
00076                   05 LINE NUMBER 7.
00077                      10 COLUMN NUMBER 6
00078                         PIC X(8)
00079                         VALUE 'SALESMAN'.
00080                      10 COLUMN NUMBER 24
00081                         PIC X(13)
00082                         VALUE 'TRANSACTION #'.
00083                      10 COLUMN NUMBER 40
00084                         PIC X(7)
00085                         VALUE 'AMOUNT'.
00086              01 TRANSACTION-LINE TYPE IS DETAIL.
00087                   05 LINE NUMBER PLUS 1.
00088                      10 COLUMN NUMBER 2
00089                         PIC X(20)
00090                         SOURCE TR-SALESMAN-NAME.
00091                      10 COLUMN NUMBER 27
00092                         PIC X(6)
00093                         SOURCE TR-NUMBER.
00094                      10 COLUMN NUMBER 41
00095                         PIC $ZZZ9
00096                         SOURCE TR-AMOUNT.
00097              01 TYPE IS CONTROL FOOTING TR-SALESMAN-NAME.
00098                   05 LINE NUMBER PLUS 1.
00099                      10 COLUMN NUMBER 4
00100                         PIC X(15)
00101                         VALUE 'SALESMAN TOTAL'.
00102                      10 SALESMAN-TOTAL
00103                         COLUMN NUMBER 48
00104                         PIC $$,999
00105                         SUM TR-AMOUNT.
00106              01 TYPE IS CONTROL FOOTING FINAL.
00107                   05 LINE NUMBER IS PLUS 5.
00108                      10 COLUMN NUMBER 10
00109                         PIC X(28)
00110                         VALUE '***FINAL TOTAL ALL LOCATIONS'.
00111                      10 COLUMN NUMBER 40
00112                         PIC $ZZZ,999
00113                         SUM SALESMAN-TOTAL.

00115              PROCEDURE DIVISION.
00116              0010-CREATE-REPORTS.
00117                   OPEN INPUT SALES-FILE
00118                        OUTPUT PRINT-FILE.
00119                   INITIATE CONTROL-BREAK.
```

Figure 3.2 *cont.*

```
00120           READ SALES-FILE INTO TRANSACTION-AREA
00121               AT END MOVE 'NO' TO WS-DATA-FLAG.
00122           PERFORM 0020-PROCESS-ALL-TRANSACTIONS UNTIL NO-MORE-DATA.
00123           TERMINATE CONTROL-BREAK.
00124           CLOSE SALES-FILE
00125               PRINT-FILE.
00126           STOP RUN.

00128       0020-PROCESS-ALL-TRANSACTIONS.
00129           GENERATE CONTROL-BREAK.
00130           READ SALES-FILE INTO TRANSACTION-AREA
00131               AT END MOVE 'NO' TO WS-DATA-FLAG.
```

Figure 3.2 *cont.*

```
                                                          PAGE    2
                   TWO LEVEL CONTROL BREAK EXAMPLE
                      SALES ACTIVITY FOR BOSTON

         SALESMAN           TRANSACTION #      AMOUNT
      JEFFRY BOROW              373737         $5000
         SALESMAN TOTAL                                  $5,000
      STEVEN GULFMAN            424242         $4300
      STEVEN GULFMAN            675432         $ 800
         SALESMAN TOTAL                                  $5,100
                                                        ----------
         LOCATION TOTAL                                 $10,100



         ***FINAL TOTAL ALL LOCATIONS   $ 31,217
```

```
                                                          PAGE    1
                   TWO LEVEL CONTROL BREAK EXAMPLE
                      SALES ACTIVITY FOR ATLANTA

         SALESMAN           TRANSACTION #      AMOUNT
      JOHN JONES                123456         $ 500
      JOHN JONES                222222         $2000
      JOHN JONES                333333         $2542
         SALESMAN TOTAL                                  $5,042
      PETER SMITH               100000         $2500
      PETER SMITH               200000         $3000
         SALESMAN TOTAL                                  $5,500
      THOMAS TAYLOR             300000         $1500
      THOMAS TAYLOR             400000         $1575
      THOMAS TAYLOR             456789         $3500
      THOMAS TAYLOR             601209         $4000
         SALESMAN TOTAL                                 $10,575
                                                        ----------
         LOCATION TOTAL                                 $21,117
```

Figure 3.3 Desired Report.

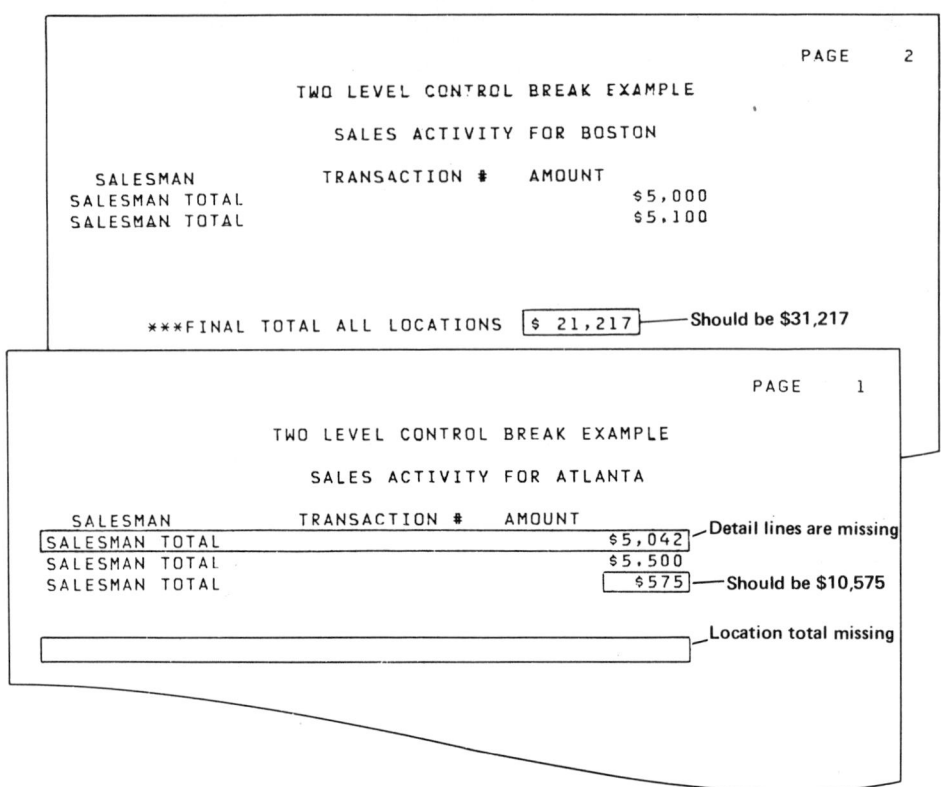

Figure 3.4 Actual Report.

As can be seen by contrasting Figures 3.3 and 3.4, three major errors occurred. In particular:
1. The detail lines for individual transactions, with salesman name, transaction number, etc., were omitted. Supply the required COBOL code, and indicate where the statements belong.
2. Location totals are missing. Supply the necessary COBOL code and indicate where the statements should go.
3. The total for the third salesman is off by $10,000, (which causes the final total to also be off by $10,000) but the totals for the other four salesmen seem correct.

Correct all errors.

Exercise 3.3: Execution Errors and Control Breaks

The program in Fig. 3.5 is designed to process an invoice file which has been *presorted* by location and by salesman. Each incoming record contains: the salesman name, amount of sale, invoice number, and location name.

There can be many records or invoices for one salesman.

The program was designed to list all invoices in the file, with salesmen in the same location appearing on the same page. Individual totals are required for each salesman. Location totals are required as well. The program was tested with the data of Fig. 3-6 and produced the output of Fig. 3-7. Indicate the necessary COBOL corrections.

```
00001           IDENTIFICATION DIVISION.
00002           PROGRAM-ID.    TWOLEVEL.
00003           AUTHOR.        R GRAUER.
00004           ENVIRONMENT DIVISION.
00005           CONFIGURATION SECTION.
00006           SOURCE-COMPUTER.      IBM-370.
00007           OBJECT-COMPUTER.      IBM-370.
00008           INPUT-OUTPUT SECTION.
00009           FILE-CONTROL.
00010               SELECT SALES-FILE ASSIGN TO UT-S-SYSIN.
00011               SELECT PRINT-FILE ASSIGN TO UT-S-SYSOUT.
00012
00013           DATA DIVISION.
00014           FILE SECTION.
00015           FD  SALES-FILE
00016               LABEL RECORDS ARE OMITTED
00017               RECORD CONTAINS 80 CHARACTERS
00018               DATA RECORD IS TRANSACTION-RECORD.
00019           01  TRANSACTION-RECORD      PIC X(80).
00020           FD  PRINT-FILE
00021               LABEL RECORDS ARE OMITTED
00022               RECORD CONTAINS 133 CHARACTERS
00023               DATA RECORD IS PRINT-LINE.
00024           01  PRINT-LINE              PIC X(133).
00025           WORKING-STORAGE SECTION.
00026           77  WS-PREVIOUS-SALESMAN    PIC X(20) VALUE SPACES.
00027           77  WS-PREVIOUS-LOCATION    PIC X(20) VALUE SPACES.
00028           77  WS-DATA-FLAG            PIC X(3)  VALUE SPACES.
00029               88  NO-MORE-DATA                  VALUE 'NO'.
00030
00031           01  INTERMEDIATE-TOTALS.
00032               05  THIS-LOCATION-SALES PIC S9(6) VALUE ZEROS.
00033               05  THIS-SALESMAN-SALES PIC S9(4).
00034
00035           01  HEADING-LINE-ONE.
00036               05  FILLER              PIC X(80) VALUE SPACES.
00037               05  FILLER              PIC X(5)  VALUE 'PAGE '.
00038               05  PAGE-NUMBER         PIC 9(4)  VALUE ZEROS.
00039               05  FILLER              PIC X(44) VALUE SPACES.
00040
00041           01  HEADING-LINE-TWO.
00042               05  FILLER              PIC X(10) VALUE SPACES.
00043               05  FILLER              PIC X(20) VALUE 'SALESMAN NAME'.
00044               05  FILLER              PIC X(10) VALUE SPACES.
00045               05  FILLER              PIC X(15) VALUE 'LOCATION'.
00046               05  FILLER              PIC X(10) VALUE SPACES.
00047               05  FILLER              PIC X(13) VALUE 'TRANSACTION #'.
00048               05  FILLER              PIC X(5)  VALUE SPACES.
00049               05  FILLER              PIC X(4)  VALUE 'SALE'.
00050               05  FILLER              PIC X(46) VALUE SPACES.
00051
00052           01  TRANSACTION-AREA.
```

Figure 3.5 Two-Level Control Break Program with Execution Errors.

```
00053            05  TR-SALESMAN-NAME       PIC X(20).
00054            05  TR-AMOUNT              PIC S9(4).
00055            05  FILLER                 PIC XX.
00056            05  TR-NUMBER              PIC X(6).
00057            05  FILLER                 PIC X(18).
00058            05  TR-SALESMAN-LOCATION   PIC X(20).
00059            05  FILLER                 PIC X(10).
00060
00061        01  SALESMAN-DETAIL-LINE.
00062            05  FILLER                 PIC X(10)   VALUE SPACES.
00063            05  DETAIL-NAME            PIC X(20).
00064            05  FILLER                 PIC X(10)   VALUE SPACES.
00065            05  DETAIL-LOCATION        PIC X(15).
00066            05  FILLER                 PIC X(12).
00067            05  DETAIL-TRANSACTION     PIC X(6).
00068            05  FILLER                 PIC X(8).
00069            05  DETAIL-SALES           PIC $Z,ZZ9.
00070            05  FILLER                 PIC X(46).
00071
00072        01  SALESMAN-TOTAL-LINE.
00073            05  FILLER                 PIC X(71) VALUE SPACES.
00074            05  FILLER                 PIC X(14) VALUE 'SALESMAN TOTAL'.
00075            05  FILLER                 PIC X(4)  VALUE SPACES.
00076            05  TOTAL-LINE-SALES       PIC $Z,ZZ9.
00077            05  FILLER                 PIC X(74) VALUE SPACES.
00078
00079        01  LOCATION-TOTAL-LINE.
00080            05  FILLER                 PIC X(81) VALUE SPACES.
00081            05  FILLER                 PIC X(15) VALUE 'LOCATION TOTAL'.
00082            05  FILLER                 PIC X(9)  VALUE SPACES.
00083            05  PRINT-LOCATION-SALES   PIC $$$$,999.
00084            05  FILLER                 PIC X(20) VALUE SPACES.
00085
00086        PROCEDURE DIVISION.
00087        0010-CREATE-REPORTS.
00088            OPEN INPUT SALES-FILE
00089                 OUTPUT PRINT-FILE.
00090            READ SALES-FILE INTO TRANSACTION-AREA
00091                AT END MOVE 'NO' TO WS-DATA-FLAG.
00092            PERFORM A000-PROCESS-ALL-LOCATIONS UNTIL NO-MORE-DATA.
00093            CLOSE SALES-FILE
00094                  PRINT-FILE.
00095            STOP RUN.
00096
00097        A000-PROCESS-ALL-LOCATIONS.
00098            MOVE TR-SALESMAN-LOCATION TO WS-PREVIOUS-LOCATION.
00099            PERFORM A300-WRITE-LOCATION-HEADER.
00100            PERFORM A100-PROCESS-ONE-LOCATION
00101                UNTIL TR-SALESMAN-LOCATION NOT = WS-PREVIOUS-LOCATION
00102                    OR NO-MORE-DATA.
00103            MOVE THIS-LOCATION-SALES TO PRINT-LOCATION-SALES.
00104            WRITE PRINT-LINE FROM LOCATION-TOTAL-LINE
00105                AFTER ADVANCING 2 LINES.
00106
00107        A100-PROCESS-ONE-LOCATION.
00108            MOVE ZEROS TO THIS-SALESMAN-SALES.
00109            MOVE TR-SALESMAN-NAME TO WS-PREVIOUS-SALESMAN.
00110            PERFORM A310-PROCESS-ONE-SALESMAN
00111                UNTIL TR-SALESMAN-NAME NOT = WS-PREVIOUS-SALESMAN
00112                    OR NO-MORE-DATA.
00113            MOVE TR-AMOUNT TO TOTAL-LINE-SALES.
00114            ADD THIS-SALESMAN-SALES TO THIS-LOCATION-SALES.
```

Figure 3.5 *cont.*

```
00115              WRITE PRINT-LINE FROM SALESMAN-TOTAL-LINE
00116                  AFTER ADVANCING 2 LINES.
00117
00118          A300-WRITE-LOCATION-HEADER.
00119              ADD 1 TO PAGE-NUMBER.
00120              WRITE PRINT-LINE FROM HEADING-LINE-ONE
00121                  AFTER ADVANCING PAGE.
00122              WRITE PRINT-LINE FROM HEADING-LINE-TWO
00123                  AFTER ADVANCING 2 LINES.
00124
00125          A310-PROCESS-ONE-SALESMAN.
00126              MOVE SPACES TO SALESMAN-DETAIL-LINE.
00127              MOVE TR-SALESMAN-NAME TO DETAIL-NAME.
00128              MOVE TR-SALESMAN-LOCATION TO DETAIL-LOCATION.
00129              MOVE TR-AMOUNT TO DETAIL-SALES.
00130              MOVE TR-NUMBER TO DETAIL-TRANSACTION.
00131              ADD TR-AMOUNT TO THIS-SALESMAN-SALES.
00132              WRITE PRINT-LINE FROM SALESMAN-DETAIL-LINE
00133                  AFTER ADVANCING 2 LINES.
00134              READ SALES-FILE INTO TRANSACTION-AREA
00135                  AT END MOVE 'NO' TO WS-DATA-FLAG.
00136
```

Figure 3.5 *cont.*

```
PETER SMITH          3000   200000        ATLANTA              10.
THOMAS TAYLOR        1500   300000        ATLANTA              11.
JEFFRY BORON         5000   373737        BOSTON               12.
STEVEN GULFMAN       4300   424242        BOSTON               13.
CHANDLER LLAVOR      8000   151100        CHICAGO              14.
CRAIG TATER          0500   050000        CHICAGO              15.
```

Figure 3.6 Test Data.

```
                                    PAGE 0003

SALESMAN NAME        LOCATION        TRANSACTION #      SALE

CHANDLER LLAVOR      CHICAGO           151100         $8,000
                                       SALESMAN TOTAL  $   500
CRAIG TATER          CHICAGO           050000         $   500
                                       SALESMAN TOTAL  $7,700
                                                LOCATION TOTAL    $27,300
```

```
                                    PAGE 0002

SALESMAN NAME        LOCATION        TRANSACTION #      SALE

JEFFRY BOROW         BOSTON            373737         $5,000
                                       SALESMAN TOTAL  $4,300
STEVEN GULFMAN       BOSTON            424242         $4,300
                                       SALESMAN TOTAL  $8,000
                                                LOCATION TOTAL    $18,800    ← Location total is cumulative over all locations.
```

```
                                    PAGE 0001

SALESMAN NAME        LOCATION        TRANSACTION #      SALE

JOHN JONES           ATLANTA           123456         $   500
JOHN JONES           ATLANTA           222222         $2,000
                                       SALESMAN TOTAL  $2,500
PETER SMITH          ATLANTA           100000         $2,500
PETER SMITH          ATLANTA           200000         $3,000
                                       SALESMAN TOTAL  $1,500    ← Salesman total is wrong.
THOMAS TAYLOR        ATLANTA           300000         $1,500
                                       SALESMAN TOTAL  $5,000
                                                LOCATION TOTAL    $9,500
```

Figure 3.7 Incorrect Output of a Double Control Break Program.

Exercise 3.4: Compilation Errors and SORT

Correct the compilation errors found in Fig. 3.8.

```
00001              IDENTIFICATION DIVISION.
00002              PROGRAM-ID. "SORT2".
00003              AUTHOR.     MARION MILGROM.
00004
00005              ENVIRONMENT DIVISION.
00006              CONFIGURATION SECTION.
00007              SOURCE-COMPUTER.    IBM-370.
00008              OBJECT-COMPUTER.    IBM-370.
00009              INPUT-OUTPUT SECTION.
00010              FILE-CONTROL.
00011                  SELECT EMPLOYEE-FILE ASSIGN TO UT-S-SYSIN.
00012                  SELECT PRINT-FILE ASSIGN TO UT-S-SYSOUT.
00013                  SELECT SORT-FILE ASSIGN TO UT-S-SORTWK01.
00014
00015              DATA DIVISION.
00016              FILE SECTION.
00017              FD  EMPLOYEE-FILE
00018                  LABEL RECORDS ARE OMITTED
00019                  RECORD CONTAINS 80 CHARACTERS
00020                  DATA RECORD IS EMPLOYEE-RECORD.
00021              01  EMPLOYEE-RECORD.
00022                  05  CARD-NAME.
00023                      10  LAST-NAME           PIC X(15).
00024                      10  FIRST-NAME          PIC X(9).
00025                      10  MIDDLE-INITIAL      PIC X.
00026                  05  CARD-TITLE              PIC X(10).
00027                  05  DATE-OF-BIRTH.
00028                      10  BIRTH-MONTH         PIC 99.
00029                      10  BIRTH-YEAR          PIC 99.
00030                  05  PRESENT-SALARY          PIC 9(5).
00031                  05  FILLER                  PIC X(4).
00032                  05  FORMER-SALARY           PIC 9(5).
00033                  05  FILLER                  PIC X(27).
00034
00035              SD  SORT-FILE
00036                  LABEL RECORDS ARE OMITTED
00037                  RECORD CONTAINS 80 CHARACTERS
00038                  DATA RECORD IS SORT-RECORD.
00039              01  SORT-RECORD.
00040                  05  CARD-NAME.
00041                      10  LAST-NAME           PIC X(15).
00042                      10  FIRST-NAME          PIC X(9).
00043                      10  MIDDLE-INITIAL      PIC X.
00044                  05  CARD-TITLE              PIC X(10).
00045                  05  DATE-OF-BIRTH.
00046                      10  BIRTH-MONTH         PIC 99.
00047                      10  BIRTH-YEAR          PIC 99.
00048                  05  PRESENT-SALARY          PIC 9(5).
00049                  05  FILLER                  PIC X(4).
00050                  05  FORMER-SALARY           PIC 9(5).
00051                  05  EMPLOYEE-AGE            PIC 99V9.
00052                  05  PERCENT-SALARY-INCREASE PIC 99V9.
00053                  05  FILLER                  PIC X(21).
00054
00055              FD  PRINT-FILE
00056                  LABEL RECORDS ARE OMITTED
```

Figure 3.8 SORT Program with Compilation Errors.

```
00057              RECORD CONTAINS 133 CHARACTERS
00058              DATA RECORD IS PRINT-LINE.
00059          01  PRINT-LINE                    PIC X(133).
00060
00061          WORKING-STORAGE SECTION.
00062          77  END-OF-DATA-FLAG              PIC XXX      VALUE SPACES.
00063          77  END-OF-SORTED-DATA            PIC XXX      VALUE SPACES.
00064          77  TOTAL-SALARY-YOUNG-PROGRAMMERS PIC 9(6)    VALUE ZEROS.
00065
00066          01  DATE-WORK-AREA.
00067              05  TODAYS-YEAR               PIC 99.
00068              05  TODAYS-MONTH              PIC 99.
00069              05  TODAYS-DAY                PIC 99.
00070
00071          01  DASHED-LINE.
00072              05  FILLER                    PIC X(57)    VALUE ALL "-".
00073              05  FILLER                    PIC X(76)    VALUE SPACES.
00074
00075          01  HEADING-LINE.
00076              05  FILLER                    PIC X(10)    VALUE SPACES.
00077              05  FILLER                    PIC X(4)     VALUE "NAME".
00078              05  FILLER                    PIC X(7)     VALUE SPACES.
00079              05  FILLER                    PIC X(3)     VALUE "AGE".
00080              05  FILLER                    PIC X(4)     VALUE SPACES.
00081              05  FILLER                    PIC X(8)     VALUE "PRES SAL".
00082              05  FILLER                    PIC X(3)     VALUE SPACES.
00083              05  FILLER                    PIC X(7)     VALUE "OLD SAL".
00084              05  FILLER                    PIC X(3)     VALUE SPACES.
00085              05  FILLER                    PIC X(6)     VALUE "% INCR".
00086              05  FILLER                    PIC X(78)    VALUE SPACES.
00087
00088          01  DETAIL-LINE.
00089              05  FILLER                    PIC X(1)     VALUE SPACES.
00090              05  PRINT-LAST-NAME           PIC X(15).
00091              05  FILLER                    PIC X(5)     VALUE SPACES.
00092              05  PRINT-AGE                 PIC 99.9.
00093              05  FILLER                    PIC X(4)     VALUE SPACES.
00094              05  PRINT-PRESENT-SALARY      PIC $99,999.
00095              05  FILLER                    PIC X(3)     VALUE SPACES.
00096              05  PRINT-FORMER-SALARY       PIC $99,999.
00097              05  FILLER                    PIC X(4)     VALUE SPACES.
00098              05  PRINT-PERCENT-INCREASE    PIC ZZ.9.
00099              05  FILLER                    PIC X(81)    VALUE SPACES.
00100
00101          01  TOTAL-LINE.
00102              05  FILLER                    PIC X(12)    VALUE SPACES.
00103              05  FILLER                    PIC X(17)
00104                  VALUE "TOTAL SALARIES =".
00105              05  PRINT-TOTAL-SALARIES      PIC $999,999.
00106              05  FILLER                    PIC X(86)    VALUE SPACES.
00107
00108          PROCEDURE DIVISION.
00109          A-SORTING SECTION.
00110              SORT SORT-FILE
00111                  ON DESCENDING KEY PRESENT-SALARY
00112                  INPUT PROCEDURE B-PROCESS-UNSORTED-RECORDS
00113                  OUTPUT PROCEDURE C-REPORT.
00114              STOP RUN.
00115
00116          B-PROCESS-UNSORTED-RECORDS.
00117              ACCEPT DATE-WORK-AREA FROM DATE.
00118              OPEN INPUT EMPLOYEE-FILE.
00119              READ EMPLOYEE-FILE
00120                  AT END MOVE "YES" TO END-OF-DATA-FLAG.
```

Figure 3.8 *cont.*

```
00121                    PERFORM B020-READ-EMPLOYEE-RECORDS
00122                        UNTIL END-OF-DATA-FLAG = "YES".
00123                    CLOSE EMPLOYEE-FILE.
00124                    GO TO B060-EXIT.
00125
00126                B020-READ-EMPLOYEE-RECORDS.
00127                    COMPUTE EMPLOYEE-AGE
00128                        = TODAYS-YEAR - BIRTH-YEAR OF EMPLOYEE-RECORD
00129                        + (TODAYS-MONTH - BIRTH-MONTH OF EMPLOYEE-RECORD) / 12.
00130                    COMPUTE PERCENT-SALARY-INCREASE
00131                        = 100 * (PRESENT-SALARY OF EMPLOYEE-RECORD
00132                                - FORMER-SALARY OF EMPLOYEE-RECORD)
00133                                / FORMER-SALARY OF EMPLOYEE-RECORD.
00134                    MOVE CORRESPONDING EMPLOYEE-RECORD TO SORT-RECORD.
00135                    RELEASE SORT-FILE.
00136                    READ EMPLOYEE-FILE
00137                        AT END MOVE "YES" TO END-OF-DATA-FLAG.
00138
00139                B060-EXIT.
00140                    EXIT.
00141
00142                C-REPORT SECTION.
00143                    OPEN OUTPUT PRINT-FILE.
00144                    PERFORM C040-WRITE-HEADINGS.
00145                    RETURN SORT-RECORD
00146                        AT END MOVE "YES" TO END-OF-SORTED-DATA.
00147                    PERFORM C020-PROCESS-SORTED-RECORDS
00148                        UNTIL END-OF-SORTED-DATA = "YES".
00149                    PERFORM C050-WRITE-TOTALS.
00150                    CLOSE PRINT-FILE.
00151                    GO TO C060-EXIT.
00152
00153                C020-PROCESS-SORTED-RECORDS.
00154                    IF CARD-TITLE OF SORT-RECORD = "PROGRAMMER"
00155                      AND EMPLOYEE-AGE OF SORT-RECORD < 30
00156                        MOVE SPACES                       TO PRINT-LINE
00157                        MOVE CARD-NAME OF SORT-RECORD     TO PRINT-LAST-NAME
00158                        MOVE EMPLOYEES-AGE OF SORT-RECORD  TO PRINT-AGE
00159                        MOVE PRESENT-SALARY OF SORT-RECORD
00160                            TO PRINT-PRESENT-SALARY
00161                        MOVE FORMER-SALARY OF SORT-RECORD TO PRINT-FORMER-SALARY
00162                        MOVE PERCENT-SALARY-INCREASE TO PRINT-PERCENT-INCREASE
00163                        WRITE PRINT-LINE FROM DETAIL-LINE AFTER ADVANCING 2 LINES
00164                        ADD PRESENT-SALARY OF SORT-RECORD
00165                            TO TOTAL-SALARY-YOUNG-PROGRAMMERS.
00166                    RETURN SORT-FILE
00167                        AT END MOVE "YES" TO END-OF-SORTED-DATA.
00168
00169                C040-WRITE-HEADINGS.
00170                    MOVE SPACES TO PRINT-LINE.
00171                    MOVE "            SALARY REPORT FOR PROGRAMMERS UNDER 30"
00172                        TO PRINT-LINE.
00173                    WRITE PRINT-LINE AFTER ADVANCING PAGE.
00174                    MOVE HEADING-LINE TO PRINT-LINE.
00175                    WRITE PRINT-LINE AFTER ADVANCING 3 LINES.
00176                    WRITE PRINT-LINE FROM DASHED-LINE AFTER ADVANCING 1 LINE.
00177
00178                C050-WRITE-TOTALS.
00179                    WRITE PRINT-LINE FROM DASHED-LINE AFTER ADVANCING 2 LINES.
00180                    MOVE TOTAL-SALARY-YOUNG-PROGRAMMERS TO PRINT-TOTAL-SALARIES.
00181                    WRITE PRINT-LINE FROM TOTAL-LINE.
00182
00183                C060-EXIT.
00184                    EXIT.
```

Figure 3.8 *cont.*

CARD	ERROR MESSAGE	
36	IKF1034I-W	LABEL CLAUSE IN SD LEVEL IS TREATED AS COMMENTS IN OS. SKIPPING TO NEXT CLAUSE.
110	IKF3002I-E	PRESENT-SALARY NOT UNIQUE. DISCARDED.
110	IKF4050I-E	SYNTAX REQUIRES SORT-KEY . FOUND SORT . STATEMENT DISCARDED.
110	IKF4054I-E	SYNTAX REQUIRES SORT-FILE NAME. FOUND INPUT . STATEMENT DISCARDED.
110	IKF4054I-E	SYNTAX REQUIRES SORT-FILE NAME. FOUND OUTPUT . STATEMENT DISCARDED.
135	IKF4066I-E	SYNTAX REQUIRES 01 LEVEL SD DATA-NAME IN RELEASE STATEMENT. FOUND DNM=2-75 . STATEMENT DISCARDED.
145	IKF4054I-E	SYNTAX REQUIRES SORT-FILE NAME. FOUND DNM=2-96 . STATEMENT DISCARDED.
158	IKF3006I-E	EMPLOYEES-AGE NOT DEFINED AS PART OF SORT-RECORD . DISCARDED.

Figure 3.8 *cont.*

Exercise 3.5: Execution Errors and SORT

The program in Fig. 3.9 is intended to process a file of employee records and select all programmers, listing them in order of *decreasing* age; that is, oldest first. As can be seen from the output (Fig. 3.10), several errors occurred. In addition, the job was cancelled by the operator because the program was in an infinite loop. Analyze and correct the errors.

```
00001           IDENTIFICATION DIVISION.
00002           PROGRAM-ID. "SORT1".
00003           AUTHOR.     MARION MILGROM.
00004
00005           ENVIRONMENT DIVISION.
00006           CONFIGURATION SECTION.
00007           SOURCE-COMPUTER.    IBM-370.
00008           OBJECT-COMPUTER.    IBM-370.
00009           INPUT-OUTPUT SECTION.
00010           FILE-CONTROL.
00011               SELECT EMPLOYEE-FILE ASSIGN TO UT-S-SYSIN.
00012               SELECT PRINT-FILE ASSIGN TO UT-S-SYSOUT.
00013               SELECT SORT-FILE ASSIGN TO UT-S-SORTWK01.
00014               SELECT ORDERED-FILE ASSIGN TO UT-S-SORTED.
00015
00016           DATA DIVISION.
00017           FILE SECTION.
00018           SD  SORT-FILE
00019               RECORD CONTAINS 80 CHARACTERS
00020               DATA RECORD IS SORT-RECORD.
00021           01  SORT-RECORD.
00022               05  FILLER                  PIC X(35).
00023               05  SORT-MONTH              PIC 99.
00024               05  SORT-YEAR               PIC 99.
00025               05  FILLER                  PIC X(41).
00026
00027           FD  EMPLOYEE-FILE
00028               LABEL RECORDS ARE OMITTED
00029               RECORD CONTAINS 80 CHARACTERS
00030               DATA RECORD IS EMPLOYEE-RECORD.
00031           01  EMPLOYEE-RECORD.
00032               05  EMP-NAME.
00033                   10  LAST-NAME           PIC X(15).
00034                   10  FIRST-NAME          PIC X(9).
00035                   10  MIDDLE-INITIAL      PIC X.
00036               05  EMP-TITLE               PIC X(10).
00037               05  DATE-OF-BIRTH.
00038                   10  BIRTH-MONTH         PIC 99.
00039                   10  BIRTH-YEAR          PIC 99.
00040               05  PRESENT-SALARY          PIC 9(5).
00041               05  FILLER                  PIC X(4).
00042               05  FORMER-SALARY           PIC 9(5).
00043               05  FILLER                  PIC X(27).
00044
00045           FD  PRINT-FILE
00046               LABEL RECORDS ARE OMITTED
00047               RECORD CONTAINS 133 CHARACTERS
00048               DATA RECORD IS PRINT-LINE.
00049           01  PRINT-LINE                  PIC X(133).
00050
```

Figure 3.9 Sort Program with Execution Errors.

```
00051          FD  ORDERED-FILE
00052              LABEL RECORDS ARE OMITTED
00053              RECORD CONTAINS 80 CHARACTERS
00054              DATA RECORD IS SORTED-EMPLOYEE-RECORD.
00055          01  SORTED-EMPLOYEE-RECORD          PIC X(80).
00056
00057          WORKING-STORAGE SECTION.
00058          77  END-OF-DATA-FLAG                PIC XXX      VALUE SPACES.
00059          77  EMPLOYEE-AGE                    PIC 99V9.
00060          77  PERCENT-SALARY-INCREASE         PIC 99V9.
00061
00062          01  WS-EMPLOYEE-RECORD.
00063              05  WS-EMP-NAME.
00064                  10  WS-LAST-NAME            PIC X(15).
00065                  10  WS-FIRST-NAME           PIC X(9).
00066                  10  WS-MIDDLE-INITIAL       PIC X.
00067              05  WS-EMP-TITLE                PIC X(10).
00068              05  WS-DATE-OF-BIRTH.
00069                  10  WS-BIRTH-MONTH          PIC 99.
00070                  10  WS-BIRTH-YEAR           PIC 99.
00071              05  WS-PRESENT-SALARY           PIC 9(5).
00072              05  FILLER                      PIC X(4).
00073              05  WS-FORMER-SALARY            PIC 9(5).
00074              05  FILLER                      PIC X(27).
00075
00076          01  DATE-WORK-AREA.
00077              05  TODAYS-MONTH                PIC 99.
00078              05  TODAYS-DAY                  PIC 99.
00079              05  TODAYS-YEAR                 PIC 99.
00080
00081          01  DASHED-LINE.
00082              05  FILLER                      PIC X(69)    VALUE ALL "-".
00083              05  FILLER                      PIC X(64)    VALUE SPACES.
00084
00085          01  HEADING-LINE.
00086              05  FILLER                      PIC X(10)    VALUE SPACES.
00087              05  FILLER                      PIC X(4)     VALUE "NAME".
00088              05  FILLER                      PIC X(7)     VALUE SPACES.
00089              05  FILLER                      PIC X(3)     VALUE "AGE".
00090              05  FILLER                      PIC X(4)     VALUE SPACES.
00091              05  FILLER                      PIC X(9)     VALUE "BIRTHDATE".
00092              05  FILLER                      PIC X(3)     VALUE SPACES.
00093              05  FILLER                      PIC X(8)     VALUE "PRES SAL".
00094              05  FILLER                      PIC X(3)     VALUE SPACES.
00095              05  FILLER                      PIC X(7)     VALUE "OLD SAL".
00096              05  FILLER                      PIC X(3)     VALUE SPACES.
00097              05  FILLER                      PIC X(6)     VALUE "% INCR".
00098              05  FILLER                      PIC X(66)    VALUE SPACES.
00099
00100          01  DETAIL-LINE.
00101              05  FILLER                      PIC X(1)     VALUE SPACES.
00102              05  PRINT-LAST-NAME             PIC X(15).
00103              05  FILLER                      PIC X(5)     VALUE SPACES.
00104              05  PRINT-AGE                   PIC 99.9.
00105              05  FILLER                      PIC X(5)     VALUE SPACES.
00106              05  PRINT-BIRTH-DAY.
00107                  10  PRINT-MONTH             PIC 99.
00108                  10  FILLER                  PIC X        VALUE "/".
00109                  10  PRINT-YEAR              PIC 99.
00110              05  FILLER                      PIC X(5)     VALUE SPACES.
00111              05  PRINT-PRESENT-SALARY        PIC $99,999.
```

Figure 3.9 *cont.*

```
00112             05  FILLER                       PIC X(3)     VALUE SPACES.
00113             05  PRINT-FORMER-SALARY          PIC $99,999.
00114             05  FILLER                       PIC X(5)     VALUE SPACES.
00115             05  PRINT-PERCENT-INCREASE       PIC ZZ.9.
00116             05  FILLER                       PIC X(69)    VALUE SPACES.
00117
00118         PROCEDURE DIVISION.
00119         0010-MAINLINE-ROUTINE.
00120             SORT SORT-FILE
00121                 ON ASCENDING KEY SORT-MONTH SORT-YEAR
00122                 USING EMPLOYEE-FILE
00123                 GIVING ORDERED-FILE.
00124
00125             OPEN INPUT ORDERED-FILE
00126                  OUTPUT PRINT-FILE.
00127             ACCEPT DATE-WORK-AREA FROM DATE.
00128             PERFORM 0040-WRITE-HEADINGS.
00129             READ ORDERED-FILE INTO WS-EMPLOYEE-RECORD
00130                 AT END MOVE "YES" TO END-OF-DATA-FLAG.
00131             PERFORM 0020-PROCESS-EMPLOYEE-RECORDS
00132                 UNTIL END-OF-DATA-FLAG = "YES".
00133             CLOSE ORDERED-FILE, PRINT-FILE.
00134             STOP RUN.
00135
00136         0020-PROCESS-EMPLOYEE-RECORDS.
00137             COMPUTE EMPLOYEE-AGE
00138                 = TODAYS-YEAR - WS-BIRTH-YEAR
00139                 + (TODAYS-MONTH - WS-BIRTH-MONTH) / 12.
00140             COMPUTE PERCENT-SALARY-INCREASE
00141                 = 100 * (WS-PRESENT-SALARY - WS-FORMER-SALARY)
00142                 / WS-FORMER-SALARY.
00143             IF WS-EMP-TITLE = "PROGRAMMER"
00144                 MOVE SPACES                  TO PRINT-LINE
00145                 MOVE WS-EMP-NAME             TO PRINT-LAST-NAME
00146                 MOVE EMPLOYEE-AGE            TO PRINT-AGE
00147                 MOVE WS-BIRTH-MONTH          TO PRINT-MONTH
00148                 MOVE WS-BIRTH-YEAR           TO PRINT-YEAR
00149                 MOVE WS-PRESENT-SALARY       TO PRINT-PRESENT-SALARY
00150                 MOVE WS-FORMER-SALARY        TO PRINT-FORMER-SALARY
00151                 MOVE PERCENT-SALARY-INCREASE TO PRINT-PERCENT-INCREASE
00152                 WRITE PRINT-LINE FROM DETAIL-LINE AFTER ADVANCING 2 LINES.
00153             READ ORDERED-FILE INTO WS-EMPLOYEE-RECORD
00154                 AT END MOVE "YES" TO END-OF-DATA-FLAG.
00155
00156         0040-WRITE-HEADINGS.
00157             MOVE SPACES TO PRINT-LINE.
00158             MOVE "            SALARY REPORT FOR PROGRAMMERS"
00159                 TO PRINT-LINE.
00160             WRITE PRINT-LINE AFTER ADVANCING PAGE.
00161             MOVE HEADING-LINE TO PRINT-LINE.
00162             WRITE PRINT-LINE AFTER ADVANCING 3 LINES.
00163             WRITE PRINT-LINE FROM DASHED-LINE AFTER ADVANCING 1 LINE.
```

Figure 3.9 *cont.*

There are three major problems; in particular:
1. Age is calculated incorrectly from the birthdate which prints correctly (the birthdates in Figure 3.10 are identical to those in the incoming data). Provide an explanation and a correction.

```
              SALARY REPORT FOR PROGRAMMERS

            NAME         AGE    BIRTHDATE   PRES SAL    OLD SAL    % INCR
       ----------------------------------------------------------------------
       DOE               24.5    01/43       $23,000    $21,000     9.5
       JOHNSON           28.5    01/47       $23,000    $22,000     4.5
       SAMSON            35.8    04/54       $10,000    $08,500    17.6
       PERSNICKETTY II   31.9    05/50       $19,000    $16,000    18.7
       MILGROM           35.9    05/54       $10,000    $08,650    15.6
       SMITH             35.9    05/54       $15,000    $14,100     6.3
       ADAMSON           39.9    05/58       $10,000    $08,500    17.6
       WILCOX            29.0    06/47       $19,000    $17,500     8.5
       LEVINE            30.0    06/48       $19,000    $17,500     8.5
       LEE               33.3    10/51       $12,000    $11,000     9.0
       CRAWFORD          27.4    11/45       $28,000    $25,000    12.0
       SUPERPROGRAMMER   37.5    12/55       $39,000    $34,000    14.7
```

Figure 3.10 Incorrect Output Produced by the Program of Fig. 3.9.

2. Employees are not listed by age, although the SORT attempted to list them by birthdate. Provide an explanation and a correction.

3. The program went into an infinite loop the first time that the employee being processed was *not* a programmer. Why? (Reader be forewarned, this error is extremely subtle and not more than one person in ten will find it.)

Exercise 3.6: Subprograms: 1

The two programs in this exercise (a main and a subprogram) process a file of employee records and print the information in a more appealing format. Much of the incoming data are stored in coded form and expanded in the subprogram prior to printing. The subprogram is also responsible for all table initialization. Consequently, it employs a COPY clause to initialize a table of location codes and values. It also reads a separate file to establish a table of job codes and expanded values.

In addition, certain calculations based on salary history are required. A maximum of three levels of historical data are kept denoting present salary, previous salary, and second previous salary. The program computes the percent salary increase, the Months Between Increase (MBI) and the annual Rate of Salary Increase (RSI). For example, a 10% increase after 6 months is equivalent to an annual RSI of 20%.

Source Level Debugging 159

To better understand the objectives of this program, consider the example of *desired* output which appears in Fig. 3.11. That is followed by the actual output produced by the programs (Fig. 3.12). Both the valid and invalid output were produced from the first line of input data shown in Fig. 3.13.

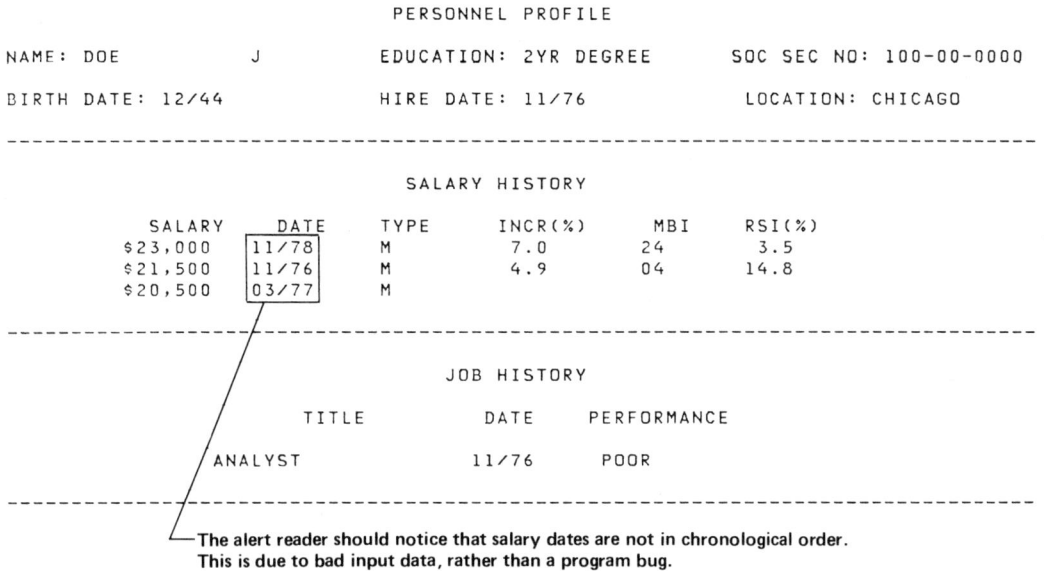

Figure 3.11 Valid Profile.

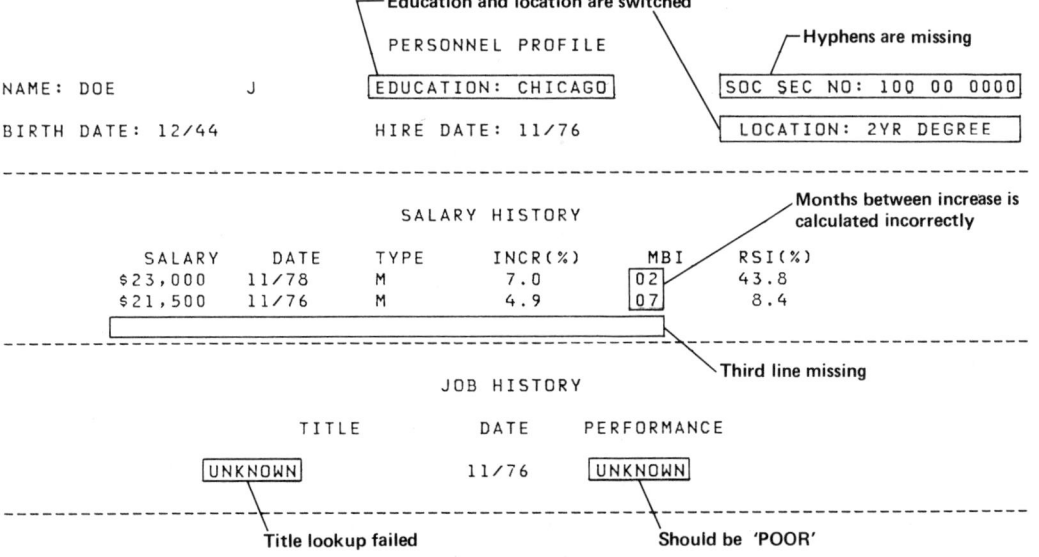

Figure 3.12 Invalid Profile.

```
100000000DOE            J  124411763031551176323000M1178721500M1176520500M03775
200000000WILCOX         P  104811773031451177319000M1178517500H1177400000
300000000SMITH          J  115507764041450776215000M0778514000M0777513200H01775
400000000LEVINE         S  015008763041450876219000H0876500000         00000
444444444LOWELL         S  015011783041451178218000H1178500000         00000
500000000CRAWFORD       M  034601724041551177228000M0876726500M0575725000M05746
600000000SUPERPROG      S  045710774051451077139000H1077900000         00000
700000000LEE            B  105302763061450277117000P0578513000H0277400000
800000000PERSNICKETY    P  085103784031450378109000H0378600000         00000
```

Figure 3.13 Test Data

Your assignment is to find and correct the errors in both the main program (Figure 3.14) and subprogram (Figure 3.15), so that the corrected version will produce the intended output.

```
00001           IDENTIFICATION DIVISION.
00002           PROGRAM-ID. "PROFILE"
00003           AUTHOR.
00004               MARION MILGROM.
00005
00006           ENVIRONMENT DIVISION.
00007           CONFIGURATION SECTION.
00008           SOURCE-COMPUTER.    IBM-370.
00009           OBJECT-COMPUTER.    IBM-370.
00010
00011           INPUT-OUTPUT SECTION.
00012           FILE-CONTROL.
00013               SELECT EMPLOYEE-FILE ASSIGN TO UT-S-SYSIN.
00014               SELECT PRINT-FILE ASSIGN TO UT-S-SYSOUT.
00015
00016           DATA DIVISION.
00017           FILE SECTION.
00018               COPY EMPLOYEE.
00019 C         FD  EMPLOYEE-FILE
00020 C             LABEL RECORDS ARE OMITTED
00021 C             RECORD CONTAINS 80 CHARACTERS
00022 C             DATA RECORD IS EMPLOYEE-RECORD.
00023 C         01  EMPLOYEE-RECORD.
00024 C             05  EMP-SOC-SEC-NUMBER          PIC X(9).
00025 C             05  EMP-NAME-AND-INITIALS       PIC X(15).
00026 C             05  EMP-DATE-OF-BIRTH.
00027 C                 10  EMP-BIRTH-MONTH         PIC 99.
00028 C                 10  EMP-BIRTH-YEAR          PIC 99.
00029 C             05  EMP-DATE-OF-HIRE.
00030 C                 10  EMP-HIRE-MONTH          PIC 99.
00031 C                 10  EMP-HIRE-YEAR           PIC 99.
00032 C             05  EMP-LOCATION-CODE           PIC 99.
00033 C             05  EMP-EDUCATION-CODE          PIC 9.
00034 C             05  EMP-TITLE-DATA.
00035 C                 10  EMP-TITLE-CODE          PIC 9(3).
00036 C                 10  EMP-TITLE-DATE          PIC 9(4).
00037 C                 10  EMP-PERFORMANCE         PIC 9.
00038 C             05  EMP-SALARY-DATA OCCURS 3 TIMES
00039 C                         INDEXED BY SAL-INDEX.
00040 C                 10  EMP-SALARY              PIC 9(5).
00041 C                 10  EMP-SALARY-TYPE         PIC X.
00042 C                 10  EMP-SALARY-DATE.
00043 C                     15  EMP-SALARY-MONTH    PIC 99.
```

Figure 3.14 Main Program.

```
00044 C              15     EMP-SALARY-YEAR        PIC 99.
00045 C          10     EMP-SALARY-GRADE           PIC 9.
00046 C      05 FILLER                             PIC X(4).
00047
00048       FD PRINT-FILE
00049           LABEL RECORDS ARE OMITTED
00050           RECORD CONTAINS 133 CHARACTERS
00051           DATA RECORD IS PRINT-LINE.
00052       01 PRINT-LINE                          PIC X(133).
00053
00054       WORKING-STORAGE SECTION.
00055       77 WS-END-OF-DATA-SWITCH     PIC X(3)   VALUE "YES".
00056           88 NO-MORE-EMPLOYEE-RECORDS         VALUE "NO ".
00057           88 STILL-MORE-EMPLOYEE-RECORDS      VALUE "YES".
00058
00059       01 SALARY-MEASUREMENT-DATA.
00060           05 WS-PCT-SALARY-INCR     PIC S99V9.
00061           05 WS-MONTHS-BETWEEN-INCR PIC 99.
00062           05 WS-RATE-SALARY-INCR    PIC S99V9.
00063
00064       01 WS-DASHED-LINE.
00065           05 FILLER                 PIC X(1)   VALUE SPACES.
00066           05 DASHES                 PIC X(80)  VALUE ALL "-".
00067           05 FILLER                 PIC X(52)  VALUE SPACES.
00068
00069       01 WS-HDG-LINE-1.
00070           05 FILLER                 PIC X(31)  VALUE SPACES.
00071           05 FILLER                 PIC X(10)  VALUE "PERSONNEL".
00072           05 FILLER                 PIC X(7)   VALUE "PROFILE".
00073           05 FILLER                 PIC X(85)  VALUE SPACES.
00074
00075       01 WS-HDG-LINE-2.
00076           05 FILLER                 PIC X      VALUE SPACES.
00077           05 FILLER                 PIC X(6)   VALUE "NAME: ".
00078           05 PRT-NAME               PIC X(15).
00079           05 FILLER                 PIC X(8)   VALUE SPACES.
00080           05 FILLER                 PIC X(11)  VALUE "EDUCATION: ".
00081           05 PRT-EDUCATION          PIC X(10).
00082           05 FILLER                 PIC X(6)   VALUE SPACES.
00083           05 FILLER                 PIC X(12)  VALUE "SOC SEC NO: ".
00084           05 PRT-SOC-SEC-NO         PIC 999B99B9999.
00085           05 FILLER                 PIC X(53)  VALUE SPACES.
00086
00087       01 WS-HDG-LINE-3.
00088           05 FILLER                 PIC X      VALUE SPACES.
00089           05 FILLER                 PIC X(12)  VALUE "BIRTH DATE: ".
00090           05 PRT-BIRTH-DATE.
00091               10 PRT-BIRTH-MONTH    PIC 99.
00092               10 FILLER             PIC X      VALUE "/".
00093               10 PRT-BIRTH-YEAR     PIC 99.
00094           05 FILLER                 PIC X(12)  VALUE SPACES.
00095           05 FILLER                 PIC X(11)  VALUE "HIRE DATE: ".
00096           05 PRT-HIRE-DATE.
00097               10 PRT-HIRE-MONTH     PIC 99.
00098               10 FILLER             PIC X      VALUE "/".
00099               10 PRT-HIRE-YEAR      PIC 99.
00100           05 FILLER                 PIC X(12)  VALUE SPACES.
00101           05 FILLER                 PIC X(10)  VALUE "LOCATION: ".
00102           05 PRT-LOCATION           PIC X(13).
00103           05 FILLER                 PIC X(52)  VALUE SPACES.
00104
00105       01 WS-SAL-HDG-1.
00106           05 FILLER                 PIC X(32)  VALUE SPACES.
00107           05 FILLER                 PIC X(14)  VALUE "SALARY HISTORY".
00108           05 FILLER                 PIC X(87)  VALUE SPACES.
```

Figure 3.14 *cont.*

```
00109
00110            01   WS-SAL-HDG-2.
00111                 05   FILLER               PIC X(12)   VALUE SPACES.
00112                 05   FILLER               PIC X(10)   VALUE "SALARY".
00113                 05   FILLER               PIC X(8)    VALUE "DATE".
00114                 05   FILLER               PIC X(9)    VALUE "TYPE".
00115                 05   FILLER               PIC X(12)   VALUE "INCR(%)".
00116                 05   FILLER               PIC X(7)    VALUE "MBI".
00117                 05   FILLER               PIC X(9)    VALUE "RSI(%)".
00118                 05   FILLER               PIC X(76)   VALUE SPACES.
00119
00120            01   WS-SAL-DETAIL-LINE.
00121                 05   FILLER               PIC X(10)   VALUE SPACES.
00122                 05   PRT-SALARY           PIC $$$,$$$.
00123                 05   FILLER               PIC X(3)    VALUE SPACES.
00124                 05   PRT-SALARY-DATE.
00125                      10   PRT-SALARY-MONTH   PIC 99.
00126                      10   PRT-SALARY-SLASH   PIC X    VALUE "/".
00127                      10   PRT-SALARY-YEAR    PIC 99.
00128                 05   FILLER               PIC X(5)    VALUE SPACES.
00129                 05   PRT-SALARY-TYPE      PIC X.
00130                 05   FILLER               PIC X(6)    VALUE SPACES.
00131                 05   PRT-SALARY-PCT-INCR  PIC -ZZ9.9.
00132                 05   FILLER               PIC X(7)    VALUE SPACES.
00133                 05   PRT-MNTHS-BETWEEN-INCR PIC 99.
00134                 05   FILLER               PIC X(4)    VALUE SPACES.
00135                 05   PRT-RATE-SALARY-INCR PIC -ZZ9.9.
00136                 05   FILLER               PIC X(83)   VALUE SPACES.
00137
00138            01   WS-TITLE-HDG-1.
00139                 05   FILLER               PIC X(35)   VALUE SPACES.
00140                 05   FILLER               PIC X(11)   VALUE "JOB HISTORY".
00141                 05   FILLER               PIC X(87)   VALUE SPACES.
00142
00143            01   WS-TITLE-HDG-2.
00144                 05   FILLER               PIC X(24)   VALUE SPACES.
00145                 05   FILLER               PIC X(14)   VALUE "TITLE".
00146                 05   FILLER               PIC X(8)    VALUE "DATE".
00147                 05   FILLER               PIC X(11)   VALUE "PERFORMANCE".
00148                 05   FILLER               PIC X(76)   VALUE SPACES.
00149
00150            01   WS-TITLE-LINE.
00151                 05   FILLER               PIC X(17)   VALUE SPACES.
00152                 05   PRT-TITLE            PIC X(18).
00153                 05   FILLER               PIC X(2)    VALUE SPACES.
00154                 05   PRT-TITLE-DATE       PIC ZZ/ZZ.
00155                 05   FILLER               PIC X(5)    VALUE SPACES.
00156                 05   PRT-PERFORMANCE      PIC X(9).
00157                 05   FILLER               PIC X(77)   VALUE SPACES.
00159            PROCEDURE DIVISION.
00160            005-MAINLINE-ROUTINE.
00161                OPEN INPUT EMPLOYEE-FILE
00162                     OUTPUT PRINT-FILE.
00163                PERFORM 010-READ-EMPLOYEE-RECORD.
00164                PERFORM 020-PROCESS-EMPLOYEE-RECORDS
00165                     UNTIL NO-MORE-EMPLOYEE-RECORDS.
00166                CLOSE EMPLOYEE-FILE PRINT-FILE.
00167                STOP RUN.
00168
00169            010-READ-EMPLOYEE-RECORD.
00170                READ EMPLOYEE-FILE
00171                     AT END MOVE "NO " TO WS-END-OF-DATA-SWITCH.
00172
00173            020-PROCESS-EMPLOYEE-RECORDS.
```

Figure 3.14 *cont.*

```
00174
00175          * EXPAND ALL CODED INFORMATION BEFORE DOING ANY OUTPUT
00176              CALL "DECODER"
00177                  USING EMP-TITLE-CODE         PRT-TITLE
00178                        EMP-LOCATION-CODE      PRT-LOCATION
00179                        EMP-EDUCATION-CODE     PRT-EDUCATION.
00180
00181              IF EMP-PERFORMANCE = "1"
00182                  MOVE "EXCELLENT" TO PRT-PERFORMANCE
00183              ELSE
00184                  IF EMP-PERFORMANCE = "2"
00185                      MOVE "AVERAGE" TO PRT-PERFORMANCE
00186                  ELSE
00187                      IF EMP-PERFORMANCE = "3"
00188                          MOVE "POOR" TO PRT-PERFORMANCE
00189                          MOVE "UNKNOWN" TO PRT-PERFORMANCE.
00190
00191          * BEGIN OUTPUT FOR PERSONAL PROFILE
00192              WRITE PRINT-LINE FROM WS-HDG-LINE-1
00193                  AFTER ADVANCING PAGE.
00194              MOVE EMP-NAME-AND-INITIALS TO PRT-NAME.
00195              MOVE EMP-SOC-SEC-NUMBER     TO PRT-SOC-SEC-NO.
00196              INSPECT PRT-SOC-SEC-NO REPLACING ALL "-" BY " ".
00197              WRITE PRINT-LINE FROM WS-HDG-LINE-2 AFTER ADVANCING 2 LINES.
00198              MOVE EMP-BIRTH-MONTH    TO PRT-BIRTH-MONTH.
00199              MOVE EMP-BIRTH-YEAR     TO PRT-BIRTH-YEAR.
00200              MOVE EMP-HIRE-MONTH     TO PRT-HIRE-MONTH.
00201              MOVE EMP-HIRE-YEAR      TO PRT-HIRE-YEAR.
00202              WRITE PRINT-LINE FROM WS-HDG-LINE-3 AFTER ADVANCING 2 LINES.
00203              WRITE PRINT-LINE FROM WS-DASHED-LINE AFTER ADVANCING 2 LINES.
00204              WRITE PRINT-LINE FROM WS-SAL-HDG-1 AFTER ADVANCING 2 LINES.
00205              WRITE PRINT-LINE FROM WS-SAL-HDG-2 AFTER ADVANCING 2 LINES.
00206              PERFORM 030-WRITE-SALARY-LINE
00207                  VARYING SAL-INDEX FROM 1 BY 1
00208                  UNTIL SAL-INDEX = 3
00209                    OR EMP-SALARY (SAL-INDEX) = 0.
00210              WRITE PRINT-LINE FROM WS-DASHED-LINE AFTER ADVANCING 2 LINES.
00211              WRITE PRINT-LINE FROM WS-TITLE-HDG-1 AFTER ADVANCING 2 LINES.
00212              WRITE PRINT-LINE FROM WS-TITLE-HDG-2 AFTER ADVANCING 2 LINES.
00213              MOVE EMP-TITLE-DATE       TO PRT-TITLE-DATE.
00214              WRITE PRINT-LINE FROM WS-TITLE-LINE AFTER ADVANCING 2 LINES.
00215              WRITE PRINT-LINE FROM WS-DASHED-LINE AFTER ADVANCING 2 LINES.
00216
00217              PERFORM 010-READ-EMPLOYEE-RECORD.
00218
00219          030-WRITE-SALARY-LINE.
00220              MOVE SPACES TO WS-SAL-DETAIL-LINE.
00221              MOVE "/" TO PRT-SALARY-SLASH.
00222              MOVE EMP-SALARY (SAL-INDEX)         TO PRT-SALARY.
00223              MOVE EMP-SALARY-MONTH (SAL-INDEX)   TO PRT-SALARY-MONTH.
00224              MOVE EMP-SALARY-YEAR (SAL-INDEX)    TO PRT-SALARY-YEAR.
00225              MOVE EMP-SALARY-TYPE (SAL-INDEX)    TO PRT-SALARY-TYPE.
00226
00227              IF SAL-INDEX < 3 AND EMP-SALARY (SAL-INDEX + 1) > 0
00228                  PERFORM 040-COMPUTE-SALARY-INCREASES.
00229              WRITE PRINT-LINE FROM WS-SAL-DETAIL-LINE.
00230
00231          040-COMPUTE-SALARY-INCREASES.
00232              COMPUTE WS-PCT-SALARY-INCR ROUNDED
00233                  = 100 * (EMP-SALARY (SAL-INDEX)
00234                  - EMP-SALARY (SAL-INDEX + 1))
00235                  / EMP-SALARY (SAL-INDEX + 1).
00236
00237              COMPUTE WS-MONTHS-BETWEEN-INCR ROUNDED
```

Figure 3.14 *cont.*

```
00238                     = (EMP-SALARY-YEAR (SAL-INDEX)
00239                        + EMP-SALARY-MONTH (SAL-INDEX))
00240                        - (EMP-SALARY-YEAR (SAL-INDEX + 1)
00241                        + EMP-SALARY-MONTH (SAL-INDEX + 1)).
00242
00243               COMPUTE WS-RATE-SALARY-INCR ROUNDED
00244                     = WS-PCT-SALARY-INCR / (WS-MONTHS-BETWEEN-INCR / 12).
00245
00246               MOVE WS-PCT-SALARY-INCR       TO PRT-SALARY-PCT-INCR.
00247               MOVE WS-MONTHS-BETWEEN-INCR   TO PRT-MNTHS-BETWEEN-INCR.
00248               MOVE WS-RATE-SALARY-INCR      TO PRT-RATE-SALARY-INCR.
```

Figure 3.14 *cont.*

```
00001          IDENTIFICATION DIVISION.
00002          PROGRAM-ID. "DECODER"
00003          AUTHOR.      MARION MILGROM.
00004
00005          ENVIRONMENT DIVISION.
00006          INPUT-OUTPUT SECTION.
00007          FILE-CONTROL.
00008              SELECT TITLE-FILE ASSIGN TO UT-S-TITLES.
00009          CONFIGURATION SECTION.
00010          SOURCE-COMPUTER.    IBM-370.
00011          OBJECT-COMPUTER.    IBM-370.
00012          DATA DIVISION.
00013          FILE SECTION.
00014          FD   TITLE-FILE
00015               LABEL RECORDS ARE STANDARD
00016               RECORD CONTAINS 80 CHARACTERS
00017               DATA RECORD IS TITLE-RECORD.
00018          01   TITLE-RECORD.
00019               05   TITLE-FILE-CODE        PIC 9(3).
00020               05   TITLE-FILE-VALUE       PIC X(18).
00021               05   FILLER                 PIC X(59).
00022
00023          WORKING-STORAGE SECTION.
00024          77   WS-NUMBER-OF-TITLES         PIC 999    VALUE 1.
00025          77   WS-ALREADY-EXECUTED-SWITCH  PIC X(3)   VALUE "NO".
00026          77   WS-TITLE-FILE-SWITCH        PIC X(3)   VALUE "NO".
00027               88   END-OF-TITLE-FILE                 VALUE "YES".
00028
00029          01   TITLE-TABLE.
00030               05   TITLES OCCURS 1 TO 999 TIMES
00031                    DEPENDING ON WS-NUMBER-OF-TITLES
00032                    ASCENDING KEY IS TITLE-CODE
00033                    INDEXED BY TITLE-INDEX.
00034                    10   TITLE-CODE        PIC 9(3).
00035                    10   TITLE-VALUE       PIC X(18).
00036
00037               COPY LOCATION.
00038 C        01   LOCATION-VALUE.
00039 C             05   FILLER         PIC X(15)  VALUE "10ATLANTA".
00040 C             05   FILLER         PIC X(15)  VALUE "20BOSTON".
00041 C             05   FILLER         PIC X(15)  VALUE "30CHICAGO".
00042 C             05   FILLER         PIC X(15)  VALUE "40DETROIT".
00043 C             05   FILLER         PIC X(15)  VALUE "50KANSAS CITY".
00044 C             05   FILLER         PIC X(15)  VALUE "60LOS ANGELES".
00045 C             05   FILLER         PIC X(15)  VALUE "70MINNEAPOLIS".
00046 C             05   FILLER         PIC X(15)  VALUE "80NEW YORK".
00047 C             05   FILLER         PIC X(15)  VALUE "90PHILADELPHIA".
00048 C             05   FILLER         PIC X(15)  VALUE "95SAN FRANCISCO".
```

Figure 3.15 Subprogram.

```
00049 C
00050 C          01  LOCATION-TABLE REDEFINES LOCATION-VALUE.
00051 C              05  LOCATIONS OCCURS 10 TIMES
00052 C                      INDEXED BY LOC-INDEX.
00053 C                  10  LOC-CODE    PIC 99.
00054 C                  10  LOC-NAME    PIC X(13).
00055
00056            01  EDUCATION-TABLE.
00057                05  EDUCATION-VALUES.
00058                    10  FILLER              PIC X(10)   VALUE "SOME HS".
00059                    10  FILLER              PIC X(10)   VALUE "HS DIPLOMA".
00060                    10  FILLER              PIC X(10)   VALUE "2YR DEGREE".
00061                    10  FILLER              PIC X(10)   VALUE "4YR DEGREE".
00062                    10  FILLER              PIC X(10)   VALUE "SOME GRAD".
00063                    10  FILLER              PIC X(10)   VALUE "MASTERS".
00064                    10  FILLER              PIC X(10)   VALUE "PH. D.".
00065                    10  FILLER              PIC X(10)   VALUE "OTHER".
00066                05  EDU-NAME REDEFINES EDUCATION-VALUES
00067                        OCCURS 8 TIMES PIC X(10).
00068
00069            LINKAGE SECTION.
00070            77  LS-TITLE-CODE           PIC 9(3).
00071            77  LS-EXPANDED-TITLE       PIC X(18).
00072            77  LS-LOCATION-CODE        PIC 99.
00073            77  LS-EXPANDED-LOCATION    PIC X(13).
00074            77  LS-EDUC-CODE            PIC 9.
00075            77  LS-EXPANDED-EDUCATION   PIC X(10).
00076
00077            PROCEDURE DIVISION
00078                USING LS-TITLE-CODE         LS-EXPANDED-TITLE
00079                      LS-LOCATION-CODE      LS-EXPANDED-EDUCATION
00080                      LS-EDUC-CODE          LS-EXPANDED-LOCATION.
00081
00082            005-MAINLINE.
00083                IF WS-ALREADY-EXECUTED-SWITCH = "NO"
00084                    PERFORM 010-INITIALIZE-TITLE-TABLE.
00085
00086           * EXPAND TITLE CODE VIA A BINARY SEARCH
00087                SEARCH ALL TITLES
00088                    AT END
00089                        MOVE "UNKNOWN" TO LS-EXPANDED-TITLE
00090                    WHEN LS-TITLE-CODE = TITLE-CODE (TITLE-INDEX)
00091                        MOVE TITLE-VALUE (TITLE-INDEX) TO LS-EXPANDED-TITLE.
00092
00093           * EXPAND LOCATION-CODE VIA LINEAR SEARCH
00094                SET LOC-INDEX TO 1.
00095                SEARCH LOCATIONS
00096                    AT END
00097                        MOVE "UNKNOWN" TO LS-EXPANDED-LOCATION
00098                    WHEN LS-LOCATION-CODE = LOC-CODE (LOC-INDEX)
00099                        MOVE LOC-NAME (LOC-INDEX) TO LS-EXPANDED-LOCATION.
00100
00101           * EXPAND EDUCATION-CODE VIA DIRECT ACCESS TO TABLE ENTRY
00102                IF LS-EDUC-CODE < 1 OR > 8
00103                    MOVE "UNKNOWN" TO LS-EXPANDED-EDUCATION
00104                ELSE
00105                    MOVE EDU-NAME (LS-EDUC-CODE) TO LS-EXPANDED-EDUCATION.
00106
00107            007-RETURN-TO-MAIN.
00108                EXIT PROGRAM.
00109
00110            010-INITIALIZE-TITLE-TABLE.
00111                MOVE "YES" TO WS-ALREADY-EXECUTED-SWITCH.
```

Figure 3.15 *cont.*

```
00112                    OPEN INPUT TITLE-FILE.
00113                    SET TITLE-INDEX TO 1.
00114                    READ TITLE-FILE
00115                        AT END MOVE "YES" TO WS-TITLE-FILE-SWITCH.
00116                    PERFORM 020-READ-FROM-TITLE-FILE
00117                        UNTIL END-OF-TITLE-FILE.
00118                    CLOSE TITLE-FILE.
00119
00120                020-READ-FROM-TITLE-FILE.
00121                    IF WS-NUMBER-OF-TITLES > 999
00122                        MOVE "YES" TO WS-TITLE-FILE-SWITCH
00123                        DISPLAY "ERROR - TOO MANY TITLES - TABLE EXCEEDED "
00124                    ELSE
00125                        MOVE TITLE-FILE-CODE TO TITLE-CODE (TITLE-INDEX)
00126                        MOVE TITLE-FILE-VALUE TO TITLE-VALUE (TITLE-INDEX)
00127                    READ TITLE-FILE
00128                        AT END MOVE "YES" TO WS-TITLE-FILE-SWITCH.
```

Figure 3.15 cont.

Exercise 3.7: Subprograms: 2

Two programs (a main and a subprogram) have been developed to process a file of student records and compute student transcripts. The main program reads an incoming record, and passes control to the subprogram to compute the grade point average. (A four-point system is used in which A, B, C, D, and F are worth 4, 3, 2, 1, and 0, respectively. The exact method of computation is explained in Section 6, Project 6.4.) The main program also expands the code for student major and proceeds to print a transcript.

Test data are shown in Fig. 3.16. (The record layout can be found by examining lines 34 through 42 of the main program).

```
BENJAMIN, L     140005111A3222A3333A3444A3555A3
SMITH, JOHN     396004666C4777C4888C4999C4
BOROW, J        396004666A4777A4888A4999B4
MILGROM, M      140006123A2456A3789A4012A3345B3678B3
```

Figure 3.16 Test Data for Student Transcripts.

The transcripts actually produced by the programs are shown in Fig. 3.17. Note that five transcripts were produced from four records, an obvious error. The grade point average for John Smith should be 2.00 rather than 0.00. Borow's average should *not* be 4.00 as he received a B in course 999. Finally, Milgrom's major should appear as Biology rather than unknown. (Both Benjamin and Milgrom have a major code of 1400.)

Find and correct all errors in the main program of Figure 3.18 and the subprogram of Figure 3.19.

```
                    TRANSCRIPT

  NAME:MILGROM, M           MAJOR:UNKNOWN

            COURSE#   CREDITS   GRADE
              123        2        A
              456        3        A
              789        4        A
              012        3        A
              345        3        B
              678        3        B

                  AVERAGE: 3.80
```

```
                    TRANSCRIPT

  NAME:MILGROM, M           MAJOR:UNKNOWN

            COURSE#   CREDITS   GRADE
              123        2        A
              456        3        A
              789        4        A
              012        3        A
              345        3        B
              678        3        B

                  AVERAGE: 3.80
```

```
                    TRANSCRIPT

  NAME:BOROW, J             MAJOR:FINANCE

            COURSE#   CREDITS   GRADE
              666        4        A
              777        4        A
              888        4        A
              999        4        B

                  AVERAGE: 4.00
```

```
                    TRANSCRIPT

  NAME:SMITH, JOHN          MAJOR:FINANCE

            COURSE#   CREDITS   GRADE
              666        4        C
              777        4        C
              888        4        C
              999        4        C

                  AVERAGE: 0.00
```

```
                    TRANSCRIPT

  NAME:BENJAMIN, L          MAJOR:BIOLOGY

            COURSE#   CREDITS   GRADE
              111        3        A
              222        3        A
              333        3        A
              444        3        A
              555        3        A

                  AVERAGE: 4.00
```

Figure 3.17 Invalid Student Transcripts.

```
00001              IDENTIFICATION DIVISION.
00002              PROGRAM-ID.    'MAINPROG'.
00003              AUTHOR.        GRAUER.
00004
00005
00006              ENVIRONMENT DIVISION.
00007
00008              CONFIGURATION SECTION.
00009              SOURCE-COMPUTER.   IBM-370.
00010              OBJECT-COMPUTER.   IBM-370.
00011
00012              INPUT-OUTPUT SECTION.
00013              FILE-CONTROL.
00014                  SELECT STUDENT-FILE ASSIGN TO UT-S-CARDS.
00015                  SELECT PRINT-FILE ASSIGN TO UT-S-SYSOUT.
00016
00017
00018              DATA DIVISION.
00019              FILE SECTION.
00020              FD  STUDENT-FILE
00021                  LABEL RECORDS ARE OMITTED
00022                  RECORD CONTAINS 80 CHARACTERS
00023                  DATA RECORD IS STUDENT-RECORD.
00024              01  STUDENT-RECORD            PIC X(80).
00025              FD  PRINT-FILE
00026                  LABEL RECORDS ARE OMITTED
00027                  RECORD CONTAINS 133 CHARACTERS
00028                  DATA RECORD IS PRINT-LINE.
00029              01  PRINT-LINE                PIC X(133).
00030              WORKING-STORAGE SECTION.
00031              77  WS-SUB                    PIC S9(4)     COMP.
00032              77  WS-END-OF-FILE            PIC X(3)   VALUE 'NO '.
00033              77  WS-GRADE-AVERAGE          PIC S9V99.
00034              01  WS-STUDENT-RECORD.
00035                  05  ST-NAME               PIC X(15).
00036                  05  ST-MAJOR-CODE         PIC 9(4).
00037                  05  ST-NUMBER-OF-COURSES  PIC 99.
00038                  05  ST-COURSE-TABLE OCCURS 8 TIMES.
00039                      10  ST-COURSE-NUMBER  PIC X(3).
00040                      10  ST-COURSE-GRADE   PIC A.
00041                      10  ST-COURSE-CREDITS PIC 9.
00042                  05  FILLER                PIC X(19).
00043              01  HEADING-LINE-ONE.
00044                  05  FILLER                PIC X(20)  VALUE SPACES.
00045                  05  FILLER                PIC X(10)  VALUE 'TRANSCRIPT'.
00046                  05  FILLER                PIC X(103) VALUE SPACES.
00047              01  HEADING-LINE-TWO.
00048                  05  FILLER                PIC X(6)   VALUE ' NAME:'.
00049                  05  HDG-NAME              PIC A(15).
00050                  05  FILLER                PIC X(5)   VALUE SPACES.
00051                  05  FILLER                PIC X(6)   VALUE 'MAJOR:'.
00052                  05  HDG-MAJOR             PIC X(10).
00053                  05  FILLER                PIC X(91)  VALUE SPACES.
00054              01  HEADING-LINE-THREE.
00055                  05  FILLER                PIC X(10)  VALUE SPACES.
00056                  05  FILLER                PIC X(9)   VALUE 'COURSE#  '.
00057                  05  FILLER                PIC X(9)   VALUE 'CREDITS  '.
00058                  05  FILLER                PIC X(5)   VALUE 'GRADE'.
00059                  05  FILLER                PIC X(100) VALUE SPACES.
00060              01  DETAIL-LINE.
00061                  05  FILLER                PIC X(13)  VALUE SPACES.
00062                  05  DET-COURSE            PIC X(3).
00063                  05  FILLER                PIC X(9)   VALUE SPACES.
00064                  05  DET-CREDITS           PIC 9.
```

Figure 3.18 Main Program.

```
00065               05  FILLER                PIC X(5)   VALUE SPACES.
00066               05  DET-GRADE             PIC A.
00067               05  FILLER                PIC X(101) VALUE SPACES.
00068           01  TOTAL-LINE.
00069               05  FILLER                PIC X(16)  VALUE SPACES.
00070               05  FILLER                PIC X(9)   VALUE 'AVERAGE: '.
00071               05  TOT-GPA               PIC 9.99.
00072               05  FILLER                PIC X(104) VALUE SPACES.
00073           01  MAJOR-VALUE.
00074               05  FILLER                PIC X(14)  VALUE '1234ACCOUNTING'.
00075               05  FILLER                PIC X(14)  VALUE '1400BIOLOGY   '.
00076               05  FILLER                PIC X(14)  VALUE '1976CHEMISTRY '.
00077               05  FILLER                PIC X(14)  VALUE '2100CIVIL ENG '.
00078               05  FILLER                PIC X(14)  VALUE '2458E. D. P.  '.
00079               05  FILLER                PIC X(14)  VALUE '3245ECONOMICS '.
00080               05  FILLER                PIC X(14)  VALUE '3960FINANCE   '.
00081               05  FILLER                PIC X(14)  VALUE '4321MANAGEMENT'.
00082               05  FILLER                PIC X(14)  VALUE '4999MARKETING '.
00083               05  FILLER                PIC X(14)  VALUE '5400STATISTICS'.
00084           01  MAJOR-TABLE REDEFINES MAJOR-VALUE.
00085               05  MAJORS    OCCURS 10 TIMES
00086                     INDEXED BY MAJOR-INDEX.
00087                 10  MAJOR-CODE      PIC 9(4).
00088                 10  MAJOR-NAME      PIC X(10).
00089           PROCEDURE DIVISION.
00090           001-MAINLINE.
00091               OPEN INPUT STUDENT-FILE,
00092                    OUTPUT PRINT-FILE.
00093               SET MAJOR-INDEX TO 1.
00094               PERFORM 020-PROCESS-CARDS
00095                   UNTIL WS-END-OF-FILE = 'YES'.
00096               CLOSE STUDENT-FILE, PRINT-FILE.
00097               STOP RUN.
00098
00099           020-PROCESS-CARDS.
00100               READ STUDENT-FILE INTO WS-STUDENT-RECORD,
00101                   AT END MOVE 'YES' TO WS-END-OF-FILE.
00102               CALL 'SUBRTN'
00103                   USING WS-STUDENT-RECORD
00104                         WS-GRADE-AVERAGE.
00105
00106           *DETERMINE MAJOR
00107               SEARCH MAJORS
00108                   AT END MOVE 'UNKNOWN' TO HDG-MAJOR
00109                   WHEN MAJOR-CODE (MAJOR-INDEX) = ST-MAJOR-CODE
00110                       MOVE MAJOR-NAME (MAJOR-INDEX) TO HDG-MAJOR.
00111
00112           *WRITE HEADING LINES
00113               WRITE PRINT-LINE FROM HEADING-LINE-ONE
00114                   AFTER ADVANCING PAGE.
00115               MOVE ST-NAME TO HDG-NAME.
00116               WRITE PRINT-LINE FROM HEADING-LINE-TWO
00117                   AFTER ADVANCING 2 LINES.
00118               WRITE PRINT-LINE FROM HEADING-LINE-THREE
00119                   AFTER ADVANCING 2 LINES.
00120
00121           *WRITE DETAIL LINES - 1 PER COURSE
00122               PERFORM 040-WRITE-DETAIL-LINE
00123                   VARYING WS-SUB FROM 1 BY 1
00124                   UNTIL WS-SUB > ST-NUMBER-OF-COURSES.
00125
00126           *WRITE GRADE POINT AVERAGE
00127               MOVE WS-GRADE-AVERAGE TO TOT-GPA.
00128               WRITE PRINT-LINE FROM TOTAL-LINE
00129                   AFTER ADVANCING 2 LINES.
```

Figure 3.18 *cont.*

```
00130
00131           040-WRITE-DETAIL-LINE.
00132               MOVE ST-COURSE-NUMBER (WS-SUB) TO DET-COURSE.
00133               MOVE ST-COURSE-CREDITS (WS-SUB) TO DET-CREDITS.
00134               MOVE ST-COURSE-GRADE (WS-SUB) TO DET-GRADE.
00135               WRITE PRINT-LINE FROM DETAIL-LINE
00136                   AFTER ADVANCING 1 LINES.
00137
```

Figure 3.18 *cont.*

```
00001           IDENTIFICATION DIVISION.
00002           PROGRAM-ID.    'SUBRTN'.
00003           AUTHOR.        GRAUER.
00004
00005
00006           ENVIRONMENT DIVISION.
00007
00008           CONFIGURATION SECTION.
00009           SOURCE-COMPUTER.   IBM-370.
00010           OBJECT-COMPUTER.   IBM-370.
00011
00012
00013           DATA DIVISION.
00014           WORKING-STORAGE SECTION.
00015           77  WS-TOTAL-CREDITS              PIC 999.
00016           77  WS-QUALITY-POINTS             PIC 999.
00017           77  WS-MULTIPLIER                 PIC 9.
00018           77  WS-SUB                        PIC S9(4)      COMP.
00019
00020          ******************************************************
00021           LINKAGE SECTION.
00022           77  LS-CALCULATED-AVERAGE         PIC S9V99.
00023           01  DATA-PASSED-FROM-MAIN.
00024               05  ST-NAME                   PIC X(15).
00025               05  ST-MAJOR-CODE             PIC 9(4).
00026               05  ST-NUMBER-OF-COURSES      PIC 99.
00027               05  ST-COURSE-TABLE OCCURS 8 TIMES.
00028                   10  ST-COURSE-NUMBER      PIC X(3).
00029                   10  ST-COURSE-GRADE       PIC A.
00030                   10  ST-COURSE-CREDITS     PIC 9.
00031               05  FILLER                    PIC X(19).
00032          ******************************************************
00033
00034           PROCEDURE DIVISION
00035               USING DATA-PASSED-FROM-MAIN
00036                     LS-CALCULATED-AVERAGE.
00037          ******************************************************
00038          * ROUTINE TO COMPUTE GRADE POINT AVERAGE
00039          * WEIGHTS:  A=4, B=3, C=2, D=1, F=0
00040          * NO PLUS OR MINUS GRADES
00041          * QUALITY POINTS FOR A GIVEN COURSE = WEIGHT X CREDITS
00042          * GRADE POINT AVERAGE = TOTAL QUALITY POINTS / TOTAL CREDITS
00043          ******************************************************
00044           001-MAINLINE.
00045               MOVE ZERO TO WS-QUALITY-POINTS.
00046               MOVE ZERO TO WS-TOTAL-CREDITS.
00047               PERFORM 010-COMPUTE-QUALITY-POINTS
00048                   VARYING WS-SUB FROM 1 BY 1
00049                   UNTIL WS-SUB = ST-NUMBER-OF-COURSES.
00050               COMPUTE LS-CALCULATED-AVERAGE ROUNDED
00051                   = WS-QUALITY-POINTS / WS-TOTAL-CREDITS.
00052           005-RETURN-TO-MAIN.
00053               EXIT PROGRAM.
00054
```

Figure 3.19 Subprogram.

```
00055          010-COMPUTE-QUALITY-POINTS.
00056              MOVE ZERO TO WS-MULTIPLIER.
00057          * NESTED IF COULD BE USED, BUT ISN'T IN ORDER TO OBTAIN
00058          * GREATER CLARITY.
00059              IF ST-COURSE-GRADE (WS-SUB) = 'A', MOVE 4 TO WS-MULTIPLIER.
00060              IF ST-COURSE-GRADE (WS-SUB) = 'B', MOVE 3 TO WS-MULTIPLIER.
00061              IF ST-COURSE-GRADE (WS-SUB) = 'C', MOVE 2 TO WS-MULTIPLIER.
00062              IF ST-COURSE-GRADE (WS-SUB) = 'D', MOVE 1 TO WS-MULTIPLIER.
00063              COMPUTE WS-QUALITY-POINTS = WS-QUALITY-POINTS
00064                  + ST-COURSE-CREDITS (WS-SUB) * WS-MULTIPLIER.
00065              ADD ST-COURSE-CREDITS (WS-SUB) TO WS-TOTAL-CREDITS.
```

Figure 3.19 *cont.*

Exercise 3.8: Sequential File Maintenance

The program in Fig. 3.20 is intended to sequentially process a transaction file against an existing master file. Output is to consist of a new master and associated error messages.

Three types of transactions are possible. A transaction code of "A" means add a new record, a code of "D" is to delete an existing record, and a code of "C" indicates a salary change in which the salary field in the transaction record is to replace the salary in the existing master record.

Two types of errors are to be checked for. The first is a "duplicate add" in which the social security number on a transaction record with a code of "A," matches that of an existing record. The second is a "no match" in which the social security number in a salary change or delete transaction is not found in the old master. In either case, the error is to be flagged and the invalid transaction record ignored. The transaction and old master files are shown in Fig. 3.21 and 3.22, respectively.

The program of Fig. 3.20 produced the *incorrect* output shown in Fig. 3.23 and Fig. 3.24, respectively. Indicate what the correct output, that is, new master file and error messages should be. Then indicate the necessary COBOL corrections to Figure 3.20.

```
00001          IDENTIFICATION DIVISION.
00002          PROGRAM-ID.      UPDATE.
00003          AUTHOR.          GRAUER.
00004          ENVIRONMENT DIVISION.
00005          CONFIGURATION SECTION.
00006          SOURCE-COMPUTER.  IBM-370.
00007          OBJECT-COMPUTER.  IBM-370.
00008          INPUT-OUTPUT SECTION.
00009          FILE-CONTROL.
00010              SELECT TRANSACTION-FILE ASSIGN TO UT-S-TRANS.
00011              SELECT ERROR-FILE ASSIGN TO UT-S-PRINT.
00012              SELECT OLD-MASTER-FILE ASSIGN TO UT-S-OLD.
00013              SELECT NEW-MASTER-FILE ASSIGN TO UT-S-NEW.
00014          DATA DIVISION.
00015          FILE SECTION.
00016          FD  OLD-MASTER-FILE
00017              LABEL RECORDS ARE STANDARD
00018              BLOCK CONTAINS 0 RECORDS
00019              RECORD CONTAINS 40 CHARACTERS
```

Figure 3.20 Sequential Maintenance Program.

```
00020              DATA RECORD IS OLD-MAST-RECORD.
00021          01  OLD-MAST-RECORD         PIC X(40).
00022          FD  NEW-MASTER-FILE
00023              LABEL RECORDS ARE STANDARD
00024              BLOCK CONTAINS 0 RECORDS
00025              RECORD CONTAINS 40 CHARACTERS
00026              DATA RECORD IS NEW-MAST-RECORD.
00027          01  NEW-MAST-RECORD         PIC X(40).
00028          FD  TRANSACTION-FILE
00029              LABEL RECORDS ARE OMITTED
00030              RECORD CONTAINS 80 CHARACTERS
00031              DATA RECORD IS TRANS-RECORD.
00032          01  TRANS-RECORD            PIC X(80).
00033          FD  ERROR-FILE
00034              LABEL RECORDS ARE OMITTED
00035              RECORD CONTAINS 132 CHARACTERS
00036              DATA RECORD IS ERROR-RECORD.
00037          01  ERROR-RECORD            PIC X(132).
00038          WORKING-STORAGE SECTION.
00039          77  WS-OLD-MAST-READ-SWITCH PIC X(3)   VALUE 'NO'.
00040          77  WS-TRANS-READ-SWITCH    PIC X(3)   VALUE 'NO'.
00041          01  WS-OLD-MAST-RECORD.
00042              05  WS-OLDMAST-ID       PIC X(9).
00043              05  WS-OLDMAST-NAME     PIC X(25).
00044              05  WS-OLDMAST-SALARY   PIC 9(6).
00045          01  WS-NEW-MAST-RECORD.
00046              05  WS-NEWMAST-ID       PIC X(9).
00047              05  WS-NEWMAST-NAME     PIC X(25).
00048              05  WS-NEWMAST-SALARY   PIC 9(6).
00049          01  WS-TRANS-RECORD.
00050              05  WS-TRANS-ID         PIC X(9).
00051              05  WS-TRANS-NAME       PIC X(25).
00052              05  WS-TRANS-SALARY     PIC 9(6).
00053              05  WS-TRANS-CODE       PIC X.
00054                  88  ADDITION                   VALUE 'A'.
00055                  88  DELETION                   VALUE 'D'.
00056                  88  SALARY-CHANGE              VALUE 'C'.
00057              05  FILLER              PIC X(39).
00058          01  WS-PRINT-RECORD.
00059              05  WS-PRINT-MESSAGE    PIC X(40).
00060              05  WS-PRINT-ID         PIC X(9).
00061              05  FILLER              PIC X(5)   VALUE SPACES.
00062              05  WS-PRINT-NAME       PIC X(25).
00063              05  FILLER              PIC X(53)  VALUE SPACES.
00064          PROCEDURE DIVISION.
00065          005-MAINLINE.
00066              OPEN INPUT TRANSACTION-FILE
00067                         OLD-MASTER-FILE
00068                   OUTPUT NEW-MASTER-FILE
00069                          ERROR-FILE.
00070              PERFORM 080-READ-TRANSACTION.
00071              PERFORM 090-READ-OLD-MASTER.
00072              PERFORM 010-COMPARE-IDS
00073                  UNTIL WS-TRANS-ID = HIGH-VALUES
00074                  AND WS-OLDMAST-ID = HIGH-VALUES.
00075              CLOSE TRANSACTION-FILE
00076                    OLD-MASTER-FILE
00077                    NEW-MASTER-FILE
00078                    ERROR-FILE.
00079              STOP RUN.
00080
00081          010-COMPARE-IDS.
00082              IF WS-OLDMAST-ID < WS-TRANS-ID
00083                  PERFORM 050-COPY-OLD-REC
00084              ELSE
```

Figure 3.20 *cont.*

```
00085                   IF WS-OLDMAST-ID = WS-TRANS-ID
00086                       PERFORM 060-MATCH-ROUTINE
00087                   ELSE
00088                       PERFORM 070-NEW-RECORD.
00089
00090               IF WS-TRANS-READ-SWITCH = 'YES'
00091                   MOVE 'NO ' TO WS-TRANS-READ-SWITCH
00092                   PERFORM 080-READ-TRANSACTION.
00093
00094               IF WS-OLD-MAST-READ-SWITCH = 'YES'
00095                   PERFORM 090-READ-OLD-MASTER.
00096
00097
00098           050-COPY-OLD-REC.
00099               WRITE NEW-MAST-RECORD FROM WS-OLD-MAST-RECORD.
00100               MOVE 'YES' TO WS-OLD-MAST-READ-SWITCH.
00101
00102           060-MATCH-ROUTINE.
00103               IF ADDITION
00104                   MOVE WS-TRANS-NAME            TO WS-PRINT-NAME
00105                   MOVE WS-TRANS-ID              TO WS-PRINT-ID
00106                   MOVE 'ERROR - RECORD ALREADY IN FILE' TO WS-PRINT-MESSAGE
00107                   WRITE ERROR-RECORD FROM WS-PRINT-RECORD
00108                   WRITE NEW-MAST-RECORD FROM WS-OLD-MAST-RECORD
00109               ELSE
00110                   IF SALARY-CHANGE
00111                       WRITE NEW-MAST-RECORD FROM WS-OLD-MAST-RECORD
00112                       MOVE WS-TRANS-SALARY TO WS-OLDMAST-SALARY
00113                   ELSE
00114                       IF DELETION
00115                           NEXT SENTENCE.
00116
00117               MOVE 'YES' TO WS-TRANS-READ-SWITCH.
00118               MOVE 'YES' TO WS-OLD-MAST-READ-SWITCH.
00119
00120           070-NEW-RECORD.
00121               IF ADDITION
00122                   MOVE WS-TRANS-NAME            TO WS-PRINT-NAME
00123                   MOVE WS-TRANS-ID              TO WS-PRINT-ID
00124                   MOVE 'ERROR - NO MATCH'       TO WS-PRINT-MESSAGE
00125                   WRITE ERROR-RECORD FROM WS-PRINT-RECORD
00126               ELSE
00127                   WRITE NEW-MAST-RECORD FROM WS-TRANS-RECORD.
00128               MOVE 'YES' TO WS-TRANS-READ-SWITCH.
00129
00130           080-READ-TRANSACTION.
00131               READ TRANSACTION-FILE INTO WS-TRANS-RECORD
00132                   AT END MOVE HIGH-VALUES TO WS-TRANS-RECORD.
00133
00134           090-READ-OLD-MASTER.
00135               READ OLD-MASTER-FILE INTO WS-OLD-MAST-RECORD
00136                   AT END MOVE HIGH-VALUES TO WS-OLD-MAST-RECORD.
```

Figure 3.20 *cont.*


```
222222222BAKER                    028000C
333333333ZIDROW                        D
400000000NEW EMPLOYEE             016000A
500000000JONES                    020000C
610000000NEW EMPLOYEE II          018000A
777777777BOROW                    055000C
888888888JAMES                    018500A
```

Figure 3.21 Transaction File.

```
111111111ADAMS              015000
222222222BAKER              025000
333333333ZIDROW             008000
444444444MILGROM            040000
555555555BENJAMIN           100000
666666666SHERRY             007500
777777777BOROW              050000
888888888JAMES              017500
999999999RENAZEV            030000
```

Figure 3.22 Old Master File.

```
ERROR - NO MATCH                    400000000    NEW EMPLOYEE
ERROR - NO MATCH                    610000000    NEW EMPLOYEE II
ERROR - RECORD ALREADY IN FILE      888888888    JAMES
```

Figure 3.23 Invalid Error Messages.

```
111111111ADAMS              015000
222222222BAKER              025000
500000000JONES              020000
777777777BOROW              050000
888888888JAMES              017500
999999999RENAZEV            030000
```

Figure 3.24 Invalid New Master File.

Exercise 3.9: Nonsequential File Maintenance

The specifications for this problem are essentially the same as the preceding program (Exercise 3.8), except that the update is *nonsequential*. There is a single master file which functions as both the old and new master. *Only* those records which actually change are rewritten, and the transaction file need not have its records in sequential order.

The COBOL program of Fig. 3.25 adheres to the ANS 74 standard for indexed files, and hence uses VSAM, rather than ISAM (for IBM systems). Test data are provided in Fig. 3.26 and 3.27. The reader may observe that the master file is the same as for the sequential exercise, but the transaction file is different.

```
00001           IDENTIFICATION DIVISION.
00002           PROGRAM-ID.    UPDATE.
00003           AUTHOR.        GRAUER.
00004           ENVIRONMENT DIVISION.
00005           CONFIGURATION SECTION.
00006           SOURCE-COMPUTER.    IBM-370.
00007           OBJECT-COMPUTER.    IBM-370.
00008           INPUT-OUTPUT SECTION.
00009           FILE-CONTROL.
00010               SELECT TRANSACTION-FILE ASSIGN TO UT-S-TRANS.
00011               SELECT ERROR-FILE ASSIGN TO UT-S-SYSOUT.
00012               SELECT VSAM-FILE ASSIGN TO DA-VSAMMAST
00013                   ACCESS IS RANDOM
00014                   ORGANIZATION IS INDEXED
00015                   RECORD KEY IS VSAM-ID-NUMBER.
00016           DATA DIVISION.
```

Figure 3.25 Nonsequential Maintenance Program.

```
00017            FILE SECTION.
00018            FD   VSAM-FILE
00019                 LABEL RECORDS ARE STANDARD
00020                 RECORD CONTAINS 40 CHARACTERS
00021                 DATA RECORD IS VSAM-RECORD.
00022            01   VSAM-RECORD.
00023                 05 VSAM-ID-NUMBER            PIC X(9).
00024                 05 VSAM-NAME                 PIC X(25).
00025                 05 VSAM-SALARY               PIC X(6).
00026            FD   TRANSACTION-FILE
00027                 LABEL RECORDS ARE OMITTED
00028                 RECORD CONTAINS 80 CHARACTERS
00029                 DATA RECORD IS TRANS-RECORD.
00030            01   TRANS-RECORD                 PIC X(80).
00031            FD   ERROR-FILE
00032                 LABEL RECORDS ARE OMITTED
00033                 RECORD CONTAINS 133 CHARACTERS
00034                 DATA RECORD IS ERROR-RECORD.
00035            01   ERROR-RECORD                 PIC X(133).
00036            WORKING-STORAGE SECTION.
00037            77   WS-EOF-INDICATOR             PIC X(3)
00038                                              VALUE 'NO '.
00039            77   WS-INVALID-SWITCH            PIC X(3).
00040                 88 NO-MATCH-OR-NEW-RECORD       VALUE 'YES'.
00041            01   WS-TRANS-RECORD.
00042                 05 WS-TRANS-ID               PIC X(9).
00043                 05 WS-TRANS-NAME             PIC X(25).
00044                 05 WS-TRANS-SALARY           PIC 9(6).
00045                 05 FILLER                    PIC X(39).
00046                 05 WS-TRANS-CODE             PIC X.
00047                    88 ADDITION          VALUE 'A'.
00048                    88 DELETION          VALUE 'D'.
00049                    88 SALARY-CHANGE     VALUE 'C'.
00050            01   WS-ERROR-MESSAGE-1           PIC X(40)
00051                                              VALUE ' RECORD ALREADY IN FILE '.
00052            01   WS-ERROR-MESSAGE-2           PIC X(40)
00053                                              VALUE ' NO MATCH '.
00054            01   WS-PRINT-RECORD.
00055                 05 WS-PRINT-MESSAGE          PIC X(40).
00056                 05 WS-PRINT-ID               PIC X(9).
00057                 05 FILLER                    PIC X(5)
00058                                              VALUE SPACES.
00059                 05 WS-PRINT-NAME             PIC X(25).
00060                 05 FILLER                    PIC X(53)
00061                                              VALUE SPACES.
00062            01   WS-VSAM-RECORD.
00063                 05 WS-VSAM-ID                PIC X(9).
00064                 05 WS-VSAM-NAME              PIC X(25).
00065                 05 WS-VSAM-SALARY            PIC X(6).
00066            PROCEDURE DIVISION.
00067                 MOVE 'NO ' TO WS-INVALID-SWITCH.
00068                 OPEN INPUT TRANSACTION-FILE
00069                      I-O VSAM-FILE
00070                      OUTPUT ERROR-FILE.
00071                 READ TRANSACTION-FILE INTO WS-TRANS-RECORD
00072                     AT END MOVE 'YES' TO WS-EOF-INDICATOR.
00073                 PERFORM 010-READ-VSAM-FILE
00074                     UNTIL WS-EOF-INDICATOR = 'YES'.
00075                 CLOSE TRANSACTION-FILE
00076                       VSAM-FILE
00077                       ERROR-FILE.
00078                 STOP RUN.
00079
00080            010-READ-VSAM-FILE.
00081                 MOVE WS-TRANS-ID TO VSAM-ID-NUMBER.
00082                 READ VSAM-FILE INTO WS-VSAM-RECORD
```

Figure 3.25 *cont.*

```
00083                    INVALID KEY MOVE 'YES' TO WS-INVALID-SWITCH.
00084            IF NO-MATCH-OR-NEW-RECORD
00085                PERFORM 070-NEW-RECORD
00086            ELSE
00087                PERFORM 060-MATCH-ROUTINE.
00088            READ TRANSACTION-FILE INTO WS-TRANS-RECORD
00089                AT END MOVE 'YES' TO WS-EOF-INDICATOR.
00090
00091        060-MATCH-ROUTINE.
00092            IF ADDITION
00093                MOVE WS-TRANS-NAME       TO WS-PRINT-NAME
00094                MOVE WS-TRANS-ID         TO WS-PRINT-ID
00095                MOVE WS-ERROR-MESSAGE-1 TO WS-PRINT-MESSAGE
00096                WRITE ERROR-RECORD FROM WS-PRINT-RECORD
00097            ELSE
00098                IF SALARY-CHANGE
00099                    MOVE WS-TRANS-SALARY TO WS-VSAM-SALARY
00100                    REWRITE VSAM-RECORD FROM WS-VSAM-RECORD.
00101
00102        070-NEW-RECORD.
00103            IF ADDITION
00104                MOVE WS-TRANS-ID         TO WS-VSAM-ID
00105                MOVE WS-TRANS-NAME       TO WS-VSAM-NAME
00106                MOVE WS-TRANS-SALARY     TO WS-VSAM-SALARY
00107                WRITE VSAM-RECORD FROM WS-VSAM-RECORD
00108            ELSE
00109                MOVE WS-TRANS-NAME       TO WS-PRINT-NAME
00110                MOVE WS-TRANS-ID         TO WS-PRINT-ID
00111                MOVE WS-ERROR-MESSAGE-2 TO WS-PRINT-MESSAGE
00112                WRITE ERROR-RECORD FROM WS-PRINT-RECORD.
```

Figure 3.25 *cont.*

```
222222222BAKER                     028000...C
400000000NEW EMPLOYEE              016000...A
500000000JONES                     020000...C
610000000NEW EMPLOYEE II           018000...A
666666666SHERRY                                D
777777777BOROW                     055000...C
888888888JAMES                     018500...A
```

Figure 3.26 Transaction File.

```
111111111ADAMS          015000
222222222BAKER          025000
333333333ZIDROW         008000
444444444MILGROM        040000
555555555BENJAMIN       100000
666666666SHERRY         007500
777777777BOROW          050000
888888888JAMES          017500
999999999RENAZEV        030000
```

Figure 3.27 Old Master File.

The update program of Figure 3.25 produced the output shown in Fig. 3.28 and Fig. 3.29. Indicate what the correct output (new master file and error messages) should be. Then indicate the necessary COBOL corrections.

```
NO MATCH                 500000000    JONES
NO MATCH                 666666666    SHERRY
NO MATCH                 777777777    BOROW
```

Figure 3.28 Invalid Error Messages.

```
111111111ADAMS              015000
222222222BAKER              028000
333333333ZIDROW             008000
400000000NEW EMPLOYEE       016000
444444444MILGROM            040000
555555555BENJAMIN           100000
610000000NEW EMPLOYEE II    018000
666666666SHERRY             007500
777777777BOROW              050000
888888888JAMES              017500
999999999RENAZEV            030000
```

Figure 3.29 New Master File.

Exercise 3.10: Two-file Merge: 1

Records from two files with identical record layouts are to be merged into a single file, also with the same layout. Both incoming files can be assumed to be in ascending sequence by social security number (positions 10-18 in each record).

This exercise and the next involve different COBOL programs to merge the two files. Note well that an additional requirement is to display any social security number which appears in both input files, and to omit these records from the merged file. A set of test data with *correct* output is shown in Fig. 3.30.

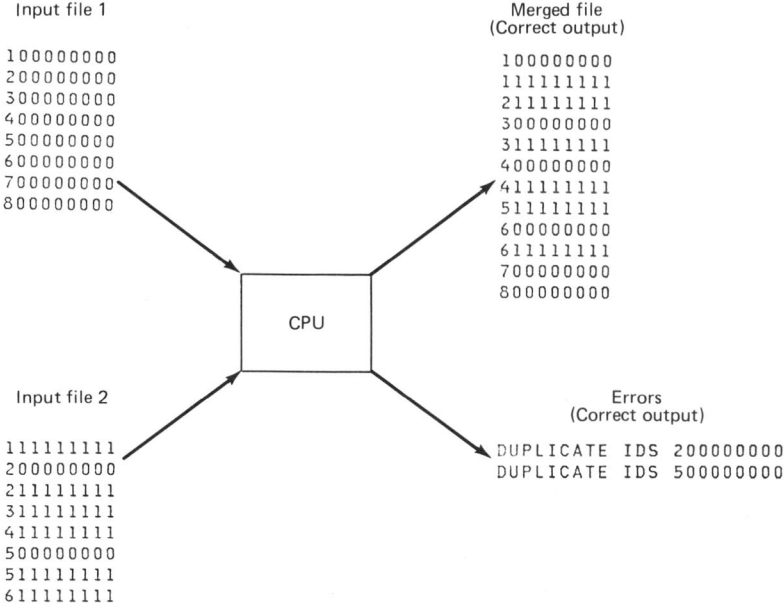

Figure 3.30 Test Data and Correct Output.

178 Section 3

The program in Fig. 3.31 produced the output in Fig. 3.32 from the original input provided with the problem statement (Figure 3.30). Find and correct the logic error(s).

```
00001              IDENTIFICATION DIVISION.
00002              PROGRAM-ID.    TWOFILES.
00003              AUTHOR.      R. GRAUER.
00004              ENVIRONMENT DIVISION.
00005              CONFIGURATION SECTION.
00006              SOURCE-COMPUTER.   IBM-370.
00007              OBJECT-COMPUTER.   IBM-370.
00008              INPUT-OUTPUT SECTION.
00009              FILE-CONTROL.
00010                  SELECT INPUT-FILE-ONE ASSIGN TO UT-S-FILEONE.
00011                  SELECT INPUT-FILE-TWO ASSIGN TO UT-S-FILETWO.
00012                  SELECT MERGED-FILE ASSIGN TO UT-S-MERGED.
00013              DATA DIVISION.
00014              FILE SECTION.
00015              FD  INPUT-FILE-ONE
00016                  LABEL RECORDS ARE STANDARD
00017                  BLOCK CONTAINS 0 RECORDS
00018                  RECORD CONTAINS 80 CHARACTERS
00019                  DATA RECORD IS INPUT-RECORD-ONE.
00020              01  INPUT-RECORD-ONE.
00021                  05   FILLER                        PIC X(9).
00022                  05   INPUT-ONE-ID                  PIC X(9).
00023                  05   INPUT-ONE-NAME                PIC X(20).
00024                  05   INPUT-ONE-SALARY              PIC 9(6).
00025                  05   INPUT-ONE-DEPARTMENT          PIC 9(4).
00026                  05   INPUT-ONE-LOCATION            PIC X(10).
00027                  05   FILLER                        PIC X(22).
00028              FD  INPUT-FILE-TWO
00029                  LABEL RECORDS ARE STANDARD
00030                  BLOCK CONTAINS 0 RECORDS
00031                  RECORD CONTAINS 80 CHARACTERS
00032                  DATA RECORD IS INPUT-RECORD-TWO.
00033              01  INPUT-RECORD-TWO.
00034                  05   FILLER                        PIC X(9).
00035                  05   INPUT-TWO-ID                  PIC X(9).
00036                  05   INPUT-TWO-NAME                PIC X(20).
00037                  05   INPUT-TWO-SALARY              PIC 9(6).
00038                  05   INPUT-TWO-DEPARTMENT          PIC 9(4).
00039                  05   INPUT-TWO-LOCATION            PIC X(10).
00040                  05   FILLER                        PIC X(22).
00041              FD  MERGED-FILE
00042                  LABEL RECORDS ARE STANDARD
00043                  RECORD CONTAINS 80 CHARACTERS
00044                  BLOCK CONTAINS 0 RECORDS
00045                  DATA RECORD IS MERGED-RECORD.
00046              01  MERGED-RECORD                      PIC X(80).
00047              WORKING-STORAGE SECTION.
00048              77  WS-READ-INPUT-ONE-SWITCH      VALUE SPACES  PIC X(3).
00049              77  WS-READ-INPUT-TWO-SWITCH      VALUE SPACES  PIC X(3).
00050              PROCEDURE DIVISION.
00051
00052              005-MAINLINE.
00053                  OPEN INPUT INPUT-FILE-ONE
00054                             INPUT-FILE-TWO
00055                       OUTPUT MERGED-FILE.
00056                  READ INPUT-FILE-ONE
00057                      AT END MOVE HIGH-VALUES TO INPUT-ONE-ID.
00058                  READ INPUT-FILE-TWO
00059                      AT END MOVE HIGH-VALUES TO INPUT-TWO-ID.
00060                  PERFORM 010-PROCESS-FILES THRU 020-PROCESS-FILES-EXIT
```

Figure 3.31 Two-file Merge: 1

```
00061                    UNTIL INPUT-ONE-ID = HIGH-VALUES
00062                      AND INPUT-TWO-ID = HIGH-VALUES.
00063              CLOSE INPUT-FILE-ONE
00064                    INPUT-FILE-TWO
00065                    MERGED-FILE.
00066              STOP RUN.
00067
00068         010-PROCESS-FILES.
00069
00070              IF INPUT-ONE-ID LESS THAN INPUT-TWO-ID
00071                   WRITE MERGED-RECORD FROM INPUT-RECORD-ONE
00072                   MOVE 'YES' TO WS-READ-INPUT-ONE-SWITCH
00073              ELSE
00074                   IF INPUT-TWO-ID LESS THAN INPUT-ONE-ID
00075                        WRITE MERGED-RECORD FROM INPUT-RECORD-TWO
00076                        MOVE 'YES' TO WS-READ-INPUT-TWO-SWITCH
00077                   ELSE
00078                        DISPLAY 'DUPLICATE IDS ' INPUT-ONE-ID
00079                        MOVE 'YES' TO WS-READ-INPUT-ONE-SWITCH
00080                        MOVE 'YES' TO WS-READ-INPUT-TWO-SWITCH.
00081
00082              IF WS-READ-INPUT-ONE-SWITCH = 'YES'
00083                   MOVE 'NO' TO WS-READ-INPUT-ONE-SWITCH.
00084                   READ INPUT-FILE-ONE
00085                        AT END MOVE HIGH-VALUES TO INPUT-ONE-ID.
00086
00087              IF WS-READ-INPUT-TWO-SWITCH = 'YES'
00088                   MOVE 'NO' TO WS-READ-INPUT-TWO-SWITCH.
00089                   READ INPUT-FILE-TWO
00090                        AT END MOVE HIGH-VALUES TO INPUT-TWO-ID.
00091
00092         020-PROCESS-FILES-EXIT.
00093              EXIT.
```

Figure 3.31 *cont.*

Merged File	Error Messages
100000000	
211111111	DUPLICATE IDS 200000000
311111111	
411111111	
500000000	
511111111	
611111111	

Figure 3.32 Incorrect Output.

Exercise 3.11: Two-File Merge: 2

The program in Fig. 3.33 produced the output in Fig. 3.34 from the original input provided with the problem statement of exercise 3.10. Find and correct the logic error(s).

```
00001         IDENTIFICATION DIVISION.
00002         PROGRAM-ID.    TWOFILES.
00003         AUTHOR.        R. GRAUER.
00004         ENVIRONMENT DIVISION.
00005         CONFIGURATION SECTION.
00006         SOURCE-COMPUTER.  IBM-370.
```

Figure 3.33 Two-File Merge: 2

```
00007              OBJECT-COMPUTER.   IBM-370.
00008              INPUT-OUTPUT SECTION.
00009              FILE-CONTROL.
00010                  SELECT INPUT-FILE-ONE ASSIGN TO UT-S-FILEONE.
00011                  SELECT INPUT-FILE-TWO ASSIGN TO UT-S-FILETWO.
00012                  SELECT MERGED-FILE ASSIGN TO UT-S-MERGED.
00013              DATA DIVISION.
00014              FILE SECTION.
00015              FD  INPUT-FILE-ONE
00016                  LABEL RECORDS ARE STANDARD
00017                  BLOCK CONTAINS 0 RECORDS
00018                  RECORD CONTAINS 80 CHARACTERS
00019                  DATA RECORD IS INPUT-RECORD-ONE.
00020              01  INPUT-RECORD-ONE                       PIC X(80).
00021              FD  INPUT-FILE-TWO
00022                  LABEL RECORDS ARE STANDARD
00023                  BLOCK CONTAINS 0 RECORDS
00024                  RECORD CONTAINS 80 CHARACTERS
00025                  DATA RECORD IS INPUT-RECORD-TWO.
00026              01  INPUT-RECORD-TWO                       PIC X(80).
00027              FD  MERGED-FILE
00028                  LABEL RECORDS ARE STANDARD
00029                  RECORD CONTAINS 80 CHARACTERS
00030                  BLOCK CONTAINS 0 RECORDS
00031                  DATA RECORD IS MERGED-RECORD.
00032              01  MERGED-RECORD                          PIC X(80).
00033              WORKING-STORAGE SECTION.
00034              01   WS-RECORD-ONE.
00035                   05   FILLER                           PIC X(9).
00036                   05   WS-REC-ONE-ID                    PIC X(9).
00037                   05   WS-REC-ONE-NAME                  PIC X(20).
00038                   05   WS-REC-ONE-SALARY                PIC 9(6).
00039                   05   WS-REC-ONE-DEPARTMENT            PIC 9(4).
00040                   05   WS-REC-ONE-LOCATION              PIC X(10).
00041                   05   FILLER                           PIC X(22).
00042              01   WS-RECORD-TWO.
00043                   05   FILLER                           PIC X(9).
00044                   05   WS-REC-TWO-ID                    PIC X(9).
00045                   05   WS-REC-TWO-NAME                  PIC X(20).
00046                   05   WS-REC-TWO-SALARY                PIC 9(6).
00047                   05   WS-REC-TWO-DEPARTMENT            PIC 9(4).
00048                   05   WS-REC-TWO-LOCATION              PIC X(10).
00049                   05   FILLER                           PIC X(22).
00050              PROCEDURE DIVISION.
00051
00052              005-MAINLINE.
00053                  OPEN INPUT INPUT-FILE-ONE
00054                             INPUT-FILE-TWO
00055                       OUTPUT MERGED-FILE.
00056                  PERFORM 020-READ-FIRST-FILE.
00057                  PERFORM 030-READ-SECOND-FILE.
00058                  PERFORM 010-PROCESS-FILES
00059                      UNTIL WS-REC-ONE-ID = HIGH-VALUES
00060                         OR WS-REC-TWO-ID = HIGH-VALUES.
00061                  CLOSE INPUT-FILE-ONE
00062                        INPUT-FILE-TWO
00063                        MERGED-FILE.
00064                  STOP RUN.
00065
00066              010-PROCESS-FILES.
00067
00068                  IF WS-REC-ONE-ID LESS THAN WS-REC-TWO-ID
00069                      WRITE MERGED-RECORD FROM INPUT-RECORD-ONE
00070                      PERFORM 020-READ-FIRST-FILE
00071                  ELSE
00072                      IF WS-REC-TWO-ID LESS THAN WS-REC-ONE-ID
00073                          WRITE MERGED-RECORD FROM INPUT-RECORD-ONE
```

Figure 3.33 *cont.*

```
00074                    PERFORM 030-READ-SECOND-FILE
00075                ELSE
00076                    DISPLAY 'DUPLICATE IDS ' WS-REC-ONE-ID
00077                    PERFORM 020-READ-FIRST-FILE
00078                    PERFORM 030-READ-SECOND-FILE.
00079
00080
00081       020-READ-FIRST-FILE.
00082           READ INPUT-FILE-ONE INTO WS-RECORD-ONE
00083               AT END MOVE HIGH-VALUES TO WS-REC-ONE-ID.
00084
00085       030-READ-SECOND-FILE.
00086           READ INPUT-FILE-TWO INTO WS-RECORD-TWO
00087               AT END MOVE HIGH-VALUES TO WS-REC-TWO-ID.
```

Figure 3.33 *cont.*

Merged File	Error Messages
100000000	
200000000	DUPLICATE IDS 200000000
300000000	DUPLICATE IDS 500000000
300000000	
400000000	
400000000	
500000000	
600000000	
600000000	
700000000	

Figure 3.34 Incorrect Output.

Exercise 3.12: Incorrect Use of a Group Move

The program in Fig. 3.35 is meant to illustrate both correct and incorrect ways of initializing counters. Explain the rather curious output of Fig. 3.36. (Note: The program failed in executing line 035 with a message indicating it could not add improper decimal data.)

```
00001       IDENTIFICATION DIVISION.
00002       PROGRAM-ID.    GROUPMV.
00003       AUTHOR.        R GRAUER.
00004       ENVIRONMENT DIVISION.
00005       CONFIGURATION SECTION.
00006       SOURCE-COMPUTER.      IBM-370.
00007       OBJECT-COMPUTER.      IBM-370.
00008       DATA DIVISION.
00009       WORKING-STORAGE SECTION.
00010       01  FIRST-GROUP-FIELD.
00011           05   FIRST-DISPLAY    PIC 9(4).
00012           05   FIRST-BINARY     PIC 9(4)    COMP.
00013           05   FIRST-PACKED     PIC 9(4)    COMP-3.
00014       01  SECOND-GROUP-FIELD.
00015           05   SECOND-DISPLAY   PIC 9(4).
00016           05   SECOND-BINARY    PIC 9(4)    COMP.
00017           05   SECOND-PACKED    PIC 9(4)    COMP-3.
00018       PROCEDURE DIVISION.
00019       *  CORRECT INITIALIZATION
00020           MOVE ZEROS TO FIRST-BINARY.
00021           ADD 1 TO FIRST-BINARY.
00022           DISPLAY 'FIRST-BINARY = ' FIRST-BINARY.
00023           MOVE ZEROS TO FIRST-DISPLAY.
```

Figure 3.35 Incorrect Use of a Group Move.

```
00024              ADD 1 TO FIRST-DISPLAY.
00025              DISPLAY 'FIRST-DISPLAY = ' FIRST-DISPLAY.
00026              MOVE ZEROS TO FIRST-PACKED.
00027              ADD 1 TO FIRST-PACKED.
00028              DISPLAY 'FIRST-PACKED = ' FIRST-PACKED.
00029         *INCORRECT INITIALIZATION
00030              MOVE ZEROS TO SECOND-GROUP-FIELD.
00031              ADD 1 TO SECOND-BINARY.
00032              DISPLAY 'SECOND-BINARY = ' SECOND-BINARY.
00033              ADD 1 TO SECOND-DISPLAY.
00034              DISPLAY 'SECOND-DISPLAY = ' SECOND-DISPLAY.
00035              ADD 1 TO SECOND-PACKED.
00036              DISPLAY 'SECOND-PACKED = ' SECOND-PACKED.
00037              STOP RUN.
```

Figure 3.35 *cont.*

```
                    FIRST-BINARY = 0001
                    FIRST-DISPLAY = 0001
                    FIRST-PACKED = 0001
                    SECOND-BINARY = 3855
                    SECOND-DISPLAY = 0001
```

Figure 3.36 Output Produced by Figure 3.35.

Exercise 3.13 Incorrect Use of the SEARCH Verb

The program in Fig. 3.37 illustrates both correct and incorrect use of SEARCH and SEARCH ALL. As can be seen from the associated output (Fig. 3.38), the SEARCH verb appeared to work sporadically. Specifically, New York was found with a binary, but *not* with a sequential search. Denver, on the other hand, was found with a sequential search, but *not* with a binary search. Why?

```
00001         IDENTIFICATION DIVISION.
00002         PROGRAM-ID.
00003             ERRORS.
00004         AUTHOR.
00005             GRAUER.
00006         ENVIRONMENT DIVISION.
00007         CONFIGURATION SECTION.
00008         SOURCE-COMPUTER.
00009             IBM-370.
00010         OBJECT-COMPUTER.
00011             IBM-370.
00012         DATA DIVISION.
00013
00014         WORKING-STORAGE SECTION.
00015
00016         01  LOCATION-VALUE.
00017             05  FILLER        PIC X(16) VALUE "010ATLANTA       ".
00018             05  FILLER        PIC X(16) VALUE "020BOSTON        ".
00019             05  FILLER        PIC X(16) VALUE "030CHICAGO       ".
00020             05  FILLER        PIC X(16) VALUE "040DETROIT       ".
00021             05  FILLER        PIC X(16) VALUE "050KANSAS CITY   ".
00022             05  FILLER        PIC X(16) VALUE "060LOS ANGELES   ".
00023             05  FILLER        PIC X(16) VALUE "070NEW YORK      ".
00024             05  FILLER        PIC X(16) VALUE "080PHILADELPHIA  ".
00025             05  FILLER        PIC X(16) VALUE "090SAN FRANCISCO ".
00026             05  FILLER        PIC X(16) VALUE "045DENVER        ".
```

Figure 3.37 Incorrect Use of a Search.

```
00027
00028            01  LOCATION-TABLE REDEFINES LOCATION-VALUE.
00029                05  LOCATION OCCURS 10 TIMES
00030                    ASCENDING KEY IS LOCATION-CODE
00031                    INDEXED BY LOCATION-INDEX.
00032                    10  LOCATION-CODE   PIC X(3).
00033                    10  LOCATION-NAME   PIC X(13).
00034        PROCEDURE DIVISION.
00035        SEARCH-ROUTINE.
00036
00037        *SHOW BINARY SEARCH WORKS FOR NEW YORK
00038            SEARCH ALL LOCATION
00039                AT END DISPLAY "*ERROR FOR NEW YORK IN BINARY SEARCH"
00040                WHEN LOCATION-CODE (LOCATION-INDEX) = "070"
00041                DISPLAY "BINARY SEARCH OK FOR NEW YORK".
00042
00043        * SHOW BINARY SEARCH FAILS FOR DENVER
00044            SEARCH ALL LOCATION
00045                AT END DISPLAY  "*ERROR FOR DENVER IN BINARY SEARCH"
00046                WHEN LOCATION-CODE (LOCATION-INDEX) = "045"
00047                DISPLAY "BINARY SEARCH OK FOR DENVER".
00048
00049        *SHOW LINEAR SEARCH WORKS FOR DENVER
00050            SET LOCATION-INDEX TO 1.
00051            SEARCH LOCATION
00052                AT END DISPLAY  "*ERROR IN LINEAR SEARCH FOR DENVER"
00053                WHEN LOCATION-CODE (LOCATION-INDEX) = "045"
00054                DISPLAY "LINEAR SEARCH OK FOR DENVER".
00055
00056        *SHOW LINEAR SEARCH FAILS FOR NEW YORK
00057            SEARCH LOCATION
00058                AT END DISPLAY  "*ERROR IN LINEAR SEARCH FOR NEW YORK"
00059                WHEN LOCATION-CODE (LOCATION-INDEX) = "070"
00060                DISPLAY "LINEAR SEARCH OK FOR NEW YORK".
00061
00062            STOP RUN.
```

Figure 3.37 *cont.*

```
BINARY SEARCH OK FOR NEW YORK
*ERROR FOR DENVER IN BINARY SEARCH
LINEAR SEARCH OK FOR DENVER
*ERROR IN LINEAR SEARCH FOR NEW YORK
```

Figure 3.38 Output.

Exercise 3.14: Incorrect Use of Signed Numbers

The program in Fig. 3.39 represents a simplistic inventory application, in which an incoming order is compared to the existing quantity on hand. If the amount of stock is sufficient, the ordered quantity is to be shipped, if not an error message is to be printed.

As can be seen from the output (Fig. 3.40), the total quanitity shipped summed to 250 units, whereas the initial quantity on hand was only 100 (line 39). Why?

```
00001            IDENTIFICATION DIVISION.
00002            PROGRAM-ID.    SIGNED.
00003            AUTHOR.        R. GRAUER.
00004            ENVIRONMENT DIVISION.
```

Figure 3.39 Incorrect Use of Signed Numbers.

```
00005              CONFIGURATION SECTION.
00006              SOURCE-COMPUTER.
00007                  IBM-370.
00008              OBJECT-COMPUTER.
00009                  IBM-370.
00010              INPUT-OUTPUT SECTION.
00011              FILE-CONTROL.
00012                  SELECT ORDER-FILE ASSIGN TO UT-S-SYSIN.
00013                  SELECT PRINT-FILE ASSIGN TO UT-S-SYSOUT.
00014              DATA DIVISION.
00015              FILE SECTION.
00016              FD   ORDER-FILE
00017                   RECORDING MODE IS F
00018                   LABEL RECORDS ARE OMITTED
00019                   RECORD CONTAINS 80 CHARACTERS
00020                   DATA RECORD IS CARD.
00021              01   CARD.
00022                   05   CUSTOMER-NAME       PIC X(20).
00023                   05   CUSTOMER-ORDER      PIC 9(2).
00024                   05   FILLER              PIC X(58).
00025              FD   PRINT-FILE
00026                   RECORDING MODE IS F
00027                   LABEL RECORDS ARE OMITTED
00028                   RECORD CONTAINS 133 CHARACTERS
00029                   DATA RECORD IS PRINT-LINE.
00030              01   PRINT-LINE.
00031                   05   FILLER              PIC X(4).
00032                   05   PRT-NAME            PIC X(20).
00033                   05   FILLER              PIC X.
00034                   05   PRT-CUSTOMER-AMOUNT PIC 9(3).
00035                   05   FILLER              PIC X(8).
00036                   05   PRT-QUANTITY-LEFT   PIC 9(3).
00037                   05   FILLER              PIC X(94).
00038              WORKING-STORAGE SECTION.
00039              77   WS-QUANTITY-ON-HAND      PIC 9(3)    VALUE 100.
00040              77   WS-EOF-SWITCH            PIC X(3)    VALUE SPACES.
00041              01   HDG-LINE.
00042                   05   FILLER              PIC X(8)    VALUE SPACES.
00043                   05   FILLER              PIC X(8)    VALUE 'CUSTOMER'.
00044                   05   FILLER              PIC X(7)    VALUE SPACES.
00045                   05   FILLER              PIC X(6)    VALUE 'AMOUNT'.
00046                   05   FILLER              PIC X(3)    VALUE SPACES.
00047                   05   FILLER              PIC X(10)   VALUE 'STOCK LEFT'.
00048                   05   FILLER              PIC X(91)   VALUE SPACES.
00049              PROCEDURE DIVISION.
00050                  OPEN INPUT ORDER-FILE
00051                       OUTPUT PRINT-FILE.
00052                  WRITE PRINT-LINE FROM HDG-LINE.
00053                  READ ORDER-FILE AT END MOVE 'YES' TO WS-EOF-SWITCH.
00054                  PERFORM 010-PROCESS-ORDERS
00055                       UNTIL WS-EOF-SWITCH = 'YES' OR WS-QUANTITY-ON-HAND < 0.
00056                  CLOSE ORDER-FILE
00057                        PRINT-FILE.
00058                  STOP RUN.
00059
00060              010-PROCESS-ORDERS.
00061                  SUBTRACT CUSTOMER-ORDER FROM WS-QUANTITY-ON-HAND.
00062
00063                  IF WS-QUANTITY-ON-HAND > 0
00064                      PERFORM 020-SHIP-ORDER
00065                  ELSE
00066                      DISPLAY 'STOCK SLIPPING BELOW 0 ' CUSTOMER-NAME.
00067                  READ ORDER-FILE AT END MOVE 'YES' TO WS-EOF-SWITCH.
00068
```

Figure 3.39 *cont.*

```
00069              020-SHIP-ORDER.
00070                  MOVE SPACES TO PRINT-LINE.
00071                  MOVE CUSTOMER-NAME TO PRT-NAME.
00072                  MOVE CUSTOMER-ORDER TO PRT-CUSTOMER-AMOUNT.
00073                  MOVE WS-QUANTITY-ON-HAND TO PRT-QUANTITY-LEFT.
00074                  WRITE PRINT-LINE.
```

Figure 3.39 *cont.*

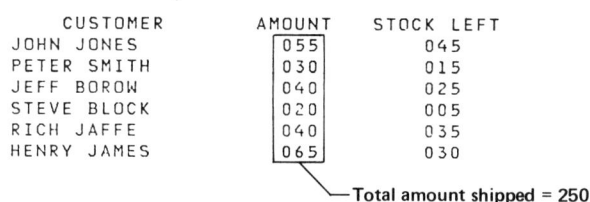

Exercise 3.15: Incorrect Use of Output Buffers

The listing of Fig. 3.41 merely displays a record before and after it is written. As can be seen, the output (Fig. 3.42) is rather unexpected. Why?

```
00001              IDENTIFICATION DIVISION.
00002              PROGRAM-ID.   ERRORS.
00003              AUTHOR.   GRAUER.
00004              ENVIRONMENT DIVISION.
00005              CONFIGURATION SECTION.
00006              SOURCE-COMPUTER.
00007                  IBM-370.
00008              OBJECT-COMPUTER.
00009                  IBM-370.
00010              INPUT-OUTPUT SECTION.
00011              FILE-CONTROL.
00012                  SELECT CARD-FILE
00013                      ASSIGN TO UT-S-SYSIN.
00014                  SELECT DISK-FILE
00015                      ASSIGN TO UT-S-DISKOUT
00016                      RESERVE 1 ALTERNATE AREA.
00017              DATA DIVISION.
00018              FILE SECTION.
00019              FD   CARD-FILE
00020                   LABEL RECORDS ARE OMITTED
00021                   RECORD CONTAINS 80 CHARACTERS
00022                   DATA RECORD IS CARD-RECORD.
00023              01   CARD-RECORD                    PIC X(80).
00024              FD   DISK-FILE
00025                   LABEL RECORDS ARE OMITTED
00026                   RECORD CONTAINS 80 CHARACTERS
00027                   DATA RECORD IS DISK-RECORD.
00028              01   DISK-RECORD.
00029                   05  DISK-NAME                  PIC X(20).
00030                   05  FILLER                     PIC X(60).
00031              WORKING-STORAGE SECTION.
00032              77   WS-END-OF-FILE                 PIC X(3)
00033                              VALUE SPACES.
00034              PROCEDURE DIVISION.
00035                  OPEN INPUT CARD-FILE
```

Figure 3.41 Incorrect Use of Output Buffer.

185

```
00036              OUTPUT DISK-FILE.
00037          PERFORM READ-AND-WRITE THRU READ-AND-WRITE-EXIT
00038              UNTIL WS-END-OF-FILE = 'YES'.
00039          CLOSE CARD-FILE
00040              DISK-FILE.
00041          STOP RUN.
00042
00043      READ-AND-WRITE.
00044          READ CARD-FILE
00045              AT END MOVE 'YES' TO WS-END-OF-FILE
00046              GO TO READ-AND-WRITE-EXIT.
00047          MOVE CARD-RECORD TO DISK-RECORD.
00048          DISPLAY DISK-NAME 'DISK-NAME BEFORE WRITING'.
00049          WRITE DISK-RECORD.
00050          DISPLAY DISK-NAME 'DISK-NAME AFTER WRITING'.
00051      READ-AND-WRITE-EXIT.
00052          EXIT.
```

Figure 3.41 *cont.*

```
PETER JONES        DISK-NAME BEFORE WRITING
JOHN SMITH         DISK-NAME AFTER WRITING
HENRY BROWN        DISK-NAME BEFORE WRITING
PETER JONES        DISK-NAME AFTER WRITING
MARION MILGROM     DISK-NAME BEFORE WRITING
HENRY BROWN        DISK-NAME AFTER WRITING
CHANDLER LAVOR     DISK-NAME BEFORE WRITING
MARION MILGROM     DISK-NAME AFTER WRITING
BENJAMIN LEE       DISK-NAME BEFORE WRITING
```

Figure 3.42 Invalid Output.

Exercise 3.16: Table Processing

This exercise illustrates various aspects of table processing. Essentially, a coded employee file is to be processed and various fields printed in an expanded format. Incoming records contain codes for employee location and title, which are to be expanded via a *sequential* and *binary* search, respectively. In addition, employee salary is to be determined as a function of both responsibility (values 1-10) and experience (values 1-5) as per Fig. 3.43. For example, an employee with a responsibility level of 4 and an experience level of 1 earns $10,000. An employee with a responsibility level of 1 and an experience level of 4 earns $9,000. The program listing is shown in Figure 3.44.

Test data for both the employee and title files are shown in Fig. 3.45 and 3.46. (Note well that in the program of Fig. 3.44 the title table is initialized by reading values from a file.)

The *intended* output is shown in Fig. 3.47 and the *actual* output in Fig. 3.48. As can be seen, there were several problems.

Correct all errors.

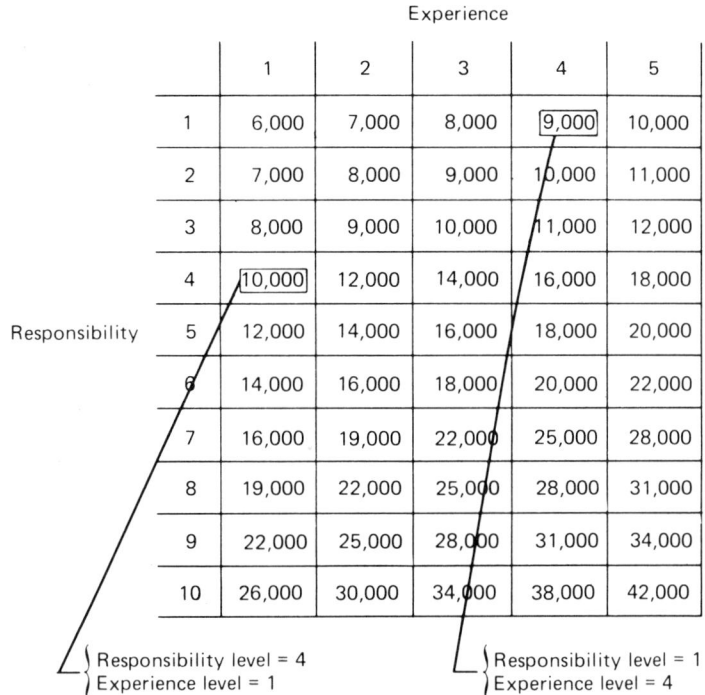

Figure 3.43 Employee Salaries.

```
00001              IDENTIFICATION DIVISION.
00002              PROGRAM-ID.
00003                  'SEARCH'.
00004              AUTHOR.
00005                  ROBERT T. GRAUER.
00006
00007              ENVIRONMENT DIVISION.
00008              CONFIGURATION SECTION.
00009              SOURCE-COMPUTER.
00010                  IBM-370.
00011              OBJECT-COMPUTER.
00012                  IBM-370.
00013
00014              INPUT-OUTPUT SECTION.
00015              FILE-CONTROL.
00016                  SELECT EMPLOYEE-FILE  ASSIGN TO UT-S-SYSIN.
00017                  SELECT PRINT-FILE ASSIGN TO UT-S-PRINT.
00018                  SELECT TITLE-FILE ASSIGN TO UT-S-TITLES.
00019
00020              DATA DIVISION.
00021              FILE SECTION.
00022              FD  TITLE-FILE
00023                  LABEL RECORDS ARE OMITTED
```

Figure 3.44 Table Processing Program.

```
00024                  RECORD CONTAINS 80 CHARACTERS
00025                  DATA RECORD IS TITLE-IN.
00026          01  TITLE-IN.
00027              05  CARD-TITLE-CODE              PIC X(4).
00028              05  CARD-TITLE-NAME              PIC X(15).
00029              05  FILLER                       PIC X(61).
00030          FD  EMPLOYEE-FILE
00031                  LABEL RECORDS ARE OMITTED
00032                  RECORD CONTAINS 80 CHARACTERS
00033                  DATA RECORD IS EMPLOYEE-RECORD.
00034          01  EMPLOYEE-RECORD.
00035              05  EMP-NAME                     PIC X(20).
00036              05  EMP-TITLE-CODE               PIC X(4).
00037              05  EMP-LOC-CODE                 PIC X(3).
00038              05  EMP-SALARY-DETERMINANTS.
00039                  10  EMP-RESPONSIBILITY       PIC 99.
00040                  10  EMP-EXPERIENCE           PIC 9.
00041              05  FILLER                       PIC X(50).
00042          FD  PRINT-FILE
00043                  LABEL RECORDS ARE OMITTED
00044                  RECORD CONTAINS 133 CHARACTERS
00045                  DATA RECORD IS PRINT-LINE.
00046          01  PRINT-LINE.
00047              05  FILLER                       PIC X.
00048              05  DET-NAME                     PIC X(20).
00049              05  FILLER                       PIC XX.
00050              05  DET-LOCATION                 PIC X(13).
00051              05  FILLER                       PIC XX.
00052              05  DET-TITLE                    PIC X(14).
00053              05  FILLER                       PIC XX.
00054              05  DET-SALARY                   PIC $ZZ,ZZZ.00.
00055              05  FILLER                       PIC X(69).
00056          WORKING-STORAGE SECTION.
00057          01  WS-END-OF-FILE-SWITCHES.
00058              05  WS-END-OF-TITLE-FILE         PIC X(3)      VALUE 'NO'.
00059                  88  NO-MORE-TITLES                         VALUE 'YES'.
00060              05  WS-END-OF-EMPLOYEE-FILE      PIC X(3)      VALUE 'NO'.
00061                  88  NO-MORE-EMPLOYEES                      VALUE 'YES'.
00062          01  TITLE-TABLE-VARIABLES.
00063              05  WS-NUMBER-OF-TITLES          PIC 999       VALUE ZEROS.
00064              05  WS-TITLE-SUB    COMP         PIC S9(4)     VALUE 1.
00065          01  LOCATION-VALUE.
00066              05  FILLER          PIC X(16)    VALUE 'ATLATLANTA      '.
00067              05  FILLER          PIC X(16)    VALUE 'BOSBOSTON       '.
00068              05  FILLER          PIC X(16)    VALUE 'CHICHICAGO      '.
00069              05  FILLER          PIC X(16)    VALUE 'DETDETROIT      '.
00070              05  FILLER          PIC X(16)    VALUE 'KC KANSAS CITY  '.
00071              05  FILLER          PIC X(16)    VALUE 'LA LOSANGELES   '.
00072              05  FILLER          PIC X(16)    VALUE 'MINMINEAPOLIS   '.
00073              05  FILLER          PIC X(16)    VALUE 'NY NEW YORK     '.
00074              05  FILLER          PIC X(16)    VALUE 'PHIPHILADELPHIA '.
00075              05  FILLER          PIC X(16)    VALUE 'SF SAN FRANCISCO'.
00076          01  LOCATION-TABLE.
00077              05  LOCATIONS OCCURS 10 TIMES
00078                  INDEXED BY LOCATION-INDEX.
00079                  10  LOCATION-CODE            PIC X(3).
00080                  10  LOCATION-NAME            PIC X(13).
00081
00082          01  TITLE-TABLE.
00083              05  TITLES OCCURS 1 TO 999 TIMES
00084                  DEPENDING ON WS-NUMBER-OF-TITLES
00085                  ASCENDING KEY IS TITLE-CODE
00086                  INDEXED BY TITLE-INDEX.
00087                  10  TITLE-CODE               PIC X(4).
00088                  10  TITLE-NAME               PIC X(15).
00089
```

Figure 3.44 *cont.*

```
00090               01  SALARY-MIDPOINTS.
00091                   05  FILLER    PIC X(25)  VALUE '06000070000800009000010000'.
00092                   05  FILLER    PIC X(25)  VALUE '07000080000900010000011000012000'.
00093                   05  FILLER    PIC X(25)  VALUE '08000090000100001100012000'.
00094                   05  FILLER    PIC X(25)  VALUE '10000120001400016000018000'.
00095                   05  FILLER    PIC X(25)  VALUE '12000140001600018000020000'.
00096                   05  FILLER    PIC X(25)  VALUE '14000160001800020000022000'.
00097                   05  FILLER    PIC X(25)  VALUE '16000190002200025000028000'.
00098                   05  FILLER    PIC X(25)  VALUE '19000220002500028000031000'.
00099                   05  FILLER    PIC X(25)  VALUE '22000250002800031000034000'.
00100                   05  FILLER    PIC X(25)  VALUE '26000300003400038000042000'.
00101               01  SALARY-TABLE REDEFINES SALARY-MIDPOINTS.
00102                   05  SALARY-RESPONSIBILITY OCCURS 10 TIMES.
00103                       10  SALARY-EXPERIENCE OCCURS 5 TIMES
00104                                             PIC 9(5).
00105
00106               PROCEDURE DIVISION.
00107
00108               005-MAINLINE.
00109                   PERFORM 010-INITIALIZE-TITLES.
00110                   OPEN INPUT EMPLOYEE-FILE
00111                        OUTPUT PRINT-FILE.
00112                   READ EMPLOYEE-FILE
00113                       AT END MOVE 'YES' TO WS-END-OF-EMPLOYEE-FILE.
00114                   PERFORM 020-PROCESS-EMPLOYEE-RECORDS
00115                       UNTIL NO-MORE-EMPLOYEES.
00116                   CLOSE EMPLOYEE-FILE
00117                         PRINT-FILE.
00118                   STOP RUN.
00119
00120               010-INITIALIZE-TITLES.
00121                   OPEN INPUT TITLE-FILE.
00122                   READ TITLE-FILE
00123                       AT END MOVE 'YES' TO WS-END-OF-TITLE-FILE.
00124                   PERFORM 015-READ-TITLE-FILE
00125                       UNTIL NO-MORE-TITLES.
00126                   CLOSE TITLE-FILE.
00127
00128               015-READ-TITLE-FILE.
00129                   MOVE CARD-TITLE-CODE TO TITLE-CODE (WS-TITLE-SUB).
00130                   MOVE CARD-TITLE-NAME TO TITLE-NAME (WS-TITLE-SUB).
00131                   READ TITLE-FILE
00132                       AT END MOVE 'YES' TO WS-END-OF-TITLE-FILE
00133                   ADD 1 TO WS-TITLE-SUB.
00134                   ADD 1 TO WS-NUMBER-OF-TITLES.
00135
00136               020-PROCESS-EMPLOYEE-RECORDS.
00137
00138                   READ EMPLOYEE-FILE
00139                       AT END MOVE 'YES' TO WS-END-OF-EMPLOYEE-FILE.
00140                   MOVE SPACES TO PRINT-LINE.
00141
00142               *DETERMINE TITLE USING BINARY SEARCH
00143                   SEARCH ALL TITLES
00144                       AT END MOVE 'UNKNOWN' TO DET-TITLE
00145                       WHEN TITLE-CODE (TITLE-INDEX) = EMP-TITLE-CODE
00146                           MOVE TITLE-NAME (TITLE-INDEX) TO DET-TITLE.
00147
00148               *DETERMINE LOCATION USING LINEAR SEARCH
00149                   SET LOCATION-INDEX TO 1.
00150                   SEARCH LOCATIONS
00151                       AT END MOVE 'UNKNOWN' TO DET-LOCATION
00152                       WHEN EMP-LOC-CODE = LOCATION-CODE (LOCATION-INDEX)
00153                           MOVE LOCATION-NAME (LOCATION-INDEX) TO DET-LOCATION.
00154
```

Figure 3.44 *cont.*

```
00155            *USE DIRECT TABLE LOOKUP - NO SEARCH
00156                 MOVE SALARY-EXPERIENCE (EMP-EXPERIENCE, EMP-RESPONSIBILITY)
00157                      TO DET-SALARY.
00158
00159            * WRITE DETAIL LINE
00160                 MOVE EMP-NAME TO DET-NAME.
00161                 WRITE PRINT-LINE AFTER ADVANCING 2 LINES.
00162
```

Figure 3.44 cont.

```
         CHARLES SHORTT      0567CHI105
         SUSAN KELTIE        2345MIN063
         PAT COWEN           0111NY 041
         DAVE CAMPBELL       0951TTT014
         DIANA HORROCKS      0999ATL011
```

Figure 3.45 Test Data (Employee File).

```
              0111ANALYST
              0567AUDITOR
              0999DIRECTOR
              1345MANAGER
              2345PROGRAMMER
```

Figure 3.46 Test Data (Title File).

```
     CHARLES SHORTT     CHICAGO         AUDITOR       $42,000.00
     SUSAN KELTIE       MINEAPOLIS      PROGRAMMER    $18,000.00
     PAT COWEN          NEW YORK        ANALYST       $10,000.00
     DAVE CAMPBELL      UNKNOWN         UNKNOWN       $ 9,000.00
     DIANA HORROCKS     ATLANTA         DIRECTOR      $ 6,000.00
```

Figure 3.47 Intended Output.

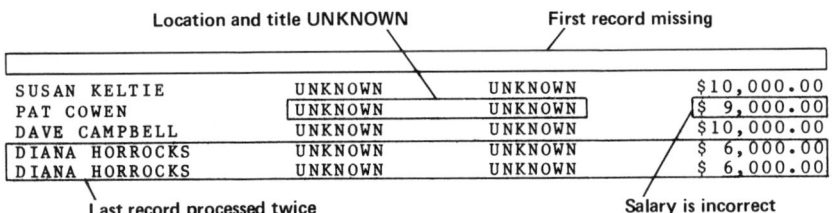

Figure 3.48 Actual Output.

Exercise 3.17: Procedure Division Potpourri

The program in Fig. 3.49 illustrates a variety of Procedure Division features in the context of a car billing problem. Processing specifications are as follows: Compute the money owed for each incoming customer record, where the amount due is a function of car type, days rented, and miles driven. Compact cars (C in column 41) are billed at 8 cents per mile and $7.00 a day, intermediate cars (I in column 41) cost 10 cents per mile and $8.00 per day, and full size cars (F in column 41) cost 12 cents per mile and $10.00 per day. Each incoming record is to be checked for valid data.

Car type must be C, I, or F, and both miles driven and days rented must be positive numbers. If any of these conditions are not met, the record should be bypassed and an appropriate error message indicated.

Each valid record is to appear on a separate line of a printed report with a maximum of 11 customers per page. An appropriate heading, including the date of execution, is to appear at the top of each page.

Test data are shown in Fig. 3.50, followed by *intended* output in Fig. 3.51, and the actual report (produced by the program) in Fig. 3.52. Correct all errors.

```
00001           IDENTIFICATION DIVISION.
00002           PROGRAM-ID.
00003               'CARS'.
00004           AUTHOR.
00005               ROBERT T. GRAUER.
00006
00007           ENVIRONMENT DIVISION.
00008           CONFIGURATION SECTION.
00009           SOURCE-COMPUTER.
00010               IBM-370.
00011           OBJECT-COMPUTER.
00012               IBM-370.
00013            SPECIAL-NAMES.
00014               C01 IS TOP-OF-PAGE.
00015
00016           INPUT-OUTPUT SECTION.
00017           FILE-CONTROL.
00018               SELECT RENTAL-RECORD-FILE
00019                   ASSIGN TO UT-S-SYSIN.
00020               SELECT PRINT-FILE
00021                   ASSIGN TO UT-S-SYSPRT.
00022
00023           DATA DIVISION.
00024           FILE SECTION.
00025
00026           FD  RENTAL-RECORD-FILE
00027               BLOCK CONTAINS 0 RECORDS
00028               LABEL RECORDS ARE OMITTED
00029               RECORD CONTAINS 80 CHARACTERS
00030               DATA RECORD IS RENTAL-RECORD.
00031
00032           01  RENTAL-RECORD            PIC X(80).
00033
00034           FD  PRINT-FILE
00035               BLOCK CONTAINS 0 RECORDS
00036               LABEL RECORDS ARE OMITTED
00037               RECORD CONTAINS 133 CHARACTERS
00038               DATA RECORD IS PRINT-LINE.
00039
00040           01  PRINT-LINE               PIC X(133).
00041
00042           WORKING-STORAGE SECTION.
00043           01  WS-END-OF-FILE-SWITCH    PIC XXX       VALUE 'NO'.
00044               88  WS-END-OF-FILE                     VALUE 'YES'.
00045           01  PAGE-AND-LINE-COUNTERS.
00046               05  WS-LINE-COUNT        PIC 99        VALUE 11.
00047               05  WS-PAGE-COUNT        PIC 99        VALUE ZERO.
00048           01  BILLINGS-CONSTANTS.
```

Figure 3.49 Car Billing Program.

```
00049              05  WS-MILEAGE-RATE       PIC 9V99.
00050              05  WS-DAILY-RATE         PIC 99V99.
00051              05  WS-CUSTOMER-BILL      PIC 9999V99.
00052
00053          01  DATE-WORK-AREA.
00054              05  TODAYS-YEAR           PIC 99.
00055              05  TODAYS-MONTH          PIC 99.
00056              05  TODAYS-DAY            PIC 99.
00057
00058          01  WS-CARD-IN.
00059              05  SOC-SEC-NUM           PIC 9(9).
00060              05  NAME-FIELD            PIC A(25).
00061              05  DATE-RETURNED         PIC 9(6).
00062              05  RENTAL-INFORMATION.
00063                  10  CAR-TYPE          PIC X.
00064                      88  COMPACT                        VALUE 'C'.
00065                      88  INTERMEDIATE                   VALUE 'I'.
00066                      88  FULL-SIZE                      VALUE 'F'.
00067                      88  VALID-CODES                VALUES ARE 'C' 'I'.
00068                  10  DAYS-RENTED       PIC 99.
00069                  10  MILES-DRIVEN      PIC 9(4).
00070              05  FILLER                PIC X(33).
00071
00072          01  WS-PRINT-LINE.
00073              05  FILLER                PIC X(4).
00074              05  SOC-SEC-NUM           PIC 999B99B9999.
00075              05  FILLER                PIC X(4).
00076              05  NAME-FIELD            PIC A(25).
00077              05  FILLER                PIC XX.
00078              05  CAR-TYPE              PIC X.
00079              05  FILLER                PIC X(4).
00080              05  DAYS-RENTED           PIC Z9.
00081              05  FILLER                PIC X(4).
00082              05  MILES-DRIVEN          PIC ZZZ9.
00083              05  FILLER                PIC X(4).
00084              05  CUSTOMER-BILL         PIC $$,$$9.99.
00085              05  FILLER                PIC X(59).
00086
00087          01  WS-HEADING-LINE-ONE.
00088              05  FILLER                PIC X(65)      VALUE SPACES.
00089              05  FILLER                PIC X(5)       VALUE 'PAGE '.
00090              05  WS-PAGE-PRINT         PIC ZZ9.
00091              05  FILLER                PIC X(60)      VALUE SPACES.
00093          01  WS-HEADING-LINE-TWO.
00094              05  FILLER                PIC X(20)      VALUE SPACES.
00095              05  TITLE-INFO            PIC X(33).
00096              05  FILLER                PIC XX         VALUE SPACES.
00097              05  TITLE-DATE.
00098                  10  TITLE-MONTH       PIC 99.
00099                  10  FILLER            PIC X          VALUE '/'.
00100                  10  TITLE-DAY         PIC 99.
00101                  10  FILLER            PIC X          VALUE '/'.
00102                  10  TITLE-YEAR        PIC 99.
00103              05  FILLER                PIC X(70)      VALUE SPACES.
00104
00105          01  WS-HEADING-LINE-THREE.
00106              05  FILLER                PIC X(8)       VALUE SPACES.
00107              05  FILLER                PIC X(11)      VALUE ' ACCT #'.
00108              05  FILLER                PIC XX         VALUE SPACES.
00109              05  FILLER                PIC X(4)       VALUE 'NAME'.
00110              05  FILLER                PIC X(19)      VALUE SPACES.
00111              05  FILLER                PIC X(4)       VALUE 'TYPE'.
00112              05  FILLER                PIC XX         VALUE SPACES.
00113              05  FILLER                PIC X(4)       VALUE 'DAYS'.
00114              05  FILLER                PIC XX         VALUE SPACES.
00115              05  FILLER                PIC X(5)       VALUE 'MILES'.
00116              05  FILLER                PIC X(4)       VALUE SPACES.
```

Figure 3.49 *cont.*

```
00117                05  FILLER              PIC X(6)      VALUE 'AMOUNT'.
00118                05  FILLER              PIC X(60)     VALUE SPACES.
00119           PROCEDURE DIVISION.
00121           A-MAINLINE.
00122               ACCEPT DATE-WORK-AREA FROM DATE.
00123               OPEN INPUT RENTAL-RECORD-FILE
00124                   OUTPUT PRINT-FILE.
00125               READ RENTAL-RECORD-FILE INTO WS-CARD-IN
00126                   AT END MOVE 'YES' TO WS-END-OF-FILE-SWITCH.
00127               PERFORM B-PROCESS-CUSTOMER-RECORDS
00128                   UNTIL WS-END-OF-FILE.
00129               CLOSE RENTAL-RECORD-FILE
00130                   PRINT-FILE.
00131               STOP RUN.
00132
00133           B-PROCESS-CUSTOMER-RECORDS.
00134               IF NOT VALID-CODES
00135                   DISPLAY 'INVALID CAR TYPE ' NAME-FIELD OF WS-CARD-IN
00136               ELSE
00137                   PERFORM C-COMPUTE-AND-WRITE
00138               READ RENTAL-RECORD-FILE INTO WS-CARD-IN
00139                   AT END MOVE 'YES' TO WS-END-OF-FILE-SWITCH.
00140
00141           C-COMPUTE-AND-WRITE.
00142               IF COMPACT
00143                   MOVE .08 TO WS-MILEAGE-RATE
00144                   MOVE 7.00 TO WS-DAILY-RATE
00145                   IF INTERMEDIATE
00146                       MOVE .10 TO WS-MILEAGE-RATE
00147                       MOVE 8.00 TO WS-DAILY-RATE
00148                   ELSE
00149                       MOVE .12 TO WS-MILEAGE-RATE
00150                       MOVE 10.00 TO WS-DAILY-RATE.
00151
00152               COMPUTE WS-CUSTOMER-BILL ROUNDED =
00153                   MILES-DRIVEN OF WS-CARD-IN * WS-MILEAGE-RATE
00154                   + DAYS-RENTED OF WS-CARD-IN * WS-DAILY-RATE
00155                   ON SIZE ERROR
00156                       DISPLAY 'RECEIVING FIELD TOO SMALL FOR BILL '
00157                           NAME-FIELD OF WS-CARD-IN.
00158
00159               IF WS-LINE-COUNT IS GREATER THAN 10
00160                   PERFORM D-PAGE-HEADING-ROUTINE.
00161               MOVE SPACES TO WS-PRINT-LINE.
00162               MOVE CORRESPONDING WS-CARD-IN TO WS-PRINT-LINE.
00163               INSPECT SOC-SEC-NUM OF WS-PRINT-LINE
00164                   REPLACING ALL ' ' BY '-'.
00165               MOVE WS-CUSTOMER-BILL TO CUSTOMER-BILL.
00166               WRITE PRINT-LINE FROM WS-PRINT-LINE
00167                   AFTER ADVANCING 2 LINES.
00168               ADD 1 TO WS-LINE-COUNT.
00169
00170           D-PAGE-HEADING-ROUTINE.
00171               ADD 1 TO WS-PAGE-COUNT.
00172               MOVE WS-PAGE-COUNT TO WS-PAGE-PRINT.
00173               WRITE PRINT-LINE FROM WS-HEADING-LINE-ONE
00174                   AFTER ADVANCING TOP-OF-PAGE.
00175               MOVE ' STACEY CAR RENTALS - REPORT DATE ' TO TITLE-INFO.
00176               MOVE TODAYS-DAY TO TITLE-DAY.
00177               MOVE TODAYS-MONTH TO TITLE-MONTH.
00178               MOVE TODAYS-YEAR TO TITLE-YEAR.
00179               WRITE PRINT-LINE FROM WS-HEADING-LINE-TWO
00180                   AFTER ADVANCING 1 LINES.
00181               WRITE PRINT-LINE FROM WS-HEADING-LINE-THREE
00182                   AFTER ADVANCING 1 LINES.
```

Figure 3.49 *cont.*

```
123456789BAKER,RG          091576C050345
987654321BROWN,PG          091476I102000
999999999JONES,PJ          091576I050345
987654555BROWNING,PJ       091776I102000
999777666ELSINOR,TR        091476C050345
987654390SMITH,PG          091776C039000
093477777BUTLER,JH         091776C050345
193456789SAMUELS,SH        091776C050345
456765456RAMSEY,ED         091776C040200
678123453SIEGEL,J          091976I060222
334422443BERGMAN,J         092076C020077
987654391SHERRY,KL         091676F109000
193456789BAKER,TT          091776C050345
```

Figure 3.50 Test Data.

```
                                                           PAGE    2
               STACEY CAR RENTALS - REPORT DATE  06/18/80
  ACCT #       NAME                    TYPE  DAYS  MILES  AMOUNT
987-65-4391    SHERRY,KL                F    10    9000   $1,180.00
193-45-6789    BAKER,TT                 C     5     345      $62.60
```

```
                                                           PAGE    1
               STACEY CAR RENTALS - REPORT DATE  06/18/80
  ACCT #       NAME                    TYPE  DAYS  MILES  AMOUNT
123-45-6789    BAKER,RG                 C     5     345      $62.60
987-65-4321    BROWN,PG                 I    10    2000     $280.00
999-99-9999    JONES,PJ                 I     5     345      $74.50
987-65-4555    BROWNING,PJ              I    10    2000     $280.00
999-77-7666    ELSINOR,TR               C     5     345      $62.60
987-65-4390    SMITH,PG                 C     3    9000     $741.00
093-47-7777    BUTLER,JH                C     5     345      $62.60
193-45-6789    SAMUELS,SH               C     5     345      $62.60
456-76-5456    RAMSEY,ED                C     4     200      $44.00
678-12-3453    SIEGEL,J                 I     6     222      $70.20
334-42-2443    BERGMAN,J                C     2      77      $20.16
```

Figure 3.51 Intended Output.

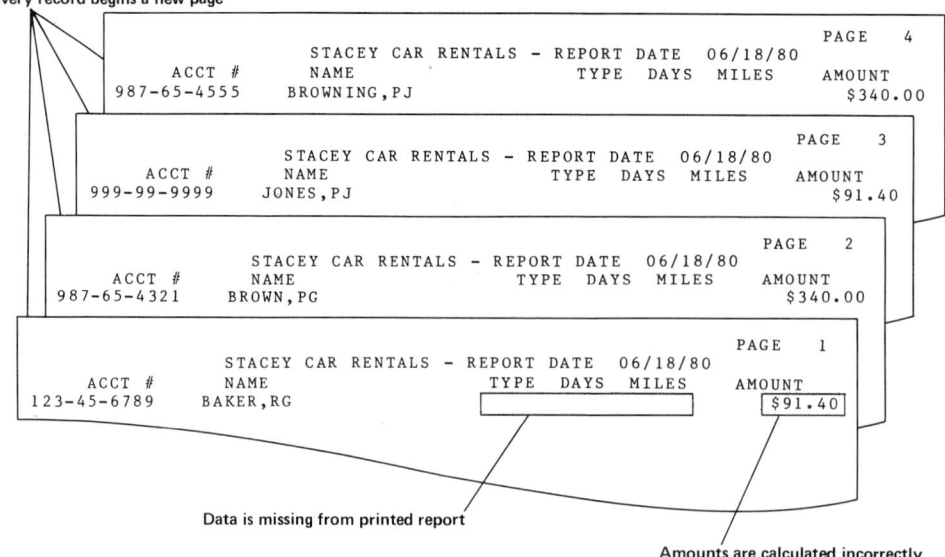

Figure 3.52 Actual (Invalid) Output.

```
INVALID CAR TYPE SHERRY,KL
INVALID CAR TYPE SHERRY,KL
INVALID CAR TYPE SHERRY,KL
INVALID CAR TYPE SHERRY,KL
INVALID CAR TYPE SHERRY,KL
INVALID CAR TYPE SHERRY,KL
INVALID CAR TYPE SHERRY,KL
INVALID CAR TYPE SHERRY,KL
INVALID CAR TYPE SHERRY,KL
INVALID CAR TYPE SHERRY,KL
INVALID CAR TYPE SHERRY,KL
INVALID CAR TYPE SHERRY,KL
INVALID CAR TYPE SHERRY,KL
INVALID CAR TYPE SHERRY,KL
INVALID CAR TYPE SHERRY,KL
INVALID CAR TYPE SHERRY,KL
INVALID CAR TYPE SHERRY,KL
  .
  .
  .
```

Display messages indicate an infinite loop the first time a full size car is encountered

Figure 3.52 *cont.*

Solutions

Exercise 3.1: Compilation Errors and Report Writer

Card 61 E PAGE-COUNT NOT DEFINED. DISCARDED . . .
Report Writer uses the COBOL reserved word PAGE-COUNTER, *not* PAGE-COUNT, to automatically increment page numbers.
Correction: Change PAGE-COUNT to PAGE-COUNTER in line 63. (Note that the entry beginning on line 61 ends on line 63.)

Card 86 E DETAIL REPORT GROUP SPECIFIED WITH NO DATA-NAME. CONTINUING . . .
As a rule, data names are not used in the Report Section. The exception is detail report groups where data names are required and tied to subsequent GENERATE statements (see line 141).
Correction: Modify line 86 to include the data name TRANSACTION-LINE (tied to line 141) after the 01 level number.

Card 88 E TR-NAME NOT DEFINED. DISCARDED . . .
Note that card 88 was flagged, whereas the actual statement extends from line 88 to line 90, with TR-NAME appearing in line 90. Collectively, these entries cause the value of the 20 position item beginning in column 2, is to be taken from a data name, TR-NAME. The problem is that TR-NAME was not previously defined.
Correction: Substitute TR-SALESMAN-NAME (defined in line 37) for TR-NAME in line 90.

Card 97 E CONTROL NAME NOT SPECIFIED IN RD. SKIPPING TO NEXT 01.
Line 97 requests a control footing whenever there is a break

on TR-SALESMAN-NAME. Unfortunately the CONTROLS clause of the RD did not specify TR-SALESMAN-NAME as a control field, hence the error.

Correction: Insert TR-SALESMAN-NAME at the end of line 50. This assumes that name is the minor field, and TR-SALESMAN-LOCATION the major field.

Card 118 E   INVALID TYPE CLAUSE. SKIPPING TO NEXT 01 . . . Line 118 indicates a control footing. The problem is that the field denoting the control break was not specified.

Correction: Judging by the literal in line 122, 'Final Total All Locations,' it appears that the control footing of line 118 is to occur only once at the end of the report. Hence, add the reserved word FINAL to the end of line 118.

Card 131 E   OPERAND FOR INITIATE NOT FOUND OR ILLEGAL. OPERAND DROPPED . . .
The INITIATE statement requires a report name which in turn is defined in the REPORT IS clause of an FD.

Correction: Change line 131 to read INITIATE CONTROL-BREAK.

Card 134 E   EXPECTING NEW STATEMENT. FOUND END. DELETING TILL NEXT VERB OR PROCEDURE-NAME . . .
The word END is in fact a COBOL reserved word, but only for use in the AT END clause of a READ statement. It has no business beginning a new sentence as on line 135.

Correction: Change line 135 to read TERMINATE CONTROL-BREAK.

Card 134 E   REPORT NAME ILLEGAL AS USED. DISCARDED . . .
A report name, CONTROL-BREAK, appears in either an INITIATE or TERMINATE statement, but not in a nonexistent END statement.

Correction: None required beside previous fix.

Card 141 E   OPERAND FOR GENERATE NOT FOUND. CLAUSE DROPPED . . .
The GENERATE statement references either a report name (for summary reporting) or a detail report group. The problem here is that TRANSACTION-LINE was not previously defined.

Correction: None required beside previous fix to line 86.

Exercise 3.2: Execution Errors and Report Writer

The first error, missing detail lines, illustrates the power of Report Writer and the ease with which changes can be made. All that is required is to modify line 129 to read GENERATE TRANSACTION-LINE, rather than GENERATE CONTROL-BREAK. Recall that the syntax of the GENERATE verb is:

$$\text{\underline{GENERATE}} \quad \begin{Bmatrix} \text{data-name} \\ \text{report-name} \end{Bmatrix}$$

If report-name is specified, as was done in Figure 3.2, then summary reporting takes palce; that is, detail records are appropriately totaled, but *not* printed. Under summary reporting, printing occurs only after a control break. If a data-name is specified in the GENERATE statement, detail report groups are printed in addition to control headings, footings, etc. (Note that a detail report group for TRANSACTION-LINE has already been defined in lines 86 through 96).

The missing location totals are a case of the programmer getting exactly what was asked, rather than what was intended. If location totals are desired, then a control footing on location must be specified. Accordingly, the following code should be included in the Report Section.

```
01    TYPE IS CONTROL FOOTING TR-SALESMAN-LOCATION.
   05    LINE NUMBER PLUS 2.
      10    COLUMN NUMBER 48
            PIC X(10)
            VALUE ALL '-'.
   05    LINE NUMBER PLUS 1.
      10    COLUMN NUMBER 4
            PIC X(14)
            VALUE 'LOCATION TOTAL'.
      10    COLUMN NUMBER 48
            PIC $$$$,999
            SUM SALESMAN-TOTAL.
```

The final error illustrates a weakness of release 2.1 of the OS/VS compiler. (Hopefully, the problem no longer exists.) Specifications for SALESMAN-TOTAL are provided in lines 102 through 105. The value of SALESMAN-TOTAL is obtained by summing TR-AMOUNT over all incoming records for each salesman. The sum will be edited and printed according to the picture clause $$,999 as specified in line 104. Hence, the *maximum* value of SALESMAN-TOTAL is $9,999. There is no problem for the first two salesmen, with totals of $5,042 and $5,500, respectively. However, the total for the third salesman is $10,575 which does *not* fit in the associated picture clause. Hence, the high order digits are truncated and $575 remains. The $10,000 is lost in the total for the third salesman as well as the final total. The solution is to expand the picture clause of line 104. The author believes that it would be desirable for the compiler to include a warning diagnostic to the effect that the picture clause of line 104 may be insufficient. No such message appeared.

Exercise 3.3: Execution Errors and Control Breaks

Control breaks are a frequent business application. *The author strongly believes they are best handled by Report Writer and encourages use of this often neglected facility.* Nevertheless, there are those, who for one reason or another, shun Report Writer and insist on developing their own logic. Although the requirements of multiple control breaks are not overpowering, they do contain several subtleties and the programmer is advised to proceed with caution.

To properly debug the program of Figure 3.3, it is necessary to precisely state the nature of the errors. These are:

1. Location total is cumulative: The total for the first location is correctly shown as $9,500. The total for the second location should be $9,300; instead it appears as $18,800 ($9,500 + $9,300). In similar fashion the total for the third location should be $8,500 and not $27,300 ($9,500 + $9,300 + $8,500). The problem results from a failure to reset the sales total for each new location to zero.

2. Salesman totals are printing incorrectly: The total of the previous salesman wrongly appears as the amount of the next transaction. For example, the total for PETER SMITH shows as $1,500, which is equal to the transaction amount for THOMAS TAYLOR.

The first error is corrected by resetting THIS-LOCATION-SALES to zero, as each new location is processed. The statement MOVE ZEROS TO THIS-LOCATION-SALES should be inserted as the first statement in the paragraph A000-PROCESS-ALL-LOCATIONS.

The problem of incorrect salesman totals is due either to improper calculation or printing the wrong field. Since salesman total prints consistently as the transaction amount of the next record, we are led to the second possibility. Accordingly, THIS-SALESMAN-SALES should be substituted for TR-AMOUNT in line 113.

Exercise 3.4: Compilation Errors and Sort

Card 36 W   LABEL CLAUSE IN SD IS TREATED AS COMMENTS IN OS. SKIPPING TO NEXT CLAUSE ...
A file defined in an SD, for example, SORT-FILE, is a *work* file that exists only for the duration of the job. Hence, the LABEL RECORDS clause has no meaning and is ignored.
Correction: Delete line 36.

Card 110 E   PRESENT-SALARY NOT UNIQUE. DISCARDED ...
PRESENT-SALARY is defined in line 30 (under EM-

PLOYEE-RECORD) and again in line 48 (under SORT-RECORD). Its use in line 111 is ambiguous and thus the error.

Correction: Qualify line 111 to read PRESENT-SALARY OF SORT-RECORD.

Card 110 E   SYNTAX REQUIRES SORT-KEY. FOUND SORT. STATEMENT DISCARDED . . .
Recall the previous error on line 110 which flagged PRESENT-SALARY as nonunique, and discarded it. PRESENT-SALARY OF SORT-RECORD was intended as a sort key and the omitted qualification caused the present diagnostic.

Correction: None required beyond the previous fix.

Card 110 E   SYNTAX REQUIRES SORT-FILE NAME . . . (appears twice)
Again a case of the compiler rubbing salt into the wound. Statement 110 was flagged four times, although only a single error, the nonunique data name used as a sort key, was made.

Correction: None required beyond the original fix. Note well, however, that when statement 110 is corrected, a *new* warning diagnostic will emerge, indicating that the Input Procedure on line 112 is a paragraph rather than a section. This error cannot be detected at present because the syntax of the SORT verb was wrecked by the nonunique data name used as a sort key.

Card 135 E   SYNTAX REQUIRES 01 LEVEL SD DATA-NAME IN RELEASE STATEMENT . . .
RELEASE is analogous to WRITE, hence one releases a record name, and not a file name.

Correction: Change line 135 to read RELEASE SORT-RECORD.

Card 145 E   SYNTAX REQUIRES SORT-FILE NAME . . .
RETURN is analogous to READ, hence one returns a file name, and not a record name.

Correction: Change line 145 to read RETURN SORT-FILE.

Card 158 E   EMPLOYEES-AGE NOT DEFINED AS PART OF SORT-RECORD. DISCARDED . . .
This error does not relate to sort per se, but is simply a case of misspelling a data name.

Correction: Change EMPLOYEES-AGE to EMPLOYEE-AGE in line 158.

Exercise 3.5: Execution Errors With SORT

This exercise illustrates execution errors associated with the SORT verb, the significance of a "missing" period, and use of the reserved word DATE.

The first problem is that age is calculated incorrectly. John Doe, the first record, was born in January 1943, yet his age shows as 24.5. (The program was run in 1979). The first thought is that the COMPUTE statement to calculate age (lines 137-139) is wrong, but that statement is *correct* as written. (The best way of verifying any statement is to plug in data. For example, using John Doe's birthdate of 1/43 and an execution date of 7/79, one should obtain an age of 36.5. Plugging these numbers into the COMPUTE statement does in fact yield 36.5 as expected (79 - 43 + (7 - 1) /12). After a while (the length of time depends on the skill of the individual), the programmer must realize that the COMPUTE statement is a dead end and look elsewhere. *If the COMPUTE itself is correct, then the data on which it operates must be incorrect, and* therein lies the problem. Any or all of the four data names used in the calculation are potential problems.

The date of execution, which includes TODAYS-YEAR and TODAYS-MONTH, is accepted into DATE-WORK-AREA from the reserved word DATE in line 127. The error is that DATE-WORK-AREA (defined in lines 76-79) does not conform to the reserved word DATE. The latter returns a six-digit field in the form yymmdd, and *not* as mmddyy as shown in lines 76 through 79. The problem is easily resolved by moving line 79 between lines 76 and 77. The second problem pertains to the order in which records appear. Since the SORT used birthdate, rather than age, the problem is *not* caused by difficulty with DATE-WORK-AREA. However, SORT-YEAR is a more important field than SORT-MONTH and should be designated as the *major* field in line 121. (Note that for employees to be listed in order of decreasing age, (oldest first), the sort on birth year must be *ascending* as correctly shown in line 121.)

The final error is that the program entered an infinite loop the first time that the record being processed was not a programmer. The Procedure Division is relatively short and straight forward, and gives no immediate indication as to why this would happen. After the sort has taken place, files are opened, a heading is written, and the first record is read. The routine 0020-PROCESS-EMPLOYEE-RECORDS will be performed until the data are exhausted, after which files are closed and the run terminated.

The only apparent way to go into an infinite loop is to somehow not read the next record and continue processing, ad infinitum, the current record. At first glance this does not seem possible, since the last statement of the performed routine is a correct READ. However, we were given one additional clue, that the loop occurred when the first *nonprogrammer* was processed.

Assume, for a second, that there were no period at the end of line 152. This would make the READ of line 153 part of the IF statement and cause its execution only if the current record were a programmer. Put another way, the READ would *not* be executed when a nonprogrammer was processed and an infinite loop would result. We have in effect explained the loop if there were no period in line 152. Unfortunately, there is a period, or is there? Count columns carefully and discover the period in line 152 is in column 73, which is ignored by the compiler and hence produces the infinite loop.

Lest this be taken as a contrived error, the author admits to inadvertently making it himself. He was preparing the exercise and had chosen to include only the first two problems. He was as surprised as anyone when the operator informed him of the infinite loop.

Exercise 3.6: Subprograms: 1

This exercise illustrates almost everything that can go wrong in a "simple" print program. Essentially the program is reading data in coded form, expanding it, doing simple calculations on specific fields, and printing the entire record in a more appealing format.

The resulting errors are adequately noted on the invalid report of Figure 3.12. Explanations are as follows:

1. Education and location are switched: The incoming codes for education and location, of 3 and 30 respectively, have been *correctly* expanded to 2 YR DEGREE and CHICAGO. The expansion was done in the subprogram in lines 102-105 for education, and lines 95-99 for location. Note well the different techniques which were used. The education code itself pointed directly to a position in a table, whereas a linear search was used for location. What then is the problem?

    The expansion was done in a subprogram. Hence, the order of the passed parameters must be *identical* in the CALL statement of the main program (lines 176 through 179) and the USING clause in the subprogram (lines 78 through 80). Closer examination will reveal that LS-EXPANDED-EDUCATION and LS-EXPANDED-LOCATION have been switched in the subprogram.

2. Title lookup failed: The incoming title code of 155 should print as ANALYST, rather than UNKNOWN. Since this expansion is done in the subprogram, attention is focused on the SEARCH ALL statement of lines 87 through 91. That statement is *correct* as written, and the order of passed parameters is also *correct,* leaving only one possible explanation. *If the statements to expand a code are proper but the expansion fails, then the data on which the statements operate must be improper.*

    Notice that the location and education tables are "hard-coded" in the subprogram, but that the title table is initialized from a file. The latter is a highly commendable practice as it eliminates the need for recompiling a program when the table changes. Unfortunately, it was not done correctly.

Execution of 010-INITIALIZE-TITLE-TABLE is properly controlled by a switch to limit its use to the first time the subprogram is entered. The routine opens the TITLE-FILE, reads the first record, and performs 020-READ-FROM-TITLE-FILE until there are no more records. The latter routine should move each new title into *successive* positions of TITLE-TABLE. TITLE-INDEX is initialized in line 113, but is never incremented as each new title is read, causing each new title to be rewritten in the same space as the previous title. The problem is solved by adding a VARYING clause to the PERFORM statement of line 116; i.e., VARYING TITLE-INDEX FROM 1 BY 1. This eliminates the need for the original SET statement. (It is also possible to retain the initial SET and add another, SET TITLE-INDEX UP BY 1 after line 126). Finally, note that the size of the table is dependent on WS-NUMBER-OF-TITLES as per the OCCURS DEPENDING ON clause of line 31. It is also necessary to insert the statement ADD 1 TO WS-NUMBER-OF-TITLES after line 126.

3. Performance should be POOR rather than UNKNOWN: The performance code is expanded in a nested IF in the main program in lines 181 through 189. The statement will correctly handle performance codes of 1 and 2, but fails if the code is 3. As the statement is presently written, POOR will be moved to PRT-PERFORMANCE whenever EMP-PERFORMANCE is 3, but it (POOR) will be immediately replaced by UNKNOWN. The correction requires insertion of the word ELSE between lines 188 and 189.

4. Hyphens missing in social security number: The social security number is invariably read as a nine-position numeric field, but printed as an 11-position field with embedded hyphens. One way of accomplishing this is to move the incoming numeric field with PIC 9(9) to an edit field with PIC 999B99B9999, and then replace the blanks with hyphens through an INSPECT statement. The problem in this instance is that the REPLACING clause in line 196 is backward; it should read REPLACING ALL ' ' BY ' –', rather than the other way around.

5. Months between salary increases are wrong: There should be 24 months shown between 11/78 and 11/76, rather than 2. This error is very straightforward and the reader should have little trouble in correcting the COMPUTE statement of lines 237 through 241 to read:

```
COMPUTE WS-MONTHS-BETWEEN-INCR ROUNDED
    = (EMP-SALARY-YEAR (SAL-INDEX)
        - EMP-SALARY-YEAR (SAL-INDEX + 1)) * 12
    + (EMP-SALARY-MONTH (SAL-INDEX)
        - EMP-SALARY-MONTH (SAL-INDEX + 1)).
```

There are, of course, equivalent ways to rewrite the COMPUTE statement. However, the reader is urged to plug in numbers by hand to assure the correctness of his solutions.
6. Third line of salary data missing: An easy error to find, provided one knows that the UNTIL condition of the PERFORM is tested *prior* to execution of the designated routine. In other words, execution ceases as soon as the UNTIL condition is met. Consequently, equal should be changed to greater than in line 208 in Fig. 3.14.

Exercise 3.7 Subprograms: 2

This exercise aptly demonstrates a major consideration in testing procedure, that *the programmer should compute expected results by hand prior to running a test.* Failure to do this can result in the program output biasing the test, especially if it "looks right."

The transcript for the first record Benjamin, is correct in every way. The second transcript for Smith, has average calculated incorrectly. It should be 2.00 (Smith received all Cs), but it shows as 0.00. There is a problem in calculating average, yet it doesn't affect every average as Benjamin's correctly printed as 4.00. A logical guess is that the problem relates to the grade of C.

The reader should turn his attention to the subprogram where grade point average is calculated. Consider lines 59-62 in which a letter grade is converted to a numerical value. All appears correct except the *period is missing at the end of line 60.* The effect of this omission is to convert the two IF statements in lines 60 and 61 to a *nested* IF. Consequently whenever a grade of B is read, 3 is moved to WS-MULTIPLIER and a test is made to see whether the current grade is a C. (It isn't because the grade is compared to C, only after it has already been determined to be a B.) *There is no way to check for a grade of C without first getting a B, an impossible situation.* Hence, WS-MULTIPLIER will always remain at zero whenever there is a grade of C. Insertion of a period in line 60 solves the problem.

Moving on to Borow's transcript, we find that average incorrectly prints as 4.00. Borow received a B in course 999, and his computed average should be 3.75. The missing period in line 60 has nothing to do with this problem.

The calculation of a 4.00 average is correct if only the first three grades are considered, as Borow did receive A's in these courses. The procedure for calculating average apparently *ignores the last* course. Look carefully at the PERFORM statement of lines 47 through 49 which invokes the routine 010-COMPUTE-QUALITY-POINTS. The PERFORM/VARYING/ UNTIL statement tests the condition *before* executing the performed routine, and execution ceases as soon as the condition is satisfied. Put another way, 010-COMPUTE-QUALITY-POINTS is performed *one less time* than the value of ST-NUMBER-OF-COURSES due to the *equal* sign in line 49. The solution is to change the equal to a greater than condition. Note that while this problem existed for the first record, Benjamin, it did not affect the calculated average as Benjamin received all As, and ignoring his last course didn't matter.

The transcript for the last record, Milgrom, M, is printed twice. This is due to mistaken use of the priming read in a structured program. The *correct* structure is to have an *initial* read in the mainline routine, and a second read as the *last* statement of the performed routine (as was shown in the skeletal COBOL outline in Sect. 1). The *incorrect* structure used here has a single read (line 100) as the first statement of the performed routine. To better understand the consequence of this *incorrect* structure, consider a file containing only a single record.

The mainline routine opens the files and performs 020-PROCESS-CARDS until there are no more records. The performed routine reads the first record from the one-record file, and proceeds to print a transcript. The perform ends but the end of file has not been sensed so 020-PROCESS-CARDS is reentered. The first statement is again the READ of line 100, which senses the end of file. However, processing is in the middle of the perform when the end of file is sensed, so it wrongly continues with the record in hand and a second transcript is printed. The problem is eliminated by adhering to the skeletal COBOL outline as explained earlier.

There is yet another problem with the Milgrom transcript. Milgrom's major code is 1400 which corresponds to Biology (line 75) and is *not* unknown. Note well that Benjamin's major is also Biology and printed as such. What happened to the table lookup between the first and last records?

The answer is simple. A linear SEARCH, lines 107-110, must be initialized with a SET statement prior to every execution. The initialization took place for the first record by the SET statement in the mainline routine, but that SET was executed only once. When subsequent searches for the second and third records moved past Biology in the table, the effect of the initialization was destroyed. When the SEARCH statement was entered for Milgrom, it began where the search for the previous record (Borow) ended, i.e., at code 3960. Consequently, Milgrom's code of 1400 could not be found. The correction is made by moving the SET statement of line 93 between lines 106 and 107, prior to the SEARCH statement.

Exercise 3.8: Sequential File Maintenance

The first requirement of the exercise is to indicate what the *correct* output should be. This is essential in any testing procedure and anticipated results are shown in Fig. 3.53 and Fig. 3.54, respectively.

```
111111111ADAMS              015000
222222222BAKER              028000
400000000NEW EMPLOYEE       016000
444444444MILGROM            040000
555555555BENJAMIN           100000
```

Figure 3.53 Valid New Master File.

```
610000000NEW EMPLOYEE II              018000
666666666SHERRY                       007500
777777777BOROW                        055000
888888888JAMES                        017500
999999999RENAZEV                      030000
```

Figure 3.53 cont.

```
ERROR - NO MATCH                500000000       JONES
ERROR - RECORD ALREADY IN FILE  888888888       JAMES
```

Figure 3.54 Valid Error Messages.

As can be seen from Figures 3.23 and 3.24, the actual results are quite different from the intended results. A good place to begin analysis is with the construction of a hierarchy chart to show how the program is intended to function. Consider the chart shown in Figure 3.55:

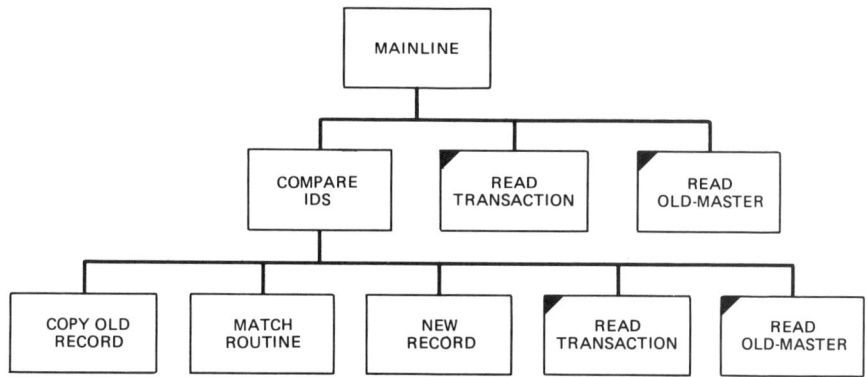

Figure 3.55 Hierarchy Chart.

The COMPARE-IDS module effectively drives the entire program by comparing social security numbers on the old master and transaction files, and deciding which lower level routine to call. Comparison of the actual and incorrect outputs indicates problems in both the MATCH and NEW-RECORD routines.

The NEW-RECORD module failed to create records in the new master file for NEW EMPLOYEE and NEW EMPLOYEE II, flagging them instead as errors. The routine appears in lines 120 through 128. It contains an IF/ELSE statement to determine whether a record should be added to the new file or flagged as a NO MATCH. The problem is that the detail lines under IF and ELSE have been *reversed*. In other words, when the social security number of a record on the transaction file is not found in the old master, *and* the transaction code is an addition, then the transaction record should be written to the new master. The correction is made by taking the WRITE statement on line 127 and moving it directly after the IF of line 121, and simultaneously placing the statements on lines 122 through 125 after the ELSE on line 126.

The incorrect IF statement also produced a second problem; incorrectly adding a record to the new master. The incoming transaction file contained an intended salary change for Jones, social security number 500000000. This should have resulted in a "No Match" as the social security number was not present in the old master. The NEW-RECORD routine was correctly entered, but because the IF statement of lines 121 through 127 was reversed, Jones was incorrectly added to the new master.

The MATCH-ROUTINE is intended to change the salary field in the new master record for a transaction code of C, provided that record already exists in the old master. Baker, for example, (social security number 222222222) should have had the salary field updated from 25000 to 28000. The program failed to do this and attention is focused on the MATCH-ROUTINE (lines 102 through 118). The nested IF determines the transaction code and takes appropriate action. The problem occurs on a transaction code of C (condition-name SALARY-CHANGE) in that lines 111 and 112 are switched. The new record is written first with the *old* salary, *after which the salary field is corrected but not written.*

A fourth and final error results in records randomly disappearing from the master file for no apparent reason, for example, Milgrom with social security number 444444444. This record existed in the old master, did not have a matching transaction, and was *not* written to the new master. Note, however, that both Adams and Renazev, with social security numbers 111111111 and 999999999, existed in the old master, did not have matching transactions either, but were correctly written to the new master. This observation leads to the conclusion that the COPY-OLD-RECORD module is correct in and of itself. The problem must reside somewhere else, and there is no immediate hint where to look. The only means of solution is to "play computer" and attempt to recreate what happened.

The program establishes two switches in Working-Storage, in lines 39 and 40, to control which file(s) will be read next. The Procedure Division opens all files, then reads the initial record from both the old master and transaction files. It performs 010-COMPARE-IDS until both input files are empty, after which processing terminates.

The first old master and transaction records have social security numbers of 111111111 and 222222222, respectively, leading to the execution of 050-COPY-OLD-RECORD. This module correctly copies Adams (social security number 111111111) to the new master and sets the switch to read another record from the old master file. Control returns from 050-COPY-OLD-RECORD to line 90. Recall the value of WS-TRANS-READ-SWITCH was initialized to NO, and further that its value has not yet been changed. Hence, no read takes place in the transaction file and the previous transaction, social security number 222222222 is retained. The value of WS-OLD-MAST-READ-SWITCH was also initialized to NO, but reset to YES in line 100 of 050-COPY-OLD-REC, causing a new record to be read from the old master.

The COMPARE-IDS routine is re-entered. This time the social security numbers are equal (both are 222222222) and 060-MATCH-ROUTINE is invoked. Both switches are set to YES in lines 117 and 118, causing new records to be taken from each file in lines 90 through 95. Coincidentally, the same social security number, 333333333, is read from each file. 060-MATCH-ROUTINE is again invoked, both switches are again set to YES, and two new records are read with social security numbers of 400000000 and 444444444 in the transaction and old master file, respectively. *Note well that WS-TRANS-READ-SWITCH is reset to NO, but that WS-OLD-MAST-READ-SWITCH remains at YES.*

When the current records are compared 070-NEW-RECORD is entered, because 400000000 is less than 444444444. This routine ends by resetting WS-TRANS-READ-SWITCH to YES (line 128) and returning control to line 90. A new transaction record is *correctly* read in lines 90 through 92. A new old master record is *incorrectly* read in lines 90 and 91, overlaying the previous record with social security number 444444444, *before this record was copied to the new master.* The problem occurred because WS-OLD-MAST-READ-SWITCH is *permanently* set to YES, causing a record to be read from the old master *every* time 010-COMPARE-IDS is entered. The solution is to reset the switch to NO by inserting MOVE 'NO' to WS-OLD-MAST-READ-SWITCH after line 94.

Exercise 3.9: Nonsequential Maintenance

Comparison of this exercise with the previous problem is an effective means of distinguishing between sequential and nonsequential file maintenance. *In sequential processing, every record in the old master is rewritten to the new master, regardless of whether it changes. In nonsequential processing, only those records which actually change are rewritten.* Sequential processing makes use of two distinct master files, an old and a new, which function as input and output files, respectively. Nonsequential processing uses a single file which serves as both input and output. Finally, sequential maintenance is driven by comparing the record key from the old master and transaction files. Nonsequential maintenance merely processes the transaction file until it is empty. With this as background, we are ready to discuss specifics of the exercise.

Analysis begins by determining what the intended output should be. Accordingly, if the program worked correctly it would have produced the new master and error messages shown in Fig. 3.56 and Fig. 3.57, respectively.

```
111111111ADAMS                      015000
222222222BAKER                      028000
333333333ZIDROW                     008000
400000000NEW EMPLOYEE               016000
444444444MILGROM                    040000
555555555BENJAMIN                   100000
```

Figure 3.56 Valid New Master File.

```
610000000NEW EMPLOYEE II            018000
777777777BOROW                      055000
888888888JAMES                      017500
999999999RENAZEV                    030000
```

Figure 3.56 *cont.*

```
NO MATCH                  500000000       JONES
RECORD ALREADY IN FILE    888888888       JAMES
```

Figure 3.57 Valid Error Messages.

The program appears to work correctly for the first four transactions, up to and including NEW EMPLOYEE II. Sherry should have been deleted and Borow was to have his salary updated. Instead both records were flagged NO MATCH, implying that their social security numbers, 666666666 and 777777777, were not found in the master file. Finally, James, with social security number 888888888, should have been flagged as a duplicate addition, but no message appeared.

These errors all have a common origin, *failure to reset WS-INVALID-SWITCH*. In line 81, the social security number of the current transaction is moved to the RECORD KEY field of the indexed file. The READ statement in line 82 attempts to find an indexed record with this value. If the record does not exist in the indexed file, then WS-INVALID-SWITCH is set to YES, implying either an addition for a new record or a miscopied social security number (a no match) for an existing record. The IF statement of lines 84 through 87 tests the value of this switch (through an 88-level entry) and invokes an appropriate lower level routine. *The problem occurs because WS-INVALID-SWITCH is never reset to NO.* Consequently, when the INVALID KEY condition is raised for the first time, it is *permanently* on. The result is that the IF statement on line 84 will *always* invoke 070-NEW-RECORD. As can be seen from lines 103 through 112, any transaction which is not an addition will result in a NO MATCH message, regardless of whether that record exists.

The solution is to insert the statement MOVE 'NO' TO WS-INVALID-SWITCH as the first line in 070-NEW-RECORD. A good rule of thumb is to immediately reset a switch whenever an action is taken because that switch has a particular value.

This correction will fully resolve the problems associated with Borow and James, but an additional change is needed to successfully delete Sherry from the new master. In sequential processing a record can be *implicitly* deleted from the new master simply by not writing it. In nonsequential maintenance, the record must be *explicitly* deleted through the DELETE verb in the ANS 74 standard. Accordingly, the nested IF of lines 92 through 100 should be expanded to include ELSE IF DELETION DELETE VSAM-FILE. (Note that ISAM files under IBM operating systems do not adhere to the ANS 74 standard and hence do not use the DELETE verb. Instead, HIGH-VALUES are moved to the first byte of an ISAM record, after which the record is rewritten.)

Exercise 3.10: Two-File Merge: 1

Our analysis begins by comparing the actual (and incorrect) output with the intended version. One should notice immediately that the actual output is considerably shorter than what was expected. The merged file contained only 7 records as opposed to the 12 that were intended, although the records which were present appeared in proper sequence. In addition, one error message, instead of two resulted.

Since there is no indication of what went wrong, we begin at the start of the Procedure Division. Files are opened, and the first record from each input file is read in the mainline paragraph. Next 010-PROCESS-FILES is performed until *both* files are out of data.

This routine is driven by the nested IF of lines 70 through 80, which compares ID-numbers from the two input files. If the first file is less than the second, then the merged record is written from the first file, and a switch is set to read a new record from the first file only. Conversely, if the second file is less than the first, the merged record is written from the second file and a switch is set for the second file. If the ID-numbers are equal, an error message is displayed and switches are set for both files. The nested IF is *correct* as written and typical of sequential file processing. The problem therefore must reside somewhere else, perhaps in either or both of the IF statements in lines 82 through 90.

The IF statement, beginning in line 82 tests the value of WS-READ-INPUT-ONE-SWITCH. If the switch is equal to "YES," it is correctly set to "NO." The indentation in line 84 *implies* that the READ will be executed only if the switch were equal to "YES," but the period in line 83 causes *the READ to be executed regardless of the value of the switch.* A similar situation exists for the IF statement beginning in line 87.

Could these two extra periods account for all our difficulty? The answer is again found by "playing computer." The initial reads cause records with IDs of 100000000 and 111111111 to be read from file 1 and 2, respectively. The nested IF causes the first merged record to be written with an ID of 100000000, and the periods cause a new record to be read from *both* files. The IDS being processed are now 200000000 for both file 1 and file 2 (note that record 111111111 has disappeared). An error message is written as the IDs are equal, and two more records are read. This time the ID on file 2, 211111111, is less than the ID on file 1, 300000000, so that record 211111111 is written to the merged file. A new record is read again from *both* files causing record 300000000 to disappear. The reader should be able to verify the rest of the output.

Exercise 3.11: Two-File Merge: 2

As in exercise 3.10, we are given a head start in that the intended output is provided. This time the merged file is seen to contain duplicate ID numbers which did not exist in the original input. Our attention therefore should be immediately focused on the statement(s) which write records to the merged file, the nested IF of lines 68 through 78.

If WS-REC-ONE-ID is less than WS-REC-TWO-ID, then the merged record is *correctly* written from the first file (lines 68 and 69). However, if WS-REC-TWO-ID is less than WS-REC-ONE-ID, the merged record is also written from the first file (lines 72 and 73). In other words, merged records are *always* written from the first file, regardless of the results of the comparison. The correction is made by changing line 73 to read FROM INPUT-RECORD-TWO.

Does this account for all the errors? The reader should notice that the correct output shows a total of 12 records in the merged file, whereas only 10 records are present in the actual output. In addition, even though records from the first file are written to the merged file, record 800000000 which is present in the first file, is missing from the output. Hence, there must be *another* error which causes processing to terminate prematurely.

The second error is not in 010-PROCESS-FILES, but rather in the statement which invokes that paragraph. Closer inspection of the PERFORM statement in lines 58 through 60 reveals that the perform will be terminated when *either* file is empty, rather than when *both* files are empty. The compound condition in the UNTIL clause should read AND, rather than OR.

Exercise 3.12: Incorrect Use of a Group Move

There are several distinct forms of internal data representation. It is the COBOL USAGE clause which determines actual storage allocation. This exercise illustrates difficulties that can arise when one loses sight of these considerations.

The program produces the expected values for FIRST-BINARY, FIRST-DISPLAY, and FIRST-PACKED. The value of SECOND-DISPLAY is also 1, but the value of SECOND-BINARY is 3855, and attempted execution of statement 35 (to calculate SECOND-PACKED) resulted in job termination and subsequent dump. Why? Simply stated, the difficulties with SECOND-BINARY and SECOND-PACKED are caused by the group move of line 30. *All group moves are treated as alphanumeric moves,* causing the "wrong" kind of zeros to be moved to SECOND-BINARY and SECOND-PACKED. In effect these fields are not initialized to zero at all.

To fully understand the ensuing explanation requires a knowledge of assembler fundamentals. SECOND-DISPLAY, SECOND-BINARY, and SECOND-PACKED will be assigned lengths of 4, 2, and 3 bytes, respectively.

The MOVE ZEROS statement in line 30 is a group move, hence alphanumeric (EBCDIC) zeros are moved to the three fields as follows:

SECOND-DISPLAY | F0 | F0 | F0 | F0 |

SECOND-BINARY | F0 | F0 |

SECOND-PACKED | F0 | F0 | F0 |

Now consider COBOL statement 31, ADD 1 TO SECOND-BINARY. The compiler generates the instructions to do "binary addition" and the contents of SECOND-BINARY, before and after, are shown in binary:

```
SECOND-BINARY (Before)      1111 0000  1111 0000
SECOND-BINARY (After)      +0000 0000  0000 0001
                            1111 0000  1111 0001
```

Since the high order bit in the sum is a "1," the sum is negative and stored in twos complement form. However, since SECOND-BINARY is defined as an *unsigned* field (COBOL line 16), the minus sign is dropped after the twos complement is obtained.

```
SECOND-BINARY (after addition)   1111 0000 1111 0001
Reverse 0's and 1's              0000 1111 0000 1110
Add 1                          +                    1
                                 0000 1111 0000 1111
```

The twos complement is converted to a hex 0F0F, then to its decimal value of 3855; the latter is the displayed value.

As to the failure of statement 35 to execute, and the resulting data exception, realize that SECOND-PACKED is designated a packed field by the clause, COMP-3. Packed fields require a sign as the low order hex digit. Valid signs are a hex "C" or "F" for positive numbers, and a hex "D" for negative numbers. Anything else is invalid as a sign and will cause problems in subsequent execution. *Specifically, any attempt to do arithmetic on a packed field with an invalid sign will invariably fail and produce a data exception.*

The field, SECOND-PACKED, has been initialized by the group move to contain F0F0F0. The low order hex digit is "0" which is invalid as a sign. Hence, attempted execution of the COBOL ADD in statement 35 failed. Complete explanation requires knowledge of base displacement addressing, and BAL instruction formats, topics which are covered in Sect. 7.

Exercise 3.13: Incorrect Use of the SEARCH Verb

A binary search requires that the table to be searched have its keys in sequence (either ascending or descending), whereas no special order is necessary for a linear search. Essentially the binary procedure eliminates half the table in each attempt at finding a match. A linear search, on the other hand, looks at one element at a time. Obviously, the larger the table, the more advantageous the binary search becomes. For example, in a table of 100 elements, the binary approach would require no more than 7 comparisons, whereas a linear search could take as many as 100! In a 1000 element table the corresponding numbers are 10 and 1000 respectively! *The key to implementing a binary search is that the incoming table have its keys in sequence.* Failure to do this could cause the binary search to fail.

In the exercise, a table of location codes has been established in lines 16-26. The ASCENDING KEY clause of line 30 requires that the codes be in ascending order. The first nine codes are fine, but the tenth code (045 for DENVER) is out of sequence. SEARCH ALL is implemented in COBOL line 38 for New York, and again in line 44 for Denver. The first search is successful, the second is not, even though a linear search for Denver in COBOL line 51 was also successful.

Admittedly, this particular example is contrived in that a cursory examination of the program quickly reveals that the location codes are out of sequence. However, the author has seen countless instances where a binary search fails because the table is not in order. This is particularly true in fluid situations where additional codes are constantly added to existing tables. The solution is obvious and easy to implement. Include a housekeeping routine to verify proper sequence of table codes in any and all programs utilizing a binary search.

The exercise also contains a common error in relation to the linear search, namely failure to initialize the associated index. A linear search is initiated in COBOL lines 51 and 57 for Denver and New York, respectively. The linear search for Denver was successful, whereas the search for New York failed. It is the responsibility of the programmer to establish an entry point within the table for a linear search. This was done for Denver, by the SET statement in line 50. It was *not* done for New York; thus the search of line 57 begins with whatever value happens to be in LOCATION-INDEX. LOCATION-INDEX was last effected by the linear search for Denver. Since Denver is past New York in the table, a match was not found and the AT END condition is reached.

Exercise 3.14: Incorrect Use of Signed Numbers

The inclusion of an "S" in a numeric picture clause significantly affects the way in which the numeric field is subsequently manipulated. Inclusion of the "S" generally results in more efficient object code, but can produce "strange" output if signed fields are printed directly. *Omission of the "S" will produce incorrect algebraic results when negative numbers are expected.*

In the problem at hand, customer orders are always shipped if the remaining quantity on hand (the amount left after subtraction of the current order) is greater than zero (see lines 63-64). Processing is terminated when the remaining stock falls below zero. Initial stock is set at 100 via the VALUE clause in line 39.

Output for six customers is shown. Note well that the total amount shipped is 250, which is 150 units more than the initial allocation! The problem stems from the COBOL definition of WS-QUANTITY-ON-HAND as PIC 9(3) in line 39. *Simply stated, COBOL does not allow an unsigned numeric field to assume a negative value;* hence, the remaining stock on hand will never fall below zero. Subtraction is done according to regular algebraic rules in line 61, but any time the result of the subtraction becomes negative, the answer is automatically made positive.

John Jones is the first customer processed. After his order of 55 is taken, WS-QUANTITY-ON-HAND is equal to 45 (100 - 55). Next the 30 units of Peter Smith are subtracted, leaving 15 as the value of WS-QUANTITY-ON-HAND. At this point, Jeff Borow enters the system with an order of 40 units. We would expect the subtraction to yield a result of -25 (15 - 40). *However, since WS-QUANTITY-ON-HAND was defined as an unsigned number, its value is always made positive.* Consequently, the expected -25 is converted to a +25 and processing continues.

The correction is simple; merely include a sign in the picture clause of line 39, PIC S9(3).

Exercise 3.15: Incorrect Use of Output Buffers

This mistake is one that most beginners make at least once. The program itself is rather simple, it reads from a card file and creates a disk file. Incoming records are read in line 44, moved in line 47, and written in line 49. Lines 48 and 50 display the contents of the output area before and after writing to the disk. What could be easier?

The output shows the display messages produced by the program. Peter Jones is the first record shown. However, when the output area is displayed immediately after writing, we see John Smith, rather than Peter Jones. Then Henry Brown is the next input record and when the output area is displayed after writing, Peter Jones reappears.

The explanation is as follows. There are two output areas or output buffers, as per the RESERVE 1 ALTERNATE AREA clause in line 16. (One alternate area is the usual default for most compilers; this problem would probably occur with or without the RESERVE ALTERNATE AREA clause.)

Execution of a WRITE automatically causes a "pointer" to switch to the alternate area. The situation is shown schematically in Fig. 3.58.

Step 1 - PETER JONES has been read and moved to I-O area. Line 48 executes PETER JONES DISK-NAME BEFORE WRITING.

| PETER JONES | JOHN SMITH |

↖ pointer

Step 2 - PETER JONES has been written in line 49 causing I-O pointer to move. Line 50 executes: JOHN SMITH DISK-NAME AFTER WRITING.

| PETER JONES | JOHN SMITH |

↗ pointer

Step 3 - HENRY BROWN has been read as next record and moved to I-O area replacing JOHN SMITH. Line 48 executes: HENRY BROWN DISK-NAME BEFORE WRITING.

| PETER JONES | HENRY BROWN |

↗ pointer

Step 4 - HENRY BROWN has been written in line 49 causing I-O pointer to move. Line 50 executes: PETER JONES DISK-NAME AFTER WRITING.

| PETER JONES | HENRY BROWN |

↖ pointer

Figure 3.58 Use of Alternate Buffers.

There is no correction per se to the exercise. One must simply know *not to reference an I/O area after a WRITE has occurred.*

Exercise 3.16: Table Processing

The table lookups for location and title appear as UNKNOWN. A logical starting point for the location error is in the SEARCH routine of lines 148 through 153. After some soul searching, the reader may conclude that there is *absolutely nothing wrong* with these statements. What then is the problem? Simply this: *if there is nothing wrong with the logic of the table lookup (lines 148 through 153) then there must be something wrong with the table itself.* Attention should shift, therefore, to lines 65 through 80, where the table is initialized. Recall the Capsule Summary of the SEARCH verb from Sect. 2, which showed one technique of table initialization. Codes and corresponding expansions are first put into memory through repeated use of VALUE clauses. Next, these entries are collectively given a new name through a single REDEFINES clause, which in turn has a table defined under it. This rather involved scheme is mandated because COBOL does not permit the same entry to contain both an OCCURS and a VALUE clause. A closer look at line 76 reveals that the *REDEFINES clause has been omitted. Hence, LOCATION-VALUE and LOCATION-TABLE do not reference the same locations, which means the table was never initialized.*

Analogous reasoning applies to the title table. The reader first turns to lines 142 through 146 where the binary search is implemented. Again, nothing is wrong with the table lookup, so the problem must reside within the table itself. This time, however, the table is not initialized in the Data Division (space is merely allocated in lines 82 through 88) but rather by reading values from a file (lines 120 through 134). The logic is intended to read a code and expanded value from TITLE-FILE, move both to the appropriate place in the table indicated by the current value of WS-TITLE-SUB, increment WS-TITLE-SUB by 1, and repeat the process. The problem is that WS-TITLE-SUB is incremented only after the end of file has been reached, rather than every time a code is read. *The ADD statement of line 133 is taken as part of the AT END clause because a period is missing at the end of line 132.*

Salary is to be determined from a two-level table, which is *correctly* defined in lines 90 through 104. Two subscripts are required for responsibility and experience *in that order*. The MOVE statement of line 156 has the subscripts in *reverse* order, causing erroneous values to be pulled from the table.

Finally, the problems of the duplicate last record and missing first record are related. A correct program structure calls for an initial (or priming) read, with the *last* statement of the performed routine as a second read. (See the Capsule Summary of Sect. 1.) The priming read is correctly placed (lines 112 and 113) but the read of lines 138 and 139 should be moved to the end of 020-PROCESS-EMPLOYEE-RECORDS, after line 161.

Exercise 3.17: Procedure Division Potpourri

The problem of every record appearing on a new page is easily solved. A page heading routine typically tests the value of a line counter (as was done in lines 159 and 160). The error is that the value of WS-LINE-COUNT is *not* reset to zero, so that D-PAGE-HEADING-ROUTINE is executed for every record. The solution is to add a statement, MOVE ZEROS TO WS-LINE-COUNT after line 170.

The missing data on car type, days rented, and miles driven is more subtle. The MOVE CORRESPONDING statement of line 162 is intended to move identical data names, *including* CAR-TYPE, DAYS-RENTED, and MILES-DRIVEN, from WS-CARD-IN to WS-PRINT-LINE. However, *the fine print in a COBOL manual states that the MOVE CORRESPONDING is effective only if the data-names in both source and receiving field have identical qualification* (excluding the names of the corresponding 01 records). Note well the presence of RENTAL-INFORMATION in the description of WS-CARD-IN (line 62) and its absence in WS-PRINT-LINE. Hence, the qualification is different and no moves take place for these fields. Note however, that SOC-SEC-NUM and NAME-FIELD do have identical qualification in both WS-CARD-IN and WS-PRINT-LINE, and those moves take place as intended.

An infinite loop resulted the first time a full size car was processed, causing the endless set of DISPLAY messages. The problem is that the READ statement of lines 138 and 139 is no longer executed once a full size car is processed, because *the READ is taken as part of the ELSE*. In other words, as long as incoming records were valid, the IF/ELSE statement beginning on line 134 invoked C-COMPUTE-AND-WRITE, and then read the next record. However, as soon as an invalid code was encountered, the DISPLAY message resulted, and the infinite loop began. A partial solution, therefore, is to insert a period at the end of line 137. This does not, however, account for the fact that a car type of F *incorrectly* registers as an invalid code. The latter problem is corrected by expanding the definition of VALID-CODES in line 67 to include the letter F.

The final error pertains to the incorrect bills which are calculated for all records. WS-MILEAGE-RATE and WS-DAILY-RATE are functions of car type, and determined in the "nested" IF of lines 142 through 150. The problem is caused by a *missing* ELSE (between lines 144 and 145). Careful analysis of the statement as written reveals that $.12 and $10 will always be used as the statement is now written. (Note that the first record processed was a compact car.)

4 Top Down Testing

OVERVIEW

Testing is like "motherhood and apple pie." Top down testing, whatever that may be, is even more fashionable. Few, if any, will disagree on the need for testing, or the desirability of the top down approach, but fewer still will offer understandable guidelines on a testing procedure. It is the purpose of this section to define and illustrate a top down approach to testing, in such fashion as to make the methodology applicable to any problem.

A case study for a personnel application is used to develop a maintenance program with nontrivial logic requirements. The techniques of pseudocode and hierarchy charts will be integrated into the presentation of top down testing. In addition, the maintenance program will be developed for both sequential and nonsequential processing. A secondary objective of this section, therefore, is to leave the reader with two model programs for sequential and nonsequential maintenance. (The reader may wish to consider Projects 6.10 and 6.20 in Sect. 6 as follow-up exercises on file maintenance.)

CASE STUDY REQUIREMENTS

Develop a COBOL program to process an existing employee master file against a transaction file, and produce a new master. The record description of the master file is shown in Fig. 4.1

As can be seen from Fig. 4.1, a substantial amount of typical personnel data is included; for example, date of birth, date of hire, and so on. In addition, historical data is kept on employee salaries as evidenced by the three occurrences of EMP-SALARY-DATA. The first occurrence corresponds to an employee's present salary, the second occurrence previous salary, and the third occurrence second previous salary. (Newer employees need not necessarily have values for all three levels of salary data.)

```
01  EMPLOYEE-RECORD.
    05  EMP-SOC-SEC-NUMBER              PIC X(9).
    05  EMP-NAME-AND-INITIALS           PIC X(15).
    05  EMP-DATE-OF-BIRTH.
        10  EMP-BIRTH-MONTH             PIC 99.
        10  EMP-BIRTH-YEAR              PIC 99.
    05  EMP-DATE-OF-HIRE.
        10  EMP-HIRE-MONTH              PIC 99.
        10  EMP-HIRE-YEAR               PIC 99.
    05  EMP-LOCATION-CODE               PIC 99.
    05  EMP-EDUCATION-CODE              PIC 9.
    05  EMP-TITLE-DATA.
        10  EMP-TITLE-CODE              PIC 9(3).
        10  EMP-TITLE-DATE              PIC 9(4).
        10  EMP-PERFORMANCE             PIC 9.
    05  EMP-SALARY-DATA OCCURS 3 TIMES
                    INDEXED BY SAL-INDEX.
        10  EMP-SALARY                  PIC 9(5).
        10  EMP-SALARY-TYPE             PIC X.
        10  EMP-SALARY-DATE.
            15  EMP-SALARY-MONTH        PIC 99.
            15  EMP-SALARY-YEAR         PIC 99.
        10  EMP-SALARY-GRADE            PIC 9.
    05  FILLER                          PIC X(4).
```

Figure 4.1 Record Description of Employee Master File.

The record description of the transaction file is similar to that of the master file and is shown in Fig. 4.2.

```
01  TRANSACTION-RECORD.
    05  TRANS-SOC-SEC-NUMBER            PIC X(9).
    05  TRANS-NAME-AND-INITIALS         PIC X(15).
    05  TRANS-DATE-OF-BIRTH.
        10  TRANS-BIRTH-MONTH           PIC 99.
        10  TRANS-BIRTH-YEAR            PIC 99.
    05  TRANS-DATE-OF-HIRE.
        10  TRANS-HIRE-MONTH            PIC 99.
        10  TRANS-HIRE-YEAR             PIC 99.
    05  TRANS-LOCATION-CODE             PIC 99.
    05  TRANS-EDUCATION-CODE            PIC 9.
    05  TRANS-TITLE-DATA.
        10  TRANS-TITLE-CODE            PIC 9(3).
        10  TRANS-TITLE-DATE            PIC 9(4).
        10  TRANS-PERFORMANCE           PIC 9.
    05  TRANS-SALARY-DATA.
        10  TRANS-SALARY                PIC 9(5).
        10  TRANS-SALARY-TYPE           PIC X.
        10  TRANS-SALARY-DATE.
            15  TRANS-SALARY-MONTH      PIC 99.
            15  TRANS-SALARY-YEAR       PIC 99.
        10  TRANS-SALARY-GRADE          PIC 9.
    05  FILLER                          PIC X(25).
    05  TRANS-CODE                      PIC X.
        88  ADDITION        VALUE "A".
        88  CORRECTION      VALUE "C".
        88  DELETION        VALUE "D".
        88  SALARY-UPDATE   VALUE "U".
```

Figure 4.2 Record Description of Transaction File.

Figure 4.2 implies that four types of transactions are possible. These are:

Additions: To add a new record to the employee master. The transaction record requires that all fields be completed.

Corrections: To change a field in an existing record. The transaction record requires the social security number and *only* the field(s) which change; i.e., if the value of a given field is correct in the old master, then that field should be left blank on the transaction.

Deletions: To delete an existing record. Only the name and social security number are required on the transaction record.

Salary Updates: To enter a new salary and retain the previous salary as historical data. The salary value on the transaction record becomes the present salary (first occurrence) on the new master, the present salary on the old master becomes the previous salary (second occurrence) on the new master, and the previous salary on the old master becomes the second previous salary on the new master. (The second previous salary on the old master, if it was present, is lost.) The transaction record requires name, social security number, and the new salary data.

It can be assumed that data in the transaction file have been validated in a *separate* edit program, thereby reducing the requirements for error processing in the maintenance program itself. Nevertheless, the maintenance program is to check (and flag) three kinds of errors which *could not* be detected in the separate edit program that processed only a transaction file. These are:

Duplicate Additions: In which the social security number of a transaction coded as an addition already exists in the old master.

No Matches: In which the social security number of a transaction coded as a correction, deletion, or salary update, does *not* exist on the old master.

Duplicate Salary Updates: In which the salary date in a salary update transaction is already the current salary date in the old master.

Sequential Versus Nonsequential Processing

In a sequential update, every record in the old master is rewritten to the new master regardless of whether it changes. In nonsequential processing only those records which actually change are rewritten. A sequential update requires *two* distinct master files, an old and a new. Its logic is driven by comparing records in the old master file with those in a transaction file, both of which are in sequential order. A nonsequential update has only a single master file, which is read from and written to. A nonsequential update is driven by the transaction file, whose records may be in any order, and by processing the transaction file until it is empty.

It is easy to say which method should be used in the *extreme* cases; sequential processing is preferred when *every* record changes and nonsequential processing when only a *single* record is altered. In general, sequential access is used when many records change and nonsequential access when only a few records are modified. Unfortunately, there is not much in the way of quantitative guidelines as to what constitutes many versus few. Programs of both sequential and nonsequential access will be developed and the decision as to which to use will be left to the reader.

SEQUENTIAL FILE MAINTENANCE

The logic inherent in sequential file maintenance will be described using the techniques of pseudocode and hierarchy charts. Pseudocode is *procedural* in nature and depicts decision-making logic as does a flow chart. Hierarchy charts are *functional* in nature and indicate *what* has to be done, rather than *when*. Both techniques are useful in the design and documentation phases of program development.

Pseudocode

Pseudocode is a convenient way of expressing a program's logic. It uses English statements in the form of instructions similar to those of a computer program, but does not have precise syntactical rules. The programmer is free to use verbs of his own choosing, employ any indentation he or she desires, and so on. Pseudocode flows from the "top down," and is therefore conducive to implementing structured design and programming concepts.

The logic of a sequential approach to the file maintenance problem is shown in Fig. 4.3. After the files are opened, an initial record is taken from both the old master and transaction files. Next a routine is executed continually until both input files are out of data. This module is driven by a nested IF which depends on the relationship between the two most recently read records.

If the social security number on the old master is less than the social security number on the transaction file, it means there is no activity for the current old master record. Hence, it should be merely copied to the new master file. If the social security numbers are equal, then additional processing is required to determine the type of transaction. Finally, if the old master social security number is greater than the transaction social security number, it means the current transaction is not on the existing master. This in turn implies either a new record is to be added, or the social security number of an existing record was miscopied.

The end of the nested IF is also the end of the performed routine. The latter is re-executed as long as data remains on *either* file, after which the files are closed and processing is terminated.

```
       Open Files
       Initial reads for OLD-MASTER and TRANSACTION files
 ┌─ PERFORM until no more data on both files
 │    ┌─ IF OLD-MASTER social security number < TRANSACTION social security number
 │    │     Copy old master record to new master record
 │    │     Read OLD-MASTER only
 │    │  ELSE IF OLD-MASTER social security number = TRANSACTION social security number
 │    │    ┌─ IF addition-write error indicating duplicate addition
 │    │    │  ELSE IF correction-change appropriate fields
 │    │    │  ELSE IF deletion-delete old master record
 │    │    │  ELSE IF update-do salary update
 │    │    └─ ENDIF
 │    │     Read OLD MASTER and TRANSACTION
 │    │  ELSE IF OLD-MASTER social security number > TRANSACTION social security number
 │    │    ┌─ IF addition-add record to NEW-MASTER-FILE
 │    │    │  ELSE write error indicating no match
 │    │    └─ ENDIF
 │    │     Read TRANSACTION-FILE only
 │    └─ ENDIF
 └─ ENDPERFORM
       Close files
       Stop run
```

Figure 4.3 Pseudocode for Sequential Update.

Hierarchy Charts

A COBOL program, capable of the logic inherent in Fig. 4.3, will consist of several readily identifiable routines. The relationship among these modules (COBOL paragraphs or sections) is best expressed in a hierarchy chart, as shown in Fig. 4.4. This figure depicts the *function* of each routine in a program and the relationship among functions. It does *not* show decision making logic or program flow, as does pseudocode.

A hierarchy chart is developed from the top down. One module, MAINLINE, sits alone at the top of the chart and controls all the others. The next lower level breaks the overall nature of the program into smaller, more readily identifiable functions, for example, COMPARE-IDS. These in turn consist of lower level routines, for example, COPY-OLD-RECORD, MATCH-ROUTINE, etc., which can be broken into still lower level modules, with increasingly clearer function; for example, UPDATE-OLD-RECORD, CORRECT-OLD-RECORD, etc.

Each module in a hierarchy chart should be *independent* of all others. This allows any module to be modified without affecting the working of any other module. Independence can be partially achieved by restricting each module to a *single* function; correcting an old record, adding a new record, comparing social security numbers, etc.

Each module in a hierarchy chart can only be called by the module immediately above it, and must in turn return control to that module. (Some modules, however, may be called by more than one module or performed from different parts of a program, and consequently appear twice in a hierarchy chart. This is indicated by shading the upper left hand corner of those modules in the chart.)

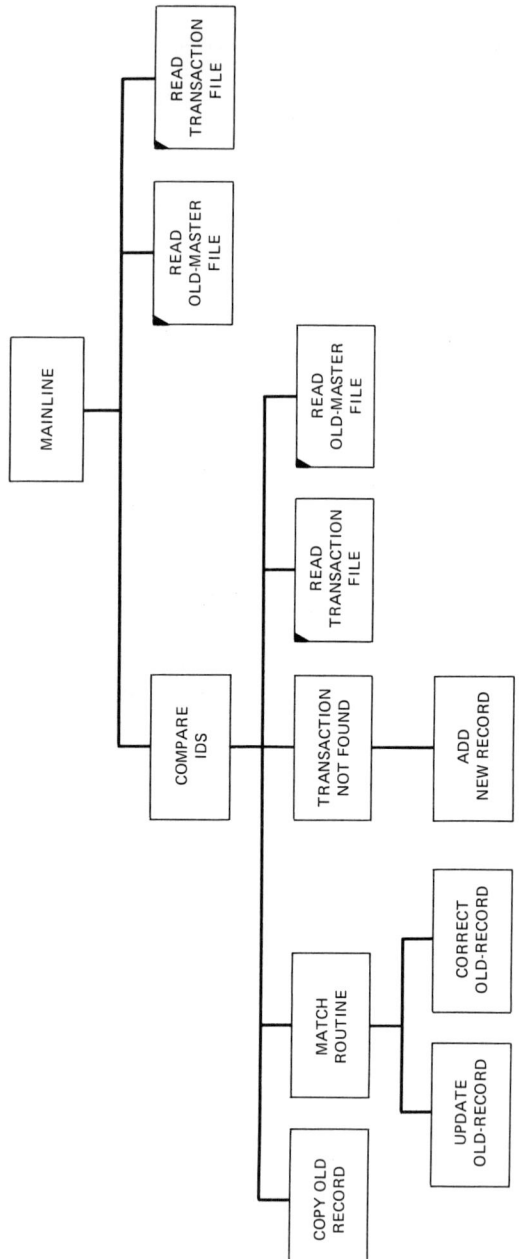

Figure 4.4 Hierarchy Chart for Sequential Update.

TESTING

The job of the programmer is to verify that his or her program does what it is supposed to do. To that end, he or she must obtain test data to run through the program. Expected results should be computed *before* testing actually begins. Otherwise, it is too easy to assume the program works, because the output "looks right."

It is also desirable that a person other than the original programmer supply some or all of the test data. The latter individual, who has no idea of how the actual program is structured, is in a better position to make up objective data. Test data can also be provided by commercial products known as test data generators. These programs are ideal for producing large volumes of objective data, a tedious and demanding task.

Finally, the programmer should realize that live data will not always be in the form expected, and the testing environment should reflect both normal and abnormal data. Initially, the program is tested with only proper data. Once it performs as expected under normal conditions, testing should be expanded to include obviously improper data. A sound program will continue to operate and include appropriate error messages.

A set of test data for the sequential update is shown in Fig. 4.5. The expected output is shown in Fig. 4.6 in the form of a new master file plus a set of associated error messages.

Finally, the crucial question occurs: when can testing begin? An obvious answer is that testing can begin only when the program is finished. A different answer, more reflective of current thought, and the author's strong personal belief, is that *testing should begin as soon as possible, and well before the program is completely finished.*

This latter philosophy is best explained by returning to the hierarchy chart of Fig. 4.4. The most complex module is MAINLINE, the one sitting alone at the top of the chart. It, in turn, calls COMPARE-IDS, which invokes COPY-OLD-RECORD, MATCH-ROUTINE, and so on. The most difficult aspect of the maintenance program is the interaction of higher level routines, such as when should COPY-OLD-RECORD be called in lieu of MATCH-ROUTINE. The easiest part of the program is the details of the *lowest* level routines such as UPDATE-OLD-RECORD or ADD-NEW-RECORD. *The top down approach to testing reasons that the relationship among the higher level routines can be tested even if the lowest level routines are not completely finished!*

In other words, top down testing argues that the highest level (and most difficult) modules be tested earlier and more often than the lower level (and often trivial) routines. This is accomplished by initially coding the lowest level modules as *program stubs*, one sentence paragraphs consisting only of a DISPLAY statement indicating that the paragraph was entered. The details of these modules are completed at a later date, after it has been determined that the routines are being properly called. This approach is discussed further in the next section.

Old master: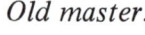

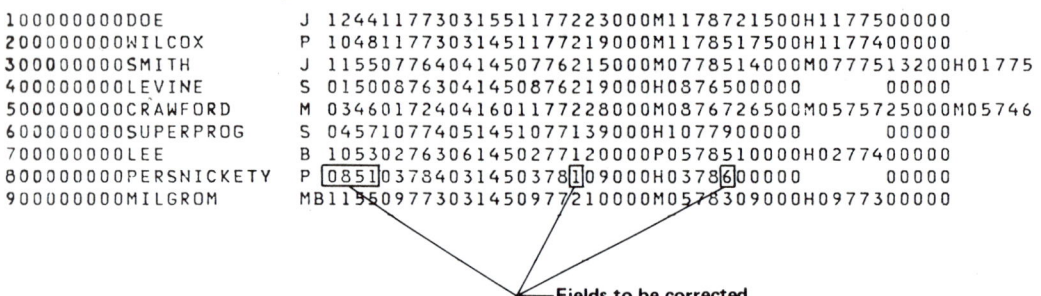

Transaction:

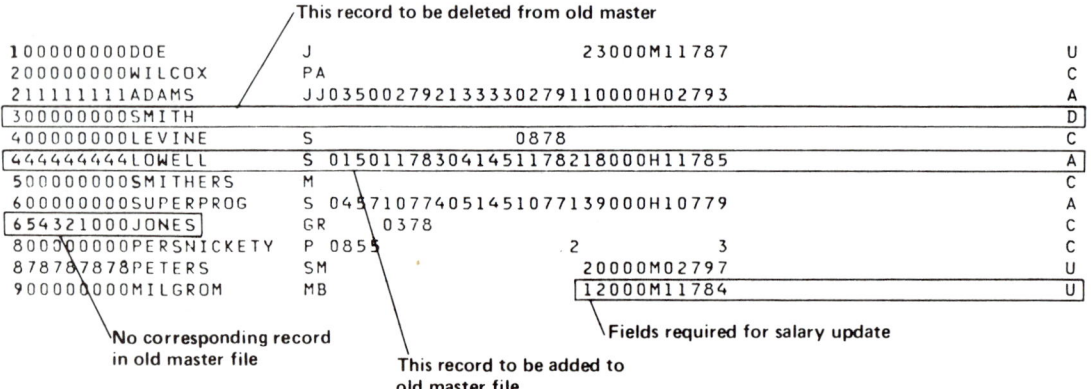

Figure 4.5 Test Data for Sequential Update.

New master:

```
100000000DOE            J  12441177303155117722300M1178721500H1177500000
200000000WILCOX         PA10481177303145117721900M1178517500H1177400000
211111111ADAMS          JJ03500279213333027911000H0279300000       00000
400000000LEVINE         S  01500876304145087621900H0876500000       00000
444444444LOWELL         S  01501178304145117821800H1178500000       00000
500000000SMITHERS       M  03460172404160117722800M0876726500M0575725000M05746
600000000SUPERPROG      S  04571077405145107713900P0578510000H0277400000
700000000LEE            B  10530276306145027712000P0578510000H0277400000
800000000PERSNICKETY    P  08550378403145037820900H0378300000       00000
900000000MILGROM        MB1155097730314509772 12000M1178410000M0578309000H09773
```

Record has been added to master file   Salary fields reflect update

Error messages:

```
ERROR - UPDATE ALREADY DONE        100000000    DOE          J
ERROR - RECORD IN FILE             600000000    SUPERPROG    S
ERROR - NO MATCH                   654321000    JONES        GR
ERROR - NO MATCH                   878787878    PETERS       SM
```

Figure 4.6 Intended Output of Completed Update.

The Sequential Maintenance Program (With Stubs)

Figure 4.7 contains a *partially* coded COBOL program designed to accomplish a sequential update. The Data Division appears somewhat long, but on closer examination is seen to consist primarily of three COPY statements (COBOL lines 17, 47, and 77) for the old master, new master, and transaction files, respectively. The new master contains identical fields in identical positions as the old master; its data names, however, use a different prefix.

The MAINLINE opens all three files and executes an initial read for the old master and transaction files. The routine 010-COMPARE-IDS is performed until both input files are out of data. It is this module which drives the entire program. In particular, lines 140-146 contain a nested IF to determine which of three lower level routines in the hierarchy chart of Fig. 4.4 is to be called.

If the current record in the old master file has a social security number lower than the current record in the transaction file, it means there is no corresponding transaction for the current old master record. Hence, the old master record is to be copied intact to the new master file. If the social security numbers match, then additional processing is required to determine the nature of the transaction. Finally, if the social security number in the old master is greater than that in the transaction, it means that the current transaction social security number does not exist in the old master. Additional processing is required to determine if the transaction should be added to the master file, or whether its social security number was coded incorrectly.

Figure 4.8 shows output produced by the program of Fig. 4.7 in conjunction with the test data of Fig. 4.5. *Critical* analysis of this figure constitutes initial program testing. As can be seen, the first record in each input file contains the social security number 100-00-0000, causing 060-MATCH-ROUTINE to be entered. The nested IF of lines 163-174 acts on the transaction code of U and invokes execution of 075-UPDATE-OLD-RECORD. So far so good.

A new record is taken from both the old master and transaction files. Again, the social security numbers match, but this time the transaction code is C. The routine 085-CORRECT-OLD-RECORD is entered as expected.

New records are read again from both input files, but this time the transaction social security number is lower than that of the old master. The routine 095-TRANSACTION-NOT-FOUND is executed and detects a transaction code of A. It in turn invokes the module 105-ADD-NEW-RECORD to add the social security number 211-11-1111 to the new master file. Note well that a new record will be read only from the transaction file, and the program holds the old master social security number of 300-00-0000. The match routine is entered (both files contain 300-00-0000) but since the transaction code is D, no other routines are called.

The reader should realize that the maintenance program is working correctly. Thus, even though the program is not yet finished, we can sense that the modules are being called in proper sequence. The testing was begun early in the cycle, so that if errors were found, they would be easy to correct. Further, early testing significantly improves both programmer morale and performance.

The remainder of Fig. 4.8 is left to the reader as an exercise.

```
00001              IDENTIFICATION DIVISION.
00002              PROGRAM-ID.      STUBS.
00003              AUTHOR.          GRAUER.
00004
00005              ENVIRONMENT DIVISION.
00006              CONFIGURATION SECTION.
00007              SOURCE-COMPUTER.  IBM-370.
00008              OBJECT-COMPUTER.  IBM-370.
00009              INPUT-OUTPUT SECTION.
00010              FILE-CONTROL.
00011                  SELECT TRANSACTION-FILE ASSIGN TO UT-S-TRANS.
00012                  SELECT EMPLOYEE-FILE ASSIGN TO UT-S-OLD.
00013                  SELECT NEW-MASTER-FILE ASSIGN TO UT-S-NEW.
00014
00015              DATA DIVISION.
00016              FILE SECTION.                ┌─COPY clause for the old master file
00017                  │COPY EMPLOYEE.│
00018 C             FD  EMPLOYEE-FILE
00019 C                 LABEL RECORDS ARE OMITTED
00020 C                 RECORD CONTAINS 80 CHARACTERS
00021 C                 DATA RECORD IS EMPLOYEE-RECORD.
00022 C             01  EMPLOYEE-RECORD.
00023 C                 05  EMP-SOC-SEC-NUMBER          PIC X(9).
00024 C                 05  EMP-NAME-AND-INITIALS       PIC X(15).
00025 C                 05  EMP-DATE-OF-BIRTH.
00026 C                     10  EMP-BIRTH-MONTH         PIC 99.
00027 C                     10  EMP-BIRTH-YEAR          PIC 99.
00028 C                 05  EMP-DATE-OF-HIRE.
00029 C                     10  EMP-HIRE-MONTH          PIC 99.
00030 C                     10  EMP-HIRE-YEAR           PIC 99.
00031 C                 05  EMP-LOCATION-CODE           PIC 99.
00032 C                 05  EMP-EDUCATION-CODE          PIC 9.
00033 C                 05  EMP-TITLE-DATA.
00034 C                     10  EMP-TITLE-CODE          PIC 9(3).
00035 C                     10  EMP-TITLE-DATE          PIC 9(4).
00036 C                     10  EMP-PERFORMANCE         PIC 9.
00037 C                 05  EMP-SALARY-DATA OCCURS 3 TIMES
00038 C                         INDEXED BY SAL-INDEX.
00039 C                     10  EMP-SALARY              PIC 9(5).
00040 C                     10  EMP-SALARY-TYPE         PIC X.
00041 C                     10  EMP-SALARY-DATE.
00042 C                         15  EMP-SALARY-MONTH    PIC 99.
00043 C                         15  EMP-SALARY-YEAR     PIC 99.
00044 C                     10  EMP-SALARY-GRADE        PIC 9.
00045 C                 05  FILLER                      PIC X(4).
00046                                              ┌─COPY clause for the new master file
00047                  │COPY NEWMAST.│
00048 C             FD  NEW-MASTER-FILE
00049 C                 LABEL RECORDS ARE OMITTED
00050 C                 RECORD CONTAINS 80 CHARACTERS
00051 C                 DATA RECORD IS NEW-MASTER-RECORD.
00052 C             01  NEW-MASTER-RECORD.
00053 C                 05  NEW-SOC-SEC-NUMBER          PIC X(9).
00054 C                 05  NEW-NAME-AND-INITIALS       PIC X(15).
```

Figure 4.7 Stubs Program for Sequential Update.

```
00055 C           05    NEW-DATE-OF-BIRTH.
00056 C                 10    NEW-BIRTH-MONTH           PIC 99.
00057 C                 10    NEW-BIRTH-YEAR            PIC 99.
00058 C           05    NEW-DATE-OF-HIRE.
00059 C                 10    NEW-HIRE-MONTH            PIC 99.
00060 C                 10    NEW-HIRE-YEAR             PIC 99.
00061 C           05    NEW-LOCATION-CODE               PIC 99.
00062 C           05    NEW-EDUCATION-CODE              PIC 9.
00063 C           05    NEW-TITLE-DATA.
00064 C                 10    NEW-TITLE-CODE            PIC 9(3).
00065 C                 10    NEW-TITLE-DATE            PIC 9(4).
00066 C                 10    NEW-PERFORMANCE           PIC 9.
00067 C           05    NEW-SALARY-DATA OCCURS 3 TIMES
00068 C                             INDEXED BY SAL-INDEX.
00069 C                 10    NEW-SALARY                PIC 9(5).
00070 C                 10    NEW-SALARY-TYPE           PIC X.
00071 C                 10    NEW-SALARY-DATE.
00072 C                       15    NEW-SALARY-MONTH    PIC 99.
00073 C                       15    NEW-SALARY-YEAR     PIC 99.
00074 C                 10    NEW-SALARY-GRADE          PIC 9.
00075 C           05    FILLER                          PIC X(4).
00076
00077              COPY TRANSACT.      ──COPY clause for transaction file
00078 C     FD    TRANSACTION-FILE
00079 C           LABEL RECORDS ARE OMITTED
00080 C           RECORD CONTAINS 80 CHARACTERS
00081 C           DATA RECORD IS TRANSACTION-RECORD.
00082 C     01    TRANSACTION-RECORD.
00083 C           05    TRANS-SOC-SEC-NUMBER            PIC X(9).
00084 C           05    TRANS-NAME-AND-INITIALS         PIC X(15).
00085 C           05    TRANS-DATE-OF-BIRTH.
00086 C                 10    TRANS-BIRTH-MONTH         PIC 99.
00087 C                 10    TRANS-BIRTH-YEAR          PIC 99.
00088 C           05    TRANS-DATE-OF-HIRE.
00089 C                 10    TRANS-HIRE-MONTH          PIC 99.
00090 C                 10    TRANS-HIRE-YEAR           PIC 99.
00091 C           05    TRANS-LOCATION-CODE             PIC 99.
00092 C           05    TRANS-EDUCATION-CODE            PIC 9.
00093 C           05    TRANS-TITLE-DATA.
00094 C                 10    TRANS-TITLE-CODE          PIC 9(3).
00095 C                 10    TRANS-TITLE-DATE          PIC 9(4).
00096 C                 10    TRANS-PERFORMANCE         PIC 9.
00097 C           05    TRANS-SALARY-DATA.
00098 C                 10    TRANS-SALARY              PIC 9(5).
00099 C                 10    TRANS-SALARY-TYPE         PIC X.
00100 C                 10    TRANS-SALARY-DATE.
00101 C                       15    TRANS-SALARY-MONTH  PIC 99.
00102 C                       15    TRANS-SALARY-YEAR   PIC 99.
00103 C                 10    TRANS-SALARY-GRADE        PIC 9.
00104 C           05    FILLER                          PIC X(25).
00105 C           05    TRANS-CODE                      PIC X.
00106 C                 88    ADDITION        VALUE "A".
00107 C                 88    CORRECTION      VALUE "C".
00108 C                 88    DELETION        VALUE "D".
00109 C                 88    SALARY-UPDATE   VALUE "U".
00110
00111        WORKING-STORAGE SECTION.
00112        01    WORKING-STORAGE-SWITCHES.
00113              05    WS-OLD-MAST-READ-SWITCH PIC X(3)   VALUE "NO".
00114              05    WS-TRANS-READ-SWITCH    PIC X(3)   VALUE "NO".
00115
00116        PROCEDURE DIVISION.
00117        005-MAINLINE.
00118              OPEN INPUT TRANSACTION-FILE
00119                         EMPLOYEE-FILE
00120                   OUTPUT NEW-MASTER-FILE.
```

Figure 4.7 *cont.*

```
00121           PERFORM 180-READ-TRANSACTION.      ──READs are performed rather
00122           PERFORM 190-READ-OLD-MASTER.          than coded inline
00123
00124
00125           PERFORM 010-COMPARE-IDS
00126               UNTIL TRANS-SOC-SEC-NUMBER = HIGH-VALUES
00127               AND EMP-SOC-SEC-NUMBER = HIGH-VALUES.
00128
00129           CLOSE TRANSACTION-FILE
00130                 EMPLOYEE-FILE
00131                 NEW-MASTER-FILE.
00132           STOP RUN.
00133                                              Nested IF determines relationship
00134       010-COMPARE-IDS.                       between old master and
00135           DISPLAY "    ".                    transaction file
00136           DISPLAY "RECORDS BEING PROCESSED".
00137           DISPLAY "   TRANSACTION SOC SEC: " TRANS-SOC-SEC-NUMBER
00138               "   TRANSACTION CODE: " TRANS-CODE.
00139           DISPLAY "   OLD MASTER SOC SEC: " EMP-SOC-SEC-NUMBER.
00140           IF EMP-SOC-SEC-NUMBER < TRANS-SOC-SEC-NUMBER
00141               PERFORM 050-COPY-OLD-RECORD
00142           ELSE
00143               IF EMP-SOC-SEC-NUMBER = TRANS-SOC-SEC-NUMBER
00144                   PERFORM 060-MATCH-ROUTINE
00145               ELSE
00146                   PERFORM 095-TRANSACTION-NOT-FOUND.
00147
00148           IF WS-TRANS-READ-SWITCH = "YES"
00149               MOVE "NO " TO WS-TRANS-READ-SWITCH
00150               PERFORM 180-READ-TRANSACTION.
00151                                                        ──Switches are tested
00152           IF WS-OLD-MAST-READ-SWITCH = "YES"              and reset
00153               MOVE "NO " TO WS-OLD-MAST-READ-SWITCH
00154               PERFORM 190-READ-OLD-MASTER.
00155
00156
00157       050-COPY-OLD-RECORD.
00158           DISPLAY "050-COPY-OLD-RECORD ENTERED".
00159           MOVE "YES" TO WS-OLD-MAST-READ-SWITCH.  ──Causes next record to be
00160                                                     read only from old
00161       060-MATCH-ROUTINE.                            master file
00162           DISPLAY "060-MATCH-ROUTINE ENTERED".
00163           IF ADDITION
00164               DISPLAY "ERROR - ADDITION TRANSACTION ALREADY IN FILE"
00165                   TRANS-SOC-SEC-NUMBER
00166           ELSE
00167               IF SALARY-UPDATE
00168                   PERFORM 075-UPDATE-OLD-RECORD
00169               ELSE
00170                   IF DELETION
00171                       NEXT SENTENCE          ──Set switches to read
00172                   ELSE                          from both files
00173                       IF CORRECTION
00174                           PERFORM 085-CORRECT-OLD-RECORD.
00175
00176           MOVE "YES" TO WS-TRANS-READ-SWITCH.
00177           MOVE "YES" TO WS-OLD-MAST-READ-SWITCH.
00178
00179       075-UPDATE-OLD-RECORD.
00180           DISPLAY "075-UPDATE-OLD-RECORD ENTERED".
00181                                                       ──Program stubs
00182       085-CORRECT-OLD-RECORD.
00183           DISPLAY "085-CORRECT-OLD-RECORD ENTERED".
00184
00185       095-TRANSACTION-NOT-FOUND.
00186           DISPLAY "095-TRANSACTION-NOT-FOUND ENTERED".
```

Figure 4.7 *cont.*

```
00187                 IF ADDITION
00188                     PERFORM 105-ADD-NEW-RECORD
00189                 ELSE
00190                     DISPLAY "ERROR - NO MATCH FOR TRANSACTION RECORD"
00191                         TRANS-SOC-SEC-NUMBER.
00192                 MOVE "YES" TO WS-TRANS-READ-SWITCH.
00193
00194             105-ADD-NEW-RECORD.
00195                 DISPLAY "105-ADD-NEW-RECORD ENTERED".
00196
00197             180-READ-TRANSACTION.
00198                 READ TRANSACTION-FILE
00199                     AT END MOVE HIGH-VALUES TO TRANS-SOC-SEC-NUMBER.
00200
00201             190-READ-OLD-MASTER.
00202                 READ EMPLOYEE-FILE
00203                     AT END MOVE HIGH-VALUES TO EMP-SOC-SEC-NUMBER.
```

Line 00192: Causes next record to be read only from transaction file

Figure 4.7 *cont.*

```
RECORDS BEING PROCESSED
   TRANSACTION SOC SEC: 100000000   TRANSACTION CODE: U
   OLD MASTER SOC SEC:  100000000
060-MATCH-ROUTINE ENTERED
075-UPDATE-OLD-RECORD ENTERED

RECORDS BEING PROCESSED
   TRANSACTION SOC SEC: 200000000   TRANSACTION CODE: C
   OLD MASTER SOC SEC:  200000000
060-MATCH-ROUTINE ENTERED
085-CORRECT-OLD-RECORD ENTERED

RECORDS BEING PROCESSED
   TRANSACTION SOC SEC: 211111111   TRANSACTION CODE: A
   OLD MASTER SOC SEC:  300000000
095-TRANSACTION-NOT-FOUND ENTERED
105-ADD-NEW-RECORD ENTERED
```
Transaction record < old master record; hence transaction record will be added

```
RECORDS BEING PROCESSED
   TRANSACTION SOC SEC: 300000000   TRANSACTION CODE: D
   OLD MASTER SOC SEC:  300000000
060-MATCH-ROUTINE ENTERED
```
Old master record remains the same, since previous transaction was an add

```
RECORDS BEING PROCESSED
   TRANSACTION SOC SEC: 400000000   TRANSACTION CODE: C
   OLD MASTER SOC SEC:  400000000
060-MATCH-ROUTINE ENTERED
085-CORRECT-OLD-RECORD ENTERED
```
Transaction record = old master record; hence match routine will be entered to determine how to process transaction

```
RECORDS BEING PROCESSED
   TRANSACTION SOC SEC: 444444444   TRANSACTION CODE: A
   OLD MASTER SOC SEC:  500000000
095-TRANSACTION-NOT-FOUND ENTERED
105-ADD-NEW-RECORD ENTERED

RECORDS BEING PROCESSED
   TRANSACTION SOC SEC: 500000000   TRANSACTION CODE: C
   OLD MASTER SOC SEC:  500000000
060-MATCH-ROUTINE ENTERED
085-CORRECT-OLD-RECORD ENTERED

RECORDS BEING PROCESSED
   TRANSACTION SOC SEC: 600000000   TRANSACTION CODE: A
   OLD MASTER SOC SEC:  600000000
060-MATCH-ROUTINE ENTERED
ERROR - ADDITION TRANSACTION ALREADY IN FILE600000000
```

Figure 4.8 Output of Sequential Stubs Program.

```
RECORDS BEING PROCESSED
  TRANSACTION SOC SEC:  654321000    TRANSACTION CODE: C     ⎤ Transaction record
  OLD MASTER SOC SEC:   700000000                            ⎦ < old master record
095-TRANSACTION-NOT-FOUND ENTERED                              but transaction code
ERROR - NO MATCH FOR TRANSACTION RECORD654321000               is not an add; hence
                                                               an error
RECORDS BEING PROCESSED
  TRANSACTION SOC SEC:  800000000    TRANSACTION CODE: C
  OLD MASTER SOC SEC:   700000000    Old master record < transaction record
050-COPY-OLD-RECORD ENTERED          hence old master record will be copied

RECORDS BEING PROCESSED
  TRANSACTION SOC SEC:  800000000    TRANSACTION CODE: C
  OLD MASTER SOC SEC:   800000000    Transaction record remains the same
060-MATCH-ROUTINE ENTERED            since previous old master record was
085-CORRECT-OLD-RECORD ENTERED       merely copied.

RECORDS BEING PROCESSED
  TRANSACTION SOC SEC:  878787878    TRANSACTION CODE: U
  OLD MASTER SOC SEC:   900000000
095-TRANSACTION-NOT-FOUND ENTERED
ERROR - NO MATCH FOR TRANSACTION RECORD878787878

RECORDS BEING PROCESSED
  TRANSACTION SOC SEC:  900000000    TRANSACTION CODE: U
  OLD MASTER SOC SEC:   900000000
060-MATCH-ROUTINE ENTERED
075-UPDATE-OLD-RECORD ENTERED
```

Figure 4.8 *cont.*

The Completed Sequential Maintenance Program

Once the skeletal update has been tested and debugged, it is relatively simple to "fill in the blanks" and complete the maintenance program. In other words, the most difficult portion of the maintenance program is the interaction between modules, such as whether to read from the old master or the transaction file, or both; and which module to call: update, correct, or add. The details of these routines are easy by comparison.

Figure 4.9 represents an expansion of Fig. 4.7. The most obvious difference between the two programs is the increased length of the latter, which has been achieved by expanding the program stubs for: 075-UPDATE-OLD-RECORD, 085-CORRECT-OLD-RECORD, and 105-ADD-NEW-RECORD.

The update routine (075-UPDATE-OLD-RECORD) tests whether the transaction salary increase is already in effect by comparing the incoming transaction salary date to the current salary date in the old master (line 193). If the dates are equal, an error message is written to that effect. If, however, the dates are different, then the update must take effect. This is accomplished by the three move statements of lines 201-203. Recall that three occurrences of salary data are maintained (lines 68-69) with indexes of 1, 2, and 3 denoting current, previous, and second previous salary, respectively. The previous salary is moved to the second previous salary (line 201), after which the current salary is moved to the previous (line 202). Finally, the incoming transaction salary is moved to the current salary in line 203. These moves are preceded by a single group move in line 200 which moves the entire old master to the new master and followed by a write to the new master file in line 204.

The correction routine, lines 207-233, moves the existing old master to the new master in line 207. Then it checks incoming transaction fields, one at a time, to determine whether any action has to be taken. Recall that the transaction is to contain data only for those fields which change. If a transaction field is blank, no action is taken, but if it is not blank, the value will be moved to the corresponding field in the new master. When all transaction fields have been checked, the new master record is written in line 233.

The routine to add a new record, lines 246-258, is even more straightforward. The new master record is initially blanked out, after which the transaction fields are moved in one at a time. Lines 254 and 255 move zeros to the previous and second previous salaries in the new master prior to writing the new record. (This is mandated because COBOL distinguishes between blanks and zeros in numeric fields; for example, salary.)

Figure 4.9 is also differentiated from Fig. 4.7 by the addition of a fourth file, ERROR-FILE, which contains various error messages. (Fig. 4.7 used DISPLAY statements instead.) The actual output produced by the program of Fig. 4.9 corresponds exactly to the intended output shown earlier in Fig. 4.6. Note the presence of new records for Adams and Lowell and the absence of Smith, which have been affected through two adds and one delete from the input of Fig. 4.5.

Figure 4.6 also contains the list of error messages. The transaction to update Doe's salary is correct in and of itself. However, the salary dates in the transaction and old master files of Fig. 4.5 and 4.6 are the same, so the attempted update is flagged in Fig. 4.6. The transactions for Jones and Peters are flagged because no corresponding master records can be found. Finally, the attempted addition for Superprog is flagged because that record already appears in the old master to Fig. 4.5.

```
00001           IDENTIFICATION DIVISION.
00002           PROGRAM-ID.       UPDATE.
00003           AUTHOR.           GRAUER.
00004
00005           ENVIRONMENT DIVISION.
00006           CONFIGURATION SECTION.
00007           SOURCE-COMPUTER.  IBM-370.          ┌─Fourth file has been
00008           OBJECT-COMPUTER.  IBM-370.           added to accommodate
00009           INPUT-OUTPUT SECTION.                error messages.
00010           FILE-CONTROL.
00011               SELECT TRANSACTION-FILE ASSIGN TO UT-S-TRANS.
00012               SELECT ERROR-FILE ASSIGN TO UT-S-PRINT.
00013               SELECT EMPLOYEE-FILE ASSIGN TO UT-S-OLD.
00014               SELECT NEW-MASTER-FILE ASSIGN TO UT-S-NEW.
00015
00016           DATA DIVISION.
00017           FILE SECTION.
00018               COPY EMPLOYEE.    ─COPY for old master
00019 C         FD  EMPLOYEE-FILE
00020 C             LABEL RECORDS ARE OMITTED
00021 C             RECORD CONTAINS 80 CHARACTERS
```

Figure 4.9 Completed Program for Sequential Update.

```
00022 C              DATA RECORD IS EMPLOYEE-RECORD.
00023 C          01  EMPLOYEE-RECORD.
00024 C              05  EMP-SOC-SEC-NUMBER           PIC X(9).
00025 C              05  EMP-NAME-AND-INITIALS        PIC X(15).
00026 C              05  EMP-DATE-OF-BIRTH.
00027 C                  10  EMP-BIRTH-MONTH          PIC 99.
00028 C                  10  EMP-BIRTH-YEAR           PIC 99.
00029 C              05  EMP-DATE-OF-HIRE.
00030 C                  10  EMP-HIRE-MONTH           PIC 99.
00031 C                  10  EMP-HIRE-YEAR            PIC 99.
00032 C              05  EMP-LOCATION-CODE            PIC 99.
00033 C              05  EMP-EDUCATION-CODE           PIC 9.
00034 C              05  EMP-TITLE-DATA.
00035 C                  10  EMP-TITLE-CODE           PIC 9(3).
00036 C                  10  EMP-TITLE-DATE           PIC 9(4).
00037 C                  10  EMP-PERFORMANCE          PIC 9.
00038 C              05  EMP-SALARY-DATA OCCURS 3 TIMES
00039 C                              INDEXED BY SAL-INDEX.
00040 C                  10  EMP-SALARY               PIC 9(5).
00041 C                  10  EMP-SALARY-TYPE          PIC X.
00042 C                  10  EMP-SALARY-DATE.
00043 C                      15  EMP-SALARY-MONTH     PIC 99.
00044 C                      15  EMP-SALARY-YEAR      PIC 99.
00045 C                  10  EMP-SALARY-GRADE         PIC 9.
00046 C              05  FILLER                       PIC X(4).
00047
00048            COPY NEWMAST.              ──COPY for new master
00049 C          FD  NEW-MASTER-FILE
00050 C              LABEL RECORDS ARE OMITTED
00051 C              RECORD CONTAINS 80 CHARACTERS
00052 C              DATA RECORD IS NEW-MASTER-RECORD.
00053 C          01  NEW-MASTER-RECORD.
00054 C              05  NEW-SOC-SEC-NUMBER           PIC X(9).
00055 C              05  NEW-NAME-AND-INITIALS        PIC X(15).
00056 C              05  NEW-DATE-OF-BIRTH.
00057 C                  10  NEW-BIRTH-MONTH          PIC 99.
00058 C                  10  NEW-BIRTH-YEAR           PIC 99.
00059 C              05  NEW-DATE-OF-HIRE.
00060 C                  10  NEW-HIRE-MONTH           PIC 99.
00061 C                  10  NEW-HIRE-YEAR            PIC 99.
00062 C              05  NEW-LOCATION-CODE            PIC 99.
00063 C              05  NEW-EDUCATION-CODE           PIC 9.
00064 C              05  NEW-TITLE-DATA.
00065 C                  10  NEW-TITLE-CODE           PIC 9(3).
00066 C                  10  NEW-TITLE-DATE           PIC 9(4).
00067 C                  10  NEW-PERFORMANCE          PIC 9.
00068 C              05  NEW-SALARY-DATA OCCURS 3 TIMES
00069 C                              INDEXED BY SAL-INDEX.
00070 C                  10  NEW-SALARY               PIC 9(5).
00071 C                  10  NEW-SALARY-TYPE          PIC X.
00072 C                  10  NEW-SALARY-DATE.     ──Three occurrences of salary data
00073 C                      15  NEW-SALARY-MONTH     PIC 99.
00074 C                      15  NEW-SALARY-YEAR      PIC 99.
00075 C                  10  NEW-SALARY-GRADE         PIC 9.
00076 C              05  FILLER                       PIC X(4).
00077
00078            COPY TRANSACT.              ──COPY for transaction file
00079 C          FD  TRANSACTION-FILE
00080 C              LABEL RECORDS ARE OMITTED
00081 C              RECORD CONTAINS 80 CHARACTERS
00082 C              DATA RECORD IS TRANSACTION-RECORD.
00083 C          01  TRANSACTION-RECORD.
00084 C              05  TRANS-SOC-SEC-NUMBER         PIC X(9).
00085 C              05  TRANS-NAME-AND-INITIALS      PIC X(15).
00086 C              05  TRANS-DATE-OF-BIRTH.
00087 C                  10  TRANS-BIRTH-MONTH        PIC 99.
00088 C                  10  TRANS-BIRTH-YEAR         PIC 99.
00089 C              05  TRANS-DATE-OF-HIRE.
```

Figure 4.9 *cont.*

```
00090 C              10   TRANS-HIRE-MONTH          PIC 99.
00091 C              10   TRANS-HIRE-YEAR           PIC 99.
00092 C         05   TRANS-LOCATION-CODE            PIC 99.
00093 C         05   TRANS-EDUCATION-CODE           PIC 9.
00094 C         05   TRANS-TITLE-DATA.
00095 C              10   TRANS-TITLE-CODE          PIC 9(3).
00096 C              10   TRANS-TITLE-DATE          PIC 9(4).
00097 C              10   TRANS-PERFORMANCE         PIC 9.
00098 C         05   TRANS-SALARY-DATA.
00099 C              10   TRANS-SALARY              PIC 9(5).
00100 C              10   TRANS-SALARY-TYPE         PIC X.
00101 C              10   TRANS-SALARY-DATE.
00102 C                   15   TRANS-SALARY-MONTH   PIC 99.
00103 C                   15   TRANS-SALARY-YEAR    PIC 99.
00104 C              10   TRANS-SALARY-GRADE        PIC 9.
00105 C         05   FILLER                         PIC X(25).
00106 C         05   TRANS-CODE                     PIC X.
00107 C              88   ADDITION         VALUE "A".
00108 C              88   CORRECTION       VALUE "C".         ── Transaction types
00109 C              88   DELETION         VALUE "D".
00110 C              88   SALARY-UPDATE    VALUE "U".
00111                                        ── ERROR-FILE has been added
00112         FD   ERROR-FILE
00113              LABEL RECORDS ARE OMITTED
00114              RECORD CONTAINS 132 CHARACTERS
00115              DATA RECORD IS ERROR-RECORD.
00116         01   ERROR-RECORD                     PIC X(132).
00117
00118         WORKING-STORAGE SECTION.
00119         01   WORKING-STORAGE-SWITCHES.
00120              05   WS-OLD-MAST-READ-SWITCH     PIC X(3)   VALUE "NO".
00121              05   WS-TRANS-READ-SWITCH        PIC X(3)   VALUE "NO".
00122
00123         01   WS-PRINT-RECORD.
00124              05   WS-PRINT-MESSAGE            PIC X(40).
00125              05   WS-PRINT-ID                 PIC X(9).
00126              05   FILLER                      PIC X(5)   VALUE SPACES.
00127              05   WS-PRINT-NAME               PIC X(25).
00128              05   FILLER                      PIC X(53)  VALUE SPACES.
00129
00130         PROCEDURE DIVISION.
00131         005-MAINLINE.
00132              OPEN INPUT TRANSACTION-FILE
00133                         EMPLOYEE-FILE
00134                    OUTPUT NEW-MASTER-FILE
00135                           ERROR-FILE.
00136
00137              PERFORM 180-READ-TRANSACTION.
00138              PERFORM 190-READ-OLD-MASTER.
00139
00140              PERFORM 010-COMPARE-IDS
00141                  UNTIL TRANS-SOC-SEC-NUMBER = HIGH-VALUES
00142                    AND EMP-SOC-SEC-NUMBER   = HIGH-VALUES.
00143
00144              CLOSE TRANSACTION-FILE
00145                    EMPLOYEE-FILE
00146                    NEW-MASTER-FILE
00147                    ERROR-FILE.          ── Nested IF determines relationship
00148              STOP RUN.                        between old master and
00149                                               transaction file
00150         010-COMPARE-IDS.
00151              IF EMP-SOC-SEC-NUMBER < TRANS-SOC-SEC-NUMBER
00152                  PERFORM 050-COPY-OLD-RECORD
00153              ELSE
00154                  IF EMP-SOC-SEC-NUMBER = TRANS-SOC-SEC-NUMBER
00155                      PERFORM 060-MATCH-ROUTINE
00156                  ELSE
00157                      PERFORM 095-TRANSACTION-NOT-FOUND.
00158
```

Figure 4.9 *cont.*

```
00159            IF WS-TRANS-READ-SWITCH = "YES"
00160                MOVE "NO " TO WS-TRANS-READ-SWITCH
00161                PERFORM 180-READ-TRANSACTION.
00162
00163            IF WS-OLD-MAST-READ-SWITCH = "YES"
00164                MOVE "NO " TO WS-OLD-MAST-READ-SWITCH
00165                PERFORM 190-READ-OLD-MASTER.
00166
00167
00168        050-COPY-OLD-RECORD.
00169            WRITE NEW-MASTER-RECORD FROM EMPLOYEE-RECORD.
00170            MOVE "YES" TO WS-OLD-MAST-READ-SWITCH.
00171
00172        060-MATCH-ROUTINE.
00173            IF ADDITION
00174                MOVE TRANS-NAME-AND-INITIALS  TO WS-PRINT-NAME
00175                MOVE TRANS-SOC-SEC-NUMBER     TO WS-PRINT-ID
00176                MOVE "ERROR - RECORD IN FILE" TO WS-PRINT-MESSAGE
00177                WRITE ERROR-RECORD FROM WS-PRINT-RECORD
00178                WRITE NEW-MASTER-RECORD FROM EMPLOYEE-RECORD
00179            ELSE
00180                IF SALARY-UPDATE
00181                    PERFORM 075-UPDATE-OLD-RECORD
00182                ELSE
00183                    IF DELETION
00184                        NEXT SENTENCE
00185                    ELSE
00186                        IF CORRECTION
00187                            PERFORM 085-CORRECT-OLD-RECORD.
00188
00189            MOVE "YES" TO WS-TRANS-READ-SWITCH.
00190            MOVE "YES" TO WS-OLD-MAST-READ-SWITCH.
00191
00192        075-UPDATE-OLD-RECORD.
00193            IF TRANS-SALARY-DATE = EMP-SALARY-DATE (1)
00194                MOVE TRANS-NAME-AND-INITIALS  TO WS-PRINT-NAME
00195                MOVE TRANS-SOC-SEC-NUMBER     TO WS-PRINT-ID
00196                MOVE "ERROR - UPDATE ALREADY DONE" TO WS-PRINT-MESSAGE
00197                WRITE ERROR-RECORD FROM WS-PRINT-RECORD
00198                WRITE NEW-MASTER-RECORD FROM EMPLOYEE-RECORD
00199            ELSE
00200                MOVE EMPLOYEE-RECORD TO NEW-MASTER-RECORD
00201                MOVE NEW-SALARY-DATA (2) TO NEW-SALARY-DATA (3)
00202                MOVE NEW-SALARY-DATA (1) TO NEW-SALARY-DATA (2)
00203                MOVE TRANS-SALARY-DATA TO NEW-SALARY-DATA (1)
00204                WRITE NEW-MASTER-RECORD.
00205
00206        085-CORRECT-OLD-RECORD.
00207            MOVE EMPLOYEE-RECORD TO NEW-MASTER-RECORD.
00208            IF TRANS-NAME-AND-INITIALS NOT = SPACES
00209                MOVE TRANS-NAME-AND-INITIALS TO NEW-NAME-AND-INITIALS.
00210            IF TRANS-DATE-OF-BIRTH NOT = SPACES
00211                MOVE TRANS-DATE-OF-BIRTH TO NEW-DATE-OF-BIRTH.
00212            IF TRANS-DATE-OF-HIRE NOT = SPACES
00213                MOVE TRANS-DATE-OF-HIRE TO NEW-DATE-OF-HIRE.
00214            IF TRANS-LOCATION-CODE IS NUMERIC
00215                MOVE TRANS-LOCATION-CODE TO NEW-LOCATION-CODE.
00216            IF TRANS-EDUCATION-CODE IS NUMERIC
00217                MOVE TRANS-EDUCATION-CODE TO NEW-EDUCATION-CODE.
00218            IF TRANS-TITLE-CODE IS NUMERIC
00219                MOVE TRANS-TITLE-CODE TO NEW-TITLE-CODE.
00220            IF TRANS-TITLE-DATE IS NUMERIC
00221                MOVE TRANS-TITLE-DATE TO NEW-TITLE-DATE.
00222            IF TRANS-PERFORMANCE IS NUMERIC
00223                MOVE TRANS-PERFORMANCE TO NEW-PERFORMANCE.
00224            IF TRANS-SALARY IS NUMERIC
00225                MOVE TRANS-SALARY TO NEW-SALARY (1).
```

Figure 4.9 *cont.*

```
00226              IF TRANS-SALARY-TYPE NOT = SPACES
00227                  MOVE TRANS-SALARY-TYPE TO NEW-SALARY-TYPE (1).
00228              IF TRANS-SALARY-DATE NOT = SPACES
00229                  MOVE TRANS-SALARY-DATE TO NEW-SALARY-DATE (1).
00230              IF TRANS-SALARY-GRADE IS NUMERIC
00231                  MOVE TRANS-SALARY-GRADE TO NEW-SALARY-GRADE (1).
00232
00233              WRITE NEW-MASTER-RECORD.
00234
00235          095-TRANSACTION-NOT-FOUND.
00236              IF ADDITION
00237                  PERFORM 105-ADD-NEW-RECORD
00238              ELSE
00239                  MOVE TRANS-NAME-AND-INITIALS  TO WS-PRINT-NAME
00240                  MOVE TRANS-SOC-SEC-NUMBER     TO WS-PRINT-ID
00241                  MOVE "ERROR - NO MATCH"       TO WS-PRINT-MESSAGE
00242                  WRITE ERROR-RECORD FROM WS-PRINT-RECORD.
00243              MOVE "YES" TO WS-TRANS-READ-SWITCH.
00244
00245          105-ADD-NEW-RECORD.          ⎯Expanded from a program stub
00246              MOVE SPACES TO NEW-MASTER-RECORD.
00247              MOVE TRANS-SOC-SEC-NUMBER     TO NEW-SOC-SEC-NUMBER.
00248              MOVE TRANS-NAME-AND-INITIALS  TO NEW-NAME-AND-INITIALS.
00249              MOVE TRANS-DATE-OF-BIRTH      TO NEW-DATE-OF-BIRTH.
00250              MOVE TRANS-DATE-OF-HIRE       TO NEW-DATE-OF-HIRE.
00251              MOVE TRANS-LOCATION-CODE      TO NEW-LOCATION-CODE.
00252              MOVE TRANS-EDUCATION-CODE     TO NEW-EDUCATION-CODE.
00253              MOVE TRANS-TITLE-DATA         TO NEW-TITLE-DATA.
00254              MOVE TRANS-SALARY-DATA        TO NEW-SALARY-DATA (1).
00255              MOVE ZEROS                    TO NEW-SALARY (2).
00256              MOVE ZEROS                    TO NEW-SALARY (3).
00257
00258              WRITE NEW-MASTER-RECORD.    Previous and second previous
00259                                          salaries are zeroed out
00260          180-READ-TRANSACTION.
00261              READ TRANSACTION-FILE
00262                  AT END MOVE HIGH-VALUES TO TRANS-SOC-SEC-NUMBER.
00263
00264          190-READ-OLD-MASTER.
00265              READ EMPLOYEE-FILE
00266                  AT END MOVE HIGH-VALUES TO EMP-SOC-SEC-NUMBER.
```

Figure 4.9 *cont.*

SEQUENTIAL MAINTENANCE—A REVIEW

The sequential maintenance program is now complete, and we will pause briefly to review what has transpired. The requirements for a nontrivial update program were presented in the section opening. The required logic was developed in pseudocode in Fig. 4.3. A hierarchy chart delineating the necessary modules was presented in Fig. 4.4. Test data were developed in Fig. 4.5 with anticipated results shown in Fig. 4.6.

The essential point of this section of the book is that significant testing can begin prior to the completion of the entire program. A *stubs* program was developed in Fig. 4.7 and testing began immediately. The relationship of this program to the hierarchy chart of Fig. 4.4 is paramount. The lowest level modules in the chart appear as one statement (DISPLAY) paragraphs in the program. Nevertheless, testing of this partially completed program provides *meaningful* results, because the programmer is assured that the lowest level routines are called in proper sequence. In addition, if any errors are uncovered, they are found early in the development cycle, when corrections are easiest.

The stubs program was expanded to a complete version in Fig. 4.9. The output produced by this program corresponded exactly to the anticipated results of Fig. 4.6.

NONSEQUENTIAL FILE MAINTENANCE

The initial presentation of the case study requirements emphasized the differences between sequential and nonsequential processing. The desired result of the nonsequential maintenance program to be developed now is virtually identical to that of the sequential program developed earlier. The difference is in the access method and number of files. The sequential program used *two* distinct master files, an old and a new, in addition to the transaction file. Every record in the old master had to be rewritten to the new master regardless of whether it changed. The nonsequential program will use a single master file, representing both the old and the new master. Records which change are *rewritten,* whereas nothing will be done to records remaining the same.

The logic of the sequential update was driven by *comparing* the social security numbers of the current old master and transaction records, as depicted in the pseudocode of Fig. 4.3. The nonsequential update will be driven solely by the transaction file. An incoming transaction is read, and an attempt made to match the transaction social security number with that of an existing record in the master file. A match on a correction, deletion, or salary update, indicates that an existing record will be rewritten. A match on an addition implies an error due to a duplicate add.

If the transaction social security number is *not* found in the master file, and the transaction code is an add, a new record will be added to the master file. A no match on a correction, deletion, or salary update indicates the transaction social security number was miscopied. Processing will cease when the transaction file is empty. The pseudocode for a nonsequential update is depicted in Fig. 4.10.

Figure 4.11 contains a hierarchy chart for the nonsequential update. As was stated earlier, the purpose of the hierarchy chart is to show the *function* of each routine in a program and the relationship among functions. It is not intended to show decision making logic which is the purpose of pseudocode.

The reader should observe that many of the module names found in Fig. 4.11 also appeared in Fig. 4.4, the hierarchy chart for sequential maintenance. The MATCH-ROUTINE calls either of two lower level modules; UPDATE-OLD-RECORD or CORRECT-OLD-RECORD. The TRANSACTION-NOT-FOUND module calls ADD-NEW-RECORD, and so on. Note well, however, the presence of COPY-OLD-RECORD in Fig. 4.4 and its absence in Fig. 4.11. This is because existing records in a sequential

```
Initialize
Open Files
READ TRANSACTION-FILE at end indicate no more data
┌─PERFORM until no more transactions
│    MOVE TRANSACTION social security number to record key
│    READ INDEXED-FILE
│       INVALID KEY means TRANSACTION record does not exist.
│  ┌─IF TRANSACTION record does not exist
│  │  ┌─IF addition-add record to INDEXED-FILE
│  │  └─ELSE write error indicating a no match
│  │  ELSE
│  │  ┌─IF correction-change appropriate fields
│  │  │ ELSE IF deletion-delete record
│  │  │ ELSE IF salary update-adjust salaries
│  │  │ ELSE IF addition-write error indicating duplicate addition
│  │  └─ENDIF
│  └─ENDIF
│  READ TRANSACTION-FILE at end indicate no more data
└─ENDPERFORM
Close Files
Stop run
```

Figure 4.10 Pseudocode for Nonsequential Update.

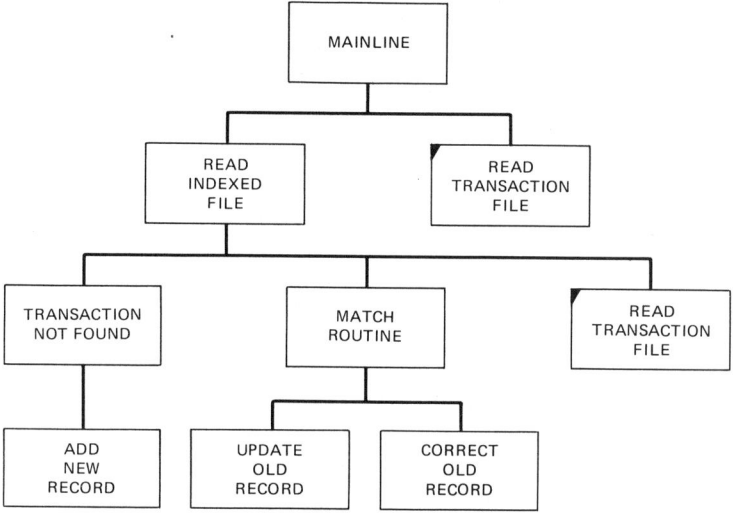

Figure 4.11 Hierarchy Chart for Nonsequential Update.

update must be copied to the new master whether or not they change. A nonsequential update, however, utilizes a single master file and rewrites only those records which actually change. It does not copy existing records with no activity, and hence, there is no need for a COPY-OLD-RECORD routine. The COMPARE-IDS module was also present in Figure 4.4, but missing from Fig. 4.11. A sequential update is driven by the relationship between *two* files and requires the module. A nonsequential update merely processes transactions until none remain.

The Nonsequential Maintenance Program (With Stubs)

The logic for nonsequential maintenance has been adequately detailed in the pseudocode of Fig. 4.10. We are now ready to develop the program itself, and assume that the reader is familiar with the COBOL requirements for indexed files. (We adhere to the ANS 74 standard which is consistent with IBM's implementation of VSAM, but differs from its ISAM version. The reader is referred to Topic 2.8 in Section 2 for exercises on indexed files and also specific differences between ISAM and VSAM.)

Of greater import is that the rationale for top down testing and development, which was presented earlier, applies equally well here. Accordingly, the initial program will contain stubs for the lowest level modules.

Figure 4.12 contains the nonsequential maintenance program. The SELECT statement for the indexed file extends from lines 12-15, and contains the clauses: ACCESS IS RANDOM, ORGANIZATION IS INDEXED, and RECORD KEY IS VSAM-SOC-SEC-NUMBER. The latter designates a data name which must be present in the indexed record itself (line 25). The record key, VSAM-SOC-SEC-NUMBER is used to build the indexes and is unique for each record in the file.

The indexed file is opened as an I-O file in line 94. The READ statement for this file uses the INVALID KEY clause, lines 111-112. It is preceded by a MOVE statement in line 109, which places the transaction social security number in the record key. Note also that the INVALID KEY condition, if activated, turns on a switch. Hence, the same switch is turned off immediately prior to the READ (line 110).

The DELETE verb is illustrated in line 130. The REWRITE verb will appear in the routines, 075-UPDATE-OLD-RECORD and 085-CORRECT-OLD-RECORD, when they are expanded from program stubs.

The program of Fig. 4.12 was tested with the data of Fig. 4.5 and produced the output shown in Fig. 4.13. The reader should compare the output of this program with that of the *sequential* stubs program in Fig. 4.8 and observe two differences.

First, the sequential program displayed the social security numbers on both the old master and transaction files, as its logic was driven by the comparison of these two data names. The nonsequential program is concerned only with the transaction file; it reads a transaction record and tries to match the incoming social security number through a *random* read. If a match is found, the appropriate routine is entered: correction, salary-update, etc. If no match is found, the INVALID KEY condition is raised and an attempt is made to add the record.

The second difference occurs when there is no change to an existing master record. The sequential approach recognizes this condition when the old master social security number is less than that of the transaction record.

It invokes a COPY-OLD-MASTER-RECORD routine, which writes the old record to the new master, even though it remains unchanged. No such requirement exists for nonsequential maintenance as unchanged records are left alone.

```
00001              IDENTIFICATION DIVISION.
00002              PROGRAM-ID.      STUBS.
00003              AUTHOR.          GRAUER.
00004
00005              ENVIRONMENT DIVISION.
00006              CONFIGURATION SECTION.
00007              SOURCE-COMPUTER.  IBM-370.
00008              OBJECT-COMPUTER.  IBM-370.
00009              INPUT-OUTPUT SECTION.
00010              FILE-CONTROL.
00011                  SELECT TRANSACTION-FILE ASSIGN TO UT-S-TRANS.
00012                  SELECT VSAM-MASTER-FILE ASSIGN TO DA-VSAM
00013                      ACCESS IS RANDOM
00014                      ORGANIZATION IS INDEXED
00015                      RECORD KEY IS VSAM-SOC-SEC-NUMBER.
00016
00017              DATA DIVISION.
00018              FILE SECTION.
00019                  COPY VSAMMAST.
00020 C         FD  VSAM-MASTER-FILE
00021 C             LABEL RECORDS ARE OMITTED
00022 C             RECORD CONTAINS 80 CHARACTERS
00023 C             DATA RECORD IS VSAM-MASTER-RECORD.
00024 C         01  VSAM-MASTER-RECORD.
00025 C             05  VSAM-SOC-SEC-NUMBER         PIC X(9).
00026 C             05  VSAM-NAME-AND-INITIALS      PIC X(15).
00027 C             05  VSAM-DATE-OF-BIRTH.
00028 C                 10  VSAM-BIRTH-MONTH        PIC 99.
00029 C                 10  VSAM-BIRTH-YEAR         PIC 99.
00030 C             05  VSAM-DATE-OF-HIRE.
00031 C                 10  VSAM-HIRE-MONTH         PIC 99.
00032 C                 10  VSAM-HIRE-YEAR          PIC 99.
00033 C             05  VSAM-LOCATION-CODE          PIC 99.
00034 C             05  VSAM-EDUCATION-CODE         PIC 9.
00035 C             05  VSAM-TITLE-DATA.
00036 C                 10  VSAM-TITLE-CODE         PIC 9(3).
00037 C                 10  VSAM-TITLE-DATE         PIC 9(4).
00038 C                 10  VSAM-PERFORMANCE        PIC 9.
00039 C             05  VSAM-SALARY-DATA OCCURS 3 TIMES
00040 C                              INDEXED BY SAL-INDEX.
00041 C                 10  VSAM-SALARY             PIC 9(5).
00042 C                 10  VSAM-SALARY-TYPE        PIC X.
00043 C                 10  VSAM-SALARY-DATE.
00044 C                     15  VSAM-SALARY-MONTH   PIC 99.
00045 C                     15  VSAM-SALARY-YEAR    PIC 99.
00046 C                 10  VSAM-SALARY-GRADE       PIC 9.
00047 C             05  FILLER                      PIC X(4).
00048
00049                  COPY TRANSACT.
00050 C         FD  TRANSACTION-FILE
00051 C             LABEL RECORDS ARE OMITTED
00052 C             RECORD CONTAINS 80 CHARACTERS
00053 C             DATA RECORD IS TRANSACTION-RECORD.
00054 C         01  TRANSACTION-RECORD.
00055 C             05  TRANS-SOC-SEC-NUMBER        PIC X(9).
00056 C             05  TRANS-NAME-AND-INITIALS     PIC X(15).
00057 C             05  TRANS-DATE-OF-BIRTH.
00058 C                 10  TRANS-BIRTH-MONTH       PIC 99.
```

Annotations:
- Line 00013: Specifies access method
- Line 00014: Required for indexed organization
- Line 00025: Data name in RECORD KEY clause must exist in indexed record
- Line 00049: COPY clause for transaction file

Figure 4.12 Stubs Program for Nonsequential Update.

```
00059 C                    10    TRANS-BIRTH-YEAR          PIC 99.
00060 C              05    TRANS-DATE-OF-HIRE.
00061 C                    10    TRANS-HIRE-MONTH          PIC 99.
00062 C                    10    TRANS-HIRE-YEAR           PIC 99.
00063 C              05    TRANS-LOCATION-CODE             PIC 99.
00064 C              05    TRANS-EDUCATION-CODE            PIC 9.
00065 C              05    TRANS-TITLE-DATA.
00066 C                    10    TRANS-TITLE-CODE          PIC 9(3).
00067 C                    10    TRANS-TITLE-DATE          PIC 9(4).
00068 C                    10    TRANS-PERFORMANCE         PIC 9.
00069 C              05    TRANS-SALARY-DATA.
00070 C                    10    TRANS-SALARY              PIC 9(5).
00071 C                    10    TRANS-SALARY-TYPE         PIC X.
00072 C                    10    TRANS-SALARY-DATE.
00073 C                          15   TRANS-SALARY-MONTH   PIC 99.
00074 C                          15   TRANS-SALARY-YEAR    PIC 99.
00075 C                    10    TRANS-SALARY-GRADE        PIC 9.
00076 C              05    FILLER                          PIC X(25).
00077 C              05    TRANS-CODE                      PIC X.
00078 C                    88    ADDITION         VALUE "A".
00079 C                    88    CORRECTION       VALUE "C".      ⎯ Transaction types
00080 C                    88    DELETION         VALUE "D".
00081 C                    88    SALARY-UPDATE    VALUE "U".
00082
00083          WORKING-STORAGE SECTION.
00084          01    WORKING-STORAGE-SWITCHES.
00085                05    WS-END-OF-TRANSACTION-SWITCH  PIC X(3)  VALUE "YES".
00086                      88    NO-MORE-TRANSACTION-RECORDS        VALUE "NO".
00087                      88    STILL-MORE-TRANSACTION-RECORDS     VALUE "YES".
00088                05    WS-INVALID-SWITCH             PIC X(3)  VALUE "NO".
00089                      88    NO-MATCH-OR-NEW-RECORD             VALUE "YES".
00090
00091          PROCEDURE DIVISION.
00092          005-MAINLINE.
00093              OPEN INPUT TRANSACTION-FILE
00094                   I-O VSAM-MASTER-FILE.          ⎯ Indexed file is opened as both input
00095                                                      and output
00096              PERFORM 180-READ-TRANSACTION.
00097
00098              PERFORM 010-READ-VSAM-FILE
00099                 UNTIL NO-MORE-TRANSACTION-RECORDS.
00100
00101              CLOSE TRANSACTION-FILE
00102                    VSAM-MASTER-FILE.
00103              STOP RUN.
00104                                       Transaction key is moved to record key prior to READ
00105          010-READ-VSAM-FILE.
00106              DISPLAY " ".
00107              DISPLAY "TRANSACTION SOC/SEC: " TRANS-SOC-SEC-NUMBER
00108                      "TRANSACTION-CODE: " TRANS-CODE.
00109              MOVE TRANS-SOC-SEC-NUMBER TO VSAM-SOC-SEC-NUMBER.
00110              MOVE "NO" TO WS-INVALID-SWITCH.
00111              READ VSAM-MASTER-FILE           Invalid switch is turned off prior to READ
00112                  INVALID KEY MOVE "YES" TO WS-INVALID-SWITCH.
00113              IF NO-MATCH-OR-NEW-RECORD
00114                  PERFORM 095-TRANSACTION-NOT-FOUND
00115              ELSE
00116                  PERFORM 060-MATCH-ROUTINE.        Invalid switch is turned on
00117                                                     if record is not found
00118              PERFORM 180-READ-TRANSACTION.
00119
00120          060-MATCH-ROUTINE.
00121              DISPLAY "060-MATCH-ROUTINE ENTERED".
00122              IF ADDITION
```

Figure 4.12 *cont.*

```
00123                DISPLAY "ERROR-ADDITION TRANSACTION ALREADY IN FILE"
00124                        TRANS-SOC-SEC-NUMBER
00125            ELSE
00126                IF SALARY-UPDATE
00127                    PERFORM 075-UPDATE-OLD-RECORD
00128                ELSE
00129                    IF DELETION                DELETE statement removes records from indexed file
00130                        DELETE VSAM-MASTER-FILE
00131                    ELSE
00132                        IF CORRECTION
00133                            PERFORM 085-CORRECT-OLD-RECORD.
00134
00135        075-UPDATE-OLD-RECORD.
00136            DISPLAY "075-UPDATE-OLD-RECORD ENTERED".
00137
00138        085-CORRECT-OLD-RECORD.
00139            DISPLAY "085-CORRECT-OLD-RECORD ENTERED".          Program stubs
00140
00141        095-TRANSACTION-NOT-FOUND.
00142            DISPLAY "095-TRANSACTION-NOT-FOUND ENTERED".
00143            IF ADDITION
00144                PERFORM 105-ADD-VSAM-RECORD
00145            ELSE
00146                DISPLAY "ERROR-NO MATCH FOR TRANSACTION RECORD"
00147                        TRANS-SOC-SEC-NUMBER.
00148
00149        105-ADD-VSAM-RECORD.
00150            DISPLAY "105-ADD-VSAM-RECORD ENTERED".
00151
00152        180-READ-TRANSACTION.
00153            READ TRANSACTION-FILE
00154                AT END MOVE "NO" TO WS-END-OF-TRANSACTION-SWITCH.
00155
```

Figure 4.12 *cont.*

```
TRANSACTION SOC SEC: 100000000TRANSACTION-CODE: U
060-MATCH-ROUTINE ENTERED
075-UPDATE-OLD-RECORD ENTERED

TRANSACTION SOC SEC: 200000000TRANSACTION-CODE: C
060-MATCH-ROUTINE ENTERED
085-CORRECT-OLD-RECORD ENTERED

TRANSACTION SOC SEC: 211111111TRANSACTION-CODE: A
095-TRANSACTION-NOT-FOUND ENTERED
105-ADD-VSAM-RECORD ENTERED

TRANSACTION SOC SEC: 300000000TRANSACTION-CODE: D
060-MATCH-ROUTINE ENTERED

TRANSACTION SOC SEC: 400000000TRANSACTION-CODE: C
060-MATCH-ROUTINE ENTERED
085-CORRECT-OLD-RECORD ENTERED

TRANSACTION SOC SEC: 444444444TRANSACTION-CODE: A
095-TRANSACTION-NOT-FOUND ENTERED
105-ADD-VSAM-RECORD ENTERED

TRANSACTION SOC SEC: 500000000TRANSACTION-CODE: C
060-MATCH-ROUTINE ENTERED
085-CORRECT-OLD-RECORD ENTERED

TRANSACTION SOC SEC: 600000000TRANSACTION-CODE: A
060-MATCH-ROUTINE ENTERED
ERROR-ADDITION TRANSACTION ALREADY IN FILE600000000
```

Figure 4.13 Output of Nonsequential Stubs Program.

```
TRANSACTION SOC SEC: 654321000TRANSACTION-CODE: C
095-TRANSACTION-NOT-FOUND ENTERED
ERROR-NO MATCH FOR TRANSACTION RECORD654321000

TRANSACTION SOC SEC: 800000000TRANSACTION-CODE: C
060-MATCH-ROUTINE ENTERED
085-CORRECT-OLD-RECORD ENTERED

TRANSACTION SOC SEC: 878787878TRANSACTION-CODE: U
095-TRANSACTION-NOT-FOUND ENTERED
ERROR-NO MATCH FOR TRANSACTION RECORD878787878

TRANSACTION SOC SEC: 900000000TRANSACTION-CODE: U
060-MATCH-ROUTINE ENTERED
075-UPDATE-OLD-RECORD ENTERED
```

Figure 4.13 *cont.*

The Completed Nonsequential Maintenance Program

As with the sequential update, once the stubs program was tested and debugged, it is relatively easy to fill in the blanks and complete the program. Fig. 4.14 contains the finished program for nonsequential maintenance. It has detailed modules for: 075-UPDATE-OLD-RECORD, 085-CORRECT-OLD-RECORD, and 105-ADD-VSAM-RECORD in lieu of program stubs. In addition, it incorporates a third file, ERROR-FILE, instead of DISPLAY messages.

The logic in the modules for updating and correcting existing records closely follows that of the sequential program (Fig. 4.9). Note, however, the use of REWRITE in lines 159 and 187 when an existing record is changed. The logic to add a new record is identical in both programs. Little more need be said about Fig. 4.14 that was not already said about its counterpart for sequential maintenance.

Figure 4.14 was tested with the identical test data of Fig. 4.5 and produced the same results as Fig. 4.6.

```
00001           IDENTIFICATION DIVISION.
00002           PROGRAM-ID.      UPDATE2.
00003           AUTHOR.          GRAUER.
00004
00005           ENVIRONMENT DIVISION.
00006           CONFIGURATION SECTION.
00007           SOURCE-COMPUTER.  IBM-370.
00008           OBJECT-COMPUTER.  IBM-370.
00009           INPUT-OUTPUT SECTION.
00010           FILE-CONTROL.
00011               SELECT TRANSACTION-FILE ASSIGN TO UT-S-TRANS.
00012               SELECT ERROR-FILE ASSIGN TO UT-S-PRINT.
00013               SELECT VSAM-MASTER-FILE ASSIGN TO DA-VSAM
00014                   ACCESS IS RANDOM
00015                   ORGANIZATION IS INDEXED
00016                   RECORD KEY IS VSAM-SOC-SEC-NUMBER.
00017                                          Required entry for indexed files
00018           DATA DIVISION.
00019           FILE SECTION.           COPY clause for indexed file
00020               COPY VSAMMAST.
```

Figure 4.14 Completed Program for Nonsequential Processing.

```
00021 C          FD  VSAM-MASTER-FILE
00022 C              LABEL RECORDS ARE OMITTED
00023 C              RECORD CONTAINS 80 CHARACTERS
00024 C              DATA RECORD IS VSAM-MASTER-RECORD.
00025 C          01  VSAM-MASTER-RECORD.
00026 C              05  VSAM-SOC-SEC-NUMBER              PIC X(9).
00027 C              05  VSAM-NAME-AND-INITIALS           PIC X(15).
00028 C              05  VSAM-DATE-OF-BIRTH.
00029 C                  10  VSAM-BIRTH-MONTH             PIC 99.
00030 C                  10  VSAM-BIRTH-YEAR              PIC 99.
00031 C              05  VSAM-DATE-OF-HIRE.
00032 C                  10  VSAM-HIRE-MONTH              PIC 99.
00033 C                  10  VSAM-HIRE-YEAR               PIC 99.
00034 C              05  VSAM-LOCATION-CODE               PIC 99.
00035 C              05  VSAM-EDUCATION-CODE              PIC 9.
00036 C              05  VSAM-TITLE-DATA.
00037 C                  10  VSAM-TITLE-CODE              PIC 9(3).
00038 C                  10  VSAM-TITLE-DATE              PIC 9(4).
00039 C                  10  VSAM-PERFORMANCE             PIC 9.
00040 C              05  VSAM-SALARY-DATA OCCURS 3 TIMES
00041 C                              INDEXED BY SAL-INDEX.
00042 C                  10  VSAM-SALARY                  PIC 9(5).
00043 C                  10  VSAM-SALARY-TYPE             PIC X.
00044 C                  10  VSAM-SALARY-DATE.
00045 C                      15  VSAM-SALARY-MONTH        PIC 99.
00046 C                      15  VSAM-SALARY-YEAR         PIC 99.
00047 C                  10  VSAM-SALARY-GRADE            PIC 9.
00048 C              05  FILLER                           PIC X(4).
00049
00050            |COPY TRANSACT.|──── COPY clause for transaction file
00051 C          FD  TRANSACTION-FILE
00052 C              LABEL RECORDS ARE OMITTED
00053 C              RECORD CONTAINS 80 CHARACTERS
00054 C              DATA RECORD IS TRANSACTION-RECORD.
00055 C          01  TRANSACTION-RECORD.
00056 C              05  TRANS-SOC-SEC-NUMBER             PIC X(9).
00057 C              05  TRANS-NAME-AND-INITIALS          PIC X(15).
00058 C              05  TRANS-DATE-OF-BIRTH.
00059 C                  10  TRANS-BIRTH-MONTH            PIC 99.
00060 C                  10  TRANS-BIRTH-YEAR             PIC 99.
00061 C              05  TRANS-DATE-OF-HIRE.
00062 C                  10  TRANS-HIRE-MONTH             PIC 99.
00063 C                  10  TRANS-HIRE-YEAR              PIC 99.
00064 C              05  TRANS-LOCATION-CODE              PIC 99.
00065 C              05  TRANS-EDUCATION-CODE             PIC 9.
00066 C              05  TRANS-TITLE-DATA.
00067 C                  10  TRANS-TITLE-CODE             PIC 9(3).
00068 C                  10  TRANS-TITLE-DATE             PIC 9(4).
00069 C                  10  TRANS-PERFORMANCE            PIC 9.
00070 C              05  TRANS-SALARY-DATA.
00071 C                  10  TRANS-SALARY                 PIC 9(5).
00072 C                  10  TRANS-SALARY-TYPE            PIC X.
00073 C                  10  TRANS-SALARY-DATE.
00074 C                      15  TRANS-SALARY-MONTH       PIC 99.
00075 C                      15  TRANS-SALARY-YEAR        PIC 99.
00076 C                  10  TRANS-SALARY-GRADE           PIC 9.
00077 C              05  FILLER                           PIC X(25).
00078 C              05  TRANS-CODE                       PIC X.
00079 C                  88  ADDITION          VALUE "A".
00080 C                  88  CORRECTION        VALUE "C".
00081 C                  88  DELETION          VALUE "D".
00082 C                  88  SALARY-UPDATE     VALUE "U".
00083
00084            |FD  ERROR-FILE|──── ERROR-FILE has been added to stubs program
00085              LABEL RECORDS ARE OMITTED
00086              RECORD CONTAINS 132 CHARACTERS
```

Figure 4.14 *cont.*

```
00087                DATA RECORD IS ERROR-RECORD.
00088            01  ERROR-RECORD                        PIC X(132).
00089
00090        WORKING-STORAGE SECTION.
00091            01  WORKING-STORAGE-SWITCHES.
00092                05  WS-END-OF-TRANSACTION-SWITCH  PIC X(3)    VALUE "YES".
00093                    88  NO-MORE-TRANSACTION-RECORDS           VALUE "NO".
00094                    88  STILL-MORE-TRANSACTION-RECORDS        VALUE "YES".
00095                05  WS-INVALID-SWITCH             PIC X(3)    VALUE "NO".
00096                    88  NO-MATCH-OR-NEW-RECORD                VALUE "YES".
00097
00098            01  WS-PRINT-RECORD.
00099                05  WS-PRINT-MESSAGE              PIC X(40)   VALUE SPACES.
00100                05  WS-PRINT-ID                   PIC X(9).
00101                05  FILLER                        PIC X(5)    VALUE SPACES.
00102                05  WS-PRINT-NAME                 PIC X(25).
00103                05  FILLER                        PIC X(53)   VALUE SPACES.
00104
00105        PROCEDURE DIVISION.
00106        005-MAINLINE.
00107            OPEN INPUT TRANSACTION-FILE
00108                 I-O VSAM-MASTER-FILE          ──── Indexed file is opened as I-O
00109                 OUTPUT ERROR-FILE.
00110
00111            PERFORM 180-READ-TRANSACTION.
00112
00113            PERFORM 010-READ-VSAM-FILE
00114                UNTIL NO-MORE-TRANSACTION-RECORDS.
00115
00116            CLOSE TRANSACTION-FILE
00117                  VSAM-MASTER-FILE
00118                  ERROR-FILE.
00119            STOP RUN.
00120                                          ── Transaction key moved to record key
00121        010-READ-VSAM-FILE.
00122            MOVE TRANS-SOC-SEC-NUMBER TO VSAM-SOC-SEC-NUMBER.
00123            MOVE "NO" TO WS-INVALID-SWITCH.
00124            READ VSAM-MASTER-FILE
00125                INVALID KEY MOVE "YES" TO WS-INVALID-SWITCH.
00126            IF NO-MATCH-OR-NEW-RECORD
00127                PERFORM 095-TRANSACTION-NOT-FOUND
00128            ELSE                                      INVALID KEY clause is used
00129                PERFORM 060-MATCH-ROUTINE.            with random read
00130
00131            PERFORM 180-READ-TRANSACTION.
00132
00133        060-MATCH-ROUTINE.
00134            IF ADDITION
00135                MOVE TRANS-NAME-AND-INITIALS   TO WS-PRINT-NAME
00136                MOVE TRANS-SOC-SEC-NUMBER      TO WS-PRINT-ID
00137                MOVE "ERROR - RECORD IN FILE" TO WS-PRINT-MESSAGE
00138                WRITE ERROR-RECORD FROM WS-PRINT-RECORD
00139            ELSE
00140                IF SALARY-UPDATE
00141                    PERFORM 075-UPDATE-OLD-RECORD
00142                ELSE                       ── Removal of inactive record
00143                    IF DELETION
00144                        DELETE VSAM-MASTER-FILE
00145                    ELSE
00146                        IF CORRECTION
00147                            PERFORM 085-CORRECT-OLD-RECORD.
00148                                      ── Expanded from a program stub
00149        075-UPDATE-OLD-RECORD.
00150            IF TRANS-SALARY-DATE = VSAM-SALARY-DATE (1)
00151                MOVE TRANS-NAME-AND-INITIALS   TO WS-PRINT-NAME
00152                MOVE TRANS-SOC-SEC-NUMBER      TO WS-PRINT-ID
```

Figure 4.14 *cont.*

```
00153              MOVE "ERROR - UPDATE ALREADY DONE" TO WS-PRINT-MESSAGE
00154              WRITE ERROR-RECORD FROM WS-PRINT-RECORD
00155          ELSE
00156              MOVE VSAM-SALARY-DATA (2) TO VSAM-SALARY-DATA (3)
00157              MOVE VSAM-SALARY-DATA (1) TO VSAM-SALARY-DATA (2)
00158              MOVE TRANS-SALARY-DATA TO VSAM-SALARY-DATA (1)
00159              REWRITE VSAM-MASTER-RECORD.         ← REWRITE statement
00160
00161      085-CORRECT-OLD-RECORD.                    ← Expanded from a program stub
00162          IF TRANS-NAME-AND-INITIALS NOT = SPACES
00163              MOVE TRANS-NAME-AND-INITIALS TO VSAM-NAME-AND-INITIALS.
00164          IF TRANS-DATE-OF-BIRTH NOT = SPACES
00165              MOVE TRANS-DATE-OF-BIRTH TO VSAM-DATE-OF-BIRTH.
00166          IF TRANS-DATE-OF-HIRE NOT = SPACES
00167              MOVE TRANS-DATE-OF-HIRE TO VSAM-DATE-OF-HIRE.
00168          IF TRANS-LOCATION-CODE IS NUMERIC
00169              MOVE TRANS-LOCATION-CODE TO VSAM-LOCATION-CODE.
00170          IF TRANS-EDUCATION-CODE IS NUMERIC
00171              MOVE TRANS-EDUCATION-CODE TO VSAM-EDUCATION-CODE.
00172          IF TRANS-TITLE-CODE IS NUMERIC
00173              MOVE TRANS-TITLE-CODE TO VSAM-TITLE-CODE.
00174          IF TRANS-TITLE-DATE IS NUMERIC
00175              MOVE TRANS-TITLE-DATE TO VSAM-TITLE-DATE.
00176          IF TRANS-PERFORMANCE IS NUMERIC
00177              MOVE TRANS-PERFORMANCE TO VSAM-PERFORMANCE.
00178          IF TRANS-SALARY IS NUMERIC
00179              MOVE TRANS-SALARY TO VSAM-SALARY (1).
00180          IF TRANS-SALARY-TYPE NOT = SPACES
00181              MOVE TRANS-SALARY-TYPE TO VSAM-SALARY-TYPE (1).
00182          IF TRANS-SALARY-DATE NOT = SPACES
00183              MOVE TRANS-SALARY-DATE TO VSAM-SALARY-DATE (1).
00184          IF TRANS-SALARY-GRADE IS NUMERIC
00185              MOVE TRANS-SALARY-GRADE TO VSAM-SALARY-GRADE (1).
00186
00187          REWRITE VSAM-MASTER-RECORD.             ← REWRITE statement
00188
00189      095-TRANSACTION-NOT-FOUND.
00190          IF ADDITION
00191              PERFORM 105-ADD-VSAM-RECORD
00192          ELSE
00193              MOVE TRANS-NAME-AND-INITIALS  TO WS-PRINT-NAME
00194              MOVE TRANS-SOC-SEC-NUMBER     TO WS-PRINT-ID
00195              MOVE "ERROR - NO MATCH"       TO WS-PRINT-MESSAGE
00196              WRITE ERROR-RECORD FROM WS-PRINT-RECORD.
00197                                             ← Expanded from a program stub
00198      105-ADD-VSAM-RECORD.
00199          MOVE SPACES TO VSAM-MASTER-RECORD.
00200          MOVE TRANS-SOC-SEC-NUMBER      TO VSAM-SOC-SEC-NUMBER.
00201          MOVE TRANS-NAME-AND-INITIALS   TO VSAM-NAME-AND-INITIALS.
00202          MOVE TRANS-DATE-OF-BIRTH       TO VSAM-DATE-OF-BIRTH.
00203          MOVE TRANS-DATE-OF-HIRE        TO VSAM-DATE-OF-HIRE.
00204          MOVE TRANS-LOCATION-CODE       TO VSAM-LOCATION-CODE.
00205          MOVE TRANS-EDUCATION-CODE      TO VSAM-EDUCATION-CODE.
00206          MOVE TRANS-TITLE-DATA          TO VSAM-TITLE-DATA.
00207          MOVE TRANS-SALARY-DATA         TO VSAM-SALARY-DATA (1).
00208          MOVE ZEROS                     TO VSAM-SALARY (2).
00209          MOVE ZEROS                     TO VSAM-SALARY (3).
00210
00211          WRITE VSAM-MASTER-RECORD.
00212
00213      180-READ-TRANSACTION.
00214          READ TRANSACTION-FILE
00215              AT END MOVE "NO" TO WS-END-OF-TRANSACTION-SWITCH.
00216
```

Figure 4.14 *cont.*

SUMMARY

The intention of this section is to leave the reader with model programs for both sequential and nonsequential maintenance. Although the specific requirements will obviously change from application to application, the underlying mechanisms, such as the comparison of the transaction and old master in sequential maintenance and the matching of transaction records to those in an indexed file, tend to remain the same. Hence, the reader may be able to apply parts of these programs to a wider variety of applications than at first imagined. Follow-up exercises are provided in Projects 6.10 and 6.20 of Sect. 6 for two different systems.

In addition to the model programs, the author hopes to have instilled an appreciation for top down testing; that a program need not be completely coded before testing can begin. The higher level modules of a program contain its most complex logic, and hence, should be tested earlier and more often than the lower level routines. The latter contain detailed, but often trivial, logic and are the easiest to code.

5 Good Practices and Bad

OVERVIEW

The professional programmer should produce a product that is easily read and maintained by someone other than the original author. It is the purpose of this section to evaluate various coding practices for inclusion in one's programming style to realize this objective. This is accomplished by postulating 18 guidelines for use in COBOL programming. These are:

- Use appropriate comments
- Eliminate 77-level entries
- Choose meaningful names
- Indent
- Space attractively
- Avoid commas
- Restrict switches and subscripts to a single use
- Use 88-level entries
- Perform paragraphs not sections
- Use the COMPUTE verb for multiple arithmetic operations
- Keep it simple
- Use the appropriate search technique
- Initialize tables dynamically
- Avoid constants
- Avoid literals
- Use READ INTO, WRITE FROM, and WS BEGINS HERE
- Pass a single 01 parameter to a subprogram
- Consider Report Writer

Some of the guidelines are purely *cosmetic;* they are concerned only with the arrangement of the COBOL code itself. Indentation, spacing, avoiding commas, and so on fall into this class. Other guidelines suggest particular COBOL features to use and/or avoid; for example, performing paragraphs rather than sections, using 88 level entries and avoiding 77s, and so on. Still others focus on the choice of algorithm, such as initializing tables dynamically.

These suggestions are *guidelines, rather than rigid standards,* and the reader is not necessarily expected to agree with all items. If you have sound reason for objecting to an element of the style presented here, so be it. You are on your way to developing your own.

USE APPROPRIATE COMMENTS

Although there is growing disillusionment with comments in structured COBOL programs, good code does not eliminate their necessity. As Yourdon* has so eloquently stated, "No programmer, no matter how wise, no matter how experienced, no matter how hard pressed for time, no matter how well intentioned, should be forgiven an uncommented and undocumented program." The mere presence of comments, however, does not ensure a well-documented program, and poor comments are sometimes worse than no comments at all. The most common fault is *redundance* with the source code. For example, in the code below:

```
*   CALCULATE NET PAY
    COMPUTE NET-PAY = GROSS-PAY - FEDERAL-TAX - VOLUNTARY-DEDUCTION
```

the comment does not add to the readability of the program. It might even be said to detract from legibility because it breaks the logical flow as one is reading. Worse than redundant, comments may be *obsolete, incorrect,* or *inconsistent with the associated code.* This happens if program statements are changed during debugging or maintenance, and the comments are not correspondingly altered. The compiler, unfortunately, does not validate comments. Comments may also be correct, but incomplete and hence misleading. In sum, the presence of comments is essential, but great care, *more than is commonly exercised,* should be applied to developing and maintaining comments in a program.

As a general rule, comments should be provided whenever you are doing something which is not immediately obvious to another person. When considering a comment, imagine you are turning the program over for maintenance, and insert comments whenever you would pause to explain

*Yourdon, Edward, *Techniques of Program Structure and Design* Prentice-Hall, (Englewood Cliffs, N.J.: 1975).

a feature in your program. Do assume, however, that the maintenance programmer is as competent in COBOL as you are. Thus, your comments should be directed to *why* you are doing something, rather than to what you are doing.

ELIMINATE 77-LEVEL ENTRIES

The next COBOL standard will apparently eliminate 77-level entries. The alternative is to group related entries under a common 01 description in Working-Storage. Consider:

Poor Code:

```
77   COUNTER-ONE                    PIC 9(3)   VALUE ZEROS.
77   COUNTER-TWO                    PIC 9(3)   VALUE ZEROS.
77   COUNTER-THREE                  PIC 9(3)   VALUE ZEROS.
```

Improved Code:

```
01   RECORD-COUNTERS.
     05   NUMBER-OF-RECORDS-READ    PIC 9(3)   VALUE ZEROS.
     05   NUMBER-OF-GOOD-RECORDS    PIC 9(3)   VALUE ZEROS.
     05   NUMBER-OF-BAD-RECORDS     PIC 9(3)   VALUE ZEROS.
```

The improved code has given the three counters more descriptive names which reflect both similarities and differences among the related items.

CHOOSE MEANINGFUL NAMES

The COBOL compiler is very lenient with its rules for programmer-chosen names. Specifically, a user-defined word may not exceed thirty characters or begin or end with a hyphen. Valid characters for inclusion in a user defined word are A through Z, 0 through 9, and the hyphen. File and data names must contain at least one alphabetic character, whereas paragraph and section names may be all numeric. It is strongly recommended that these rules be amended as follows:

1. Data names should be mnemonically significant. Although COBOL allows up to thirty characters, two and three character cryptic names are used too frequently. It is impossible for the maintenance programmer, or even the original author, to determine the meaning of abbreviated data names. On first reading, it may seem that this guideline adds unnecessarily to the burden of writer's cramp. Ex-

perience has shown, however, that meaningful data names significantly ease the job of the maintenance programmer. Some examples:

Poor Choice:

    SWITCH-ONE
    TOTAL-1
    TRANS-ID

Improved Choice:

    END-OF-TRANSACTION-FILE-SWITCH
    TOTAL-EMPLOYEE-GROSS-PAY
    TRANSACTION-ID-NUMBER

2. All data names within the same 01 record should have a common two-or three-letter prefix. The utility of this guideline becomes apparent in the Procedure Division if it is necessary to refer back to the definition of a data name.

Poor Choice:

    01 EMPLOYEE-RECORD.
        05 SOC-SEC-NUMBER
        05 NAME
        05 ADDRESS

Improved Choice:

    01 EMPLOYEE-RECORD.
        05 EMP-SOC-SEC-NUMBER
        05 EMP-NAME
        05 EMP-ADDRESS

3. File names should fully indicate the purpose of the file and include the suffix-FILE. A file name should never be tied to a physical device. Some examples:

Poor Choice:

    CUSTOMER-MASTER
    PRINT-FILE
    CARD-FILE

Improved Choice:

```
CUSTOMER-MASTER-FILE
EMPLOYEE-EXCEPTION-REPORT-FILE
```

4. Paragraph names should be *functional* in nature, and reflect the purpose of the paragraph. A guiding principle of structured design is that a paragraph be strongly *cohesive;* every statement in a paragraph should be related to the *single* task that the paragraph is to perform. A paragraph name should consist of a verb, an adjective or two, and an object: READ-TRANSACTION-FILE, ADD-NEW-RECORD, and so on. If a paragraph cannot be named in this manner, it is probably not functional, and consideration should be given to redesigning the program and/or paragraph.

   Paragraph names should also be sequenced. Programmers and managers alike accept the utility of this guideline to quickly locate paragraphs in the Procedure Division. There is, however, considerable disagreement on just what sequencing scheme to use; all numbers, a single letter followed by numbers, etc. We make no strong argument for one scheme over another, other than to insist a consistent sequencing rule be followed. Some examples:

Poor Choice:

```
0005-MAINLINE
A010-READ-AND-WRITE
READ-TRANSACTION-FILE
```

Improved Choice:

```
A010-WRITE-NEW-MASTER-RECORD
1000-PRODUCE-ERROR-REPORT
2000-READ-TRANSACTION-FILE
```

INDENT

Virtually no one will argue against indenting successive level numbers within a record description in the Data Division. Why then do so few employ indentation in the Procedure Division? Consider:

Poor Code:

```
PERFORM INITIALIZE-TABLE VARYING LOCATION-SUB FROM 1
BY 1 UNTIL LOCATION-SUB > 3 AFTER DEPARTMENT-SUB
FROM 1 BY 1 UNTIL DEPARTMENT-SUB > 5.
```

```
WRITE ISAM-RECORD INVALID KEY
    MOVE 'YES' TO INVALID-ISAM-KEY-SWITCH
PERFORM WRITE-ERROR-MESSAGE.

IF EMPLOYEE-AGE > 65 MOVE EMP-NAME TO
PRINT-RETIREMENT-NAME, ADD 1 TO
NUMBER-OF-RETIREEES, PERFORM WRITE-RETIREE-REPORT.
```

Improved Code:

```
PERFORM INITIALIZE-TABLE
    VARYING LOCATION-SUB FROM 1 BY 1
      UNTIL LOCATION-SUB > 3
    AFTER DEPARTMENT-SUB FROM 1 BY 1
      UNTIL DEPARTMENT-SUB > 5.

WRITE ISAM-RECORD
    INVALID KEY
      MOVE 'YES' TO INVALID-ISAM-KEY-SWITCH
      PERFORM WRITE-ERROR-MESSAGE.

IF EMPLOYEE-AGE > 65
    MOVE EMP-NAME TO PRINT-RETIREMENT-NAME
    ADD 1 TO NUMBER-OF-RETIREES
    PERFORM WRITE-RETIREE-REPORT.
```

As can be seen from the improved code, subservient clauses should always be indented under the main verbs. The legibility of PERFORM, for example, is improved immeasurably by indenting VARYING under PERFORM, and UNTIL under VARYING. Other examples in the same vein include:

```
AFTER (BEFORE) ADVANCING under WRITE
AT END and WHEN under SEARCH
AT END and INVALID KEY under READ
SIZE ERROR under COMPUTE
GIVING under ADD, MULTIPLY, SUBTRACT, and DIVIDE
```

Indentation should always be *consistent* with compiler interpretation. The INVALID KEY clause, for example, is terminated by a period and the indentation should reflect this. INVALID KEY is written on a line by itself in the improved code with two subservient statements (MOVE and PERFORM) indented under it. All actions taken as a result of an IF should be indented as well, as shown in the last example.

The nested IF statement is worthy of special mention. The compiler does not interpret ELSE clauses as the programmer writes them but associates the ELSE clause with the closest unpaired previous IF. Consider:

Poor Code:

```
IF CD-SEX IS EQUAL TO 'M'
   IF CD-AGE IS GREATER THAN 30
      MOVE CD-NAME TO MALE-OVER-30
      ADD 1 TO NUMBER-QUALIFIED-MALES
   ELSE MOVE CD-NAME TO PRT-NAME
   ADD 1 TO MALE-UNDER-30.
```

The indentation implies that CD-NAME will be moved to PRT-NAME if CD-SEX is not equal to 'M.' This is *not* the compiler interpretation. The ELSE clause is associated with the closest previous IF which is not already paired with another ELSE. Therefore, the compiler will move CD-NAME to PRT-NAME if CD-SEX equals 'M' but CD-AGE is not greater than 30.

Nested IFs should be coded as follows:

1. Indent successive IFs four columns
2. Put the word ELSE on a line by itself, and directly under its associated IF
3. Indent detail lines for both IF and ELSE four columns

The previous nested IF statement is rewritten to reflect these guidelines:

Improved Code:

```
IF CD-SEX IS EQUAL TO 'M'
    IF CD-AGE IS GREATER THAN 30
        MOVE CD-NAME TO MALE-OVER-30
        ADD 1 TO NUMBER-QUALIFIED-MALES
    ELSE
        MOVE CD-NAME TO PRT-NAME
        ADD 1 TO MALE-UNDER-30.
```

SPACE ATTRACTIVELY

The adoption of various spacing conventions can go a long way toward improving the appearance and legibility of a program. We believe very strongly in the insertion of blank lines throughout a program to highlight important statements. Specific suggestions include a blank line before all paragraph and/or section headers, before all FDs and/or 01 entries, and even before specific verbs.

The reader can also cause various portions of a listing to begin on a new page. This is accomplished in the ANS 74 standard by putting a slash in column 7 of a separate card prior to the source statement.

Vertical spacing is also important. The Data Division, for example, is enhanced significantly by beginning all picture clauses in the same column.

AVOID COMMAS

The compiler treats a comma as noise, it has no effect on the generated object code. Many programmers, have acquired the habit of inserting commas to increase legibility. While this works rather well with prose, it can have just the opposite effect in COBOL. This is because of blurred print chains which make it difficult to distinguish a comma from a period. As we have already seen, the presence or absence of a period is critical. Hence, the inability to distinguish a period from a comma becomes rather annoying. The best solution is to try to avoid commas altogether.

RESTRICT SWITCHES AND SUBSCRIPTS TO A SINGLE USE

Data names defined as switches and/or subscripts should be restricted to a single use. Consider:

Poor Code:

```
77    SUBSCRIPT                    PIC S9(4)    COMP.
77    EOF-SWITCH                   PIC X(3)     VALUE SPACES.
 .
 .
      PERFORM INITIALIZE-TITLE-FILE
         UNTIL EOF-SWITCH = 'YES'.

      MOVE SPACES TO EOF-SWITCH.

      PERFORM PROCESS-EMPLOYEE-RECORDS
         UNTIL EOF-SWITCH = 'YES'.

      PERFORM COMPUTE-SALARY-HISTORY
         VARYING SUBSCRIPT FROM 1 BY 1
            UNTIL SUBSCRIPT > 3.

      PERFORM FIND-MATCHING-TITLE
         VARYING SUBSCRIPT FROM 1 BY 1
            UNTIL SUBSCRIPT > 100.
```

Improved Code:

```
01  PROGRAM-SUBSCRIPTS.
    05  TITLE-SUBSCRIPT            PIC S9(4)   COMP.
    05  SALARY-SUBSCRIPT           PIC S9(4)   COMP.

01  END-OF-FILE-SWITCHES.
    05  END-OF-TITLE-FILE-SWITCH       PIC X(3)   VALUE SPACES.
    05  END-OF-EMPLOYEE-FILE-SWITCH    PIC X(3)   VALUE SPACES.
      .
      .
    PERFORM INITIALIZE-TITLE-FILE
        UNTIL END-OF-TITLE-FILE-SWITCH = 'YES'.

    PERFORM PROCESS-EMPLOYEE-RECORDS
        UNTIL END-OF-EMPLOYEE-FILE-SWITCH = 'YES'.

    PERFORM COMPUTE-SALARY-HISTORY
        VARYING SALARY-SUBSCRIPT FROM 1 BY 1
        UNTIL SALARY-SUBSCRIPT > 3.

    PERFORM FIND-MATCHING-TITLE
        VARYING TITLE-SUBSCRIPT FROM 1 BY 1
        UNTIL TITLE-SUBSCRIPT > 100.
```

At the very least, the improved code offers superior documentation. By restricting data names to a single use, one automatically avoids such nondescript entries as EOF-SWITCH or SUBSCRIPT. Of greater impact, the improved code is more apt to be correct in that a given data name is modified or tested in fewer places within a program. Finally, if bugs do occur, the final values of the unique data names (TITLE-SUBSCRIPT and SALARY-SUBSCRIPT) will be of much greater use than the single value of SUBSCRIPT.

USE 88-LEVEL ENTRIES

Condition names (88-level entries) are useful to improve documentation. They facilitate program changes and can reduce the need for compound conditions in an IF statement. Consider the case of a political candidate seeking the names of registered Democrats in three Florida cities.

Poor Code:

```
IF (LOCATION-CODE = 48 OR 65 OR 93)
    AND POLITICAL-PARTY = 'D' . . .
```

Improved Code:

```
05  LOCATION-CODE           PIC 99.
    88 MIAMI                VALUE 48.
    88 TAMPA                VALUE 65.
    88 FT-LAUDERDALE        VALUE 93.
    88 FLORIDA              VALUES ARE 48, 65, 93.

05  POLITICAL-PARTY         PIC X.
    88 DEMOCRAT             VALUE 'D'.
    88 REPUBLICAN           VALUE 'R'.

IF FLORIDA AND DEMOCRAT . . .
```

When 88-level entries are *not* used, the IF statement is considerably harder to read. Moreover, the chances for error are greater as the condition portion is more complex to code. In the example shown, the parentheses are required, and the meaning will change if they are removed. The improved code defines the city and political party codes in the Data Division, resulting in an easier to read Procedure Division.

Condition names also facilitate maintenance in that changes to existing codes, and/or addition of new codes is done in only one place, the Data Division. When 88-level entries are not used, and the value of a given data name is tested more than once in the Procedure Division, changes are required in several places.

PERFORM PARAGRAPHS, NOT SECTIONS

The motivation behind this guideline is best demonstrated by example. Given the following Procedure Division, what will be the final value of X?

```
PROCEDURE DIVISION.
MAINLINE SECTION.
    MOVE ZEROS TO X.
    PERFORM A.
    PERFORM B.
    PERFORM C.
    PERFORM D.
    STOP RUN.
A SECTION.
    ADD 1 TO X.
B.
    ADD 1 TO X.
C.
    ADD 1 TO X.
D.
    ADD 1 TO X.
```

The *correct* answer is 7, *not 4*. A common error made by many programmers is a misinterpretation of the statement PERFORM A. Since A is a section and not a paragraph, the statement PERFORM A invokes *every* paragraph in that section, namely, paragraphs B, C, and D, in addition to the unnamed paragraph immediately after the section header.

A PERFORM statement specifies a *procedure,* which is *either* a section or a paragraph. Unfortunately, there is no way of telling the nature of the procedure from the PERFORM statement itself. Consequently, when a section is specified as a procedure, the unfortunate result is too often execution of unintended code. Can't happen? Did you correctly compute the value of X?

USE THE COMPUTE VERB FOR MULTIPLE ARITHMETIC OPERATORS

The COMPUTE verb should always be used when multiple arithmetic operators are involved. Consider two sets of equivalent code:

Poor Code:

```
MULTIPLY B BY B GIVING B-SQUARED.
MULTIPLY 4 BY A GIVING FOUR-A.
MULTIPLY FOUR-A BY C GIVING FOUR-A-C.
SUBTRACT FOUR-A-C FROM B-SQUARED GIVING RESULT-1.
COMPUTE RESULT-2 = RESULT-1 ** .5.
SUBTRACT B FROM RESULT-2 GIVING NUMERATOR.
MULTIPLY 2 BY A GIVING DENOMINATOR.
DIVIDE NUMERATOR BY DENOMINATOR GIVING X.
```

Improved Code:

```
COMPUTE X = (-B + (B ** 2 - (4 * A * C)) ** .5) / (2 * A).
```

Both sets of code apply to the quadratic formula,

$$X = \frac{-B + \sqrt{B^2 - 4AC}}{2A}$$

It is fairly easy to determine what is happening from the single COMPUTE statement. It is next to impossible to realize the cumulative effect of the eight individual arithmetic statements. Interpretation of the unacceptable code is further clouded by the mandatory definition of data names for intermediate results, RESULT-1, RESULT-2, etc.

Note well that parentheses are often required in COMPUTE statements to alter the normal hierarchy of operations. For example, parentheses are *required* around 2 * A in the denominator. If they had been omitted, the numerator would have been divided by 2 and then the quotient would have been multiplied by A. Sometimes the parentheses are optional to the compiler, but should be used to clarify things for the programmer. The parentheses around 4 * A * C do not alter the normal order of operations and hence are optional.

KEEP IT SIMPLE

Procedure Division code should be kept as straightforward as possible, and efforts at being cute or fancy should be discouraged. Beginning programmers, especially, are notorious for trying to impress their peers with "clever" code, which too often confuses the issue.

Consider the following payroll specification for hourly employees: all employees receive straight time for the first forty hours worked, time and a half for the next 8 hours, and double time for any hours over 48. For example, an employee who worked 50 hours with an hourly rate of $5.00 should receive $280.00 (40 hours at $5.00, 8 hours at $7.50, and 2 hours at $10.00).

The following, *logically equivalent* IF statements, are partial solutions:

```
IF HOURS-WORKED > 48
    COMPUTE GROSS-PAY
        = 40 * HOURLY-RATE
        + 8 * HOURLY-RATE * 1.5
        + (HOURS-WORKED - 48) * HOURLY-RATE * 2.

IF HOURS-WORKED > 48
    COMPUTE GROSS-PAY
        = 52 * HOURLY-RATE
        + (HOURS-WORKED - 48) * HOURLY-RATE * 2.
```

The first statement is a line longer, but is the preferred solution as it more closely represents the physical problem. It is easy to see that individuals working more than 48 hours receive straight time for the first 40 hours, time and a half for the next 8 hours, and double time for any hours over 48. Although the second statement produces equivalent results, it deviates significantly from the physical situation. A maintenance programmer would be hard pressed to understand the meaning of the constant 52. Lest the reader think that this is a concocted example, we credit it to a math major in COBOL 1. The student was an accomplished mathematician and FORTRAN programmer. His solution may be elegant in a mathematical sense, but it is certainly undesirable in a commercial environment.

USE THE APPROPRIATE SEARCH TECHNIQUE

Three common techniques are used for table lookups. These are a linear (or sequential) search, a binary search, and direct access to table entries. The particular technique chosen depends on the length of the table and the type of code (numeric or alphabetic) on which the search is performed.

The *linear or sequential* search is always applicable, but often the least efficient. It examines entries in a table in sequence, beginning with the first entry, until a match is found. This technique becomes rather time consuming when the table is large and/or the code in question is near the end of the table. For example, a table of 1000 entries could require as many as 1000 guesses.

A *binary* search requires that keys in a table be in sequence. It begins in the middle of a table, and eliminates half of the remaining entries with each subsequent guess. The maximum number of guesses is far less than with a linear search; for example a maximum of

- 9 guesses are required in a table with up to 511 entries
- 10 guesses are required in a table with up to 1023 entries
- 11 guesses are required in a table with up to 2047 entries

However, because of the additional effort in computing each guess, binary searches should not be used on tables with less than 25 entries.

A third technique, *direct access to table entries,* requires no comparisons at all. Rather it uses the value of the incoming code as a direct pointer to the expanded table entry. This technique requires consecutive numeric codes. All three techniques are illustrated in Fig. 5.1.

```
01  DEPARTMENT-VALUES.
    05   FILLER                      PIC X(15)    VALUE '001ACCOUNTING'.
    05   FILLER                      PIC X(15)    VALUE '002ADVERTISING'.
         .
         .
         .
    05   FILLER                      PIC X(15)    VALUE '100WAREHOUSE'.

01  DEPARTMENT-TABLE REDEFINES DEPARTMENT-VALUES.
    05   DEPARTMENT-ENTRIES OCCURS 100 TIMES
              ASCENDING KEY IS DEPARTMENT-CODE
              INDEXED BY DEPARTMENT-INDEX.
         10   DEPARTMENT-CODE         PIC 9(3).
         10   DEPARTMENT-EXPANSION    PIC X(12).

*LINEAR SEARCH
    SET DEPARTMENT-INDEX TO 1.
```

Figure 5.1 Illustration of Search Techniques.

```
    SEARCH DEPARTMENT-ENTRIES
        AT END MOVE 'NO MATCH' TO OUTPUT-FIELD
        WHEN INCOMING-DEPARTMENT-CODE = DEPARTMENT-CODE (DEPARTMENT-INDEX)
            MOVE DEPARTMENT-EXPANSION (DEPARTMENT-INDEX) TO OUTPUT-FIELD.

*BINARY SEARCH
    SEARCH ALL DEPARTMENT-ENTRIES
        AT END MOVE 'NO MATCH' TO OUTPUT-FIELD
        WHEN DEPARTMENT-CODE (DEPARTMENT-INDEX) = INCOMING-DEPARTMENT-CODE
            MOVE DEPARTMENT-EXPANSION (DEPARTMENT-INDEX) TO OUTPUT-FIELD.

*DIRECT ACCESS TO DEPARTMENT ENTRIES
    MOVE DEPARTMENT-EXPANSION (INCOMING-DEPARTMENT-CODE) TO OUTPUT-FIELD.
```

Figure 5.1 cont.

INITIALIZE TABLES DYNAMICALLY

Change is perhaps the most fundamental law of data processing. Nowhere is change more apparent than in the constant addition of new codes to various tables. It is highly desirable to make the implementation of table changes as easy as possible. Consider three alternative methods for table initialization.

The least desirable technique is hard coding a table within a program. The main problem with hard coding is that the program has to be recompiled and retested every time a new code is added. Moreover, since the table is apt to be used in several programs, the same change has to be made in *many* places, in *every* program which references the table. This leads to various problems in data integrity because some programs will not be changed, or changed incorrectly, or changed at different times, etc.

An improved technique is to use a COPY statement. Every program requiring a table has access to it, through the same COPY statement. Use of the COPY facilitates change in that additions to the table are made in only one place, the COPY library. The disadvantage to this technqiue is that all programs utilizing the COPY statement still have to be recompiled and retested.

The optimal method is to initialize a table by dynamically reading values from a file. Changes to the table are made in only one place, the file itself. Programs accessing the file need not be recompiled or retested. Sample code is shown below. (Note well the check to ensure that the table size of 500 elements is not exceeded.)

```
        READ LOCATION-CODE-FILE
            AT END DISPLAY 'LOCATION FILE EMPTY'.
        PERFORM 010-INITIALIZE-LOCATION-TABLE
            VARYING LOCATION-INDEX FROM 1 BY 1
                UNTIL LOCATION-FILE-SWITCH = 'YES'.
```

```
010-INITIALIZE-LOCATION-TABLE.
    ADD 1 TO NUMBER-OF-LOCATIONS.
    IF NUMBER-OF-LOCATIONS > 500
        DISPLAY 'LOCATION TABLE TOO SMALL'
        MOVE 'YES' TO LOCATION-FILE-SWITCH
    ELSE
        MOVE INCOMING-FILE-CODE TO LOCATION-CODE (LOCATION-INDEX)
        MOVE INCOMING-FILE-NAME TO LOCATION-NAME (LOCATION-INDEX).
    READ LOCATION-CODE-FILE
        AT END MOVE 'YES' TO LOCATION-FILE-SWITCH.
```

AVOID CONSTANTS

A significant portion of maintenance programming (and headaches) could probably be avoided if the original program were written with an eye toward future change. Consider:

Poor Code:

```
05  STATE-TABLE OCCURS 50 TIMES.
    10  STATE-POPULATION     PIC 9(8).
    10  STATE-NAME           PIC X(15).
    .
    .
    PERFORM COMPUTE-STATE-TOTALS
        VARYING STATE-SUBSCRIPT FROM 1 BY 1
        UNTIL STATE-SUBSCRIPT > 50.

    COMPUTE AVERAGE-POPULATION = TOTAL-POPULATION / 50.
```

Improved Code:

```
05  STATE-POPULATION OCCURS 1 TO 55 TIMES
                DEPENDING ON NUMBER-OF-STATES.
    10  STATE-POPULATION     PIC 9(8).
    10  STATE-NAME           PIC X(15).
    .
    .
    PERFORM COMPUTE-STATE-TOTALS
        VARYING STATE-SUBSCRIPT FROM 1 BY 1
        UNTIL STATE-SUBSCRIPT > NUMBER-OF-STATES.

    COMPUTE AVERAGE-POPULATION = TOTAL-POPULATION / NUMBER-OF-STATES.
```

Admittedly, it has been some twenty years since Alaska and Hawaii became states. Nevertheless, if and when another state is admitted, the improved code is decidedly easier to modify. All that needs to be changed is the value of NUMBER-OF-STATES. The poor code, however, requires changes in several places: the constant 50 has to be changed to 51 three times. The possibility of error is much greater, as the programmer is required to track down all instances where the value changes. (Remember, constants do not appear on a cross reference listing.)

A second benefit of avoiding constants in favor of variable data names is increased legibility. Consider:

Poor Code:

      ADD .04 .04 GIVING SALES-TAX-PERCENTAGE.

Improved Code:

      ADD NEW-YORK-STATE-SALES-TAX NEW-YORK-CITY-SALES-TAX
         GIVING TOTAL-SALES-TAX-PERCENTAGE.

The reader is hard pressed to determine the meaning of either occurrence of .04 in the first example, whereas the meaning is obvious in the second example. True, the latter requires definition of additional data names in the Data Division and extra pencil strokes in the Procedure Division. This is a small price to pay, however, for the increased legibility and ease of maintenance.

AVOID LITERALS

The constant (literal) portion of a print line should be defined in Working-Storage, rather than being moved to the print line in the Procedure Division. Consider:

Poor Code:

```
MOVE 'STUDENT NAME        SOC SEC NUM     CREDITS    TUITION
   'SCHOLARSHIP    FEES' TO PRINT-LINE.
WRITE PRINT-LINE.
```

Improved Code:

```
01      HEADING-LINE.
   05   FILLER      PIC X(12)     VALUE 'STUDENT NAME'.
   05   FILLER      PIC X(10)     VALUE SPACES.
   05   FILLER      PIC X(11)     VALUE 'SOC SEC NUM'.
   05   FILLER      PIC X(2)      VALUE SPACES.
   05   FILLER      PIC X(7)      VALUE 'CREDITS'.
   05   FILLER      PIC X(2)      VALUE SPACES.
```

```
            05   FILLER       PIC X(7)       VALUE 'TUITION'.
            05   FILLER       PIC X(3)       VALUE SPACES.
            05   FILLER       PIC X(11)      VALUE 'SCHOLARSHIP'.
            05   FILLER       PIC X(2)       VALUE SPACES.
            05   FILLER       PIC X(4)       VALUE 'FEES'.
            05   FILLER       PIC X(62)      VALUE SPACES.

        WRITE PRINT-LINE FROM HEADING-LINE.
```

The improved code may appear unnecessarily long in contrast to the poor code. However, it is an unwritten law that users will change column headings and/or spacing at least twice before being satisfied. Such changes are easily accommodated in the improved code, but often tedious in the original solution. Assume, for example, that four spaces are required between CREDITS and TUITION, rather than the two that are there now. Modification of the poor code requires that *both* lines in the MOVE statement be completely rewritten, whereas only a picture clause changes in the improved version.

Definition of literals in the Data Division, rather than in the Procedure Division, should be extended to tables of error messages as well. Consider:

Poor Code:

```
        MOVE 'TRANSACTION CODE IS NOT A, C, OR D' TO PRINT-MESSAGE.
        PERFORM WRITE-ERROR-MESSAGE.
             .
             .
        MOVE 'TRANSACTION ID IS NOT FOUND ON MASTER FILE' TO PRINT-MESSAGE.
        PERFORM WRITE-ERROR-MESSAGE.
             .
             .
        MOVE 'TRANSACTION ID IS ALREADY ON MASTER FILE' TO PRINT-MESSAGE.
        PERFORM WRITE-ERROR-MESSAGE.
```

Improved Code:

```
        01   ERROR-MESSAGES.
             05   TRANSACTION-CODE-ERROR           PIC X(45)
                  VALUE 'TRANSACTION CODE IS NOT A, C, OR D'.
             05   MISSING-TRANSACTION-ERROR        PIC X(45)
                  VALUE 'TRANSACTION ID IS NOT FOUND ON MASTER FILE'.
             05   DUPLICATE-TRANSACTION-ERROR      PIC X(45)
                  VALUE 'TRANSACTION ID IS ALREADY ON MASTER FILE'.
                  .
                  .
        MOVE TRANSACTION-CODE-ERROR TO PRINT-MESSAGE.
        PERFORM WRITE-ERROR-MESSAGE.
```

.
.
    MOVE MISSING-TRANSACTION-ERROR TO PRINT-MESSAGE.
    PERFORM WRITE-ERROR-MESSAGE.
.
.
    MOVE DUPLICATE-TRANSACTION-ERROR TO PRINT-MESSAGE.
    PERFORM WRITE-ERROR-MESSAGE.

The improved code is again significantly longer than the poorer version. However, it enables the programmer to see at a glance the various error checks because they are grouped together in the Data Division. Of equal importance is the ease with which the text of an existing message can be changed, and/or a new message added.

USE READ INTO, WRITE FROM, AND WS BEGINS HERE

If a program ABENDS, the first task is to identify the record being processed at the instant the problem occurred. Unfortunately, I/O areas are difficult to find in a dump. The problem is further compounded with blocked records when the entire physical record is in storage and one has to isolate the logical record within the physical record. The following technique is helpful:

```
WORKING-STORAGE SECTION.
01   FILLER                          PIC X(14)
        VALUE 'WS BEGINS IIERE'.
01   WS-EMPLOYEE-RECORD.
     05   EMP-NAME                   PIC X(25).
     05   EMP-SOC-SEC-NUMBER         PIC 9(9).
          .
          .
01   WS-HDG-LINE-1.
          .
          .
     READ EMPLOYEE-FILE INTO WS-EMPLOYEE-RECORD
          AT END...
     WRITE PRINT-LINE FROM WS-HDG-LINE-1
          AFTER ADVANCING...
```

The start of Working-Storage is found by scanning the alphabetic interpretation of the dump, searching for WS BEGINS HERE. The technique is not sophisticated, but it does work. Once the Working-Storage Section is found, one can easily identify the record in question as well as the values of all other data names defined in Working-Storage, e.g., switches, subscripts, etc.

PASS A SINGLE 01 PARAMETER TO A SUBPROGRAM

The *order* or arguments in the CALL USING and PROCEDURE DIVISION USING clauses of the calling and called program is critical. One can *guarantee* that the order and picture clauses will be identical in both calling and called program by passing only a single 01 record which is *copied* into both programs. Consider:

Poor Code:

```
CALL 'DECODER'
     USING TITLE-CODE, EXPANDED-TITLE,
           LOCATION-CODE, EXPANDED-LOCATION.
  .
  .
  .
PROCEDURE DIVISION
     USING LS-TITLE-CODE, LS-EXPANDED-TITLE,
           LS-LOCATION-CODE, LS-EXPANDED-LOCATION.
```

Improved Code:

```
              COPY ARGUMENTS
C      01     PARAMETER-LIST.
C              05  TITLE-CODE          PIC 9(3).
C              05  EXPANDED-TITLE      PIC X(15).
C              05  LOCATION-CODE       PIC XX.
C              05  EXPANDED-LOCATION   PIC X(12).
                .
                .
              CALL 'DECODER'
                  USING PARAMETER-LIST.

              LINKAGE SECTION.
              COPY ARGUMENTS
C      01     PARAMETER-LIST.
C              05  TITLE-CODE          PIC 9(3).
C              05  EXPANDED-TITLE      PIC X(15).
C              05  LOCATION-CODE       PIC XX.
C              05  EXPANDED-LOCATION   PIC X(12).
              PROCEDURE DIVISION
                  USING PARAMETER-LIST.
```

Use of the single 01 parameter facilitates coding in the USING clauses, and also makes them immune to change. Use of the same COPY member in both programs eliminates any problem with listing arguments in the wrong order, and/or inconsistent definition through different pictures.

CONSIDER REPORT WRITER

Report Writer is one of the most powerful features in COBOL, yet many programmers will not even consider using it. We view this situation as extremely unfortunate, and due primarily to notoriously poor vendor manuals. Nevertheless, Report Writer is well worth learning because it provides automatic formation of heading, detail, and footing lines. Of greater import, it automatically and *correctly* totals, and subtotals, over various levels of control breaks.

Report Writer produces a report by describing its physical characteristics in the Data Division, rather than by specifying its logic in the Procedure Division. Once this philosophy is understood, it is a routine matter to learn how to use the facility. The desired appearance of a report is specified by describing various *report groups* in the Report Section of the Data Division. Every line in every report belongs to one of seven such groups. These are:

1. *Report Heading:* one or more lines appearing once at the beginning (initiation) of a report.
2. *Report Footing:* one or more lines appearing once at the conclusion (termination) of a report.
3. *Page Heading:* one or more lines appearing at the beginning of each page after the report heading
4. *Page Footing:* one or more lines appearing at the end of each page.
5. *Control Heading:* one or more lines appearing prior to each control break, such as when the contents of a designated field change.
6. *Control Footing:* one or more lines appearing after each control break
7. *Detail:* one line (or lines) for each record in the file

It is not necessary that a given report contain all seven kinds of report groups, and there may be more than one occurrence of a particular report group. The format of the desired report is completely specified through the designated report groups. The logic is generated automatically, and consequently the Procedure Division is quite short.

This discussion was intended only as the briefest of introductions to Report Writer. The reader may want to refer to Topic 2-9, to Exercises 3-1 and 3-2, and to a COBOL text for additional material.

6 Programming Projects

OVERVIEW

The purpose of this section is to provide *two* sets of related projects to provide necessary programming experience. The projects are grouped into two systems, with which individuals can easily identify. The first is a student information system for a university, the second is a personnel system for a medium-sized company.

We believe that a unified set of projects, with common COPY clauses and data files, promotes a sense of continuity and, hence, is superior to isolated assignments. Since this book is designed to augment a two-semester COBOL sequence, the projects range from a simple "on and off the machine" program in the first assignment, to nonsequential maintenance of an indexed file in the last assignment. In between, all major aspects of COBOL are covered including: table handling, subprograms, sorting, and Report Writer. *Either* set of 10 projects should provide ample material for a two-semester sequence.

A COBOL Book of Practice and Reference is designed for use with *any* COBOL text. Consequently, the programming projects are not tied to specific chapters in a particular book, but are linked instead to COBOL topics. Because different books have different learning sequences, the projects need not be done in the order listed. Tables 6.1 and 6.2 summarize the projects for the Student and Personnel Systems, respectively. The instructor should note carefully the objectives and COBOL material associated with each assignment.

Finally, in order to further promote a sense of continuity, each project is presented in a uniform format as follows:

> *Objectives:* Describes the particular goals of the project in terms of the COBOL language, and ties the assignment to specific topics.
>
> *Problem Statement:* Contains the programming specifications and logical requirements.

Incoming Data: Describes the incoming record(s) and contains test data for the system. Test data should be keypunched *exactly* as shown, even if obviously invalid. Improper data are *deliberately* included to test that programs work correctly under all conditions.

Suggested Extra: Contains suggestions for extra credit to accommodate the student or trainee seeking an additional challenge.

Variations: Presents modifications in the problem statement to allow the instructor and/or student greater flexibility.

Table 6.1: Summary of Programming Projects for the Student Information System

Project 6.1: Student Selection	Introduction to COBOL to get "on and off" the machine
Project 6.2: Grade Point Listing	Basic arithmetic, implied decimal point, simple editing, and use of the IF statement
Project 6.3: Tuition Billing	Heading, detail and total lines, simple arithmetic, and detailed report formats
Project 6.4: Student Transcipts	One-dimensional tables, signed numbers, nested IF and PERFORM; optional use of SORT, subprograms and table lookups
Project 6.5: Student Course Cards	One-dimensional tables, multiple record formats in a single file, complex logic
Project 6.6: Student Profiles	Implied decimal points, page headings, date of execution, and one-dimensional tables; optional use of SORT
Project 6.7: Student Profiles with Table Lookups	Indexing, SEARCH, and SEARCH ALL, table initialization, and subprograms
Projects 6.8: Grade Distributions	Two-dimensional tables, nested IF, PERFORM VARYING, and data validation
Project 6.9: Student Credit Hours	SORT, Report Writer, and control breaks; optional use of table lookups and subprograms
Project 6.10a: Sequential File Maintenance	Concepts of file maintenance, presentation of a program with nontrivial logic, top down testing, pseudocode, and hierarchy charts
Project 6.10b: Nonsequential File Maintenance	Same specifications and objectives as Project 6.10a except access of the master file is nonsequential

Table 6.2: Summary of Programming Projects for the Personnel Information System

Project 6.11 Employee Selection	Introduction to COBOL to get "on and off" the machine
Project 6.12: Annual Compensation Analysis	Basic arithmetic, implied decimal point, simple editing, and use of the IF statement
Project 6.13: Payroll	Heading, detail and total lines, simple arithmetic, and detailed report formats
Project 6.14: Benefit Statement	Use of DATE, 88-level entries, and more complex logic
Project 6.15: Employee Profiles	Implied decimal points, page headings, date of execution, and one-dimensional tables; optional use of SORT
Project 6.16: Employee Profiles with Table Lookup	Indexing, SEARCH, and SEARCH ALL, table initialization, and subprograms
Project 6.17: EEO Reporting	Multiple input files, complex logic, nested IF and PERFORM statements
Project 6.18: Salary Distributions	Two-dimensional tables, nested IF, PERFORM VARYING, and data validation
Project 6.19: Salary Totals	SORT, Report Writer, and control breaks; optional use of table lookups and subprograms
Project 6.20a: Sequential File Maintenance	Concepts of file maintenance, presentation of a program with nontrivial logic, top down testing, pseudocode, and hierarchy charts
Project 6.20b: Nonsequential File Maintenance	Same specifications and objectives as Project 6.20a except access of the master file is nonsequential

STUDENT INFORMATION SYSTEM

Project 6.1: Student Selection

Objectives

To introduce COBOL and to get students "on and off" the machine.

Problem Statement

Process a file of student records and print the names of all students who are: business majors with at least 90 credits.

Incoming Data

Incoming cards are punched as follows:

Field	Columns	Picture
Student name	10-29	X(20)
Major	30-44	X(15)
Credits	45-47	9(3)

Use the test data of Fig. 6.10 on page 289.

Required Output

Use the report format shown in Fig. 6.1.

Suggested Extra

Count the number of students who meet both qualifications, and print this number in a total line at the end of the report.

Variation

Prepare a second program that will list freshmen (less than 30 credits) majoring in engineering.

Project 6.2: Grade Point Listing

Objectives

To do simple arithmetic using implied decimal points for totals and averages, to introduce simple editing, to gain proficiency with the IF statement. (The suggested extra requires knowledge of the SORT verb.)

Problem Statement

Read a file of student records, and for *every* student print social security number, grade point average, and year in school. (The latter is determined from cumulative credits; freshmen have fewer than 30, sophomores between 30 and 59, juniors between 60 and 89, and seniors 90 or more.) Students with a GPA of 3.00 or higher are on the dean's list. Students with a GPA of less than 1.50 are on probation; however, incoming freshmen with GPA of 0.00 should not be considered on probation.

When all students have been processed, print the total number of students on the Dean's List and the total number on probation. Compute and print the average GPA for students on both lists.

Incoming Data

Use the record description of Fig. 6.9 and the test data in Fig. 6.10, on page 289.

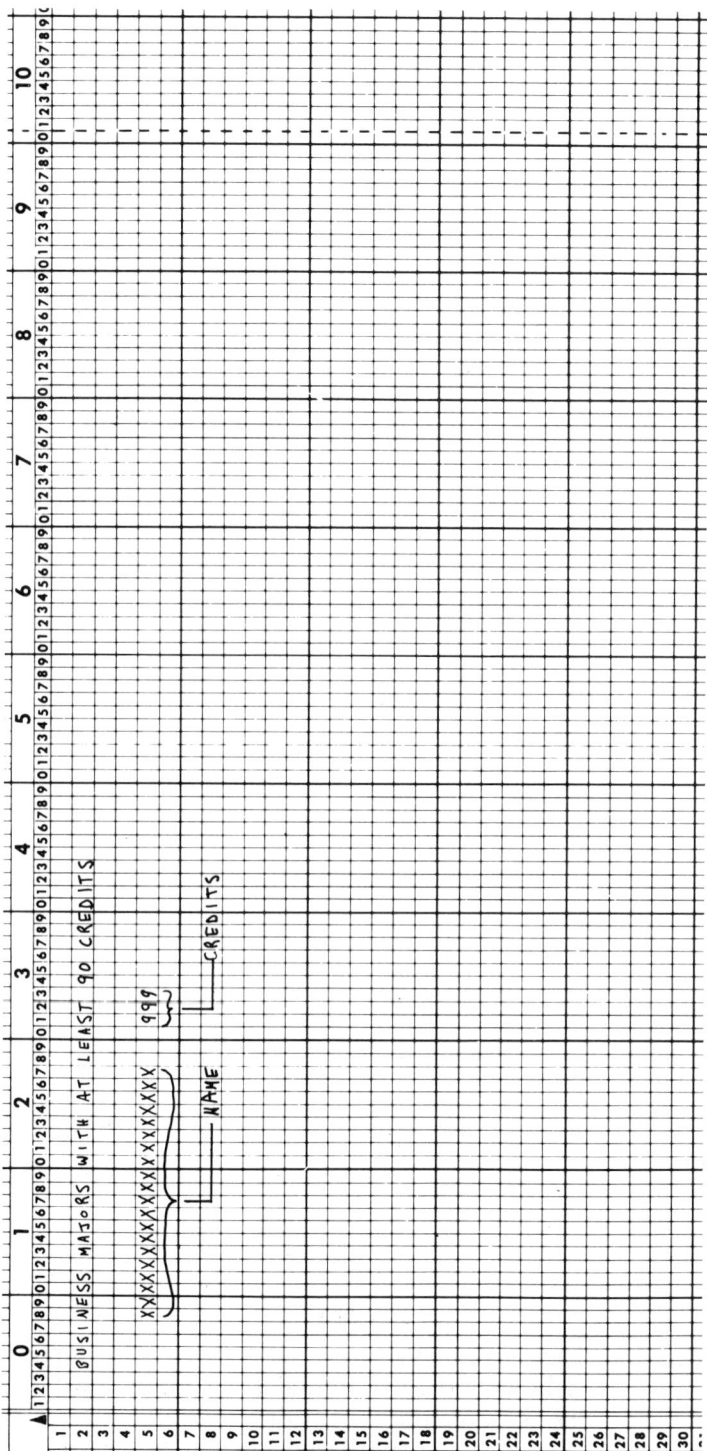

Figure 6.1 Report Format for Student Selection.

Required Output

Use the report format shown in Fig. 6.2.

Suggested Extra

Print students in alphabetical order, rather than the order in which they appear in the input file.

Variations

Print three distinct lists, each with its appropriate heading, and beginning on a new page. The first is to contain only students on academic probation, the second those who are neither on probation nor the Dean's List, and the third only those on the Dean's List. Compute the same totals and averages as previously, and print them at the end of their respective lists.

One way of printing three distinct lists is to have incoming records prearranged in order of increasing GPA; knowledge of SORT is required.

The problem can also be solved by defining three "print" files and writing each record to its appropriate file. (This is easily accomplished on an IBM OS system by supplying additional DD statements.)

Project 6.3: Tuition Billing

Objectives

To cover heading, detail, and total lines; to introduce simple arithmetic through the COMPUTE statement, to produce a formatted report with elementary editing. Suggested extras include a page heading routine and use of DATE.

Problem Statement

Process a file of student records to compute individual bills *and* university totals as follows:

Tuition	$100 per credit
Union Fee	$75 for members, $0 for nonmembers (Members have a Y punched in column 50)
Activity Fee	$10 for 3 credits or less $50 for 4 to 8 credits $95 for 9 credits or more
Scholarship	Only students with a GPA of 3.00 or higher can receive a scholarship. The actual amount of a scholarship is given as a percentage of tuition, from 0 to 100, in columns 51-53 as per the description of incoming data. (Note well

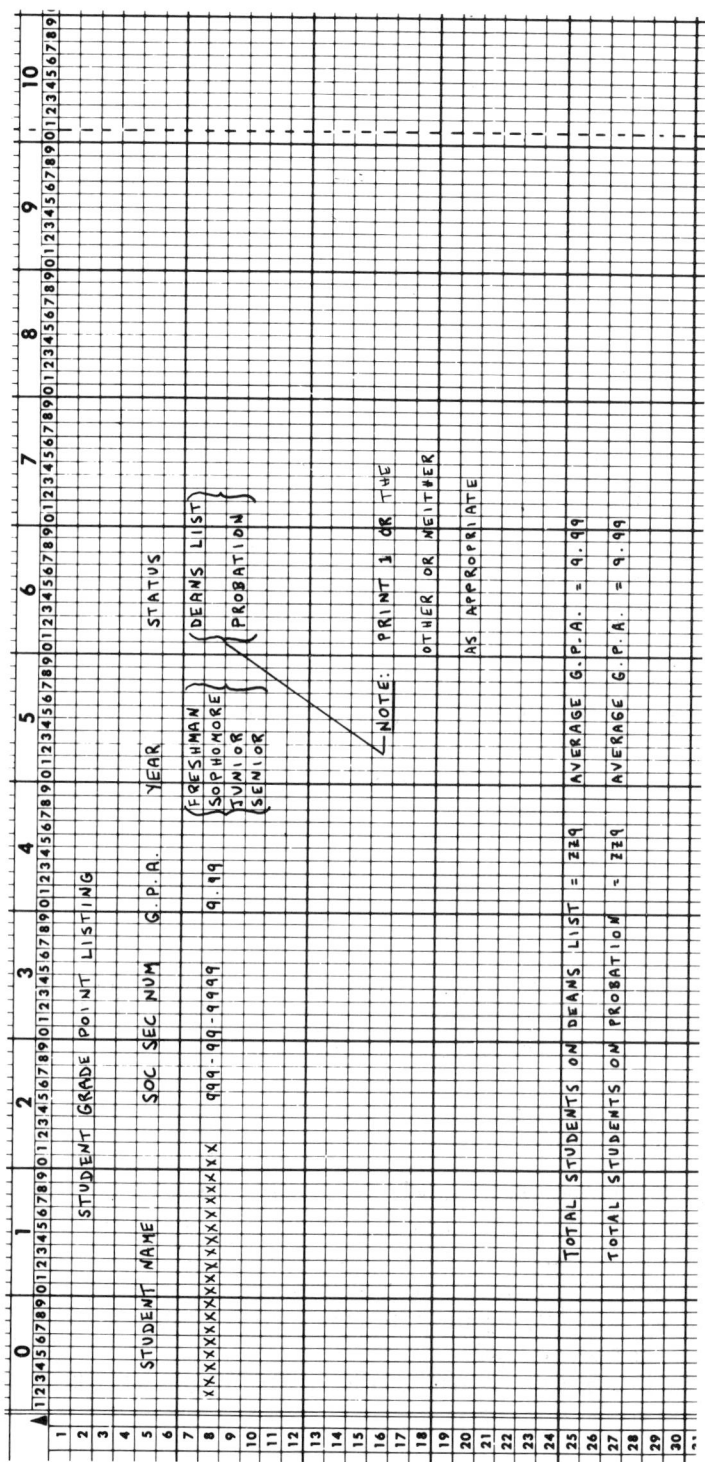

Figure 6.2 Report Format for Grade Point Listing.

that a student with a GPA of less than 3.00 is *not* to receive a scholarship regardless of the percent indicated.)

Net Amount   Tuition plus Union and Activity Fee minus Scholarship

Incoming Data

Use the record description of Fig. 6.9 and the test data of Fig. 6.10 on page 289.

Required Output

A suitable heading is to appear at the beginning of the report, and university totals at the end. Figure 6.3 contains the report specifications. Pay particular attention to the indicated editing.

Suggested Extras

1. Limit the number of students to 10 per page. This modification requires that the heading routine is executed an indeterminate number of times; once for each 10 students. The heading routine is to include a page number and the date of execution.
2. Determine the average number of credits, and average scholarship amount, for *full-time* students (those with 12 credits or more). Print these two numbers, with appropriate descriptive information, after the total line. Do *not* include part-time students (11 credits or less) in the averages.

Project 6.4: Student Transcripts

Objectives

To present one-dimensional tables, to optionally use signed numbers in arithmetic and editing, to gain proficiency with nested IF and PERFORM statements. The suggested extras include use of SORT and/or subprograms.

Problem Statement

Process a file of student records to calculate student transcripts. A four-point system is used in which the GPA varies from 0.00 to 4.00. Accordingly, A, B, C, D, and F are worth 4, 3, 2, 1, and 0, respectively.

The grade point average is calculated by dividing a student's quality points by the total number of credits. Quality points in a given course are computed by multiplying the numerical value of the grade in that course by the credits for that course.

As an illustration, consider the following grades which were received by John Smith.

STUDENT NAME	SOC SEC NUM	G.P.A.	TUITION	UNION FEE	ACT FEE	SCHOLARSHIP	CREDITS	TOTAL
XXXXXXXXXXXXXXX	999 99 9999	2.22	$$,$$9	$$9	$99	$$,$$9	Z9	$$,$$9
XXXXXXXXXXXXXXX	999 99 9999	2.22	$$,$$9	$$9	$99	$$,$$9	Z9	$$,$$9
XXXXXXXXXXXXXXX	999 99 9999	2.22	$$,$$9	$$9	$99	$$,$$9	Z9	$$,$$9
*** UNIVERSITY TOTALS ***			$$$,$$9	$$,$$9	$$,$$9	$$$,$$9	ZZ,ZZ9	$$$,$$9

Figure 6.3 Report Format for Tuition Billing Project.

Course Number	Grade	Credits	Quality Points	
111	A	4	16	← Obtained by multiplying
222	B	3	9	the value of an A (4) by
333	C	4	8	the number of credits in
444	D	3	3	that course (4)
555	F	2	0	
TOTALS		16	36	

John Smith's GPA is obtained by dividing his total quality points (36) by his total credits (16) to obtain a GPA of 2.25.

Note well that any course with a grade other than A, B, C, D, or F is required to appear in the transcript but should not affect the GPA. Hence, if John Smith received an I (incomplete) in a sixth course, his GPA would be unchanged.

Incoming Data

Use the record layout of Fig. 6.11 and the test data in Fig. 6.12 on page 290.

Required Output

Print a transcript for every student in the file according to your own report specifications. You must, however, include all of the following fields in each transcript: student name and social security number (with hyphens), major code, and school code. In addition, for every course taken, print the course code, number of credits, and grade.

Suggested Extras

1. Incorporate a sort into the program and present a separate list of students making the Dean's List (those with a GPA of 3.00 or higher). Include the student's name, major code, school code, and GPA. Print the students in order of *decreasing* GPA.

2. Include a call to a subprogram which will expand the major, school, and course codes to meaningful descriptions. Modify the individual transcripts to reflect the expanded information. (See Project 6.7, Student Profiles with Table Lookups, for guidelines.)

Variations

1. To introduce signed numbers, use a four point system which varies from -2.00 to 2.00 in which A, B, C, D, and F are worth +2, +1, 0, -1, -2, respectively. The GPA for John Smith, whose grades were presented in the problem statement should now work out to +.25 (+4/16).

2. Modify the use of SORT (see the first Suggested Extra) to print a separate list of students on probation; i.e., those with a GPA below -.5 (or below 1.5 in the four point system).

Project 6.5: Student Course Cards

Objective

To present multiple record formats in a single file, to develop a one-dimensional table, and to introduce a program with more complex logic requirements. Suggested extras cover the SORT verb and variable length records.

Problem Statement

Process a file containing multiple course cards for each individual student, to produce a single student record. There is a distinct course card, containing the course number, grade, and course credits for *every* course in which a student is enrolled. In addition, there is a single master card for every student containing additional information. Thus, a student enrolled in five courses should have a total of six cards (one master and five course cards). The master and course cards are distinguishable by a code in column 80 of M and C, respectively.

The problem, in essence, is to take the individual master and multiple course cards for an individual, and produce a single output record. Two distinct errors can occur and must be flagged. A master record may have no corresponding course cards or course cards may have no corresponding master. In either case, DISPLAY an appropriate error message and do *not* produce the output record.

You may assume that the input file has been presorted by social security number, by code (either M or C), and in ascending and descending order, respectively; the master card precedes the course cards. You may also assume that all data cards contain either a M or C in column 80.

Incoming Data

Figure 6.15 on page 291 contains the record description for incoming course cards. (Note well the DATA RECORDS ARE clause to indicate the multiple record types; M and C.) Use the test data of Fig. 6.16 on page 292.

Required Output

This program does not produce a report per se, but rather a file which can be used as input to Projects 6.4 and 6.9, Student Transcripts and Student Credit Hours. The record layout of the output file is supplied in Fig. 6.11 on page 289.

The choice of output medium (punched cards, disk, printer, etc.) is left to the student and/or instructor. Error messages, if any, may be simply displayed.

Suggested Extras

1. Modify the record description of Fig. 6.11 to accommodate variable length records; the number of courses taken can vary from 1 to 7. Also, modify the FD to block output records by a factor of 3.
2. Input to your program is no longer in order. Accordingly, the USING/OUTPUT PROCEDURE option of the SORT verb is now required in your project.

Project 6.6: Student Profiles

Objectives

To format a detailed print report, to introduce the OCCURS clause and one-dimensional tables, to do elementary data editing and introduce the INSPECT verb, to further develop arithmetic with implied decimal points, to introduce page headings and date of execution. (The suggested extras require material on sorting. Table lookups are covered in the next project.)

Problem Statement

Develop a program to print a set of student profiles which provide detailed information on each student. The precise print format is shown under Required Output. Student profiles are to appear two per page, with a page heading on every new page. Note well the following requirements and/or specifications:

1. Student age is to be calculated from date of birth and date of program execution.
2. The social security number requires the insertion of hyphens; accomplish this by defining an output picture containing blanks in appropriate positions and then replace the blanks through the INSPECT verb.
3. Part-time students take fewer than 12 credits per semester.
4. Grade point average is defined as the cumulative points divided by the cumulative credits and does not include credits taken this semester. Calculate this field to two decimal places.
5. Year in school is a function of cumulative credits; freshmen have fewer than 30, sophomores between 30 and 59, juniors between 60 and 89, and seniors 90 or more.

Incoming Data

Use the record description of Fig. 6.13 on page 290 and the test data of Fig. 6.14 on page 291.

Required Output

Profiles are to appear *two per page* and are to follow the format of Fig. 6.4.

Suggested Extra

Sort the incoming file so that profiles appear in alphabetical order.

Project 6.7: Student Profiles with Table Lookups

Objectives

To introduce SEARCH, SEARCH ALL, and direct access to table entries, to cover indexing, variable length tables, and REDEFINES, to initialize tables through the VALUE clause and by reading values from a file, to present subprograms.

Problem Statement

The registrar has decided that the student profiles, as presently written (in Project 6.6) with codes for major, school, and course names, are somewhat irritating. Accordingly, he wants the profiles rewritten to print *expanded,* rather than *coded* values.

This program is to be written as a *subprogram,* as its use is anticipated in future projects as well. It is to accept codes passed from a calling program and return expanded values. The first four arguments are major code (PIC X(3)), expanded major (PIC X(15)), school code (PIC 9), and expanded school (PIC X(12)). Next comes a *table* of seven course codes, each with (PIC X(3)), followed by a *table* of seven expanded course names, each with (PIC X(15)).

School code is to be expanded via a *direct lookup* (the code itself indicates the position in the table of the expanded value). Use the following table:

Code	School
1	BUSINESS
2	LIBERAL ARTS
3	ENGINEERING
4	EDUCATION

Major code is to be expanded through a *sequential search* using the table on page 281. (The table of major codes is to be established using the OCCURS, VALUE, and REDEFINES clauses.)

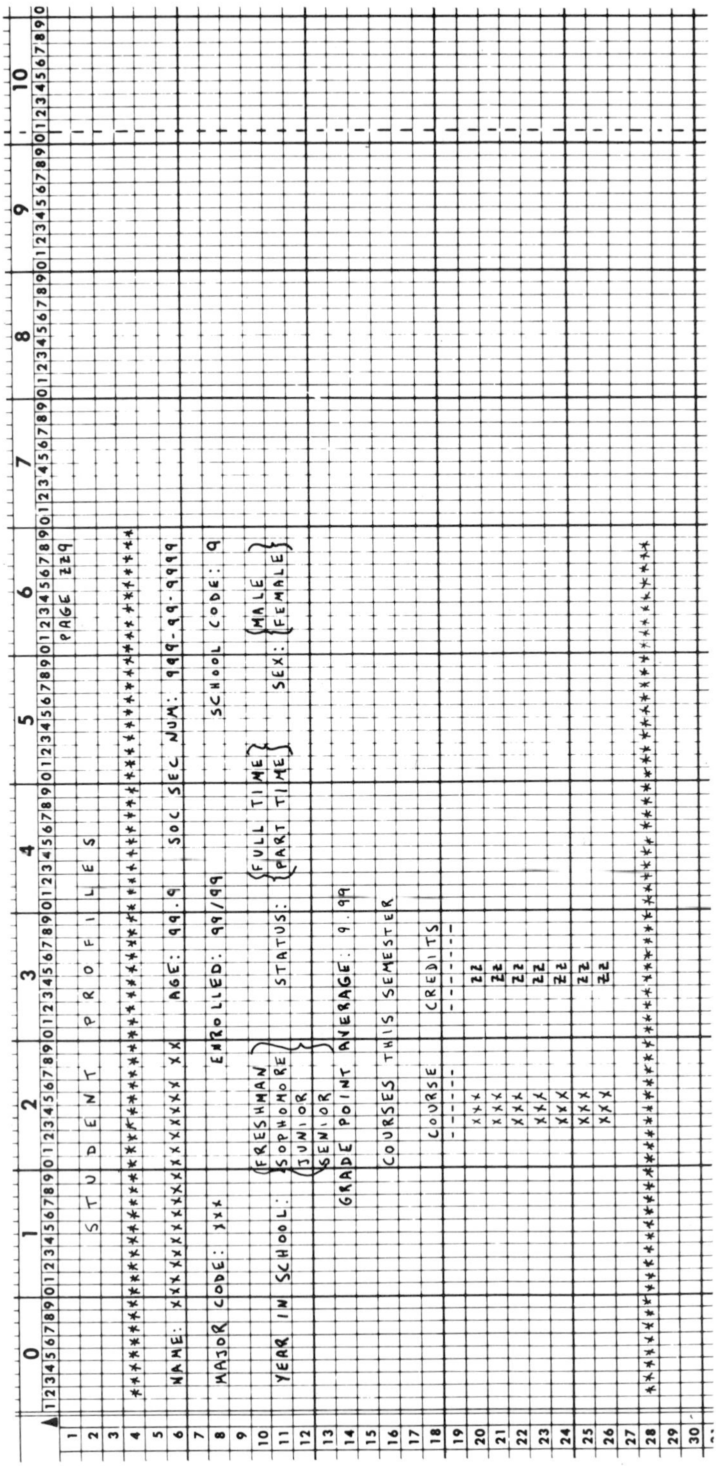

Figure 6.4 Report Format for Student Profile Project.

Code	Major	Code	Major
STA	STATISTICS	ECO	ECONOMICS
FIN	FINANCE	FRL	FOREIGN LANG
MKT	MARKETING	EEN	ELECTRICAL ENG
MAN	MANAGEMENT	MEN	MECHANICAL ENG
EDP	DATA PROCESSING	CEN	CHEMICAL ENG
PHY	PHYSICS	IEN	INDUSTRIAL ENG
ENG	ENGLISH	ELE	ELEMENTARY EDUC
BIO	BIOLOGY	SEE	SECONDARY EDUC
HIS	HISTORY	SPE	SPECIAL EDUC

The table of seven course codes is to be expanded using a *binary search*. (However, if any of the seven course codes is blank, no expansion is to be done for that code; instead the corresponding code name is to be returned as blank as well.) The table of course codes itself is to be established from a file, with the following format: course code in columns 1-3, and course name in columns 4-18. The maximum table length is 100 courses. Finally, your program is to contain sufficient logic so that the file of course codes and expanded names is *read only once;* the first time the subprogram is called.

Incoming Data

There are no input files for this project other than the file of course codes. (The previous project on student profiles reads a student record and passes the necessary parameters to this program through a CALL statement.) The table of course codes is shown:

Course Code	Course Name
100	ENGLISH 1
111	COMPUTER SCI
140	SPANISH I
150	MUSIC
160	ART APPREC
200	BIOLOGY
222	CHEMISTRY
300	CALCULUS
333	ELECT ENG 1
400	STAT INFERENCE
444	REGRESSION
501	AM HISTORY
503	EUR HISTORY
504	ECONOMICS
505	POL SCIENCE
506	CREATIVE WRIT
555	EDUC THEORY
600	FORTRAN
601	COBOL
666	PSYCHOLOGY
675	SPECIAL EDUC
700	THESIS

Required Output

No specific report is produced by this program as its output is returned to the calling program of Project 6.6. The latter in turn will print the expanded values in a report. Use the format of Fig. 6.4 modified to print expanded rather than coded values.

Suggested Extra

Find the proper utility program to create a COBOL copy member. Invoke this utility to establish an entry for major codes and values, then initialize the table in the project through a COPY clause.

Project 6.8: Grade Distributions

Objectives

To use two-dimensional tables, to introduce the date of program execution and an age calculation, to gain proficiency with the nested IF and PERFORM, to introduce data validation.

Problem Statement

Professor Milgrom in the Statistics Department is trying to determine whether grade point average is affected by a student's sex and/or age. Accordingly, he would like a two-by-two contingency table developed which presents the average GPA for various age and sex combinations. The table is to take the format shown in Fig. 6.5 with *hypothetical* data as illustration:

	Male	Female
21 and older	2.85	2.75 —Average GPA for women 21 and older
Under 21	2.40	2.50

Figure 6.5 Report Format for Grade Distribution Project.

From the data given, women 21 and older have an average GPA of 2.75, whereas men under 21 have an average GPA of 2.40. Develop a program that will process a file of student records and compute the four numbers the professor is looking for.

Incoming Data

Use the record description of Fig. 6.9 on page 288 and the test data of Fig. 6.10 on page 289.

Required Output

Professor Milgrom also needs to know the number of students in each of the four categories, in addition to the average GPA. He would like computer output in the format shown in Fig. 6.7 on page 284.

Suggested Extras

1. Data Validation: Unfortunately incoming records cannot be assumed to contain valid data. In particular, sex is often left blank, or coded incorrectly (other than M or F). In addition, the birthdates of many students were entered incorrectly. Hence, students with calculated ages older than 70 or younger than 15 should be disregarded from the averages. The names of students with invalid data, and the associated error, should be displayed.
2. Print the tables side by side rather than one under the other. If you are really ambitious, box in the numbers with lines of asterisks.

Variations

The good professor has decided that year in school is apt to be a better discriminator than age, and hence, is interested in a four by two contingency table shown in Fig. 6.6:

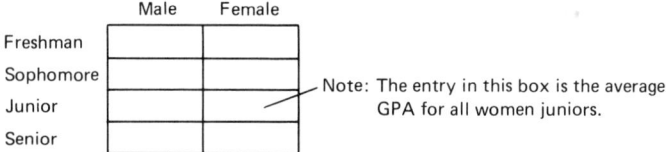

Figure 6.6

Freshmen are considered to have fewer than 30 credits, sophomores between 30 and 59, juniors between 60 and 89, and seniors over 90. Do *not* include freshmen with zero credits in your computations.

Project 6.9: Student Credit Hours

Objectives

To present control breaks, the SORT verb, and Report Writer. Options associated with this problem include subprograms and table lookups.

Problem Statement

The administration is planning for the hiring and/or termination of faculty over the next three years. In order to plan more effectively, it needs

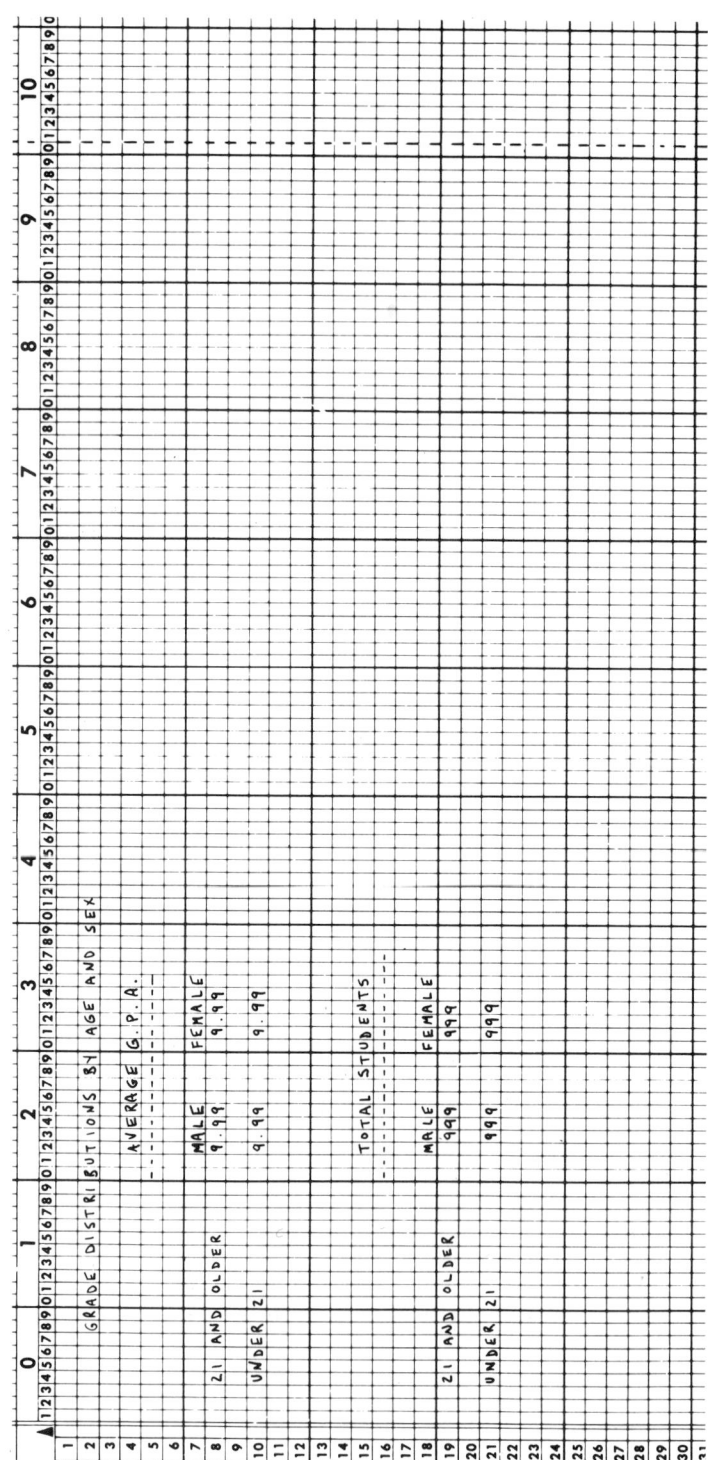

Figure 6.7 Report Format for Grade Distribution Project.

to know which majors are most in demand. Accordingly, the Provost has requested a report which will provide a listing of student credit hours by school by major. Develop a program which will process a file of student records and compute these totals.

Incoming Data

Use the record description of Fig. 6.11 on page 289 and the test data of Fig. 6.12 on page 290. Note that *all* courses in a student record are credited to the major code appearing in that record, even though the courses may be outside of the major. Note well that the incoming data are *not* sorted.

Required Output

Use the report layout in Fig. 6.8 as a guide. Begin the output for each school on a new page.

Suggested Extras

1. Expand the output to print *expanded* values for major and school. Do this by including a call to the subprogram for code expansion (originally described in Project 6.7, Student Profiles with Table Lookups).
2. It is assumed that this problem will be solved using Report Writer. However, the rather involved logic of a double control break problem provides an excellent opportunity to use techniques of stepwise refinement and top down program development. Accordingly, solve the problem both ways and compare.

Projects 6.10a and b: File Maintenance
(Sequential and Nonsequential)

Objectives

To present concepts of file maintenance, as well as a problem with more complex logic requirements.

Problem Statement

Update the student master file by including information on last semester's grades. (See the Incoming Data Section for specifications of the old master and transaction files.) Your program is to accommodate *all* of the following:

1. Update the EXP-CUMULATIVE-POINTS and EXP-CUMULATIVE-CREDITS fields in the master file. Allow 4, 3, 2, 1, and 0 points for an A, B, C, D, or F respectively. An A in a three credit course adds 12 points and 3 credits to EXP-CUMULATIVE-POINTS and EXP-

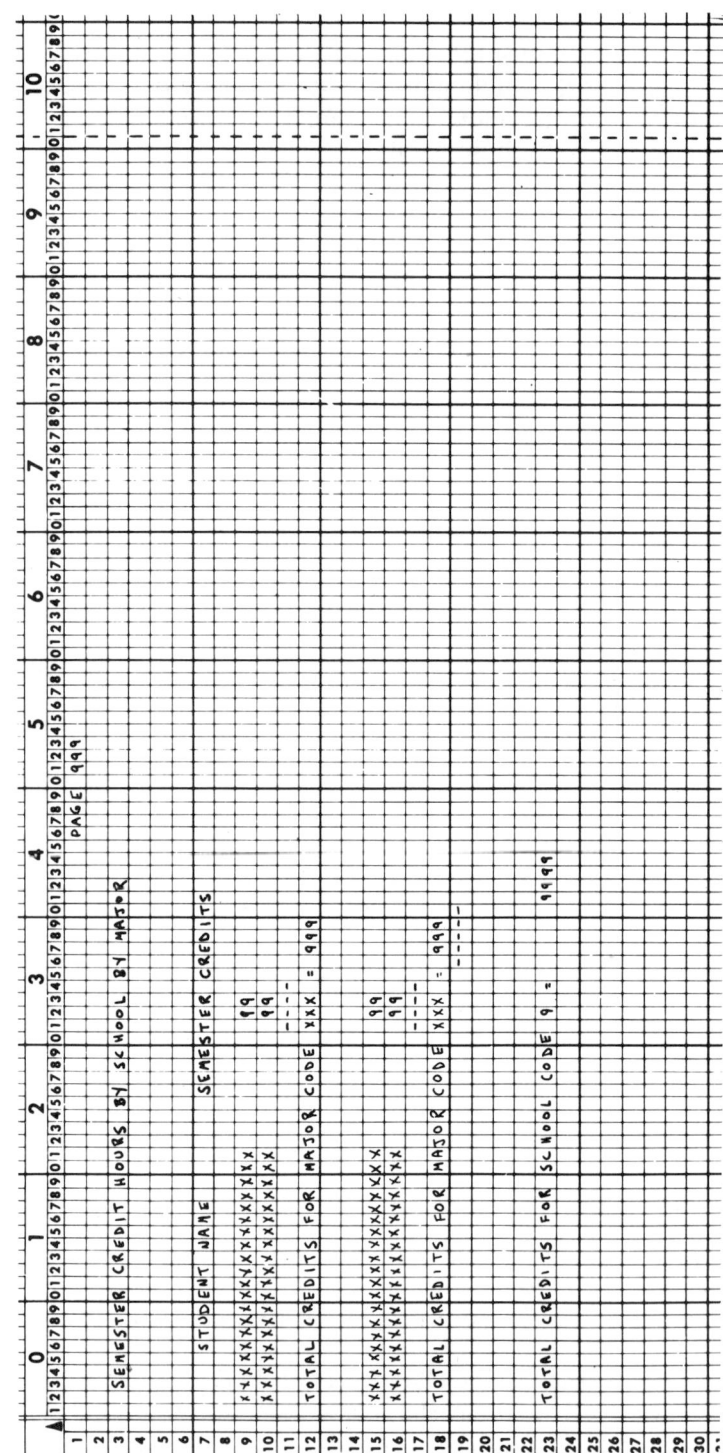

Figure 6.8 Report Format for Student Credit Hours Project.

CUMULATIVE-CREDITS, respectively. Do *not* increment either field if the grade is other than A, B, C, D, or F.

2. Delete students reaching 120 or more cumulative credits from the new master file. Display their names as graduating seniors.
3. Check that every course appearing in a student's master record (in the table EXP-COURSES-THIS-SEMESTER) appears in the corresponding transaction record. If a course is missing from the transaction file, display the error message, 'NO GRADE FOR COURSE NO XXXX' with the student's name and social security number.
4. Check that every course appearing in a transaction record appears in the student's master record. If a course is missing from the master record, display the message 'GRADE RECEIVED FOR NON-REGISTERED COURSE' with the student's name and social security number. Do not update the EXP-CUMULATIVE-POINTS and EXP-CUMULATIVE-CREDITS fields in the master record for this course.
5. Blank out any entry in the table EXP-COURSES-THIS-SEMESTER of the new master record if the course was present in a matching transaction record, *and* if the course had a valid grade; A, B, C, D, or F. If either of these conditions is not met, retain only the course(s) with invalid data but blank out all others.
6. Display the transaction social security number and error message 'NO CORRESPONDING MASTER RECORD' if a social security number in the transaction file does not match an existing master record.
7. Display the old master social security number and the error message 'NO GRADES FOR LAST SEMESTER' if a social security number in the old master does not have a matching record in the transaction file. Write a new master record identical to the existing record.
8. If *either* the major or school code is different in the transaction record than in the master record, change the new master record to reflect the code of the transaction record.

Incoming Data

Use the EXPANDED-STUDENT-FILE of Fig. 6.13 on page 290 as the record layout for the old (and new) master file. Realize, however, that if sequential access is used there will be *two* distinct master files and a unique prefix will be required for each. Use the test data of Fig. 6.14 as the original old master.

The transaction file consists of the test data in Fig. 6.12 and conforms to the record layout of Fig. 6.11.

Required Output

Various DISPLAY messages are required as detailed in the problem statement. In addition, the new master file must appear as hard copy in order for the student and/or instructor to check results. (The means of achieving printed output is left to the student. Ideally, the new master should be created on disk and its contents printed through a utility program. Less advanced students may choose to create the new master directly as a print file.)

Suggested Extras

1. Provide documentation for the program in the form of pseudocode and hierarchy charts.
2. Develop the maintenance program in two phases. The first version is to include program stubs and utilize top down testing, the second version will be the completed program.

Variation

Do the project two ways, utilizing both sequential and nonsequential access of the master file.

Record Descriptions and Test Data for Student Information System

Record Description and Test Data for Student Selection, Tuition Billing, Grade Point Listing, and Grade Distribution Projects

```
FD  STUDENT-FILE
    LABEL RECORDS ARE OMITTED
    RECORD CONTAINS 80 CHARACTERS
    DATA RECORD IS STUDENT-RECORD.
01  STUDENT-RECORD.
    05  STU-SOC-SEC-NUMBER           PIC 9(9).
    05  STU-NAME-AND-INITIALS        PIC X(20).
    05  STU-MAJOR                    PIC X(15).
    05  STU-CUMULATIVE-CREDITS       PIC 999.
    05  STU-CREDITS-THIS SEMESTER    PIC 99.
    05  STU-UNION-MEMBER             PIC X.
    05  STU-SCHOLARSHIP-PERCENT      PIC 9(3).
    05  STU-GRADE-POINT-AVERAGE      PIC 9V99.
    05  STU-BIRTH-DATE.
        10  STU-BIRTH-MONTH          PIC 99.
        10  STU-BIRTH-YEAR           PIC 99.
    05  STU-SEX                      PIC X.
    05  FILLER                       PIC X(19).
```

Figure 6.9 Record Description.

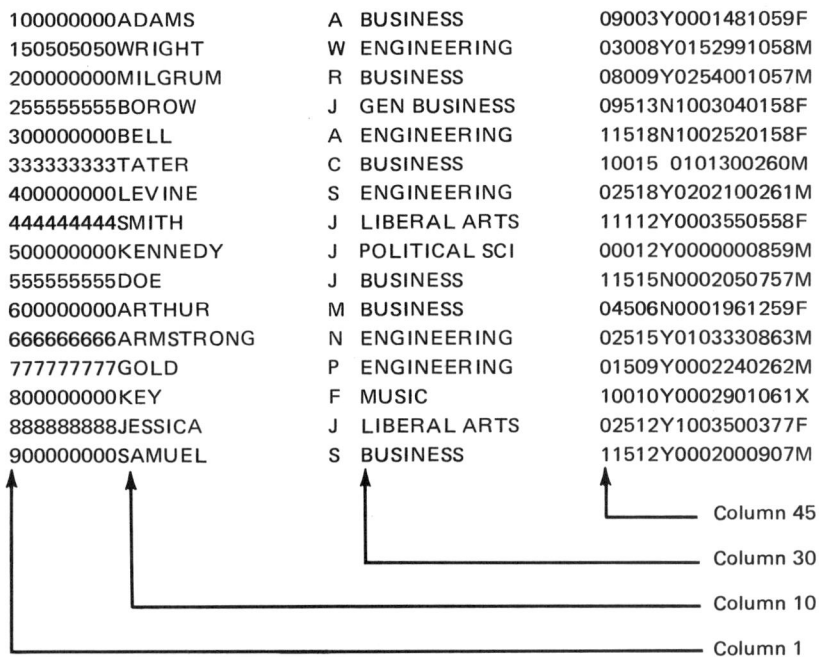

```
100000000ADAMS          A  BUSINESS         09003Y0001481059F
150505050WRIGHT         W  ENGINEERING      03008Y0152991058M
200000000MILGRUM        R  BUSINESS         08009Y0254001057M
255555555BOROW          J  GEN BUSINESS     09513N1003040158F
300000000BELL           A  ENGINEERING      11518N1002520158F
333333333TATER          C  BUSINESS         10015 0101300260M
400000000LEVINE         S  ENGINEERING      02518Y0202100261M
444444444SMITH          J  LIBERAL ARTS     11112Y0003550558F
500000000KENNEDY        J  POLITICAL SCI    00012Y0000000859M
555555555DOE            J  BUSINESS         11515N0002050757M
600000000ARTHUR         M  BUSINESS         04506N0001961259F
666666666ARMSTRONG      N  ENGINEERING      02515Y0103330863M
777777777GOLD           P  ENGINEERING      01509Y0002240262M
800000000KEY            F  MUSIC            10010Y0002901061X
888888888JESSICA        J  LIBERAL ARTS     02512Y1003500377F
900000000SAMUEL         S  BUSINESS         11512Y0002000907M
```

                          Column 45
                    Column 30
              Column 10
        Column 1

Figure 6.10 Test Data.

Record Description and Test Data for Student Transcripts, Credit Hours, and File Maintenance Projects

```
FD  STUDENT-GRADE-FILE
    LABEL RECORDS ARE OMITTED
    RECORD CONTAINS 80 CHARACTERS
    DATA RECORD IS STUDENT-GRADE-RECORD.
01  STUDENT-GRADE-RECORD.
    05  STU-SOC-SEC-NUMBER                  PIC 9(9).
    05  STU-NAME-AND-INITIALS               PIC X(20).
    05  STU-MAJOR-CODE                      PIC X(3).
    05  STU-SCHOOL-CODE                     PIC 9.
    05  STU-NUMBER-OF-COURSES-TAKEN         PIC 9.
    05  STU-COURSE-CREDITS-GRADE OCCURS 7 TIMES.
        10  STU-COURSE-NUMBER               PIC X(3).
        10  STU-COURSE-GRADE                PIC X.
        10  STU-COURSE-CREDITS              PIC 9.
    05  FILLER                              PIC X(11).
```

Figure 6.11 Record Description.

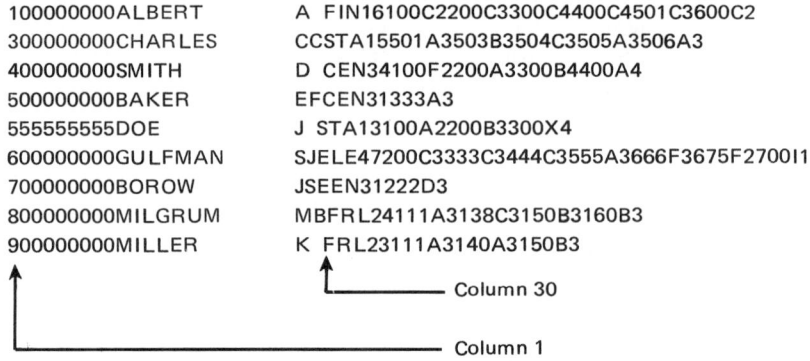

Figure 6.12 Test Data.

Record Description and Test Data for Student Profiles, Table Lookups, and File Maintenance Projects

```
FD  EXPANDED-STUDENT-FILE
    LABEL RECORDS ARE OMITTED
    RECORD CONTAINS 80 CHARACTERS
    DATA RECORD IS EXPANDED-STUDENT-RECORD.
01  EXPANDED-STUDENT-RECORD.
    05  EXP-SOC-SEC-NUMBER                      PIC 9(9).
    05  EXP-NAME-AND-INITIALS.
        10  EXP-LAST-NAME                       PIC X(18).
        10  EXP-INITIALS                        PIC XX.
    05  EXP-DATE-OF-BIRTH.
        10  EXP-BIRTH-MONTH                     PIC 99.
        10  EXP-BIRTH-YEAR                      PIC 99.
    05  EXP-SEX                                 PIC X.
    05  EXP-MAJOR-CODE                          PIC X(3).
    05  EXP-SCHOOL-CODE                         PIC 9.
    05  EXP-CUMULATIVE-CREDITS                  PIC 999.
    05  EXP-CUMULATIVE-POINTS                   PIC 999.
    05  EXP-UNION-MEMBER-CODE                   PIC X.
    05  EXP-SCHOLARSHIP                         PIC 999.
    05  EXP-DATE-OF-ENROLLMENT                  PIC 9(4).
    05  EXP-COURSES-THIS-SEMESTER OCCURS 7 TIMES.
        10  EXP-COURSE-NUMBER                   PIC XXX.
        10  EXP-COURSE-CREDITS                  PIC 9.
```

Figure 6.13 Record Description.

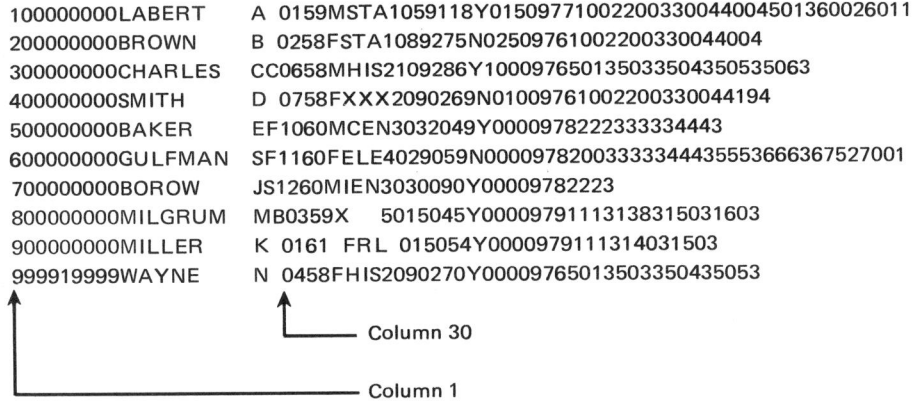

```
100000000LABERT    A 0159MSTA1059118Y01509771002200330044004501360026011
200000000BROWN     B 0258FSTA1089275N02509761002200330044004
300000000CHARLES   CC0658MHIS2109286Y10009765013503350435053506 3
400000000SMITH     D 0758FXXX2090269N01009761002200330044194
500000000BAKER     EF1060MCEN3032049Y00009782223333344 43
600000000GULFMAN   SF1160FELE4029059N000097820033333444355536663675 27001
700000000BOROW     JS1260MIEN3030090Y00009782223
800000000MILGRUM   MB0359X   5015045Y00009791113138315031603
900000000MILLER    K 0161 FRL 015054Y00009791113140 31503
999919999WAYNE     N 0458FHIS2090270Y00009765013503350435053
```

Figure 6.14 Test Data

Record Description and Test Data for Student Course Cards Project

```
FD   STUDENT-COURSE-FILE
     LABEL RECORDS ARE OMITTED
     RECORD CONTAINS 80 CHARACTERS
     DATA RECORDS ARE MASTER-RECORD, COURSE-RECORD.
01   MASTER-RECORD.
     05   MAST-SOC-SEC-NUMBER              PIC 9(9).
     05   MAST-NAME                        PIC X(22).
     05   MAST-MAJOR-CODE                  PIC X(3).
     05   MAST-SCHOOL-CODE                 PIC 9.
     05   FILLER                           PIC X(44).
     05   MAST-CODE                        PIC X.
          88   MASTER-CARD      VALUE 'M'.
          88   COURSE-CARD      VALUE 'C'.
01   COURSE-RECORD.
     05   COURSE-SOC-SEC-NUMBER            PIC 9(9).
     05   COURSE-NUMBER                    PIC X(3).
     05   COURSE-GRADE                     PIC X.
     05   COURSE-CREDITS                   PIC 9.
     05   FILLER                           PIC X(65).
     05   COURSE-CODE                      PIC X.
```

Figure 6.15 Record Description.

```
          100000000ALBERT           A STA1          M
          100000000100C2                            C
          100000000200C3                            C
          100000000300C4                            C
          100000000400C4                            C
```

Figure 6.16 Test Data.

291

```
100000000501C3                          C
100000000600C2                          C
100000001601C2                          C
200000000BROWN          B  STA1         M
200000001100A2                          C
200000001200B3                          C
200000001300C4                          C
200000001400D4                          C
300000000CHARLES        CCSTA2          M
300000000510A3                          C
300000000503B3                          C
300000000504C3                          C
300000000505A3                          C
300000000506A3                          C
400000000SMITH          D  CEN3         M
400000000100F2                          C
400000000200A3                          C
400000000300B4                          C
400000000400A4                          C
500000000BAKER          EFCEN3          M
500000000333A3                          C
555555555DOE            J  STA1         M
555555555100A2                          C
555555555200B3                          C
555555555300X4                          C
600000000GULFMAN        SJELE4          M
600000000200C3                          C
600000000333C3                          C
600000000444C3                          C
600000000555A3                          C
600000000666F3                          C
600000000675F2                          C
60000000070OI1                          C
700000000BOROW          JSCEN3          M
700000000222D3                          C
800000000MILGRUM        MBFRL2          M
800000000111A3                          C
800000000138C3                          C
800000000150B3                          C
800000000160B3                          C
900000000MILLER         K  FRL2         M
900000000111A3                          C
900000000140A3                          C
900000000150B3                          C
```

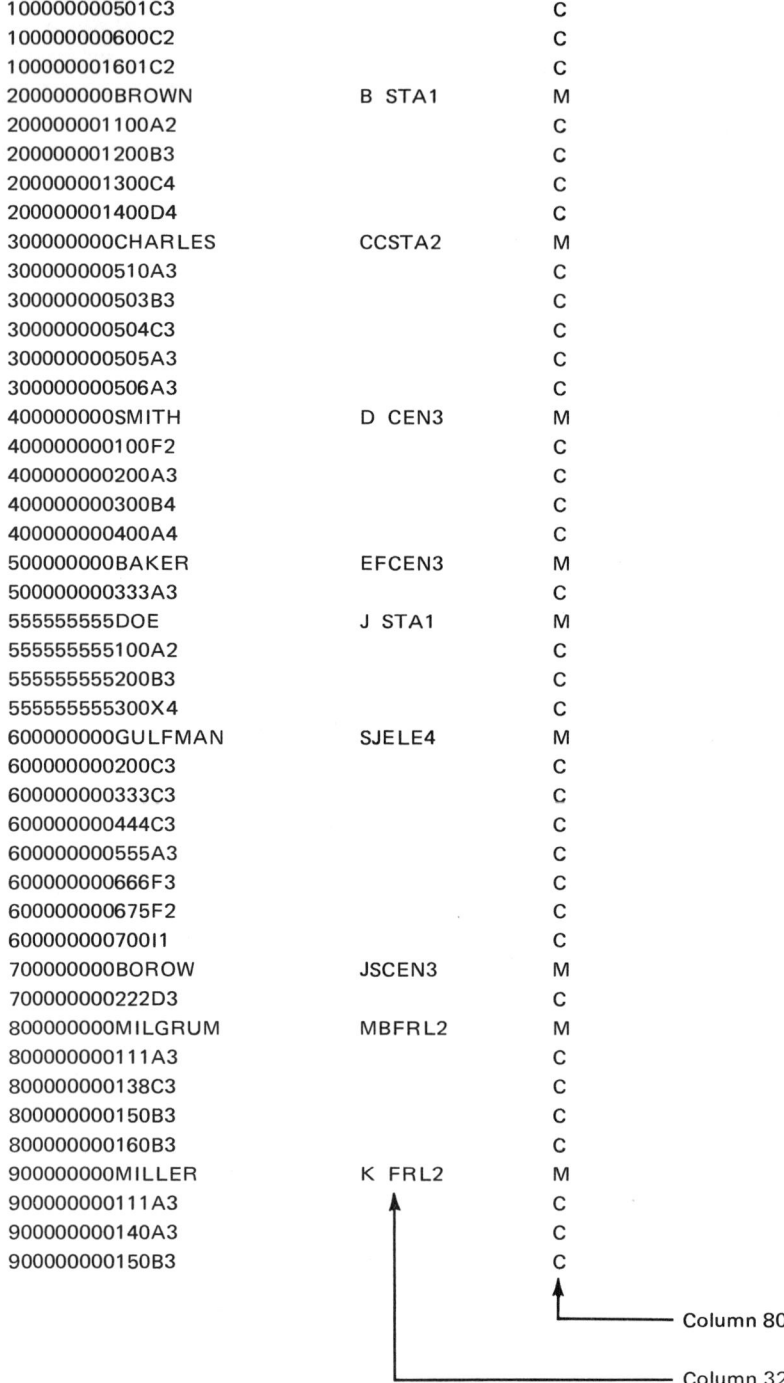

Figure 6.16 *cont.*

PERSONNEL INFORMATION SYSTEM

Project 6.11: Employee Selection

Objectives

To introduce COBOL and to get students "on and off" the machine.

Problem Statement

Process a file of employee records and print the names of all employees who have the job title "programmer" and earn at least $15,000.

Incoming Data

Incoming records have the following format:

Field	Columns	Picture
Employee Name	10-25	X(16)
Job Title	26-35	X(10)
Salary	36-40	9(5)

Make up your own test data.

Required Output

Use the report format of Fig. 6.17 as shown.

Suggested Extras

1. Count the number of employees who meet both qualifications and print this number in a total line at the end of the report.
2. Include elementary editing to print a dollar sign and comma in appropriate positions in employee salary.

Variation

Modify the program to list programmers *and* operators who earn at least $15,000.

Project 6.12: Annual Compensation Analysis

Objectives

To do simple arithmetic on fields containing implied decimal points, to calculate totals and averages, to introduce simple editing, and to gain proficiency with the IF statement. (Suggested extras include use of the SORT verb, page headings, and condition names.)

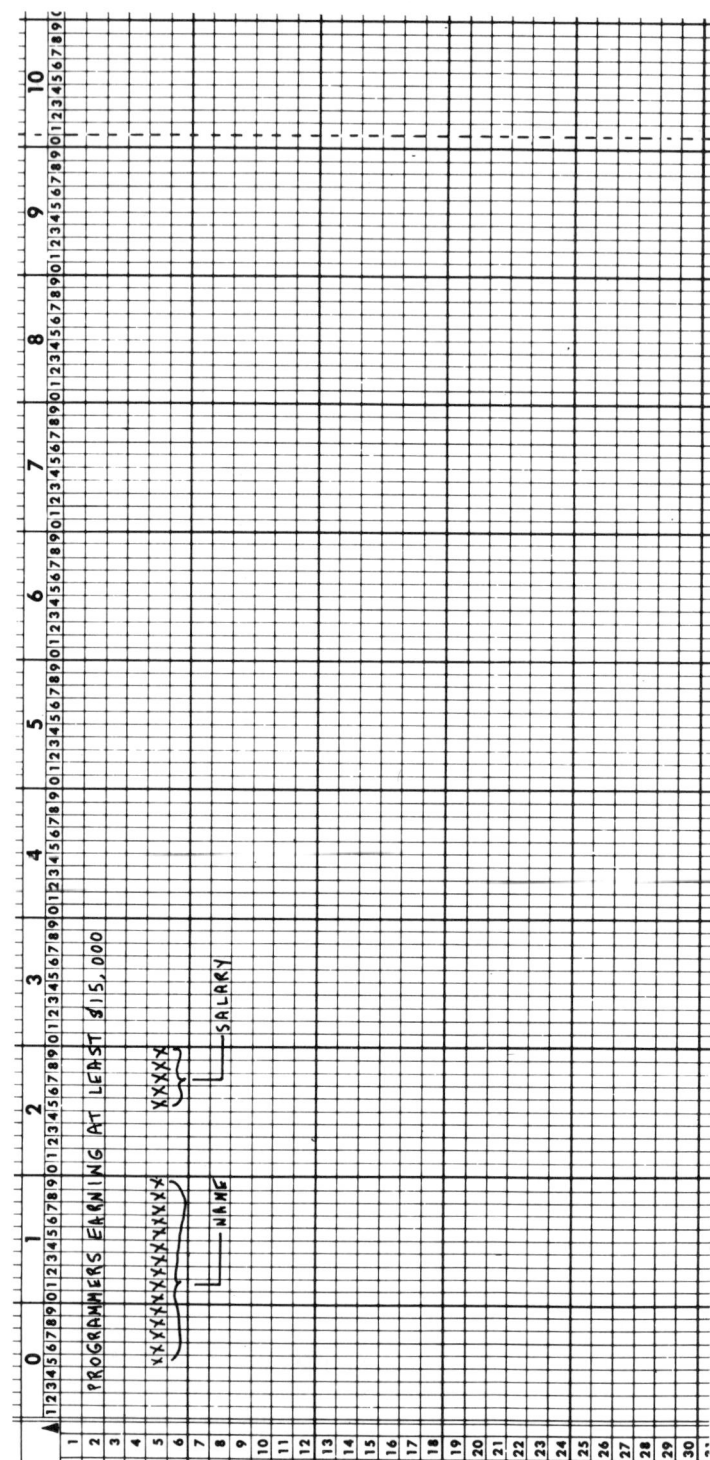

Figure 6.17 Report Format for Employee Selection.

Problem statement

Process a file of employee records, and for every employee, calculate his or her *annual* earnings. The method of compensation is specified in one of two ways according to the compensation code on the employee record. Codes of H and M denote hourly and monthly, respectively. Use 40 hours/week and 52 weeks/year in determining the annual figure.

When all the records have been processed, print the average annual earnings in each of the two compensation categories.

Incoming Data

Use the record description of Fig. 6.24 and the test data of Fig. 6.25, both on page 311.

Required Output

Use the report format of Fig. 6.18.

Suggested Extras

1. Use 88-level entries in the record description to define the method of compensation.
2. Use the SORT verb to group employees by compensation type, H or M, and alphabetically within type. Begin each group of employees on a new page.

Project 6.13: Payroll

Objectives

To cover heading, detail, and total lines, to gain further practice in arithmetic, and to produce a formatted report with reasonable editing. Suggested extras include a page heading routine and use of DATE.

Problem Statement

Process a file of employee records to compute individual pay and company totals as follows:

1. Computations are to be performed only for hourly employees, i.e., those with EMP-COMPENSATION-CODE of H. All other employees are to be excluded from this report.
2. Gross pay is computed as follows:
   a. Straight time for the first 40 hours
   b. Time and a half for the next 8 hours (between 40 and 48 hours)
   c. Double time for anything over 48 hours

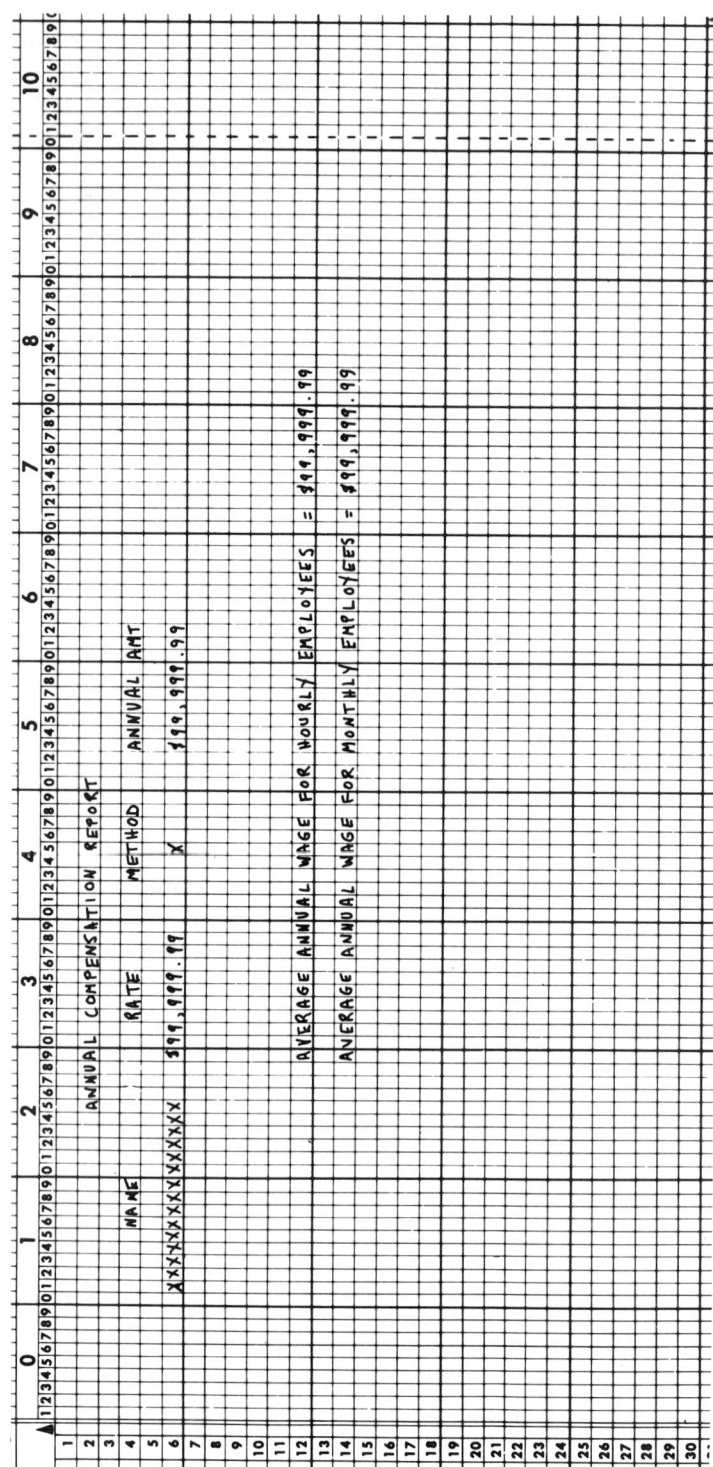

Figure 6.18 Report Format for Compensation Analysis.

3. Federal withholding tax is calculated as follows:
   a. 18% on first $200 of gross
   b. 20% on amounts between $200 and $240
   c. 22% on amounts between $240 and $280
   d. 24% on anything over $280
4. Net pay is simply gross pay minus federal withholding tax
5. Company totals are required for gross pay, federal withholding taxes, and net pay.

Incoming Data

Use the record description of Fig. 6.24 and the test data of Fig. 6.25, both on page 311.

Required Output

A suitable heading is to appear at the beginning of the report and company totals at the end. Fig. 6.19 contains the report specifications. Pay particular attention to the indicated editing.

Suggested Extra

Limit the number of employees to 4 per page. This requires that the heading routine be executed an indeterminate number of times, once for each 4 employees. The heading routine should include a page number and date of execution.

Project 6.14: Benefit Statement

Objectives

To do more complex arithmetic, to introduce DATE of execution in an age calculation, to further develop editing capability and the IF statement, and to present a program with more complex logic requirements. The suggested extra introduces the PERFORM/VARYING statement.

Problem Statement

Process a file of employee records, and for each employee print a benefit statement showing the value of fringe benefits. Benefit information is to be calculated in two areas:

Sick Pay: An employee is entitled to one week of full pay and an additional two weeks of half pay, for every year (or fraction thereof) of employment. The *maximum* benefit, however, is 10 weeks of full salary and 20 of half salary, which is reached after 10 years. (An employee with two years service, for example, is entitled to two weeks full pay and an additional four weeks of half pay.)

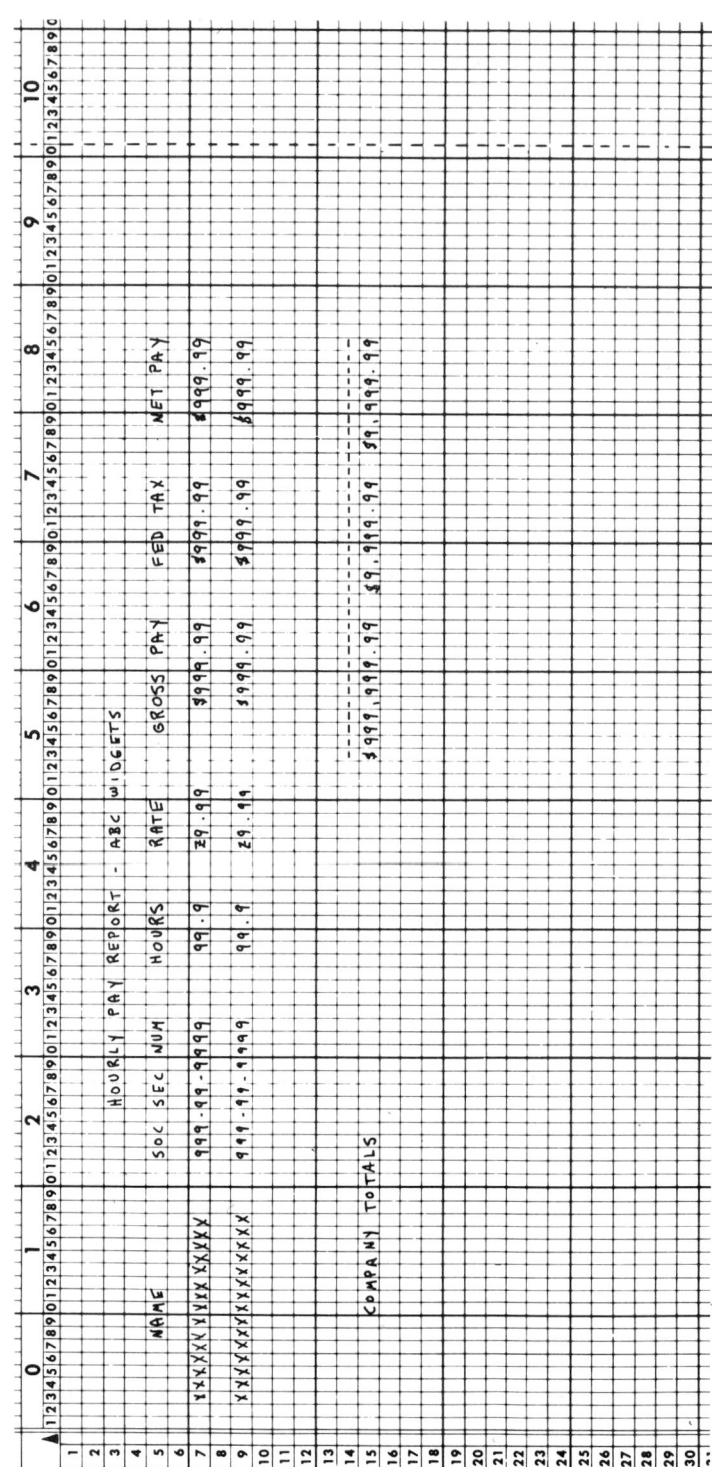

Figure 6.19 Report Layout for Payroll Project.

Retirement: The company has just announced a pension plan in which it will make an annual contribution for each employee based on salary. The contribution is equal to 5% of the first $10,000 of salary plus 3% on any salary in excess of $10,000. Hence, the company would contribute $560 annually for an employee earning $12,000 (5% of 10,000 = 500, plus 3% of 2000 = $60). The money is invested for the employees and assumed to earn 8% annually. Your program is to compute and print the amount the employee will have at age 65. Use the following formula:

$$\text{Amount at age 65} = \frac{((1 + i)^n - 1)}{i} * \text{Annual Contribution}$$

where i = interest rate; for example, .08,
and n = years till age 65

Incoming Data

Use the record description of Fig. 6.24. (Note that an employee's salary is not necessarily expressed as an annual amount, and consequently, it is necessary to first determine an annual salary as per the specifications of Project 6.12). Use the test data in Fig. 6.25 on page 311.

Required Output

Begin each benefit statement on a new page. Use the format shown in Fig. 6.20.

Suggested Extras

1. Include a life insurance benefit where the amount of insurance is determined by the type of compensation. Hourly employees receive an amount of insurance equal to one year's salary, whereas monthly employees receive an amount equal to twice their annual salary.
2. Expand the retirement portion of the benefit statement to show the amount accumulated at age 65 with various interest rates: 8, 9, 10, 11, and 12 percent. Use a PERFORM/VARYING statement.

Project 6.15: Employee Profiles

Objectives

To format a detailed print report, to introduce the OCCURS clause and one-dimensional tables, to do elementary editing and introduce the INSPECT verb, to further develop arithmetic with implied decimal points; to introduce

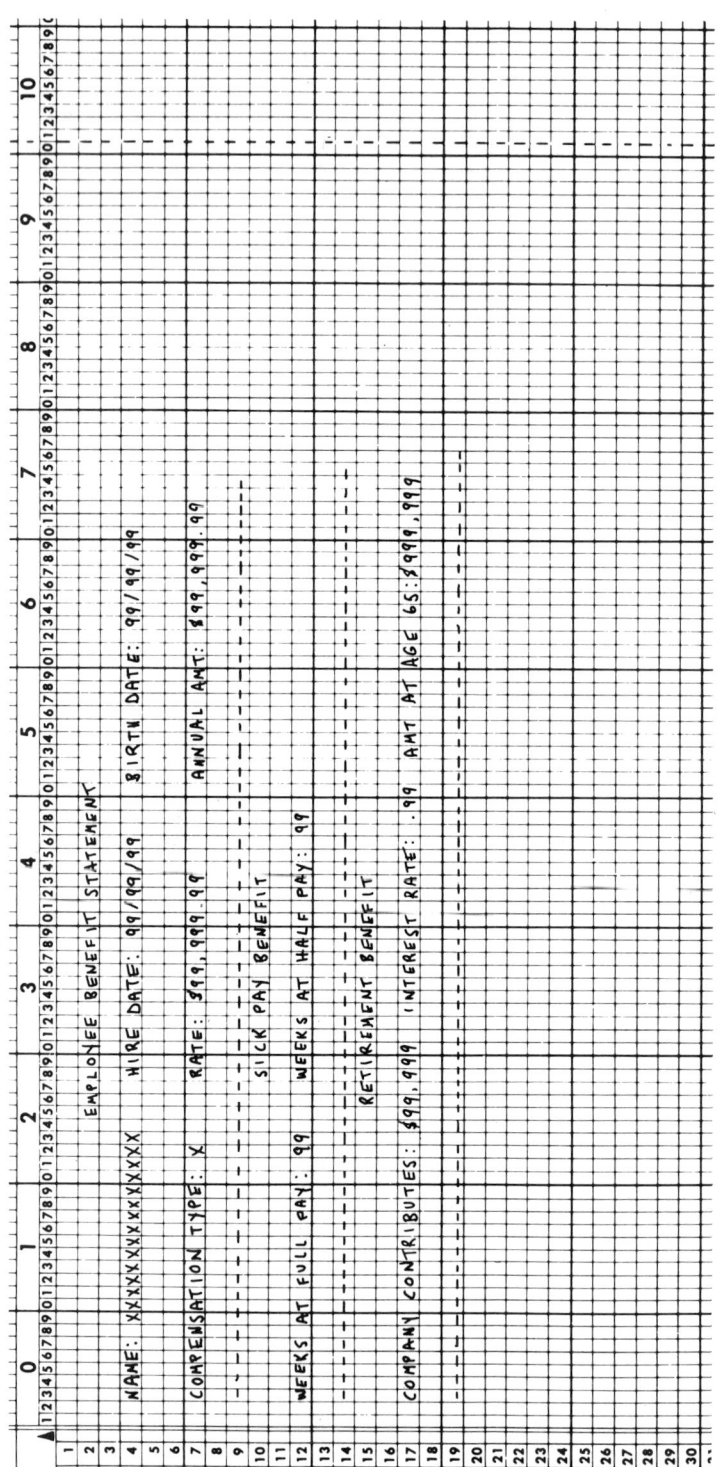

Figure 6.20 Report Format for Compensation Analysis.

page headings and date of execution. (The suggested extras require material on sorting.)

Problem Statement

Develop a program to prepare a set of employee profiles which provide detailed information on each employee. An approximate report format is shown in the Required Output section. Employee profiles are to appear two per page with a page heading on every new page. Note well the following requirements and/or specifications:

1. Employee age is to be calculated from date of birth and date of program execution.
2. The social security number requires the insertion of hyphens; accomplish this by defining an output picture containing blanks in appropriate positions, and then replace the blanks through the INSPECT verb.
3. Percent salary increase, months between increase, and annual rate of salary increase all require two sets of salary data; present and previous, or previous and second previous. Do not attempt a calculation when there are insufficient data.
4. Percent salary increase is found by subtracting the old salary from the new salary, dividing the result by the old salary, and multiplying by 100. For example, new and old salaries of $11,000 and $10,000, respectively, yield a percent increase of 10 percent.
5. Months between increase is simply the number of months between two salary dates.
6. Annual rate of salary increase is found by converting the percent salary increase to a 12 month basis; 10 percent after 6 months is equivalent to an annual rate of 20 percent, 10 percent after two years is an annual rate of 5 percent.
7. The salary midpoint measures the average salary for all employees at a particular grade level. (All employees are assigned a grade of from 1 to 9 to indicate their level of responsibility in the company; for example, a janitor might have a grade of 1, and the president a grade of 9.) The salary midpoint is found by multiplying the grade level by $4,000 (for example, a grade of 4 has a midpoint of $16,000).
8. The percent of grade midpoint is found by dividing an individual's salary by his grade midpoint and multiplying by 100.

Incoming Data

Use the record description of Fig. 6.26 and the test data of Fig. 6.27, both on page 312.

Required Output

Use Fig. 6.21 as a guide in both report format and definition of terms.

		PERSONNEL PROFILE							
NAME:	JONES, A.B.		EDUCATION:	2 YR. DEGREE*		SOC–SEC–NO.:	123-45-6789		
AGE:	21.4 YEARS		HIRE DATE:	1/79		LOCATION: NEW YORK*			
			SALARY HISTORY						
SALARY	DATE	TYPE	PERCENT INCREASE	MONTHS BETWEEN INCREASE	ANNUAL RATE OF INCREASE	GRADE	GRADE MIDPOINT	PERCENT GRADE MIDPOINT	
$12,100	7/80	P	10.0	6	20.0%	4	$16,000	75.6	
$11,000	1/80	M	10.0	12	10.0%	3	$12,000	91.6	
$10,000	1/79	H				3	$12,000	83.3	
			JOB DESCRIPTION						
			TITLE	DATE					
			JR. PROGRAMMER*	7/80					
			TRAINEE	1/79					

*Note: In this project coded values will appear for education, location, and title. The codes will be expanded in Project 6.16.

Figure 6.21 Employee Profile Report Format.

Suggested Extra

Sort the incoming file so that profiles appear in alphabetical order.

Project 6.16: Employee Profiles With Table Lookups

Objectives

To introduce SEARCH, SEARCH ALL, and direct access to table entries, to cover indexing, variable length tables, and REDEFINES, to initialize tables through the VALUE clause and by reading values from a file, to present subprograms.

Problem Statement

The employee profiles of Project 6.15, with codes for job title, location, and education, have been rejected by Personnel. Project 6.15 is to be modified to print *expanded,* rather than coded data for these fields.

This project is to be written as a subprogram, as its use is anticipated in future projects as well. It is to accept codes passed from a calling program and return expanded values. There are a total of eight parameters as follows: location-code (PIC 99), expanded location (PIC X(15)), title-code (PIC XX), expanded title (PIC X(15)), previous title code (PIC XX), previous title (PIC X(15)), education code (PIC 9), and expanded education (PIC X(17)).

Education code is to be expanded via a *direct* lookup (the code itself indicates the position in the table of expanded values). Use the following table:

Code	Education
1	Some H.S.
2	H.S. Diploma
3	Two Year Degree
4	Four Year Degree
5	Some Grad School
6	Master's Degree
7	Ph.D.
8	Other Grad Degree

Location code is to be expanded through a *sequential search,* using the table provided. The location table is to be established, using the OCCURS, VALUE, and REDEFINES clauses. Use the following data:

Code	Location
05	Atlanta
10	Boston
15	Chicago
20	Detroit
25	Kansas City
30	Los Angeles
35	Minneapolis
40	New York
45	Philadelphia

Title code is to be expanded, using a *binary search* unless the code (present or previous) is spaces, in which case the expanded title should be spaces also. The table itself is to be initialized by dynamically reading values from a file in the following format: title code in columns 1 and 2, expanded title in columns 3 through 17. The maximum table length is 100 titles. Finally, your program is to contain sufficient logic so that the file of title codes (shown in the Incoming Data Section) is read only once, the first time the subprogram is called.

Incoming Data

There are no input files for this project other than the file of title codes. (The previous project on employee profiles reads an employee record and passes the necessary parameters to this program through a CALL statement.) The title file is listed below:

Code	Title
18	Sr. Accountant
20	Auditor
35	Jr. Programmer
45	Sr. Programmer
55	Analyst
60	Manager

Required Output

No specific report is produced by this program as its output is returned to the calling program of Project 6.15. The latter in turn will print the expanded values in a report. Use the format of Fig. 6.21 modified to print expanded rather than coded values.

Suggested Extra

Find the proper utility program to create a COBOL COPY member. Invoke this utility to establish an entry for location codes and values, then initialize the location table in the project through a COPY clause.

Project 6.17: EEO Reporting

Objectives

To introduce a program with multiple input files and consequently more complex logic, to fully utilize nested IF and PERFORM statements.

Problem Statement

Write a COBOL program to merge two files and create a third. The first is the employee master file of Projects 6.15 and 6.16. The second is a new EEO file containing only social security numbers and EEO codes.

Both input files have been sorted by social security number. Ideally, every record contained on the employee file should have a matching social security number on the EEO file, but your program must test for two possible errors:

1. A social security number present in the employee file, but missing in the EEO file, and
2. A social security number present in the EEO file, but missing in the employee file.

If the same social security number is found on both files, the two records are to be combined into a new merged record as described in the Required Output section. The merged record is to extract all fields from the original employee record and append two new fields from the EEO record.

Incoming Data

Use the record descriptions of Fig. 6.26 and 6.31 and the test data of Fig. 6.27 and 6.32. (see pages 312 and 314.)

Required Output

Two distinct error messages are required as detailed in the problem statement. These messages can appear in DISPLAY statements, and consequently no report formatting is necessary.

The format for the merged file is provided in Fig. 6.30. Records in this file must appear as hard copy in order for the student to check results. Ideally, the merged file should be created on disk, and its contents printed through a utility program. Less advanced students may choose to create the new master directly as a print file.

Suggested Extra

Include additional logic to verify that the incoming files are in sequence, and terminate processing if either file is out of order.

Project 6.18: Salary Totals

Objectives

To present control breaks, the SORT verb, and Report Writer. Options associated with this problem include subprograms and table lookups.

Problem Statement

The compensation analyst in Personnel requires summary statistics on location salaries, and the job titles within a location. Develop a COBOL program which will process a master file of employee records and compute these totals.

Incoming Data

Use the record description of Fig. 6.26 and the test data of Fig. 6.27. Note well that the incoming records are in social security sequence, rather than the location, and title within location, order which is required for this problem.

Required Output

Use the report layout of Fig. 6.22 as a guide. Begin the output for each location on a new page.

Suggested Extras

1. Expand the output to print expanded values for title and location. Do this by including a call to the subprogram for code expansion

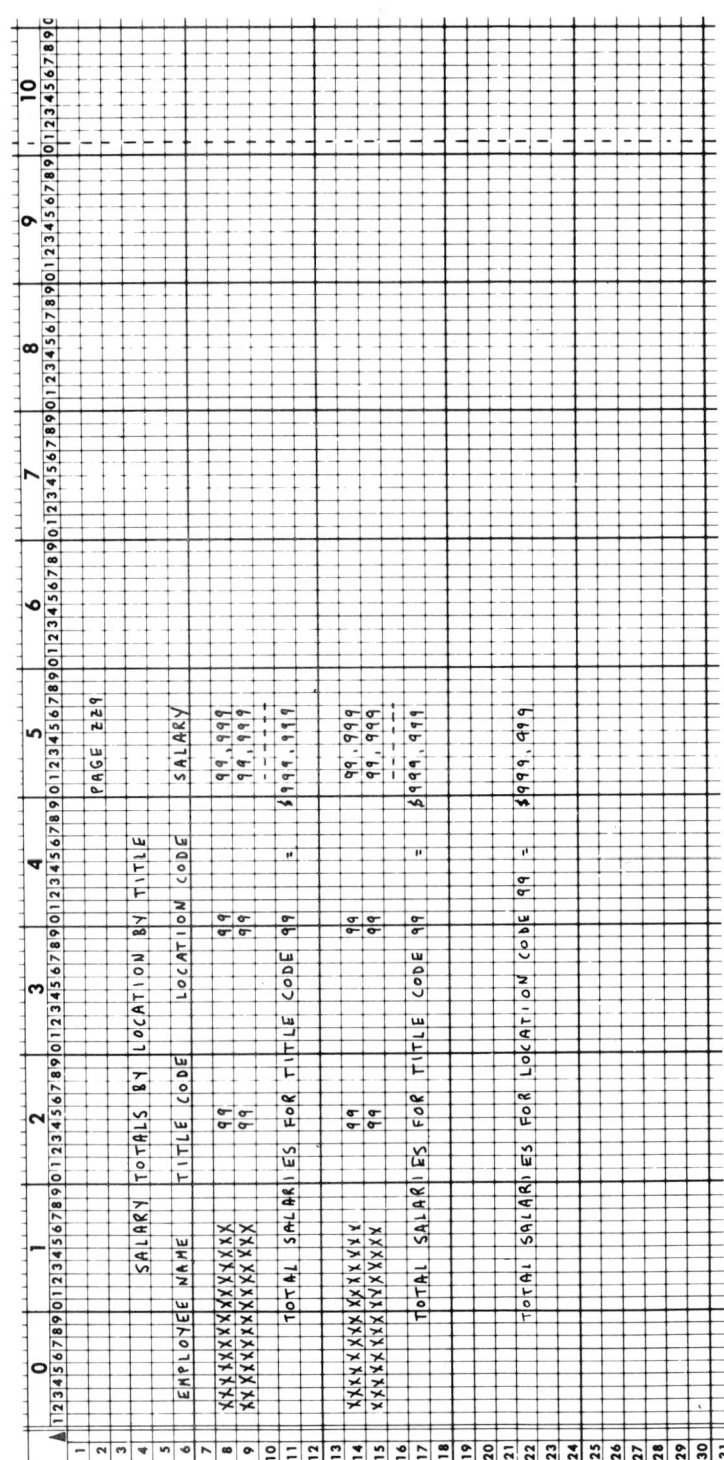

Figure 6.22 Report Format for Salary Totals.

(originally described in Project 6.16, Employee Profiles with Table Lookups).

2. It is assumed that this problem will be solved using Report Writer, However, the rather involved logic of a double control break problem provides an excellent opportunity to use techniques of top down program development and stepwise refinement. Accordingly, solve the problem both ways and compare.

Project 6.19: Salary Distributions

Objectives

To use two-dimensional tables, to extend PERFORM VARYING to manipulate two subscripts, to introduce anticipatory error processing, and optional use of SORT.

Problem Statement

Personnel is trying to evaluate its compensation policies on a national basis. The office has requested comparative data for the cities of Atlanta, Boston, Chicago, Los Angeles, and New York, and for men and women. Develop a COBOL program which will process the master employee file and produce a two-level table such as the one shown in the Required Output section. Each entry in the table is to be the *average* salary for the particular sex-location combination. Realize that in order to calculate the average salary it is necessary to count the number of employees in each combination, and use that number as a divisor. Be sure to include a check which will prevent division by zero if there are no employees in a particular combination.

Incoming Data

Use the record description of Fig. 6.26 modified to include 88-level entries to define the cities of interest. Use the first occurrence of salary data in each record for inclusion in the summary statistics. Use the test data in Fig. 6.27. (Both figures are on page 312.)

Required Output

Print the two-dimension table as shown in Fig. 6.23.

Suggested Extras

Prepare a companion detail report which will list the name, sex, location, and salary for each employee whose data is included in the summary report. Employees should be listed by location, and by sex within location, on the detail report.

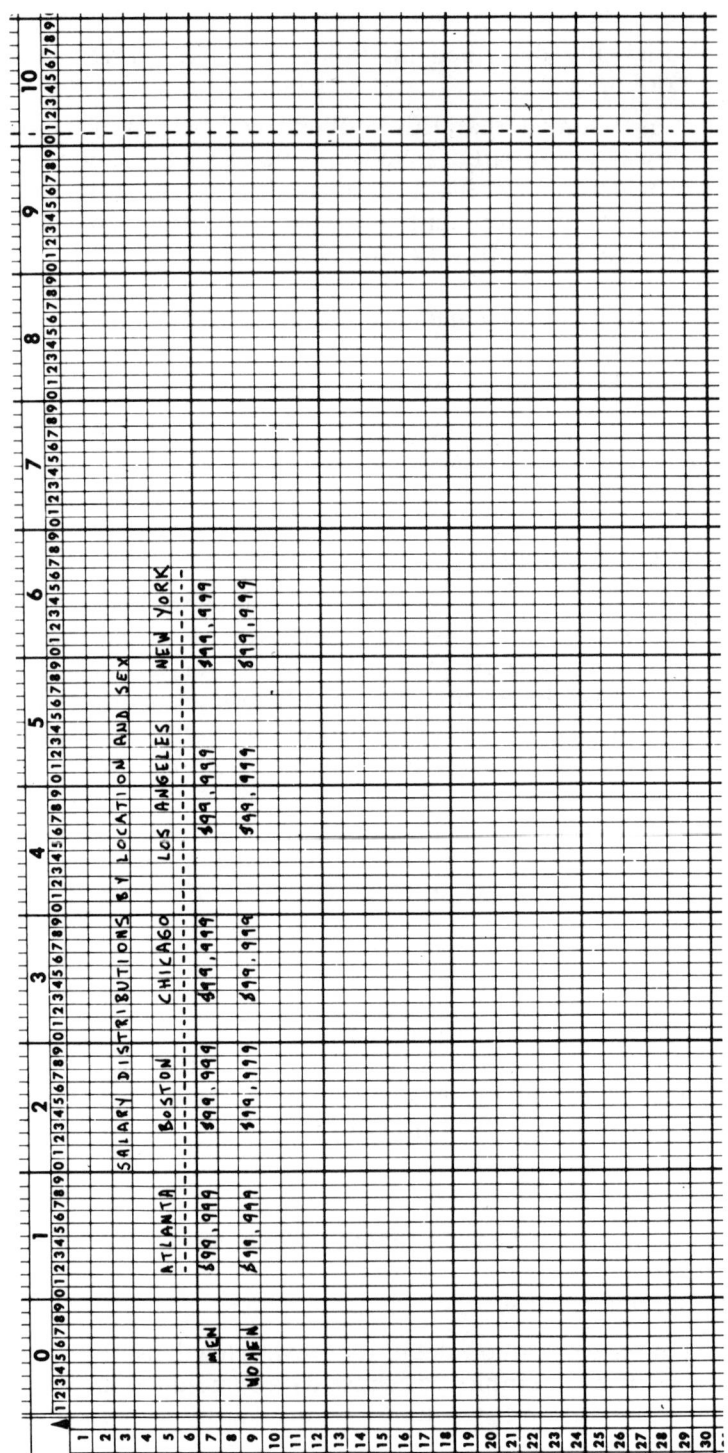

Figure 6.23 Report Format for Salary Distribution.

Variation

Prepare an additional two-dimension table which will show average percent salary increase, rather than average salary. Realize, however, that in order to compute percent salary increase, two occurrences of salary (present and previous) must be present in the individual employee records. Finally, prepare the table for location-age (over and under 30) rather than location-sex combinations.

Projects 6.20a and b: File Maintenance (Sequential and Nonsequential)

Objectives

To present concepts of file maintenance, data validation, and a problem with more complex logic requirements.

Problem Statement

Update the employee master file by merging it with a transaction file. Your program is to accommodate all of the following:

1. Five transaction types are possible: A (addition), C (correction), D (deletion), T (title change), and U (salary update). Flag any transaction whose transaction code is not one of these five values.
2. *Additions* require all of the following fields: social security number, name, date of birth, date of hire, location code, education code, title code and date, salary, salary type, and date. An attempted addition which is missing any of these fields should be flagged. Attempted duplicate additions, such as a transaction record whose social security number is already on the old master, should also be flagged.
3. *Corrections* apply to the following fields: name, date of birth, date of hire, location, education, and the *first* occurrence of title and salary data. The transaction record contains only the social security number and any field(s) which are to be corrected. This transaction type should cause data from the transaction record to be moved to the corresponding field in the new master record. All other fields are to be copied as is from the old master record. If the transaction social security number does not exist in the old master file, the transaction record should be flagged as a "no match."
4. *Deletions* require that the transaction social security number exist on the old master file; if this is not the case, the transaction record should be flagged as a "no match." A deletion removes an existing record.

5. *Title changes* require both a title code and a date. If either field is not present, the record should be flagged accordingly. Given a valid transaction, the title data on the transaction record becomes the present title data on the new master. The first occurrence of title data on the old master becomes the second occurrence on the new master. This transaction type also requires that the transaction social security number exist on the old master file, otherwise the transaction is to be flagged as a "no match."

6. *Salary updates* indicate an increase in salary. This transaction code requires: salary, date, and type. If any of these fields are missing, the transaction is to be flagged as incomplete. Given a valid transaction, the salary data on the transaction record is to become the first occurrence of salary data on the new master, the first occurrence of salary data in the old master is to become the second occurrence in the new master, and the second occurrence in the old master is to become the third occurrence in the new master. However, if either the salary amount or salary date on the transaction record matches either field on the old master, the transaction is to be flagged as a duplicate update and no updating is to be done. Finally, the transaction social security number must be present in the old master file, otherwise the transaction should be flagged as a "no match."

Incoming Data

Use the record layout of Fig. 6.26 as the employee file record layout for both the old and new master files. Note that if sequential access is used, there will be two distinct master files and a unique prefix will be required for each. Use the test data of Fig. 6.27.

The transaction file consists of the test data in Fig. 6.29 and conforms to the record layout of Fig. 6.28 on page 313.

Required Output

Various error messages are required as detailed in the problem statement. All error messages are to be printed by the *same* print module which is called from various points in the program. This is best accomplished by establishing a *table* of error messages and codes in Working-Storage, and then passing the proper error number to the print module.

In addition, the new master file must appear as hard copy in order for the student and/or instructor to check results. (The means of achieving printed output is left to the student. Ideally, the new master should be created on disk and its contents printed through a utility program. Less advanced students may choose to create the new master directly as a print file.)

Suggested Extras

1. Provide documentation for the program in the form of pseudocode and hierarchy charts.
2. Develop the maintenance program in two phases. The first version is to include program stubs and utilize top down testing, the second version will be the completed program. (Use the examples in Sect. 4 as a guide.)

Variation

Do the project two ways, utilizing both sequential and nonsequential access of the master file.

Record Descriptions and Test Data for the Personnel Information System

Record Description and Test Data for Compensation Analysis, Payroll, and Benefit Projects

```
01   EMPLOYEE-RECORD.
     05   EMP-SOC-SEC-NUMBER                 PIC 9(9).
     05   EMP-NAME-AND-INITIALS.
          10   EMP-LAST-NAME                 PIC X(13).
          10   EMP-INITIALS                  PIC XX.
     05   EMP-COMPENSATION-RATE              PIC 9(5)V99.
     05   EMP-COMPENSATION-CODE              PIC X.
     05   EMP-HIRE-DATE.
          10   EMP-HIRE-MONTH                PIC 99.
          10   EMP-HIRE-YEAR                 PIC 99.
     05   EMP-BIRTH-DATE.
          10   EMP-BIRTH-MONTH               PIC 99.
          10   EMP-BIRTH-YEAR                PIC 99.
     05   EMP-HOURS-WORKED-LAST-WEEK         PIC 99.
     05   FILLER                             PIC X(38).
```

Figure 6.24 Record Description.

```
111111111DOE              JR0000700H0180016038
222222222MARSHAL          CC0120000M01700450
333333333MILGROM          MB0100000M04770930
444444444LEE              BG0000500H0678114550
555555555BENJAMIN         LG0000650H0965034845
666666666CRAWFORD         MA0000650H0827104940
777777777BOROW            JB0130000M09740250
888888888JONES            EM0001000H0872034548
999999999TATER            CJ0000950H0676105036
                                ↑
                                └─column 23
```

Figure 6.25 Test Data.

Record Description and Test Data for Employee Profiles, Salary Totals, Salary Distributions, Data Validation, and File Maintenance Projects

```
01   EMPLOYEE-RECORD.
     05   EMP-SOC-SEC-NUMBER              PIC X(9).
     05   EMP-NAME-AND-INITIALS           PIC X(14).
     05   EMP-DATE-OF-BIRTH.
          10   EMP-BIRTH-MONTH            PIC 99.
          10   EMP-BIRTH-YEAR             PIC 99.
     05   EMP-DATE-OF-HIRE.
          10   EMP-HIRE-MONTH             PIC 99.
          10   EMP-HIRE-YEAR              PIC 99.
     05   EMP-LOCATION-CODE               PIC 99.
     05   EMP-EDUCATION-CODE              PIC 9.
     05   EMP-TITLE-DATA OCCURS 2 TIMES.
          10   EMP-TITLE-CODE             PIC X(2).
          10   EMP-TITLE-DATE             PIC 9(4).
     05   EMP-SEX                         PIC X.
     05   EMP-SALARY-DATA OCCURS 3 TIMES.
          10   EMP-SALARY                 PIC 9(5).
          10   EMP-SALARY-TYPE            PIC X.
          10   EMP-SALARY-DATE.
               15   EMP-SALARY-MONTH      PIC 99.
               15   EMP-SALARY-YEAR       PIC 99.
          10   EMP-SALARY-GRADE           PIC 9.
```

Figure 6.26 Record Description.

```
100000000DOE           J  12441177103551178451177  M23000M1178721500M1177500000
200000000WILCOX        PA 10481177303451177        M19000M1178517500H1177400000
400000000LEVINE        S  01500876304450878        F19000H0876500000           00000
444444444LOWELL        S  01501178304451178        M18000H1178500000           00000
500000000SMITHERS      M  03460172404601177        M28000M0876726500M0575725000M05746
600000000SUPERPROG     S  04571077405451077        M39000H1077900000           00000
700000000LEE           B  10530276306450277        F20000P0578510000H0277400000
800000000PERSNICKETY   P  08550378403450378        M09000H0378300000           00000
900000000MILGROM       MB 11550977103450977        F12000M1178410000M0578309000H09773
910000000BAKER         AA 01460877056550877        M60000M1179955000M1178950000H08779
920000000MARKS         BB 02470679056550680450679 F22000M0880920000H0679800000
930000000GOLDEN        CC 03480980156550980        M30000H0980900000
940000000SUGRUE        DD 04491079155181079        M24000H1079600000
950000000GITLOW        FF 05501079408201079        F28000H1079700000
                          ↑
                          └─ column 22
```

Figure 6.27 Test Data.

312

*Transaction Record Description and Test Data
for File Maintenance Project*

```
01  TRANSACTION-RECORD.
    05  TRANS-SOC-SEC-NUMBER              PIC X(9).
    05  TRANS-NAME-AND-INITIALS           PIC X(14).
    05  TRANS-DATE-OF-BIRTH.
        10  TRANS-BIRTH-MONTH             PIC 99.
        10  TRANS-BIRTH-YEAR              PIC 99.
    05  TRANS-DATE-OF-HIRE.
        10  TRANS-HIRE-MONTH              PIC 99.
        10  TRANS-HIRE-YEAR               PIC 99.
    05  TRANS-LOCATION-CODE               PIC XX.
    05  TRANS-EDUCATION-CODE              PIC 9.
    05  TRANS-TITLE-DATA.
        10  TRANS-TITLE-CODE              PIC XX.
        10  TRANS-TITLE-DATE              PIC 9(4).
    05  TRANS-SEX                         PIC X.
    05  TRANS-SALARY-DATA.
        10  TRANS-SALARY                  PIC 9(5).
        10  TRANS-SALARY-TYPE             PIC X.
        10  TRANS-SALARY-DATE.
            15  TRANS-SALARY-MONTH        PIC 99.
            15  TRANS-SALARY-YEAR         PIC 99.
        10  TRANS-SALARY-GRADE            PIC 9.
    05  FILLER                            PIC X(27).
    05  TRANS-CODE                        PIC X.
        88  ADDITION           VALUE 'A'.
        88  CORRECTION         VALUE 'C'.
        88  DELETION           VALUE 'D'.
        88  TITLE-CHANGE       VALUE 'T'.
        88  SALARY-UPDATE      VALUE 'U'.
```

Figure 6.28 Record Description.

```
100000000DOE           J                                            U
200000000WILCOX        PA       1149             25000   11787      C
211111111ADAMS         JJ       03500279213330279F10000H02793       A
300000000SMITH                                                      D
400000000LEVINE        S        0876                                C
444444444LOWELL        S                         19000M11795        U
500000000SMITHERS      M                                            C
600000000SUPERPROG     S        04571077405451077F39000H10779       A
654321000JONES         GR       0378                                C
800000000PERSNICKETY   P        0859             F           4      C
878787878PETERS        SM                        20000M02797        U
900000000MILGROM       MB                        12000M02797        U
910000000BAKER         AA                        600180             T
920000000MARKS         BB                        600180
                                                              ↑
                                                              └─ column 80
```

Figure 6.29 Test Data.

313

Record Description and Test Data for EEO Reporting Project

```
01  MERGED-RECORD.
    05  MGD-SOC-SEC-NUMBER                    PIC X(9).
    05  MGD-NAME-AND-INITIALS                 PIC X(14).
    05  MGD-DATE-OF-BIRTH
        10  MGD-BIRTH-MONTH                   PIC 99.
        10  MGD-BIRTH-YEAR                    PIC 99.
    05  MGD-DATE-OF-HIRE.
        10  MGD-HIRE-MONTH                    PIC 99.
        10  MGD-HIRE-YEAR                     PIC 99.
    05  MGD-LOCATION-CODE                     PIC XX.
    05  MGD-EDUCATION-CODE                    PIC 9.
    05  MGD-TITLE-DATA OCCURS 2 TIMES.
        10  MGD-TITLE-CODE                    PIC X(2).
        10  MGD-TITLE-DATE                    PIC 9(4).
    05  MGD-SALARY-DATA OCCURS 3 TIMES.
        10  MGD-SALARY                        PIC 9(5).
        10  MGD-SALARY-TYPE                   PIC X.
        10  MGD-SALARY-DATE.
            15  MGD-SALARY-MONTH              PIC 99.
            15  MGD-SALARY-YEAR               PIC 99.
        10  MGD-SALARY-GRADE                  PIC 9.
    05  MGD-EEO-LEVEL                         PIC X.
    05  MGD-ETHNIC-BACKGROUND                 PIC X.
```

Figure 6.30 Merged Record Description.

```
01  EEO-RECORD.
    05  EEO-SOC-SEC-NUMBER                    PIC X(9).
    05  EEO-LEVEL                             PIC X.
    05  EEO-ETHNIC-BACKGROUND                 PIC X.
    05  FILLER                                PIC X(69).
```

Figure 6.31 EEO Record Description.

```
20000000010
40000000010
50000000010
55555555520
60000000020
70000000010
80000000035
90000000030
91000000040
92222222210
93000000010
94000000010
```

Figure 6.32 Test Data for EEO File.

7 ABEND Debugging

OVERVIEW

Errors in execution fall into two general classes: those where the computer is able to execute the entire program, but produces results which are different from what the programmer expects or intends, and errors where the computer is unable to execute a particular instruction, such as a division by zero, and comes to a premature or abnormal end of job, that is ABENDs.

Execution errors of the first kind are often more difficult to find and correct. The computer gives no indication that anything is amiss, and it is up to the programmer to realize that the output is not what it should have been. Then and only then can he or she proceed to debug the program. Abundant exercises of this kind were provided in Sect. 3.

Despite any preconceived ideas about dumps, errors of the second type are often easier to find than those which do not ABEND. This is because a dump provides a hint of where to look. The computer was instructed to do something it could not do; hence, it objects and gives a reason for its objection. Analysis of the subsequent dump may be trivial or complicated, but in any event, one knows that a bug exists, and has a lead as to its nature and location.

This section provides several problems in ABEND debugging. These are preceded by a series of "warm-up" exercises in prerequisite topics: instruction formats, base/displacement addressing, internal data representation, and hexadecimal arithmetic. Solutions for all exercises are provided.

Warmup Exercises

Hexadecimal Arithmetic

Do the following additions and subtractions:

1. $(1234)_{16}$
   $+ \underline{(ABCD)_{16}}$

2. $(ABCD)_{16}$
   $+ \underline{(FACE)_{16}}$

3. $(ABCD)_{16}$
   $- \underline{(1234)_{16}}$

4. $(FACE)_{16}$
   $- \underline{(ABCD)_{16}}$

Number System Conversion

Fill in the blanks as appropriate.

1. $(789)_{16} = (\ ?\ )_{10} = (\ ?\ )_2$
2. $(\ ?\ )_{16} = (789)_{10} = (\ ?\ )_2$

Base/Displacement Addressing

Assume the contents of register 4 is $(00001234)_{16}$ and the contents of register 11 is $(00005678)_{16}$. Given the instruction: F2124123B500

1. What is the effective address of the *second* operand?
2. What is the effective address of the *first* operand?
3. What is the nature of the instruction?

Use the contents of registers 4 and 11 as given above, and assume the contents of register 8 is $(00000123)_{16}$. Given the instruction: 4A4B8123

4. What is the base register associated with the *second* operand?
5. What is the index register associated with the *second* operand?
6. What is the effective address of the second operand?
7. What is the nature of this instruction?

Instruction Formats

Indicate the instruction type which:

1. Has an operand contained in the instruction itself.
2. Uses two registers to calculate a storage address.
3. References two storage locations.
4. Is 6 bytes long.

5. Does not reference a storage location.
6. Is 2 bytes long.
7. Contains one length code.
8. Contains two length codes.

Internal Data Representation

1. Show internal representation for the following COBOL entries:

    a. 77 FIELD-A PIC 9(4)   DISPLAY   VALUE 31.
    b. 77 FIELD-B PIC 9(4)   VALUE 31.
    c. 77 FIELD-C PIC 9(4)   COMP   VALUE 31.
    d. 77 FIELD-D PIC 9(3)   COMP   VALUE 31.
    e. 77 FIELD-E PIC 9(5)   COMP   VALUE 31.
    f. 77 FIELD-F PIC 9(10) COMP   VALUE 31.
    g. 77 FIELD-G PIC 9(10) COMP-3   VALUE 31.
    h. 77 FIELD-H PIC 9(5)   COMP-3   VALUE 31.
    i. 77 FIELD-I PIC 9(9)   COMP-3   VALUE 31.

2. Assume the following are internal representations for a binary field defined as follows:

    05 BINARY-FIELD COMP PIC S9(4).

    Express the decimal equivalents of the following binary numbers:

    a. | 0000 0101 | 1101 0010 |
    b. | 1111 1111 | 1111 1111 |
    c. | 0111 1111 | 1111 1111 |
    d. | 1000 0000 | 0000 0000 |

3. Assume the following are internal (hex) representations for a packed field defined as follows:

    05 PACKED-FIELD COMP-3 PIC S9(5).

    Express the decimal equivalents of the following packed numbers:

    a. | 12 | 34 | 5F |
    b. | 12 | 34 | 5C |
    c. | 54 | 32 | 1D |

4. What is the largest positive binary number which can be stored in a full word?

Self-Checking Examination

Circle the most correct answer.

1. All of the following are valid instruction formats *except:*
   a. SS.
   b. RR.
   c. XX.
   d. RS.

2. All of the following are true about a displacement *except:*
   a. It requires 12 bits in an instruction.
   b. It can express a binary value up to 4095.
   c. At least one displacement is specified in every instruction.
   d. It generates an effective address of 24 bits in conjunction with a base register.

3. A four-digit numeric field; e.g., PIC 9(4), requires:
   a. 3 bytes of storage if USAGE IS COMP-3.
   b. 4 bytes of storage if USAGE IS DISPLAY.
   c. 2 bytes of storage is USAGE IS COMP.
   d. 4 bytes of storage if no usage is specified.
   e. All of the above.

4. The sign of a binary number:
   a. Is denoted by its leftmost (high order) bit.
   b. Is denoted by its rightmost (low order) bit.
   c. Is invalid.
   d. Either (a) or (b) above.

5. Two bytes will be required for a one-two-three-or four-digit number if:
   a. USAGE IS COMP is specified.
   b. USAGE IS COMP-3 is specified.
   c. USAGE IS DISPLAY is specified.
   d. No usage is specified.

6. (123) is a valid number in every base shown *except:*
   a. Base 10.
   b. Base 16.
   c. Base 8.
   d. Base 3.

7. All of the following are true *except:*
   a. $(15)_{10} = (1111)_2$
   b. $(15)_{10} = (F)_{16}$
   c. $(15)_{10} = (30)_5$
   d. $(15)_{10} = (15)_{16}$
   e. $(15)_{10} = (23)_6$

8. The instruction type which does *not* reference a location in storage is:
   a. RR.
   b. RX.
   c. SI.
   d. RS.
   e. SS.

9. The instruction: D2 05 A 010 3 050:
   a. Is a PACK instruction.
   b. Has an op code of 05.
   c. Is 3 bytes in length.
   d. Will move a total of 5 bytes.
   e. None of the above.

10. A valid instruction length is everything *except:*
    a. 2 bytes.
    b. 4 bytes.
    c. 6 bytes.
    d. 8 bytes.

11. A binary (COMPUTATIONAL) number may be stored in all of the following *except:*
    a. 2 bytes.
    b. 4 bytes.
    c. 6 bytes.
    d. 8 bytes.

12. $(101)_2 + (101)_2 = $:
    a. $(1010)_2$
    b. $(A)_{16}$
    c. $(202)_5$
    d. Both (a) and (b) above.
    e. All of the above.

13. $(AB)_{16} + (AB)_{16} = $:
    a. $(156)_{16}$
    b. $(146)_{16}$

c. Impossible to determine.
d. $(10101011)_2$

14. A byte:

    a. Contains 256 bits.
    b. Is the smallest addressable unit of storage.
    c. Can contain 128 unique combinations of zeros and ones.
    d. Contains 9 parity bits.

15. The character string 'IBM':

    a. Would require three bytes of internal storage.
    b. Would appear as C9 C2 D4 in EBCDIC.
    c. Cannot be represented in EBCDIC.
    d. Both (a) and (b) above.

16. Assume that the three bytes 000004 were found in storage. The data they represent:

    a. Are valid as a packed field.
    b. Indicate a string of blanks.
    c. Could represent a string of blanks after packing.
    d. None of the above.

17. The sign of a packed field:

    a. May be C, D, or F.
    b. Is found in the high order four bits of the high order byte.
    c. Is never checked.
    d. None of the above.

18. The entry point address of a COBOL program:

    a. Is likely to change every time the program is executed under the MVT operating system.
    b. Is likely to remain the same every time the program is executed under the MVS operating system.
    c. Is three bytes long and found in the CDE portion of a dump.
    d. All of the above.

Solutions to Warm-Up Exercises

Hexadecimal Arithmetic

```
1.   1 2 3 4         2.   A B C D
   + A B C D           + F A C E
   ─────────           ─────────
     B E 0 1           1 A 6 9 B

3.   A B C D         4.   F A C E
   - 1 2 3 4           - A B C D
   ─────────           ─────────
     9 9 9 9             4 F 0 1
```

Number Systems

1. $(789)_{16} = (1929)_{10} = (0111\ 1000\ 1001)_2$
2. $(315)_{16} = (789)_{10} = (0011\ 0001\ 0101)_2$

Base/Displacement Addressing

1. 005B78
2. 001357
3. It packs the data found in the *three* bytes, beginning at location 005B78 into the *two* bytes beginning at 001357.
4. Register 8
5. Register 11
6. 0058BE (The contents of register 8, plus the contents of register 11, plus the displacement of 123).
7. It adds the halfword beginning at location 0058BE, to the contents of register 4, and leaves the result in register 4.

Instruction formats

1. SI
2. RX
3. SS
4. SS
5. RR
6. RR
7. SS
8. SS

Internal Data Representation

1. a. F0 F0 F3 F1
   b. F0 F0 F3 F1
   c. 00 1F
   d. 00 1F
   e. 00 00 00 1F
   f. 00 00 00 00 00 00 00 1F
   g. 00 00 00 00 03 1C
   h. 00 03 1C
   i. 00 00 00 03 1C

2. a. 1490
   b. −1
   c. 32,767
   d. −32,768
3. a. 12,345
   b. 12,345
   c. −54,321
4. $2^{31} - 1 = 2,147,483,647$

Self-Checking Examination

1. C	6. D	11. C	16. C
2. C	7. D	12. D	17. A
3. E	8. A	13. A	18. D
4. A	9. E	14. B	
5. A	10. D	15. D	

Capsule Summary: Elementary ABEND Debugging Procedure

A program ABENDs, or aborts, because the computer was instructed to do something it couldn't, such as divide by zero, read a file that isn't there, and so on. When an event like this occurs, the computer in effect "gives up." It does, however, provide a *dump,* as a clue for the programmer. ABEND debugging requires the programmer to relate the internal contents displayed in a dump to the source program.

Before proceeding further, it is useful to define several terms associated with ABEND debugging. These include:

Dump: A picture of the computer's memory at the time the ABEND occurred.

PMAP or Procedure Division Map: A listing of the machine language instructions generated by the COBOL compiler from each COBOL instruction.

DMAP or Data Division Map: A listing of all the data names in a COBOL program showing where and how they are stored internally.

PSW or Program Status Word: 64 bits which provide abundant information on the current status of the CPU. Of greatest significance are the right most 3 bytes (24 bits) which, under OS, contain the machine address of the next sequential instruction that would have executed if the dump had not occurred.

EPA or Entry Point Address: The machine address at which the COBOL program was loaded.

Relative Address: The address within the COBOL program where the

> **Capsule Summary, cont.**
>
> ABEND occurred. The relative address is found by subtracting the entry point address from the address contained in the PSW. The COBOL instruction causing the problem is found by relating the relative address to the PMAP.
>
> Completion Code: An IBM code describing the nature of the ABEND. The examples in this section center on a completion code of 0C7; the programming tip which follows lists 19 of the most common completion codes, reasons for their occurrence, and possible corrections.
>
> A dump is quite overwhelming to the uninitiated. However, if the programmer approaches the problem in a calm and rational manner, fruitful results can often be obtained quite quickly. The first step is to identify the nature of the completion code, and to extract the EPA and PSW addresses. Subtraction of the EPA from the PSW address yields the relative address, which in turn is tied to a particular COBOL instruction through the PMAP. At this point, the programmer may well be able to identify the problem.
>
> If the solution is not forthcoming, one is usually required to analyze the machine language instruction which failed to execute. This entails identification of specific COBOL variables in memory to ascertain their values at the time of the problem. It may be necessary to backtrack and review the effects of several other instructions which immediately preceded the one in question.
>
> It should be emphasized that while a dump reveals the technical cause of an ABEND, it is still up to the programmer to relate this knowledge to the source program. Debugging is part art and part science, and there are no "guaranteed" debugging procedures. Bugs do not leap from amidst pages in a dump, but are coaxed out by a combination of experience, skill, perseverance, and luck. Knowing what to look for helps a great deal. Accordingly, consider the ensuing Programming Tip "A List of Common ABENDs."

> **Programming Tip: A List of Common ABENDS**
>
> Although the exercises in this section pertain almost exclusively to the 0C7 (data exception) and related materials, a more complete list of ABENDs is provided for on the job reference.
>
> 0C1:-Operation exception, an invalid operation code. The first byte of any instruction contains the op code. An operation exception results if this byte is unknown to the system.

Programming Tip, cont.

Common Causes:

1. A missing (or misspelled) DD statement. (Missing DD statements can sometimes be caused by an inadvertent duplication of an EXEC statement where the duplicated statement would have no DD statements.)
2. Attempting to read from a data set which has not been opened; for example, a misplaced OPEN statement.
3. A subscript or index error which caused a portion of code to be overlaid, resulting in an attempt to "execute" data.

Corrective Action:

1. A very low address for the interrupt indicates that the error occurred in a data management routine, rather than in the COBOL program per se. Check the JCL messages carefully for indication of missing DD statement.
2. If the JCL messages are not helpful, register 2 plus hex 28 should point to the TIOT offset of the DDname in question.
3. If the interrupt address is within the program (or close to it), chances are the 0C1 was caused by a subscript (or index) problem. A careful review of program logic is called for with particular attention to any routines which fill tables.

0C4:-Protection exception, attempting to overwrite a protected area in storage.

Common Causes:

1. Invalid subscript or index.
2. Inclusion of a STOP RUN statement in the INPUT or OUTPUT PROCE-DURE of the SORT verb.
3. SELECT statement missing.
4. Missing or misspelled DD statement.
5. Block size and record size specified as equal in a variable length file.

Corrective Action:

1. An interrupt at a low address indicates a missing DD statement or attempt to read an unopened file.
2. If the interrupt is within the COBOL program, it is probably a subscript

Programming Tip, cont.
(index) error. A *thorough* review of program logic is required. Subscript errors are often the most difficult to find.
0C5: Addressing exception, an address has been calculated outside the bounds of available storage. *Common Causes:* 1. Invalid subscript or index. 2. Attempting to close an already closed file. 3. An attempt to reference an I/O area before READ or OPEN was issued. 4. Improper exit from a performed routine; remember, "GO TO" out of a PERFORM is strictly prohibited. 5. Invoking a subprogram with a Linkage Section, but with no associated USING clause, or too few parameters, or parameters listed in the wrong order, etc. *Corrective Action:* 1. Review program logic to determine if a subscript error exists. 2. Register 1 contains the DCB address of the last referenced file. Register 14 should contain the next sequential instruction in the COBOL program.
0C6: Specification exception, an address was generated which does not fall on the proper boundary. *Common Causes:* 1. Invalid subscript or index. 2. Incorrect or missing DD statement. 3. Improper exit from a performed routine; remember, "GO TO" out of a PERFORM is strictly prohibited. *Corrective Action:* 1. Register 2 contains the DCB address of the last file referenced prior to the ABEND. 2. Review program logic to determine if a subscript error exists.
0C7: Data exception, invalid "decimal" data. This error can result only after

Programming Tip, cont.

attempted execution of an instruction to process packed data. Specifically, the sign or digits of an operand in a decimal arithmetic, editing, or CVB instruction are invalid.

Common Causes:

1. Failure to initialize a counter.
2. Invalid incoming data, such as blanks, decimal points, or commas in a numeric field.
3. Exceeding a table via a subscript (index) error causing a reference to invalid data. This can also result in an 0C4, 0C5, or 0C6.
4. Moving zeros or low values to a group field defined as numeric.
5. An omitted or erroneous USAGE clause.
6. Passing parameters between programs in the wrong order.

Corrective Action:

1. Subtracting the EPA from the PSW address, or the STATE option will identify the COBOL statement causing the ABEND. The error may be immediately obvious, as in the case of an uninitialized counter or erroneous USAGE clause. If not, a check of the program's logic is necessary to determine if invalid data is referenced.
2. Register 2 will point to the DCB for the last referenced file.

0CB: Decimal Divide Exception (division by zero). This error results from attempted execution of a DP (Divide Packed) Assembler instruction where the divisor is zero.

Common Causes:

1. A COBOL DIVIDE or COMPUTE statement has a divisor of zero.

Corrective Action:

1. The STATE option can identify the COBOL statement in error. Review program logic to determine how the divisor is calculated.

001: An uncorrectable I-O error which is sometimes attributable to DCB conflicts.

Programming Tip, cont.

Common Causes:

1. Attempting to read from a file after the AT END condition has been encountered.
2. WRITE FROM area is not equal to the FD record length.
3. A device malfunction or a damaged (dirty) tape or disk.
4. Wrong length record of physical block.

Corrective Action:

1. Check the JCL message for an indication of the file in question.
2. Register 2 points to the DCB.

013: Unsuccessful attempt to OPEN a file usually due to a DCB conflict. An error message will appear in the JCL to indicate the exact nature of the error. The return code mentioned in the error message specifies the error. Some common return codes are:

18   System was unable to find specified member of a partitioned data set.

20   BLKSIZE is not a multiple of LRECL.

34   BLKSIZE not specified; the system knows it has to allocate buffers, but is unable to do so.

60   BLKSIZE is not equal to LRECL for unblocked (RECFM = F) records.

68   BLKSIZE specified as greater than 32,767.

Corrective Action:

1. Check the JCL messages to determine the file in question. Look for any immediately obvious inconsistencies.
2. Register 2 contains the DCB address of the file in question. Use the table of DCB offsets to determine DCB information. (See parts 35 to 39 in Exercise 7.4).

122: Job cancelled by operator for unspecified reason.

Common Causes:

1. Program in an apparent endless loop.
2. Program is producing an "abnormal" number of error messages.

Programming Tip, cont.

3. Program requested an unavailable resource.
4. A "panic" job required immediate processing and needed resources assigned to your job.
5. A mistake on the part of operations.

Corrective Action:

1. It is definitely possible that nothing is wrong with your job. Find out why the operator cancelled. Make the necessary corrections and resubmit.

213: An error in opening a file on a direct access device; the system cannot locate the data set specified in the DSNAME parameter.

Common Causes:

1. The DSNAME parameter is misspelled.
2. The wrong volume was specified.
3. The data set no longer exists because it was accidentally scratched.
4. The DISP parameter specified OLD or SHR for an output data set.

Corrective Action:

1. Register 2 contains the DCB address. Add hex 28 to locate the two byte TIOT offset. Determine the DDname from the TIOT offset.
2. Register 4 plus hex 64 contains the DSNAME as specified in the JCL.
3. Register 4 plus hex DA contains the volume serial number as specified in the JCL or catalog.

322: CPU time limit for a step or job was exceeded.

Common Causes:

1. An error in program logic causing an endless loop.
2. A switch to a slower CPU.
3. A switch to a different operating system.
4. The time requested was insufficient.

Corrective Action:

1. Check to see if a slower CPU was used. This can happen in large shops with multiple CPU's where for some reason your job was switched to a

Programming Tip, cont.

different CPU.

2. Review program logic to insure that no endless loops are present. Structured programs will not contain traditional loops, those induced by backward GO TO statements. However, they can well contain problems brought about by improper setting (resetting) of switches. Some advice: do *not* use a switch for more than one purpose, and do use meaningful names; TRANSACTION-FILE-SWITCH as opposed to SWITCH-1.

3. The subtraction technique can be used to determine the next sequential instruction. This may be useful in determining the endless loop if one exists.

4. The READY TRACE statement and/or FLOW option may be useful in identifying the loop. Use of READY TRACE should be carefully controlled with ON and RESET TRACE statements to avoid needless volumes of paper. (READY TRACE has been deleted from the ANS 74 standard, but is still supported by various IBM compilers.)

513: An attempt was made to open more than one data set on the same tape volume.

Common Causes:

1. Attempting to open a second file before closing the first.
2. Assignment of two data sets to the same tape device.
3. Transferring data sets from direct access devices which may have more than one data set open simultaneously.

Corrective Action:

1. This type of error may be easily corrected at the source level. Examine all OPEN and associated CLOSE statements to determine where the problem exists.
2. The JCL allocation messages can also be studied to determine which devices are used for which files.
3. Register 2 contains the address of the DCB in question.

80A, 804: More storage was requested than is currently available in the region.

Common Causes:

1. The REGION parameter was omitted and the installation's default is too small.

Programming Tip, cont.
2. The REGION parameter on the JOB or EXEC statement did not specify sufficient storage. Realize that if REGION is specified on the JOB card it *overrides* any subsequent specification on EXEC cards, the REGION parameter of EXEC statements is ignored. 3. Blocking factors were increased without corresponding increase in REGION parameter. *Corrective Action:* 1. Review JCL to insure that REGION parameters are not omitted and/or overridden.
806: A requested program could not be found. *Common Causes:* 1. Missing JOBLIB or STEPLIB statements. 2. Misspelled module name. *Corrective Action:* 1. The system messages will typically contain the module name. (A list of commonly called I/O subroutines and their function can be found in the *IBM Programmer's Guide* by looking under ILB subroutines in the index.) 2. The address in Register 12 plus 4 may point to the missing module. 3. Register 15 will contain 00000004 if the requested module could not be found in the private, job, or link library. It will contain 00000008 if an I/O error occurred in searching the directory of the indicated libraries.
813: An error in label processing for tape; specifically the data set name on the header label does not match the specification in the JCL. *Common Causes:* 1. The DSNAME parameter is misspelled. 2. The wrong volume was called for and mounted. 3. The data set no longer exists. *Corrective Action:* 1. Add 64 to the address contained in register 4 to determine the DSNAME

Programming Tip, cont.
parameter in storage obtained from the DD statement. 2. Add 4 to the address contained in register 4 to determine the data set name as it appears on the header label. Attempt to resolve the conflict between this and the JCL entry from step 1. If more than a misspelling, then a review of file logs, etc., is probably called for.
B37, D37, E37: Space problems, insufficient space available for an output data set. *Common Causes:* 1. An infinite loop containing a WRITE statement. 2. The space requested was insufficient. This may happen if a secondary allocation was not specified in the SPACE parameter, or if specified, then it was not large enough to accommodate the data set. 3. Sufficient space was requested but was not available on the volume specified. *Corrective Action:* 1. The possibility of an infinite loop should be eliminated through review of program logic. 2. Check the SPACE parameter for a secondary allocation on the file in question. Register 2 plus hex 28 will supply the TIOT offset from where the DDname can be determined. 3. The DCB/DEB relationship can be used to determine the number of extents (i.e. secondary allocations) actually made. Register 2 plus hex 2D contains the DEB address of the file in question. The first byte of the 5th word in the DEB contains the number of extents used. If this value is less than 15, then the system did not have sufficient space.

PROBLEM STATEMENT: EMPLOYEE SELECTION

The COBOL listing (Fig. 7.1) Data (Fig. 7.2) and Procedure (Fig. 7.3) Division Maps, Memory Map (Fig. 7.4) and Register Assignments (Fig. 7.5) are to be used in exercises 7.1 *and* 7.2 beginning on page 337. (Other versions of this program appeared in exercises 1.3 and 1.4 in Sect. 1).

```
00001              IDENTIFICATION DIVISION.
00002              PROGRAM-ID. "SECOND"
00003              AUTHOR.
00004                  MARION MILGROM.
00005
00006              ENVIRONMENT DIVISION.
00007              CONFIGURATION SECTION.
00008              SOURCE-COMPUTER.    IBM-370.
00009              OBJECT-COMPUTER.    IBM-370.
00010
00011              INPUT-OUTPUT SECTION.
00012              FILE-CONTROL.
00013                  SELECT CARD-FILE ASSIGN TO UT-S-SYSIN.
00014                  SELECT PRINT-FILE ASSIGN TO UT-S-SYSOUT.
00015
00016              DATA DIVISION.
00017              FILE SECTION.
00018              FD  CARD-FILE
00019                  LABEL RECORDS ARE OMITTED
00020                  RECORD CONTAINS 80 CHARACTERS
00021                  DATA RECORD IS EMPLOYEE-CARD.
00022              01  EMPLOYEE-CARD.
00023                  05  CARD-NAME.
00024                      10  LAST-NAME           PIC X(15).
00025                      10  FIRST-NAME          PIC X(9).
00026                      10  MIDDLE-INITIAL      PIC X.
00027                  05  CARD-TITLE              PIC X(10).
00028                  05  DATE-OF-BIRTH.
00029                      10  BIRTH-MONTH         PIC 99.
00030                      10  BIRTH-YEAR          PIC 99.
00031                  05  PRESENT-SALARY          PIC 9(5).
00032                  05  FILLER                  PIC X(4).
00033                  05  FORMER-SALARY           PIC 9(5).
00034                  05  FILLER                  PIC X(27).
00035              FD  PRINT-FILE
00036                  LABEL RECORDS ARE OMITTED
00037                  RECORD CONTAINS 133 CHARACTERS
00038                  DATA RECORD IS PRINT-LINE.
00039              01  PRINT-LINE                  PIC X(133).
00040
00041              WORKING-STORAGE SECTION.
00042              77  END-OF-DATA-FLAG            PIC XXX     VALUE SPACES.
00043              77  EMPLOYEE-AGE                PIC 99V9.
00044              77  PERCENT-SALARY-INCREASE     PIC 99V9.
00045              77  TOTAL-SALARY-YOUNG-PROGRAMMERS PIC 9(6)  VALUE ZEROS.
00046              01  DATE-WORK-AREA.
00047                  05  TODAYS-YEAR             PIC 99.
00048                  05  TODAYS-MONTH            PIC 99.
00049                  05  TODAYS-DAY              PIC 99.
00050              01  DASHED-LINE.
00051                  05  FILLER                  PIC X(57)   VALUE ALL "-".
00052                  05  FILLER                  PIC X(76)   VALUE SPACES.
00053              01  HEADING-LINE.
00054                  05  FILLER                  PIC X(10)   VALUE SPACES.
00055                  05  FILLER                  PIC X(4)    VALUE "NAME".
00056                  05  FILLER                  PIC X(7)    VALUE SPACES.
00057                  05  FILLER                  PIC X(3)    VALUE "AGE".
00058                  05  FILLER                  PIC X(4)    VALUE SPACES.
00059                  05  FILLER                  PIC X(8)    VALUE "PRES SAL".
00060                  05  FILLER                  PIC X(3)    VALUE SPACES.
00061                  05  FILLER                  PIC X(7)    VALUE "OLD SAL".
```

Figure 7.1 COBOL Listing.

```
00062              05  FILLER                      PIC X(3)    VALUE SPACES.
00063              05  FILLER                      PIC X(6)    VALUE "% INCR".
00064              05  FILLER                      PIC X(78)   VALUE SPACES.
00065          01  DETAIL-LINE.
00066              05  FILLER                      PIC X(1)    VALUE SPACES.
00067              05  PRINT-LAST-NAME             PIC X(15).
00068              05  FILLER                      PIC X(5)    VALUE SPACES.
00069              05  PRINT-AGE                   PIC 99.9.
00070              05  FILLER                      PIC X(4)    VALUE SPACES.
00071              05  PRINT-PRESENT-SALARY        PIC $99,999.
00072              05  FILLER                      PIC X(3)    VALUE SPACES.
00073              05  PRINT-FORMER-SALARY         PIC $99,999.
00074              05  FILLER                      PIC X(4)    VALUE SPACES.
00075              05  PRINT-PERCENT-INCREASE      PIC ZZ.9.
00076              05  FILLER                      PIC X(81)   VALUE SPACES.
00077          01  TOTAL-LINE.
00078              05  FILLER                      PIC X(12)   VALUE SPACES.
00079              05  FILLER                      PIC X(17)
00080                      VALUE "TOTAL SALARIES =".
00081              05  PRINT-TOTAL-SALARIES        PIC $999,999.
00082              05  FILLER                      PIC X(86)   VALUE SPACES.
00083
00084          PROCEDURE DIVISION.
00085          MAINLINE-ROUTINE.
00086              OPEN INPUT CARD-FILE
00087                   OUTPUT PRINT-FILE.
00088              ACCEPT DATE-WORK-AREA FROM DATE.
00089              MOVE SPACES TO PRINT-LINE.
00090              MOVE "            SALARY REPORT FOR PROGRAMMERS UNDER 30"
00091                   TO PRINT-LINE.
00092              WRITE PRINT-LINE AFTER ADVANCING PAGE.
00093              MOVE HEADING-LINE TO PRINT-LINE.
00094              WRITE PRINT-LINE AFTER ADVANCING 3 LINES.
00095              WRITE PRINT-LINE FROM DASHED-LINE AFTER ADVANCING 1 LINE.
00096              READ CARD-FILE
00097                   AT END MOVE "YES" TO END-OF-DATA-FLAG.
00098              PERFORM PROCESS-EMPLOYEE-RECORDS
00099                   UNTIL END-OF-DATA-FLAG = "YES".
00100              WRITE PRINT-LINE FROM DASHED-LINE AFTER ADVANCING 2 LINES.
00101              MOVE TOTAL-SALARY-YOUNG-PROGRAMMERS TO PRINT-TOTAL-SALARIES.
00102              WRITE PRINT-LINE FROM TOTAL-LINE.
00103              CLOSE CARD-FILE, PRINT-FILE.
00104              STOP RUN.
00105
00106          PROCESS-EMPLOYEE-RECORDS.
00107              COMPUTE EMPLOYEE-AGE
00108                  = TODAYS-YEAR - BIRTH-YEAR
00109                  + (TODAYS-MONTH - BIRTH-MONTH) / 12.
00110              COMPUTE PERCENT-SALARY-INCREASE
00111                  = 100 * (PRESENT-SALARY - FORMER-SALARY) / FORMER-SALARY.
00112              IF CARD-TITLE = "PROGRAMMER" AND EMPLOYEE-AGE < 30
00113                  MOVE SPACES              TO PRINT-LINE
00114                  MOVE CARD-NAME           TO PRINT-LAST-NAME
00115                  MOVE EMPLOYEE-AGE        TO PRINT-AGE
00116                  MOVE PRESENT-SALARY      TO PRINT-PRESENT-SALARY
00117                  MOVE FORMER-SALARY       TO PRINT-FORMER-SALARY
00118                  MOVE PERCENT-SALARY-INCREASE TO PRINT-PERCENT-INCREASE
00119                  WRITE PRINT-LINE FROM DETAIL-LINE AFTER ADVANCING 2 LINES
00120                  ADD PRESENT-SALARY TO TOTAL-SALARY-YOUNG-PROGRAMMERS.
00121              READ CARD-FILE
00122                  AT END MOVE "YES" TO END-OF-DATA-FLAG.
```

Figure 7.1 *cont.*

LVL	SOURCE NAME	BASE	DISPL	INTRNL NAME	DEFINITION
FD	CARD-FILE	DCB=01		DNM=1-086	
01	EMPLOYEE-CARD	BL=1	000	DNM=1-109	DS 0CL80
02	CARD-NAME	BL=1	000	DNM=1-138	DS 0CL25
03	LAST-NAME	BL=1	000	DNM=1-160	DS 15C
03	FIRST-NAME	BL=1	00F	DNM=1-179	DS 9C
03	MIDDLE-INITIAL	BL=1	018	DNM=1-202	DS 1C
02	CARD-TITLE	BL=1	019	DNM=1-226	DS 10C
02	DATE-OF-BIRTH	BL=1	023	DNM=1-246	DS 0CL4
03	BIRTH-MONTH	BL=1	023	DNM=1-272	DS 2C
03	BIRTH-YEAR	BL=1	025	DNM=1-293	DS 2C
02	PRESENT-SALARY	BL=1	027	DNM=1-313	DS 5C
02	FILLER	BL=1	02C	DNM=1-337	DS 4C
02	FORMER-SALARY	BL=1	030	DNM=1-348	DS 5C
02	FILLER	BL=1	035	DNM=1-371	DS 27C
FD	PRINT-FILE	DCB=02		DNM=1-385	
01	PRINT-LINE	BL=2	000	DNM=1-409	DS 133C
77	END-OF-DATA-FLAG	BL=3	000	DNM=1-429	DS 3C
77	EMPLOYEE-AGE	BL=3	003	DNM=1-455	DS 3C
77	PERCENT-SALARY-INCREASE	BL=3	006	DNM=1-477	DS 3C
77	TOTAL-SALARY-YOUNG-PROGRAMMERS	BL=3	009	DNM=2-000	DS 6C
01	DATE-WORK-AREA	BL=3	010	DNM=2-040	DS 0CL6
02	TODAYS-YEAR	BL=3	010	DNM=2-067	DS 2C
02	TODAYS-MONTH	BL=3	012	DNM=2-088	DS 2C
02	TODAYS-DAY	BL=3	014	DNM=2-113	DS 2C
01	DASHED-LINE	BL=3	018	DNM=2-133	DS 0CL133
02	FILLER	BL=3	018	DNM=2-157	DS 57C
02	FILLER	BL=3	051	DNM=2-171	DS 76C
01	HEADING-LINE	BL=3	0A0	DNM=2-185	DS 0CL133
02	FILLER	BL=3	0A0	DNM=2-210	DS 10C
02	FILLER	BL=3	0AA	DNM=2-224	DS 4C
02	FILLER	BL=3	0AE	DNM=2-238	DS 7C
02	FILLER	BL=3	0B5	DNM=2-252	DS 3C
02	FILLER	BL=3	0B8	DNM=2-266	DS 4C
02	FILLER	BL=3	0BC	DNM=2-280	DS 8C
02	FILLER	BL=3	0C4	DNM=2-294	DS 3C
02	FILLER	BL=3	0C7	DNM=2-308	DS 7C
02	FILLER	BL=3	0CE	DNM=2-322	DS 3C
02	FILLER	BL=3	0D1	DNM=2-336	DS 6C
02	FILLER	BL=3	0D7	DNM=2-350	DS 78C
01	DETAIL-LINE	BL=3	128	DNM=2-364	DS 0CL135
02	FILLER	BL=3	128	DNM=2-388	DS 1C
02	PRINT-LAST-NAME	BL=3	129	DNM=2-402	DS 15C
02	FILLER	BL=3	138	DNM=2-427	DS 5C
02	PRINT-AGE	BL=3	13D	DNM=2-441	DS 4C
02	FILLER	BL=3	141	DNM=2-469	DS 4C
02	PRINT-PRESENT-SALARY	BL=3	145	DNM=3-000	DS 7C
02	FILLER	BL=3	14C	DNM=3-041	DS 3C
02	PRINT-FORMER-SALARY	BL=3	14F	DNM=3-055	DS 7C
02	FILLER	BL=3	156	DNM=3-095	DS 4C
02	PRINT-PERCENT-INCREASE	BL=3	15A	DNM=3-109	DS 4C
02	FILLER	BL=3	15E	DNM=3-150	DS 81C
01	TOTAL-LINE	BL=3	1B0	DNM=3-164	DS 0CL123
02	FILLER	BL=3	1B0	DNM=3-187	DS 12C
02	FILLER	BL=3	1BC	DNM=3-201	DS 17C
02	PRINT-TOTAL-SALARIES	BL=3	1CD	DNM=3-215	DS 8C
02	FILLER	BL=3	1D5	DNM=3-256	DS 86C

Figure 7.2 Abbreviated Data Division Map.

```
106      *PROCESS-EMPLOYEE-RECORDS          PN=01
         000C16                             EQU   *
         000C16  53 F0 C 014                L     15,014(0,12)      V(ILBOFLW1)
         000C1A  05 1F                      BALR  1,15
         000C1C  0000006A                   DC    X'0000006A'
107      COMPUTE
         000C20  F2 71 D 210 7 025          PACK  210(8,13),025(2,7)    TS=01           DNM=1-293
         000C26  F2 71 D 218 6 010          PACK  218(8,13),010(2,6)    TS=09           DNM=2-67
         000C2C  FB 11 D 21E D 216          SP    21E(2,13),216(2,13)   TS=015          TS=07
         000C32  F2 71 D 210 7 023          PACK  210(8,13),023(2,7)    TS=01           DNM=1-272
         000C38  F2 71 D 220 6 012          PACK  220(8,13),012(2,6)    TS=017          DNM=2-88
         000C3E  FB 11 D 226 D 216          SP    226(2,13),216(2,13)   TS=023          TS=07
         000C44  FD 20 D 225 D 001          DP    225(3,13),001(0),0    TS=022
         000C4A  FD 41 D 223 C 09A          DP    223(5,13),09A(2,12)   TS=C20          LIT+10
         000C50  F8 72 D 220 D 223          ZAP   220(8,13),223(3,13)   TS=017          TS=020
         000C56  F0 20 D 21D D 001          SRP   21D(3,13),001(0),0    TS=014
         000C5C  FA 22 D 225 D 21D          AP    225(3,13),21D(3,13)   TS=022          TS=014
         000C62  F3 22 6 005                UNPK  003(3,6),225(3,13)    DNM=1-455       TS=022
         000C68                             OI    005(6),X'F0'          DNM=1-455+2
110      COMPUTE
         000C6C  F2 74 D 220 7 030          PACK  220(8,13),030(5,7)    TS=017          DNM=1-348
         000C72  F2 74 D 218 7 027          PACK  218(8,13),027(5,7)    TS=09           DNM=1-313
         000C78  FB 32 D 21C D 225          SP    21C(4,13),225(3,13)   TS=013          TS=022
         000C7E  FC 51 D 21A C 09C          MP    21A(6,13),09C(2,12)   TS=011          LIT+12
         000C84  F2 74 D 220 7 030          PACK  220(8,13),030(5,7)    TS=017          DNM=1-348
         000C8A  FD 40 D 21B D 001          SRP   21B(5,13),001(0),0    TS=012
         000C90  FD 72 D 213 D 225          DP    213(8,13),225(3,13)   TS=09
         000C96  F8 74 D 218 D 218          ZAP   218(8,13),218(5,13)   TS=09
         000C9C  F3 24 6 006 D 21B          UNPK  006(3,6),21B(5,13)    DNM=1-477
         000CA2  96 F0 6 008                OI    008(6),X'F0'          DNM=1-477+2
112      IF
         000CA6  58 20 C 05C                L     2,05C(0,12)           GN=010
         000CAA  D5 09 7 019 C ODA          CLC   019(10,7),0DA(12)     DNM=1-226
         000CB0  07 72                      BCR   7,2
         000CB2  F2 72 D 220 6 003          PACK  220(8,13),003(3,6)    TS=017          LIT+74
         000CB8  F8 71 D 21D D 09E          ZAP   21D(8,13),09E(2,12)   TS=09           DNM=1-455
         000CBE  FB 21 D 21D D 226          SP    21D(3,13),226(2,13)   TS=014          LIT+14
         000CC4  58 F0 C 05C                L     15,05C(0,12)          GN=010          TS=023
         000CC8  07 DF                      BCR   13,15
```

Figure 7.3 Abbreviated Procedure Division Map.

335

```
                MEMORY MAP

            TGT                         00590

        SAVE AREA                       00590
        SWITCH                          005D8
        TALLY                           005DC
        SORT SAVE                       005E0
        ENTRY-SAVE                      005E4
        SORT CORE SIZE                  005E8
        RET CODE                        005EC
        SORT RET                        005EE
        WORKING CELLS                   005F0
        SORT FILE SIZE                  00720
        SORT MODE SIZE                  00724
        PGT-VN TBL                      00728
        TGT-VN TBL                      0072C
        RESERVED                        00730
        LENGTH OF VN TBL                00734
        LABEL RET                       00736
        RESERVED                        00737
        DBG R14SAVE                     00738
        COBOL INDICATOR                 0073C
        A(INIT1)                        00740
        DEBUG TABLE PTR                 00744
        SUBCOM PTR                      00748
        SORT-MESSAGE                    0074C
        SYSOUT DDNAME                   00754
        RESERVED                        00755
        COBOL ID                        00756
        COMPILED POINTER                00758
        COUNT TABLE ADDRESS             0075C
        RESERVED                        00760
        DBG R11SAVE                     00768
        COUNT CHAIN ADDRESS             0076C
        PRBL1 CELL PTR                  00770
        RESERVED                        00774
        TA LENGTH                       00779
        RESERVED                        0077C
        PCS LIT PTR                     00784
        DEBUGGING                       00788
        CD FOR INITIAL INPUT            0078C
        OVERFLOW CELLS                  00790
        BL CELLS                        00790
        DECBADR CELLS                   0079C
        FIB CELLS                       0079C
        TEMP STORAGE                    007A0
        TEMP STORAGE-2                  007B8
        TEMP STORAGE-3                  007C8
        TEMP STORAGE-4                  007C8
        BLL CELLS                       007C8
        VLC CELLS                       007D0
        SBL CELLS                       007D0
        INDEX CELLS                     007D0
        SUBADR CELLS                    007D0
```

Figure 7.4 Memory Map.

```
            REGISTER ASSIGNMENT

            REG 6       BL =3
            REG 7       BL =1
            REG 8       BL =2
```
Figure 7.5 Register Assignments.

Exercise 7.1: Dump Reading

Determine why the dump of Fig. 7.6 occurred. The questions below are provided as a guide. Use the COBOL Program, Data, Procedure, and Memory Maps of Fig. 7.1 through Fig. 7.5. as necessary.

Determine where the ABEND occurred.

1. What is the meaning of the completion code?
2. What is the address contained in the PSW?
3. At what location was the program located?
4. What is the relative location within the COBOL program of the instruction?
5. What machine instruction is at that location?
6. What is the corresponding COBOL instruction?

Examine the machine instruction which failed to execute. The instruction which actually produced the ABEND is the one immediately before the instruction determined in part 5.

7. What is the machine instruction which actually caused the ABEND?
8. What is its op code?
9. Which base register is associated with the first operand?
10. What is the displacement of the first operand?
11. What is the effective address of the first operand?
12. How many bytes are associated with the first operand? (Careful)
13. What are the internal contents of the first operand; are they valid as a decimal number?
14. Which base register is associated with the second operand?
15. What is the displacement of the second operand?
16. How many bytes are associated with the second operand?
17. What are the internal contents of the second operand; are they valid as a decimal number?

Determine the record which contained the invalid data.

18. Which base register is associated with CARD-FILE?

```
JOB SSTBERN1           STEP GO              TIME 081141    DATE 79081    ID = 000                             PAGE 0001

COMPLETION CODE       SYSTEM = 0C7

PSW AT ENTRY TO ABEND  078D1000 000968D6        ILC 6    INTC 0007

CDE
        80C000      NCDE 00000000  RBP 0080C918  NM MAIN      EPA 00095C58  XL/MJ 0080C1E8  USE 00010000  ATTR 0B20000
        FD4168      NCDE 00FCCA68  RBP 00000000  NM IGG019DK  EPA 00F9A000  XL/MJ 00FD4188  USE 00040000  ATTR B122000
        FBA580      NCDE 00FBC1A0  RBP 00000000  NM IGG019AQ  EPA 00ED0A70  XL/MJ 00FBA5A0  USE 00060000  ATTR B122000
        FF8110      NCDE 00FF9C80  RBP 00000000  NM IGG019DJ  EPA 00ADE488  XL/MJ 00FF8130  USE 00100000  ATTR B922000

REGS AT ENTRY TO ABEND

    FLTR 0-6    0000000000000000    0000000000000000    0000000000000000    0000000000000000

    REGS 0-7    00096EEC  50096874  00096350 00000000  000966FE  00800634  00000000  00096A20  000095CF8  000944F0
    REGS 8-15   00096160  00096A7C  00000000 00000000  00095C58  00095C58  00000000  000961E8  00096678   00097A8E
        LINES 094300-094320 SAME AS ABOVE
094340   00000000 00000000  00000000 00000000  00000000 00000000  00000000 00000000    *                                *
094360   00000000 00000000  00000000 00000000  000943D8 00000000  00000000 00000000    *                                *
        LINES 094350-0943A0 SAME AS ABOVE
0943C0   00000000 00000000  00000000 00000000  00000000 00000000  00094460 00000000    *                            Q   *
0943E0   0C000000 00000000  00000000 00000000  00000000 00000000  00000000 00000000    *                                *
        LINES 094400-0944C0 SAME AS ABOVE
094440   00000000 00000000  000944F0 00050050  E6C9D3C3 D6E74040  40404040 40404040    *          0....WILCOX           *
094500   40404040 40404040  40D7D9D6 C7D9C1D4  D4C5D9F0 F6F4F7F1  F9F0F0F0 40404040    *    PROGRAMMER06471900          *
094520   40404040 40404040  40404040 40404040  40404040 40F1F3F1  4B404040 00000000    *                131.            *
094540   00094590 40404040  40404040 40404040  40404040 28000000  5C5C5C5C 00000000    *                ****            *
```

Figure 7.6 Dump for Exercise 7.1.

Figure 7.6 cont.

19. What is the address contained in that base register when the ABEND occurred?

20. What is the displacement of FORMER-SALARY?

21. What is the internal location of FORMER-SALARY?

22. What value was read from the card for FORMER-SALARY?

23. Which employee had the invalid data?

Summarize why the dump occurred.

Deeper Analysis

24. What is the address of the BL cells (use the Memory Map)?

25. Add the answer from part 24 to the entry point address (the answer given in part 3).

26. What hex characters are contained in the First Word (bytes 1, 2, 3, and 4) beginning at the address computed in part 25?

27. What is the significance of the answer to part 26?

28. What hex characters are contained in the third word (bytes 9, 10, 11, and 12) from the address in part 25?

29. What is the significance of the answer to part 28?

30. Circle the machine instruction which caused the dump in core?

Exercise 7.2: Dump Reading

Determine why the dump of Fig. 7.7 occurred. The questions below are provided as a guide. Use the COBOL Program, Data, Procedure, and Memory Maps of Fig. 7.1 through 7.5 as necessary.

Determine where the ABEND occurred.

1. What is the meaning of the completion code?

2. What is the address contained in the PSW?

3. At what location was the program located?

4. What is the relative location within the COBOL program of the instruction?

5. What machine instruction is at that location?

6. What is the corresponding COBOL instruction?

Examine the machine instruction which failed to execute. The instruction which actually produced the ABEND is the one immediately before the instruction determined in part 5.

7. What is the machine instruction which actually caused the ABEND?
8. What is its op code?
9. Which base register is associated with the first operand?
10. What is the displacement of the first operand?
11. What is the effective address of the first operand?
12. How many bytes are associated with the first operand? (Careful)
13. What are the internal contents of the first operand; are they valid as a decimal number?
14. Which base register is associated with the second operand?
15. What is the displacement of the second operand?
16. How many bytes are associated with the second operand?
17. What are the internal contents of the second operand; are they valid as a decimal number?

Determine the record which contained the invalid data.

18. Which base register is associated with CARD-FILE?
19. What is the address contained in that base register when the ABEND occurred?
20. What is the displacement of BIRTH-YEAR?
21. What is the internal location of BIRTH-YEAR?
22. What value was read from the card for BIRTH-YEAR?
23. Which employee had the invalid data?

Summarize why the dump occurred.

Deeper Analysis

24. What is the address of the BL cells (use the Memory Map)?
25. Add the answer from part 24 to the entry point address (the answer given in part 3).
26. What hex characters are contained in the first word (bytes 1, 2, 3, and 4) beginning at the address computed in part 25?
27. What is the significance of the answer to part 26?
28. What hex characters are contained in the third word (bytes 9, 10, 11, and 12) from the address in part 25?

```
JOB SSTBERN1        STEP GO           TIME 074332    DATE 79107    ID = 000                           PAGE 0001
COMPLETION CODE     SYSTEM = 0C7
PSW AT ENTRY TO ABEND  078D1000 0009688A        ILC 6    INTC 0007

CDE
     80C000      NCDE 00000000   RBP 007DB088  NM MAIN      EPA 00095C58   XL/MJ 0080CAF0   USE 00010000   ATTR 0B20000
     FCD200      NCDE 00FCD230   RBP 00000000  NM IGG019DK  EPA 00F9A000   XL/MJ 00FCD220   USE 00030000   ATTR B122000
     FD4018      NCDE 00FE6170   RBP 00000000  NM IGG019AQ  EPA 00ED0A70   XL/MJ 00FD4038   USE 00050000   ATTR B122000
     FE8150      NCDE 00FF9C90   RBP 00000000  NM IGG019DJ  EPA 00ADE488   XL/MJ 00FE8170   USE 000E0000   ATTR B122000

REGS AT ENTRY TO ABEND

FLTR 0-6     0000000000000000      0000000000000000      0000000000000000      0000000000000000
REGS 0-7     000966EC  50096874  000966FE  00800634  00000000  00096048  00096A20  000944F0
REGS 8-15    00096160  00096A7C  00095C58  00095C58  00000000  00096468  000961E8  00097A8E

0942C0  LINE 0942A0 SAME AS ABOVE
0942E0  40404040  40000000  00094350  00000000  00000000  00000000  00000000  00000000   *                              *
        LINES 094300-094320 SAME AS ABOVE
094340  00000000  00000000  00000000  00000000  000943D8  00000000  00000000  00000000   *                              *
094360  00000000  00000000  00000000  00000000  00000000  00000000  00000000  00000000   *           .Q.                *
        LINES 094380-0943A0 SAME AS ABOVE
0943C0  00000000  00000000  00000000  00000000  00000000  00094460  00000000  00000000   *                              *
0943E0  00000000  00000000  00000000  00000000  00000000  00000000  00000000  00000000   *                              *
        LINES 094400-0944C0 SAME AS ABOVE
```

Figure 7.7 Dump for Exercise 7.2.

Address							
0944E0	00000000	00000000	00000000	00000000	E2D4C9E3	C8404040	40404040	*........................SMITH *
094500	40404040	40404040	40D7D9D6	C7D9C1D4	D4C5D940	404040F1	F5F0F0F0	* PROGRAMMER 15000*
094520	F1F4F1F0	F0404040	40404040	40404040	40404040	40F1F3F2	4B404040	*14100 132. *
094540	00094590	28000000	40404040	40404040	40404040	5C5C5C5C	00000000	*........ ****....*
094560	00000200	80000000	00000000	4F006B00	00000000	00420000	00000000	*............|,.......... *
094580	00004000	90000050	00500000	00094550	00004040	40404040	40404040	*... ....&.. *
0945A0	40404040	40404040	40404040	40404040	40404040	40404040	40404040	* *
0945C0	00000000	00000100	00000000	D1C5E2F2	4BD1D6C2	F0F0F6F7	F74BE2D6	*............JES2.JOB00677.SO*

095D00	F5F0F0F0	F0F0F000	F7F9F0F4	F1F70000	60606060	60606060	60606060	*5000000.790417..----------------*
095D20	60606060	60606060	60606060	60606060	60606060	60606060	60606060	*--------------------------------*
095D40	40404040	40404040	40404040	40404040	40404040	40404040	40404040	* *
095D60	40404040	40404040	40404040	40404040	40404040	40404040	40404040	* NAME AGE *
095D80	4040D5C1	D4C54040	40404040	4040C1C7	C5404040	40E2C1D3	404040D6	* LD SAL INCR PRES SAL O*
095DA0	D3C440E2	C1D34040	406C40C9	D5C3D940	40404040	40404040	40404040	* *
095DC0	40404040	40404040	40404040	40404040	40404040	40404040	40404040	* *
095DE0	40404040	40404040	40404040	40404040	40404040	40404040	40404040	* *

096300	00000000	00000000	00000000	00000000	00010F88	00000000	8F096080	*..........................h....*
096320	00096080	00800634	00096048	50096ACC	00000000	00097A26	00000000	*........&...............8.......*
096340	00095C58	00095C58	000096468	00000000	00000000	00000000	00096160	*................................*
096360	00000000	00000000	00000000	00000000	00000000	40095982	00000000	*............................0...*
096380	00000000	00000000	00000000	C1000000	00000000	00095C58	000007F8	*........SYSOUT A.............8*
0963A0	00099760	E2E8D2D6	E4E34040	000944F0	00000000	00000000	00000000	*................................*
0963C0	00000000	00000000	00000000	00000000	00000000	00000000	00000004	*........................0....8*
0963E0	00000000	00000000	00000000	0000079F	00000000	F1F7030C	00000000	*.............0.........790417.*
096400	00000000	00000000	00000000	00096A26	000966EC	00095F64	8F096080	*................................*
096420								

096820	40084110	10000A0A	58100C084	00096080	C0B658F0	C02405EF	5840C074	*................................*
096840	91012017	07145810	20149601	20171B44	43401005	4C401006	41101000	*...K.......0....0.....2.K..2*
096860	0ACA58F0	C01805EF	58F0C02C	07FF58F0	C014051F	0000006A	7025F271	*...K......0.K...2.K..K.K.0.K..2*
096880	D2186010	FB11D21E	D216D271	D216D216	F271D210	6012FB11	7025F271	*..K.K..8.K..K..K.2.K..K.K.0.K..2*
0968A0	0001FD41	D223C09A	F872D220	FA22D225	D21DF322	6012FB11	F020D225	*....K..0.K..2.K..K..K.3..K..K.2*
0968C0	96F6005	F274D220	F274D220	D225FC51	D21AC09C	D21B96F0	6003D225	*.0K...2.K..2.K..2.K..K..0..K.2*
0968E0	7030F040	D21B0001	FD72D218	FD72D218	F3246006	D21B96F0	F274D220	*..0 .K....K..K..3..K..0.2.K.2*
096900	C05CD509	7019C0DA	0772F272	D2206003	F871D218	C09EFB21	58F0C05C	*...N....2.K..8.K....K..0.K.*

Figure 7.7 cont.

343

29. What is the significance of the answer to part 28?

30. Circle the machine instruction which caused the dump in core?

31. Why is the Entry Point Address in this exercise identical to the value in exercise 7.1?

32. What was the date of execution?

PROBLEM STATEMENT: EMPLOYEE PROFILES

A variation of the COBOL listing of Fig. 7.8 first appeared in exercise 3.6 to illustrate debugging in a subprogram. Accordingly, note the presence of two distinct programs, PROFILE and DECODER, representing the main and sub (or calling and called) programs, respectively. Note also *two* sets of associated material (DMAPs, PMAPs, etc.,) for use in the debugging exercises. This material appears in Fig. 7.8 through 7.18.

The two problems associated with this program, exercises 7.3 and 7.4, cover more material than the previous exercises (exercises 7.1 and 7.2). The reader is now forced to consider BL and BLL cells, and is introduced to the TCB, DCB, and DEB control blocks.

```
00001              IDENTIFICATION DIVISION.
00002              PROGRAM-ID. "PROFILE".
00003              AUTHOR.
00004                   MARION MILGROM.
00005
00006              ENVIRONMENT DIVISION.
00007              CONFIGURATION SECTION.
00008              SOURCE-COMPUTER.     IBM-370.
00009              OBJECT-COMPUTER.     IBM-370.
00010
00011              INPUT-OUTPUT SECTION.
00012              FILE-CONTROL.
00013                   SELECT EMPLOYEE-FILE ASSIGN TO UT-S-SYSIN.
00014                   SELECT PRINT-FILE ASSIGN TO UT-S-SYSOUT.
00015
00016              DATA DIVISION.
00017              FILE SECTION.
00018                   COPY EMPLOYEE.
00019 C            FD   EMPLOYEE-FILE
00020 C                 LABEL RECORDS ARE OMITTED
00021 C                 RECORD CONTAINS 80 CHARACTERS
00022 C                 DATA RECORD IS EMPLOYEE-RECORD.
00023 C            01   EMPLOYEE-RECORD.
00024 C                 05   EMP-SOC-SEC-NUMBER          PIC X(9).
00025 C                 05   EMP-NAME-AND-INITIALS       PIC X(15).
00026 C                 05   EMP-DATE-OF-BIRTH.
00027 C                      10   EMP-BIRTH-MONTH        PIC 99.
00028 C                      10   EMP-BIRTH-YEAR         PIC 99.
00029 C                 05   EMP-DATE-OF-HIRE.
```

Figure 7.8 Calling Program for Exercises 7.3 and 7.4.

```
00030 C              10  EMP-HIRE-MONTH           PIC 99.
00031 C              10  EMP-HIRE-YEAR            PIC 99.
00032 C          05  EMP-LOCATION-CODE            PIC 99.
00033 C          05  EMP-EDUCATION-CODE           PIC 9.
00034 C          05  EMP-TITLE-DATA.
00035 C              10  EMP-TITLE-CODE           PIC 9(3).
00036 C              10  EMP-TITLE-DATE           PIC 9(4).
00037 C              10  EMP-PERFORMANCE          PIC 9.
00038 C          05  EMP-SALARY-DATA OCCURS 3 TIMES
00039 C                          INDEXED BY SAL-INDEX.
00040 C              10  EMP-SALARY               PIC 9(5).
00041 C              10  EMP-SALARY-TYPE          PIC X.
00042 C              10  EMP-SALARY-DATE.
00043 C                  15  EMP-SALARY-MONTH     PIC 99.
00044 C                  15  EMP-SALARY-YEAR      PIC 99.
00045 C              10  EMP-SALARY-GRADE         PIC 9.
00046 C          05  FILLER                       PIC X(4).
00047
00048       FD  PRINT-FILE
00049           LABEL RECORDS ARE OMITTED
00050           RECORD CONTAINS 133 CHARACTERS
00051           DATA RECORD IS PRINT-LINE.
00052       01  PRINT-LINE                        PIC X(133).
00053
00054       WORKING-STORAGE SECTION.
00055       77  WS-END-OF-DATA-SWITCH    PIC X(3)  VALUE "YES".
00056           88  NO-MORE-EMPLOYEE-RECORDS      VALUE "NO ".
00057           88  STILL-MORE-EMPLOYEE-RECORDS   VALUE "YES".
00058
00059       01  SALARY-MEASUREMENT-DATA.
00060           05  WS-PCT-SALARY-INCR   PIC S99V9.
00061           05  WS-MONTHS-BETWEEN-INCR PIC 99.
00062           05  WS-RATE-SALARY-INCR  PIC S99V9.
00063
00064       01  WS-DASHED-LINE.
00065           05  FILLER               PIC X(1)  VALUE SPACES.
00066           05  DASHES               PIC X(80) VALUE ALL "-".
00067           05  FILLER               PIC X(52) VALUE SPACES.
00068
00069       01  WS-HDG-LINE-1.
00070           05  FILLER               PIC X(31) VALUE SPACES.
00071           05  FILLER               PIC X(10) VALUE "PERSONNEL".
00072           05  FILLER               PIC X(7)  VALUE "PROFILE".
00073           05  FILLER               PIC X(85) VALUE SPACES.
00074
00075       01  WS-HDG-LINE-2.
00076           05  FILLER               PIC X     VALUE SPACES.
00077           05  FILLER               PIC X(6)  VALUE "NAME: ".
00078           05  PRT-NAME             PIC X(15).
00079           05  FILLER               PIC X(8)  VALUE SPACES.
00080           05  FILLER               PIC X(11) VALUE "EDUCATION: ".
00081           05  PRT-EDUCATION        PIC X(10).
00082           05  FILLER               PIC X(6)  VALUE SPACES.
00083           05  FILLER               PIC X(12) VALUE "SOC SEC NO: ".
00084           05  PRT-SOC-SEC-NO       PIC 999B99B9999.
00085           05  FILLER               PIC X(53) VALUE SPACES.
00086
00087       01  WS-HDG-LINE-3.
00088           05  FILLER               PIC X     VALUE SPACES.
00089           05  FILLER               PIC X(12) VALUE "BIRTH DATE: ".
```

Figure 7.8 *cont.*

```
00090            05  PRT-BIRTH-DATE.
00091                10  PRT-BIRTH-MONTH     PIC 99.
00092                10  FILLER              PIC X        VALUE "/".
00093                10  PRT-BIRTH-YEAR      PIC 99.
00094            05  FILLER                  PIC X(12)    VALUE SPACES.
00095            05  FILLER                  PIC X(11)    VALUE "HIRE DATE: ".
00096            05  PRT-HIRE-DATE.
00097                10  PRT-HIRE-MONTH      PIC 99.
00098                10  FILLER              PIC X        VALUE "/".
00099                10  PRT-HIRE-YEAR       PIC 99.
00100            05  FILLER                  PIC X(12)    VALUE SPACES.
00101            05  FILLER                  PIC X(10)    VALUE "LOCATION: ".
00102            05  PRT-LOCATION            PIC X(13).
00103            05  FILLER                  PIC X(52)    VALUE SPACES.
00104
00105        01  WS-SAL-HDG-1.
00106            05  FILLER                  PIC X(32)    VALUE SPACES.
00107            05  FILLER                  PIC X(14)    VALUE "SALARY HISTORY".
00108            05  FILLER                  PIC X(87)    VALUE SPACES.
00109
00110        01  WS-SAL-HDG-2.
00111            05  FILLER                  PIC X(12)    VALUE SPACES.
00112            05  FILLER                  PIC X(10)    VALUE "SALARY".
00113            05  FILLER                  PIC X(8)     VALUE "DATE".
00114            05  FILLER                  PIC X(9)     VALUE "TYPE".
00115            05  FILLER                  PIC X(12)    VALUE "INCR(%)".
00116            05  FILLER                  PIC X(7)     VALUE "MBI".
00117            05  FILLER                  PIC X(9)     VALUE "RSI(%)".
00118            05  FILLER                  PIC X(76)    VALUE SPACES.
00119
00120        01  WS-SAL-DETAIL-LINE.
00121            05  FILLER                  PIC X(10)    VALUE SPACES.
00122            05  PRT-SALARY              PIC $$$,$$$.
00123            05  FILLER                  PIC X(3)     VALUE SPACES.
00124            05  PRT-SALARY-DATE.
00125                10  PRT-SALARY-MONTH    PIC 99.
00126                10  PRT-SALARY-SLASH    PIC X        VALUE "/".
00127                10  PRT-SALARY-YEAR     PIC 99.
00128            05  FILLER                  PIC X(5)     VALUE SPACES.
00129            05  PRT-SALARY-TYPE         PIC X.
00130            05  FILLER                  PIC X(6)     VALUE SPACES.
00131            05  PRT-SALARY-PCT-INCR     PIC -ZZ9.9.
00132            05  FILLER                  PIC X(7)     VALUE SPACES.
00133            05  PRT-MNTHS-BETWEEN-INCR  PIC 99.
00134            05  FILLER                  PIC X(4)     VALUE SPACES.
00135            05  PRT-RATE-SALARY-INCR    PIC -ZZ9.9.
00136            05  FILLER                  PIC X(83)    VALUE SPACES.
00137
00138        01  WS-TITLE-HDG-1.
00139            05  FILLER                  PIC X(35)    VALUE SPACES.
00140            05  FILLER                  PIC X(11)    VALUE "JOB HISTORY".
00141            05  FILLER                  PIC X(87)    VALUE SPACES.
00142
00143        01  WS-TITLE-HDG-2.
00144            05  FILLER                  PIC X(24)    VALUE SPACES.
00145            05  FILLER                  PIC X(14)    VALUE "TITLE".
00146            05  FILLER                  PIC X(8)     VALUE "DATE".
00147            05  FILLER                  PIC X(11)    VALUE "PERFORMANCE".
00148            05  FILLER                  PIC X(76)    VALUE SPACES.
00149
```

Figure 7.8 *cont.*

```
00150            01  WS-TITLE-LINE.
00151                05  FILLER              PIC X(17)   VALUE SPACES.
00152                05  PRT-TITLE           PIC X(18).
00153                05  FILLER              PIC X(2)    VALUE SPACES.
00154                05  PRT-TITLE-DATE      PIC ZZ/ZZ.
00155                05  FILLER              PIC X(5)    VALUE SPACES.
00156                05  PRT-PERFORMANCE     PIC X(9).
00157                05  FILLER              PIC X(77)   VALUE SPACES.
00159        PROCEDURE DIVISION.
00160        005-MAINLINE-ROUTINE.
00161            OPEN INPUT EMPLOYEE-FILE
00162                 OUTPUT PRINT-FILE.
00163            PERFORM 010-READ-EMPLOYEE-RECORD.
00164            PERFORM 020-PROCESS-EMPLOYEE-RECORDS
00165                UNTIL NO-MORE-EMPLOYEE-RECORDS.
00166            CLOSE EMPLOYEE-FILE PRINT-FILE.
00167            STOP RUN.
00168
00169        010-READ-EMPLOYEE-RECORD.
00170            READ EMPLOYEE-FILE
00171                AT END MOVE "NO " TO WS-END-OF-DATA-SWITCH.
00172
00173        020-PROCESS-EMPLOYEE-RECORDS.
00174
00175        *  EXPAND ALL CODED INFORMATION BEFORE DOING ANY OUTPUT
00176            CALL "DECODER"
00177                USING EMP-TITLE-CODE         PRT-TITLE
00178                      EMP-LOCATION-CODE      PRT-LOCATION
00179                      EMP-EDUCATION-CODE     PRT-EDUCATION.
00180
00181            IF EMP-PERFORMANCE = "1"
00182                MOVE "EXCELLENT" TO PRT-PERFORMANCE
00183            ELSE
00184                IF EMP-PERFORMANCE = "2"
00185                    MOVE "AVERAGE" TO PRT-PERFORMANCE
00186                ELSE
00187                    IF EMP-PERFORMANCE = "3"
00188                        MOVE "POOR" TO PRT-PERFORMANCE
00189                    ELSE
00190                        MOVE "UNKNOWN" TO PRT-PERFORMANCE.
00191
00192        *  BEGIN OUTPUT FOR PERSONAL PROFILE
00193            WRITE PRINT-LINE FROM WS-HDG-LINE-1
00194                AFTER ADVANCING PAGE.
00195            MOVE EMP-NAME-AND-INITIALS TO PRT-NAME.
00196            MOVE EMP-SOC-SEC-NUMBER     TO PRT-SOC-SEC-NO.
00197            INSPECT PRT-SOC-SEC-NO REPLACING ALL " " BY "-".
00198            WRITE PRINT-LINE FROM WS-HDG-LINE-2 AFTER ADVANCING 2 LINES.
00199            MOVE EMP-BIRTH-MONTH      TO PRT-BIRTH-MONTH.
00200            MOVE EMP-BIRTH-YEAR       TO PRT-BIRTH-YEAR.
00201            MOVE EMP-HIRE-MONTH       TO PRT-HIRE-MONTH.
00202            MOVE EMP-HIRE-YEAR        TO PRT-HIRE-YEAR.
00203            WRITE PRINT-LINE FROM WS-HDG-LINE-3 AFTER ADVANCING 2 LINES.
00204            WRITE PRINT-LINE FROM WS-DASHED-LINE AFTER ADVANCING 2 LINES.
00205            WRITE PRINT-LINE FROM WS-SAL-HDG-1 AFTER ADVANCING 2 LINES.
00206            WRITE PRINT-LINE FROM WS-SAL-HDG-2 AFTER ADVANCING 2 LINES.
00207            PERFORM 030-WRITE-SALARY-LINE
00208                VARYING SAL-INDEX FROM 1 BY 1
00209                UNTIL SAL-INDEX > 3
00210                    OR EMP-SALARY (SAL-INDEX) = 0.
00211            WRITE PRINT-LINE FROM WS-DASHED-LINE AFTER ADVANCING 2 LINES.
```

Figure 7.8 *cont.*

```
00212           WRITE PRINT-LINE FROM WS-TITLE-HDG-1 AFTER ADVANCING 2 LINES.
00213           WRITE PRINT-LINE FROM WS-TITLE-HDG-2 AFTER ADVANCING 2 LINES.
00214           MOVE EMP-TITLE-DATE          TO PRT-TITLE-DATE.
00215           WRITE PRINT-LINE FROM WS-TITLE-LINE AFTER ADVANCING 2 LINES.
00216           WRITE PRINT-LINE FROM WS-DASHED-LINE AFTER ADVANCING 2 LINES.
00217
00218           PERFORM 010-READ-EMPLOYEE-RECORD.
00219
00220       030-WRITE-SALARY-LINE.
00221           MOVE SPACES TO WS-SAL-DETAIL-LINE.
00222           MOVE "/" TO PRT-SALARY-SLASH.
00223           MOVE EMP-SALARY (SAL-INDEX)          TO PRT-SALARY.
00224           MOVE EMP-SALARY-MONTH (SAL-INDEX)    TO PRT-SALARY-MONTH.
00225           MOVE EMP-SALARY-YEAR (SAL-INDEX)     TO PRT-SALARY-YEAR.
00226           MOVE EMP-SALARY-TYPE (SAL-INDEX)     TO PRT-SALARY-TYPE.
00227
00228           IF SAL-INDEX < 3 AND EMP-SALARY (SAL-INDEX + 1) > 0
00229               PERFORM 040-COMPUTE-SALARY-INCREASES.
00230           WRITE PRINT-LINE FROM WS-SAL-DETAIL-LINE.
00231
00232       040-COMPUTE-SALARY-INCREASES.
00233           COMPUTE WS-PCT-SALARY-INCR ROUNDED
00234               = 100 * (EMP-SALARY (SAL-INDEX)
00235                  - EMP-SALARY (SAL-INDEX + 1))
00236                  / EMP-SALARY (SAL-INDEX + 1).
00237
00238           COMPUTE WS-MONTHS-BETWEEN-INCR ROUNDED
00239               = (EMP-SALARY-YEAR (SAL-INDEX) * 12
00240                  + EMP-SALARY-MONTH (SAL-INDEX))
00241                  - (EMP-SALARY-YEAR (SAL-INDEX + 1) * 12
00242                  + EMP-SALARY-MONTH (SAL-INDEX + 1)).
00243
00244           COMPUTE WS-RATE-SALARY-INCR ROUNDED
00245               = WS-PCT-SALARY-INCR / (WS-MONTHS-BETWEEN-INCR / 12).
00246
00247           MOVE WS-PCT-SALARY-INCR      TO PRT-SALARY-PCT-INCR.
00248           MOVE WS-MONTHS-BETWEEN-INCR  TO PRT-MNTHS-BETWEEN-INCR.
00249           MOVE WS-RATE-SALARY-INCR     TO PRT-RATE-SALARY-INCR.
```

Figure 7.8 *cont.*

```
00001       IDENTIFICATION DIVISION.
00002       PROGRAM-ID. "DECODER".
00003       AUTHOR.     MARION MILGROM.
00004
00005       ENVIRONMENT DIVISION.
00006       INPUT-OUTPUT SECTION.
00007       FILE-CONTROL.
00008           SELECT TITLE-FILE ASSIGN TO UT-S-TITLES.
00009       CONFIGURATION SECTION.
00010       SOURCE-COMPUTER.   IBM-370.
00011       OBJECT-COMPUTER.   IBM-370.
00012       DATA DIVISION.
00013       FILE SECTION.
00014       FD  TITLE-FILE
00015           LABEL RECORDS ARE STANDARD
00016           RECORD CONTAINS 80 CHARACTERS
00017           DATA RECORD IS TITLE-RECORD.
00018       01  TITLE-RECORD.
00019           05  TITLE-FILE-CODE          PIC 9(3).
00020           05  TITLE-FILE-VALUE         PIC X(18).
00021           05  FILLER                   PIC X(59).
```

Figure 7.9 Called Program for Exercises 7.3 and 7.4.

```
00022
00023              WORKING-STORAGE SECTION.
00024                  77  WS-NUMBER-OF-TITLES          PIC 999     VALUE ZEROS.
00025                  77  WS-ALREADY-EXECUTED-SWITCH   PIC X(3)    VALUE "NO".
00026                  77  WS-TITLE-FILE-SWITCH         PIC X(3)    VALUE "NO".
00027                      88  END-OF-TITLE-FILE                    VALUE "YES".
00028
00029                  01  TITLE-TABLE.
00030                      05  TITLES OCCURS 1 TO 999 TIMES
00031                          DEPENDING ON WS-NUMBER-OF-TITLES
00032                          ASCENDING KEY IS TITLE-CODE
00033                          INDEXED BY TITLE-INDEX.
00034                          10  TITLE-CODE           PIC 9(3).
00035                          10  TITLE-VALUE          PIC X(18).
00036
00037                      COPY LOCATION.
00038 C                  01  LOCATION-VALUE.
00039 C                      05  FILLER           PIC X(15)   VALUE "10ATLANTA".
00040 C                      05  FILLER           PIC X(15)   VALUE "20BOSTON".
00041 C                      05  FILLER           PIC X(15)   VALUE "30CHICAGO".
00042 C                      05  FILLER           PIC X(15)   VALUE "40DETROIT".
00043 C                      05  FILLER           PIC X(15)   VALUE "50KANSAS CITY".
00044 C                      05  FILLER           PIC X(15)   VALUE "60LOS ANGELES".
00045 C                      05  FILLER           PIC X(15)   VALUE "70MINNEAPOLIS".
00046 C                      05  FILLER           PIC X(15)   VALUE "80NEW YORK".
00047 C                      05  FILLER           PIC X(15)   VALUE "90PHILADELPHIA".
00048 C                      05  FILLER           PIC X(15)   VALUE "95SAN FRANCISCO".
00049 C
00050 C                  01  LOCATION-TABLE REDEFINES LOCATION-VALUE.
00051 C                      05  LOCATIONS OCCURS 10 TIMES
00052 C                          INDEXED BY LOC-INDEX.
00053 C                          10  LOC-CODE  PIC 99.
00054 C                          10  LOC-NAME  PIC X(13).
00055
00056                  01  EDUCATION-TABLE.
00057                      05  EDUCATION-VALUES.
00058                          10  FILLER           PIC X(10)   VALUE "SOME HS".
00059                          10  FILLER           PIC X(10)   VALUE "HS DIPLOMA".
00060                          10  FILLER           PIC X(10)   VALUE "2YR DEGREE".
00061                          10  FILLER           PIC X(10)   VALUE "4YR DEGREE".
00062                          10  FILLER           PIC X(10)   VALUE "SOME GRAD".
00063                          10  FILLER           PIC X(10)   VALUE "MASTERS".
00064                          10  FILLER           PIC X(10)   VALUE "PH. D.".
00065                          10  FILLER           PIC X(10)   VALUE "OTHER".
00066                      05  EDU-NAME REDEFINES EDUCATION-VALUES
00067                              OCCURS 8 TIMES PIC X(10).
00068
00069              LINKAGE SECTION.
00070                  77  LS-TITLE-CODE                PIC 9(3).
00071                  77  LS-EXPANDED-TITLE            PIC X(18).
00072                  77  LS-LOCATION-CODE             PIC 99.
00073                  77  LS-EXPANDED-LOCATION         PIC X(13).
00074                  77  LS-EDUC-CODE                 PIC 9.
00075                  77  LS-EXPANDED-EDUCATION        PIC X(10).
00076
00077              PROCEDURE DIVISION
00078                  USING LS-TITLE-CODE           LS-EXPANDED-TITLE
00079                        LS-LOCATION-CODE        LS-EXPANDED-LOCATION
00080                        LS-EDUC-CODE            LS-EXPANDED-EDUCATION.
00081
00082              005-MAINLINE.
00083                  IF WS-ALREADY-EXECUTED-SWITCH = "NO"
```

Figure 7.9 *cont.*

```
00084                PERFORM 010-INITIALIZE-TITLE-TABLE.
00085
00086           * EXPAND TITLE CODE VIA A BINARY SEARCH
00087               SEARCH ALL TITLES
00088                   AT END
00089                       MOVE "UNKNOWN" TO LS-EXPANDED-TITLE
00090                   WHEN LS-TITLE-CODE = TITLE-CODE (TITLE-INDEX)
00091                       MOVE TITLE-VALUE (TITLE-INDEX) TO LS-EXPANDED-TITLE.
00092
00093           * EXPAND LOCATION-CODE VIA LINEAR SEARCH
00094               SET LOC-INDEX TO 1.
00095               SEARCH LOCATIONS
00096                   AT END
00097                       MOVE "UNKNOWN" TO LS-EXPANDED-LOCATION
00098                   WHEN LS-LOCATION-CODE = LOC-CODE (LOC-INDEX)
00099                       MOVE LOC-NAME (LOC-INDEX) TO LS-EXPANDED-LOCATION.
00100
00101           * EXPAND EDUCATION-CODE VIA DIRECT ACCESS TO TABLE ENTRY
00102               IF LS-EDUC-CODE < 1 OR > 8
00103                   MOVE "UNKNOWN" TO LS-EXPANDED-EDUCATION
00104               ELSE
00105                   MOVE EDU-NAME (LS-EDUC-CODE) TO LS-EXPANDED-EDUCATION.
00106
00107           007-RETURN-TO-MAIN.
00108               EXIT PROGRAM.
00109
00110           010-INITIALIZE-TITLE-TABLE.
00111               MOVE "YES" TO WS-ALREADY-EXECUTED-SWITCH.
00112               OPEN INPUT TITLE-FILE.
00113               SET TITLE-INDEX TO 1.
00114               READ TITLE-FILE
00115                   AT END MOVE "YES" TO WS-TITLE-FILE-SWITCH.
00116               PERFORM 020-READ-FROM-TITLE-FILE
00117                   UNTIL END-OF-TITLE-FILE.
00118               CLOSE TITLE-FILE.
00119
00120           020-READ-FROM-TITLE-FILE.
00121               ADD 1 TO WS-NUMBER-OF-TITLES.
00122               IF WS-NUMBER-OF-TITLES > 999
00123                   MOVE "YES" TO WS-TITLE-FILE-SWITCH
00124                   DISPLAY "ERROR - TOO MANY TITLES - TABLE EXCEEDED "
00125               ELSE
00126                   MOVE TITLE-FILE-CODE TO TITLE-CODE (TITLE-INDEX)
00127                   MOVE TITLE-FILE-VALUE TO TITLE-VALUE (TITLE-INDEX)
00128                   SET TITLE-INDEX UP BY 1
00129                   READ TITLE-FILE
00130                       AT END MOVE "YES" TO WS-TITLE-FILE-SWITCH
00131                   SET TITLE-INDEX DOWN BY 1.
```

Figure 7.9 *cont.*

LVL	SOURCE NAME	BASE	DISPL	INTRNL NAME	DEFINITION
FD	EMPLOYEE-FILE	DCB=01		DNM=1-188	
01	EMPLOYEE-RECORD	BL=1	000	DNM=1-215	DS 0CL80
02	EMP-SOC-SEC-NUMBER	BL=1	000	DNM=1-243	DS 9C
02	EMP-NAME-AND-INITIALS	BL=1	009	DNM=1-271	DS 15C
02	EMP-DATE-OF-BIRTH	BL=1	018	DNM=1-302	DS 0CL4
03	EMP-BIRTH-MONTH	BL=1	018	DNM=1-332	DS 2C

Figure 7.10 Abbreviated Data Division Map for Main Program (PROFILE).

03	EMP-BIRTH-YEAR	BL=1	01A	DNM=1-357	DS	2C	
02	EMP-DATE-OF-HIRE	BL=1	01C	DNM=1-381	DS	0CL4	
03	EMP-HIRE-MONTH	BL=1	01C	DNM=1-410	DS	2C	
03	EMP-HIRE-YEAR	BL=1	01E	DNM=1-434	DS	2C	
02	EMP-LOCATION-CODE	BL=1	020	DNM=1-457	DS	2C	
02	EMP-EDUCATION-CODE	BL=1	022	DNM=2-000	DS	1C	
02	EMP-TITLE-DATA	BL=1	023	DNM=2-028	DS	0CL8	
03	EMP-TITLE-CODE	BL=1	023	DNM=2-055	DS	3C	
03	EMP-TITLE-DATE	BL=1	026	DNM=2-079	DS	4C	
03	EMP-PERFORMANCE	BL=1	02A	DNM=2-106	DS	1C	
	SAL-INDEX			DNM=2-131			
02	EMP-SALARY-DATA	BL=1	02B	DNM=2-147	DS	0CL11	
03	EMP-SALARY	BL=1	02B	DNM=2-175	DS	5C	
03	EMP-SALARY-TYPE	BL=1	030	DNM=2-198	DS	1C	
03	EMP-SALARY-DATE	BL=1	031	DNM=2-226	DS	0CL4	
04	EMP-SALARY-MONTH	BL=1	031	DNM=2-257	DS	2C	
04	EMP-SALARY-YEAR	BL=1	033	DNM=2-286	DS	2C	
03	EMP-SALARY-GRADE	BL=1	035	DNM=2-314	DS	1C	
02	FILLER	BL=1	04C	DNM=2-343	DS	4C	
FD	PRINT-FILE	DCB=02		DNM=2-354			
01	PRINT-LINE	BL=2	000	DNM=2-378	DS	133C	
77	WS-END-OF-DATA-SWITCH	BL=3	000	DNM=2-398	DS	3C	
88	NO-MORE-EMPLOYEE-RECORDS			DNM=2-432			
88	STILL-MORE-EMPLOYEE-RECORDS			DNM=2-469			
01	SALARY-MEASUREMENT-DATA	BL=3	008	DNM=3-000	DS	0CL8	
02	WS-PCT-SALARY-INCR	BL=3	008	DNM=3-036	DS	3C	
02	WS-MONTHS-BETWEEN-INCR	BL=3	00B	DNM=3-064	DS	2C	
02	WS-RATE-SALARY-INCR	BL=3	00D	DNM=3-096	DS	3C	
01	WS-DASHED-LINE	BL=3	010	DNM=3-125	DS	0CL133	
02	FILLER	BL=3	010	DNM=3-152	DS	1C	
02	DASHES	BL=3	011	DNM=3-166	DS	80C	
02	FILLER	BL=3	061	DNM=3-182	DS	52C	
01	WS-HDG-LINE-1	BL=3	098	DNM=3-196	DS	0CL133	
02	FILLER	BL=3	098	DNM=3-222	DS	31C	
02	FILLER	BL=3	0B7	DNM=3-236	DS	10C	
02	FILLER	BL=3	0C1	DNM=3-250	DS	7C	
02	FILLER	BL=3	0C8	DNM=3-264	DS	85C	
01	WS-HDG-LINE-2	BL=3	120	DNM=3-278	DS	0CL133	
02	FILLER	BL=3	120	DNM=3-304	DS	1C	
02	FILLER	BL=3	121	DNM=3-318	DS	6C	
02	PRT-NAME	BL=3	127	DNM=3-332	DS	15C	
02	FILLER	BL=3	136	DNM=3-350	DS	8C	
02	FILLER	BL=3	13E	DNM=3-364	DS	11C	
02	PRT-EDUCATION	BL=3	149	DNM=3-378	DS	10C	
02	FILLER	BL=3	153	DNM=3-401	DS	6C	
02	FILLER	BL=3	159	DNM=3-415	DS	12C	
02	PRT-SOC-SEC-NO	BL=3	165	DNM=3-429	DS	11C	
02	FILLER	BL=3	170	DNM=3-466	DS	53C	
01	WS-HDG-LINE-3	BL=3	1A8	DNM=3-480	DS	0CL133	
02	FILLER	BL=3	1A8	DNM=4-000	DS	1C	
02	FILLER	BL=3	1A9	DNM=4-014	DS	12C	
02	PRT-BIRTH-DATE	BL=3	1B5	DNM=4-028	DS	0CL5	
03	PRT-BIRTH-MONTH	BL=3	1B5	DNM=4-055	DS	2C	
03	FILLER	BL=3	1B7	DNM=4-080	DS	1C	
03	PRT-BIRTH-YEAR	BL=3	1B8	DNM=4-094	DS	2C	
02	FILLER	BL=3	1BA	DNM=4-118	DS	12C	
02	FILLER	BL=3	1C6	DNM=4-132	DS	11C	
02	PRT-HIRE-DATE	BL=3	1D1	DNM=4-146	DS	0CL5	
03	PRT-HIRE-MONTH	BL=3	1D1	DNM=4-172	DS	2C	
03	FILLER	BL=3	1D3	DNM=4-196	DS	1C	
03	PRT-HIRE-YEAR	BL=3	1D4	DNM=4-210	DS	2C	
02	FILLER	BL=3	1D6	DNM=4-233	DS	12C	
02	FILLER	BL=3	1E2	DNM=4-247	DS	10C	

Figure 7.10 *cont.*

176	CALL	000EF0	000000AD		DC	X'000000AD'	
		000EF4	41 10 7 023		LA	1,023(0,7)	DNM=2-55
		000EF8	50 10 D 29C		ST	1,29C(0,13)	PRM=1
		000EFC	41 10 6 501		LA	1,501(0,6)	DNM=6-110
		000F00	50 10 D 2A0		ST	1,2A0(0,13)	PRM=2
		000F04	41 10 7 020		LA	1,020(0,7)	DNM=1-457
		000F08	50 10 D 2A4		ST	1,2A4(0,13)	PRM=3
		000F0C	41 10 6 1EC		LA	1,1EC(0,6)	DNM=4-261
		000F10	50 10 D 2A8		ST	1,2A8(0,13)	PRM=4
		000F14	41 10 7 022		LA	1,022(0,7)	DNM=2-0
		000F18	50 10 D 2AC		ST	1,2AC(0,13)	PRM=5
		000F1C	41 10 6 149		LA	1,149(0,6)	DNM=3-378
		000F20	50 10 D 2B0		ST	1,2B0(0,13)	PRM=6
		000F24	96 80 D 2B0		OI	2B0(13),X'80'	
		000F28	41 10 D 29C		LA	1,29C(0,13)	PRM=1
		000F2C	58 F0 C 018		L	15,018(0,12)	V(ILBDDBG4)
		000F30	05 EF		BALR	14,15	
		000F36	96 40 D 049		OI	049(13),X'40'	
		000F3A	05 EF		L	15,02C(0,13)	V(DECODER)
		000F3C	94 BF D 049		BALR	14,15	
		000F40	40 F0 D 05C		NI	049(13),X'BF'	
		000F44	58 F0 D 1B8		STH	15,05C(0,13)	
		000F48	50 D0 F 080		L	15,1B8(0,15)	
					ST	13,080(0,15)	
181	IF	000F4C	58 20 C 05C		L	2,05C(0,12)	
		000F40	58 10 D 2A0		ST	1,2A0(0,13)	
		001443	41 10 D 29C		L	1,29C(0,13)	
		001443	58 F0 2 0D4		L	15,0D4(0,2)	
		00144C	05 EF		BALR	14,15	
		00144E	58 10 D 280		EQU	*	
		001452	07 F1		L	1,280(0,13)	
					BCR	15,1	
232	*040-COMPUTE-SALARY-INCREASES					GN=028	
		001454	58 F0 C 014		L	15,014(0,12)	V(ILBOFLW1)
		001453	05 1F		BALR	1,15	
233	COMPUTE	00145A	000000E8		DC	X'000000E8'	
		00145E	41 40 7 02B		LA	4,02B(0,7)	DNM=2-175
		001462	5A 40 D 248		A	4,248(0,13)	INX=1
		001466	41 20 7 02B		LA	2,02B(0,7)	DNM=2-175
		001534	5A 20 D 248		A	2,248(0,13)	INX=1
		001534	96 F0 6 00C		OI	00C(6),X'F0'	DNM=3-64+1
244	COMPUTE	001533	F2 71 D 228 6 0DB	PACK	228(8,13),00B(2,6)	DNM=3-64
		001553	FC 20 D 228 0 002	SRP	22D(3,13),002(0),0	TS=025
		001554	FD 41 D 22B D 11A	DP	22B(5,13),11A(2,12)	TS=030
		00154A	F8 72 D 228 D 22B	ZAP	228(8,13),22B(3,13)	LIT+42
		001550	F2 72 D 220 6 008	PACK	220(8,13),008(3,6)	TS=028
		001556	F0 30 D 224 0 003	SRP	224(4,13),003(0),0	DNM=3-36
		001555	FD 62 D 221 D 22D	DP	221(7,13),22D(3,13)	TS=017
		001562	F8 73 D 220 D 221	ZAP	220(8,13),221(4,13)	TS=018
		001568	F0 35 D 224 0 03F	SRP	224(4,13),03F(0),5	TS=017
		00156E	F3 22 6 00D D 225	UNPK	00D(3,6),225(3,13)	TS=021
247	MOVE	001574	F2 72 D 228 6 008	PACK	228(8,13),008(3,6)	DNM=3-96
		00157A	D2 07 D 230 C 11C	MVC	230(8,13),11C(12)	TS=025
		001580	DE 07 D 230 D 22D	ED	230(8,13),22D(13)	LIT+44
		001586	50 30 D 258		ST	3,258(0,13)	TS=030
							TS=022
							DNM=3-36
							TS=025
							TS2=1
							TS2=1
							SBS=4
							TS=030

Figure 7.11 Abbreviated Procedure Division Map for Main Program (PROFILE).

```
                       MEMORY MAP

                TGT                      008D8

            SAVE AREA                    008D8
            SWITCH                       00920
            TALLY                        00924
            SORT SAVE                    00928
            ENTRY-SAVE                   0092C
            SORT CORE SIZE               00930
            RET CODE                     00934
            SORT RET                     00936
            WORKING CELLS                00938
            SORT FILE SIZE               00A68
            SORT MODE SIZE               00A6C
            PGT-VN TBL                   00A70
            TGT-VN TBL                   00A74
            RESERVED                     00A78
            LENGTH OF VN TBL             00A7C
            LABEL RET                    00A7E
            RESERVED                     00A7F
            DBG R14SAVE                  00A80
            COBOL INDICATOR              00A84
            A(INIT1)                     00A88
            DEBUG TABLE PTR              00A8C
            SUBCOM PTR                   00A90
            SORT-MESSAGE                 00A94
            SYSOUT DDNAME                00A9C
            RESERVED                     00A9D
            COBOL ID                     00A9E
            COMPILED POINTER             00AA0
            COUNT TABLE ADDRESS          00AA4
            RESERVED                     00AA8
            DBG R11SAVE                  00AB0
            COUNT CHAIN ADDRESS          00AB4
            PRBL1 CELL PTR               00AB8
            RESERVED                     00ABC
            TA LENGTH                    00AC1
            RESERVED                     00AC4
            PCS LIT PTR                  00ACC
            DEBUGGING                    00AD0
            CD FOR INITIAL INPUT         00AD4
            OVERFLOW CELLS               00AD8
            BL CELLS                     00AD8
            DECBADR CELLS                00AE4
            FIB CELLS                    00AE4
            TEMP STORAGE                 00AE8
            TEMP STORAGE-2               00B08
            TEMP STORAGE-3               00B18
            TEMP STORAGE-4               00B18
            BLL CELLS                    00B18
            VLC CELLS                    00B20
            SBL CELLS                    00B20
            INDEX CELLS                  00B20
            SUBADR CELLS                 00B24
```

Figure 7.12 Memory Map for Main Program (PROFILE).

```
REGISTER ASSIGNMENT

   REG 6      BL =3
   REG 7      BL =1
   REG 8      BL =2
```

WORKING-STORAGE STARTS AT LOCATION 000A0 FOR A LENGTH OF 00578.

Figure 7.13 Register Assignments for Main Program (PROFILE).

LVL	SOURCE NAME	BASE	DISPL	INTRNL NAME	DEFINITION	USAGE
FD	TITLE-FILE	DCB=01		DNM=1-140		QSAM
01	TITLE-RECORD	BL=1	000	DNM=1-164	DS 0CL80	GROUP
02	TITLE-FILE-CODE	BL=1	000	DNM=1-189	DS 3C	DISP-NM
02	TITLE-FILE-VALUE	BL=1	003	DNM=1-214	DS 18C	DISP
02	FILLER	BL=1	015	DNM=1-240	DS 59C	DISP
77	WS-NUMBER-OF-TITLES	BL=2	000	DNM=1-251	DS 3C	DISP-NM
77	WS-ALREADY-EXECUTED-SWITCH	BL=2	003	DNM=1-280	DS 3C	DISP
77	WS-TITLE-FILE-SWITCH	BL=2	006	DNM=1-316	DS 3C	DISP
88	END-OF-TITLE-FILE			DNM=1-349		
01	TITLE-TABLE	BL=2	010	DNM=1-379	DS VLC=1	GROUP
	TITLE-INDEX			DNM=1-403		INDEX-NM
02	TITLES	BL=2	010	DNM=1-421	DS 0CL21	GROUP
03	TITLE-CODE	BL=2	010	DNM=1-440	DS 3C	DISP-NM
03	TITLE-VALUE	BL=2	013	DNM=1-463	DS 18C	DISP
01	LOCATION-VALUE	BL=7	208	DNM=2-000	DS 0CL150	GROUP
02	FILLER	BL=7	208	DNM=2-027	DS 15C	DISP
02	FILLER	BL=7	217	DNM=2-041	DS 15C	DISP
02	FILLER	BL=7	226	DNM=2-055	DS 15C	DISP
02	FILLER	BL=7	235	DNM=2-069	DS 15C	DISP
02	FILLER	BL=7	244	DNM=2-083	DS 15C	DISP
02	FILLER	BL=7	253	DNM=2-097	DS 15C	DISP
02	FILLER	BL=7	262	DNM=2-111	DS 15C	DISP
02	FILLER	BL=7	271	DNM=2-125	DS 15C	DISP
02	FILLER	BL=7	280	DNM=2-139	DS 15C	DISP
02	FILLER	BL=7	28F	DNM=2-153	DS 15C	DISP
01	LOCATION-TABLE	BL=7	208	DNM=2-167	DS 0CL150	GROUP
	LOC-INDEX			DNM=2-194		INDEX-NM
02	LOCATIONS	BL=7	208	DNM=2-213	DS 0CL15	GROUP
03	LOC-CODE	BL=7	208	DNM=2-235	DS 2C	DISP-NM
03	LOC-NAME	BL=7	20A	DNM=2-256	DS 13C	DISP
01	EDUCATION-TABLE	BL=7	2A0	DNM=2-277	DS 0CL80	GROUP
02	EDUCATION-VALUES	BL=7	2A0	DNM=2-305	DS 0CL80	GROUP
03	FILLER	BL=7	2A0	DNM=2-334	DS 10C	DISP
03	FILLER	BL=7	2AA	DNM=2-348	DS 10C	DISP
03	FILLER	BL=7	2B4	DNM=2-362	DS 10C	DISP
03	FILLER	BL=7	2BE	DNM=2-376	DS 10C	DISP
03	FILLER	BL=7	2C8	DNM=2-390	DS 10C	DISP
03	FILLER	BL=7	2D2	DNM=2-404	DS 10C	DISP
03	FILLER	BL=7	2DC	DNM=2-418	DS 10C	DISP
03	FILLER	BL=7	2E6	DNM=2-432	DS 10C	DISP
02	EDU-NAME	BL=7	2A0	DNM=2-446	DS 10C	DISP
77	LS-TITLE-CODE	BLL=3	000	DNM=2-464	DS 3C	DISP-NM
77	LS-EXPANDED-TITLE	BLL=4	000	DNM=3-000	DS 18C	DISP
77	LS-LOCATION-CODE	BLL=5	000	DNM=3-030	DS 2C	DISP-NM
77	LS-EXPANDED-LOCATION	BLL=6	000	DNM=3-056	DS 13C	DISP
77	LS-EDUC-CODE	BLL=7	000	DNM=3-086	DS 1C	DISP-NM
77	LS-EXPANDED-EDUCATION	BLL=8	000	DNM=3-108	DS 10C	DISP

Figure 7.14 Abbreviated Data Division Map for Subprogram (DECODER).

```
  67  SEARCH ALL  0058EE                                EQU   *                          GN=03
              0058F2  07 F1                              BCR   15,1
  89  MOVE      0058F4                                   EQU   *
              0058F4  58 10 C 054                        L     1,054(0,12)                        GN=05
              0058F8  53 10 D 254                        MVC   14,254(0,13)                       BLL=4         LIT+12
              0058FE  D2 06 E 007 C 0D4                  MVC   000(7,14),0D4(12)                  DNM=3-0
              005902  92 40 E 008                        MVI   007(14),X'40'                      DNM=3-0+7
              005908  D2 09 E 008 C 007                  MVC   008(10,14),007(14)                 DNM=3-0+8
              005908  58 10 C 060                        L     1,060(0,12)                        GN=08         DNM=3-0+7
              00590C  07 F1                              BCR   15,1
  89  MOVE      00590E                                   EQU   *                          GN=06
              00590E  41 00 6 010                        LA    0,010(0,6)                         DNM=1-421
              005912  50 00 D 238                        ST    0,238(0,13)                        TS4=1
              005916  F2 72 D 230 6 000                  PACK  230(8,13),000(3,6)                 TS2=1
              00591C  4F 00 D 230                        CVB   0,230(0,13)                        TS4=5
              005920  50 00 D 23C                        ST    0,23C(0,13)                        TS4=5
              005924  D2 03 C 240 C 058                  MVC   240(4,13),058(12)                  TS4=9
              00592A  D2 01 D 246 C 0C8                  MVC   246(4,13),0C8(12)                  TS4=15
              005930  58 10 C 250                        L     14,250(0,13)                       BLL=3
              005934  D2 02 D 230 C 000                  MVC   230(3,13),000(14)                  TS2=1
              00593A  96 F0 D 232                        OI    232(13),X'F0'                      TS2=1+2
              00593E  92 01 D 244                        MVI   244(13),X'01'                      TS4=13
              005942  41 00 D 230                        LA    0,230(0,13)                        TS2=1
              005946  41 10 D 238                        LA    1,238(0,13)                        TS4=1
              00594A  58 F0 C 018                        L     15,018(0,12)                       V(ILBODBG4)
              00594E  05 EF                              BALR  14,15
              005950  0 0                                DC    0,0
              005952  58 F0 C 01C                        L     15,01C(0,12)                       V(ILBOSCH0)
              005956  05 EF                              BALR  14,15
              005958  9003000                            DC    X'90030000'
              00595C  1B 01                              SR    0,1
              00595E  50 00 D 270                        ST    0,270(0,13)                        INX=1
              005962  41 40 6 013                        LA    4,013(0,6)                         DNM=1-463
  91  MOVE      005A22                                   EQU   *                          GN=012
              005A22  07 F1                              BCR   15,1
 102  IF        005A24                                   EQU   *
              005A24  58 E0 D 260                        L     14,260(0,13)                       BLL=7         DNM=3-86
              005A28  F2 70 D 228 E 000                  PACK  228(8,13),000(1,14)                TS=09         LIT+2
              005A2E  F9 00 D 22F C 0CA                  CP    22F(1,13),0CA(1,12)                TS=016
              005A34  58 F0 C 078                        L     15,078(0,12)                       GN=014
              005A38  07 4F                              PACK  4,15
 103  MOVE      005A3A                                   EQU   *
              005A3A  F2 70 D 223 E 000                  PACK  22B(8,13),000(1,14)                TS=09         DNM=3-86
              005A40  F9 00 D 22F C 0CB                  CP    22F(1,13),0CB(1,12)                TS=016        LIT+3
              005A46  58 F0 C 07C                        L     15,07C(0,12)                       GN=015
              005A4A  07 DF                              BCR   13,15
 105  MOVE      005A4C                                   EQU   *
              005A4C  58 E0 D 264                        L     14,264(0,13)                       BLL=8         LIT+12
              005A50  D2 06 E 000 C 0D4                  MVC   000(7,14),0D4(12)                  DNM=3-108
              005A56  92 40 E 007                        MVI   007(14),X'40'                      DNM=3-108+7
              005A5A  D2 01 E 008 E 007                  MVC   003(2,14),007(14)                  DNM=3-108+8
              005A60  58 10 C 034                        L     1,034(0,12)                        PN=01         DNM=3-108+7
              005A64  07 F1                              BCR   15,1
              005A66                                     EQU   *
              005A66  58 E0 D 218                        L     14,218(0,13)                       BL =7
              005A6A  41 40 E 2A0                        LA    4,2A0(0,14)                        DNM=2-446
```

Figure 7.15 Abbreviated Procedure Division Map for Subprogram (DECODER).

355

```
                MEMORY MAP

         TGT                           054B0

         SAVE AREA                     054B0
         SWITCH                        054F8
         TALLY                         054FC
         SORT SAVE                     05500
         ENTRY-SAVE                    05504
         SORT CORE SIZE                05508
         RET CODE                      0550C
         SORT RET                      0550E
         WORKING CELLS                 05510
         SORT FILE SIZE                05640
         SORT MODE SIZE                05644
         PGT-VN TBL                    05648
         TGT-VN TBL                    0564C
         RESERVED                      05650
         LENGTH OF VN TBL              05654
         LABEL RET                     05656
         RESERVED                      05657
         DBG R14SAVE                   05658
         COBOL INDICATOR               0565C
         A(INIT1)                      05660
         DEBUG TABLE PTR               05664
         SUBCOM PTR                    05668
         SORT-MESSAGE                  0566C
         SYSOUT DDNAME                 05674
         RESERVED                      05675
         COBOL ID                      05676
         COMPILED POINTER              05678
         COUNT TABLE ADDRESS           0567C
         RESERVED                      05680
         DBG R11SAVE                   05688
         COUNT CHAIN ADDRESS           0568C
         PRBL1 CELL PTR                05690
         RESERVED                      05694
         TA LENGTH                     05699
         RESERVED                      0569C
         PCS LIT PTR                   056A4
         DEBUGGING                     056A8
         CD FOR INITIAL INPUT          056AC
         OVERFLOW CELLS                056B0
         BL CELLS                      056B0
         DECBADR CELLS                 056CC
         FIB CELLS                     056CC
         TEMP STORAGE                  056D0
         TEMP STORAGE-2                056E0
         TEMP STORAGE-3                056E8
         TEMP STORAGE-4                056E8
         BLL CELLS                     056F8
         VLC CELLS                     0571C
         SBL CELLS                     05720
         INDEX CELLS                   05720
         SUBADR CELLS                  05728
```

Figure 7.16 Memory Map for Subprogram (DECODER).

```
REGISTER ASSIGNMENT

    REG  6     BL  =2
    REG  7     BL  =1
    REG  8     BL  =3
    REG  9     BL  =4
    REG 10     BL  =5
    REG 11     BL  =6

WORKING-STORAGE STARTS AT LOCATION 000A0 FOR A LENGTH OF 052F0.
```

Figure 7.17 Register Assignments for Subprogram (DECODER).

```
CONTROL SECTION                        ENTRY

NAME      ORIGIN    LENGTH             NAME       LOCATION     NAME       LOCATION     NAME       LOCATION     NAME       LOCATION
PROFILE   00        17F3
DECODER   17F8      5F4E
ILBODBG   7748      E58                ILBODBG0   777A         ILBODBG1   777E         ILBODBG2   7782         ILBODBG3   7786
                                       ILBODBG4   778A         ILBODBG5   778E         ILBODBG6   7792         ILBODBG7   7796

ILBOEXT * 85A0      68                 ILBOEXT0   85A2         ILBOEXT1   85A6

ILBOFLW * 8608      54C                ILBOFLW0   860A         ILBOFLW1   860E         ILBOFLW2   8612

ILBOQIO * 8B58      6E8                ILBOQIO0   8B5A         ILBOQIO1   8B5E

ILBOSPA * 9240      6C4                ILBOSPA0   9242         ILBOSPA1   9246         ILBOSPA2   924A

ILBOSRV * 9908      4DC                ILBOSRV0   9912         ILBOSR5    9912         ILBOSR3    9912         ILBOSR     9912
                                       ILBOSRV1   9916         ILBOSTP1   9916         ILBOST     991A         ILBOSTP0   991A

ILBOBEG * 9DE8      158                ILBOBEG0   9DEA

ILBOCMM * 9F40      399                ILBOCMM0   9F42         ILBOCMM1   9F46

ILBOCOM*  A2E0      169                ILBOCOM    A2E0

ILBOCVB * A450      428                ILBOCVB0   A452         ILBOCVB1   A456

ILBODSP * A878      A08                ILBODSP0   A87A         ILBODSS0   A87A

ILBOINS * B280      6DA                ILBOINS0   B282

ILBOMSG * B960      100                ILBOMSG0   B962

ILBOSCH * BA60      40A                ILBOSCH0   BA62

ILBOWTB * BE70      11A                ILBOWTB0   BE72

ILBOACS * BF90      10A                ILBOACS0   BF92         ILBOACS1   BF96

ENTRY ADDRESS    00

TOTAL LENGTH     C0A0
****MAIN  DOES NOT EXIST BUT HAS BEEN ADDED TO DATA SET
AUTHORIZATION CODE IS    0.
```

Figure 7.18 Link-Edit Map.

Exercise 7.3: Dump Reading

Determine why the dump of Fig. 7.19 occurred. Use the COBOL programs, Data, Procedure and Memory Maps of Fig. 7.8 through Fig. 7.18 as necessary. The questions below are provided as a guide.

Analyze the completion code.

1. What is the completion code?
2. What does the completion code mean?

Determine where the ABEND occurred.

3. What address is contained in the PSW?
4. At what location was the program loaded?
5. Subtract the address in part 4 from the one in part 3.
6. Is the relative location obtained in part 5 contained in the main program?
7. What is the origin of the subroutine within the load module?
8. Subtract the address in part 7 from the one in part 5.
9. To which program does the relative location in part 8 refer?
10. What machine instruction is at that location?
11. What is the actual machine address of the instruction in part 10?
12. What is the corresponding COBOL instruction?

Examine the machine instruction that failed to execute. The instruction that actually produced the ABEND is the one immediately before the instruction determined in part 11.

13. What is the machine instruction that actually caused the ABEND?
14. What is its op code?
15. Which base register is associated with the first operand?
16. What is the displacement of the first operand?
17. What is the effective address of the first operand?
18. How many bytes are associated with the first operand? (Careful)
19. What are the internal contents of the first operand? Are they valid as a decimal number?
20. Which base register is associated with the second operand?

```
JOB SSTBERN1            STEP GO              TIME 081602     DATE 79212     ID = 000                                      PAGE 0001
COMPLETION CODE         SYSTEM = 0C7
PSW AT ENTRY TO ABEND  078D2000 0009D18C         ILC 6    INTC 0007

CDE
  78C310   NCDE 00000000   RBP 007570A0   NM MAIN       EPA 00095F60   XL/MJ 007BC7F0   USE 00010000   ATTR 0B20000
  FCADB8   NCDE 00FCAE30   RBP 00000000   NM IGG019DK   EPA 00F9A000   XL/MJ 00FCADD8   USE 00030000   ATTR B122000
  FF8080   NCDE 00FFF0108  RBP 00000000   NM IGG019DJ   EPA 00AD2438   XL/MJ 00FF80A0   USE 00070000   ATTR B122000
  FEF628   NCDE 00FEF658   RBP 00000000   NM IGG019CU   EPA 00ED18C8   XL/MJ 00FEF648   USE 00090000   ATTR B023000
  FC75B8   NCDE 00FCADB8   RBP 00000000   NM IGG019CU   EPA 00ED1000   XL/MJ 00FEF673   USE 00A0000    ATTR B122000
  FC6478   NCDE 00FECD50   RBP 00000000   NM IGG019CZ   EPA 00EDFF10   XL/MJ 00FC75D8   USE 00020000   ATTR B122000
  FC7640   NCDE 00FC7640   RBP 00000000   NM IGG019AA   EPA 00ED0938   XL/MJ 00FC6498   USE 00050000   ATTR B122000
           NCDE 00FEF628   RBP 00000000   NM IGG019AQ   EPA 00ED0A70   XL/MJ 00FC7660   USE 00050000   ATTR B122000

SAVE AREA TRACE
MAIN   WAS ENTERED VIA LINK
SA  094FB30  WD1 00000000   HSA 00000000   LSA 00096838   RET 00010880   EPA 00095F60   R0  0078C800
             R1  00094FF8   R2  00000040   R3  00780634   R4  00780610   R5  0078C9A8   R6  0078C013
             R7  FD000000   R8  0074B030   R9  8078CC38   R10 00000000   R11 0078CB10   R12 70D6A1A2

MAIN   WAS ENTERED VIA CALL
SA  096338  WD1 0030C4C2   HSA 00094FB0   LSA 0009CC08   RET 50096E9C   EPA 00097758   R0  00096E4A
             R1  00096AD4   R2  00096D22   R3  60097F8    R4  0009490E   R5  00096E44   R6  00096000
             R7  00094838   R8  000967B0   R9  00097A8    R10 00095F60   R11 00095F60   R12 00096B10

MAIN   WAS ENTERED VIA CALL   AT EP %&<Q" WE"ILBOSCH VSREL2.1UP10966  ¢R%Q_  <$#QA  <H  QQ>QB  I  HH  Q!&AS
SA  09CC08  WD1 0030C4C2   HSA 00096838   LSA 00094B90   RET 5009D0B0   EPA 000A19C2   R0  0009CE38
             R1  0009CE40   R2  0009D046   R3  0000001E   R4  00096AD4   R5  80096149   R6  000977F8
             R7  000A2E70   R8  000987F8   R9  0009977F8  R10 0009A7F8   R11 0009B7F8   R12 0009CEC0

REGS AT ENTRY TO ABEND
FLTR 0-6    0000000000000000      0000000000000000      0000000000000000      0000000000000000
REGS 0-7    00000087   0009D17C   0009CA20   0000001E   0009CA1E   80096149   000977F8   000A2E70
REGS 8-15   000937F8   000997F8   0009A7F8   0009B7F8   0009CEC0   0009CC08   0009485A   0009CA20
```

Figure 7.19 Dump for Exercise 7.3.

```
0947A0   00000004  0009479C  0D000000  00000000  00000000  0000B09  *................H...............*
0947C0   92094803  60000005  86094888  0009479C  88094828  22094828  00000001  *....-..........Q.............*
0947E0   00094750  00000000  00094773  60000000  40094820  88094820  00094778  *.&.............-. ........... *
094800   22094828  00000000  0000B07  92094773  60000050  F9F0F0F0  F0F0F0F0  90000000  *............-..90000000.90000000*
094820   22094828  00000050  0E000000  F9F0F0F0  F0F0F0F0  F0F0F0F0  *............9000000000000000*
094840   F0D4C9D3  C7D9D6D4  4040D4C2  F1F1F5F5  F0F9F7F7  F3F0F1  F4F5F609  *0MILGROM  MB1155097730 1459*
094860   F7F7F2F1  F2F0F0F0  D4F1F7F8  F3F1F0F0  F0F5F7F8  F3F0F0F0  D6C74040  4040F240  *7721000M117831000057830000HO   2*
094880   F9F7F7F3  40404040  F6F0F0F0  F0F0F0F0  C5E4D7C5  D9D7D9D6  C7404040  F7F9F0F0  *9773     60000000SUPERPROG  S*
0948A0   F0F4F5F7  F1F0F7F7  F4F0F5F1  F4F0F5F7  F7F1F3F0  F0F0F0F4  F1F0F7F7  F9F0F0F0  *045710774051077139000H10779000*
0948C0   F0F0F0F0  40404040  4B404040  F8F0F0F0  F0F0F0F0  C8F1F0F7  F7F9F0F0  00000000  *0000    1322.   80000000H1077900*
0948E0   D9D7C5D9  E2D5C9C3  D2C5E3E8  4040D7F7  F0F6F5F1  F0F3F7F8  F4F0F5F3  *OPERSNICKETY P 0651037840314503*
094900   F7F8F1F0  F9F0F0F0  C8F0F3F7  F8F6F0F0  00000000  40404040  0200000  00000000  *78109000H03786000    00000     *
094920   F1F3F2F2  4B404040  4040D7B  00094740  4040F0F0  *1324.        Q   00*
094940   00000000  00000000  000000A3  00000000  00000000  00000000  *...........................*
         LINES 094960-094980 SAME AS ABOVE
0949C0   00000000  00000000  00000000  00000000  00000000  00094AD8  00000100  00000000  *................Q...*

095F60   90ECD000  C64D7D9D6  185D5F0  4580F010  C9D3C540  7D9D6C6  0709989F  F02407FF  *.......C.}}.PROFILE VSR1....0.*
095F80   96021034  07FE41F0  0009754A  0001097FE  0000000  00000000  0709989F  00096B10  *......0.......................*
095FA0   00096C64  0009754A  0000000  0000000  00000000  00000000  00000000  00000000  *..............................*
095FC0   00000000  00000000  00000000  00000000  00000000  00000000  00000000  00000000  *................................*
095FE0   00000000  00000000  40F84BF1  D1E4D340  F3F14040  F1F9F7F9  F1F9F7F9  00000000  *..... .8.1.JUL 31. 1979        *
096000   E8C5E200  00000000  F0F6C0F1  F3F16340  F0F6F0F0  F1F9F7F9  *YES      .06.1206.  1979*

096020   60606060  60606060  6060606  60606060  60606060  60606060  60606060  60606060  *-------------------------------*
         LINE 096040 SAME AS ABOVE

096060   40404040  40404040  40404040  40404040  40404040  40404040  40404040  40404040  *                                *
096080   40404040  40404040  40404040  40404040  40404040  40404040  40404040  40404040  *                                *
0960A0   4DD7D9D6  C6C9D3C5  40404040  40404040  40404040  40404040  40404040  40404040  *PROFILE                         *
0960C0   40404043  0009754A  40404040  40404040  40404043  C5D9E2D6  D5D5C5D3  40404040  *.........          PERSONNEL    *
0960E0   40404040  00000000  00000000  40404040  40404040  40404040  40404040  40404040  *                                *

096100   00000000  00000000  40F84BF1  D1E4D340  F3F14040  F1F9F7F9  F1F9F7F9  00000000  *..... .8.1.JUL 31. 1979        *
```

```
0977E0   40F84BF1 F54BF3F9 D1E4D340 F3F16B40   F1F9F7F9 00000000 E3C1D5E3 C5E2E8C5   * 8.15.39JUL 31, 1979....OIIYESYE*
097800   E2000000 00000000 F0F1F5D1 D9404003   C3D64BD5 F5C1E4C4 C3C3D6E4 D5E3C1D5   *S.....015JR ACCOUNTANT  025AUDITOR 020*
097820   E2D94DC1 C3C3D6E4 D5E3C1D5 E3404040   4040D6F2 F5C1E4C4 C9E3D6D9 40404040   *SR ACCOUNTANT  025AUDITOR     *
097840   40404040 404040F1 F4F0D1D9 4007D9D6   C7D9C1D4 D4C5D940 F1F4F5D7 F1F4F507   *         140JR PROGRAMMER  145P*
097860   D9D6C7D9 C1D4D4C5 D9404040 40404040   40F1F5F0 E2D940D7 D9D6C7D9 C1D4D4C5   *ROGRAMMER         150SR PROGRAMME*
097880   D9404040 404040F1 F5F5C1D5 C1D3E8E2   F1F7F7C3 D3C5D9D2 40404040 40404040   *R         155ANALYST    170CLERK*
0978A0   E2E340D4 C7D94040 40404040 40404040   F1F7F7C3 D3C5D9D2 40404040 40404040   *ST MGR             170CLERK*
0978C0   40404040 40F1F7F5 E3C5C3C8 D5C9C3C9   C1D54040 4C40F1F6 F0D4C1D5 00000000   *     175TECHNICIAN   160MAN*
0978E0   C1C7C5D9 40404040 40404040 40404040   00000000 00000000 00000000 00000000   *AGER                            *
097900   00000000 00000000 00000000 00000000   00000000 00000000 00000000 00000000   *                                *
         LINES 097920-09C9E0 SAME AS ABOVE
09CA00   F1F0C1E3 D3C1D5E3 C1404040 404040F2   E3D6D540 40404040 4040F0F0 4040F3F0   *10ATLANTA          20BOSTON    30*
09CA20   C3C3C9C3 C1C7D540 40404040 40F4F0C4   C5E3D9D6 C9E34040 4040F6F0 F5D6D2C1   *CHICAGO          40DETROIT    50KA*
09CA40   D5E2C1E2 40C3C3E3 E84040F6 F0D3D6E2   40C1D5C7 C5D3C5E2 404077F0 D4C9D9D5   *NSAS CITY   60LOS ANGELES  70MINN*
09CA60   C5C1D7D6 D3C3E240 40F8F0D5 C5E640E5   D6D9D240 40404040 F9F0D7C8 C9D3C1C4   *EAPOLIS   80NEW YORK     90PHILAD*
09CA80   C5D3D7C8 C9C140D9 F9F5E2C1 D5406DC6   D5C3C9E2 C3D60000 E2D6D4C5 40C8E240   *ELPHIA 95SAN FRANCISCO. SOME HS *
09CAA0   404008E2 40C4C9D7 D3D6D4C1 F2E8D940   C4C5F4E8 D7C84B40 D9406CD5 C7D9C5C5   *HS DIPLOMA2YR DEGREE4YR DEGREE*
09CAC0   E2D64DC5 40C7D9C1 C4404040 00000000   E2404040 D7C84B40 C4484040 4040D6E3   *SOME GRAD MASTERS    PH. D.   OT*
09CAE0   C8C5D940 0009777E 00000000 00000001   00000000 000A2E69 00098506 00000000   *HER                  . V.         *
09CB00   00000000 00000000 00000000 00000000   00000000 00000000 00000001 00000000   *                                *
09CB20   80000000 00000000 00000000 00000000   00000000 00000000 00000000 00000000   *                                *
09CB40   00000000 46079E52 00000000 000A2E70   C5E24040 02004800 00000050 00004000   *  . . .    .M2 .                *
09CB60   00080050 05EF0700 00000000 000A2E60   000A2E70 00000000 00000001 00000000   *         .-.                    *
09CB80   00000000 02000001 00500014 00000000   00000000 00000000 00000000 00000000   *                                *
09CBA0   00000030 00000001 0500001A 000EC76   0009EC76 00000000 00000000 00009D440   *                                *
09CBC0   00000000 00000000 00000000 00000000   00000000 00000000 00000000 00000000   *                                *
09CBE0   00000000 00000000 00000000 0009EC76   0009EC76 00000000 00000000 00000000   *                                *
09CC00   00000000 00000000 0030C4C2 00096B38   50009D030 0009EC76 00000000 00009CE33   *        .DB.   .B.              *
09CC20   0009CE40 00090046 0004 2E70 0009ADA4   000A2E70 0009ADF8 0009787F0 0009987F0   *                        .8. .B.*
09CC40   00099F78 0009A7F0 0009B7F8 0009CEC0   24228040 00000001 00000015 00009CFD4   *                                *
09CC60   00000000 00000002 00000000 00000000   00000000 00097F80 01090B24 00009D5C0   *             145.L.       .M   *
09CC80   50094F2 000097BD A 70090D2F4 6009EACC   000A2E70 00097F8 000097F8 00009D46   *     .M2 .K4 .8. . .8. . .N.   *
09CCA0   000978F0 000CE CO 00000000 00000030   00000000 0009CB24 0009D46 400907F8   *                                *
09CCC0   03F0F060 00000000 00000000 00000C00   00000000 00000000 00000000 00000000   *                                *
         LINE 09CD00 SAME AS ABOVE
09CD20   00000000 00098C24 40090SC0 0009CAEC   00000000 00008506 00000000 00008C24   *                                *
09CD40   00000000 00008A1E 00008CA0 00008CEC0   00000000 00000000 000097F8 00008977F3   *                                *
09CD60   00087F6 00098B78 00000000 01000000   00000000 00000000 00000000 00000000   *                                *
09CD80   00000000 00000000 00000000 05000000   C1000000 00000000 00005750 00000000   *            SYSOUT A           *
09CDA0   000A02A0 E2E8E2D6 E4E34040 C1000000   00000000 00000000 00097758 00000000   *   SYSOUT A                     *
09CDC0   00000000 00000000 00000000 0009EC76   00000000 0009778 000097BD0 00000010F   *                                *
09CDE0   00097F8 0009D46 0009D04C 01000015   00000000 0009AFB 0009A7F8 000008978   *                                *
09CE00   0009C620 000000 00 0009D04C 80096149   00000000 00086149 00000AFB 000008977FB   *                                *
09CE20   0009 6346 0009485A 00096149 00000000   00009658 F1F4F500 0000011F 00000000   *                 .8.   .8.  .B.*
09CE40   00097603 000961EC 000SCAEC 80086149   00000000 00008054 000009651 00006501   *                      .145.    *
09CE60   0009CA1E 0009D372 00090054 0000540E   00000000 0009D5A 0009D5A 00000001E   *                                *
09CE80   000CB24 0009D5A 0009D5A 00000000   00000000 0009D6C 00009D06 00005750   *                                *
09CEA0   0009EB06 0009DEA6 0009556A 0009EEE   00000000 00057DE 00009EA 00000190C2   *                   .L. .M. .NY.O.*
09CEC0   00087872 00095ADA 0009040 AF1040F6   00000000 00008D6C 0009070A 00009D372   *              .V. .B..V..O..B *
09CEE0   000A1002 000900300 00D8F054 00008D54   00000000 000079D1 0009A150 00009D066   *                  .K. .JO..K..L.*
09CF00   00005E06 0009EABA 000A07DA 0009EEC   00000000 0009740 000D904A 0009D1BE   *           .U..J. .O. .M..J.   *
09CF20   0009D22A 0009D168 0009D46C 0009D20F   00000000 00087064 0009010A 000901FA   *                                *
09CF40   0009D24E 0009C540 0009D24A 0009D066   00000000 000F74 0009D46 00009D1A   *           .K. .K. .LO.K..L.  *
09CF60   0009D2AE 0009D36C 0009D643 00009D4EA   00000000 00019454 0009D306 00009D1BE   *           .K..L..M..MW..L.. J. *
09CF80   0009D45A 00000000 00151C8C 00000000   00000000 00000000 00000000 00000000   *      .M          NUNKNOWNYES. *
```

361

21. What is the displacement of the second operand?
22. How many bytes are associated with the second operand?
23. What are the internal contents of the second operand? Are they valid as a decimal number?
24. Technically, why did the ABEND occur?

Relate the technical cause of the ABEND to the COBOL program.

25. Which data name in the main program contains the description of the invalid employee record?
26. Which base locator is associated with that data name?
27. What is the displacement of the BL cells in the main program?
28. Add the entry point address of the main program to the answer in part 27.
29. What is contained at the four bytes beginning at the address found in part 28?
30. What is the value of Base Locator 1?
31. Which employee had the invalid data? Identify his record in core.
32. Add the displacement associated with EMP-EDUCATION-CODE to the answer from part 30.
33. What is contained in the location obtained in part 32?

Verify the solution using the BLL cells.

34. Which data name in the subprogram contains the description of the invalid education code?
35. Which Base Linkage Locator is associated with that data name?
36. What is the displacement of the BLL cells in the subprogram?
37. Add the Entry Point Address of the main program, plus the origin of the subprogram, plus the answer from part 36.
38. What is contained at the 4 bytes beginning at the address found in part 37?
39. What is the value of Base Linkage Locator 7?
40. What is the relationship between the answers in parts 32 and 39?

Using the SAVE AREA TRACE:

41. What are the linkage conventions for registers 14 and 15?
42. What is the entry point in the main program?
43. What return address is specified in the first called program in the save area trace?
44. Subtract the address in part 42 from that in part 43. Examine the assembler instruction in the main program immediately before this one and explain its significance.

Exercise 7.4: Dump Reading

Determine why the dump of Fig. 7.20 occurred. Use the COBOL programs, Data, Procedure, and Memory Maps of Fig. 7.8 through Fig. 7.18 as necessary. The questions below are provided as a guide.

Analyze the completion code.

1. What is the completion code?
2. What does the completion code mean?

Determine where the ABEND occurred.

3. What address is contained in the PSW?
4. At what location was the program loaded?
5. Subtract the address in part 4 from the one in part 3.
6. What is the origin of the subroutine within the load module?
7. Is the relative location obtained in part 5 contained in the main or subprogram?
8. What machine instruction is at the location obtained in part 5?
9. What is the corresponding COBOL instruction?

Examine the machine instruction that failed to execute. The instruction that actually produced the ABEND is the one immediately before the instruction determined in part 8.

10. What is the machine instruction that actually caused the ABEND?
11. What is its op code?

```
JOB SSTBERN1          STEP GO           TIME 081504   DATE 79212   ID = 000                            PAGE 0001

COMPLETION CODE            SYSTEM = 0CB

PSW AT ENTRY TO ABEND   078D0000 000974C2       ILC 6    INTC 000B

TCB  757210
  +0    RBP   0078E6E0   PIE    00000000   DEB  00763D00   TIO 00758020   CMP  900CB000   TRN  00000000
  +18   MSS   0078F0E0   PK-FLG 80010000   FLG  0000FFFF   LLS 0076C850   JLB  0078C288   JPQ  0078C310
  +70   FSA   01094FB0   TCB    00000000   TME  00000000   JST 0075C210   NIC  00000000   QTC  0078C9A8
  +33   LTC   00000000   IQE    00000000   ECB  0074B054   TSF 20000000   D-PQE 0078F548  AQE  007573C0
  +A0   STAB  0078CEE4   TCT    3078CC33   USER 007C02CC   SDF 00000000   MDID 00000000   JSCB 0078C09C
  +B8   RESV  00000000   IOBRC  00000000   XCPD 00000000   EXT 00000000   BITS 00000000   DAR  00000000
  +D0   EXT2  00757338   AECB   00000000   TIRB 00000000   BAK 00000000   RTMWA 0074BC30  IOTM 00000000
  +E8   TMSAV 00000000   ABCR   00000000   XSCT 80000040   FOE 00000000   SWA  0078C530   STAW 00000000
  +100  BID   E3C3C240   RTM1   00000000   ESTA 80000000   UKY 0078C560   CPVI 0000FFFF   BYT1 08040000
  +118  RPT   00000000   DBTB   00000000   SWAS 00769E90   SCB 00000000   RESV 00000000   RESV 00000000
  EXT2         00000000  SVAB   00000000   EVNT 00000000   RES 00000000   RESV 00000000   RESV 00000000

CDE
  78C310     NCDE 00000000  RBP 007570A0  NM MAIN      EPA 00095F60   XL/MJ 0078C7F0   USE 00010000   ATTR 0B20000
  FCADB8     NCDE 00FCAE30  RBP 00000000  NM IGG019DK  EPA 00F9A000   XL/MJ 00FCADD8   USE 00030000   ATTR B122000
  FF8080     NCDE 00FF0103  RBP 00000000  NM IGG019DJ  EPA 00AD2483   XL/MJ 00FF30A0   USE 000A0000   ATTR B122000
  FEF628     NCDE 00FCADB8  RBP 00000000  NM IGG019CW  EPA 00ED18C8   XL/MJ 00FEF648   USE 000A0000   ATTR B023000
  FEF658     NCDE 00FCADB8  RBP 00000000  NM IGG019CU  EPA 00ED1000   XL/MJ 00FEF673   USE 000F0000   ATTR B122000
  FC75B3     NCDE 00FECD50  RBP 00000000  NM IGG019CZ  EPA 00EDFF10   XL/MJ 00FC75D8   USE 00030000   ATTR B122000
  FC6478     NCDE 00FC7640  RBP 00000000  NM IGG019AA  EPA 00ED0988   XL/MJ 00FC6493   USE 00060000   ATTR B122000
  FC7640     NCDE 00FEF628  RBP 00000000  NM IGG019AQ  EPA 00ED0A70   XL/MJ 00FC7660   USE 00060000   ATTR B122000

TIOT 758020
  OFFSET       JOB SSTBERN1 STEP GO     TYR-ST      STB-UC
  + 0018       LN-STA   DDNAME          76BIC000    80765 9E0
  + 002C       14010100 STEPLIB         76ADC000    80002DA0
  + 0040       14010100                 76578000    80002C50
  + 0054       14010100 SYS00024        76AC4000    80000000
  + 0068       14010102 SYSDBOUT        76AAC000    80000000
  + 007C       14010102 SYSOUA          76A94000    80000000
  + 0090       14010102 SYSUDUMP        76A7C000    80000000
  + 00A4       14010102 TITLES          76A64000    80000000
  + 00B8       14010100 SYSOUT          76A4C000    80002F20
                        SYSIN
```

Figure 7.20 Dump for Exercise 7.4.

```
-DEB------------------------AT LOCATION 00763D00
-----
 -8              EXTNSION 00763010 LENGTH   10       AMTYPE   81       TBLOF    0003
 +0     TCBADR   00757210 NEXTDEB  00763258 IRBADR   08766CA0 PATB     0F000900
        USRPG    00000000 RRQ      0074DE08 DCBADR   8F094198 APPADR   00E28774
+20     00002B90 E2E2C9C2 00240000 DIC5E2F2
+30     00000000 00000000 00000000 00140010
+40     00000000 00000000 E2E2D6C2 00140010
+50     00763D24 00000000 00763D5C 00180000
+60     00000000 00763DFC 00763D00 00766CA0
+70     00000000 00000000

*** FOR THIS DEB THERE IS NO DCB, THE CONTROL BLOCK POINTED TO BY THE DEB IS AN ACB ***

-DEB------------------------AT LOCATION 00763253
-----
 -8              EXTNSION 007632D0 LENGTH   10       AMTYPE   81       TBLOF    0002
 +0     TCBADR   00757210 NEXTDEB  007637BC IRBADR   08766A60 PATB     0F000900
        USRPG    00000000 RRQ      000966D0 DCBADR   8F0945D0 APPADR   00E28774
+20     00002B90 E2E2C9C2 00240000 DIC5E2F2
+30     00000000 00000000 00000000 00000000
+40     00000000 00000000 E2E2D6C2 00140010
+50     0076327C 00000000 007632B4 00180000
+60     00000000 007633F4 00763258 00766A60
+70     00000000 00000000

*** FOR THIS DEB THERE IS NO DCB, THE CONTROL BLOCK POINTED TO BY THE DEB IS AN ACB ***

-DEB------------------------AT LOCATION 007637BC
-----
-24     DEBAVT   00EDFF10 0001566E DEBPCIA  00015666E DEBCEA  00ED1004 DEBXCEA  00ED1004
-10     PREFIX   00000000 00000103 EXTNSION 00763820 LENGTH   11       AMTYPE   20       TBLOF  0001
 +0     TCBADR   05757210 NEXTDEB  10000000 IRBADR   68000000 PATB     00000100
+10     USRPG    01000000 RRQ      FF000000 DCBADR   8F0965B4 APPADR   04763798
+20     53002F20 00000000 00B00000 00B00001
+30     00010001 00000000 00000000 00000050
+40     C1D8C1C1 C3E9C3E4 C3E60000 00000000
+50     00000000 00000000 00000000 00000000
+60     00000000 00000000

-DCB-   (QSAM)                              AT LOCATION 000965B4
-----
+10     002B4B36 03094830 00004000 000946F8 4609EC52 8009657C 00B84800 007637BC
+30     12ED0988 00EDDA70 09000001 10DD0050 00003000 00094 7E0 00094928 000948D8
+50     00000050 00000000 00000000 00ED18C8

365
```

```
SAVE AREA TRACE

MAIN     WAS ENTERED VIA LINK

SA  094FB0  WD1 00000000    HSA 00000000    LSA 00096838    RET 00010880    EPA 00095F60    R0  0078C800
            R1  0094FF8     R2  00000040    R3  00780634    R4  00780610    R5  0078C9A8    R6  00758018
            R7  FD000000    R8  0074B030    R9  8078CC38    R10 00000000    R11 0078CB10    R12 70D6A1A2

MAIN     WAS ENTERED VIA CALL                   AT EP 02=G04:&%%<Q03BJ¢kDG 3DQE 8A< -&EB%E-2UQ 40ANBMAVB%Q'QN 8G00< I=S&A   K

SA  096838  WD1 0030C4C2    HSA 00094FB0    LSA 00094F90    RET 0009738E    EPA 0009E56E    R0  00097372
            R1  600973BA    R2  00094909    R3  6009722CC    R4  00094908    R5  00094908    R6  00096000
            R7  000948D8    R8  000967B0    R9  0009758A    R10 00095F60    R11 00095F60    R12 00096B10

REGS AT ENTRY TO ABEND

FLTR 0-6      0000000000000000    0000000000000000    0000000000000000    0000000000000000    00094908   00094508
                                                                                               00094916   0009E56E
REGS 0-7    00000000 00097372 0000000 00094909E 00094916 00000000 00094594 00000000
REGS 8-15   00000000 0009678D 0000000 0009758A  00095F60 00000000 00094909 52000000

094580  00000000 00000000 00000000 00000100 00000030 00094590 40000000 00094594
094540  00000000 00000000 00000000 00000000 00096600 A000004C 00000000 0E28774 52000000
094550  92000000 00000000 42840008 00000000 00000000 00000001 00A40041 00763258
094560  F1F9C1C8 00000000 0009440C 00000000 00850085 00000000 00002000 00000001 C9C7C7F0
094600  00094650 00094590 80096610 00094268 00000000 C0000000 C0100001 00094650
094620  00094269 92AD2494 4009F1B8 00094268 00000006 000014C 4000000 00000034
094640  00000400 00094268 00094268 00094500 00094B0 00000000 000002009 00000000
094680  00000000 00000085 00000000 00000000 00010499 03000000 000942AC 00094590
094680  00000000 00000000 00000000 00000000 00094268 00000000 00000000 00094530
094660  08000000 00000000 04000000 00000000 00000100 00000000 00000000 41000000
094680  00000000 00000000 02000000 41094600 00000000 00000050 00003800 40000005
094700  00000000 00947ED 00947700 00000004 4109460C 00000000 40000061 00000000
094720  00000000 00000000 00000000 00000000 00000000 40000061 31094728 40000000
094740  08094738 00094738 02000000 00000000 00000000 00094798 70000000 00000000
094760  00094793 0C000000 00094778 00000000 00000000 00000000 00003000 60000005
094780  06094333 40000050 68094790 00947CB 00000000 00000001 00094730 41000000
094740  00000000 00094790 00000000 00000000 40000050 00000000 00094730 00000B09
094700  92094803 60000005 86094683 00094268 0D000000 86094708 22094322 00000001
094720  00094750 7F000000 00000000 00094764 00000000 83000000 00094308 80000020
094800  00000000 00000007 10000000 92094773 60000005 86094848 40000050 58094820 00094778
094820  22094828 00000000 10000000 40404042 00000000 F1F1F555 F0F9F777 F3F0F3F1 F4F5F0F9
094840  F0D4C9D3 C7D9D6D4 40404040 F2F0F0F0 F0F3F0F3 F0F0F0F0 F0F0F0F0 F0F0F0F0
094860  F7F7F2F1 F2F0F0F0 40404040 D4F1F1F7 F8F3F1F0 F0F0F0D4 F0F5F7F8 F4F5F0F9
094880  F9F7F7F3 40404040 F4F0F0F0 F0F0F0F0 F2E2E4D7 C5D9D7D9 D6C74040 4040E240
094840  F0F4F5F1 F1F0F7F7 F4F0F3F0 F4F0F0F0 F0F0F0F0 C8C1E7 E7F9F0F0 00000000
094800  F0F0F040 40404040 40404040 40404040 4B404040 F8F0F0F0 F0F0F0F0 11.
094860  F0D7C5D9 F2E2D5C9 D2C5E3E8 404D7040 F0F0F3F1 F0F0F0F0 F0F3F1F4 F5F0F3
094800  F7F8F1F0 F9F0F0F0 F0F0F0F0 D4C3F7F8 F6F0F0F9 F0F0F0D4 F0F3F8F6 F0F0F0F0
094920  404F1F3 4B404040 000949D8 00000030 00000000 00000048 02000000 00000000
094940  00000000 00000000 00000000 00000000 00000000 00000000 00000000 00000000
```

```
*................................*
*................................*
*................S...............*
*................................*
*................................IGG0*
*...19AH.........................*
*..Y..............Y..............*
*....Z...........Y...............*
*................................*
*................................H...*
*................................*
*............................H...*
*................................*
*................................*
*................................*
*................................*
*...........................Q....*
*................................*
*..................U.............*
*................Q..........90000000*
*............MB1155097730314509*
*.MLGROM..................*
*............M1173100000H05783090000H0*
*.773..60000000SUPERPROG    S*
*046571077405145107713900H01077900*
*........0000...11..800000000*
*OPERSNICKETY P 0851037840314503*
*78109000MC378603000M0378600000*
*................................*
*........Q.......................*
```

366

```
ACTIVE LOAD MODULES

LPA/JPA MODULE      MAIN
095F60  90ECD00C 185DD5F0 4580F010 D7D9D6C6 C9D3C540 E5E2D9F1 0700989F F02407FF  *....0...0.PROFILE VSR1...0....*
095F80  96021034 07FE41F0 000107FE 0009758A 00095F60 00095F60 00096B10 00096838  *................*
095FA0  00096C64 00097544 00000000 00000000 00000000 00000000 00000000 00000000  *................*
095FC0  00000000 00000000 00000000 00000000 00000000 00000000 00000000 00000000  *................*
095FE0  E8C5E200 00000000 F0F0C0F0 F0F6F0F9 D1E4D340 F3F16B40 F1F9F7F9 00000000  *YES.....8.14,09JUL 31,1979....*
096000  60606060 60606060 F0F0F6F0 F0F6F0F9 60606060 60606060 60606060 60606060  *.........00.0006...........*
096020  60606060 60606060                                                        *........*
    LINE 096040 SAME AS ABOVE
096060  40404040 40404040 40404040 40404040 40404040 40404040 40404040 40404040  *.                              *
096080  40404040 40404040 40404040 40404040 40404040 40404040 D5D5C5D3 5BD5D5D3  *                   PERSONNEL*
0960A0  40D7D9D6 C6C9D3C5 40404040 40404040 40404040 40404040 C5D9E2D6 5BD5D5D3  *  PROFILE                   *
0960C0  40404040 40404040 40404040 40404040 40404040 40404040 40404040 40404040  *                                *
096100  40D5C1D4 C57A40D7 C5D9E2D5 C9C3D2C5 E3E84040 D7404040 40E2D6C3 40E2C5C3  *  NAME. PERSNICKETY P   SOC SEC*
096120  E4C3C1E3 C9D6D57A 40F2E5D9 4004C5C7 D9C5C540 40404040 40E2D6C3 40E2C5C3  *UCATION. 2YR DEGREE     SOC SEC*
096140  40D5D67A 40F8F0F0 4B4FE0F0 40404040 40404040 40404040 40404040 40404040  *  NO. 800.00.0000               *
096160  40404040 40404040 40404040 40404040 40404040 40404040 40404040 40404040  *                                *
0961A0  40404040 40404040 40400C2C9C9 D9C54DC4 C1E3C57A 40F0F8B6 4BF5F140 40404040  *           BIRTH DATE. 08.51    *
0961C0  40F0F361 4040C8C9 D6C57A40 D6C5E3D9 40F0F661 F5F1F040 D6C5E3D9 40404040  *  03       HIRE DATE.03.78      *
0961E0  4040D3D6 C3C1E3C9 D6D57A40 C4C5E3D9 40F8F40E0 40404040 40404040 40404040  *    LOCATION,DETROIT            *
096200  40404040 40404040 40404040 40404040 40404040 40404040 40404040 40404040  *                                *
096220  40404040 40404040 40404040 40C2C909 D6C54DC4 C9E2E3D6 D9E84040 40404040  *              SALARY HISTORY    *
096260  40404040 40404040 40404040 40404040 40404040 40404040 40404040 40404040  *                                *
    LINE 096280 SAME AS ABOVE
0962A0  40404040 40404040 40404040 40404040 40404040 40404040 40404040 40404040  *                                *
0962C0  40404040 E2C1D3C1 D9E84040 E3C54040 40404040 D7C54040 40404040 40404C1  *  SALARY   DATE       TYPE    I*
0962E0  D5C3D94D 6C5D4040 40404040 4040D4C2 C94C5D40 40404040 40404040 40404040  *NCR...   MBI RSI...             *
096300  40404040 40404040 40404040 40404040 40404040 40404040 40404040 40404040  *                                *
    LINE 096320 SAME AS ABOVE
096340  40404040 40404040 40404040 40404040 40404040 4040405B F96BF0F0 F0404040  *              *3  M    .9.000   *
096360  F8404040 40404040 40404040 4040C24C1 404C4040 40404040 40404040 40404040  *                                *
096380  40404040 40404040                                                        *        *
    LINE 0963A0 SAME AS ABOVE
0963C0  40404040 40404040 40404040 40404040 40404040 40404040 40404040 40404040  *                                *
0963E0  E3C9E3D3 C5404040 40000000 D9E84040 40404040 C4C1E3C5 40404040 40404040  *TITLE          JOB HISTORY      *
096400  C5404040 40404040 40404040 40404040 40404040 40404040 40404040 40404040  *E                               *
096420  40404040 40404040 40404040 40404040 40404040 40404040 40404040 40404040  *                                *
    LINE 096440 SAME AS ABOVE
096460  40404040 40404040 40404040 40404040 40404040 40404040 40404040 40404040  *                                *
096480  E3C9E3D3 C5404040 40000000 D9E84040 40404040 C4C1E3C5 40404040 40404040  *TITLE          DATE PERFORMANC*
0964A0  C5404040 40404040 40404040 40404040 40404040 40404040 40404040 40404040  *E                               *
0964C0  40404040 40404040 40404040 40404040 40404040 40404040 40404040 40404040  *                                *
0964E0  40D7D9D6 C7D9C1D4 D4C5D940 40404040 40404040 40F1F061 F7F74040 40404040  *  PROGRAMMER          10.77    *
096520  E7C3C5D3 D3C5D5E3 40404040 40404040 40404040 40404040 40404040 40404040  *XCELLENT                       *
096540  40404040 40404040 40404040 40404040 40404040 40404040 40404040 40404040  *                                *
096560  40404040 40404040 40404040 40404040 40404040 40404040 40404040 40404040  *                                *
096580  40404040 40404040 40404040 00000000 0509E506 00000001 00000000 0000000B  *              V                 *
0965A0  0002D30C 0002B436 03094830 00000000 52000000 D9C6D6D9 D4C1D5C3 00B84800  *  L           8                 *
0965C0  007637BC 12ED0988 00EDDA70 00000001 46090EC52 8090657C 00094728 00094928  *    Q   .H                      *
0965E0  00094BD8 00000050 00000000 09000000 00000000 05EF0700 000947E0 00000000  *                                *
096600  00000000 00000000 00000000 00000000 00000001 00500804 00000000 00000000  *                                *
096620  00000000 00000000 00000000 00800000 02000000 00000000 00000000 00000000  *                                *
096640  00000000 000949E0 00000000 00000000 00000000 00000000 00000000 00000000  *                                *
096660  00000000 00000000 00000000 000096E3E 00000000 00000000 00000000 0009EC44  *                                *
```

367

```
096760   00094930  0009F1A2  00000000  00000000  00000000  00000000  00000000  00000000   *....1...........................*
096780   0009EBC4  0009EBE6  00000000  00000000  00000000  00009EC76 0009EC76  E2C1D3C1   *..D...W.........................SALA*
0967A0   0009E84040  4040C4C1  E3C54040  00000000  40404040  40404040  D5C3D94D  6C5D4040   *.RY  DATE  TYPE      INCR..*
0967C0   40404040  C2C94040  404DD9E2  C94D6C5D  40404040  40404040  40404040  40404040   *     MBI   RSI...               *
0967E0   40404040  40404040  40404040  40404040  40000000  00000000  0030C4C2  00C94FB0   *                         ..DB...*
096800   00094390  000973BE  0009E56E  00094909  00094909  00094909  00094909  00C94909   *................................*
096820   00094908  00097758A  000E90D0  00095F60  000095F60  00095F60  00096810  00009490E   *......................S..l..*
096840   34223048  00000000  00000000  00000000  00000000  00000000  00000000  0009F1AA   *................................*
096860   000960CC  00094AD4  000096B10  00095F60  00094E44  0009E5F60  00094800  0009F1AA   *......M..8...........Q.*
096880   000960CC  00097558A  00000000  0000100C1  00009EACC  00000000  00000000  00000000   *........Q.........OO..........R*
0968E0   00000000  8F096660  00000000  00000000  02F0F000  00096838  00000040  00000000   *................................*
096900   00000000  00000000  00000000  00000000  0609DD50  000096EDO 00009068B 00000000   *................................*
096920   00000000  00000000  00000000  00000000  00000000  00000000  00000000  00000000   *................................*
         LINE 096940 SAME AS ABOVE
096960   00010830  0009E506  000096D0  8F0966D0  00009666D0  00786634  00096698  500375DA   *.........SYSOUT A.*
096980   000095F60  000975BA  00095F60  00000000  00095F60  00096B10  00096B10  00010000   *........V............*
         LINE 0969A0 SAME AS ABOVE
0969C0   000D7094  40095C8A  00000000  00000000  0000A240  E2E8E2D6  E4E34040  C1000000   *.........Y....SYSOUT A..*
09649A0  0009SFE8  00000000  00000000  00000000  00000000  00000000  00000000  00000000   *................................*
096A20   00000000  00000000  00000000  00000000  00000000  0000939C  00000000  00000000   *................................*
096A40   00096D00  00000000  0000000C  F0F0F0F0  00000000  00000000  00000000  00000000   *.............Q..*
096A80   00000000  8F096600  6BF0F0F0  00094916  00094DE0B 00007298  00097298  00009734   *................................*

097760   4580F010  C4C5C3D6  C4C5D940  E5E2D9F1  07098939F  F0249F7FF  96021034  07FE41F0   *....DECODER VSR1.....0.*
097780   0011007FE  0009D534  00097758  00000001E 0009CCC8  0009CFD4  0009CFD4  00094F4   *..........J6...8...8..M..M4*
0977A0   00096838  6009D1F6  00000000  00009B7F8  0009CAAC  80096149  0009DIFA  0004A2E70   *.........8..8..8..J..8.*
0977C0   00009F87F8 0009A7F8  0004A7FB  000A7F8  0009CCC8  0009CCC8  0009CE58  *................................*
0977E0   40F84BF1  F448F3F3  D1E4D340  F3F16B43  F1F9F7F9  4040404B  F0F1F1E5  C5E2E8C5   *.14.33JUL 31, 1979...011YESYE*
097800   E2000000  000A7FB  F0F1F5D1  D9400103  E3D0404  00009E4  C9E3D6D9  40404040   *S...015JR ACCOUNTANT 020*
097820   E2D40C1  C3C3D6E4  D5E3C1D5  E3404040  40404040  40404040  C9E3D6D9  40404040   *SR  ACCOUNTANT  025AUDITOR*
097840   40404040  C3C5D6E4  F4F0D1D9  40D7D906  C7D9C1D4  D4C5D940  F1F4F5D7  *       140JR PROGRAMMER 145P*
097860   D906C7D9  C1D4D4C5  D9404040  40404040  40F1F5F0  E2D407  D9D6C7D9  C1D4D4C5   *ROGRAMMER         150SR PROGRAMME*
097880   D9404040  4040F1F5  F5C1D5C1  D3E8E2E3  40404040  40404040  F6F0C4C9  C1D4D4C5   *R    155ANALYST            160DI*
0978A0   E2E340D4  C7D94040  40404040  40404040  F1F7FOC3  D3C5D9D2  40404040  F040C1D5   *ST MGR           170CLERK    160MAN*
0978C0   40404040  40F1F7F5  E3C5C3C8  D5C9C3C9  C1D54040  40404040  40404040  F0D4C1D5   *      175TECHNICIAN          160MAN*
0978E0   C1C7C5D9  40404040  40404040  40404040  00000000  00000000  00000000  00000000   *AGER                            *
097900   00000000  00000000  00000000  00000000  00000000  00000000  00000000  00000000   *                                *
         LINES 097920-09C9E0 SAME AS ABOVE
09CA00   F1F0C1E3  D3C1D5E3  C1400040  404040F2  E3D6D540  40404040  4040F3F0  *10ATLANTA       20BOSTON       30*
09CA20   C3C8C9C3  C1C7D640  40404040  40F4F0C4  C5E3D9D6  C9E34040  F5F0D2C1  *CHICAGO         40DETROIT     50KA*
09CA40   D5E2C1E2  40C3C9E3  E840D0F6  F0D3D6E2  40C1D5C7  C5D3C5E2  404D4F7F0  D4C9D5D5  *NSAS CITY   60LOS ANGELES   70MINN*
09CA60   C5C1D7D6  D3C9E240  F840D5C5  E640F8D5  C5E640D9  C9D3C1C4  F9FD7C8  *EAPOLIS    80NEW YORK        90PHILAD*
09CA80   C5D3D7C8  C9C140F9  F5E2C1D5  40C6D9C1  D5C3C9E2  C3D60240  C9D3C5C5  *ELPHIA 95SAN FRANCISCO.SOME HS*
09CAA0   4040F082  C4C9D7D3  D6D4C1E2  C9D4C5C5  D5C5E640  C5C3E8C5  C7D9C5C5  *HS DIPLOMA2YR DEGREE4YR DEGREE*
09CAC0   E2D6D4C5  40C7D9C1  C4404041  C44D0C1  F2E8D940  E2E3C5D9  C4404040  *SOME GRAD MASTERS  PH. D.  OT*
09CAE0   C8C5D940  00097F7E  00000000  00000001  00000000  00000000  00000000  0509E506  *HER.............................V*
09CB00   80000000  00000000  02004800  00000000  00000000  00000000  00000000  00000000   *................................*
09CB20   00000001  4609EC52  00000000  00000000  00000001  00000001  00000001  00000001   *................................*
09CB40   00000000  0009CAEC  00000000  00A2E69  00000000  00000050  00000001  00000000   *........TITLES..................*
09CB60   0000A2E70 000A2E70  00000000  0000A2E70  00000000  00000000  00000000  00000000   *................................*
09CB80   00000000  05EF0700  00000000  00000000  00000000  00000000  00000000  00800000   *................................*
```

ABEND Debugging

12. Which base register is associated with the first operand?
13. What is the displacement of the first operand?
14. What is the effective address of the first operand?
15. How many bytes are associated with the first operand? (Careful)
16. What are the internal contents of the first operand? Are they valid as a decimal number?
17. Which base register is associated with the second operand?
18. What is the displacement of the second operand?
19. How many bytes are associated with the second operand?
20. What are the internal contents of the second operand? Are they valid as a decimal number?
21. Technically, why did the ABEND occur?

Relate the technical cause of the ABEND to the COBOL program.

22. Which data name in the main program contains the description of the invalid employee record?
23. Which base locator is associated with that data name?
24. What is the displacement of the BL cells in the main program?
25. Add the entry point address of the main program to the answer in part 24?
26. What is contained in the four bytes beginning at the address found in part 25?
27. What is the value of Base Locator 1?
28. Which employee had the invalid data? Identify his record in core and explain why the ABEND occurred.

Although the ABEND has now been solved, we will continue probing the dump to learn about various control blocks.

Locate the control blocks:

29. What is the address of the TCB?
30. What is the address of the first DEB in the chain?
31. What address is contained in the first word of the DEB from part 30?
32. What is the address of the second DEB?

370 Section 7

33. What is the address of the third DEB?
34. How is the end of the DEB chain indicated?

Supply DCB displacements for the following:

35. Address of the current record.
36. TIOT offset.
37. Logical record length.
38. Maximum block size.
39. Address of the associated DEB.

Using the DCB for EMPLOYEE-FILE:

40. Which DEB is associated with EMPLOYEE-FILE?
41. What is the DCB address contained in the DEB from part 40?
42. Add the answer from parts 39 and 41. What is the significance of the result?
43. Add the answer from parts 36 and 41. What are the hex contents of the two bytes beginning at that address?
44. Convert the hex contents of the two bytes from part 43 to decimal.
45. Use the answer from part 44 to find a line in the TIOT table. Show how the TIOT entry relates to EMPLOYEE-FILE.
46. Add the answer from parts 35 and 41. To what does this address refer? How do the contents of the 80 bytes beginning at this address support the conclusion from part 27?
47. Add the answer from parts 37 and 41. What is contained at the two bytes beginning at that address? How does this relate to a COBOL FD?

Solutions

Exercise 7.1: Dump Reading

1. 0C7–Data Exception
2. 0968D6
3. 095C58
4. C7E

5. FC 51 D 21A C 09C
6. COMPUTE (statement #110)
7. FB 32 D 21C D 225 (at location C78)
8. FB (subtract packed)
9. D
10. 21C
11. 96404 (961E8 + 21C)
12. 4 (one more than the length code)
13. 00 19 00 0F (yes)
14. D
15. 225
16. 3
17. 00 00 04 (No)–(Found in the 3 bytes beginning at 9640D)
18. Register 7 (BL = 1)
19. 0944F0
20. 030
21. Begins at 094520 and extends a total of 5 bytes
22. 40 40 40 40 40 (blanks)
23. WILCOX had the invalid data. The value of FORMER-SALARY was blank so that a data exception resulted when this field was used in a computation.
24. 790
25. 0963E8
26. 00 09 44 F0
27. It is the value of BL = 1 or register 7. (See part 19.)
28. 00 09 5C F8
29. That is the value of BL = 3 or register 6
30. FB 32 D2 1C D2 25 is found in the six bytes beginning at 968D0. The contents of these bytes look more like an instruction after they are regrouped according to the SS instruction format as was done in question 7.

Exercise 7.2: Dump Reading

1. 0C7–Data Exception
2. 09688A
3. 095C58

4. C32
5. F2 71 D 210 7 023
6. COMPUTE (statement 107)
7. FB 11 D 21E D 216 (at location C2C)
8. FB (Subtract Packed)
9. D
10. 21E
11. 96406 (961E8 + 21E)
12. 2 (One more than the length code)
13. 079F (Yes)
14. D
15. 216
16. 2
17. 00 04 (No)–(Found in the 2 bytes beginning at 963FE)
18. Register 7 (BL = 1)
19. 0944F0
20. 025
21. Begins at 094515 and extends a total of 2 bytes
22. 40 40 (blanks)
23. Smith had the invalid data. The value of BIRTH-YEAR was blank so that a data exception resulted when this field was used in a computation.
24. 790
25. 0963E8
26. 00 09 44 F0
27. It is the value of BL = 1 or register 7.
28. 00 09 5C F8
29. This is the value of BL = 3 or register 6.
30. Find FB 11 D2 1E D2 16 in the six bytes beginning at 96884. The contents of these six bytes can be regrouped as was done in part 7.
31. The programs were run under MVS (as opposed to MVT) in which the problem program is always loaded in the same locations.
32. From the DMAP, DATE-WORK-AREA is located $(010)_{16}$ from BL = 3, at 95D08. The value of the six bytes beginning at that location is F7 F9 F0 F4 F1 F7 or 4/17/79.

Exercise 7.3: Dump Reading

1. 0C7
2. Invalid decimal data were used in a numeric computation.
3. 09D18C
4. 095F60
5. 722C
6. No—(See Link-Edit Map (Fig. 7.18))
7. 17F8—(See Link-Edit Map (Fig. 7.18))
8. 5A34
9. The subprogram DECODER.
10. 58 F0 C 078 (A load instruction)
11. 09D18C (The address in the PSW)
12. IF (statement 102 in DECODER)
13. F9 00 D 22F C 0CA (at location 5A2E)
14. F9 (compare packed)
15. D
16. 22F
17. 09CE37 (09CC08 + 22F)
18. 1 (One more than the length code)
19. 04 (No)
20. C
21. 0CA
22. 1 (One more than the length code)
23. 1C (Yes)
24. A decimal comparison was made to a field containing 04, an invalid decimal field due to an improper sign.
25. EMPLOYEE-RECORD
26. BL = 1
27. AD8
28. 96A38
29. 00094838 (The value of BL = 1)
30. 00094838
31. MILGROM
32. 09485A

33. 40 (A blank)
34. LS-EDUC-CODE
35. BLL = 7
36. 56F8
37. 9CE50
38. 00000000 (The value of BLL = 1)
39. 0009485A
40. They are the same, both specify the address of the education code.
41. Register 15 contains the address in a subprogram where control is transferred. Register 14 contains the return address in the calling program.
42. 95F60
43. 96E9C
44. F3C (The instruction at F3A is BALR 14, 15. The effect of that instruction is to store the address of the next sequential instruction, the return point, into register 14 and branch to the address in register 15. In other words, it is implementing a subroutine call through the standard linkage conventions.)

Exercise 7.4: Dump Reading

1. 0CB
2. Attempt to divide by zero
3. 0974C2
4. 095F60
5. 1562
6. 17F8
7. In the main program.
8. F8 73 D 220 D 221
9. COMPUTE (at COBOL line 244)
10. FD 62 D 221 D 22D (at location 155C)
11. FD (Divide Packed)
12. D
13. 221
14. 96A59 (96838 + 221)
15. 7 (One more than the length code)

ABEND Debugging 375

16. 000000 0000000C (Yes)
17. D
18. 22D
19. 3
20. 00000C–Yes
21. The ABEND occurred because an attempt was made to divide by zero.
22. EMPLOYEE-RECORD
23. BL = 1
24. AD8
25. 96A38
26. The value of BL = 1
27. 000948D8
28. PERSNICKETY–The first two salary dates are both 0378. Hence, the value of WS-MONTHS-BETWEEN-INCR is 0, and the 0CB occurs in COBOL line 244 when an attempt is made to divide by this quantity.
29. 757210
30. 763D00
31. 757210; the address of the TCB
32. 763258
33. 7637BC
34. When the address of the next DEB in the chain is all zeros.
35. 4D
36. 28
37. 52
38. 3E
39. 2D
40. The last one, with DEB address 7637BC (DEBs appear in the reverse order in which files were opened)
41. 965B4
42. 965E1; it contains the address where the address of the associated DEB can be found. The contents of the three bytes beginning at 965E1 should be 7637BC.
43. 965DC; the contents of the two bytes beginning at this location are 00B8, the TIOT offset for the file in question.
44. $(184)_{10}$

45. The TIOT has a 24-byte header, plus 20 bytes for each entry. Subtracting 24 from 184, and dividing the balance by 20, leaves a quotient of 8. This means that we have completed 8 entries in the TIOT, and the file in question is found on the 9th line. Going to the TIOT we find a DD name of SYSIN in the 9th line which in turn points to EMPLOYEE-FILE.

46. 96601; the contents of this byte and the next two contain the address of the next record. The contents are 948D8, the same answer as in part 27.

47. 96606; the contents of 96606 and 96607 are $(0050)_{16} = (80)_{10}$ = record length in the COBOL FD.

Index

A

ABEND debugging, 315-76
ACCEPT, 200
ACCESS IS DYNAMIC, 116
ACCESS IS RANDOM, 238
ACCESS MODE, 114
ADD, 55-58
Addressing exception, 325
AFTER ADVANCING (*see* WRITE)
ALL, 49
Alphabetic class test, 75
ALTERNATE RECORD KEY, 117
A margin, 3
AND, 210
ANS Standard, 45
Arithmetic in COBOL, 55-63
ASCENDING KEY:
    in MERGE statement, 103, 107
    in OCCURS clause, 93, 96, 212
    in SORT statement, 106, 200
ASCII, 111
Assumed decimal point, 270, 278, 293
Asterisk:
    as comment, 139
    in PICTURE, 64, 66
    in arithmetic expression, 57
AT END:
    in READ, 137, 215, 252
    in SEARCH, 252

B

B:
    in PICTURE clause, 64, 66, 202
Base/displacement addressing, 316
Binary number, 316, 317
Binary search (*see* SEARCH ALL)
Blank line, 253
BL cells, 362, 369
BLL cells, 362
BLOCK CONTAINS, 120
Braces, 46
Brackets, 46
Byte, 320

C

CALL (*see* Subprogram)
Called program (*see* Subprogram)
Calling program, 138, 158-70
Capsule summaries:
    ABEND debugging, 322-23
    arithmetic statements, 56
    COBOL Syntax, 46
    editing, 66, 67
    MOVE, 65
    MOVE CORRESPONDING, 68, 69
    program guidelines, 3
    skeletal COBOL outline, 2
Check protection (*see* Asterisk)

C level diagnostic, 8
CLOSE, 47, 48
Coding standards (*see* Standards)
Cohesive paragraph, 251
COLLATING SEQUENCE, 103, 111
COLUMN, 125, 129
Comma:
   in editing, 64, 66-67
   in listing, 254
Comments, 139, 248-49
COMP (*see* COMPUTATIONAL)
COMP-3 (*see* COMPUTATIONAL-3)
Compilation errors, 7-15, 19-21, 23-26,
     30-32, 34-37, 41-42
Completion codes, 323
   0C1, 323
   0C4, 324
   0C5, 325
   0C6, 325
   0C7, 325
   0CB, 326
   013, 327
   122, 327
   213, 328
   322, 328
   513, 329
   804, 329-30
   806, 330
   80A, 329-30
   813, 330-31
   B37, 331
   D37, 331
   E37, 331
COMPUTATIONAL, 317, 318
COMPUTATIONAL-3, 211, 317, 318
COMPUTE, 57-59, 200, 202, 257, 272
Condition name (*see* IF, condition name)
Conditional diagnostic (*see* C level diagnostic)
CONTROL, 124, 125, 126
Control area, 116
Control breaks, 283 (*see also* Report
     writer)
   execution errors, 146-50, 198
Control interval, 116
COPY, 265, 282, 304
CORRESPONDING (*see* MOVE COR-
     RESPONDING)

CR:
   in PICTURE clause, 64, 67
Currency symbol (*see* Editing)
Cylinder index (*see* ISAM)

D

Data division map, 322, 334, 351, 354
Data exception, 325
Data-name, 249-50
Data-name qualification (*see* Qualification)
DATA RECORDS ARE, 291
Data validation, 307
DATE, 200, 272, 295, 297
DB:
   in PICTURE clause, 64, 67
DEB, 369
Debugging, 7-11
   ABEND errors, 315-16, 322-76
   compilation errors, 7-11
   logical errors, 134-216
Decimal alignment (*see* MOVE)
Decimal point (*see* Editing)
DELETE, 117, 208, 238
DEPENDING ON (*see* OCCURS DEPENDING
     ON)
DESCENDING KEY:
   in MERGE statement, 103
   in OCCURS clause, 93, 99
   in SORT statement, 103, 106, 107
Detail report group, 125, 131
Direct access to table entries, 259, 260
Disaster diagnostic (*see* D level diagnositc)
Displacement (*see* Base/displacement ad-
     dressing)
DISPLAY:
   as COBOL statement, 235
   in USAGE clause, 317, 318
DIVIDE, 55-58
D level diagnostic, 8
DMAP (*see* Data division map)
Dollar sign (*see* Editing)
Double spacing (*see* AFTER ADVANCING)
Dump (*see* ABEND debugging)
Duplicate data-names (*see* Qualification)

E

EBCDIC, 111
Editing, 64-73, 270
Elementary item, 49, 50
E level diagnostic, 8
ELSE, 77, 202 (*see also* IF)
End-of-file condition, 138
Entry point address, 322
Error diagnostic (*see* E level diagnostic)
Error processing (*see* Data validation)
Execution error, 134-216
EXIT PROGRAM, 165, 170
Exponentiation, 57, 59

F

FD, 47
File maintenance:
    nonsequential, 219, 236-46, 285, 287, 309
    sequential, 219-35, 285, 287, 309
File name, 250, 251
Floating dollar sign (*see* Editing)
Floating minus sign (*see* Editing)
Floating plus sign (*See* Editing)
FOOTING, 125, 126
FROM (*see* SUBTRACT, WRITE)

G

GENERATE, 126, 128, 197
GIVING:
    with SORT verb, 105, 107
GO TO, 137
Group item, 49, 50
Group move, 210

H

HEADING, 125, 126
Hexadecimal arithmetic, 316
Hierarchy:
    between group and elementary items, 49
    chart, 205, 221-22, 237, 288

    of arithmetic operations, 57
HIGH-VALUES, 117, 209

I

IF, 75-84
    compound, 76
    condition name, 76, 255-56
    implied conditions, 76
    indentation, 253
    nested, 78, 79, 203, 253, 274
Implied conditions (*see* IF, implied conditions)
Implied decimal point (*see* Assumed decimal point)
IN (*see* Qualification)
Indentation, 251-53
Independent overflow (*see* ISAM)
INDEXED BY, 93, 96
Indexed files, 114-23
Indexed sequential access method (*see* ISAM)
Infinite loop, 158, 195, 200, 216
Initial read, 2, 22, 204
INITIATE, 126, 128
INPUT PROCEDURE, 104
Input validation (*see* Data validation)
INSPECT, 202, 278, 299
Installation standards (*see* Standards)
Instruction formats (BAL), 316-17
Internal data representation, 317, 321
INVALID KEY, 137, 238, 252
ISAM, 115-18, 174, 208

L

Linear search (*see* SEARCH)
LINKAGE SECTION (*see* Subprogram)
Link edit map, 357
Loading a table (*see* Table)
Logical operator (*see* AND, OR)
Logic error (*see* Execution error)
LOW-VALUES, 117

M

Major sort key, 106
MERGE, 103, 107

380 Index

Merging files:
    errors in execution, 177-81
Minor sort key, 106
Minus sign:
    in PICTURE clause, 64, 67
MOVE, 64, 65, 136
    problem with group MOVE, 181-82, 210
MOVE CORRESPONDING, 68-70
    errors in execution, 215
Multilevel table (*see* Table)
MULTIPLY, 55-58

N

Negative data (*see* Signed number)
Nested IF (*see* IF)
NEXT SENTENCE, 75, 81
NOMINAL KEY, 117
Nonsequential file maintenance, 219, 236-46, 285, 287, 309
    errors in execution, 174-77, 207-9
NOT, 76
Notation, in COBOL statements, 46
Number systems, 316, 319
Numeric class test, 75

O

OCCURS, 95, 215
OCCURS DEPENDING ON, 93, 261
OF (*see* Qualification)
OPEN, 47, 48
Optional reserved word, 46
OR, 210
ORGANIZATION IS INDEXED, 120, 238
OUTPUT PROCEDURE, 104
Overflow (*see* ISAM)

P

Packed data, 211
Padding (*see* MOVE)
PAGE LIMIT, 124
Paragraph name, 251
PERFORM: 85-93
    errors in coding, 136, 203
    sections, 85, 86, 256

    THRU, 85
    UNTIL, 203
    VARYING, 87, 88, 203, 299, 307
Period:
    in IF statement, 200
    missing or extra, 77, 137, 200 203, 209
Plus sign:
    in PICTURE clause, 64-67
PMAP (*see* Procedure division map)
Prefixing (of data name), 250
Primary sort key, 106
Prime area, 229
Priming read (*see* Initial read)
PROCEDURE DIVISION USING, 265
    (*see* Subprogram)
Procedure division map, 322, 335, 352, 355
Programmer supplied name, 249-51
Programming projects, 267-314
Programming style, 247-66
Program Status Word (*see* PSW)
Program stub, 223-30, 238-42
Programming Tips:
    ABEND Debugging, 323-30
    common compilation errors to avoid, 9-11
    execution errors to avoid, 135-39
Protection exception, 325
Pseudocode, 220-21, 288, 311
PSW, 322

Q

Qualification, 64, 69, 216

R

RD, 124
READ, 47, 48
    INTO, 264
    INVALID KEY, 238, 252
Receiving item (*see* MOVE)
RECORD CONTAINS, 10
RECORD KEY, 117
REDEFINES, 96, 215
Register assignments, 352, 356
RELEASE, 103, 199
REPLACING:
    in INSPECT, 202

Report group, 126-27
Report writer, 124-33, 266, 283, 305
    compilation errors, 139-42, 195-96
    execution errors, 143-46, 196-97
RESERVE ALTERNATE AREAS, 121, 213-14
Reserved word, 10, 46
RETURN, 103, 199
REWRITE, 238
ROUNDED (*see* Arithmetic in COBOL)

S

S:
    in PICTURE (*see* Signed number)
SD, 103
SEARCH, 96, 136, 204, 259-60, 279, 302
    execution errors, 182-83, 212
SEARCH ALL, 96, 136, 259-60, 281, 302
    execution errors, 182-83, 212
Secondary sort key, 106
Section, 85, 86
Sequencing paragraph names, 251
Sequential file maintenance, 219-35, 285, 287, 309
    errors in execution, 171-74, 204-7
Sequential search (*see* SEARCH)
Sequential update (*see* Sequential file maintenance)
SET, 93, 96, 204, 212
Signed number, 61, 64, 276
    errors in coding, 136, 183-84, 212-13
    in packed field, 211
SIZE ERROR, 137, 252
Slash:
    as editing character, 64
    in column 7, 254
SORT, 103-14, 276
    compilation errors, 151-54, 198-99
    execution errors, 155-57, 199-200
SOURCE, 125
Specification exception, 325
Standards, 247-66
START, 115, 119
Stepwise refinement, 285
STOP RUN, 105, 324
Stub (*see* Program stub)

Structured design, 251
Structured walkthrough, 44
Subprogram, 138, 158-70, 201-4, 265, 276, 279, 302-4
Subroutine (*see* Subprogram)
Subscript (*see* OCCURS)
SUBTRACT, 55-58
Summary reporting, 197
Switches, 137, 206, 208, 209, 254-55
Syntax of COBOL statements, 46

T

Tables: 93-102
    initialization, 96, 202, 260-61
    lookup, 201
    one dimension, 96, 274
    two dimension, 186-87, 215, 282, 307
    three dimension, 94, 95
    variable length (*see* OCCURS DEPENDING ON)
TCB, 369
TERMINATE, 126, 128
Testing, 217-46
Three-level table (*see* Table)
TIMES, 93
TIOT, 324
Top down testing, 217-46, 288
Track index (*see* ISAM)
Truncation (*see* MOVE)
Two's complement, 211
Two-level table (*see* Table)
TYPE, 124, 126

U

UNTIL (*see* PERFORM)
Update program (*see* File maintenance)
USAGE, 210, 318
USING:
    in CALL statement (*see* Subprograms)
    in MERGE statement, 103, 107
    in Procedure Division header (*see* Subprograms)
    in SORT statement, 105, 107

V

V:
    as assumed decimal point, 270, 278, 293
Variable-length record, 278
VARYING: *(see* PERFORM)
Virtual sequential access method *(see* VSAM)
VSAM, 116-18, 174

W

WHEN *(see* SEARCH)
W level diagnostic, 8
WRITE, 47, 48, 252
    FROM, 264
WS BEGINS HERE, 264

X

X:
    in PICTURE clause, 65

Y

Yourdon, E., 248

Z

Z:
    in PICTURE clause, 64, 66